Leonardo da Vinci

THE TRAGIC PURSUIT OF PERFECTION

Martha C Hustad,

Michael J Heier   May 1 1999

Leonardo da Vinci. Self-portrait

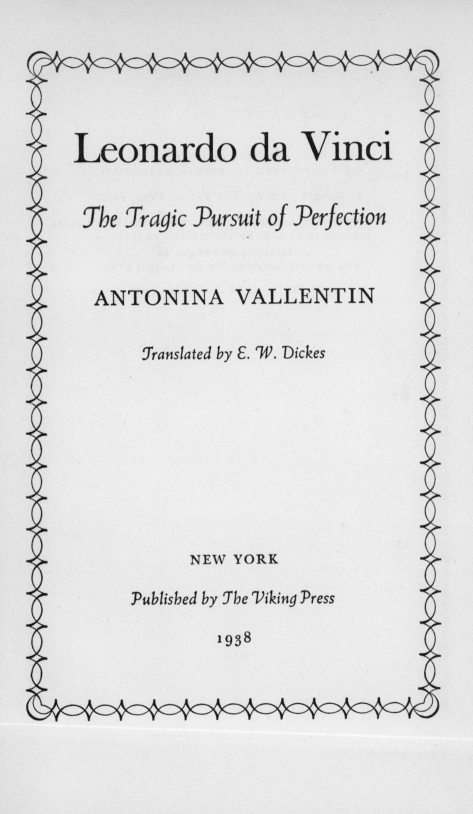

Leonardo da Vinci

The Tragic Pursuit of Perfection

ANTONINA VALLENTIN

Translated by E. W. Dickes

NEW YORK

Published by The Viking Press

1938

TO

VISCOUNT D'ABERNON

TRANSLATOR'S NOTE

The quotations in this book have unavoidably, in a few cases, been retranslated from the German version, but wherever possible they have been taken direct from the Italian. A large number of the quotations from the *Codex Atlanticus* have been taken bodily from the English versions in Dr. J. P. Richter's *Literary Works of Leonardo da Vinci*, published in 1883 (of which a second edition, revised by Miss S. A. Richter, is to be issued by the Oxford University Press). These were the work of Mrs. R. C. Bell, with the occasional help of her brother Sir Edward Poynter, and are very beautifully done, as anyone may see for himself by comparing the passage on page 404, a just rebuke from Leonardo for our own times, with the Italian given in the footnote.

Occasional advantage has been taken of the works of Professor E. McCurdy and Mr. Ivor B. Hart. The translator desires to acknowledge valuable technical assistance given by Mr. Lawrence Haward, Mr. O. S. Griffiths, and Mr. Arnold Bender. Thanks are due to Messrs. Ulrico Hoepli, Milan, for permission to take photographs from their facsimile edition of the *Codex Atlanticus*.

E. W. D.

Contents

CONTENTS

Illustrations

IN FULL COLOUR

IN ONE COLOUR

Leonardo da Vinci

THE TRAGIC PURSUIT OF PERFECTION

CHAPTER ONE

The Dream of the Great Bird

*Deh non m'avere a vil ch'io non son povero: povero
è quel che assai cose desidera.*

Despise me not, for I am not poor—Poor is he only
who has material desires.
(*Codex Atlanticus,* 71 recto.)

AT THE beginning of Leonardo's life came the omen of the
great bird. His memories reached back to his earliest childhood, and in the first of them all, *la prima ricordatione della mia
infantia,* he saw himself actually in the cradle. He was probably
two or three years old, but still, like many another peasant's son,
rocked to sleep by his mother. As the boy lay in the cradle, blink-
ing at the hard blue infinity above, he saw coming swiftly down
towards him a black spot that grew and grew, alarmingly, until it
became two powerful wings with the bird's sharp beak projecting
in front of them. The fan of its tail swished through the air, and
the shadow of the broad pinions hovered above the cradle, like
a darkness that had engulfed the sun—"and it seemed to me," said
Leonardo in retrospect, "while I lay in the cradle, as though a kite
had come down to me, opened my mouth with its tail, and struck
me with it several times between my lips." [1]

It was an age that held firmly to the belief in dreams and omens,
interpreting them as shadows which coming events cast before
them. The great philosopher of the day, Marsilio Ficino, inculcated a belief in dreams and in warnings from the dead: his own
mother, he said, foresaw in a daydream all the deaths and disasters
that came upon her family. Michelangelo, at the mere mention of
a dream which had come to one of Lorenzo de' Medici's lute-
players, fled from Florence to escape the storm gathering over the
heads of the Medici. Leonardo himself, for all his scepticism of the

3

supernatural, held fast to this childish memory, unable to make up his mind whether it was an actual experience or simply a dream. At a time when he was occupied with the boldest and most momentous plan he had dared to conceive in his whole lifetime, he recalled from his store of memories this picture of the great bird that had plunged down to the child in his cradle, and remarked, half in pride and half in resignation, "and this seems to be my destiny—*par che sia mio destino.*"

It may be that he held so fast throughout his life to this first childish recollection simply because, in the midst of commonplace realities, it seemed to promise escape and summons to a high destiny.

On his father's side Leonardo came from a world with narrow horizons, a world of stolid industry and thrift, firmly rooted in tradition and custom. His forefathers, as far back as could be remembered, had been lawyers and upright, respectable dignitaries of the village of Vinci, accounted its foremost citizens and bearing the name of the place. There is documentary evidence of the Vinci family as far back as the middle of the thirteenth century, and they had always been notaries and law officers of the Florentine republic, and had married into the families of legal colleagues. But with their faithfulness to the family profession they retained their close concern with the land; they liked to get away from their sober offices to the countryside, letting forms and documents lie idle while they planted olive trees and vines on their own farms. They clung to their land with the tenacity of peasants, and took every opportunity of adding to it here a field and there a vineyard: they invested half their liquid resources in the loan office at Florence and half in real estate, gradually buying land at various spots in Vinci. Being lawyers, they knew how to make profitable bargains, and knew also how to conceal their growing prosperity from the tax-gatherer. Whenever Leonardo's grandfather or father bought a piece of land with a cottage on it, he would enter the property in his taxation return as more or less dilapidated—a heap of ruins scarcely worth including in the return.

Leonardo's grandfather, Ser Antonio, had all this love of country life; he preferred the life of a farmer to his professional work, and spent more time on his fields than in his office. As a family closely bound together by their profession and their property, the Vinci lived under a single roof, father and mother and grown-up sons together, with the sons' wives and the children as they came. It was a simple, routine existence that they led in the roomy house with its big garden; like most of the people of their own station in life, they worked hard and had few wants; they liked ample, nourishing, uncomplicated food, avoided ostentation in dress, and economized on the pleasures of the moment for the sake of the morrow. They had the education appropriate to their profession, an education that did not allow them to degenerate into dilettantism: they might quote Dante on occasion, but their letters were plain, precise lawyers' letters for all that.

At times one of them would burst the bonds of this secure and ordered middle-class existence, but these were only rare happenings. There was Leonardo's uncle Francesco, who had no occupation and of whom all the taxation returns stated that he lived at home and did nothing: *stassi in villa e non fa nulla*. Leonardo's father, Ser Piero, was not of that sort. He had been in business since his twenty-first year. For a time he had been at Pisa; then his connexions with Florence grew steadily closer and more permanent. But neither his industry and pushfulness and ambition nor the steady middle-class traditions he had inherited prevented him from threatening, in the impulsiveness of his ardent youth, to throw all considerations of social standing to the winds, letting sentiment triumph over sense. At twenty-three he was already self-supporting, though still under family authority; but he was overflowing with vitality, with strong lustful senses (as he remained to the end of his life), and, at the very outset of his career, there came a brief adventure that clouded its respectability, an adventure with a simple peasant girl, with no family connexions and no dowry, a girl he could not possibly bring into his parents' house.

Leonardo came into the world as a love-child, or an unwanted one.

In the same year, 1452, Ser Piero was hurriedly married off by his family, to prevent any further follies; a girl of sixteen, of good family, Albiera di Giovanni Amadori, was to console him for the spoiling of his romance.

The girl Caterina, who bore to Ser Piero this healthy, fair-complexioned boy, was herself "of good blood"—*di buon sangue*—according to contemporary biographers, writing when Leonardo had become famous; but that was all they could tell of her origin and her obscure life. The blood was, at all events, not good enough for marriage with Ser Piero; some years later Leonardo's unwedded mother closed her short romance by marriage with a plain countryman of Vinci, Piero di Vacca di Accattabriga. Nevertheless, it was probably either that "good blood," or the exultant animal joy with which two young people in the prime of their vigour had come together, that brought to this family of lawyers, which went on producing notaries thereafter, the miracle of Leonardo's birth.

Long after this, when Leonardo was no longer among the living, and his career had become a legend of the purest radiance, his half-brother Bartolommeo, Ser Piero's youngest son, determined to make another test of the family's capacity to bring a creative genius into the world. He gathered every detail of the story of his father's association with the girl Caterina, and sought out from among the women of Vinci a daughter of the same robust and healthy stock; he induced in himself a feeling of passion for her, and prayed to God that the miracle might be repeated in the womb of his wife.

When she bore him a son he would have liked to call him Leonardo, but was prevented by his veneration for his half-brother; he called the boy after his and Leonardo's father. So great was his admiration for his famous brother, whom he had scarcely known in his life, and so ardent his ambition to give Leonardo a spiritual heir, that the boy, whose handsome features and light hair and lively character recalled those of Leonardo as a child, was infected with the same feelings, and with a love for art. Chance or some obscure working of heredity reinforced the influence of the Leonardo legend, and Pierino da Vinci became a sculptor of no mean quality. His short life, and the product of his epigonous gift, were like a last momentary flicker of glory on the dried-up Vinci stock.

About the time when Leonardo's mother Caterina was setting her own existence in order, Ser Piero brought his natural son into his parents' home. The young girl of good family whom he had married had remained childless, and the big house in which his ageing parents lived—his father was eighty-five and his mother seventy-four years old—had room and to spare for a merry, fair-haired, handsome child. At five years of age Leonardo counted already as one of the members of the family. The taxation return for 1457 for his grandfather's house, in the Santa Croce quarter, includes him as the natural son of Ser Piero—*figlio di Piero non legittimo*. In those days the taint of illegitimacy involved no injury to a boy's future. The success of illegitimate dynasties, the triumph of famous bastards seated on princely thrones, had gone far to destroy the significance of marriage formalities in this broadened fifteenth-century Italy, and only foreigners coming from a world of strict orthodoxy and adherence to tradition, like, for instance, the Frenchman Commines, still saw anything unusual in children born in and out of wedlock being brought up together in Italian families, treated exactly alike, and given the same opportunities in life.

The young stepmother, then scarcely twenty-one years old, readily accepted the beautiful and attractive child, and mothered him with all the care and understanding possible in a childless woman. Her family, too, were devoted to the boy, and up to his early manhood Leonardo was on terms of warm friendship with his stepmother's brother, Alessandro Amadori. His father's brother Francesco, the Uncle Francesco who lived at home and had nothing to do, was particularly fond of the boy, and continued to the end of his life to show his attachment to Leonardo and his preference for him over Ser Piero's legitimate children.

But the child was carefully kept away from his own mother. Leonardo's development was permanently influenced by the fact that he grew up as a motherless child, bereft of the primitive, irreplaceable tenderness and natural warmth of mother love. The child must have had an obscure intuition, too, that, unreservedly as he had been admitted in all external respects into the middle-class environment of the family, in some way he nevertheless was not one of them. This incomplete acceptance, this sense of admittance only with reservations, coloured Leonardo's whole personal development and outlook on life. From early childhood the boy was thrown back upon himself; he had lost the happiness and the tyranny of mother love, and gained unfettered liberty to reap impressions from the world around him.

The first deep impression was made on him by the landscape amid which he had come into the world. The little town of Vinci seems to cling to the slopes of Monte Albano; its houses, grouped on a spur of the mountain, as on a levelled socle, are dominated by the castle with its campanile. The gaze may wander freely far into the distance. The slopes of Monte Albano descend, spur after spur, into the valley, and seem powdered with silver when the wind stirs the leaves of the olive trees. Beyond is the rich green valley of Lucca, flecked by the brightness of saplings like little points of flame; between the trees the white houses gleam cheerfully. On the other side the Albano range towers up, a mysterious but attractive and tempting mountain world. Between the crags mountain streams rush down, carrying with them sharp stones which are slowly ground away as they roll and rub down stream, ultimately to form the pebbly bed of rivers that have grown sluggish.

Many years later, when Leonardo was engaged on the problem of the formation of rivers, his thoughts went back to the mountain stream by his home, of which he had retained a vivid memory, and in the midst of his theoretical argument he wrote the name of his birthplace—and then struck it out, as though he wanted to avoid anything too personal.[2]

In this period of his early youth the boy acquired a community with nature which helped to compensate him for the lack of intimate human relationships. Like all youthful emotions and enthusiasms, Leonardo's love of nature was of the engrossing sort that shut out all other interests; he tried to escape from everything that interfered with it. For the sake of his journeyings through the countryside he neglected the little schooling that was to be had at Vinci. He had learnt to read and write, had been taught the elements of mathematics, and had gained a very rudimentary notion of Latin, but his curiosity did not extend beyond the elements he was made to acquire. His father was away more and more on business in Florence, and there was no one to urge the boy to show more industry. Leonardo was to suffer throughout his life from the defective educational grounding of these early years. The immense store of knowledge he accumulated later was self-taught, and he had painfully to acquire first elements at a time when he was concerned with final results. All his life he was to regret his lack of a formal education.

But the boy growing up at Vinci did not know what he was losing when he neglected his wearisome and unintelligible school books for the sake of direct observation and experience, of the independent research which became the dominant passion of his life. Leonardo climbed up the slopes of Monte Albano between precipitous rocks that threw deep shadows on the slippery mountain tracks. Cliffs of strange shapes standing out from the undergrowth tempted the wanderer, when he had tired of climbing, further and further into their jagged labyrinth. One day he was brought to a stop by the dark and yawning entrance of a cave. No human voice broke the breathless stillness, no sound came of distant shuffling footsteps; the silence came suddenly upon the boy like an enemy. But stronger than the desire for flight, more overpowering than the dread of some undefined peril, was his eagerness to probe the secret of this cavern, of whose existence he had never heard, and into which no one had gone before him. He had to bend his tall frame to slip through the overhanging rocks. Scarring his hand as he groped, he felt his way between the dank walls. He had to shade his light-drenched eyes and to close them to narrow slits before he could get used to the darkness. But a strong impulse urged him on, in spite of the uneasiness that crept over him and of his physical tiredness. "Drawn by my eager desire to see the mighty [strata] of strange and manifold shapes that creative nature has produced, I ventured among the gloomy rocks." The impenetrable darkness of the cave was like a curtain that shut him out from view of a strange spectacle; he bent one way and the other in order to gain glimpses of vague outlines within it, and his gaze sought ardently, painfully, to pierce the darkness. "And after I had remained there awhile, suddenly two emotions arose in me, fear and desire: fear of the threatening dark cavern, desire to see whether there were any marvellous thing within." [3] It was the young Leonardo who told of this experience, explaining himself in the dramatizing style of his early years. "Like an eddying wind," he wrote, "that sweeps along a sandy, sinuous valley, and in its swift course catches up everything that it meets into its centre ... Not otherwise does the north wind rage in its tempestuous progress ... nor Stromboli nor Mount Etna, when the sulphurous flames rend asunder the great mountains, which fulminate stones and earth through the air with the vomited fire. . . ." He knew his own nature to this extent, that he recognized the search for knowledge as his overmastering passion, a passion akin to the north wind and the volcano, which overcome and devour all that stands in their way. He was tormented by so many enigmas, beset by so many questions to which he could give no answer! What was the explanation of these shells, far from the ocean, in the lower stratum of rock—had Earth "plunged beneath the ocean in indignation"? [4] How had the vestiges of a mighty monster come into one of the caves he explored, caught there in the stone and with its bare bones helping to form the framework of the mountain? [5]

There must be men and books that could satisfy his desire to solve the astonishing problem—and at the thought he became unsettled; he was no longer content with the pettier interests that had filled his mind in the past. And his studies aroused in him the desire to create. His first sketches were made on his journeys in order to record memorable things for his own pleasure. He sketched everything of note that he came upon, striking species of flowers, strangely formed rocks, and peculiar animals. He had suddenly discovered the joy of portrayal, felt the strong impulse to capture things seen. The others took it merely for a boy's pastime, but he had found his life's path.

From an early age he permitted none of the family to enter his room; he used to shut himself up in it, entrenching himself behind a mystery—a foible that remained with him throughout his life. In this room the strange produce of his journeys lay scattered about; the high odour of animals he had caught and the stench of dried and decaying fish and larvæ mingled with the heavy scent of fading flowers.

To these early years must belong the anecdote told later in Florence in proof of Leonardo's precocity; Vasari gives it at length. One day a peasant brought Leonardo's father a round panel which he had carved out of a felled fig tree, and asked him to have a picture painted on it by some artist in Florence. The peasant had often been useful to Ser Piero; no other was so skilled in trapping game or catching fish to provide for the notary's big family, and accordingly Ser Piero readily agreed to do what he wanted. The panel lay about in the house, however, for some time, until the wood began to warp and the poorly carved surface grew rough. It was in this state when it came into Leonardo's hands. He had an admiration for beautiful material, for gleaming surfaces and finely grained wood, and he began to prepare the board, damping it and bending it straight under heat, polishing and priming it, until it had a perfectly smooth surface to take the colours.

At this stage Ser Piero invited his son to try his new accomplishment on this board. He may have done so in jest, and there must have been some roughness in the jesting, and a scornful hint of doubt of the boy's skill, to give Leonardo the idea of providing the panel with a design that should change his father's mood. He went morosely to work on his task. He brought home from his wanderings every strange creature he found, lizards and snakes, crickets and butterflies, bats and grasshoppers, and watched for the most startling element in each, the element best calculated to arouse horror and disgust. It was a strange occupation for a youngster, almost a sort of vengeance wreaked on his fellow-creatures. He painted on the panel the dank obscurity of the cave that had struck terror into him; and, emerging from the darkness, a mythical monster with fiery red eyes, frightful wide-open jaws vomiting flame, and distended nostrils emitting poisonous fumes. The world around him was forgotten while he worked at his symbol of horror, the choking smell of putrefaction filled the room and he hardly noticed it, while there rose around him all the dark dreams of his youth, all the real and imagined sufferings and all the nightmares of his childhood, to guide his brush.

The peasant had forgotten his panel and Ser Piero his jesting challenge when Leonardo, suppressing a smile of triumph, asked his father to come to his room. With the sure instinct for effect which he had had from childhood, the boy had half covered the window and had so placed the easel that the painted circle was all that was fully lit. It had its effect. Ser Piero had no time to recall his commissioned panel; he imagined that he saw the fire-belching monster itself leaping at him, and he made precipitately for the

door. There stood Leonardo with his arms stretched out, an enigmatic smile flickering at the corners of his mouth; with a composure and a depth of meaning beyond his years, he said: "Well, I
see that the work has achieved its purpose."

On recovering from the shock, Ser Piero regained his innate
business sense. He quietly took the grotesque to Florence, bought
there a garish wood panel showing a heart pierced by an arrow,
which delighted the peasant, and sold his son's work—sold it,
without the knowledge of the young artist, for ten ducats to a
Florentine art-dealer, who did well out of it himself, since he
passed it on to the neurotic duke of Milan for three hundred
ducats.

Leonardo must have thought of this macabre experience of his
youth when, many years later, in his *Treatise on Painting,* he gave
these directions for the representation of a dragon: "Take the
head of a mastiff or a setter, the eyes of a cat, the ears of a porcupine, the nose of a greyhound, the eyebrows of a lion, the temples
of an old cock, and the neck of a turtle." [6]

2

His commercial success with his son's work induced Ser Piero to
give up the idea of putting him to the family profession, and to
send him to study with a painter. He first took the precaution of
surreptitiously submitting some of Leonardo's sketches to Andrea
del Verrocchio, and the master's enthusiasm confirmed him in his
decision. It fitted in conveniently with the plans Ser Piero was
then considering. His first wife, who had taken the place of a
mother to Leonardo, had died a year or two before, and as Ser
Piero was unable to bear single blessedness for long he married
again in 1465. His new wife, Francesca Lanfredini, hardly more
than a child, was again of good birth, and, following the family
tradition, a notary's daughter.

But Ser Piero was not only full of animal energy; he was ambitious to extend his business activities beyond his modest provincial
connexion. Latterly he had been called in more and more fre-

quently to prepare notarial documents for the Badia (abbey) at
Florence, and he hoped now to be able to find full occupation in
the city. To minimize his risk he went into partnership with a
notary of Florence, and in October 1468 he rented an office from
the Badia on advantageous terms—*una bottega con fondachetto,*
"a shop with a little vault," suitable for the work of a notary, cen-
trally situated opposite the Bargello, the palace of the Podestà or
chief magistrate.

So Leonardo, now sixteen, came to Florence. To the boy the
city seemed bewildering with its abundance of surging life. It was
a rich city, then at the height of its prosperity, and a city in which
wealth and the consciousness of power were everywhere in evidence. The merchants of Florence had spread the network of their
commerce over the whole world; they had placed agents in every
important city, in palaces of their own with private chapels; they
imported materials in their own ships and sent their wares to the
farthest ends of the earth. They had undermined the almost legendary power of the Venetian community and had challenged the
primacy of Venetian trade in the Orient.

At this time, around 1470, a man who later became a friend
of Leonardo, and to whom he sent humorous letters, Benedetto
Dei, was describing to the Venetians the power and magnificence
of Florence. Dei had travelled in many countries and had the wildest tales to tell of his experiences; now he had discovered the
charm of his native city. "We have two trades," he told the Venetians, "which are wealthier and more extensive than the four
trades of Venice—woollens and silks. The court of Rome is a cus-
tomer of ours, and the Sultan, and the king of Spain, and the king
of Naples. Constantinople and Pera, Brusa and Adrianople, Salo-
nica and Gallipoli, Chios and Rhodes, take more silkstuffs and gold
and silver brocades from us than they do from Venice, Genoa, and
Lucca together." Benedetto Dei was going about the streets of his
native city at about the time when Leonardo first made its acquaintance; Dei counted its enterprises: the woollen guild had 270
booths within the precincts of the city, the silk weavers 83 splendid shops, and the bankers 33 *palazzi;* and this, he added with
pride, by no means exhausted the tale of the city's activities. In 54
workshops the stone masons and marble-workers plied their mal-

lets, in 84 booths the cabinet-makers fitted together the famous in-
tarsia work of inlaid coloured wood—and what gleaming and glittering there was in the 44 jewellers' shops, crowded with buyers
from all countries!

Leonardo, used to the solitude of the open country, watched
wide-eyed as the stream of humanity flowed past him—for "in
Florence," as Villani wrote, "it may be said every day that there is
a fair on." He saw buyers from the East, majestic in their raiment
of many colours, handling the cascades of glittering brocade, or
the bales of soft cloth made by Florentine weavers from English
wool, and given by the dyers the unsurpassable peach shade, or a
rich scarlet or dark violet. He saw also the beautiful women of the
city, slender and young-looking, carrying their heads high like
precious flowers; they bargained with the jewellers over the price
of rings and brooches, and bought from the gold- and silver-chasers
the delicate garlands, from which Ghirlandaio takes his name, for
their fair or bright brown hair. The shops had customers also of
another sort; they were crowded with devotees from all the world,
buying ex-votos from the goldsmiths and silversmiths for saints of
whom they had a special favour to ask or to whom they wanted to
show their gratitude.

The city with its busy craftsmen and traders was fed by the
countryside from far around, like a vast and insatiable belly; it
drew its flour and meat, its wine and oil, its vegetables and fruit
and cheese, from 30,000 farms—so Benedetto Dei calculated—to
which it paid out 900,000 ducats in ready money in the year; and
a ducat, the Florentine ducat, officially weighed and measured, had
a metallic content worth approximately a dollar and a half, and
the purchasing power of about ten dollars. The carts coming in
from the countryside, laden with vegetables or wood or hay, rolled
heavily through the city. The slaughtered cattle were unloaded
outside the butchers' shops, of which there were 70; game and
fowl were piled up on the market stalls. The peasants who brought
the Florentines their food fortified themselves with the sparkling
white wine from San Giovanni, wine that, in Dei's phrase, "could
wake the dead," and they filled the streets with their cheerful
bawling.

Every member of a guild, every merchant, every artisan, and

every hired man had his share in this wealth that poured into Florence. And it was a wealth that sought to express itself in externals and had already changed the face of the city. As he wandered through the streets of Florence, Leonardo had before him the triumph of the new art in all its splendour. Brunelleschi's cupola had already crowned the cathedral for more than thirty years past, piercing the clear, deep blue sky as a feature of the city; but the lantern had only recently been completed. Building was still in progress on the vast plan for San Lorenzo; the spacious pillared hall of the Innocenti had been completed some time before, as had the cloisters and the Pazzi chapel in Santa Croce; but Santa Annunziata was only in process of building, and the façade of Santa Maria Novella, designed by Alberti, was still in scaffolding. The Palazzo Medici had been completed barely ten years earlier, with the splendid rustication in its surface, finer and more delicate in its granulation the higher it went. The Palazzo Rucellai, with its perfect accord of hewn surfaces and pilasters, was only a few years old; the architects were still busy with the enormous Palazzo Pitti, and were just completing its court.

But if much was still unfinished, the new architecture had already taken possession of Florence. In the sharp contrasting of brightness and shadow, in the emphasis on profiles, and in the full exploitation of sun-wreathed pillars in the clear Florentine light, art was at home, as though that crystal-clear atmosphere, *aero cristallino,* the pride of all Florentines, stood in intimate relationship to the new sense of space.

The architectural style of the period was the outcome of the discovery of the classic art of the ancients, but the rebirth of the classic style had produced not so much a completely new feeling for art as a liberation of native elements whose organic development had been interrupted by the invasion of the alien Gothic style from the north. The men of that day imagined, however, that they were merely emulating a mighty past, as heirs to a noble cultural heritage. The humanism that was intellectually revolutionizing the century had not yet become common property; at the time it had the effect of segregating the social strata and dividing men intellectually from one another. In democratic Florence, living in her magnificent present, humanism limited the growth of civic consciousness more than it did in kingdoms and principalities, and its cultivation by the Medici prepared the way for their seizure of autocratic power. The intellectual élite was backward-looking, engrossed in a distant past, and remote from contemporary events and from realities.

The patricians of Florence, in their sober raiment, discussing together in the piazze and at the crossroads or on the stone seats in front of the churches, with the quick gestures of their expressive hands and their dogmatic forefingers, would grow heated over the relative merits of classical authors, or engage in furious controversy over the spelling of a word, or would fight over the interpretation of a line or verse with the blood mounting to their intolerant heads. When they threw the folds of their cloaks over their shoulders they imagined themselves to be draped in Roman togas; if they mentioned Cato or Cincinnatus, Mucius or Cicero, they seemed to be speaking of their forefathers; they reeled off classical quotations, and liked to refer to themselves as "we Latins."

The educated class shut itself off with pitiless arrogance from any contact with the life of the mass of the people. Humanism was a tyrannical intellectual discipline, monopolizing a man's thoughts; it called for concentration on classical studies from his earliest youth, confining his interests to a single field; and it presupposed his possession of the means of existence during the period of his studies. A handful of scholars, largely poor clergy who owed their success to immense industry backed by the favour of a patron, had the monopoly of knowledge; it was imparted under less rigorous conditions only to the patrician children, the sons and daughters of the rich. As Alberti said: "A nobleman by birth who is without education—*sanza lectere*—is reputed no more than a peasant."

In virtue of his descent and of the prestige of his father's profession, Leonardo belonged to the social stratum from which the intellectual élite was drawn; but his poor Latin and his unfamiliarity with the classical authors shut him out from a society which often used Latin for ordinary conversation and considered it necessary to be able to make great play with classical quotations. Moreover, in spite of the lively appreciation of art in Florentine society, the profession he had chosen stood only on the fringe of the respectable middle-class world. At the time of Leonardo's apprenticeship, the fine arts had not yet been entirely weaned from the handicrafts. Many of the painters and sculptors of the time—Ghirlandaio, Pollaiuolo, Botticelli, and Verrocchio among them—had worked in the goldsmith's craft, and many of them had been so intimately associated with their old masters in the art of chasing that they had allowed their own bourgeois names to be sacrificed, making famous instead the name of some respectable goldsmith. It was in Leonardo's own generation that the transfer of the creative artists to a higher social stratum took place. The older painters among whom he moved could tell of many a humiliation: they were addressed with a condescending "thou" by their patrons, and were given a monthly payment that often was scarcely a lackey's wage. The brothers Ghirlandaio were given the scraps from the table at the monastery of Passignano. Art was as yet no profession for sons of good families. Michelangelo's vainglorious, narrow-minded father, who was to be a burden on him throughout his life, was wild with anger when his son entered Ghirlandaio's studio, and was not mollified even by the patronage of Lorenzo de' Medici. A full generation later, at the outset of the sixteenth century, when the fame of Leonardo, Michelangelo, and Raphael had spread all over Europe, Baldassare Castiglione wrote in his *Cortegiano* that the complete courtier should try his skill in art, but that the artist's profession was not a fit one for a nobleman. When Leonardo had reached the summit of his fame he still complained of this belittlement of art by his contemporaries: "You have set painting among the mechanical arts."

Unlike the humanists, whose minds dwelt entirely in a distant past—fruitful though the treasure they unearthed might be for their own day—the artists proceeded from the very heart of contemporary life. The great event in the art of this period was the discovery of reality. From the moment when art was liberated from its subjection to religious ideas, and was no longer merely a means of expression of religious devotion, it had taken thought for its own independent existence. It owed its liberation to humanism, but, in the main, indirectly. The humanism of this age had not yet disturbed the sources of belief; on the contrary, it had been engaged in the effort to harmonize the paganism of the ancients with the Christian faith, and in Florence itself there lived a man, Marsilio Ficino, who had made it his life's task to reconcile Plato with Jesus Christ. But humanism had broken the fetters of the medieval idea of art and had given the fine arts an independent justification for existence.

After this first revolution, however, humanism and creative art had parted ways for the time being. The humanists had given to the artists of their day as models the ancient gods they had disinterred, as they had commended to the architects for imitation the ruins of classic temples and triumphal arches. Artists and architects alike were mainly interested in copying antique types of ornament from the ancient world; but while the architects found their own feeling for space confirmed, the artists realized for the first time when the figures of the gods were brought up out of the earth that these were representations of living human beings, three-dimensional creatures with both feet firmly planted on the ground.

Within a surprisingly short time the knowledge of the human figure came from all sorts of sources to the artists who were painting or carving in Florence. In their enthusiasm as innovators they went so far as to deny all merit to their predecessors; they rejected the subordination of detail to the general effect, the mutual dependence of forms, and even the monumental construction of their immediate forerunner and teacher Masaccio, because he stood in the way of their fanatical realism. This art, so deeply rooted in reality, was the product of contemporary life; it was helped by the new civic consciousness of the people of Florence, whose prosperity enabled them to see their brief earthly pilgrimage immortalized in marble or bronze, panel or fresco.

The art of this early Florentine period was an apotheosis of everyday life. The saints concealed behind the flicker of the altar candles were artisans or shopkeepers from the neighbourhood; the Madonnas bending over their chubby-faced children displayed the mother's pride of young Florentine women; the angels or young Biblical heroes were youths who stripped off their fashionable clothes when they were brought into the studio and given David's sling. The bearded prophets sat in the Grand Council of Florence; the little *amoretti* played in the streets. The scene of some episode from the lives of the saints would be the Florentine parlour of the day, with its new sense of space, its new furniture, its modern household utensils: all brightened up for the occasion, since visitors were coming, but a room that could be put to everyday uses in any age. In this homage to the ruling bourgeoisie everyone took part, the guild of craftsmen that ordered statues or altarpieces, the curly-haired boy who posed for model, or the rich merchant who had his portrait painted as a donor to some pious foundation, or as one of the Three Wise Men from the East, or as a worshipper at the manger, or as a spectator at the Crucifixion.

3

The master with whom Leonardo was placed as apprentice was a thoroughly typical product of his time. His name was Andrea di Michele di Francesco de' Cioni, but he had adopted the name of his instructor, the goldsmith Verrocchio; and he was an embodiment of the transition from craftsmanship to art, from sound workmanship to deliberate creative activity, from contentment with mastery of material to the new intellectual unrest. His square head, with its broad, domed brow, its flabby cheeks, its coarse and prominent nose, and its complacent double chin, was seated firmly on his strong shoulders. It might equally well have been the head of a Florentine woollen manufacturer, or a Florentine banker. The eyes were clear and sharp, slanting a little and with raised wondering eyebrows; unlike the suggestion of satiety in the face, the eyes had a look of covetous, unsatisfied watching. The thin, hard mouth, parting the fat surfaces of the face with a narrow slit that might have been made by a knife, seemed to lock up the unrest revealed by the eyes, as if it were a secret. According to his contemporaries, Andrea del Verrocchio was "one of the most highly esteemed instructors in every branch of the arts." He was a tireless worker; he had mastered every method of representation and was skilled in the use of every material. His firm hands, the patient hands of a gold-chaser, were ceaselessly creating with brush or mallet, palette knife or file. "Andrea was never unoccupied," writes Vasari, "he was always at work on some sculpture or painting; he went frequently from one work to another, so as not to become stale through devoting too much time to any one task."

Industry and perseverance, an ardent and honest endeavour to secure a mastery of form—such was the atmosphere Leonardo found in Verrocchio's studio. He had as fellow-pupil a young man six years his senior, Pietro Perugino, who laboured with the pertinacity of a peasant. Perugino had endured severe privations in order to become an artist. For a time he had done without a bed and had contented himself with a hard wooden chest to lie on, in order to get together the money to pay for his training. He had undertaken any sort of menial labour and put up with any hardship in his determination to fight his way through to success; and in the end his pluck had its reward. Perugino had the simple wants of the man who has made his way in life, and he took in no useless ballast: he was not troubled by his lack of education, for he was out not to write properly spelt letters, but to paint pictures that could attract a buyer. Nor could he be tempted to take an interest in other branches of art: he had set out to get his living as a painter, and he had no other ambition. When he had equipped himself for that, he made his way to middle-class comfort and prosperity, quite content with what he had achieved, and rather proud of it.

Leonardo found among all his fellow-pupils the same industry combined with the same limited outlook—the same ambition to acquire just as much skill as would bring in good earnings. Lorenzo di Credi, who was seven years younger than Leonardo, was satisfied with learning whatever came easily, and made up for lack of artistic temperament by facility in acquiring a superficial grasp of anything and everything. Now and again he would devote himself entirely to the imitation of other artists, so far as his limited intelligence permitted; Leonardo loomed over him for a time like a gigantic shadow, and Lorenzo assimilated his comrade's method of painting so well that, as Vasari says, it was impossible to distinguish his copies from the originals.

In this world of easy-going contentment with small things, Leonardo found that he and his master were alike engaged in the endeavour to explore new realms of knowledge. Verrocchio was the older of the two by seventeen years, but there was no difference of generation between them, as Michelangelo later imagined that there had been between himself and his teacher, Ghirlandaio. At the time when Leonardo entered Verrocchio's studio the big commissions that were to pave the way to fame for the older man had not yet begun to come in; Verrocchio was still testing his own powers, applying his proved abilities as a craftsman to the solution of new problems. A theoretical knowledge of the human form and of perspective was becoming essential for the painter and the sculptor, who had often begun work in the studio as little more than children, with little or no formal education. In the early period of Florentine art the laws of perspective were in the forefront of the problems exercising the minds of artists. The old painter Paolo Uccello had found them a fascinating study from which he could not tear himself. His wife would summon him crossly, late at night, from his desk, and he would sigh ecstatically as he got up: "Really, perspective is delightful!" It was the Italian painters, not the mathematicians, who pushed ahead with the study of the laws of three-dimensional space, just as it was they and not the anatomists who started experimental research into the structure of the human body.

Determined at all costs to force himself to master things that seemed beyond his grasp—for, says Vasari, his industry was greater than his natural gifts—Verrocchio had thrown himself into the study of geometry. Leonardo's innate thirst for knowledge was redoubled by the infection of his master's zeal. He felt now how much he had lost through neglecting his schooling. He procured mathematical textbooks, and sought help in his difficulties from the mathematicians he knew. For many years, even when the time came for him to warn his readers that his works were intelligible only to mathematicians, he turned to friends for help with mathematical problems—"Let Maestro Luca show you how to multiply roots." [7] It was in the very rudiments that he felt the want of a grounding to the end of his life, and when he was wrestling with some difficult problem his calculations would be upset by a mistake in dealing, perhaps, with fractions.

During this early period in Florence, Leonardo came into touch with the most prominent scholar of the time, Benedetto Aritmetico, a man busy with practical affairs, interested in industry and

commerce, and probably the one who directed the young Leonardo's attention to engineering problems and to the needs of the
industries of their day. Leonardo began very early to busy himself
with machinery. He began to make labour-saving tools of his own
invention. He designed machines for turning and grinding, and
pondered over the association of parts and the engaging of joints.
Thus he was brought up against general problems such as that of
the transmission of power, or the strength of materials; he tried to
solve them at first by the laborious method of practical tests, until
at last he would arrive at a design of which he could remark lacon-
ically: "This is simple and good. Better." [8]

The young Leonardo became more and more acutely aware of
his inadequate knowledge of the principles of physics, and he was
led once more to the classic sources, discovering the natural history
of the humanists—a thinly trickling tributary of the main stream of
their culture. He borrowed books from acquaintances, translations
of scientific works into the vernacular, or from Greek into Latin,
through which he would struggle painfully. One of the representatives of the classical school of natural history, which disseminated
the teachings of Aristotle and had become involved in a fanatical
rivalry, a sort of war of religion, with the much more influential
Neoplatonic school, was teaching then at the Studium Generale of
Florence—the Greek John Argyropoulos. He had come to Florence after the fall of Constantinople, and lectured there on the
"natural philosophy" of Aristotle, until he left for Rome at the
end of 1471. He had translated Aristotle's *Physics* and *De Cœlo*.
Leonardo attended these lectures—the Greek scholar's name occurs among his notes of the time. But the man who exerted the decisive influence over Leonardo (who was still little more than a
boy) was Paolo del Pozzo Toscanelli, physician and philosopher,
investigator of natural phenomena and mathematician. Old Toscanelli was much in men's mouths in the impressionable but vola-
tile Florence of this time: in 1468 he had traced in the cathedral
the famous meridian line which was to serve for determining the
dates of the movable feasts of the Church. The old man liked
plenty of company, and sought out travellers and adventurers from
distant parts of the earth: he would extract from their rodomon-
tades some crumb of truth. He was sparing of words himself; only

now and then his tired old eyes, which had been poring for so long over books and maps, would sparkle youthfully, and he would begin to speak, with the pregnancy of the man of few words—"and he spoke always of strange things," says Vasari.

Toscanelli never left his native city. But in front of him in his study there stood a globe showing countries still unexplored, and oceans not yet traversed, and strange races of mankind. From the confusing mass of fantastic reports that reached him, and from his measurements, made with inadequate resources, he drew with more and more certainty the conclusion that it must be possible to reach India by a westward route. He could no longer search for that passage himself, but he wanted to see it found by bolder and younger men, and he gave them maps and advice. When Columbus began to dream of the untraversed sea route to India, the Florentine physician sent a chart of the ocean to him at Lisbon; in it he had lovingly set down all his little fragments of knowledge. Ten years after Toscanelli's death, in the midst of the sinister solitude of the ocean, Columbus bent over this map and compared the indications the old man had given him with the new world, with its unsolved riddles, which was rising on the horizon.

Leonardo's talks with Toscanelli awoke in him a longing to see distant countries with their strange peoples and curious customs, and later he was to try, like old Toscanelli, to construct maps to give definition to his dreams of lands no man had seen and routes by which no man had ventured, filling in the fragmentary picture of the earth with clear outlines and variously tinted spaces.

Leonardo learned also of the appearance and disappearance of lands, of changes effected in the course of ages in the earth's surface; and now he understood that centuries had passed since the bones of the mysterious monster in the cave he had explored at Vinci were bleached. This experience of his childhood came back vividly to him, and he wrote in the enthusiastic style of his youth: "How many kings, how many peoples, how many changes of states and various events have happened since the wondrous form of this fish came to its end in the dark recess of that cave. . . . Now, destroyed by time, you lie patiently in this confined space, with your bones stripped and bare; serving as a framework and support for the superimposed mountain." [9]

Toscanelli turned the young Leonardo's gaze also to the skies, explaining to him the nature of the heavenly bodies, as he and his age understood them, and the iron laws that govern the mechanism of the universe. Leonardo looked up to the heavens, overpowered, as though in mystical adoration. He would watch the clouds piling up in a storm and the lightning that tore down "with rapid quiverings of its wings and coiled tail," amazed at the workings of a mysterious force: "O mighty and once living instrument of formative nature, unable to avail yourself of your vast strength you have to abandon a life of stillness and to obey the law which God and time gave to procreative nature." [9]

Filled with the sense of the new knowledge that was being revealed to him, Leonardo set out to attempt measurements himself, and to observe the positions of the stars; but he had not the means with which to procure the needed apparatus. The scientific instruments of the time were thoroughly primitive, showing scarcely any advance beyond the level reached by the ancients. There was the astrolabe, the "star-taker," used by Columbus on his great voyage of discovery, a round copper plate with a rotating pointer, which required three men for its manipulation: one to hold it, one to set it, and a third to read off the results; there was a ring adjusted to the equator which could be made by the addition of other rings into a model of the celestial sphere; there was the cross-staff, with its movable short arm fitted to the measuring-stick, for measuring angles; the quadrant, fixed to the wall, and directed through a movable sight to the object to be observed; and the dioptra, with cogwheel, ratchet, and elevator, and a measuring-plate from which differences of level could be read off—almost in the same form in which it was used by Hero of Alexandria.

These instruments were also rare and costly, for they made up for what they lacked in scientific precision by their elaborate decoration, with a wealth of reliefs and ornamental chasing. Thus young Leonardo had to borrow from his friends not only books but apparatus. There is a note made by him that he was able to borrow a quadrant from a certain Carlo Marmocchi, an astronomer and mathematician of no particular note. Leonardo also made instruments for himself, including those for time measurements in his own experiments: he made a water-clock, of which he said that it would be of special service on a journey, and another timepiece, with a lead weight, which worked by means of compressed air. He notes on his sketches: "There is no lack of ways and means of dividing and measuring these wretched days of ours, which we should try not to live in vain and squander without leaving any fame, any lasting memory of us in the minds of mortals. So that our poor passage through life shall not be in vain." [10] Here was a very young man philosophizing over life and death, with a seriousness in which a borrowed pessimism was combined with youthful dreams of fame and aspirations for achievement. This ambition to leave a lasting memory of his activities on earth lived in the young Leonardo side by side with his keen interest in research for its own sake. These two motives pulled him to and fro, now one dominating and now the other, and he made feverish efforts to make up for lost time.

4

His work in Verrocchio's studio brought him frequently into touch with a world of wealth and rank, which impressed him at first with its splendour, but gradually became a matter of course. Soon after settling in Florence, while still dazzled by the multitude of new impressions and experiences the city brought him, he met for the first time the man who incorporated in himself the pride and ambition of this city, its intellectual activity and its appreciation of art, its calculating business sense and its joy in life— Lorenzo de' Medici. The bank of the Medici was the outward and visible sign of the economic power of Florence, which had been built up by the mass of the people in their independent individual enterprises. It negotiated with the envoys of legitimate and illegitimate princes, bolstered up emperors and kings, swayed the issue of wars, helped new states into the world, granted or refused loans of crucial importance to every ambitious adventurer out to conquer a new empire by force of arms. The heir to this power, Lorenzo de' Medici, son of Piero the Gouty, had inherited with it the forceful temperament of his mother and the shrewdness and the insight into human nature of his grandfather, old Cosimo.

The year 1468 had been darkened by the war with the Venetian condottiere Colleoni and by an epidemic of plague in Florence; Lorenzo followed the conclusion of peace with a great tourney, in order to disperse the depression and discontent that filled the city. Verrocchio's studio was kept busy with preparations for the festival; standards were painted, costumes designed. On the day of the festivities Verrocchio's pupils were among the watching crowds in the piazza of Santa Croce. The procession was heralded by the cheerful blare of trumpets; a red and white banner waved in the sharp wind; the sound of the hoofs of heavily laden horses announced the approach of foreign knights in full armour of shining steel. After them came noblemen in their gayest costumes, heirs of the oldest Florentine families, whose names the crowd whispered to one another with respectfully possessive familiarity. Behind the knights and noblemen came a solitary horseman, a slender youth with a sharp-featured, amber-coloured face and silky black hair—Piero's younger son Giuliano de' Medici. He had the prominent eagle nose of his grandfather, narrow, contemptuous lips, and the dreamy look of a poet or lover, a look that destroyed the energy of the boy's features. This youth, of Leonardo's own age or even younger, was enveloped entirely in silver, like a relic on some shrine, as he rode past, his proud head thrown back under the burden of his shining hair; his silk stomacher was embroidered with pearls and silver, and the pale gold winter sunlight that poured over the piazza was caught in the woven gold of which the feathers of his velvet cap were made, and flamed up in the giant rubies that held together the velvet and gold.

"Eight thousand ducats has that suit cost," said the experts in the crowd, half in pride and half appalled.

Then came more trumpets and the roll of drums; the beating of the drums grew louder and faster, while the enthusiastic acclamations of the crowd surged round the elder brother Lorenzo as his horse ambled past with him. Lorenzo de' Medici, now twenty, seemed a squat, hunched-up figure on his high horse; his square head and short neck and straight hair accentuated his stocky, ungainly appearance. His embroidered cap threw shadows over his irregular features—the formidable nose, deeply indented between the sunken eyes, the big, fleshy mouth, and the strong square chin that transformed the ugliness of the face into power. His sallow complexion was made yet more ashy in appearance by contrast with the brightness of the red and white sash that crossed the young man's broad breast. His flag was also red and white; on it Verrocchio had painted the portrait of Lorenzo's mistress, Lucrezia dei Donati, weaving a wreath of laurel branches which were blossoming in her hands, under a rainbow on which there stood in golden letters the inscription: *"Le tems revient."* It was the first time that the young Leonardo had set eyes on the French motto— or the French lilies on Lorenzo's escutcheon, the gold lilies on a blue field on which his gaze was to rest in his dying hour.

The spectators packed in the Piazza Santa Croce declared excitedly to one another that the pearl in Lorenzo's cap alone cost five hundred ducats, and that the diamond sparkling on his shield, called Il Libro, was valued at two thousand ducats. After his victory in the tourney Lorenzo de' Medici, as a good business man and a true Florentine, noted in his diary that the occasion had cost him ten thousand gold florins, and it is evident that he regarded the money as usefully expended.

Leonardo was not a Florentine business man, and not a rising politician; he knew little about banking or about the influencing of public opinion. But it must have been his presence as a spectator at this festival in Florence, the first in his experience, that awoke in him the hunger for luxury, the love of fine clothing, of the undulation of the folds of brocade and the soft hang of velvet, of the proud stepping of horses, and of the haughty indifference which the great of this earth are able to assume as they go past the admiring crowd.

This feeling for luxury, born of his sense of beauty and existing alongside his innate personal abstemiousness, remained with Leonardo from then on, stimulating him in his efforts to secure recognition. But as yet he had no clear vision of the ways and means to this end; he was still in search of the best method of making his way. For the present he learned from Verrocchio everything that his master could teach him. He modelled in clay the chubby children and the smiling girls' heads, with the unconscious radiance of the spring of life, that were most to the taste of the Florentine citizens—vanished early works of which only the accounts of con-

temporaries remain. It was almost as if at times he forgot that he
had set out to become a painter. He was engrossed in everything
that went on in the studio. There was painting in tempera, and
there were cautious experiments with the new oil technique; there
was modelling in clay and gypsum and wax, carving and hammering, filing and soldering—and Leonardo was determined to miss
nothing of it all. When Verrocchio's assistants poured into its
mould the copper ball that was to be gilded and placed at the top
of the cathedral dome, and when Verrocchio, with the utmost care,
soldered the cross to the ball, so that it should resist every sort of
inclement weather, Leonardo took his full share of the manual
work; and he looked on when the ball was lifted, amidst wild
acclamations from the watching crowd, into its place above the
lantern of the Duomo. Half a century later, when engaged on a
difficult soldering experiment, he recalled this experience of his
prentice days: "Remember the soldering material with which the
palla of Santa Maria del Fiore was soldered." [11]

"But, since painting was the profession he intended to follow,
he devoted much of his studies to drawing from nature." So writes
Vasari of Leonardo's prentice years, not without an undertone of
criticism of the squandering of a unique gift on soldering and such
things. But Leonardo went steadily through every stage leading up
to the complete mastery of form. He laboriously painted the sharp
folds of cloths that had been stiffened with clay, as Verrocchio advised his pupils to do—a method which Leonardo roundly condemned later in his *Treatise on Painting*. He sketched the old
men with furrowed features whom Verrocchio employed as models. He copied the sketches that revealed Verrocchio's love of ornamentation, curiously wound plaits of hair on women's heads, elaborately decorated helmets and suits of armour with cocks' combs
that ended in the tendrils of plants, winged dragons, screaming
heads of Medusa, and roaring lions—all of them a legacy which
many years later he was to display almost intact.

But the young Leonardo did not confine himself to investigating and representing the human form: he had climbed every rocky
path around Vinci, he was familiar with woodlands in every season and at every time of day, and his gaze had closely followed the
undulating land and the moving clouds too often for him to be

content with the conventional scheme of mountain, tree, and water. "That painter," he declared later in his *Treatise,* "is not versatile who has not as much taste for one branch of painting as for another." During this early time, however, his fellow-painters objected that nature was only a foil for the human form. Botticelli maintained that it was a waste of time to study nature, since it was sufficient to throw a sponge filled with pretty shades of wet paint against a wall in order to produce the loveliest landscapes. Leonardo recalls this studio controversy of his youth in the *Treatise,* and adds the scathing comment: "and this painter painted wretched landscapes." [12]

The earliest extant sketch made by Leonardo in his youth is a pen-drawing in the Uffizi gallery in Florence which is carefully dated at the top—"Day of Saint Mary of the Snows, August 2, 1473." In this drawing Leonardo has captured with a feathering outline a bit of mountain landscape—a recollection of the loved scenes of his childhood. The wide stretch of valley that undulates away to the horizon between rocky cliffs, a spacious prospect, full of light and air, with not a human being to be seen, is the first landscape in the history of European art that dispenses entirely with any sort of narrative and exists simply for its own sake.

About the time when Leonardo drew this landscape he had reached his twenty-first year and the end of his period of training, and had already been for a year a member of the guild of painters. But while he had the courage for any innovation, he had not yet acquired either artistic or material independence. He was in such narrow circumstances that he was unable to find the money for his membership subscription to the guild, or even the small sum for the candles which every painter had to contribute to the feast of Saint Luke, the patron of the guild. His father, meanwhile, had successfully started as a notary in Florence; he occupied, for a rent of twenty-four florins a year, the greater part of the house in the Piazza Firenze, a few steps from his office. But, although Ser Piero's second marriage had remained childless, there seems to have been no room for his own son in his substantial dwelling, for Leonardo continued to live with Verrocchio after the completion of his training. He had been left to look after himself, and was entirely without means.

Messer Andrea was himself in financial straits. He had constantly to help his many relatives, and was forced to sell one after another of the properties he had inherited from his father. Before long he had to sell the family home because he could not pay his debts. He had remained a bachelor, and his widowed sister kept house for him; he had taken her to live with him with her three children. But though Verrocchio would complain of the burden of his big family and "a good deal of poverty," Leonardo found food and shelter at his home.

5

For an ambitious young man, who dreamed of leaving behind him a lasting trace of his earthly activities, this continued dependence after the completion of his prentice years, this position of anonymous assistant in his master's work, was not altogether satisfactory; but the manifold interests of life left him little time for considering these things, and for a while he seems to have been ready to content himself with the simple fact of being alive and active. Nature herself, by the profusion of gifts with which she launched him on an unending stream of work, might seem to have set out to prevent him from developing in the direction of any definite goal. The experimenting and searching for the best means of expression of an artistic temperament, the best employment of every sensed but untried power, which for a time cripples the efforts of every young man who feels that he is destined to greatness, was the more distracting for Leonardo, since when he tested the limits of his capacities he found them extending almost infinitely. Whatever he attempted he achieved without effort. His vision was as accurate as his touch was sure. He mastered the problems of representation with ease, and his quick intelligence penetrated with the same ease the most difficult paths in abstract knowledge. Anything he had once examined remained fixed for all time in his extraordinarily retentive memory.

And, as though a young man had not enough to do in coping with this wealth of intellectual gifts, he was given also a dangerous power over men, though as yet he was not quite sure what to do with it. The lovely pink-faced, curly-haired child had grown into a youth with the beauty of a young god. Not a single portrait remains of this period of his glory. The age was lavish in its records of every type of character; it transmitted to posterity numberless portraits of unknown citizens by mediocre artists, well-fed, cynical, uninteresting faces, lives with no high destiny; but it failed to transmit any lasting record of Leonardo's youthful charm. Only an old tradition couples his name with the picture of an archangel painted by a pupil of Verrocchio (at one time it was attributed to Botticelli); and Leonardo's one later self-portrait in Turin speaks for the credibility of the tradition. The young Leonardo lived in the memory of his contemporaries as an archangel clad in armour —tall, with narrow hips and broad shoulders, the lithe body erect, the head thrown back a little as though he wanted to capture the full sunlight. A broad, almost square forehead, with a cloud of gleaming auburn hair swept back from it; under the strong yoke of the eyebrows, big, lustrous eyes with a leaping, penetrating glance; a straight, masterful nose broadly and strongly constructed and with sensitive nostrils; a mouth that contradicted itself, the upper lip a firmly outlined, narrow bow above the rounded and full-blooded lower lip; and a square chin that gave to a face of too much beauty the stamp of the heroic. "It was the most beautiful face in the world," declared a contemporary historian, Paolo Giovio; and over that face there floated a smile that went out to all like a dispensation, forgiving the wickednesses of this world. "With the splendour of his mien he brought refreshment to every downcast spirit"—so Vasari was told by those who had known that smile, of which they preserved the memory as a priceless treasure.

Leonardo had not known much of human love in his early life; his childhood had passed in a fruitless longing for affection; now the sense of the influence that proceeded from him was intoxicating. His past deprivation was now made good by warm friendships which began suddenly to be of enormous significance in his life. Among his earliest sketches there appear again and again the names of young Florentines, each described as *compare*—"comrade"; and there is a fragment of a letter to an unknown youth, his "own dearest friend"—"*amantissimo quanto mio*." As though he could not have enough of success, of the enthusiasm that surrounded him, he exerted all his powers to captivate this circle of young men of his own age. He was left-handed, drawing and writing with his left hand, but able to use either arm equally well; and he had muscles of steel. He used to exhibit their strength. One of his young comrades told later how Leonardo would catch the reins of horses driven furiously past him. With his firm, slender hands he could bend horseshoes and door-knockers as though they were of lead. He would show his friends how a stout blade could be wrapped in handkerchiefs at two points and then broken like touchwood.

The carefree young fellows he gathered round him would go through the streets shouting in their exuberance:

Ciascun grida per godere
E muoia chi non vuol cantare.

"Each one shouts aloud for joy, And death to those who will not sing," as an early poet, Sacchetti, wrote. Above all the noise Leonardo's voice would emerge victoriously, "that voice of captivating timbre," as Giovio says, which those who heard it remembered ever after. He would accompany himself on instruments of his own making, instruments of specially rich tone, and made—since he was out not only to please but to amaze—in the queerest possible shapes, resembling the skull of some animal or the belly of a fish.

There was an element of frivolity in the life of the young Leonardo, entering even into his work, and sometimes upsetting all the seriousness of his scientific experiments. While he was preparing his colours, mixing some particularly vivid green or a flaming red, he would distil perfumes from orange blossom or jasmine, or mix scented water for the hands; among his sketches for foundry furnaces and grinding mills he would make notes of conjuring tricks he intended to show to his friends. In the evening he would put a saucer of boiling oil on the table, pour red wine on top, and enjoy the leaping iridescent flames.[13] He conscientiously prepared his surprises, with almost pedantic seriousness. He made notes of all sorts of tricks—how to drop three lire into a glass filled with water to the brim, without spilling a drop of the water; how a reed laid on top of two glasses filled with water can be broken without damaging the glasses—things calling for the steady hand and the sure eye of the born conjurer.

He noted down also the jokes and riddles he would pass on; he copied poems—and sometimes, when they were by unknown authors, he would take credit for them as improvisations of his own. One of these copied verses is the authentic utterance of any young man who is content with the simple joy of being on this earth:

> Let him who cannot do the thing he would
> Will to do that he can. To will is foolish
> Where there's no power to do. That man is wise
> Who, if he cannot, does not wish he could.

Leonardo, however, was engaged throughout his manhood in extending the limits of his powers; only during this short early period, when he was so full of enjoyment of the life he was living, did he accept this easy-going philosophy of contentment with modest aims.

The comrades who had intoxicated him with the sense of fellowship and association were young men of whom some, like himself, belonged to good families, and were living then on the fringe of society—handsome young men with plenty of time to waste, outdoing one another in extravagant notions, and working off on one another the love of a hoax which was so strong in Leonardo himself. In Leonardo's earliest sketches there appear again and again the same faces, half imaginary, half dreamily evoked from memory. They have the same pure Greek profile, the nose running straight on from the brow, the long curly hair sweeping past the gentle oval of the cheeks, a sensuous mouth, too small, with too short an upper lip, and an empty gaze from great round eyes.

One of his friends, Atalante Miglioretti, a few years older than Leonardo, was like him in being the illegitimate son of a respected Florentine notary. He had a particularly fine voice, and took lessons from Leonardo in lute-playing. He would use instruments of Leonardo's making, fitted with frets and possessing a volume of tone unaccustomed at the time. Another friend, Tomaso Masini, was the son of a gardener of Peretola, a village near Florence. Tomaso was an enterprising youth, dabbling a little in painting but devoting himself more thoroughly to the goldsmith's art; he had great mechanical aptitude. The young man liked to pose as a soothsayer. He felt that his family name was not imposing enough, and later assumed the name of Zoroastro da Peretola; he disowned his honest father and claimed to be the illegitimate son of Bernardo Rucellai, a relative of the Medici family. He was a long-legged youngster with a sharp, sallow face and a piercing glance from under the tangle of his black hair. He shared Leonardo's interest in juggling and conjuring and was a master of the art of hoaxing, which he developed in later years into swindling and extortion. Leonardo treated him as a butt; Tomaso put up with this with a good grace, since, for all his studied pose of fantasticalness, his practical sense was well enough developed to enable him to appreciate the advantages of his friendship with young men of good family.

Leonardo himself had a liking for human oddities, for the will-o'-the-wisps that hover on the fringes of established society, as though the mysteries of human nature of which he had but a vague conception had some sinister hold over him. It may be that he was the readier to yield to this passing allurement of the seamy side because he knew the strength of his own self-control, his sound mental and moral balance. He would give full vent to his high spirits in the company of young men of his own age, but in his own conduct he showed a sobriety and prudence beyond his years, as though a sure instinct held him back from any sort of over-indulgence or excess. It was an age in which strongly spiced stories passed from mouth to mouth, in which the coarsest songs were sung aloud in the streets by venerable guild members; but in his collection of anecdotes for the amusement of social gatherings Leonardo did not include a single one of doubtful taste. He was restrained by an innate revulsion from ever making play with erotic ideas. And in this city in which wine-bibbing was elevated, under the influence of the classic poets, to a cult of Bacchus, Leonardo avoided every drinking-party, in disgust at the fuddling effect of the fumes of alcohol, which "revenges itself on the drinker." [14]

He was equally moderate in eating; he lived mainly, and later in his life exclusively, on vegetables and fruit. He was no less careful in attention to externals, maintaining the utmost personal cleanliness and neatness. As a young man he once broke off from his eager labours, after he had been handling tools, in order to note down the way to prevent getting black nails. Later he summed up this innate love of order in the following sentence: "If anyone would see how the soul lives in its body, let him see how the body makes use of this daily tenancy: if the soul is disorderly and in confusion, the body will itself be maintained in disorder and confusion by its soul." [14a]

Generations of lawyers had bequeathed him a slightly pedantic tendency; sometimes a cold wind blew from his father's office across his piled-up papers, and in his flourishy, almost copperplate handwriting he would write unthinkingly the formula he saw so often on his father's documents—"In Dei nomine, amen." This hereditary trait appears again and again: he carefully notes down his small receipts, and suddenly enters a date in the midst of the thicket of sketches. These sporadic outbreaks of business-like attention to details continued throughout his life. In between the rapids of his thoughts he would set down details of date and hour like islands of recollection; he would enter his expenditure to the exact soldo, and again and again the impulse would come to give account of things done or not done, so as to have everything neatly and properly recorded.

He came under all sorts of conflicting influences, but in himself they became perfectly harmonized. For a time his ambition was stilled by a boy's easily satisfied vanity, his thirst for knowledge quenched to little purpose by undiscriminating curiosity; he was almost still at the stage of the swimmer who balances himself on tiptoe, tautens his muscles, stretches up his arms, and takes a deep breath, before he dives. For a time he was a radiant archangel flying in the cloudless, eventless sky of his youth.

But his unconcerned acceptance of the society of all sorts and conditions of men brought down on him a savage penalty. Doubtful characters, men who had slipped the leash of ordered society, wormed their way into the easily accessible circle of his friends, and took advantage of their trustfulness and their ignorance of the world. In the midst of his carefree existence Leonardo received a smashing blow that made an end of his lightheartedness. In the heart of this respectable city of Florence there was an institution

that gave free play to envy and malignancy, enabling dark intrigues to take cover under a show of indignation against secret
vice—a system of anonymous denunciation to the police responsible for the control of vice, the Ufficiali di Notte e dei Monasteri.
There was a box for these denunciations, called the *tamburo,* outside the Palazzo Vecchio—a standing invitation to calumny. On
April 8, 1476, there was found in the *tamburo* an accusation
against an ill-famed creature, the seventeen-year-old Jacopo Saltarelli, of homosexual relations, *sodomia* in the language of that
day, with four young Florentines; one of them was stated to be
Leonardo, the son of Ser Piero da Vinci, living in the house of
Andrea del Verrocchio.

Such charges were no uncommon event in those days. The Platonic group of the humanists had taken over the Athenian cult of
the beauty of the ephebus (the young Athenian of eighteen to
nineteen years of age), and its exaltation of friendship and comradeship; their enemies had charged them in consequence with
immoral practices. The Florentine philosopher Marsilio Ficino
headed the last chapter of his Life of Plato *"Apologia de moribus
Platonis,"* and in it he replied indignantly to the dogs, as he called
them, who were trying to besmirch the fame and the moral teaching of Plato, whose heart was indeed drawn toward the young, but
simply and purely in the world of ideas. The head of the Platonic
Academy at Rome, Pomponio Leto, had also been accused of un-
natural relations with one of his pupils, a young Venetian, whose
beauty he praised in his verses; while in prison in Rome he wrote
a defence in which he recalled that Socrates had used language
similar to his own.

A charge from which even the idolized humanists were not
strong enough to secure immunity was bound to be most serious
for an unknown youth with no influential protector. The confusion in his family circumstances added to Leonardo's desolation.
His father's second child-wife had been unable to stand the strain
of life with Ser Piero and had died not long after their marriage.
The widower must have been inconsolable for a time, and must
have had thoughts of death, for he secured a burial place in the
Badia at Florence. But the man was bursting with physical energy,
his grief did not last long, and again he found single life hard to

endure; he made yet another attempt to build up his life anew. His third wife, Margherita di Guglielmo, was once more almost a child, but in spite of the evil omens she had found the courage to wed Ser Piero; moreover, she brought him a dowry of some four hundred florins, a very substantial sum for that time. Leonardo was now more estranged than ever from his father, especially since in this year 1476 the father, now nearly fifty, was overcome with joy at the birth of his first legitimate child.

For the respectable notary, whose reputation and prosperity were increasing so much that about this time he separated from his Florentine partner and set up in business independently, the public pillorying of his eldest son was a heavy blow. Filled with the sense of the injury he himself was suffering, and boiling over with virtuous wrath, he found nothing better to do than to up-braid the desperate Leonardo with the disgrace he had brought upon his name. In his distress Leonardo turned to everyone who could help him out of his dreadful plight—to members of his family, to his uncle in Pistoia, husband of a sister of Ser Piero, and ap-parently through a friend to his mother, with whom he was no longer in touch. "Tell me," he wrote to his friend, "how things are going there; and can you tell me whether Caterina would do anything?" And again and again in his despairing notes of this time, written in the frantic search for help, there comes the name of his uncle Francesco, his father's brother; he writes down the name over and over again, as though it was his sheet anchor, and then crosses it out, as if after all the uncle failed him. Leonardo, the cynosure, intoxicated with the shouting over his achievements, and so sure of his personal success, found himself now without a friend. Suddenly he saw, like an abyss revealed by a flash of light-ning, his own utter isolation.

He saw how helpless a man is against calumny—against the in-sidious calumny launched from some undiscoverable hiding-place. "More are killed by word of mouth than by the sword" (la boccha a ne' morti più che'l coltello)—so he wrote on one of his unfinished letters. Thus early in his life he had felt the firm ground of his faith in men quake beneath him; and never again could he trust it. Never afterwards was he free from alert suspicion, a dread, never quite allayed, of human baseness.

He addressed petitions to influential Florentines of his acquaintance; and among these there was one who was a ready helper of all
who were unjustly persecuted, "a brother in the search for truth,"
as Ficino calls him—Bernardo di Simone Cortigiani, who on one occasion came to the aid of Ficino himself in a fight against calumny.
Cortigiani was at that time one of the gonfalonieri or heads of the
Florentine guilds. To this compassionate man Leonardo disclosed
the whole depth of his distress and despair: "You know—I have
said so to you before—that I have no one at my side. . . . And if
there is no such thing as love, what is left of life?—Friend!" he
added, surrounding the word with scornful flourishes.[15]

The *police des mœurs* summoned the accused persons at once
for interrogation, and there was a merciless examination of their
private lives. Youthful dreams, inclinations perhaps scarcely consciously felt, were brutally dragged forth and exposed; young and
sensitive beings were treated as though they were on a par with
professionals in the life of vice: they were bombarded with un-
savourinesses of which they had scarcely known the existence.
After the interrogation the proceedings were suspended for two
months—two long, terrible months. Then at last the charge was
dropped.

This affliction of his youth permanently poisoned Leonardo's
young spirit. He was suddenly bereft of all the comradeship that
had made up to him for the emotional starvation of his childhood.
Could it be alleged that some dark desire underlay the thirst for
beauty which drew him to young men with a slightly effeminate
grace? Could his cultivation of their friendship be liable to be
blackened with so ugly a name, and misinterpreted by a preco-
ciously corrupted boy as lust for his dissolute body? Leonardo was
almost as deeply revolted by the inexpressible ugliness of the affair
as by the wrong done to him. A cold wind froze his soul, crippling
him emotionally. Never again could he feel personal affection to
be harmless; relations with man or woman were irremediably distorted and spoilt for him. His inborn chastity of spirit built up
out of this bitter experience an inhibition which no passionate desire could overcome. The bald and coarse discussion of the sexual
act in a bare police office had stamped the act in Leonardo's sensitive mind with an ineradicable hideousness. He never ceased in

after years to feel that it was disgusting, and no less so in normal than in vicious relations. Many years later he wrote: "The act of coitus and the members that serve it are so hideous that, if it were not for the beauty of faces and craftsmen's ornamentation and the liberation of the spirit, the human species would lose its humanity." [16]

At first, however, the young man was still utterly at a loss, and in a turmoil of apprehensions. Was he actually arrested, or was it only his excited imagination that played with the possibility? A mysterious sentence from a later period adds to the obscurity in which the incident is shrouded. Was he thinking of the young artists' model Jacopo Saltarelli when he wrote this?—"When I represented the Almighty as a boy, you put me in prison; now if I represent him as a man you will do yet worse to me." He was obsessed by the horror of imprisonment, and, as though he meant to protect himself by every possible means from the loss of freedom, he sketched on a sheet dating from this early period a tool "for opening a prison from within," [17] an iron jack provided with a screw for drawing nails—a so-called "draw tongs" such as is used nowadays for tightening electric wires.

He seems also to have considered wild plans of revenge, for he began suddenly to devote a good deal of attention to methods of spraying fruit trees with poison, so as to produce fruit that looked and smelt good but would bring death.[18] For whom was this carefully prepared murder intended—for some adversary, or was Leonardo thinking of himself departing unostentatiously from life? He was certainly planning some frightful deed at that time, and hinted at it in a quotation from Ovid's *Metamorphoses*—he was still young enough to express his feelings in quotations: " 'I do not think, O Greeks, that my deeds need to be recounted to you, since you have seen them,' said Ulysses to his people, 'and equal deeds are done without witnesses and are seen only by the dark night.' " [19] Whatever he may have planned, he dreamed now of frightful cataclysms, as though he were calling them down in order that his personal suffering might come to an end in their midst; he pictured the end of the world to himself with grim satisfaction, as though he would find pleasure in the destruction of the whole evil race of mortal men.

Nature, too, was evil, for she had ordained that many animals should be food for others; "and, since this does not satisfy her desire, she frequently sends forth poisonous and pestilential vapours upon the vast increase and congregation of animals; and most of all upon men, who increase vastly because other animals do not feed upon them." [20] And the day would come when spendthrift Nature would be without water, which would sink into the interior of the earth; "the rivers will be deprived of their waters, the fruitful earth will put forth no more her light verdure; all the animals, finding no fresh grass for pasture, will die, and food will then be lacking to the lions and wolves and other beasts of prey, and to men, who after many efforts will be compelled to abandon their life, and the human race will die out. And then the earth's surface will be burnt up to cinder, and this will be the end of all terrestrial nature." [21]

Even after the agitation of the first months had abated, the young Leonardo continued to philosophize about death, the eternal accompaniment of life. "Consider! The hope of returning home and to one's former state is like the moth's fascination with the light, and the man who with constantly renewed desire looks forward to the new spring, the new summer, each new month and new year, feeling that the things he hopes for are a long time coming, does not perceive that he is longing for his own destruction." [22] It may be that Leonardo really thought that his great trial had destroyed all desire and all ambition in him, and that he could now laugh at the poor people who looked forward to every coming day with pleasure. A friend wrote to him about this time in sympathy for his trouble, and sent him a long poem exhorting him to take courage. Leonardo preserved the poem among his papers, but it is almost completely obliterated by an inkstain which leaves only one line legible: "My Lionardo, why dost thou so torment me?" This Florentine friend, who used the Florentine form of Leonardo's name, must have expressed deep and sincere sympathy, for Leonardo replied with a poem of his own, in which he proudly rejects compassion and gives vent to his new and bitter knowledge of the world:

> Despise me not, for I am not poor—
> Poor is he only who has material desires. . . .

Dead to all feelings and desires, he was at a loss what to do. He did not intend to remain in his own city, but did not know whither he could go. "Where shall I settle?" he wrote to the same friend. "You will know before long." [23] As yet he had neither means nor reputation, and could expect little success if he left the field in which he had struck root. Thus life went on and the wound the young man had suffered gradually healed. But for a while his bitter experience seemed to have crippled his creative talent and prevented the emergence of his individuality.

6

The anonymous collaboration with Verrocchio, which continued through these years, brought unexpected results, though not for the younger man, who had not yet found himself, but for the older, who now came rapidly to the fullness of his powers. This year, 1476, so fatal for Leonardo, was a year of triumph for Verrocchio, for it was in this year that his bronze statue of David was exhibited in the Palazzo Vecchio. Verrocchio had now risen above the glittering charm of his past work, with its curious mixture of strength and fragility. He had thrown off the niggling style of the jeweller, and his sureness of touch and command of his material were united with a mastery that he owed to a new grasp of intellectual content and to a purpose that transcended the mere copying of reality.

A strange mutual dependence, such as has rarely bound two creative workers to one another, existed between Verrocchio and Leonardo. The master, while still instructing and still serving as example, acquired from the still immature pupil much of the essence of the pupil's later individual achievement. In particular he acquired from him a grasp of a principle to which Leonardo had not yet been able to give articulate expression, that of securing the predominance of the permanent essential values in a work of art and excluding accidental elements. It was almost as if Verrocchio already possessed the insight of the ripe Leonardo, and he might have been regarded as the actual originator of the new elements in

his work, were it not that they give the impression of something
alien, of borrowings from the store of another, from the store of
this young man as yet unconscious of his rich endowment.

A face needs hands to give expression to the whole portrait, said
Leonardo later in his life. But before ever a portrait was ordered
from Leonardo, Verrocchio gave his marble bust of a woman in
the Bargello crossed hands—wonderful, spiritual hands, contrasting in their new repose and fullness with the severe, angular contours of the woman's face. Andrea del Verrocchio stood at the
meeting-point of two worlds, the transition from one view of art to
a new one. The next group on which he worked, showing Saint
Thomas placing his hand in Christ's wound, was to be a milestone
on the way from the art of the fifteenth century, which seemed
drunk with reality, to the school of the following period, which
aimed at increasing fidelity to appearance.

This psychological event in Verrocchio's studio was noted by his
discriminating fellow-artists and talked of in all the studios of
Florence. In the course of years it took shape as a legend, of which
Vasari gives a rather crude version. He tells at length how his hero
Leonardo, maturing early, like all heroes, lent his hand while
hardly more than a child to the completion of an unfinished painting by Verrocchio, a *Baptism of Christ,* and the angel he painted
revealed such superiority in the pupil that Messer Andrea was
overwhelmed with the realization of his own inadequacy and renounced the brush for ever.

The angel exists—the earliest extant work to which Leonardo's
name is attached. An untrained observer would perhaps scarcely
feel that the angel kneeling on the left in this *Baptism of Christ* is
in any way more remarkable than the rest. It takes its place in the
design with a wealth of contrasting masses, but the double twists
and turns of the body are robbed of their effect by the fullness of
the material gathered round the thighs and the heavy, angular
folds of the drapery. The upturned face, seen in profile, has more
life than the insipid look of the other angel, but the pronounced
hook of the nose, the eyeball protruding from tightly drawn lids,
and the sharply defined folds of the neck are evidences of a continued dependence on Verrocchio's style and formulæ, as are the
aureoles crowning hair that seems like coils of bright wire. Only

the mouth with its moist upturned corners tells of the pulse of a new life.

Yet this angel is Leonardo's own, surrounded with a chiaroscuro that suggests a sudden rush of fresh air into a closed room. The new painting technique contributed to this effect, the technique of oil colours, introduced from the north and still surrounded with mystery, which had come as a revelation to the artists in Florence with the exhibition in 1476 of the Portinari altarpiece by the Flemish painter Hugo van der Goes. Michelangelo rejected oil painting as too complicated, as an art for "women and mules," but Leonardo adopted it with enthusiasm and acquired its depth and its wealth of nuances. He enriched Verrocchio's big tempera panel with his angel painted in oil and gave retouches in oil to the landscape in the background.

No document exists that throws any light on the date of the painting of this *Baptism of Christ,* but it is not the work of a child prodigy, and it is not true that Messer Andrea never again painted a picture. A casual sketch of Leonardo's on a sheet dated 1478 in the Uffizi gallery has been described as a sketch for the angel's head. This would place the picture at the end of 1478; but this is difficult to believe, since by then Leonardo had passed out of the anonymity of his collaboration with Verrocchio.

The cruel incident of the denunciation gradually drifted into oblivion, and the injustice done to Leonardo even stood him, in some measure, in good stead; for those who had left him in the lurch at the time began to exert themselves to make amends to him, and to use their influence with official persons to help him on. Ser Piero was professionally employed by the city authorities, and must himself have moved on his son's behalf, for the Signoria, the governing body of the republic, gave Leonardo the first official commission in his life, for an altarpiece for the chapel of Saint Bernard in the Palazzo Vecchio. The work had been entrusted shortly before to Piero Pollaiuolo, but the order was cancelled, and in March 1478 Leonardo received his first payment on account, twenty-five florins.

The altarpiece, however, was never finished. A political whirlwind broke suddenly, without a moment's warning, over Florence. The peaceful progress of the city was bound sooner or later to be jeopardized by its dependence on Lorenzo de' Medici. "The Medici," says Guicciardini, "had at all times more regard for their personal advantage than for the common weal. Since, however, they were unsupported either by external resources or by the Signoria, their interest was bound up with the general interest of the community, whose greatness and fame was their own greatness and fame." But the moment personal interests, personal sympathies or antipathies, or personal ambition came into play, they inevitably came into conflict with other personal interests. The nephews of Pope Sixtus IV had the same ambition as the Medici, to capture supreme power for their own family, and in the narrow and insecure field of temporal and spiritual ownership on Italian soil either group could succeed only at the cost of the other. Lorenzo de' Medici found a determined opponent in Girolamo Riario, the nephew or son of the Pope and husband of Caterina Sforza, and resentful rivals in the Pazzi, bankers of Florence. Lorenzo trusted for safety to his financial strength, and felt that he could defy the Pope's ambition; he supported the operations of condottieri against the papal territory, and refused to give Girolamo Riario the loan he wanted for the conquest of Imola.

Only conspiracy could get the inconvenient Lorenzo out of the way. Francesco de' Pazzi and Archbishop Francesco Salviati, who shared his hatred of Lorenzo, and Girolamo Riario, an unscrupulous adventurer, associated themselves in the conspiracy with hired condottieri, wolves in priests' clothing, and desperate cut-throats. The Pope had no objection to the plot so long as it did not involve bloodshed, "for," he said, "it is not a part of my office to occasion the death of a man." Riario gave him his promise, with a cynical smile. He was well aware that the Pope would be compelled to yield to the pressure of accomplished facts.

On Sunday, April 16, 1478, the bells pealed loudly for the celebration of high mass in the Duomo in Florence, by the Pope's eighteen-year-old nephew, Cardinal Raffaello Sansoni-Riario, Girolamo's unconscious instrument. It was a glorious spring day of sparkling sunshine and blue sky, with a boisterous young wind that had raced down from the fresh green hills. Around the portico of the Duomo there moved figures who were indifferent to the brilliant sunshine as they whispered excitedly to one another;

their hasty movements were accompanied by a suspicious clanking as of weapons. But it was a day that filled the heart with joy, and none of the uninitiated passers-by noticed them. Carefully as the plot had been prepared down to the last detail, it was nearly wrecked by a chance alteration at the last moment: Giuliano de' Medici, ill and lethargic, cancelled the banquet that was to have taken place after high mass. Accordingly, with the consent of Archbishop Salviati, the scene of action was transferred from the banqueting-hall to the cathedral. It was left to a hired condottiere, inured though he was as a soldier to violence and slaughter, to refuse to stain the Duomo with murder. Two priests offered at once to take his place—familiarity with the sacred building had made them less scrupulous. Two others agreed to visit Giuliano to induce him, in spite of his sickness and of the dark premonitions that weighed on him, to go to the cathedral.

Mass had begun when Francesco de' Pazzi and Bernardo de Bandino Baroncelli, the adventurer son of a high official of the Neapolitan courts of justice, entered the cathedral with Giuliano, affectionately supporting the pale young man as he came in with unsteady steps, and meanwhile passing their murderous hands over his slender form to discover whether the velvet jerkin concealed a shirt of mail. The mass proceeded to its end; the cardinal turned to the congregation to speak the words of dismissal, *"Ite, missa est"*—the prearranged signal for the conspirators. Then a short, sharp cry pierced the silence, and Giuliano fell to the ground, struck down by the dagger of the hired murderer Bandino. Francesco de' Pazzi, a man of slight build and poor physique, struck blindly at the fallen Giuliano; agitated by the dark glance that shot from the eyes, already becoming glazed, in the waxen-white face, he hit out so wildly that he cut his own thigh. At the same moment the two priests set on Lorenzo with their daggers; but they inflicted nothing worse than a scratch on Lorenzo's arm as he sprang instantly aside. He might miscalculate and come to grief at times in his intrigues, but his instinctive movements were rapid and accurate, and he now rushed like a hunted animal up the steps to the choir and round the altar. Behind him came Bandino, in wild pursuit of the conspicuous cloak which Lorenzo had wound round his bleeding arm.

Shouts rang out, crowds swayed this way and that, men with no notion of what was in progress were squeezed up against conspirators; chairs were overturned, candelabra knocked down, daggers brandished in the air—and through the uproar there came insistently, like the humming of a conch, the pealing of the cathedral bells under a blazing blue sky. Lorenzo, chased through the nave by Bandino, reached the sacristy; Politian, Lorenzo's young tutor and friend, panting breathlessly after him, banged the heavy iron door behind the two of them and tremblingly pushed the bolt home. Lorenzo was saved. Giuliano's murderer rushed up the dark, steep staircase of the campanile; he climbed on and on, to save his life, and crouched at the top among the great metal tongues of the bells.

The cathedral was filled with tumult and shouting. Women shrieked, imagining that the dome was falling in upon them. The cardinal had sunk down at the foot of the altar; his crumpled purple vestments spread out round him like running blood, and he was sobbing like a child, despairingly reiterating that he had had no knowledge, not the slightest suspicion of this. Frantic, animal fear chased all the blood from his still unformed young face, and it was said that his features retained to his last day the pallor they were given by this hour of horror.

While the cathedral bells were still pealing, Archbishop Salviati went to the Palazzo Pubblico to visit the Priori or members of the Signoria. He assumed an air of innocence, but his behaviour was so strange that the Priori grew suspicious and closed and locked the entrance to the palace. Already there was wild rioting in the streets of Florence. The partisans of the Pazzi attacked the palace of the Signoria, to rescue the archbishop who had become its prisoner; the palace door gave way under the blows they rained on it, but they were themselves overwhelmed by the crowd that poured into the building with them—militia and mob, respectable citizens in Sunday garb and ruffianly characters. The foremost among the crowd shouted the news of the assassination of Giuliano de' Medici, and there were infuriated cries of *"Palle, palle,* death to the traitors!" *

The Signoria at once held an improvised council meeting, but

---

* The Medicean arms showed six balls (*palle*) on a gold field.

the crowd took the law into its own hands. The archbishop, in spite of his priestly robes, was roughly seized and held, and at the same moment there came up a furious group of men dragging after them the half-lifeless body of Francesco de' Pazzi, his face streaming with blood but his eyes still flashing wildly. The mangled bodies of the conspirators were suspended from the window-bars, amid the howls of the onlookers, and while the rope was tightening on Salviati's neck, the prelate, in a last spasmodic effort, threw himself against Pazzi's bared breast and furiously tore it with his teeth, seeing in Pazzi the cause of his own dreadful end.

In those hours of terror, in which eighty victims lost their lives, the man who was sought most eagerly of all escaped—Bernardo de Bandino Baroncelli, who was crouching under the ringing bells of the campanile. After days without food he crept out of his hiding-place, and fled, on and on, through country after country, until he reached the Bosporus. In Constantinople he imagined himself to be safe. But Lorenzo's arm was long. His trade connexions reached as far as the Turks, and Mahomet II arrested the murderer. A cousin of Lorenzo, Antonio de' Medici, personally received the prisoner and brought him back in chains to Florence. On December 29, 1479, Bandino was hanged outside the Palazzo del Capitano.

7

The tower of the palace of the Podestà, the chief magistrate, is decorated to this day with the portraits of the other persons hanged, Francesco and Jacopo de' Pazzi, Salviati, and others—faithfully depicted by Maestro Sandro Botticelli (but hanging heads down—a touch, perhaps, of contemporary humour) for the sum of forty florins apiece. Forty florins seemed a large sum to a painter who had recently been deprived by the turn of events of his first official commission; and Leonardo accordingly went to see the execution of Bandino, and sketched the man as he swung on the gallows, sketched him carefully down to the buttons on his fur-lined cloak, sketched once more the head with mouth awry and jaws clenched, and noted down in his gracefully curved right-

to-left writing the colours of the Turkish jacket, the mantle, the
fur lining, and even the shoe-leather (Bonnat collection, Bayonne).
His hand was firm as he entered all these macabre details at the
foot of the gallows. Yet this conscientious observer did not secure
the commission he wanted.

The fact, however, that he tried to get this commission shows
that he was still none too well off, although he had emerged by
then from the obscurity of his early years. But if material success
had not yet come, Leonardo had already achieved complete artistic independence and unfettered individuality.

On a fragment of a sketch now in the Uffizi, Leonardo entered in
an access of method the memorandum: "——ber 1478 I began the
two Virgin Marys." One of these is the so-called Benois Madonna,
now in the Hermitage at Leningrad. The motif of the Madonna
with the child in her lap, a robust, chubby-faced child, is still of
the fifteenth century; the round head of the Madonna, with the
very high forehead, the thin, curved eyebrows, and the small round
childish chin, is Florentine; the Gothic window in the background, here giving no view beyond (copies reveal a tiny glimpse
of landscape), is early Florentine *quattrocento* (fifteenth century).
But this is all there was of conventional work in the painting.

What Leonardo has captured in this picture is a transitory
mood, an intimate scene such as he may have chanced to witness
when his young stepmother, with a schoolgirl's playfulness, rocked
her first-born in her lap, breaking into hearty laughter at the awkward play of the child's little arms. The laugh shakes the girl-
mother's round neck and flows in delicate waves to the round, half-
exposed breast. The eyelids flutter above the happy distant gaze
as the long, straight Florentine fingers hold cautiously, between
thumb and forefinger, the flowerstalk which the child is making a
tremendous effort to reach with his fat little hand. Mother and
child are so entirely alone and so wrapped up in one another that
the observer begins to feel that he has been an uninvited spectator of an enclosed and self-contained world not intended for the
gaze of a stranger. In the twinkling of an eye the laugh will pass,
the girl will turn to look in surprise at the intruder, and the child's
soft little hand will crush the stalk.

The effect of spontaneity in this picture, which seems born of

Drawing of Bernardo
de Bandino Baroncelli

PHOTO GIRAUDON

BONNAT COLLECTION, BAYONNE

PHOTO ANDERSON   Caricatures   ROYAL ACADEMY, VENICE

the moment and concentrated entirely on the moment, is the result of careful thought and calculation, like a sum laboriously worked out. From the broad basis provided by the parted knees and the slipping folds of the cloak, the picture rises into an obtuse-angled triangle; from the round, plump face a line runs on one side, like an invisibly drawn architectural curve, over the bent elbow to the broad basis of the knee, and on the other side from the high bent forehead along the top of the child's head, above the mother's hand, and on to the other out-turned knee. Nothing has been left here to chance or sacrificed to the dictation of reality. The observer's eye is deliberately controlled and guided by this invisible structural design. It is not allowed to wander from the centre of the picture, but is firmly directed from the folds of the dress to the child and from the child to the central subject of the picture, the child-mother's laugh.

Deep, full colours harmonize in this picture. The dress, of a greenish blue, is fastened at the neck-opening with gold braid; the cloak, blue-green and lined with yellow velvet, absorbs all the light except where it is allowed to blaze out in gold at the folds. The strong harmonies of the colours serve in their turn only as a composition to lead up to the lovely mother-of-pearl hue of the face, through which the delicate blue veins faintly show themselves.

In this earliest of all Leonardo's extant paintings there are to be found already all the elements of his creative genius. It radiates the magic that is his own secret, as though only he could awake indescribable emotions that combine like harmonies, emotions that may be sung but not defined, as though only he could paint pictures of saints or men with which the observer may contend for ever without fathoming the secret they hold—pictures which at each new encounter are so full of surprises that everything we thought we knew of them seems wrong. But, alongside the inscrutable, this picture of the laughing Virgin Mary had enough in it that is both amazing and within every man's grasp to set every imitator furiously to work—and it attracted countless imitators down to the time of Raphael's *Madonna with the Pink*.

The second Madonna that Leonardo began at the same time has left its bright traces only in more or less faithful, more or less routine repetitions by fellow-artists in Florence. It was the *Madonna with a Pitcher*, a pitcher containing flowers, of which Vasari relates that they were covered by a dew as slight as breath, "more living than life itself"—*più vive che vivezza*.

The artists of his time would play endless variations on a subject painted by Leonardo, as though they could not get away from it, although its only novelty might consist in the treatment he gave it. The persistency with which they did so shows that from the first his art had in it an inescapable finality, of which the uniqueness only gradually wore away, as a coin may with long use. He painted about this time a little *predella* or picture for the foot of an altarpiece, perhaps an altarpiece by a fellow-student—the *Annunciation* now in the Louvre. The design dictated by the shape of the tiny picture seems at once to be inevitable, with its equally balanced spaces between and on either side of the two kneeling figures, like a deep silence around the mystery of a message of eternal import brought from heaven to earth. The Virgin, who has just heard the angel's message, bows her head with the resignation of the chosen instrument, her hands crossed on her breast in an attitude of self-effacing devotion—a woman's mature, full-fleshed hands, lifted up like a burden. The angel has raised his arm in a hieratical greeting; his head is bowed, at the same angle as Mary's, and he glances down as she has done, as if the miracle announced stands already between the two.

The figure of the angel, like that of the Virgin Mary, is built up from the broad basis of the folds of his garment, but the weight of the folds that fall round him is balanced by the lifting energy of his great wings, which reach far out toward the visible horizon. The wings are no mere symbols to indicate the heavenly messenger, but powerful pinions, with strong remiges, which could lift a heavy body into the air, as though Leonardo were already dreaming of flight above the clouds.

The scene, the enclosed garden, *hortus clausus*, in which the mystical event takes place, with the stone balustrade slanting across the design, takes up the diagonal formed by the angel's hands in their gesture of contrary motion; the line is emphasized by the bent head and the line of the back, and is repeated by the wings. All subsidiary features are subordinated, even the objects in the foreground being prevented by their dark colouring from obtruding in any way on the attention. The eye follows the isosceles triangle formed by the two figures bent towards one another, up to the blue hills, which undulate toward the silvery sky, in which a small pink cloud floats like the promise of a new day.

Leonardo deliberately worked for this simplicity of effect, this touching and eloquent reposefulness, and at a later period he wrote in strong terms of the melodramatic style of the painters of his time: "I have seen in our days an angel of the Annunciation who looked as if he meant to chase our dear Lady out of her room, with gestures suggesting such a volume of abuse as could only be poured out over the most contemptible of enemies. And our dear Lady looked as if she were in utter despair and wanted to throw herself out of the window." [24]

The suggestions that Leonardo crowded into the narrow space of this *predella* were adopted by others and developed in big panels, including an *Annunciation* in the Uffizi which contains so many evidences of his influence that it might be taken for a work of his own. Did his teacher Verrocchio paint this *Annunciation?* The splendidly carved lectern, with its wealth of antique ornamentation, which stands so boldly in the foreground, might well have been the dream of a sculptor. Or was the painting the work of Lorenzo di Credi, who at this time was under Leonardo's influence? In any case it was done by someone who had been able to see Leonardo's preliminary study for the Louvre *Angel of the Annunciation.* (This study is now at Christ Church College, Oxford; Leonardo has simplified the figure in the *predella.*) It was done by someone whom Leonardo may have helped with the work, perhaps himself touching up the angel's head. But the painter of this Uffizi *Annunciation* has not grasped the inner significance of the event; what he has painted is not the lowly servant of the Lord who has just heard the tidings, but a high-born Florentine lady, with her small aristocratic head, who has had a surprise while reading and throws up her hands in astonishment, beautiful academic fifteenth-century hands, which seem to be telling off her arguments on their finger-tips as she looks vacantly out of the picture. Leonardo's fellow-artist has also failed to grasp the special composition; he has let the balustrade run into the frame of the picture, has got the Madonna's hands out of perspective, and has made her flat face seem even more lifeless by contrasting it with the prominent masonry.

The fact that Leonardo's early works found so many imitators shows that success was beginning to smile on him. About this time he received from the king of Portugal, the richest prince in the world, a commission for tapestry which was to be woven in gold and silk in Flanders. Leonardo's cartoon, in black and white, represented the Fall—Adam and Eve in the meadows of Eden, under trees with foreshortened boughs, in the midst of flowers and grasses and grazing animals; and the landscape was "so lovingly carried out," says Vasari, "that the very idea that a man could have so much patience was amazing." The realistic treatment of the detail, which so impressed Vasari, was combined once more with a new conception of the subject of the composition. (The cartoon lives on only in descriptions; it is not now extant.) Leonardo no longer had our first parents one on each side of the Tree: he represented Eve reaching into the boughs with one arm, with a careless, sinuous movement that resembled the Serpent's coiling round the trunk, and with the other arm handing the apple to Adam. Her outstretched arms provided a formal bond between the two figures, a sort of magic circle of guilt in which they were caught. And once more there was an inevitability about the conception, and at a stroke all earlier ones had been put out of date. The new representation of the Fall became generally accepted; later Raphael adopted it as a matter of course. Once more a now vanished work of Leonardo's led men into new paths.

By this time Leonardo had discovered that his easiest way to the approbation of his contemporaries was through the touching charm of his Madonnas, and he made studies of a new one, which once more aimed at a balance between the accidental and the universal. It was again to be a representation of an everyday occurrence, the child Christ trying to get away from his mother in order to play with a cat, a picture to touch every mother's heart with its reminder of her own child's familiar actions; at the same time the intensity of feeling and the formal unity of the composition were to place a sort of zone of piety round the work. Leonardo made studies of the little round bodies of children with soft little arms

PHOTO GIRAUDON   *The Benois Madonna*   HERMITAGE, LENINGRAD

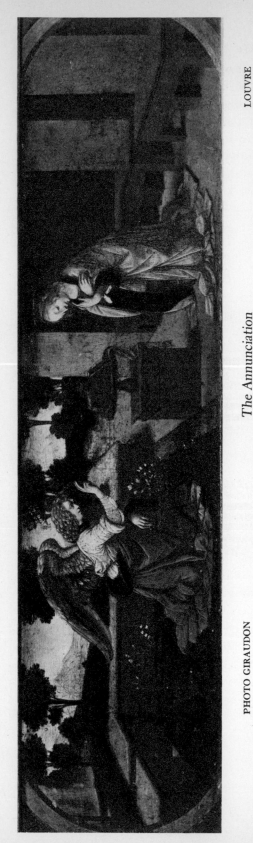

The Annunciation

closing round a coiled-up cat's body; he caught the playfulness and the mutual attraction of child and animal; but he worked yet harder on the task of producing a completely self-contained design. The first sketches (the washed pen-drawing in the British Museum is one of them) were in the form of a tall isosceles triangle; he went on to the charming idea of the child enclosed in his mother's arms as in a circle, and finally to the rectangular scheme of composition of a Madonna kneeling on the ground, bending over in profile to draw the child to her side (British Museum).

8

But it was not only this painstaking search for a complete solution that delayed the progress of his work. He was caught up into the whirl of contemporary events, and overwhelmed with personal cares. The abortive conspiracy of the Pazzi plunged Florence into war and poverty and a mass of troubles, and it forced every peaceful citizen to identify himself with the cause of the family of the Medici. The Pope, enraged by the execution of the archbishop and the imprisonment of his nephew the cardinal, and forgetting the part he had himself played in instigating the crime, turned against Florence every instrument of his spiritual and temporal power—arms and excommunication. He found an ally in King Ferdinand of Naples, who welcomed the opportunity of reducing Florentine arrogance. The king sent his son, the duke of Calabria, into the field; the duke of Urbino, Federigo da Montefeltro, took over the command of the papal army. The Florentine merchants and artisans were not born soldiers—"one of these people from beyond the mountains was bound to come some day to bring war upon us," sighed Luca Landucci.[25] Their just fury against the offenders after the outrage in the Duomo, which had sent them pouring through the streets of Florence, thirsting for blood, had soon evaporated; they no longer felt any impulse to carry their own bones to market, and were now out to make sure of their profits from the provisioning of their army. Philippe de Commines, the envoy of Louis XI (the king was too old and exhausted to intervene in the war, and was trying to calm the Pope by diplomacy), grasped the situation at once with his practised eye. "The Florentines have nothing to compare with our knowledge of the way to capture strongholds and defend them," he wrote.

But in this city of men indifferent to the arts of warfare there was one man who was keenly interested in military technique and who followed events with burning interest—the rising young painter of laughing Madonnas, Leonardo da Vinci. He was no more bellicose than his compatriots, nor had he the adventurousness that leads a man to stake his own life for the sport of it; and the cause of the Medici did not appeal to him any more than to other young men of this city, who preferred to let hired soldiers look after their safety. But the period was one in which the technique of warfare was undergoing a transformation, in which the new inventions, man's new mastery over iron and steel, offered new means of destroying human lives; and this new military art, still in its infancy, held Leonardo enthralled, like everything that was new and unexplored and capable of development. He had already filled pages of his sketchbooks with designs for grinding and rolling machinery; now he plunged into the study of the new problems to the exclusion of all else, as though his life depended on them. He filled up the pages between old sketches and studies for pictures with drawings of arms and war material—as on a sheet in the Uffizi dating from the end of 1478. The enthusiasm for technical discovery with which Leonardo was to be filled, as a son of his transitional age, began as an enthusiasm for the mechanism of war. It was a vast and profitable field, much more so even than the flourishing industries of the day, which were still tied to manual operation, and were unwilling to abandon old methods that had been justified by success.

Artillery engagements were complicated in those days by the laborious manipulation of heavy cannon. In order to increase the freedom of movement in the field, Leonardo designed a three-wheeled gun-carriage with a huge screw terminating in gigantic forceps which gripped the gun barrel.[26] He gave increased mobility to another gun-carriage, for light guns, by interlocking the joints. He devoted a great deal of time to the problem of the connexion between the various machine parts, and also to methods of putting together beams in siege structures, "so as to keep them firm." [27] But gun-making was what principally interested him. He designed "a bombard which will not recoil when it is fired," [28] and a light multiple-barrelled gun, a sort of machine-gun,[29] mounted on a carriage provided with gearing to make the gun mobile and give it multiple action [30]; and he placed on a tumbril thirty-three light gun barrels, "of which eleven will be fired at once." [31] Leonardo does not seem to have aroused much interest with his plans—Lorenzo de' Medici was employing another Florentine artist, Giuliano da Sangallo, as military engineer—but he continued to follow the course of the war with passionate interest, and to adapt his designs to the changed requirements of the fighting.

In the summer of 1479 the papal troops drove the Florentine army into an inglorious flight—"so cowardly and poor-spirited that army was become," writes Machiavelli in contempt, "that the turning of a horse's head or tail gave either victory or defeat." The papal forces advanced to within eight miles of Florence, and laid siege to the fortresses on the Florentine hills. Some Latin verses written by an unknown hand on a sheet in Leonardo's possession [32] sing the praises of the heroic defence of the fortress of Colle against Federigo of Urbino, who had brought up heavy artillery to the attack. During the long siege Leonardo devised all sorts of means of preventing the enemy troops from approaching the bastions of the fortress. He designed a system of beams to be pushed suddenly out of the embrasures in order to overturn the ladders laid by the besiegers against the battlements.[33] Another apparatus for protecting the bastions was a huge cogwheel placed outside to set in motion a great beam with horizontal sails like those of a windmill, which could be continually turned so as to prevent rams or ladders from being brought up against the bastions.[34]

The longer Leonardo occupied himself with apparatus of war, the finer and more careful his drawings became, as though he were more and more in love with his work, and were bringing to bear all his artistic skill in order to arouse interest in his plans. But his projects, however beautifully worked out, brought him no commissions as a military engineer. The war did not continue long enough for an applicant unknown in this field to secure attention. The papal commanders and the duke of Calabria satisfied them-

selves with the capture of the fortress of Colle, and then agreed to
a three months' truce, in order not to expose their troops, who had
been weakened by the long investment of the fortress, to the hardships of a winter campaign. Lorenzo de' Medici took advantage of
this breathing-space to bring the inglorious war to an end; for, in
spite of all the traps his own ambition laid for him, he was a good
judge of a contest and knew when he was beaten. He knew also,
at such a moment, how to bring to bear the weight of his personality. In order to win over his dangerous opponent King Ferdinand, he made a sudden journey in person to Naples, where he
brought into play all his resources of charm and wealth in order
to procure a settlement, with which the Pope, left in the lurch by
the king, was forced to rest content. The treaty of peace was like
any other treaty imposed on the vanquished, but the traders of
Florence considered a bad peace better than the best of wars, and
men and women fell laughing and crying into one another's arms
in the streets of the city when the incubus of war was lifted off
them.

9

The Florentines went back to business with renewed courage,
and began again to give commissions to their artists—and Leonardo carefully stowed away his war papers and designs for any
later opportunity, in order to devote himself to a big commission
on which at last he could put all his powers to the test. At the
beginning of this year of peace, 1480, the monks of San Donato a
Scopeto entered into possession of a property in Valdelsa which
had been bequeathed to them by the bast-dealer Simone, who had
become a monk; in a codicil to his will he required that a dowry of
a hundred and fifty florins should be paid to his granddaughter,
the tailoress Lisabeta. The monks determined to make use of this
legacy to have a fine altarpiece painted for their monastery, and as
they were clients of Ser Piero, the notary proposed that the work
should be commissioned from his son. The monks entered into a
formal contract with the young painter; they offered him one-third
of the property, but he was not to sell it for three years to come,

and within that period they were to be free to repurchase it from him for three hundred florins. But he was at once to be responsible to the young tailoress for her dowry, must pay for his own colours, and must even, contrary to the custom then prevailing, pay for any gold needed. He was also to forfeit any claim in respect of the painting if it was not delivered within at most thirty months.

It was a strange contract that he had concluded, under the auspices of Ser Piero—well aware as he was of his long searches and slow tentative approaches to complete expression, and of the further circumstance that he had no means out of which to pay the tailor girl her dowry; but he must have been so glad to get his first big commission that he signed whatever was put before him. He failed, of course, to meet his obligation toward Signorina Lisabeta, and the monks had themselves to advance part of her dowry, since "he says he has no means of doing so," as the disgusted monks wrote in their ledger.

Meanwhile Leonardo went ardently to work on his studies for the painting. The subject he first chose for his altarpiece was an *Adoration of the Shepherds,* an intimate scene of the touching anecdotal simplicity which the Florentines of the fifteenth century loved: Mary kneeling with folded hands before the Child, and Saint Joseph sinking onto a bench, as though overcome, and telling the shepherds of the miracle as they arrive in haste. The shepherds stand looking on, bending forward in order to see the babe better, or raising their hands to heaven (Bonnat collection, Bayonne). Another study (Kunsthalle, Hamburg) develops Joseph's story into an old man's circumstantial narrative; alongside is a sketch of the Christ Child rocking comfortably on the floor. It is again a charming and touching picture, a folk song sung *sotto voce* to soft harmonies. An ox chews in stolid contentment in the background and an ass grazes alongside it, a clumsy and wooden animal, almost like a child's toy (Windsor collection). It may be that a circle of angels was to float above the picture, as in the sketch at Venice, a bright wreath of many colours wound about the peaceful scene and rising from earth to heaven.

For a while Leonardo worked on this theme, searching for the types of his simple shepherds, credulous youngsters alongside grave and thoughtful men; he collected details for the background, shepherds dismounting from their horses and tying them up by the side of the ox and the ass. But, though he went on with his work, he was no longer content with his choice. His mind was too full of problems and ideas, he was not at rest, was torn with ambition to make his way, and the static shepherds' idyll offered him no scope. It may be that he had already begun to occupy himself with the idea of a *Last Supper*, for there is a sheet at the Louvre, dating from this period, on which he has sketched youths and men assembled in eager conversation round a narrow table, while a small sketch alongside shows Jesus Christ, with pointing forefinger, revealing the betrayal. But this is no more than an isolated spark that blazed up and went out. Perhaps Leonardo felt that he was not yet equal to the great drama of the betrayal, or he wanted to make use of the preparatory work he had done, for he settled down now to the subject of an *Adoration of the Magi*.

It was a favourite *quattrocento* subject, providing the opportunity for depicting the Florentine scene at its gayest, with rich merchants from the East and magnificent horsemen from foreign countries, and for introducing famous contemporaries, who would gaze with dignity out of the picture. Thus Botticelli had recently painted the *Adoration of the Magi* for Santa Maria Novella as a thank-offering for Lorenzo's escape and a demonstration of the temporal power of the Medici. But the element in the subject that appealed so strongly to Leonardo had nothing to do with his contemporaries' simple love of a spectacle. He wanted to fathom the inner meaning of the incident, to reveal its intrinsic significance, to paint an experience, not a procession. A miracle had happened, a star had risen above Bethlehem, a light shone in the dark night, the Son of God had been born. The news spread through the world; old and young, poor and rich, came to wonder and worship, to doubt and be overwhelmed with faith. The joy over the thing that had happened surged now round the mother, who had got up from her sickbed and sat holding up the Child on her lap.

The scene reveals in the background a pillared hall through which is to be seen a press of men and women hastening forward. There is a staircase from which observers look down with emotion (Gallichon collection, Louvre). Everything is drawn into the circle of love and worship; even the animals, warned by their vague instinct, have got on their feet. Leonardo explained in his mature years what he had tried to represent in his early *Adoration of the Magi:* "All who are present at any remarkable happening look on at it with wonder in their faces . . . and if it is a sacred occurrence, those who are standing round turn their gaze on it, giving various expression to their adoration, as though the Host were being shown to them." [35]

On countless sheets of sketches Leonardo drew the attitudes and gestures men might be expected to reveal in face of a supernatural happening, according to their age and temperament, their mental equipment and their receptivity. One youth can scarcely believe his eyes, and shades them with his hand in order to get a better view of this incomprehensible happening. Another has opened his arms, and his body is thrust forward, following the motion of the raised hands like a wave (sketch in the Louvre). He sketched one figure with the handsome head averted and the hands making a gesture of expostulation, as if to say that the hour was too portentous and his poor human soul was unequal to it. Another, with hands folded in devotion, would have that moment prolonged to eternity (Wallrat Museum, Cologne). An old man has sunk down with the motion of legs that drag and knees that are stiff; another stands in thought, his head resting on his hand (British Museum); a third is arguing with raised forefinger: any who will not hear and understand, who refuse to accept the miracle, have the message blared into their recalcitrant ears in trumpet tones (Malcolm collection, British Museum). Riders hasten up from the far distance, on horses with rounded panting flanks, and the animals that Leonardo now sketched on countless sheets (in the Windsor collection), as though he were particularly fascinated by this subsidiary subject, quickly ripen from hesitating studies to a mastery of each separate attitude—the arched neck, the strong curve of the belly—until the rearing animals fit perfectly into the current of excitement that flows through the picture.

Leonardo went to work with equal ardour and perseverance on the scene in which the sacred event took place, in order to increase the effect of depth at which he aimed from the first study for the whole picture. He worked separately on the design for the background (sketch in the Uffizi), a complicated design, eloquent of his youthful pleasure in his mastery of perspective, with a double flight of stairs, and intersecting series of arches which pass into the depth of the picture, out of which riders hasten, while a great camel lies resting on the landing between the steps in the foreground and the first of the two flights.

In the course of these laborious studies, this meditation and research, this finding and rejecting, Leonardo himself grew steadily in freedom and mastery of execution. He gained fluency in the indication of movements, and in place of the careful silverpoint he resorted more and more frequently to pen and ink, in order to capture an impression quickly. His stroke was of infinite delicacy; he would carry it without a break round a curve of the limbs, flowing down along the wave of back and thigh, to break off in a zigzag when following the jerks of a rapid movement.

But these preliminary studies went on for so long that the monks began to lose patience. "The time has gone by and we have been the losers through it," they noted in complaint in their ledger—*il tempo passava e a noi ne veniva prejudicio.* In order to appease them Leonardo made himself useful in the monastery. He painted its old clock with blue and yellow colours which the monks procured for him; for this extra work he received an advance of a lira and six soldi. At last, in the autumn of 1481, he had reached the stage at which he could make a beginning with the groundwork of the altarpiece. The monks were delighted to see progress made, and sent some sacks of corn to his home as a special reward. The things they saw when they looked over his shoulder aroused their enthusiasm, and soon Leonardo received a further gift of a cask of red wine.

Now at last there began to separate in the hard grey the outlines of brown shadow and yellow light, and a splendid vision arose, like a waking dream which one who dreamed of things beyond the scale of this life, beyond the power of man to represent, was trying to force onto his canvas. The central group of the Madonna and Child became the motionless pole of a world in commotion. By means of a turn given to the lower part of her body Leonardo secured the quiet emergence of the Virgin's narrow, raised shoulders, as though she too were holding her breath. She sat erect; only the head was bent to one side, with a flower-like droop of the high dome of the brow, as though it were weighed down with the burden of foreknowledge of tragic things. The glance from under the lowered eyelids passed sadly over the Christ Child, who with playful gravity raised his little arm in benediction. Round her mouth there hovered the shadow of a smile full of sad tenderness; her hand, bent well round at the wrist, tightly held the child's legs to protect him.

Around the still figure there was motion on all sides. Adoration surged round it and broke into foam at its feet in the form of the kneeling figures of the Wise Men from the East. The head of one of them was bowed so low that his beard almost swept the ground. For a while the movement came to rest in the two corner figures in the foreground; then it was resumed in outstretched arms, in attentive young faces and the ecstatic expressions of old men, and in the rearing bodies of horses that filled the background. The flush of yellow light that radiated from the central group, throwing into contrast the darkness around, heightened the element of the visionary, the quality of a waking dream, that distinguished the picture.

But what appeared to be an effect of spontaneity, of magnificent chance strokes, of fevered inspiration, was in reality the product of a carefully pondered, almost dialectical construction of mathematical precision. The various elements which Leonardo had laboriously assembled interlocked like the wheels of a machine, successively carrying on the movement. Two immense diagonals, crossing one another above the Madonna's head, give the picture a shoreless horizon that seems like a plunge into the abyss. The space around the principal figures is delimited by a triangle of which one side runs from the crown of Mary's head past the outstretched arms of the Christ Child, falling over the back of the kneeling king to the earth; the other zigzags down along the outline of the Virgin's brightly lit shoulder and over the head of the prostrate king. The stairs in the background carry one diagonal further from right to left; the other diagonal rises past the galloping horses to the distant hills. Everything in the picture, every figure of man or animal or tree, is subordinated to the domination of this scheme of composition. Every motif, however relatively unimportant, every figure, however modest its part, contributes to the same focusing on the principal group.

There is a worshipper in the third row, looking up with his head thrown back and his arm stretched out as though he were dazzled by the miracle. His pure profile with the straight, Grecian nose, his half-opened mouth with the short bow, abruptly falling away, of the lip, his out-thrust chin, all are irradiated with the will to believe and serve. The man and his emotion are inseparably united; it is the expression of a unique psychological happening. Yet from the point of view of the composition this youth is there only to take up the diagonal that proceeds from the corner figure over the sunken head of a man in meditation and to lead it on with the outstretched hand to the silhouette of the tree that rises like a note of exclamation on the edge of the central group.

Leonardo was scarcely thirty when he painted the *Adoration of the Magi,* but already he was familiar with every means of attaining final perfection; and, since perfection floated before his mind's eye with such inexorable clearness, he was no longer able to content himself with anything short of it. But at the moment when he solved the first great problem of his life in a masterpiece, there began the tragedy of his life, the wrecking of his search for perfection on material obstacles. As though an envious destiny had determined to set limits to men's creative power, Leonardo again and again found external circumstances conspiring to block his path. Fulfilment and frustration lay already closely interwoven on the threshold of his existence. The *Adoration of the Magi* never got beyond its brown and gold groundwork. The deep tragedy of this fragment of a miracle seems to be incorporated in one of the corner figures, the youth in armour, the only figure which looks out of the picture. Leonardo's fellow-painters used to use that position, in that attitude, for their own portraits, as though they wished to give the spectacle they were offering an expositor and interpreter who addressed himself straight to the observer. Following this tradition, Leonardo may have intended to capture for all time his own youth and strength—but he did not get beyond the outlines. From the twilight of the groundwork this figure, turning with its collected sideward glance, looks out like a ghostly shadow from the border of a world of shadows unredeemed.

10

What was it that led Leonardo to abandon his picture unfinished? Was it flight from responsibility, sudden fear that the task was beyond his powers? Or did it seem to have lost its attraction, once he had overcome the main difficulties? The actual reason that led him to throw up his uncompleted work has remained an unsolved mystery; but there is much that suggests that life in Florence had become more and more distasteful to him. About the same time when he was contenting himself with the modest recognition of his work by the monks of San Donato a Scopeto in the form of payments in kind, there fell to fellow-artists of his in Florence, Domenico Ghirlandaio, Cosimo Rosselli, and Sandro Botticelli, and his fellow-student Perugino, the most important commission the world of his day had to offer, the decoration of the papal chapel which was to immortalize the name of Sixtus IV. It was with the indignation of one who has been passed over, who has failed to secure the recognition due to him, that Leonardo saw his friends leave for Rome, the goal of all desire, the holy place of art.

He became painfully sensitive to the way the time of his full powers was slipping between his fingers. "Nothing is more fleeting," he wrote, "than the years, the sons of time." [36] This fear of the passage of time took strange possession of the young man again and again, as though he felt already that neither his creative gift nor his ardent pursuit of knowledge could bring forth its fruit within the short span of a man's life. People thought him spendthrift of time, but he was filled with the panic fear of being too late, of being robbed of the achievements and experiences for which he was striving, a fear that usually comes only to the ageing: "O time, consumer of all things, O envious old age . . . When Helen looked in her mirror, and saw how old age had rendered her face wrinkled and flabby, she wept and thought to herself, Why had she been twice carried off?" [37] Tired of waiting, and no longer comforting himself with the thought that his opportunity would come, he wrote: "He who has an opportunity and waits for another loses his friend and never has any money." [38]

And yet there was no lack in his own city even of the most splendid commissions, nor was there lacking a patron of the arts with particularly keen discrimination and with pride in his patronage. Lorenzo de' Medici, Il Magnifico, was no less persevering in his recruitment of outstanding personalities than in his cultivation of popular favour; he was an impassioned collector of ancient works of art, sending his agents to the ends of the earth to secure them; he set up later the first academy of art for young artists, in his palace and park, and he started the first museum. But in his collection he had not a single picture of Leonardo's, and not a single commission came to Leonardo directly from him.

Even more irritating to Leonardo than Lorenzo's indifference to his work was the arrogance of the intellectual élite who stood like a wall between Il Magnifico and his contemporaries. The company of the Platonic Academy had the intolerance of every clique, and their insistence on their own eminence was often carried to comic lengths. Like other men who take themselves too seriously, they burdened their proceedings with a mass of solemn absurdities. Their discussion evenings sometimes revealed a strong resemblance to the hair-splittings of the medieval Schoolmen whom they so despised. One evening a friend brought a greeting from an absent member to which Marsilio Ficino simply replied in the same terms; a pettifogging member objected that it would not do to pay back in the same coin, for the person concerned might think that his gift was being rejected. A hot controversy arose over the bright idea; finally Marsilio Ficino made this pronouncement: "If my right hand gives back to my left hand something the left has given it, this something, even if it is no longer in my right hand, is nevertheless not lost to me—and do not my friend and I belong like two hands to the same body?"

The poet Luigi Pulci was as determined as Leonardo to have no dealings with this wise company; he poked fun at the humanists' endless discussions over the nature of the soul, "whence it comes and whither it goes," at their mania for quoting Plato and Aristotle, their banquets with music and song, and their continual babble of discussion, "enough to turn your brain." Leonardo was conscious of the superiority of his own research to the book-learning of the humanists, of his own practical work to their idle war of words. His work aimed at providing increased security for humanity in a still unexplored environment. He went on with it in the midst of his studies for the *Adoration*. One of his sheets in the Louvre shows alongside splendid figures of young men a sketch of an instrument "for weighing the air and determining when the weather will break"—a disk with a pointer weighted at one end with a small sponge.

But the scholars ignored Leonardo's efforts. The humanists, clubbing together in mutual admiration, prevented all unauthorized access to the patrons on whom they depended for their reputation and their prosperity. Leonardo attributed to them his inability to obtain recognition in his own city. "They go about, puffed up and pompous, in fine raiment and bejewelled, not from the fruits of their own labours but from those of others; my own labours they refuse to recognize. They despise me, the inventor, but how much more are they to blame for not being inventors, but trumpeters and reciters of the works of others. They are little indebted to nature, for it is only by the chance that they wear clothes that they can be distinguished from herds of animals." [39]

Leonardo never forgot the wrong done to him at this period, the injury he suffered at the hands of these people. Many years later, when he was preparing his works for publication, he recalled the affront of long since: "I know well that because I have not had a literary education there are some who will think in their arrogance that they are entitled to set me down as uncultured—the fools! They will say that because I am uncultured I am not able adequately to express myself on the subject of which I wish to treat." [40] The cry of "uncultured"—*omo sanza lettere*—was raised against the man who had set out to acquire a range of knowledge such as no living man ever possessed before or after him.

He was now thirty years old; against the omnipotence of the pedants he had nothing to set but his faith in himself; he was sick of living in Florence and longed to get away from the city. Rome had offered him nothing, but might not Milan offer a field, rich Milan, which had been paying court to the artists of Florence? He had nothing left that tied him to Florence, and was waiting only for the opportunity of getting away. An amusement of his took him, perhaps by pure chance, farther than all his efforts had done. Where he had failed as a painter he succeeded as a lute-player—"for he was without an equal in the playing of the lute," says his anonymous biographer. The humanists regarded music, that "soul-medicine," as a peculiarly elegant art; as Ficino said, it "can be pursued only by cultured persons." This philosopher used to pretend to himself that he was a Greek man of learning of the classic period; at every banquet of the Platonic Academy he brought with him a lyre copied from an ancient pattern, and sang to its accompaniment in his cracked, untuneful voice; Lorenzo de' Medici would join in raucously, plucking his lute with hard and ungentle touch.

For all that, Il Magnifico was a very good judge of music. Once a gifted organ-builder, Antonio Squarcialupi, was belittled in his presence; Lorenzo warmly defended him: "If you knew what it means to be supreme in any field, you would be more lenient in your judgment of him." One day Lorenzo heard that the painter Leonardo had made a lyre of silver in the form of a horse's skull, the animal's teeth serving as frets to indicate the notes. He was delighted with the rich tone of the instrument and with its bizarre form, and as at the moment he had political reasons for cultivating the goodwill of a man who was also a lover of music and of the unusual, Lodovico Sforza, the new ruler of Milan, he decided to present the instrument to him. Leonardo declared his readiness to deliver the gift himself, and Lorenzo de' Medici had not the slightest objection to his leaving Florence, to seek abroad the good fortune his own city had denied him. "Florence," wrote Vasari, "treats its artists as time its creatures: it creates them and then slowly destroys and consumes them." Furnished with a letter of recommendation from Lorenzo de' Medici, with the musical horse's skull of silver, and with a boxful of sketches and drawings and unfinished pictures, and accompanied by his friend, the singer Atalante Miglioretti, Leonardo set out for Milan.

Into one of these pictures, now in the Vatican, a picture which he never completed, Leonardo had introduced all the bitterness, all the disgust that precedes perfection, all the revulsion from life before life's experiences are gathered, that festered in him. At the entrance to a grotto there kneels Saint Jerome, a horribly emaciated old man, holding in his outstretched hand a stone with which he is beating his sunken breast. The silhouette of the kneeling saint is broadly laid in; his cloak, caught up in wide asymmetrical folds, is done only in ground colour, but the shoulder, with the muscles roped over it, is sharply and fully modelled, and so also are the lean neck, a bundle of wiry sinews, and the bald head and fleshless cheeks, all skin and bone, a mummy's head, lifeless save for the screeching of the big twisted mouth and the flickering glance of a man in an ecstasy of self-immolating contrition. The withered body is set against the jagged rock of the grotto like one block of stone against another, light against dark. The steep diagonal of the extended arm is emphasized by the parallels of the heavily built frame of a lion in the foreground; it cuts the side of a triangle which runs from the head of this roaring lion and falls backward from the saint's brow, which is thrust forward, over the elbow. Thus the observer's gaze is led into the depth, into the obscurity of the dismal grotto which the saint called the confidant of his secret. The rocky wilderness stretches round the saint's mortified body like a silence into which his fervent cry penetrates without echo. Every carnal appetite has left this emaciated face, the skeleton of this breast, the havoc of this body. The saint is alone with his suffering; and still he ravages his own body, as though he were intent on destroying the last twitch of feeling, the last vestige of rebellion in the martyred flesh. But the anguish that surrounds his widely parted lips is allied to blessedness and has almost become a smile, and the gaze that seeks to wrest compassion from Heaven is already softened with the consolation of Heaven's mercy.

Never had surfeit of life been so depicted by any man, or suffering in all its hopeless hideousness, as though the artist meant utterly to repudiate the pleasures of the senses, to cauterize every living desire with the glowing iron of martyrdom. The unfinished Saint Jerome, like a fragment from the broken vessel of Leonardo's youth, remained by the side of his path, which was strewn with such fragments.

CHAPTER TWO

Years of Waiting

Non si volta chi a stella è fisso.

He turns not back who is bound to a star.
(W. L., 198 recto.)

IT WAS a dark, immobile, inscrutable face, the expressionless face of a man used to dissembling, that Leonardo scanned to see the effect of what he was saying. Lodovico Sforza listened with the feigned interest of a sovereign. His official biographer Corio describes him as showing uniform readiness to listen to anything. But he could also affect to be deaf and dumb, and stupid, when he did not want to understand, and the envoy from the Este family, who could permit himself many liberties, had told Sforza laughingly to his face, only a little time before this, that he could not play these tricks on him.

Leonardo, however, regarded himself as an excellent psychologist, able to read men like an open book, a diplomat, perhaps a better diplomat than the envoy of the Este family, with the gift of charming an unwilling ear. A good deal later, when he had accumulated much experience from intercourse with princes and kings, he wrote down for his pupils and young friends rules for dealing with the mighty ones of this earth—naïve and elementary rules, such as could be laid down only by one who had communed too much with himself and, in the pride of his own intellectual powers, underestimated the intelligence of other people. Toward the end of his life, forgetting his own disappointments, he wrote: "At all times the words that do not please the ear of a listener fill him with tedium or even annoyance: you may see the sign of it in that such listeners emit copious yawns. Accordingly, in talking to men whose goodwill you desire to enlist, when you see such signs of annoyance, cut short your words and change the subject;

otherwise, instead of gaining their goodwill you will incur their dislike and enmity. And if you want to discover a man's tastes without directly asking him, talk to him on many different subjects, and when you see that one of them has arrested his attention, so that he no longer yawns or frowns or the like, you may be certain that this subject on which you are talking is the one in which he takes pleasure." [1] In all this Leonardo was already sufficiently practised, and he sought for subjects that might arrest the attention of the man on whose favour so much depended.

This interview, of such crucial importance to Leonardo, took place at about the end of 1482 or the beginning of 1483. Lodovico was then in the early days of his power. He had waited long and patiently for the opportunity of seizing the dukedom of Milan, to which he was not the lawful heir. His position as a younger son, heir only in the event of death or disaster, had increased and intensified his natural adaptability, his patience and tenacity, his closeness and cunning. His education, which had been entirely in the hands of his mother, the energetic Bianca Visconti, had accentuated his natural disinclination for contention and preference for accommodation and ingratiation. She was the illegitimate heir of the long line of the Visconti, and the upstart Francesco Sforza, who owed his dominion to his rough soldier's hands, had entrusted her with the bringing up of his children to be real princes and princesses. The eldest boy and heir to the throne, Galeazzo Maria, had been headstrong, capricious, and brutal, "a youth of poor intelligence," in his mother's words, and she had no influence over him; she had devoted herself to the younger son, lavishing on him her care and energy, her affection and her love of domination: with his plastic nature he had been a ready and appreciative pupil. Mother and son were so bound up in one another that Lodovico came to her with all his troubles and wants, confessed his sins to her as a boy, asked her permission before he bought new clothes, and, when they were parted, wrote to her almost every day.

The tutor whom Bianca chose for her children, the humanist Francesco Filelfo, also found Lodovico a particularly responsive pupil; with his quick perception and his never-failing memory he acquired a knowledge of the ancient languages and literature so rapidly that at the age of eleven he was able to compose long Latin speeches. This ambitious, contentious, unreliable teacher also initiated Lodovico into his dialectical artifices, his mastery of sophistical arguments, and his delight in the speech that disguises thought. Thanks to his air of decorous modesty, to the mask of immobility which his features wore from early youth, and to the shrewdness with which he insisted on the limitations of his own position, Lodovico was so successful in winning the confidence of his hot-tempered and suspicious brother that after their journey together to Florence in 1471 Duke Galeazzo made Lodovico his heir in the event of the duke's sons' dying without issue.

At that time the duke was hurrying home from his triumphal journey to Florence, passing incognito through his own states, beset by vague fears; and already Lodovico knew that his brother's rule would come to a violent end. He was familiar with the uncontrolled covetousness that distorted the duke's pale, handsome, wild face; he was well aware of the duke's many and furious amorous pursuits, and had even put up with his own name being used as a cover for the duke's presents to his lady-loves. He knew of the fits of bloodthirstiness to which his nerve-racked brother gave way, and of the stories that seeped out through the thick walls of the duke's castle in Milan and circulated among the population, stories that made him shudder. The duke had had his favourite nailed alive into a chest, and had listened to the victim's death-rattle; another victim he had mutilated with his own hands, and watched the hot red blood trickle from the wounds; he went down into the vaults and remained for hours alongside the corpses, breathing the stench of putrefaction that sent the diseased blood faster through his veins. It was an age that set little value on human lives, but Lodovico, in spite of a streak of ferocity, was a man of normal healthy instincts, and he had been so revolted by the things he witnessed during his life with his brother that he conceived a horror of bloodshed, and in later years always shrank back from witnessing any violent death.

Lodovico had set out on a diplomatic mission to France when, in 1476, the duke fell beneath the daggers of young idealists who regarded themselves as successors of the ancient tyrannicides. Lodovico hurried home, but before he could arrive his sister-in-law Bona of Savoy already had a firm hold of the government of Milan as regent for her young son Gian Galeazzo. Under pressure from his brothers he departed prematurely from his favourite Fabian tactics and attempted a revolt against the duchess. The revolt was crushed, his brother Ottaviano fled and was drowned in the Adda, and Lodovico was exiled to Pisa. He complained bitterly of the waste of the years of his youth in exile, and from Pisa he made frequent journeys to Florence, not only in search of allies but for the sake of Florentine culture. He was attracted by the intellectual atmosphere of the city, and he liked its cultivated speech, in contrast with the rough Milanese dialect; later he brought the poet Bernardo Bellincioni from Florence in order that the example of "his ornate Florentine diction" might help "the city to smooth and polish its rather rough speech."

Lodovico himself began to get glimpses in Florence of something beyond the crude and banal luxury by which he set store; he began to appreciate the value of the artistic activities that had brought fame to the city. He learned from Lorenzo de' Medici the advantages to be gained from the encouragement of the fine arts, and was especially able to realize the usefulness as elements in prestige of such works of art as fine buildings and monuments to princely families. During these days in Florence he took up again the plan which Galeazzo Maria had been considering, of erecting a colossal monument to their famous father, the founder of the ducal house. He began to negotiate with Florentine sculptors, enjoying, as is the way of the exiled great, the discussion of ambitious plans for the days of his return; and it may be that Leonardo met him at this time and gained some hope of securing that important commission.

Lodovico took the opportunity of the fighting and disorders that followed the conspiracy of the Pazzi to appear on the frontier of Milan and offer aid to his sister-in-law, and he made such a display of loyal submission that Bona of Savoy, disarmed and flattered, placed faith in him—*par sottise,* "out of stupidity," was Philippe de Commines's blunt comment. Her gouty old chancellor, Cicco Simonetta, had been Francesco Sforza's adviser and knew the quality of that princely family. He could see behind Lodovico's smiling mask, and he warned the duchess: "I shall lose my head, and before long Your Serene Highness will lose your state." Three days later, on October 10, 1480, the old man was got out of Milan, hidden in a cask—the new ruler had not the courage for a public execution in his capital. At dawn of the thirtieth the ex-chancellor knelt in a damp meadow in Pavia, and as he saw the glistening axe of the executioner he shook his wise grey head at the thought of the rapid fulfilment of his prophecy. Bona of Savoy was soon an exile from the territory of Milan, going from one to another of her castles, and spending her days in the vain effort to enlist the aid of the most powerful princes in the world. She had still before her a long life in obscurity in which to reflect on the unheeded wisdom of her beheaded chancellor.

"Contrary to what has been reported to Your Magnificence," wrote Lodovico Sforza to his ally Lorenzo de' Medici, who had expressed doubts of the solidity of the new regime in Milan, "I have never, since my return by the grace of God to my own house and to the head of the government, seen this state so secure and firmly established as at the present moment. . . . In these matters I keep to the facts, and I am more trustworthy than those who are unable to talk of them without spleen. Others may prefer to build castles in the air; I have no intention of leaving the firm ground."

His easy triumph and the success of his simple little ruse had given Lodovico the feeling that he was a consummate politician. "Il Moro has something of the fox in him, and something of the lion," said his court poet and flatterer Bellincioni; but Lodovico gave no evidence at all of leonine quality, and contented himself with the cunning of the fox. He had not even enough of the lion to face the fact of his usurpation of power; at a time when open usurpation was more frequent than legitimate succession, this tyrant of Milan clung to constitutional forms and legal subterfuges. He contented himself at first with exercising absolute power as regent for his nephew, then a minor.

With an upstart's prudence, he tried to win over the strongest princely houses by matrimonial alliances. He betrothed his eleven-year-old nephew to the granddaughter, then eight years old, of King Ferdinand of Naples; the king conferred on Lodovico the title of duke of Bari. He offered himself in marriage to the daughter of the duke of Ferrara, and, failing to secure the hand of the elder daughter Isabella, who had been promised to the margrave of Mantua, he betrothed himself to the five-year-old Beatrice. But these alliances soon dragged him into hostilities which, although he owed his power to a war, he had been anxiously trying to evade. Once more it was the ambition of the Pope's nephew or son, Girolamo Riario, that divided Italy into two enemy camps—out of nothing more serious than a dispute between Venice and Ferrara over the working of salt deposits—and war was raging already up to the gates of Rome.

Warlike cares were weighing their heaviest on Lodovico at the moment when he received the Florentine painter who had come to his court with a silver lute. He could spare no thought for his plans for fine monuments: his ally Alfonso of Calabria, son of King Ferdinand, had just been utterly defeated by the Venetian army commander, Roberto Malatesta di Rimini, and thousands of dead lay on the pestilential battlefield of Campo Morto. Lodovico's ambitious projects for the display of his newly won power had had to give place to anxious thought for its preservation. Leonardo, following his own precept, soon observed that of all the proposals which he laid before the ruler of Milan it was those concerned with innovations in the art of war that aroused most interest. He concentrated on the opening Lodovico seemed to offer here. This, he must have said to himself, was a good opportunity for him to secure rapid recognition in this foreign court—for, like many men whose interest is confined almost entirely to general problems, he was inclined to be unpractical in everyday matters. He brought all his eloquence and characteristic persistence into play.

From time to time he looked searchingly at the big impressive man enthroned in the bare domed hall of the castle of Milan. The man's figure rose squarely against the hard back of his seat, clad in stiff brocade. He wore broad sleeves, richly embroidered and puffed out round his big, heavy shoulders; across his breast there slanted the glistening device, embroidered in pearls, of two clasped hands, with a motto of the primitive aggressiveness that Lodovico particularly affected—*Tale a ti quale ad mi*, "As thou dost to me, so shall I do to thee." A heavy gold chain buried itself in the rigid folds of the brocade and the pearl patterning, clinking as it fell against the stiff silk and sending at every breath a sparkle from a great pendant of rough-cut brilliants. The richly coloured, gold-worked clothes accentuated the olive sallowness of the duke's face. His complexion had won him at an early age the slightly mocking nickname of Il Moro, the Moor, which he readily accepted, with a sure instinct for the advertising value of a peculiarity if it fixed upon him an effective popular name.

His face was a strange product of contradictory features, some indicating greatness and some weakness. The pointed head was covered with very smooth and very dark hair, like a polished helmet; the hair, carefully singed, came down over the forehead to the eyebrows, and shaded the little round eyes; it was allowed to grow in profusion round the short neck, which thus seemed still shorter. The narrow nose of the Visconti, inherited from his mother, with its thin, sensitive nostrils, contrasted with the fleshy Sforza chin. The firm little mouth, with red coquettish lips, came as a surprise in this dark, heavy face, like a seal of sensuality.

But at this moment Leonardo penetrated no further into the mystery of these features, for he was under the influence of his own "terrible gift of exposition," as Vasari calls it, and when after this long conversation, he sat down to write a memorandum containing the substance of what he had been saying to the lord of Milan, he had great difficulty in getting his manifold proposals into shape.

2

This famous document[2] is a strange mixture of courtierly deference and lofty pride. It abounds in mysterious allusions, but in essentials it is of the utmost lucidity—the work of an able man who knew his value, though he had not yet had the opportunity of demonstrating it.

"Having sufficiently seen and considered by now, most illustrious Sir, the experiments of all those who are reputed masters and contrivers of instruments of war, and having found that in character and working the said instruments do not differ in any way from those which are in general use, I shall now endeavour, without interfering with anyone else, to divulge and explain my secrets to Your Excellency; and so soon as you deign to command it I undertake to carry into execution in due course all the things which I am about to enumerate briefly and summarily to you."

What he now enumerated—briefly, as he said, but with the circumstantiality of a period that had not yet made a fetish of specialization or developed a jargon of the initiated, still allowing free play to the intellect in every field—was the result of his theoretical and practical studies of recent years, a combination of the military science of his age with his own experiments and inventions. Leonardo owed his knowledge of the history of military technique to his careful study, witnessed by many extracts in the MS B, of the treatise of Roberto Valturio, *De Re Militari;* and he took over from Valturio the many references to ancient weapons and classical campaigns with which he interlarded his statement, in order to lend additional authority to his own proposals. These were:

"1. I have methods of construction of very light and strong bridges, which can be transported with the greatest ease, offering the means of pursuing an enemy and also, if necessary, of fleeing from him; and others which are safe and immune from damage from fire or in an engagement, and are at the same time easy to take to pieces and set up again. I also know how to fire and destroy the bridges of the enemy."

For each of these proposals more or less fully worked out drafts exist among Leonardo's papers, some of earlier date and some of later, as if the ideas have been thrashed out in the course of placing them before other persons. There are plans for flying bridges with wooden sides that would give protection against enemy guns; for use between high banks there are double tracks, one for cavalry and guns and the other for infantry.[3] There is a plan for a series of bridges that could be rapidly put together, using rope instead of nails [4]; and one for bridges made of long poles lying on forked pegs in strong frames.[5]

"2. In laying siege to a fortress I know how to empty the water out of moats, and how to construct the most varied types of siege bridges, mantlets, scaling-ladders, and other instruments required for such work."

In connexion with his system of transportable bridges, Leonardo sketched gangways that could be moved at an inclination against bastions or towers,[6] and covered footways on rollers which could be run out by means of cables and windlasses across a moat and raised against a wall. He went on to describe methods of climbing fortifications, first considering the simplest and most practical method, by securing the assistance of one of the besieged soldiers. "But if you are unable to make terms with one of the men inside to pull up the rope ladder, you must climb by driving irons of this shape" (giving a sketch) "into the joints between the stones, an ell apart. And when you have reached the top, fasten the rope ladder with an iron which is swathed in cloth, so as to make no noise." A very lively drawing is added in explanation [7]—it might well be taken for a modern "second-story" burglar at work.

To protect the besieging forces from being fired on, he suggested transportable bastions "filled with hay, and pointed in front, so that the shots from the artillery can do no damage" [8]; and wheeled protective roofs (*manteletti*) which could be moved from one point to another.[9] He showed, on the other hand, how the besieged troops could overturn the storming-ladders with horizontal beams pushed out from within the fortress by means of windlass and ropes.[10] He advised the besiegers to bribe soldiers within the fortress, and at the same time gave the besieged advice, "for times when there is ground for suspicion," on preventing treasonable activities among the defenders and correspondence with the enemy.

If the attempt was made to storm a fortress, "casks must be fetched and filled with earth. When these are rolled down the slope against the enemy they will prove of great service." [11] But the attacking party could protect itself from these casks by driving in slanting piles with beams between them.

"3. Item. If, owing to the height of the ramparts or the strength of the position, it is impossible for the besiegers to make use of bombards, I have methods of detroying any citadel or fort which is not built on rock."

The methods Leonardo had in view—he gave no details lest he should play into the hands of rivals—were underground passages and galleries, with mining-chambers, some round, some rectangular, dug in the thickness of the walls, especially in towers which might be expected to have powder magazines in their cellars.

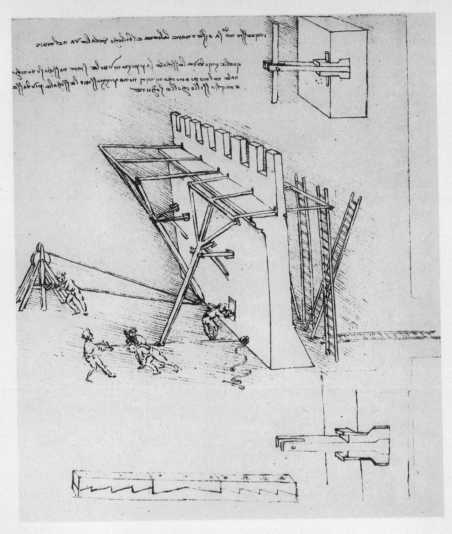

Beams for overturning scaling ladders

CODEX ATLANTICUS

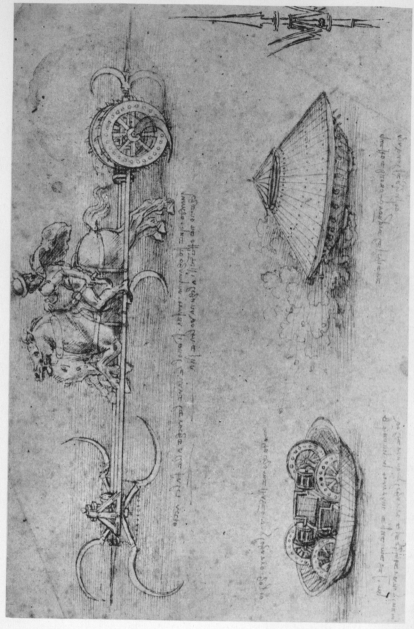

Scythed car and armoured car

Many years later Leonardo carefully studied the diversion of streams to an enemy's disadvantage; at this time he was already recommending the destruction of walls "without bombards, if you have a stream available." At an agreed signal all sluices should be opened and a vast inundation would carry all before it and rush in cascades over the fortress walls.[12] This was the first recorded suggestion of the use of water power for purposes of destruction. Leonardo went on to say that in this way a battlefield could be submerged—a foreshadowing of the desperate measure resorted to in 1672 by the Dutch against the French army, when they destroyed dikes and let the Zuider Zee inundate their country.

"4. I also have methods of making bombards which are very easily and conveniently transported. They can send out a hail of shot, and at the same time terrify the enemy with the accompanying smoke, to his great injury and confusion."

In a fine sketch in a private collection in Paris, Leonardo has represented the operation of a bomb made with hemp and fish-glue, with tubes attached like spokes to a copper ball filled with powder. "Ball, propelling itself and throwing out sheaves of fire six ells long," Leonardo wrote at the foot of the sheet; and he carefully drew the "sheaves" of flame shooting out in every direction, as though this were an innocent piece of pyrotechnics. Even when he went on to show soldiers in flight, their round steel helmets suggested nothing less Arcadian than shepherds' caps, and the men were light-footed classical heroes. Leonardo's death-dealing mechanisms are steeped in this air of beauty and antiquity, as though his interest in his subject were entirely dissociated from its purpose, or as though he kept his sense of realities out of the way lest it should spoil his pleasure in invention. This sketch with its classic harmony of form gave, moreover, a glimpse into the distant future, for it anticipated a weapon of modern times, the rotatory rocket invented by the American Hale in 1846, which was to give proof of its terrible efficacy.

"This is the most lethal machine that exists," wrote Leonardo under his design[13] of a spherical projectile filled with gunpowder and balls. "The centre ball bursts and scatters the rest, which it sets on fire, within a period of time no longer than an Ave Maria," he cheerfully added at the end of his description of this engine of

destruction. He called it Clotonbrot, and it was the first of modern
gas shells, since, in order to increase its effectiveness, he recommended that the projectiles should be filled with pieces of sulphur, the fumes of which would "produce stupor." Leonardo was
familiar not only with fuses but with the principle of percussion
firing, for he drew projectiles with a heavy conical base which,
when the projectile hit its object, penetrated a thin copper parti-
tioning and fired the explosive contents.

Leonardo's contemporaries were already acquainted with the
powder-shell, *pila pulvere plena bombardæ;* Santini mentions it
about the middle of the fifteenth century; but it was little more
than a primitive rocket. They knew of hollow glass shells, invented by Leonardo's rival, the military engineer Francesco di
Giorgio Martini, which were probably ignited by means of a sulphur fuse introduced through the neck; and they were familiar
with metal shells, supposed to be an invention of Sigismondo
Malatesta and consisting of two halves bound together by hinges
and iron bands. But these latter, like the shell used by Charles
VIII before Naples in 1495, by Maximilian of Padua in 1509, and
by Alfonso d'Este at Ravenna in 1512, were fire-balls rather than
actual explosive shells. The first recorded use of true bombs,
metal containers cast in a single piece and filled with gunpowder,
was at the siege of Wachtendock in 1588, and their invention
dates back at the earliest to 1562. Leonardo's idea of firing explosive shells from heavy guns (bombards) was also new; most surprising, however, of all was his attempt to use the metal container
to carry a bursting charge. The idea came up again for a short
time at the beginning of the seventeenth century, but was first
brought to its present horrible effectiveness by Shrapnel at the end
of the eighteenth century.

Leonardo's projects ran through the whole gamut of the human
desire to destroy, which has persisted unabated from ancient days
to our own. On the lines of the ancient fire-arrows mentioned by
Valturio, he invented a weapon similar in form to the medieval
javelin, but fitted with a powder capsule in the middle of the
shaft. On the outside were two spikes or horns, which were pressed
together by the impact of the weapon, thus setting fire to the powder and the whole fabric, which was impregnated with pitch [14]—

a weapon aiming at the same effect as the modern flame-thrower. For infantry engagements, the murderous hand-to-hand fighting, he recommended, as particularly effective, disks of which the shape was apparently borrowed from the ancients, but which consisted of explosive tubes fitted radially into the framing, to be lit with a fuse before throwing—the hand-grenades of recent wars of annihilation.

Leonardo was concerned at all times to make his weapons of the most inflammable material, so that they should burn up "rapidly, before the enemy can benefit by learning the idea of the invention," [15] or even see what it was. Thus, a shell to be thrown by a ballista had cartridges arranged radially round its centre—"there is no means of stopping its pestilential activitity," he writes with satisfaction. "And if you have thrown six to eight of these shells among your enemies, you will certainly be victorious." [16]

"5. Item. I have methods of reaching an indicated point by secret winding passages, excavated without a sound. They can be led if necessary beneath moats or a river."

The mine galleries, which he had already mentioned in connexion with the storming of fortresses, were known in ancient and medieval times in the form of tunnels, secretly dug, into which highly inflammable material was brought, together with explosives, in order to bring down whatever stood above. About the middle of the fifteenth century, Santini and the Sienese engineer Jacopo Mariano Taccola proposed the laying of powder mines in addition to the tunnels, but only as an elaboration of the old procedure. This was tried on the suggestion of Francesco di Giorgio Martini at the siege of Serezanella by the Genoese in 1487, but without success, as the points of application had been miscalculated. The powder mines were more successful at the siege of the Castel Nuovo at Naples in 1495, but it was not until the beginning of the sixteenth century that full success was attained by Pedro Navarro, in the attack on the citadel of Cephalonia (1500) and the siege of Naples (1503). It was so difficult, however, to calculate the effect of this new method that Navarro, who had failed with it in 1512 through using too little powder, returned in 1515, at the siege of the castle of Milan, to the old tunnelling.

Leonardo, however, was already acquainted with the physical

laws that determine the limits and the possibilities of the use of explosives. Subsequently, in working out his proposals, he went into them so thoroughly that he included a fully detailed specification of excavating tools required [17]—hooks, rakes, shovels, a two-handled plough, miners' shallow wheelbarrows which could be quickly made out of staves and withies, and so on, down to small and large drills with the appropriate handles. He sketched naked figures in the attitude of classic caryatides, lifting a beam; and a figure that might be taken for a sketch for a David is merely a navvy with his spade held in the proper way. There is a particularly fine rapid sketch, showing a chain of naked men with the frames of gods, handing on the excavated stones from man to man; at its foot Leonardo has put the pedantic explanation: "The way to carry out a task with speed." [18]

Leonardo had further strange proposals to make in his memorandum:

6. "I shall build covered wagons, safe and unassailable; when they penetrate with their artillery among the enemy, there are no ranks in such close array that the wagons cannot break them. And behind the wagons numbers of infantrymen can follow, unharmed and without impediment."

He dwelt for some time on this idea of an armoured car. He had found in Valturio's work a mention of a car fitted with projecting sickles, which the Romans had employed. While he was developing this idea, furnishing the vehicle with modern mechanism and already inclined to suspect the uselessness of the whole idea in practice, he sketched an apocalyptic vision of death and horror (now in the Turin Museum). He began with a sketch of a car provided with cogwheels and with four enormous sickles set in motion by a huge screw; then he drew another, resembling a modern mowing machine, except that its frightful harvest consisted of mutilated human bodies. The horses are plunging ahead, with a splendid energy in their extended limbs; the driver is bending forward. The curve of his back forms a parallel with the bend of the horses' necks, and the short fluttering cloak continues the wave motif. Bent rods lead to the cogwheels, and the sickles sprout like flowers out of the screw—one graceful curve after another, in vertical and horizontal layers. Where the sickles have passed, a victim is falling, battling with death; another, his legs severed, is writhing in agony; a third is reduced to a torso, with his severed arms and legs whirling through the air. Yet there is such an atmosphere of peace and harmony in the sketch that it seems as if the artist cannot for a moment have been conscious of what the scene he was drawing meant in reality.

Another battle car is fitted with knouts instead of sickles; another wields spiked maces—weapons of primeval savagery united with modern mechanism (Windsor collection). The artistry seems finer than ever as Leonardo grows less satisfied with his technical idea, as though he were trying to use his art to deceive himself. But this self-deception did not last long: soon he rejected his idea, realizing that the cars "will do no less harm to friends than to enemies, since they will bring fear and demoralization among your own men, and are easily put out of action." [19] He tendered this objection exactly as if he had never himself been mistaken on the subject.

The final and the only satisfactory solution of the problem of a protected car, which Leonardo promised Lodovico Sforza in his memorandum, had none of these drawbacks. With its overlapping sheets it resembles a huge tortoise (sketch in the British Museum). The armour panelling is pierced by a circle of loopholes for sharpshooters; the pointed roof has similar loopholes, and an opening at the top to admit air. Most striking of all in this early forecast of a modern tank is the fact that Leonardo had thought out a new means of locomotion for it, in order to avoid the use of draught animals, which could easily be wounded. The car was set in motion by man-power, by means of crank handles attached to horizontal trundle wheels which turned the circular spindles of pinwheels that drove the wheels of the car. "Eight men are required for moving the car; they will have to turn it this way and that in pursuit of the enemy," added Leonardo.

It was a remarkable idea for his day. He was soon to develop it further in order to adapt it to peaceful purposes; but at this moment his interest was thoroughly concentrated on the technique of warfare, to the exclusion of everything else. And among the technical problems of warfare he devoted most attention to that of gun-making. The models he invented showed an enormous advance over the artillery of his day. The most famous of contemporary cannon, such as the Scottish Mons Meg, which shot granite balls weighing three hundred pounds at the siege of Dumbarton in 1489, could be moved only with the aid of enormous handspikes, and the "reinforces" containing the powder chambers were screwed in from the mouth of the barrel, the "long chase." Leonardo announced proudly in his memorandum:

"7. Item. If occasion should arise, I shall manufacture bombards, mortars, and catapults of the most beautiful and serviceable forms, differing from those in common use."

One of these new models was a great bombard "which is loaded from the rear, and a single person can screw it in and out." [20] But, as in so many other instances, Leonardo does not seem to have succeeded in carrying out this project, for the breech-loading gun did not make its appearance until later; it was invented at Nuremberg in 1515.

In the course of his very thorough study of the subject of light and heavy guns Leonardo came into contact, almost by accident, with a power that was to revolutionize the world—steam. He must have been conscious of the novelty of his discovery, for, whenever he was getting too far away from well-established traditions, he would make his peace with the humanist training of the rulers of his day by covering himself with the authority of the Greeks or Romans; and he did so in this case. He put forward his steam bombard as an invention of Archimedes, and with his characteristic pleasure in mystification he expressed the weights in talents and the distances in stadia. "The architronite," he wrote,[21] "is a copper engine invented by Archimedes, which fires heavy iron balls with great force." He drew a water vessel connected to a copper tube which was heated by a coal fire. The water flowed into the red-hot tube and turned into steam, which drove the ball out of the mouth of the tube. "It will seem a miracle to those who see the force and hear the noise." Leonardo returned on various occasions to this great motive power of the future, but his experiments passed unnoticed, and the coming of the new world of which he had had a vision was deferred by the slumber of centuries.

The guns used in Leonardo's time were almost exclusively of

cast bronze; the older cannon had been made with iron bars. The guns Leonardo designed were in most cases intended to be produced from bronze or pure copper, either by casting around a core or by solid casting followed by boring. He gave precise instructions for both processes, calculated the thickness of metal for the "bore walls," which were to be of the length of six or eighteen balls, according as the ball was of lead or stone; with light guns the length was carried as far as thirty balls.

In addition to bronze casting Leonardo employed the old method of hooping together iron staves; he devised special machines that substantially improved the fitting together of the separate parts, and used boring-machines to produce complete smoothness in the bore. There is mention in a note of later date of a machine for profiling cannon staves, to be driven by a turbine; a carefully finished sketch accompanies the note.[22] In connexion with this return to the older process, Leonardo came to a method of construction of gun barrels which he specially recommended for a *cerbottana*, a light gun, "which shoots with remarkable force." [23] In this process he anticipated Armstrong's invention of wrought-iron coils, of trapezium section, wound spirally round a mandrel and welded together.

In the years that followed, Leonardo was continually occupied with gun-making, but he was attracted by general mechanical problems outside this special field, and grew more and more engrossed in the technique of engineering. Methodically, with his characteristic close attention to every detail, he designed a huge wagon for the transport of his great guns. He drew the forecourt of a foundry in which gun barrels were being loaded up. As he sketched he fell in love with this world of metal monsters, with the result that the drawing (now at Windsor) has become a pæan on the brotherhood of man and machine. The forecourt, with a store in the background in which gun barrels of various sizes are piled on one another, might pass for a modern engineering-shop but for its crenellated frieze. The gun wagon is placed under a mighty crane in the middle of the scene, with its giant wheels and the brightly polished gun barrel that is being gradually lowered. Naked figures are pulling or actually hanging in groups amid the confusion of iron levers and bars; backs bent in strenuous effort, arms frenziedly reaching upward, men bending their whole weight on a cable, their bodies sweeping back like a wave, all show the insignificance of man contrasted with the hugeness of machines. The impact is shown of mobile human masses on the stolidity of the iron monsters, with man and machine inextricably woven together in this first temple of the mechanical godhead of a new age. So, by this roundabout path, the first modern picture of the age of industry made its entry into the world of art.

"8. Where the bombards would fail of their effect, I shall make catapults, ballistas, blunderbusses, and other engines of marvellous efficacy, unknown to customary practice; and, in general, to suit the manifold variety of occasions, I shall construct all sorts of different things for purposes of attack and defence."

One of the most remarkable of the many portable firearms that Leonardo designed, improved, or invented was the novel pistol which he furnished with a wheel-lock instead of a matchlock. A steel wheel, turned with a key, winds up the big spiral spring. As soon as the ratchet-lever fitted on the right is dropped, the wheel is liberated. It rubs against the flint, a spark is produced, and the powder in the pan is fired.[24] The wheel-lock pistol became known to the public only in 1517, through the invention of a Nuremberg watchmaker, and its technical finish was so inferior that the matchlock continued in use until the end of the seventeenth century.

As his ninth point Leonardo wrote:

"9. And for combats at sea, I have methods of making many instruments, excellently adapted for attack and defence, and ships that can resist the fire of the most enormous bombards and powder and smoke."

Leonardo's elaboration of his plans for naval fighting belongs to a later period, but at the time of this memorandum he was already making drawings of boats with flat, box-like mortars (Windsor collection), which threw a sort of Greek fire against ships, or fired powdered and poisoned lime. He went thoroughly into the question of the poison powder, as though this insidious lethal device had a special fascination for him. He would "throw among enemy ships, by means of a catapult," lime, sulphide of arsenic (*orpimento sottile*), and verdigris, in the form of powders; "and all those who breathe the powder will perish." He did not lose sight

PHOTO ANDERSON *The Adoration of the Magi* UFFIZI GALLERY, FLORENCE

Saint Jerome

of the possibility that the wind might send the powder back, and recommended the assailant to provide himself with a sort of protective mask, "a thin, damp cloth, bound over the nose and mouth, so that the powder shall not penetrate."

This long memorandum, drawn up with an eye to the existing hostilities, might have been the work of a military engineer, summoned to Milan for no other purpose than the defence of the country. At the last moment it must have occurred to Leonardo that he had allowed himself to be influenced too much by the circumstances of the moment and by his own interest in the technique of warfare; for he added, almost as an afterthought:

"10. In time of peace I think I can give the best of satisfaction, well bearing comparison with anyone else, in architecture, in the designing of buildings, whether public or private, and in the conducting of water from one place to another.

"Item. I shall carry out sculptures, in marble, bronze, and clay, and similarly paintings, of every possible kind, to stand comparison with anyone else, be he who he may.

"It will also be possible to put in hand the bronze horse, which will be an immortal glory and eternal honour to the happy memory of your honoured father and of the illustrious house of Sforza. And if any of the aforesaid works should appear to anyone to be impossible of execution, I am ready at any time to put it to the test in your park or at whatever place shall be convenient to Your Excellency, to whom I most humbly commend myself."

3

When Leonardo handed this memorandum to Lodovico Sforza, he was unaware that it was his hard fate to be dealing with the one man who, more than any other of the manifold types of his spacious epoch, was his temperamental opposite. Lodovico Sforza was a man concerned only with the fleeting moment, greedily pursuing life's pleasures, thinking and planning only for the passing day and its brief satisfactions. It was with this man, living wholly in the present, that Leonardo had to deal—Leonardo, who could think and plan only for great stretches of future time, who would have needed many lives in order to think out his thoughts to the end and to carry his plans into execution; a despiser of the transitory, as though he lived not in time but in an enclave of eternity. One day in these first years in Milan, Leonardo looked down at the river flowing past him, and was overwhelmed by the sense of the transiency of his life: "The water you touch in the rivers is the last of the waters that have passed and the first of those that are to come. So it is with the present moment." [25]

Not only in their way of living but in their whole mental cast, these two men were poles apart in type. The Sforzas were born Philistines. Their sense of beauty found expression only in a greed for banal luxuries, in the pursuit of the most earthly of pleasures, and in a passion for extravagant display. Lodovico Sforza was more adaptable and more ready to learn than most of his family, and fell in with the contemporary fashion of cultivating art and science because he considered this to be one of the duties of a ruler and a means of impressing the public. But he never acquired an artistic taste of his own; he allowed his estimate of other men's creative work to be imposed on him by those around him. All he had learned had come to him as the finished product of other men's thinking. This fact, together with his humanist education, had given him a strong faith in authority, and alongside this faith in authority he felt a mistrust of everything new and difficult of comprehension, everything not yet tested and proved by experience.

Even, however, if Lodovico had been a man of less narrowly limited intellect, the method Leonardo employed to win his favour would still have failed. Leonardo was a newcomer into an unfamiliar field; and the things he put before the lord of Milan were too varied and too far-fetched to inspire confidence. The range of his suggestions was too wide for him to be credited with the power to carry them out, even by a man with a less strictly practical outlook than Lodovico's. The fat, firm, stubby-fingered hand that received the memorandum, a brown, heavy hand on which a ruby ring incised with Cæsar's head flamed darkly, was the hand of an unimaginative man who could make little of all these proposals.

Leonardo, however, went full of great hopes through the streets of this city, imagining that he had found a new and responsive environment. It was a great city and a wealthy one, one of the greatest and wealthiest of the continent. It stretched far into the plain of Lombardy, with its 18,000 houses (Paris then had no more than 13,000), its 14,000 shops, and its 300,000 inhabitants. The country round it was watered by many Alpine streams; the air was filled with a silvery shimmer by the rising mists; it was a country of effortless luxuriance and profusion. About 1470, the mulberry tree was first planted in its rich and fruitful soil, bringing the region a new source of wealth, and the silk industry, introduced about the middle of the century, quickly made an end of the importation of fabrics. Fifteen thousand workpeople owed their livelihood to it, and the demand for Milanese silks was so great that the ambassadors had to ask Lodovico's aid to enable them to procure a few ells of the costly brocades, for which they would pay from a dozen to twoscore ducats the ell. This city, in its competition with Venice and Florence, had caught the infection of the new commercialism, and the names of members of the oldest families of the Lombard nobility are found in the trade registers of the day—especially among the woollen manufacturers, who successfully maintained their business alongside the great new houses of the silk weavers.

This rich soil responded to all sorts of experiments. Rice was introduced by Greek traders, and sold at first at high prices by the drysalters, with sugar and pepper and exotic spices. Galeazzo Maria Sforza had tried the experiment of sowing it in his ducal parks, with such success that wide stretches of country were planted, and soon decrees had to be issued to prohibit the importation of rice into the Milanese. Yet it was neither to this rich soil nor to its textile industries that Milan owed its commercial fame. Since the thirteenth century it had prospered above all as a centre of arms manufacture. In its hundred great workshops armour and hand-weapons were hammered and filed, forged and sharpened. In the Via degli Armorai the shops were crowded together, inundating the street with shining, headless knights, legless trunks of horses in armour, a forest of lances and pikes and halberds that seemed to melt into one vast shining army.

This industry only reinforced the military character of the city of these peaceful plains. A girdle of battlemented walls bade defiance from fifteen towers to the soft and shimmering skies, and within the seven gates was an entirely medieval fortified city. The nobles' palaces, heavy square battlemented buildings with squat towers, were firmly entrenched on their sites and seemed to be showing their teeth. And on the border of the city, at the Porta Giovia, the castle which Duke Francesco had hurriedly built frowned down like an incubus of stone and steel. From its deep moats with their lazily lapping water the naked walls of the castle rose precipitously; round towers jutted out at the sides, and at the entrance the tall rectangular tower erected by Filarate for Bona of Savoy loomed up menacingly. The walls, of a fleshy red, challenged the verdant countryside, and the battlements stood out like purple fingers against the blue sky. The vast inner courtyard, the Piazza d'Armi, with its clatter of armed retainers and visitors, looking like an encampment about to be broken up, climbed toward the steep cliff of the Rocchetta, the most impregnable part of the fortress; a circumvallation bound this with the ducal wing into a single windowless stronghold, up which the eye travelled with instinctive apprehension to the evilly squinting embrasures.

The whole city might have seemed armed and mail-clad, stern and dreary, but the luxuriant soil and the bright, limpid atmosphere combined to destroy this impression. The predominance of Gothic in the buildings had softened the city's severity and drawn its fangs. The salmon-pink shade of the burnt clay, and the blood-red tiles, that dominated the street scene, seemed to fill out the profiles of the walls and the long Gothic windows. The variety of the colouring and the mass of decoration—wreaths and arabesques of flowers and fruit, symbolic animals, landscapes—further helped to soften the hard smooth surfaces; sometimes the decoration covered a whole building, as in the palazzo of the Missaglia, a famous family of armourers, who anticipated modern publicity methods by covering the façade with the arms and mottoes of the most famous and powerful of their clients.

The people were like their homes—they had the same defiant character mixed with softer elements of relaxation and indulgence. The women walking in the streets were fair, with plump figures and broad hips that moved lazily under their wide skirts; their slender waists seemed yet slimmer by contrast with their puffed sleeves, which were richly embroidered. On their broad, milk-white throats there would shimmer a red ruby like a drop of blood, and the gold chains clinked gently on their firm breasts as they went languorously, sensuously, provocatively on their way. They were impolitely compared to stuffed capons by a country-man of Leonardo's, the poet Antonio Cammelli, known as Il Pistoia, himself born at Vinci. Cammelli was fond of strolling about the streets of Milan, just killing time, always on the lookout for a pretty woman to follow, and ready to squander his last soldo and his last vestige of health in any amorous adventure. And watching these ladies of Milan as they feasted and swilled at table, with their fine dresses and pearl necklaces and with heavy rings coruscating on every finger, he exclaimed that they looked like German stalls afoot.*

These women were a symbol of the indolent life of this city with its crude pleasure-seeking, its delight in primitive luxury, its gross feeding, and its carefree enjoyment of the passing hour. Contemporaries regarded Milan as the most self-indulgent city of Italy, "where men's main concern," says Matteo Bandello, "is to load their table with rich supplies of food. The Milanese consider that they are not living unless they are eating and drinking and making merry." The city's materialistic philosophy was summed up in a proverb: "The cloak may be in rags if the plate is full." (*Straziato sia il mantello e grasso il piatello.*)

To Leonardo, used to the most frugal living, all this feasting and revelling, this coarse and noisy enjoyment of life, was entirely

---

* *Belle donne a Milan ma grasse troppe.*
  Il parlar tu lo sai, sai che son bianche,
  strette nel mezzo, ben quartate in l'anche,
  paion capon pastati in su le groppe.
  Portan certe giornee e certe gioppe
  che le fan parer ampie nel petto anche,
  basse hanno le pianelle, vanno stanche . . .
  Le veste lor di seta e di rosato,
  le scoffie d'oro e nel petto el gioiello,
  maniche di ricamo e di broccato.
  Il spalla hanno il balasso ricco e bello,
  tutto il collo di perle incatennati
  cum un pendente o d'intaglio o di niello:
  ogni dita ha lo annello.
  Quando le vedi poi mangiare ai deschi,
  paion tutte boteghe da Theredeschi.

alien. The people were alien to him, and the face of the city was alien; only here and there did he find a stray echo of the familiar tones of Florentine art. The Bank of the Medici, with its richly adorned portico, built by Michelozzo, and the vast façade of the Ospedale Maggiore, dating back to Filarate, came as unexpected breaks in the rows of Gothic houses; a Renaissance loggia erected for Duke Galeazzo Maria in the inner courtyard of the castle broke into the austere unity of the building as though a window had been timidly cut to look out on a new world; and the spacious chapel built by Michelozzo for Portinari, the Medici agent, lay embedded like a jewel of pure Florentine *quattrocento* in the church of Sant' Eustorgio.

Yet the new art of the Renaissance, already world-famous, was unable to strike root in Milan. The city was no lover of strangers, and resisted the penetration of foreign influences with a tenacity born of its indolence. Its own artists stood together in determined hostility to all outsiders; they had trouble enough to maintain their own precarious position. This city, with its pride of wealth and its luxurious living, became stingy and avaricious when it had to pay out money to its artists. Its aristocratic families had no ambition for immortalization in marble or bronze, and the artists vegetated as simple handicraftsmen. Masons and woodcarvers, miniaturists and painters of frescoes were dependent on the caprice of this materialist Philistine society—and on commissions from the court.

At this period the court of Milan was the richest in the world. The country yielded to its princes without effort half a million ducats or more a year; Lodovico's revenues reached 600,000. Their magnificence was legendary. Six months' revenues would be spent on retainers and their clothing, and on travels with armed retinue and secretaries, singers and tailors, trumpeters and cooks, falconers and grooms. A hunt was organized for jewels of great size, for unique diamonds and rubies, for precious stones of any sort, cut or uncut, so long as they had value—as though this court had constantly to be prepared for the necessity of handing out at any moment a handful of diamonds or pearls to save its bare life. But the moment it was merely a question of giving commissions to artists, these extravagant princes became aware at once of the gaps in their finances, and would haggle with a poor craftsman as though their solvency were at issue. As a rule the artists employed were not the most skilled but those who offered to work for the smallest pay. The court itself preferred to employ Milanese workers, since they could be beaten down, supervised by the court officials, and their charges checked by rival experts. Every consideration of art was subordinated to this insistence on cheapness; thus the ducal registers make mention of a painter to whom the decoration of one-sixth of the dome of a chapel was entrusted. The company of musicians at the court of the Sforzas was paid five thousand ducats a year, but the architect Danesio Maineri, who had worked for forty-two years for the Sforza family, a sick man and in danger of dying of starvation, had to wait for payment until he was reduced to imploring Duke Galeazzo Maria for help to save him from having to "enter the service of the Turks"; and the painter Costantino da Vaprio offered, "under pressure of dire need," to work without the customary advance for paints if he could be given even a part of the payment due to him for works completed years before.

The many singers at the court were all Flemings, and the harp- and lute-players, flutists and trumpeters, were mostly Germans. Nobody complained of that. But when the architect Nexemberger was brought from Graz to build the campanile of the cathedral, the Milanese masons and their assistants put so many difficulties in his way that he was soon driven from the field. When Filarate came to Milan as chief architect of the cathedral, even Francesco Sforza's iron will failed to break the resistance of the Milanese to the employment of this foreign interloper; the great hospital, Ospedale Maggiore, which he began was completed by Milanese architects, and transformed into the Gothic style. There was chuckling over every mistake that could be alleged against the "foreigners." "These Florentines want to do everything out of their own head, and sometimes they do not know what they are about" —so wrote, in malice, the director of public works to the chancellor.

Two or three years before Leonardo came to Milan, Donato d'Agnolo, called Bramante, had come to the city. Il Moro offered him five ducats a month. Singers and lute-players received twelve to fifteen ducats a month, but Bramante, the future builder of St. Peter's at Rome, was "a patient son of poverty," in the words of his pupil Cesariano; his clothing was threadbare and his shoes worn-out, but he only wrote pathetic sonnets about them. He waited patiently, in this first period of his life in Milan, hoping for important architectural commissions to come, and contented himself meanwhile with painting frescoes, of more than life size, representing young knights at court as warrior heroes in full armour.

One branch of art flourished in a modest way in this stony soil of Milanese Philistinism—portrait-painting. Portraits were commissioned not for the admiration of future generations, but in the desire to please a family, or to show civility to some neighbouring prince, or to get a daughter married. Francesco Sforza had sent his court painter, Zanetto Bugato, "who painted from nature with remarkable perfection," to Brussels in 1460, to study with Roger van der Weyden; he remained there three years, perfecting himself in the new art of oil painting. After his return Bugato went conscientiously to work, painting the duke's portrait over and over again, and portraits of the family, of the duchess and the sons, and even of the duke's favourite dog, Bareta. But he, too, had to wait a long time for payment, complaining and entreating, until at last, when overwhelmed with debts, he appealed to the duke and reminded him personally that he had so far received nothing.

Leonardo, when he set foot on the soil of Lombardy, knew nothing of the uncomfortable conditions in Milan. At first he probably hoped to take the place of the old and incapable military engineer to the duke, Bartolommeo Gadio—an illusory hope; the post was given to Ambrogio Ferrari. And there soon came a change in the menacing political situation on which he had built in placing his proposals before Lodovico Sforza. At the very moment when Lodovico was an apparently interested listener, he had given up the idea of serious warfare, which might endanger his already precarious situation, and had made up his mind to rely instead on his diplomatic skill. Leonardo had referred in his memorandum to times of peace in which he could take in hand the grandiose project of a monument to Francesco Sforza; but when these times of peace came he found them to be times of waiting, years of flickering hopes, of promises deferred, of fulfilment constantly postponed—years that were all the more devastating since every day and every hour there was the possibility of a change for the better, with fortune always on the threshold of a door never quite open and never quite closed.

Leonardo's ultimate success obscured for later observers the darker picture of his first years in Milan; success appeared to them to have smiled on him from the start. Vasari, misled by the renown that came later, writes that "when the duke heard Leonardo's marvellous proposals, he fell in love with his virtues in a measure that was beyond belief." In reality these all too marvellous proposals fell at first on deaf ears. Every day Leonardo was forced to shed something of his first illusions. Every day he saw more plainly the painful realities of the life of an artist in Milan. The savings he brought from Florence steadily melted, and soon he was no longer able to rent separate apartments, or even a single room, in one or another of the many hostelries for visitors to the city. His ambitious dreams and great plans dwindled daily, until there was nothing left of them but a struggle for the barest existence. He was a stranger in a world of petty rivalries and of bitterly humiliating struggles to get payments that were due, a world in which success required stronger elbows and a sterner practical sense than he possessed.

He learned that even his Lombard fellow-artists frequently joined in groups of two or three for mutual protection. It thus seemed best to look round for someone familiar with the conditions in Milan, shrewd and enterprising enough to make the best of the few opportunities that came, and also ambitious enough to be alive to the advantage of association with Leonardo da Vinci. He found the man he wanted in Ambrogio de Predis, who was able also to provide him with lodging and a studio.

Giovanni Ambrogio de Predis, or da Preda, was the youngest son of Leonardo (or Lorenzo) da Preda, who, like Ser Piero, had three times sought a life's happiness in marriage. Giovanni's half-brother Evangelista was a woodcarver; another half-brother, Cristo-foro, a deaf-mute, was well known as a miniaturist, uninspired but skilful and conscientious. From him Ambrogio learned his sharp, careful line and metallic elaboration of detail, with hard, pronounced outlines. An elder brother, Bernardino, was a minter of coin and a weaver of Gobelin tapestries, and the industrious Ambrogio acquired from him the technique of both callings. Their father was not sufficiently prosperous to maintain his large family, and the sons learned their trades at an early age; Ambrogio was already at work on miniatures for books of hours before he was eighteen, and as this did not bring in a living he minted coin to order with his brother Bernardino. His ambition and energy, born not of poverty but of the business sense of a solid burgher, and his efforts to rise out of the narrow routine of handiwork in which his brothers lived, brought him rapidly forward, and by the time Leonardo reached Milan, Ambrogio, a young man of twenty-eight, had become a court painter to the Sforza family; his reputa-tion had even spread beyond the Milanese, for he had worked also for the duchess of Ferrara, who had paid him with ten ells of silk-stuff.

By this time he had learned all that Lombard art could teach him. The Lombard tradition was, indeed, second nature to him; it was much more akin to his careful and painstaking industry than was the new spirit which was moving outside the borders of Milan. But he was aware that his honest but pedestrian style would bring him no further toward the fame and wealth of which he dreamed.

The mysterious newcomer from Florence represented a new world to this ambitious Milanese, and a world he meant to con-quer. His ambition was unhindered by any of the vanity which might have deterred him from accepting subordination, so long, at all events, as was necessary for outward success. Leonardo's need was Ambrogio's opportunity, and so there began this strange col-laboration between a man of genius and an industrious medioc-rity, which was to provide so many enigmas for art historians in centuries to come. Ambrogio de Predis was a resourceful and technically well-equipped artist, and he was ready to sink his individuality for a while, to become the mere reflection of another and a greater man—so entirely so that the works of the two are almost indistinguishable, though he betrays himself in details in which he was thrown upon himself. Later, when he had achieved his purpose, he reverted to his own personal style, as though he had never come under the broadening influence of a very great man.

In partnership with Ambrogio de Predis and his half-brother Evangelista, the indifferent woodcarver, Leonardo negotiated for a commission which the fraternity of the Immaculate Conception had to offer. After long negotiations the contract was signed on April 25, 1483, in the office of a Milanese notary, Antonio de' Capitani. The prior of the community, Bartolommeo degli Scarlione, came accompanied by eight of its members for this solemn legal act; they kept watch to see that none of the important clauses of the contract was overlooked. Everything was thought of and discussed in advance, and not the slightest play allowed to the initiative of the contracting artists. The altarpiece was to fit into a richly carved wood framework which the fraternity had already had made by Giacomo del Mayno. The arrangement of the carved and painted reliefs in the upper part of the altarpiece was determined by the theological zeal with which the fraternity espoused the dogma of the Immaculate Conception. God the Father was to be shown everywhere surrounded by the Seraphim, the Blessed Virgin was to wear an angel's halo, and the cradle was to be in the centre of a mountainous landscape. They also laid down the colours of the clothing, which were to shimmer through the gold brocade patterning; they laid down everything with the nicest precision, down to the dangling ends of the folds of the garments of the Seraphim. Even Maestro Leonardo (he was the only one to whom the title "Master" was conceded; the Milanese seem to have had no exaggerated respect for their own artists) was told what he was to paint. The central panel, "to be painted in oil by the Florentine," was to show the Blessed Virgin with the Child, surrounded by angels and prophets. Ambrogio de Predis was entrusted with the altar wings; he was to paint on each of them four angels, singing and playing musical instruments. The payment for the altarpiece was fixed at two hundred ducats, but the fraternity promised to make an extra payment for satisfactory execution of the work, which, in accordance with Milanese custom, was to be submitted to expert opinion. The long document ended with an agreed date of delivery—December 8, 1484.

The Florentine master signed the agreement; probably he merely shrugged his shoulders over its tiresome clauses. Then he made his way through the streets of Milan to the Ticino gate, where he was living with the de Predis brothers. It was spring— his first spring in Milan. Nothing would keep him in the town, cooped up between houses and among the artificialities of society, while the countryside glowed in the haze of the well-watered plain, or shone under brilliant blue skies. The fields were an unbroken mass of luxuriant young shoots and scented blossom, and as he roamed through them he was filled with the intoxicating charm of this spring. From childhood he had been a keen observer of the flowers and grasses around his home; now he revelled anew in the multiplicity of forms and shades, the different feel of each leaf, dry or moist, smooth or rough, the infinite variety of contours, each stalk winding in its own individual arabesque. There was something to attract and fascinate him at every step; he would bend his tall frame or kneel in the grass, carefully part the tangle of blades, and then note in his sketchbook a little bunch of leaves springing from the earth like a miniature palm crown, or follow some creeper's windings through the mossy maze; he would try to capture the emerald gleam of slender shoots and the silvery sheen of grasses; he would patiently copy the curvings of the delicate field irises, whose fragile stalks rose out of the matted foliage to support the flowers which swayed to and fro, light as butterflies, beneath the faintest breath of wind. "Many flowers drawn from nature," wrote Leonardo at the head of a list of sketches [26] which, in one of his fits of method, he made at this time, when all the Milanese was new to him.

He rode farther and farther into the country, past cliffs and crags, to "shady valleys watered by merry winding streams." He sketched the channelled face of jagged conical peaks, the broken folds of stratified rocks, precipitous ravines with glimmering walls, deep hollows in which water had collected, with the soft gleam of satin on its motionless surface. Once when he was caught in a rainstorm he sketched the streams of rain bursting from the clouds and beating down on a sheet of water. "What moves you, O man, to abandon your natural shelters in the city, and to leave relatives and friends, and to go into the open country, past mountains and valleys, if it is not the natural beauty of the world?" So he wrote later in his *Trattato della Pittura*. This natural beauty of the world inspired Leonardo's creative work in that spring of 1483. He was disillusioned and embittered, vexed by the meannesses of the contract imposed on him, depressed by the necessity of partnership with a fellow-artist who was not of his own calibre, and hampered by his narrow means; but all personal troubles were forgotten while his eyes could feast on this glorious spring.

And suddenly, in the midst of the instinctive joy in Nature's awakening, there came to him a radiant vision, his *Madonna of the Rocks*. The picture he conceived and recorded was like the daydream of one who lies stretched on moss and blinks at the sun until its radiance takes shape and colour and becomes a smiling human face. It is a picture light as air and brimming over with life. The Blessed Virgin, moved by the gentleness of the spring day, has fallen on her knees, and is stretching her arms protectively round the playing children, who are untouched as yet by any shadow of the suffering of the world. Gravely, and inwardly radiant, she turns her face to the child John. He has bent his little round knee in the midst of flowers and grasses in their springtime glory, and is lifting up his fat little clasped hands to the divine Child, who is unsteadily raising his soft, helpless little body; the little pink foot on which the light burden weighs is bent round in a touchingly awkward position as he opens his tiny fist in benediction.

Leonardo's vision is still quite close to the charming early Florentine paintings in which a slender, maidenly Madonna in the midst of a thicket worships the doll-like little body of the Christ Child. And yet there is a spirit in his picture that has nothing in common with conventional piety. A strange darkness fills the grotto in which the Virgin is kneeling. Shadows play amid the dank and trickling cliffs, and the plants and stones glisten mysteriously in the velvety hollow, which suddenly opens out to admit the entrance of light in the far distance. These rocky ledges that

overhang the darkness of the hollow, this medley of flowers springing from the rich moss, might equally well be the resting-place of
heathen gods; light-footed nymphs might emerge in alarm from
the golden twilight, fleeing from the god Pan in this enchanted
wilderness. There is more, too, of a heathen god than a heavenly
messenger in the angel who has come down by the side of the
Christ Child, the flaming red satin of his garment spreading out
as he suddenly kneels; an ecstatic glance comes from his almond-
shaped eyes between their fleshy and sensual lids, a glance laden
with mystery, and in the damp corners of his blood-red lips there
trembles as though in surrender a desire that has learnt nothing
of self-denial.

The *Madonna of the Rocks* is born of a joy in life that is entirely of this world, a worship of nature so passionate that it affords
no room for the thought of the snares and delusions of our vale of
woe. Landscape and figures are bathed in a magic of shadow and
light, and light is the most strongly active element in this picture.
A slanting stream of illumination touches the bent head of the
Virgin; it flows unresisted past her heavy eyelids, but her hand is
thrust out of the folds of the cloak in order to protect the head of
the Christ Child. Leonardo himself painted once again this lightly
moving hand with its bold foreshortening, and made it the centre
and focus of his masterpiece, the *Last Supper;* and from now on it
was to be found in every saint portrayed by his imitators, until it
became a routine gesture and lost all significance.

The strong radiance seems to stream from the domed brow of
the Christ Child, on which the reddish-gold locks mingle in the
shimmer of the skin; it embraces mother and Child in the same
powerful light. The two corner figures of the picture, the angel
and the young John, are placed in a secondary field of illumination, as though they merely receive the radiance that falls on them
from the principal figures. The diminution of light progresses by
stages into the shadows, and even the deepest gloom is transparent
and animated, throbbing with a mysterious life.

In addition to the distribution of parts through the lighting,
Leonardo again carries through the formal construction with almost mathematical precision in an equilateral triangle. One steeply
sloping line leads from the Virgin's bent head past her hand—that

Detail from the *Virgin of the Rocks* (Angel and Christ Child)

The Virgin of the Rocks

wonderful hand with its long contour carried through from the wrist, resting tenderly on the child's soft shoulder—to the boy John's firmly planted foot. The sides of the triangle meet in the dark waving hair of the Madonna's head, which is turned slant-wise; the outstretched hand makes a break in one side at the extreme margin; this side rises rapidly above the angel's head, while the other falls along the curve of the wing and parallel to it down the fold of the angel's garment. In the interior of the picture the triangle motif is taken up again: the lines pass upward from the inner fold of the Madonna's deep blue cloak to the glittering brooch on her breast, and fall past her elbow beneath the shaded surface of her hand and steeply over the back of the Christ Child to the ground.

The angel's pointing hand breaks into the inner triangular space from the right, almost as an alien element. Imprisoned, as it were, between the Virgin's and the Child's hand, it seems at first sight to introduce needless confusion into the picture. But when, under the changed sense of space of a later period, it was omitted from the replica which is now in the National Gallery, London, the striking gap produced by the omission showed the important function of the gesture both in its intellectual and its formal aspect. It is the hand of a clever ephebus, pointing forensically, and is still entirely a product of the Florentine spirit, which in these early years in Milan Leonardo maintained intact—a slender, thoroughly spiritual hand, brought into the centre of the picture firmly and confidently like a decisive argument. The whole rhythm of the picture proceeds through this sharp gesture of the angel's hand; the picture is at its most telling at this point; the gesture, which serves as a connecting link between the two halves of the picture, carries on the rhythm into the diagonals of the background, which lead on the left by the zigzag path between the cliffs into the radiant blue distance, and to a rich golden harmony through the breach in the gloom on the right.

Leonardo had paid little respect to his patrons' particularity. No bearded Old Testament prophet intruded into the company of the divine children, although his presence had been expressly stipulated by the fraternity. Leonardo was well enough acquainted, moreover, with theological issues to know how little his representation harmonized with the doctrine adhered to by the fraternity, the dogma of the Immaculate Conception. The very fact of the presence of the angel, emphasizing with his hand the Christ Child's gesture of benediction, could be interpreted as supporting the rival doctrine of the Thomists, or followers of St. Thomas Aquinas, of the Sanctification of the Birth. All this might suggest an artist's random pursuit of his own paths, in a man working less purposefully than Leonardo, but in his case it could not be mere capriciousness: it was his subtle defence against subtleties, his way of evading troublesome prescriptions.

Ambrogio de Predis was infected with Leonardo's independence, and on each of the narrow panels of the altarpiece he painted, not four angels singing and playing instruments, but one —one "big one," as he said later in self-defence. He painted his figures in uncouth attitudes, with hard detail, and with the spinelessness and the carelessness of general structure that are common to the whole of the Lombard school.

The composition must have been fairly rapidly completed in its broad outlines, and even in some of the figures, which are so close to the Florentine types of the period. But it certainly was not finished by the date for delivery. A long dispute ensued between the painter and his patrons; it dragged out for more than twenty years, and at some time during this period the London replica came mysteriously into existence. Did the fraternity object to the unconcerned way in which Leonardo had disregarded their instructions, had they theological scruples with respect to his work, or did they really consider that the altarpiece was worth no more than a final payment of twenty-five ducats while Leonardo demanded a hundred? Ten years after the signing of the contract Leonardo and Ambrogio de Predis sent a petition to Lodovico Sforza asking him to end the troublesome dispute, and ten years after Lodovico's fruitless intervention the king of France himself intervened. The dispute over seventy-five ducats endured through the convulsions of war, through the change of masters, and through the coming and going of foreign conquerors. It was probably about the turn of the century that the secret agreement was arrived at under which the painters regained possession of the original altarpiece and replaced it by a replica. The exchange must have been made in the utmost secrecy, perhaps to please a powerful purchaser; for generations of art historians have tried in vain to solve the mystery of the Paris picture, which came through unknown channels into France, and of the London one, which was acquired in Milan from the inheritors of the property of the fraternity of the Immaculate Conception.

Scarcely more than twenty years of change in artistic feeling separates the two pictures, but they belong in reality to two different epochs of artistic development. Leonardo's own picture in the Louvre belongs to the final years of the early Renaissance, while the London replica, for all its agreement with it in details, belongs to the fully developed Renaissance style of composition. At the time when the London panel probably came into existence, Leonardo was overwhelmed with commissions for the completion of which the mightiest princes were waiting in vain; his partner Ambrogio de Predis had attained the goal of his ambition, had become court painter to the Emperor Maximilian I, and must have felt sufficient confidence in himself to undertake a work of this sort, on the basis of sketches of Leonardo's and with the advantage of his former association with him. But with the best will to keep as close as possible to the original, Ambrogio de Predis was unable to extend the boundaries of his own art. The soft curves that dissolve into one another have become in his work a solid padding of flesh, while in addition to his own characteristic style his work shows the prevalent fashion of his period, which demanded development of form and a stronger emphasis on relief.

It was certainly not the first time that Ambrogio de Predis had finished a work of which Leonardo had provided the sketch or groundwork. Leonardo's business-like partner was in the habit of engaging assistants, thus making full use of his studio, but Leonardo himself was hampered in doing so by his painstaking method and fitful progress. With Leonardo the idea of a picture ripened slowly: a multitude of tentative sketches brought him gradually closer to its ultimate form; then he held fast to the result of his long meditation—only to be disappointed, to find his interest flagging, to be caught by other and keener interests, as though he had got out of touch with his own work. At this stage he would permit other men to bring it to completion. On one occasion a contemporary saw assistants busy in his studio on two pictures he had begun. Then he would find his way back to his own work, would give a liquid, moving glance to dull eyes, would vivify pale, life-less lips, and by touches with his brush would bring a flush of colour into bloodless skin. It was this method of working that produced the borderline pictures which may have been not entirely his, pictures which are not altogether free from the hardness of good capable craftsmanship, but are tantalizingly half inspired with such life as only a very great painter could put into them—pictures which nevertheless go under his name. One of these is the so-called *Madonna Litta* (Hermitage, Leningrad): the dry grey of the skin and the hard and abrupt red and blue of the clothes belong to the style of colouring of Ambrogio de Predis, but in the gentle droop of the lovely head there is a music that reveals the hand of Leonardo. In the early days of that strange association between the thinker to whose broodings there was no end and the self-confident mediocrity who was his partner, there came also into existence in the studio they shared a whole series of portraits which are art hybrids of the type of the *Madonna Litta*.

Portrait commissions were the easiest to secure in Milan, and the business-like Ambrogio knew how to make the most of his connexions with the ducal court. One of the musicians who stood in such high favour with Lodovico had his portrait painted by Ambrogio, in a black suit, with a little red cap resting on his luxu-riant auburn hair, which is trained in curls like copper wire. His profession of musician is naïvely indicated by the sheet of music held stiffly between his finger-tips. His handsome face with its broad cheekbones is sharply modelled, as in the other portrait of a man by de Predis in the Brera gallery; the eyes are surrounded by the whitish rim of light which always betrays the work of Ambrogio; but from between these hard lids there comes the am-ber gleam of a faraway glance, the nostrils suddenly twitch in the midst of the tight skin, and the mouth, which seems trapped between the hard surfaces, is full of life, with moist red lips that seem to be just closing after saying something.

A young princess of the Sforza line ordered her portrait from Ambrogio de Predis. Her challenging look betrays her noble station even more than her rich strings of pearls and the ruby on her breast. Ambrogio has painted her narrow, upturned little nose and her round, girlish chin with the same conscientiousness as her stiff brown hair, its gold net with pearl fastenings, and the embroidery on her black dress. Only the short, steep bow of the little mouth, gently overshadowed by the soft curve of the cheeks, is instinct with a life not of his giving (profile portrait in the Ambrosiana).

5

Another portrait represents the first demonstrable connexion between Leonardo and Lodovico Sforza—the portrait of Cecilia Gallerani. Cecilia was about fourteen years old when Il Moro became her lover. The regent of Milan was then in his early thirties. Up to that time he had lived the wild life of indiscriminate passion that fitted his position and the indulgent morality of his environment. He had shared with his brother the duke the beautiful Lucia Marliani. Galeazzo Maria, with cynical frankness, had put into a deed of gift a clause providing that Lucia should have no sexual intercourse with her husband without Galeazzo Maria's written consent, but the duke had no objection to his lady-love's bearing children to his younger brother as well as himself. Lodovico had brief adventures with aristocratic Milanese ladies, and with young unnamed girls for whom he provided well, and whom he then forgot. But with all its promiscuity, Lodovico's amorous life was hedged about, like all he did or thought, with careful and even anxious consideration for consequences. He was a man divided between cynical candour and a liking for secrecy; and a man of coarse and undiscriminating sensuality, never soaring to any great passion or venturing on any formidable challenge of orthodox morality. He legitimized the son whom Lucia Marliani bore him by passing him off as the child of one of his courtiers by an unnamed mother; only years later, when he felt sufficiently secure in his power, did he acknowledge his parentage and provide for his son's future: he obtained for him, while the boy was still young, the position of a papal protonotary.

Cecilia too, whom he had seduced when she was little more than

a child, bore him a handsome son, who died, like many of Lodovico's children, at a very early age from the consequences of his
father's diseased condition. But Cecilia did not allow herself to be
disposed of and forgotten as easily as others of his *innamorate*. She
came of a good Milanese family, and made good use of her advantage in education; she supported with dignity the rank of a prince's
mistress. She spoke Latin fluently, composed pleasant poems in
Italian, played and sang; the flatterers at the court of Il Moro
called her the modern Sappho. In culture she was ahead of her
years, and she was able to surround herself with an intellectual
atmosphere which filled her princely lover with pride. She knew
also how to hold his uncertain affection, to work on his easily excited and easily satiated sensuality, and to make herself indispensable to him, until he dismissed all doubts and hesitations and
fell more and more deeply under her influence. In writing to the
archbishop of Milan to recommend a younger brother of Cecilia's
for priestly office, he cynically described the candidate as the brother
of a girl with whom he was "enjoying" himself, "a young girl of
distinguished Milanese blood, highly honourable, and all that man
could desire." She was like a flower, wrote the ambassador of the
Este family, who faithfully reported all the gossip of the Milanese
court: Lodovico, he added, was very devoted to her; she lived in
the castle and accompanied him wherever he went.

Leonardo painted the portrait of Cecilia when she was seventeen
years old. Her name has been attached to a picture now at Cracow;
the identity is not absolutely demonstrable, but the tradition has
been preserved with the tenacity of those which rest more on psychological probability than on documents. The picture is the
Lady with the Weasel, in the Czartoryski gallery. It shows a long,
oval woman's face, with the pointed chin which the later Lombard
school took over from Leonardo; great eyes which look almost rectangular under the straight eyebrows; a long, narrow nose, altogether unclassical, which suggests unlimited curiosity, and small
soft lips, a child's mouth with an almost uncurved upper lip. This
tiny mouth, so much too small, conflicts with everything else in
this enigmatical face. It is younger than the experienced eyes and
the compelling, purposeful gaze, much younger than the rounded,
slanting shoulders, and most incompatible of all with the energetic

chin. A smile, or rather the ghost of a smile, hovers round the lips, escaping from the corners of the mouth although they are firmly pressed together: the face has put on a mask of gravity, but this half-suppressed smile has managed to pass over the cheeks; attractive, elusive, it flits as far as the corners of the eyes, and wrestles with the firm, straightforward gaze. There is a fraction of a second between the incipient movement of this face and the full soft smile that floods the face of Mona Lisa. The woman at Cracow is a younger sister of Mona Lisa, a sort of spoilt schoolgirl who has ripened prematurely to womanhood. There is vigorous life in the sudden leftward turn of her head; she is full of a curiosity and alertness that have been set at rest in Mona Lisa, but she is as unmistakably as her famous sister a being made up of contradictions, with the mysterious fascination of conquering womanhood. The hands, too, are younger, more expectant, more excitable in this strange being—the long hands of a lute-player, with loose fingers, thoroughly intellectual and thoroughly sensuous; the tips of the fingers are passing over the soft fur of the little ermine. Leonardo shared the liking of his time for symbols; ermine was the symbol of innocence and was Lodovico's own favourite emblem, but Leonardo may also have placed the weasel in Cecilia's arm because someone with humanist culture told him that the little carnivore belonged to a genus of which the Greek name resembles Gallerani. In painting the animal's pointed head as it turned toward the stroking fingers, he gave the sensitive little snout and the gleaming eyes a sinister community of type with the beautiful face of the woman.

The *Lady with the Weasel* is one more of the enigmas of which Leonardo's collaboration with Ambrogio de Predis has provided so many. Did Ambrogio get possession of an unfinished picture of Leonardo's, and then conscientiously paint the background right up to the oval of the face and the slanting shoulders, as he was in the habit of doing in his own pictures; was it he who spread out the fingers, and made the smooth hair surround the face like a dark coif, cutting into the curve of the cheeks? Was the over-painting the work of later restorers, or Ambrogio's, and a concession to one of the contemporary follies of fashion, which used gum arabic, brought from the East, for the hair until it was fairly pasted to the head? This made the face seem, in Leonardo's phrase, "glazed"; he inveighed with special energy against the fashion. Or has Leonardo's portrait of the young Cecilia disappeared, and is the Cracow picture a replica painted jointly with Ambrogio de Predis, at a time when Leonardo had become very famous and Cecilia's portrait was famous on his account? At that period Bernardo Bellincioni wrote a sonnet on the "Portrait of Madonna Cecilia, painted by the *maestro* Leonardo," in which he represented Nature as envious of Leonardo's work, because he had painted so lifelike a picture of the lovely woman that she seemed to be listening and all but speaking.

Later still, when it was becoming more and more difficult to secure any work of Leonardo's, Isabella d'Este wrote to Cecilia and asked her to let her have the portrait for a short time, so that she might compare it with the portraits by Giovanni Bellini. Cecilia, honoured by the request, handed the picture to the special envoy who had come on horseback from Mantua; but she remarked, with a touch of melancholy, that the picture was so unlike her—this was in April 1498—that nobody would take it for her portrait. This was not through any fault of the *maestro,* who had no equal—*in-vero credo non se trova a lui uno paro.* But it had been painted when she was "at so immature an age," and since then she had altered completely.

When Leonardo began to paint Cecilia's portrait, he may have calculated that this powerful favourite of a prince would be able to help him to secure a connexion more quickly. But then he was caught by this engrossing problem of her nature, half child's and half woman's, the mixture in her of seriousness and wantonness, the big eyes that had learnt much of life but wanted to see a great deal more, and the soft lips, still with a suggestion of innocence about them. Among Leonardo's papers there is the opening of a letter to the Magnifica Cecilia, offering thanks for a "charming message" from "my beloved *diva*"—*amantissima mia diva.* It does not seem to be in Leonardo's handwriting. Did Leonardo dictate this, or was he the confidant of another's outpourings of love—or was he merely engaging in a play with emotions and superlatives, such as his age enjoyed?

"Love conquers all things"—*amor onni cose vince*—this was another of the mottoes current in his day which Leonardo noted on a sheet of paper about this time,[27] and he followed it with a number of the puzzle pictures of which his contemporaries were especially fond, and of which in Renaissance stories couples secretly in love made use in order to pass to one another innocent-looking messages with an agreed special meaning. Leonardo conscientiously went on with this game, stringing together long passages in which the word *amore* continually recurred in the form of two mulberries (*more*) preceded by the letter A; for instance: "I should be happy if of the love I bring you you would be the beautiful resting-place," or "If fortune befriends me I will let you know." Leonardo pursued this dallying with sentiments with an exuberance which had a touch of pedantry in it. In one place he represents in this naïve language of pictures that he has burnt his fingers: *ora sono fritto*. In another he writes a lament for the guilt of misplaced love—*colpa dell' amore mal colocato*—and it seems almost as if his impregnable peace of mind, his release from all emotions, had been shaken by Cecilia's devastating glance. But whether Leonardo the man was merely playing or was pursuing a daydream of amorous longing, Leonardo the artist was unable to escape from the thrall of the eyes of the *Lady with the Weasel;* and he gave the angel of the *Madonna of the Rocks,* which he was painting at that time, her long oval face and pointed chin and her air of unhallowed expectancy.

If Leonardo hoped that Cecilia Gallerani would speak for him he had miscalculated—as always when he imagined that he was being particularly shrewd. It is very probable that it was only when he had become famous that Cecilia discovered that the *maestro* had no equal. In any case, further months and years passed without his name appearing anywhere in the official registers, in however modest a capacity, among the painters to the court. Commissions for pictures and portraits provided him with a living and kept him from despair, but the collapse of his high hopes had so discouraged him that he was unable to nerve himself to try his fortune elsewhere. He may have thought regretfully of his old home; he tried to get again into touch with old acquaintances or relatives; he inquired whether his stepmother's brother, the priest Alessandro Amadori, was still living. But with no success achieved he could not return to Florence; he went on waiting, forged new plans, and hoped for a turn of fortune and for practical evidence of the favour of Lodovico.

During this period of waiting he made an inventory of the pictures he had by him, a survey which reveals the varied nature of his gifts. Among the pictures and drawings begun were several sketches for a *Saint Jerome in the Desert,* one of them showing the kneeling saint with his back to the observer, to whom his head turns sharply—a much more gentle and genial conception than that of the picture of which he completed the groundwork. There were no less than eight sketches for a *Saint Sebastian.* One of the earliest of them, now in the Bayonne collection, shows the saint in the attitude which Sodoma later took over from Leonardo. A later one—he seemed unable to get away from the subject of the beautiful youth, half Greek god, half Christian martyr, bound to the stake—is now at Hamburg; here the saint is much more violent in gesture and more rebellious in expression. There were four sketches made in preparation for the later picture of the *Angel of the Annunciation,* and "many compositions of angels"; a pen-drawing of a head of Christ, a completed picture of the Madonna, another Madonna, seen in profile, and a head of the Blessed Virgin for a picture of the *Ascension.* There also stood in his studio one of his sculptures, a *Crucifixion* in relief—*una storia di passione fatta in forma.* Among the many studies was one of the upraised head of his friend Atalante Miglioretti. There were numbers of heads of ephebi, with the soft mass of curly hair through which, in Leonardo's phrase, "an artificial wind seems to be passing," and girls' heads with heavy coils of plaited hair. He was already attracted by everything curious in human faces, every unusual type; he had sketched a gipsy girl and many heads of old men, one with a very long, lean neck, and had been particularly interested in old women's fleshy, ravaged chins.[28] He was promised by Lodovico over and over again that he should be entrusted with the commission for the memorial to Francesco Sforza, and he had taken the promise sufficiently seriously to have already among his sketches one for the duke's head.

Leonardo made efforts during the years of waiting to fill the gaps in his education—touching efforts of a self-taught man to acquire the foundations he lacked, to gain the rudimentary knowledge he needed in order not to be held up on his path at every step. In using his mother tongue he was hampered by the lack of precision of scientific terms. The words with which the monopoly of Latin as the language of science was being broken down were still new and unfamiliar, and the conceptions inspired by the new spirit were not yet clearly defined. With the aid of contemporary dictionaries—one was Luigi Pulci's *Vocabolista*—he compiled long lists of words, adding brief definitions which are particularly characteristic of his own mental processes. "A *syllogism*," he writes— "ambiguous language" (*parlare dubbioso*); "*sophism*—involved language, falsity issued for truth; *ostentation*—setting out to be what one is not; *science*—knowledge of the things that may come." He also compiled endless lists of synonyms, in the effort to enrich his vocabulary and master every shade of expression; and he made comparative lists of nouns and of verbs, showing degrees of meaning.[29] But among the seven to eight thousand words in these lists there are often groups of expressions that seem to be there merely because of their unfamiliarity, or to be included like little heaps of paint on a palette, placed ready for future use. He worked so thoroughly on this instrument of speech—continuing these exercises throughout his life—that he was able later to declare with pride that "I possess so many words in my mother tongue that I am more likely to have trouble with the right understanding of things than from the lack of words with which to express my mind's conception of them." But what an infinity of patient labour he had expended on this mastery of expression! A labour which few men, even if they had only words as their medium of creative activity, would have carried through.

Yet Leonardo loved this labour for its own sake; for "as iron rusts when it is not used and water gets foul from standing or turns to ice when exposed to cold, so the intellect degenerates without exercise." [30] He repeats in another passage that he practises this mental gymnastic largely for its own sake: "The acquisition of any sort of knowledge is always useful to the intellect, because it will be able to dispense with useless things and preserve the good. For it is impossible to love or hate anything without first having cognizance of it." [31]

In this added clause there is a suggestion of the influence of the German philosopher Cardinal Nicholas of Cusa, or Cusanus, in whose works Leonardo was burying himself about this time. Cusanus, who died in the second half of the fifteenth century, builds up his system of philosophy from the principle that no one can love anything unless he has first comprehended it. Like Leonardo, he had come under the influence of Paolo del Pozzo Toscanelli. As a seventeen-year-old monk he was initiated by Toscanelli into the new world of the phenomena of natural science, and like Leonardo he was faced with the choice between Plato and Aristotle, and decided in favour of the mathematical and physical sciences. "We have nothing certain in our science but our mathematics," he wrote—since, just as only that which is known can be loved, only that which is measurable can be known. Leonardo was drawn to Cusanus by their common love for the measurable, and, like Cusanus, he declares that "The man who discredits the supreme certainty of mathematics is feeding on confusion, and can never silence the contradictions of sophistical sciences, which lead to an eternal quackery." [32]

But the German cardinal belonged to the transition between two epochs, and was more deeply rooted in medieval mysticism than in the new world of empiricism. His philosophic system was an attempt, carried through with the closest of logical argumentation, to reconcile his fervent and unalterable religious faith with observed facts in physics and natural science. The knowledge he gained of this world brought him no problems and raised no doubts: all knowledge was, in his view, a way to God, and cognition was simply the means of acquiring knowledge of God.

Under the inspiration of Cusanus, Leonardo began to meditate on the basis of our comprehension and perception; he felt the need to get his ideas clear on the laws and limitations of mental activity. He went back to the writings from which Cusanus had himself drawn. His daily notes reflect his unresting search for books which he had not yet read. But the sources he consulted in his philosophical research cannot all be identified. It is only rarely that the excerpts from the works of classical, medieval, or contemporary writers which are to be found among his papers bear any indication of their origin; he went to work at once on them, and thought their ideas out to the end, in his own highly individual way.

As a man relying exclusively on the evidence of his eyes, Leonardo accorded to sight the highest rank in the hierarchy of the senses; he was never tired of insisting on the primacy of the eye. And since "the eye is the window of the soul," men are always fearful of losing it. In evidence of the supreme value set, without realizing it, on the eye, Leonardo adduces the instinctive gesture often made by a man when suddenly alarmed. He does not place his hands before his heart, "the source of life," or his head or ears; he holds one hand before his averted eyes, and with the other wards off the sight of the object of horror.[33] "This is the real miracle," he exclaims, "that all shapes, all colours, all images of every part of the universe are concentrated in a single point!" And, deeply impressed by this miracle, he ends his hymn to the eye with these words: "O wonderful, O astounding necessity, by your law you compel all effects to proceed along the shortest path from their causes." [34]

Leonardo realized that this attribution of prime importance to the visual, the shifting of the basis of his general outlook to the impressions conveyed to him from without, fitted ill with the philosophical doctrine of inner contemplation, and he parries this objection: "And if you say that contemplation hinders the concentrated reflection by means of which we find our way to the knowledge of God . . . I reply that the eye, as prince of the senses, does its part by putting a stop to muddled and mendacious—not sciences, but definitions." And when Leonardo heard, or read, that a philosopher had put out his own eyes, in order not to be disturbed in meditation by things seen, he was as indignant at this folly, to him incomprehensible, as a pious man would be who has heard a blasphemy.[35]

But Leonardo was never quite at ease in the field of abstract thought, and, during this period of his first attempts to build up a system of philosophy, he was continually divided between principles he had adopted from others and his own intellectual outlook, between the desire to round off a complete system of philosophy and his innate dependence on concrete presentation. He took over the Schoolmen's conception of the position of man in the universe: "Our body is subordinate to heaven, and heaven is subordinate to the spirit." [36]

This gradation of the universe into lower and higher, material and spiritual, had its counterpart in man in the division between senses and reason. "The senses are earthly; the reason stands outside them during contemplation," writes Leonardo.[37] The four forces that govern the soul were divided into forces of reason and forces of feeling; but where the classical school described reason and will as the two rational forces, Leonardo put in their place memory and intellect. This may have been under the influence of Saint Augustine, who held that the intellect was created by the memory and that the will proceeds from both. But it was in consonance with his own intellectual make-up, his capacity of plastic thought and recollection, that he should give memory a higher rank than will and reason. Depending on the eye for all that he assimilated, he regarded memory as man's only defence against time the destroyer, and man's most precious possession, of which only death could rob him. "Men do wrong to lament the flight of time, complaining that it passes too quickly and failing to perceive that its period is sufficiently long; but a good memory, with which nature has endowed us, causes everything that is long past to appear to us to be present." [38]

In his dependence at this period on the medieval Schoolmen, Leonardo went so far as to take from them the conception of the vast effort of all living and dead things that proceeds throughout the universe; but he did not describe this as an effort to unite with God; he seemed only to want to indicate the movement and its direction, without mentioning its ultimate outcome, setting up a theology without a god. As a young man, in giving expression to his wonder at the workings of natural forces, Leonardo had spoken of the law given to creative nature by God and time. But his silent release from orthodoxy had proceeded so far since then that he broke off his account of his outlook on the world shortly before he would have had to make mention of God.

In a widely published work, *The Theology of Aristotle,* and in the works of Nicholas of Cusa, Leonardo found descriptions of the force of attraction in the universe, which works toward the harmonious union of matter with form and of power with action; he also found descriptions, corresponding to this mutual attraction of the spiritual and material elements in the universe, of the mutual attraction of body and soul in human beings. Cusanus built his system on the following trinity: the subject, which loves; the loved object; and love, which unites the two; and under his influence Leonardo wrote: "Just as the senses are awakened by that which is sensible, so the lover is moved by the loved object, uniting with it and becoming one with it. . . . When the lover has attained the loved one, he is at rest; when the weight has fallen, it is at rest." [39] In the midst of these abstract formulations he would introduce others, based on simple perception, which had reference to a field more familiar to him—that of ethics, which for him was so closely associated with æsthetics. "If the loved object is base, the lover becomes base."

From this excursion into the territory of metaphysics Leonardo ultimately retained the conception of movement in the universe, the association of cause with effect, and the hypothesis of a power of a higher order which dictates the laws of nature. This power he called necessity. Everything else he threw overboard as of no further interest to him. The problem of cognition occupied him only for a short time, and later, as though he had never devoted himself to abstract speculation, he mocked at the old philosophers who set out to define soul and life—things of which there could be no proof.[40]

During these first years in Milan he meditated on the soul, comparing it with the wind passing through organ pipes, which produces a discord if the pipes are broken; and he proclaimed the immortality of the soul, which could not decompose with the decomposition of the body.[41] At a later period he dismissed these conceptual distinctions with a shrug of the shoulders, and wrote ironically: "The rest of the definition of the soul I will leave in the minds of the monks, fathers of peoples, who know all secrets by inspiration." [42] He also declared later that no inquiry that begins and ends in the intellect is worth treating seriously: "It seems to me that those sciences which are not born of experience, the mother of all certainty, and which do not end in known experience —that is to say, those sciences whose origin or process or end does not pass through any of the five senses—are vain and full of

errors." [43] With the confidence of a man who at last feels firm
ground beneath his feet, he then contrasted the certainty of his
experimental research with the deductive method of mental science: "Here" (in mathematics and geometry) "there is no controversy over whether twice three makes more or less than six, or
whether the sum of the three angles of a triangle is greater or less
than two right angles, but all controversy is destroyed by eternal
silence and peace subsists between the followers of these sciences,
a peace such as the mendacious mental sciences can never attain." [43]

But in these years of fruitless waiting, spent in fruitless speculation, years in which Leonardo devoted his involuntary leisure to
the study of philosophy, he had not yet attained this intellectual
confidence.

6

The indignation over the wrong that had destroyed his youth
went on festering in him, his accumulated disappointments
weighed on him, and a bitterness, which every day that brought
no harvest increased, ate more and more deeply into his soul. He
had loved social intercourse, he had been warmed in the past by
the response to his eloquence, had spoken his whole mind and
heart to all whom he met, and had seen his power to move them;
and in these years he must have had to endure long stretches of
solitude and joylessness, until his desire for sympathy and understanding gave place to a misanthropic inaccessibility. With his
acute sensitiveness he was at the mercy of every blunder of the
stupid or thoughtless, every unkindness inflicted in malice or indifference. He was a man who bore his troubles in silence and
deep reserve, not admitting them even to the blank sheets on his
table which received his secret thoughts; but he could be so
deeply wounded that a half-suppressed cry of avowal was wrung
from him in this period of trial: "Where there is most capacity for
feeling there is the greatest suffering in sufferers." [44]

In these years Leonardo looked on at the victory of mediocrities,
the triumph of the mean and conscienceless. The underside of life
was revealed to him, until contempt for humanity poisoned his

spirit and he imagined himself planted in a world of human ugliness. There began to appear on the pages of the notebook devoted to his philosophical studies the first of those caricatures which became the most widely known of all his drawings, the most widely copied and forged, broadcast in seventeenth-century engravings, so that they won popularity earlier than his ideal figures. In his solitary wanderings through the streets of Milan he came across toothless old men, quarrelsome old women, fat, foxy people with loose, corroded lips. The sight of their ill-favoured, rapacious features, their expressionless mouths, their loosely hanging cheeks, and their unhealthy suppurating flesh troubled him like a nightmare. Such is man, said Leonardo to himself, and—himself tall, handsome, and in radiant health—he would follow these monsters, watching them with cold disgust and analysing their hideousness. "He was so pleased," says Vasari, "at the sight of certain bizarre faces . . . that he would follow one that had taken his fancy for a whole day; and he would so impress it on his memory that on arriving home he would draw it as though he had it in front of him."

How these women with corroded noses or wry mouths, with hanging breasts, or with goitre or warts, must have stared in surprise at the distinguished foreigner with his chin in the air who followed so persistently at their heels! One, no doubt, would give him a poisonous look, which he would commit to memory; another would meet his gaze with a lascivious smile on her wrinkled, animal face. But what he drew on returning home was not the living image Vasari imagined. "Such is man," Leonardo would think, and from components of what he had observed he would piece together his monsters—the nose of one person and the mouth of another, the chin of one and the lupus of another, pocketed eyelids and greedy mouths. No normal, ordinary, unimpressive feature would be left standing by his silver pencil; not the slightest trace of good nature or sympathy or intelligence would be discoverable in these faces. With a malicious zest he brought out in them everything that was bestial and disgusting, here another wrinkle, here a deeper shadow, here a stronger light, until a prodigy of hell emerged, vividly alive, unmistakably human.

A note of Leonardo's on Valturio's *De Re Militari* belongs to this period. After reading the work he wrote: "Demetrius used to

say that there was no difference between the words and voice of the
unlearned and ignorant and the sounds or noises from a belly full
of superfluous wind. And he said, not without justice, that it seemed
to him to make no difference from which part they emitted their
voice, from the mouth or from below, since both were of the same
value and substance." [45] Such is man! This refrain recurred constantly throughout Leonardo's life, and his caricatures grew
constantly more savage, an expression of continually growing contempt. "There are men who deserve to be called nothing else than
passages for food, augmenters of filth, and fillers of privies; because nothing else in the world is effected through them and they
are without any virtue, since nothing is left of them but filled
privies."

His one outlet from depression and misanthropy lay through
dreams of great achievements, of foreign lands, of important posts,
and of nature in turmoil—his habitual recourse in his dark venge-
fulness against an inimical world. His irresolute spirit was both
tempted and frightened by the unknown; but he pondered over
plans of vast journeys through unknown lands, far, far from the
scenes of his past and present life. He sought out travellers who
could tell strange stories of men and events in the East. One of
these travellers, now sunning himself in the glory of his experiences, was Leonardo's countryman Benedetto Dei, a frequent guest
in Milan and at the court of the Sforzas. Benedetto Dei was a man
possessed by the craving for travel and adventure, and had seen
many strange things. He had travelled in Africa, and was equally
well informed about conditions in Tunis, personalities and events
at the court of the Sultan, happenings in Asia, and the political
struggle for power in Europe. His self-confidence was no less vast
than his experience of the world: "I have brought honour," he
would say, "upon my house and my people, and this is known by
all the world, by every people in Italy and outside Italy among
whom I have as much as set foot."

On his return from his travels Benedetto Dei went from city to
city and prince to prince in Italy, carrying the latest news from
near and far, informing his patrons of the latest events, giving his
interpretation of what was going on in foreign courts and his as-
sessment of the outstanding personalities of the moment. He was

the typical journalist of an epoch which had not yet heard of news-
papers; and neither age nor illness, neither bad roads nor wind
and weather could deter him from the pursuit of his profession. In
his talk or his letters each story of an adventure gained colour and
vigour in the retelling, each experience grew more important and
more interesting in his own eyes; one of his friends and admirers
nicknamed him *tuba del bene,* "the shouter of good stories."

Leonardo kept up a correspondence with Benedetto Dei whenever Dei left Milan; and, knowing his weakness and having still
as much as ever of his own old liking for a hoax, he adopted Dei's
portentous style and sent him news of entirely impossible things
as having happened to himself. This was something more than
mere parodying; in his humorous exaggerations there was an element of his own readiness to indulge in dreams; and his liking for
the macabre would carry a story begun in jest far from the occasion that had prompted it. "News of events in the East?" he wrote
in jest in a draft letter. "Know that in the month of July there
came a giant from the Libyan desert"; and he proceeded to tell of
a black-faced giant whose glance flamed red from the depth of the
sockets of his eyes. He had dark and frightful eyebrows which he
needed only to contract in order to cloud the sky and shake the
earth. It was a borrowed picture, from Antonio Pucci's romance of
chivalry *La Reina d'Oriente;* but Leonardo furnished his formidable hero with a mass of characteristics of his own imagining.
With the utmost gravity he proceeded: "Believe me, the man did
not live who would have had the courage to withstand that glance
and not long for wings with which to flee."

So great was Leonardo's constructive power that even the wildest creations of his fancy would still contain some small intimate
touch, a sort of involuntary admixture of the observed with things
beyond conception. Thus his giant was given puffy, curling lips
surmounted by a moustache that bristled like a cat's whiskers.
Leonardo told at length of the terror the giant spread among the
population, and then of how he slipped on the muddy soil, and
fell like a mountain collapsing; the people swarmed over him like
ants and struck at him with their knives, until under the tickling
sensation this produced he got up, growling like a clap of thunder,
and shook his vast head, so that many of the pigmy humans were

hurled through the air; others held onto the strands of his tangled
hair like sailors clinging to a ship's rigging in a storm. "Really,
really, my dear Benedetto, I do not think that ever since the world
was made there was such a wailing, such universal weeping wrung
from so vast a volume of terror."

A similar admixture of the unrestrained impulse to hoaxing
with a vain longing for faraway things is to be found in the long
fragments of letters, the notes, and the drawings on pages 145 r.a.,
145 v.a., and 145 v.b. of the *Codex Atlanticus*. The letters purport
to be addressed to the Devetdar or palace governor of Syria, the
lieutenant of the "sacred Sultan of Babylon," and tell of a journey
to the East. Leonardo accompanies the story with drawings of
landscapes as though he had been on the spot. He must certainly
have long dreamed of abandoning his inhospitable native soil,
though he was perhaps well aware that he would never summon up
the resolution to do so. He invited fellow-countrymen who had
risen to eminence in the service of oriental rulers to tell him their
story; he collected maps of distant regions, and devoured the nar-
ratives and descriptions of contemporaries and of classical writers,
until his study walls opened before him and he saw himself on his
travels through fancied regions and involved in great adventures.

Did Leonardo intend to lead a later generation to suppose that
he had actually undertaken these journeys? The pains he took to
lend credibility to his story might seem to indicate that he did. Or
did he merely want to give the product of his dreams the form of
an illustrated story of adventure, as might be inferred from the
rather confused list of chapters—*divisione del libro*—which he ap-
pended to one series of letters? The threads are continually crossed
and tangled; now a purely literary purpose seems to gain the upper
hand, now there comes a tone that seems to declare the story to be
one of actual experiences. The final result is an enigma, a mystification successfully maintained through centuries.

According to the *divisione del libro*, Leonardo intended to
write the story of a prophet seeking adherents for a new faith.
(Was he thinking of Mahomet, whom he often quotes?) A terrible
inundation destroys his city, with almost every living soul in it.
The survivors drive away the prophet; then, apparently on account
of some fresh disaster, they bring him back from exile. The newly

accepted prophet shows to the people that this latest disaster was
sent to vindicate him. This series of imaginative sketches is con-
fusingly interspersed with personal touches, which give his letters
the appearance of autobiographical intention.

Leonardo added drawings of mountain landscapes, of rivers
rushing between precipitous rocks, in the attempt to give the impression of a narrative of actual experience; he even added maps
which, for all their sketchiness, were so exact that the most serious
students imagined that he had drawn them on the spot. But the
place-names which he entered on these maps were not those current in his day; they were borrowed from the ancients, and in one
note he gave his source: "Mount Cepsis is in Ptolemy's map of
Asia." [46] He seems to have used an edition printed in Ulm in 1482.
Other details he took from Aristotle's *Meteorology*.

The mystery in which Leonardo deliberately shrouded his life
hangs still over his papers; what they seem to intend to convey
cannot be quite credited, but they do surround him with an exotic
and enigmatical atmosphere. He turned his eyes away from the
narrow commonplaceness of life and from the unprepossessing
qualities of his fellow-men, and there rose before him the Taurus
range, which no other in the universe could overtop; its shining peaks, of the whitest stone, climbed into the skies, and when
the sun lit them up, four hours before dawn, their radiance
streamed like gentle moonlight through the night. So vast was the
shadow cast by this range that in summer it reached to Sarmatia,
which was distant twelve days' journey, and in winter as far as
the Hyperborean mountains, a month's journey. And suddenly
on a day of terror its mountains of snow crumbled and fell into a
luxuriant valley abounding in springs and running water, a valley
overflowing with the good things of the earth and inhabited by a
thriving population. A tornado broke over this peaceful country
with its great and magnificent city, the sluices of heaven opened,
the rivers overflowed and flooded the city; torrents in spate drove
mire and stones before them, mixed with roots and branches and
grass; the wind tore trees from the earth and flung them through
the air. And as if the unleashing of wind and flood were not
enough, the rainstorm was followed by a raging conflagration,
which seemed to be the work not of the storm but of "ten thousand

devils." And that which the waters had spared was destroyed by the flames; within ten hours the green and fertile land had become a charred desert. Among the ruins of the city, amid the frightful glare of the flames, the few survivors wandered, dumb with terror, scarcely in command of their senses. Women and children, rich and poor, crowded like flocks of sheep into the ruined churches and envied the dead their dissolution; "for," Leonardo added, as though he too had been present, "all these sufferings are as nothing in comparison with those which still await us within a very short time."

Such were his dreams when he dreamed. He was not content with the falling mountains and the inundations and the conflagration carried by ten thousand devils; his fancy rested only for a while, and he began to imagine fresh unprecedented disasters. As though he sought compensation for all that life had refused him, for his timidity that recoiled from the opportunity of adventures in sentiment, for his caution at every step, and for his slowness in extending sympathy to others, he spent his passion and his contempt, his sympathy and his misanthropy, his secret suffering and the tragedy of his vast aspirations, on an imaginary catastrophe of nature, a "weeping such as the world has never before seen."

His story of disaster in the Orient remained a fragment. The everyday life imposed its claims again on him, and was for a while full enough and varied enough to leave no more room for dreams. But the fascination of the horrible remained on the margin of his consciousness, latent when life ran smoothly, flaming up in times of disappointment, like a dark glow persisting always under the surface of a tenacious struggle for self-preservation.

CHAPTER THREE

The Triumph of the Colossus

*O dormiente, che cosa è sonno? Il sonno ha simi-
litudine colla morte. O perchè non fai adunque tale
opera, che dopo la morte tu abbi la similitudine di
perfetto vivo, che vivendo farti col sonno simile ai
tristi morti?*

O sleeper, what is sleep? Sleep resembles death.
Why, then, do you not achieve a work through
which you may have after death the semblance of
one who is living and perfect, instead of giving your
living self in sleep the semblance of the unhappy
dead?

(Codex Atlanticus, 76 recto.)

ONE day in February 1489 Milan suddenly assumed an entirely changed appearance. The long stretch from the cathedral to the castle—seventeen hundred paces if you strode it on
foot—was roofed over with white fabrics, for the weather was capricious in Milan in winter. The house-fronts had been hung with
precious tapestries, and with wreaths of broom picked out with
bright pomegranates. The young Duke Gian Galeazzo was to be
married to the granddaughter of the king of Naples, Isabella
d'Aragona.

The Florentine ambassador rode in the procession behind the
ducal couple as they left the cathedral, and he described the scene
in a letter to Lorenzo de' Medici. "Nothing more lovely has ever
been seen," he said; he feasted his eyes on the spectacle of the wedding guests in their velvets and brocades, and on the jewels worn by
the princesses and ladies of the court. He set out to give a conscientious description of all this magnificence, but abandoned the attempt: it would have taken too long, for, he said, the very cooks
were going about in silks and satins.

121

A blaze of huge diamonds and a shimmer of cloth of gold surrounded Gian Galeazzo's pale face and the long fair hair that fell round his thin cheeks. Timidly he held the hand of the tall and lovely girl by his side, and the two went hand in hand across the drawbridge and through the gateway of the castle, like two children clinging together because a fairyland has opened out before them. The great courtyard of the castle, prisoner of its bare and gruesome walls, had also lost its menacing everyday aspect; the deep red of the walls was varied with streamers of sky-blue linen, which bore painted coats of arms alternating with centaurs, and along their dull surface there ran the dark metallic sheen of thick plaits of laurel boughs and ivy. Through the centre of the spacious courtyard there went a colonnade which had sprung from the earth as if by a miracle; for the pillars were spirals of broom twigs and the arched roofing was woven of leaves and gold, and not a twig or a leaf stood out from the smooth curving surfaces; pillars and roofing might have been painted, as an enthusiastic eyewitness reported.

This perfect smoothness had been attained at the cost of a great deal of pains on Leonardo's part. He had had the twigs bound in bundles round a core of poles; the bundles had been patiently laid on from the bottom upwards, and then pressed tightly together with wickerwork and carefully trimmed. Leonardo entered in the notebook he had in use at this time all sorts of instructions for "carrying out decorations in the form of buildings," [1] and for lining tent roofs with fabrics; with his native thrift he entered also a recipe for substituting for the expensive blue paint, when large surfaces had to be covered, a paint that could be cheaply produced.[2]

This leafwork colonnade was only the prelude to the marvels he had prepared for the wedding festivities. But news came from Naples that the bride's mother, Ippolita Maria Sforza, duchess of Calabria, had died suddenly. The projected festivities were abruptly abandoned, and the young duke and duchess drove away to the castle of Pavia. Leonardo returned to the work from which the festal preparations had brought him away. The colonnade withered and was soon taken down; and Leonardo told himself with a sigh that, though architecture was occupying his thoughts to the exclusion of almost every other subject, he was privileged to carry out his plans only in perishable materials.

His passionate, all-absorbing interest in architecture in these years was probably connected with the work in progress on the cathedral of Milan. In any case, his name appears for the first time in the Milanese registers in connexion with the competition for the building of the cupola. The cathedral authorities had been busy for years with the question of the consummation of their architectural plan. They had brought a succession of architects from Germany. One of these was dismissed after five months, having "done great damage to the building." Johann Nexemberger, of Graz, had also departed, in 1486, with nothing achieved; he and his assistants had felt unable to overcome the difficulties made for them by the Milanese craftsmen.

Was Leonardo invited to give his opinion, or did he owe his part in the competition to the long communication which he addressed to the cathedral authorities, and which reached them at a moment of perplexity? This letter bore many traces of Leonardo's metaphysical studies, and was written in the same style of philosophical generalization:

"Just as it is necessary for physicians and for nurses and healers of the sick to know the nature of man and of life and of health, and to know how a balance and harmony of the elements preserves them, and how their disharmony endangers and destroys them . . . in the same way all this is needed also for the sick cathedral; it needs a physician-architect, who understands the nature of a building, the rules from which a correct method of building proceeds, and the source and divisions of these rules, and the causes which hold a building together and give it permanence."

It is rather surprising to find that the cathedral authorities were not frightened off by this opening; on the contrary, the display of learning seems to have impressed them. Still more were they impressed when Leonardo promised to go back to the ancient architects and to demonstrate from the evidence of extant buildings the causes of their endurance or their fall into ruin; "first explaining effects from causes and then proving the causes from experience." This time Leonardo showed himself a good psychologist, offering, entirely in the spirit of the Milanese enslavement to tradition, to prepare a model which "will have the symmetry, the logical consistency, and the harmony which mark the building already begun. . . . I shall be at pains," he added, "to offer no criticism of anyone and to bring no charge against anyone," and he asked the authorities to give an entirely dispassionate decision.[3]

Now, however, Lodovico Sforza took the matter into his own hands. He began by sending for an architect from Florence, Luca Fancelli, following his old method, alike in art and in politics, of consulting as many persons as possible, playing off rival ambitions against one another, spreading suspicions, administering flatteries, and never for a moment dreaming that great works of art are the product of an individual inspiration. He shared, moreover, the mistrust of the easily accessible which all men feel who have no genuine confidence in their own judgment. While Lodovico sought a competent architect from afar, Leonardo was waiting to learn the decision of the cathedral authorities, and Bramante was hoping that the summons might come to him. Bramante, after his long wait for commissions that never came, was on the point of bringing into existence, in the church of Santa Maria di San Satiro, the first full expression of the new art, the new sense of space.

Luca Fancelli, the Florentine expert, followed the example of his predecessors by declaring on his arrival in Milan that what had been done so far was all wrong. "This building," he reported to Lorenzo de' Medici, "has no backbone and is all out of proportion; it will be difficult to get it right." Accordingly so much of the substructure as had been built began to be pulled down again, without any definite idea of what was to be put in its place or whether the dome should be round or octagonal, as in the design dating back to the Milanese architect Guiniforte Solari. The Florentine went away again and returned some months later, but the issue was still unsettled, for Lodovico had to overcome Milanese lethargy and to face the determination of the neglected Milanese artists to look after their own interests. This they were so well able to do that even a Bramante found himself compelled to leave the completion of the façade of Santa Maria di San Satiro to the Lombard Amadeo, subject to exact compliance with his instructions.

While the negotiations with Luca Fancelli were still in progress, Leonardo completed the project mentioned in his letter, and at the

end of July 1487 the cathedral authorities made the first payment
on account for the wooden model which the woodcarver Bernardo
da Abbiate was making to Leonardo's design. It is plain that in
the many studies Leonardo made before arriving at a solution
with which he was satisfied he had been trying, as he pointed out
in his letter to the authorities, to reconcile the Gothic elements in
the construction with the new style of a domed cathedral, and to
provide a natural transition. In most of his sketches he kept to the
octagonal design, sometimes with a high melon-like superstructure and sometimes with an octagonal drum supported by eight
buttresses resting on eight pillars. A number of sketches show an
inner dome, which later was abandoned; on one sheet [4] this second
dome was composed of curiously formed stones which dovetailed
so exactly into one another that they gave the dome a perfectly
smooth surface. In his sketches Leonardo exhausted the various
potentialities of dome construction; he worked out every combination, represented every variation; it might be supposed that he had
lost sight of the immediate purpose of his studies and was preparing to write a special treatise on the building of cupolas.

In the midst of his sketches and calculations, adapted though
they were to the Lombard style, there crept in again and again, as
if involuntarily, as if charmed onto the paper, the great mass of
Brunelleschi's masterpiece, the cupola of Florence cathedral. It
seems almost as if Leonardo could leave his native country without
regret, could live on without home and human associations, but
could not forget that sign and token of Florence, as if he had contracted the nostalgia which Ridolfo Ghirlandaio called the "cathedral sickness," *la malattia del duomo,* and which set every native
of Florence longing to be within sight of the cathedral dome.

Leonardo's project was no more to the liking of the experts of
the cathedral building authorities than was the work of the other
competing architects. Years were to pass before a decision could be
reached. Leonardo, who was eternally dissatisfied with his own work,
tried in vain to get back his model to make improvements in it. The
cathedral authorities were continually of two minds, and unable
either definitely to reject his plan or to accept it. Ultimately Lodovico had to intervene once more in person; in the summer of 1490
he presided at a formal sitting in the castle and forced a decision.

This, as was to be expected, went in favour of the Lombard Giovanni Antonio Amadeo. By then Leonardo had already withdrawn from the competition, feeling that it was no longer worth while to trouble about the commission. He contented himself with a message which was conveyed to Lodovico by the ducal secretary—"Maestro Leonardo has told me that he holds himself at your disposal at all times in case he should be needed."

2

What did Leonardo care about the building of a cathedral dome, amid tiresome squabbles and the bitter envy of competitors, now that he had for the first time experienced the intoxicating delight of three-dimensional composition, and been seized with the passion for constructional design? His desire now was to raise new cities out of the soil, to provide a new and happier environment for humanity, in which men should move to and fro amid joy and beauty, saturated with light and air, far from disturbing noise and evil odours. How disgusting was the world in which his fellow-men lived, save for the churches in which they prayed and the few palaces of the rich. The poor were crowded like sheep into dark and airless rooms; a ragged multitude hung about the streets and squares; prostitutes lay in wait for passers-by outside the churches; gamesters settled down on the benches, shouting and cursing, immersed in their play; street sellers took possession of the pavement, shopkeepers lugged out the contents of their vaults right up to the roadway; offal and remains of food were unconcernedly thrown out of the windows on the heads of passers-by; the rain swept together a viscous conglomeration of dust, dirt, and garbage, and the rubbish heaps were left to decompose as they grew. Lodovico Sforza, as the responsible head of the community, tried in vain to improve matters by issuing regulations, which were shouted out by a trumpeter and so were called *gride*, "cries." He tried to regulate the street traffic, to keep the road surface clean, and to divorce the inhabitants from their insanitary habits by imposing penalties. In spite of him, the rubbish heaps went on fouling the atmosphere, and men and boys relieved themselves at any street corner or stairway; even in castle and palace the evil smell from kitchens and latrines penetrated to the magnificently decorated reception rooms.

Leonardo, with his acute sensitiveness, suffered from the stench which his contemporaries accepted as in the natural order of things—they combated it by an enormous consumption of perfumes. He suffered from the noise of the carts rumbling over the uneven streets, from the nagging of the women and the cursing of the porters, as from all sorts of ugliness and discordance which went unnoticed by duller senses. Only now and again did rulers become conscious of the wretched sanitary conditions and of the way the neglected houses and dirt-clogged streets became breeding-places for every sort of disease; and it needed a widespread epidemic to bring this home to them. Then they would tremble for their own lives. Between 1484 and 1486 the Black Death raged in many cities of Italy, and with special severity in Milan. Like all hedonists, Lodovico Sforza was easily frightened about his health; he consulted physicians and astrologers, who pointed to the influence of the stars and advised him not to eat oysters. He hurriedly issued order after order, introducing strict quarantine regulations, directing that the sick should be isolated and their beds and clothes burned, and setting apart a yearly sum of thirty thousand ducats for the hospital for the poor, the Ospedale Maggiore, which had accommodation, including the nursing-staff, for 1600 persons. But the plague continued unabated, and Lodovico fled from Milan. He was pale with fright, and allowed no one to approach him; the most important state documents were allowed to be sent to him by his secretary only after a period of waiting and after being heavily perfumed.

"Courage endangers life, fear preserves it," remarked Leonardo.[5] He considered ways of making use of Lodovico's life-preserving fear in the furtherance of his own big plans. In order to divert the stream of humanity from the capital cities, he proposed that ten towns should be built with five thousand houses each, to house not more than thirty thousand inhabitants; for in this way "you will distribute the masses of humanity, who live crowded together like herds of goats, filling the air with stench and spreading the seeds of plague and death." However ambitious his schemes, Leonardo never left their economic side out of account, and he proposed that the cost of the new settlements should be borne jointly by the municipalities and the state, which was to have its share of the profit: "The municipality of Lodi will meet the cost and receive the revenue, which it will hand over once a year to the duke. . . . Give me authority," he added, "for all this to be done without cost to you, and for all districts to obey those in charge of them." [6]

Leonardo proposed that his new towns should be erected along river banks (he had the Ticino in mind) or along the seashore; for he proposed nothing less than the introduction of a sewerage system on modern lines; its installation would be facilitated by the proximity of water supplies. All privies and stables, all garbage and street sweepings, were to be emptied into underground conduits—*vie sotterrane*—from which the flow of water would carry them into canals and so back to the river. All paths were provided with gutters to prevent the accumulation of rainwater and dirt; public conveniences were to be provided. But it would not be easy to wean people from their insanitary habits, and Leonardo proposed that all stairways should be spiral, for he had remarked that people generally relieved themselves on the landings between flights. He banished evil smells from his cities; and smoke was not allowed to hang in the air or be driven back by the wind down chimneys and into hearths; it was to be taken up the broad shafts of chimneys and driven out above the roofs by a special attachment, a non-return "wind cowl." [7] His cities were to be full of space and air, for the width of the streets was to be proportioned to the height of the houses. Light and air would flow through round bay-windows into every room; the rooms would be like islands, protected from the noise and bustle of the day's work.

Leonardo's dream cities were for the rich and the aristocrats of this world. There were to be two cities, one on top of the other; the upper one was for nobles and the lower one for the common people. No carts or porters were to be permitted to carry goods along the streets of the upper city. The workpeople were to pant and sweat in the arcaded ways of the lower one; in that city were to be carried on the labours that served "the needs and the convenience" of the inhabitants of the upper city, who were spared the sight and the odour of the toiling masses. It looks very much as if the one and only purpose of all the sanitary arrangements Leonardo planned was to save the mighty of this earth from the smell of the poor and the risk of infection from them. This son of the peasant girl Caterina no longer had any sense of solidarity with the social class which carried burdens and drove carts in a city. In his sensitiveness, his horror of dirt and poverty, his need of luxury, and his refinement of feeling he felt himself to be akin to the élite who went clothed in satin doublets and silken cloaks, surrounded by a cloud of perfume, and who carefully kept out of the way of the ragged and unkempt mob. His passionate adoration of beauty left no room for other feelings and considerations. All that interested him was the beauty of his clean and shining city, its arcades harmonizing with its broad and airy streets, the rhythm of the decorated façades, the gentle inclines from the upper to the lower quarter. He ended with an eloquent appeal: "The city will be a synonym for beauty; it will be of value to you in its yield and in its growth, and it will bring you everlasting fame."

This recommendation, however, went unheard, as its predecessors had done. Leonardo's dream of life in a finer and better environment remained with him for some considerable time, until its place was taken by new gleams of hope which in turn brought fresh disappointments.

Since he was not to be allowed to build ten new cities, he set out to remove the everyday nuisances from which his sense of smell suffered; he tried to improve the arrangement of privies and stables. He invented a closet seat which would drop back against the wall; the privies were also to have a covered outlet channel, with holes in its covering, "for the vapours to escape." "The seat of the latrine must turn round like the little window in monasteries, being brought back to its original position by a counterweight," he explained.[8] It was equally unnecessary, he considered, for a stable to be filled with the usual stench, but "in order to attain what I promise, this place must, contrary to usual practice, be kept clean and sweet." His clean stable was divided into three arched compartments; the middle one was for the groom, the two side ones for horses. The hay was stored on the floor and was pushed into the mangers through funnel-shaped openings. Beneath the floor of the middle compartment ran two channels into which the refuse was emptied.

Leonardo had a special reason for interesting himself in stables at this time, since he was spending a good deal of time on studies of horses. The stable he designed may have been suggested for Galeazzo da Sanseverino, who owned the most famous horses in Milan, magnificent Arabs with long bodies and thin legs that seemed almost too delicate for their strong necks and short heads. Leonardo spent many days on end sketching the beautiful animals and studying the play of the muscles that twitched beneath their silky skin. Again and again he speaks of Messer Galeazzo's "Sicilian" and his big Berber stallion, as though they are old friends.

3

Leonardo had at last reached the turning-point in his life, the opportunity for which he had waited so long. At last he had been entrusted with the commission for the monument to Francesco Sforza, for which he had been hoping for years. The road to good fortune seemed suddenly to lie open before him; and he knew that he must grasp his opportunity with both hands: "When Fortune comes, seize her firmly—by the forelock, I say, for behind she is bald." [9] All his unrealized dreams, all his wrecked plans, and his faculty for seeing everything on a broad and ample and heightened scale, poured like a torrent into the planning of the Sforza monument. When Duke Galeazzo Maria, about 1470, negotiated with the Florentine sculptors for the production of the monument, Leonardo's older colleagues were aware of the limit of their capacity, and they calculated for a maximum weight of about one thousand pounds (Florentine measure) for the whole work. But Leonardo dreamed of a colossus of such proportions as no one before him had dared to contemplate; he was determined to throw into the shade all that had ever before been done. His contemporaries were breathless with astonishment when they heard of the enormous scale on which he proposed to carry out this symbol of the power of the Sforza family. The horse was to be twelve ells high—seventy hands; Leonardo intended to cast it of one hundred thousand pounds of bronze in five furnaces.[10] As the work proceeded his ambition grew until the total weight was brought up in the end to two hundred thousand pounds.

But the statue was to be unprecedented in other ways as well as in scale. Past conquerors had been set in armour on bronze horses gently trotting; this equine colossus was to be rearing up on its hind legs, the huge momentum of its vast frame held in check by its armed rider, with his left hand, while his right arm, stretched to full length with the staff he held, provided a backward counterthrust to the movement. In one of his earliest sketches for this work—now in the Windsor collection—Leonardo proposed to support the forelegs of his colossus by placing a tree-stump beneath its hoofs, but he soon rejected this rather feeble idea for that of supporting the horse on the fallen body of an enemy warrior. Now everything was full of life, with a counterplay of forces and boldly rising diagonals; only no monument on these lines could be cast in bronze. The bold idea was worked out in a little wax model that revealed no weakness; but Leonardo quickly realized that his model was in conflict with the law of gravity. Yet he struggled on for a while, against his better knowledge, trying to achieve the impossible.

Leonardo's tentative method, his doubts and hesitations, did not escape the notice of Lodovico Sforza, who had a sharper eye for human weaknesses than for human endowments; and Lodovico's mistrust came into play with full force, the practical man's mistrust of the dreamer. He secretly asked the Florentine ambassador, Pietro Alemanni, to look round for a sculptor. In July 1489 the ambassador wrote to Lorenzo de' Medici suggesting that he should send to Milan one or two *maestri* who might be equal to the commission, since Lodovico was planning a tremendous enterprise, *una cosa in superlativo grado,* and had not much confidence in the ability of Leonardo, who had been entrusted with it, to carry it through.

The Florentine sculptors were delighted to compete for so important a commission, and Antonio Pollaiuolo made two sketches for the monument, one with conquered Verona at the rider's feet, and the other, like Leonardo's design, with a defeated warrior under the horse's hoofs. Lodovico had carefully kept his plans secret, but Leonardo noticed his patron's ill-humour, and at the moment when Lodovico was looking out for a competitor from Florence, Leonardo asked the poet and savant Piattino Piatti for an epigram for the proposed statue. He knew the value of a well-turned Latin phrase. Piatti hastened to send the required verse, written by his uncle: *"Non sum Lysippus nec Apelles nec Polycletus"* and so on—"I am no Lysippus or Apelles or Polycletus or Zeuxis, or Myron noble in bronze: I am the Florentine Leonardo, a son of Vinci, admirer and grateful pupil of the ancients. All that I lack is the ancient symmetry: I have done what I could: may posterity grant me its indulgence." [11]

In spite of the rhythmical Latin prayer for indulgence, however, Lodovico might in his dissatisfaction have withdrawn the big commission, if Leonardo had not registered a triumph which recovered for him Lodovico's precarious favour. The young duchess's year of mourning had come to an end, and the interrupted wedding festivities, for which elaborate preparations had already been made, were to be resumed at the beginning of 1490. There was a special reason for staging them with the utmost magnificence: a heavy cloud had come over the young couple's marriage and needed to be banished. The pale young Gian Galeazzo had passed through furious storms in his short life—his father's terrible death, his separation from his mother, and Lodovico's ruthless seizure of power, and all this had destroyed his self-confidence. He was still a child, without any desire for the match into which he had been forced, and he had been rather intimidated by the strong, robust foreign girl who was his wife. In her pride as a daughter of Aragon she demanded of him that he should bear himself like the ruler of a mighty state; and he had not yet even the ways of a grown man. He was extremely sensitive and nervous, and was thrown into confusion in Isabella's presence. In the end he suffered one of the attacks of fever to which he was liable, with high temperatures alternating with excessively low ones; for a time, in his youthful timidity, he took refuge in this ailment. But old King Ferdinand had no sympathy with a boy's erotic inhibitions, and pressed for the consummation of the marriage, which alone would render the marriage contract valid and binding. After a few months he sent an envoy to Milan to discover how matters were progressing, and soon every court was full of the story. The duchess of Ferrara told the queen of Hungary, who in her remote exile thirsted for any sort of gossip, "that Her Highness the duchess is still the same chaste virgin who came from Milan, and from what we see and hear she seems likely to remain so for some time yet."

More and more infuriating was the news that reached Naples; Isabella wrote agitated letters complaining of the vexations she met with in her marriage, and also in her social standing: Gian Galeazzo was but a shadow ruler, and all the power was Lodovico's; if the young duke appeared in public with his uncle the people shouted "Moro, Moro," instead of "Duca."

Lodovico grinned to himself, well satisfied with a nephew whose debility removed the risk of heirs to come. But the Neapolitan wrath must not be tempted too far, and the festivities now to be held in Isabella's honour would serve to placate her family. Bernardo Bellincioni, the facile rhymester, had put Lodovico's ideas for a tribute to the bride into the form of a stage-play.

Shortly before the festivities were due, King Ferdinand dispatched the brutal declaration that he would not part with the balance of the dowry, a sum of twenty thousand ducats, until the young duke had fulfilled his marital duty. Lodovico reproached his young nephew, and, instead of talking confidentially to him as a man in his prime to an inexperienced youth, he spoke to him in the presence of the archbishop of Milan and various prominent citizens: it was a useful opportunity for contrasting his own robust manhood with the callowness of the young ruler. "He stoked up hell for him," wrote the envoy from the Este family. Lodovico improved on King Ferdinand's threat by declaring that the dowry already paid over would have to be returned, and the bride with it.

The boy stood in helpless humiliation before these grown men who sat grinning in judgment on him. But if his uncle imagined that he had cleverly fostered the boy's inhibitions and added to his own chances of continuing the line of Sforza, he was mistaken. He had been too clever, and with his exaggerated threats he had spoilt his own game. A new expression came into the boy's troubled eyes. He knew now that he was to lose the one being who really belonged to him; and for all his shrinking from this girl who was still a stranger to him, he shrank still more from a return to his past solitude. The ambassador of the Esti, who was watching him, rightly interpreted the new fire in the pale eyes. "The thing that threatens to escape from us always arouses our desire," he murmured sententiously; he saw that this fear of deprivation had turned the boy into a man.

Thus a strange atmosphere filled the vast hall into which the aristocratic guests streamed on January 13, 1490—Gian Galeazzo's ill-concealed discomfort, Lodovico's sly satisfaction, Isabella's grief and wrath, the guests' prurient curiosity. The guests of honour took their places on a wide central dais; the ladies spread out their broad farthingales on cushions. On the left of the hall a "mountain" of benches had been arranged, banked up to allow all the spectators, from front to back row, to look on in comfort. The domed roof of the hall was like a huge green arbour, a cupola woven of green twigs—"A framework for a festal dome," Leonardo wrote in his notes.[12]

The trumpeters blared, the pipers played merrily, and at intervals there were loud bursts of drumming. Along the rows of seats there was a rustling and crackling of cloaks and dresses of velvet or stiff brocade, with their rich gold and silver embroidery; chains and pearl necklaces clinked softly, and great diamonds and rubies blazed at every movement among the rows of guests. Zigzag gleams came from the folds of cloth of gold, and the satins shone broadly; the velvets were of soft deep red, leaf green, and the deepest blue. The women's faces looked very white above their wide puffed sleeves. The hall was filled with hot, heavy waves of perfume, for Milan possessed the one perfumers' university in Italy, and its citizens, men and women alike, had a passion for heavy, exotic scents. From their underlinen, from their shoes and stockings, and from the folds of their clothes there came a mixture of all sorts of perfumes, musk and myrtle, cinnamon and aloe; their hair and their gloves emitted strong whiffs of ambergris; all this, mixed with the aromatic scent of the wreathed foliage, made up an atmosphere that took the breath away.

The sharp jingle of tambourines began to fill the hall. Isabella

of Aragon had opened the ball with a Neapolitan dance. She was
still full of the stiff dignity of a princess as she stepped down from
the dais, her white satin cloak falling in heavy folds round her
dress of gold brocade; her child's face with its naturally merry lips
was tense with a precocious wounded pride. But in spite of her
trials in the year that had passed she had not lost a young girl's
love of a spectacle; and her big eyes sparkled as the masked dancers
brought her homage from all the princes of the earth. Fantastic
costumes from all countries, foreign national costumes such as
could scarcely have been imagined by a child who had never left
her own land, whirled across the hall—Spanish masks in cloaks of
green and gold, Polish dancers with garlands of leaves in their hair
and tufts of feathers rising above the garlands, Hungarian masks
with caps hung with ornaments. Four couples in German dress,
slashed and beribboned, the women with coiffures piled high,
danced up to her on their long pointed shoes. A dancer disguised
as a knight in armour led the French masked procession. The
men's black velvet cloaks were hung crosswise with gold chains—
just like dogs, said one onlooker disrespectfully. The women wore
ermine-lined trains which pages carried behind them, and on their
heads they wore coils of pearls, with strips of black cloth under
them, which fell to their shoulders.

Suddenly there resounded through the hall, in the midst of the
dancing, the clatter of horses' hoofs. Riders in brilliantly vari-
coloured Turkish costume dismounted in front of the dais, and the
one most gorgeously attired of all, carrying a golden sceptre, bowed
before Isabella and declared to her in a well-turned speech that
the Grand Turk was not accustomed to honour festivals of Christians, and least of all in Italy, but so great was Isabella's fame that
he had sent an envoy to do homage to her. In order to maintain
his part this greatly admired Turkish envoy then sat down with
crossed legs at Isabella's feet. The magnificence of his costume
was too much for the vanity of Lodovico, who left his guests for
a while in order to exchange his brown Moorish jerkin for a
golden one in the Turkish style.

All the masks danced a great cosmopolitan dance together; all
the peoples of the earth were united in pleasure. Among them
rushed the court dancer and court jester, Piero da Sarano, with

his wild leaps; the bells that edged his suit tinkled merrily, and his wild and noisy frolics led all the dancing couples into a mad whirl. With the patience of their day in the pursuit of pleasure, the spectators watched the dancing until shortly before midnight, showing no sign of flagging interest. Only one here and there would cast a curious glance from time to time at the heavy satin curtain which was stretched across the full width of the hall, covering the entrance to a room used by the duke as his private chapel.

At last, about midnight, the real spectacle began. While the heavy curtain was being rolled up, a child wearing angel's wings came forward and announced in his shrill treble voice that the guests would now see and hear something that had never before been presented to them. Before the childish voice had finished reeling off its verses, they were drowned in loud shouts of enthusiasm from the men and little shrieks from the women guests. One of those present reported that at first he imagined he was looking at a real paradise. Before the dazzled eyes of the onlookers there spread a representation of the heavens, constructed by Leonardo. It was a huge hemisphere, richly gilded on the inner surface. Its horizon was sprinkled with stars; above the horizon the twelve signs of the zodiac were outlined by flickering lights behind panes of glass; and seven planets were arranged in their niches in accordance with the celestial hierarchy. The spoken lines, following Lodovico's indications, consisted of crudely framed flattery and courtierly hyperbole; they described Apollo's jealousy of Isabella's beauty and Jupiter's personal intervention in her honour, and ended with the dispatch of Mercury, who brought three pagan Graces and seven Christian Virtues to accompany her on her earthly journey.

Amid the diamond-powdered radiance that streamed out from the hemisphere the seven planets moved in their orbits, the Olympian gods swept down, Jupiter himself rushed from his seat in the heavens to a mountain top, the Virtues and Graces floated by, stars flickered up and went out, and dancing nymphs waved their white Chinese lanterns. Soft music sung by the crystal voices of the ducal choirs masked the sound of the mechanism, so that it almost seemed as if supernatural forces were at work. One of the diplomats present reported that when the three Graces and seven

Virtues conducted Isabella of Aragon to the door of her sleeping-chamber her childish face was so lit up "that she looked to us like a sun." The young Duke Gian Galeazzo caught some of this radiance, and in an access of self-confidence new to him he straightened his thin, frail figure in emulation of the proud and defiant attitude he had seen in the portraits of his father.

A year later Isabella had given birth to an heir to the throne of Milan. But some time before this, friendly courts had learnt that the young Gian Galeazzo had discovered in himself the forceful spirit of the line of Sforza. The envoy from the court of Este wrote cynically to his exalted mistress that the duchess of Milan was pregnant, and the duke was suffering from stomach trouble through "working the field too hard."

4

The "paradise festival" had completely reconciled Lodovico with his painter. Il Moro had a special liking for ingenuities of mechanism, though he had no understanding of them. This close, cunning man had, moreover, an element of frivolity in him; his short outbreaks of hearty merriment were often the result of childish jokes played with new mechanical inventions; and he shared Leonardo's love of hoaxing. One day he had three crimson jackets made, for the young duke, for Galeazzo da Sanseverino, and for himself, and had them embroidered with Spanish proverbs; then he appeared arm in arm with the two in the great hall of the castle. Suddenly a tinkling began on the breasts of his two companions; silver clockwork which had been sewn into their jackets began to turn. The two youths started, and Lodovico broke into his loud braying laugh.

Leonardo too was interested in clockwork; as a boy he had invented various sorts of timepieces. He now designed an apparatus for lengthening the run of clockwork. Four separate spring barrels were fixed obliquely on top of one another, each connected by catgut with its fusee. As the lower fusee turned, the next one above screwed into it, and as soon as one spring had run down the next springbox came into play. Another invention of his was aimed against his own habit of getting up late. He would work far into the night, and then would be only too glad to sleep until late in the morning, or lie in bed between waking and dreaming, conjuring up with his inventive genius schemes that took little or no account of the conditions of everyday life. So he invented for his own use and for that of other late sleepers a tall wooden trestle, to be placed a few paces from the bottom of the bed; this held up a water-pipe, from which drops trickled slowly into a basin on a tubular lever, which reached to the foot of the bed and was held down by a shallow basin of water. As soon as the basin into which the water trickled reached a certain weight it sank, lifting the other end of the tubular lever; the shallow water vessel then emptied, and the lever suddenly pushed up the sleeper's feet. "This is a clock for the use of those who watch jealously over the use of their time," wrote Leonardo at the end of his description of his invention.[13] The invention was unlikely to be of much practical value, but it reveals a particularly interesting idea, familiar in modern times under the name of "mechanical relay" or power switch, the principle of which is that a trifling application of power is so reinforced by switching over that it produces a substantial effect.

Many of Leonardo's technical discoveries of this period give the impression that he was fascinated by the potentialities of mechanical invention, and less interested in practical results than in the release of power and its augmentation and multiplication. The mechanism of the revolving, humming, glistening cogwheels was a miracle to him; he was continually experimenting with it. He took pleasure in the precise interlocking of the cogs, and in watching their infallible working he was drawn into one of those almost lyrical outbursts which showed that he had been deeply moved. "This comes next after printing; it is no less useful and used by men, and is still more profitable and a most beautiful and subtle invention." [14] From the time when he made this comment Leonardo set out to fulfil all sorts of everyday purposes by means of gearing; he used it to set everything conceivable in motion. Many of his inventions remained no more than ideas, to be forgotten or laughed at, right down to modern times, and then worked out anew. He set spits in motion with gearing, the first mechanical turnspits; and in doing so he came accidentally upon the effect of heated air. In one of his designs he arranged for uniform turning of the spit by a vane fitted in the chimney, a small turbine wheel set circulating rapidly by the heat. "This," he declared, "is the right way to roast meat, because the joint turns slowly or quickly according as the fire is moderate or fierce." [15]

An oil-press driven by gearing was claimed by him to assure a much higher yield to the Lombard olive culture. "I promise you," he declared, "that the olives will be pressed so thoroughly that they will be left almost dry." [16] In addition to these small practical improvements, Leonardo hit on the tremendous idea for his day of using mechanical means for human conveyance. The traffic facilities of his age were rudimentary, and the idea of overcoming distance was one of the earliest on which he dwelt, remaining with him until his interest was caught by the dream of the conquest of the air. In a very early drawing of his there is already a reference to a mechanism "for setting the wheels of a wagon in motion." [17] And during his Milan period he invented, in connexion with his studies of military technique and his project of a covered battle car, the first self-propelling vehicle for private use. It was a light cart made of wooden frames with linen stretched over them; its motor consisted of a system of springs which set in motion two great horizontal cogwheels connected together by a toothed crown wheel, thus giving a compensated drive, a mechanism known in modern motoring language as a differential gear, and aimed at securing a differentiated revolution for the wheels at curves. This was a particularly difficult problem for the first steam cars, and was not overcome until Pacqueur solved it about the middle of the nineteenth century. Leonardo's first mechanically propelled vehicle, which probably could travel only a few yards, was fitted with a steering-bar with transmission gear, which gave it a certain similarity to early models of tricycles.

Amid the countless ideas which he sketched out at this period, Leonardo did not forget that it was his silver lute that had brought him first into contact which Lodovico Sforza; and he now applied the "most beautiful and subtle" invention of gearing to the making of a musical instrument, a combination of violin and clavicem-

balo (harpsichord), which he called "viola organista." In this instrument the tone was produced by an endless band. A broad
notched wheel in the centre was driven by a weight or a spiral
spring; it struck on right and left against little plates fixed in
couples on perpendicular axes. The axes, which had cogwheels at
their ends, conveyed its slow, jerky movement to the endless
band.[18] About a century later the violin-clavicembalo made its
entry into the world of music under the name of Nuremberg dulci-
mer, as the invention of Hans Haydn the elder.

In Leonardo's day drums were especially popular. Every event,
every procession or festival, opened with the roll of the drums.
Leonardo set out to mechanize the drum. One design of his [19] set
the drumsticks in motion by means of cogwheels; but this did not
satisfy him, as it required the use of a hand crank. He invented an
enormous drum on a wheeled trestle; as soon as the trestle was
pushed along, cylinders with pegs set in them began to revolve,
and drumsticks attached to the pegs beat the drumhide at a regular tempo.

Leonardo had set his stage mechanism in motion and his Olym-
pians and planets circling and floating by means of a complicated
set of gearing. The guests at the "paradise festival" regretted that
this elaborately constructed spectacle was to be exhibited on only
a single evening. But it appears that the gilded firmament was
made to serve once more before the linen rotted and the gold leaf
peeled off, though Leonardo's name was no longer mentioned in
connexion with it. On November 12 of the same year the wedding
of Eleonora da Sanseverino with Giovanni Adorno, a Venetian
aristocrat, was celebrated at Genoa, and at the end of the wedding
celebrations a tableau was staged. A huge hemisphere had been
erected on the stage; Jupiter was enthroned on high with Apollo
below him; planets surrounded them. Then the roof, which was
magnificently illuminated, and decorated in "an almost heavenly
way," opened, and four figures of angels floated down to the four
Cardinal Virtues. This time, however, the pagan Olympus, the
angels, and the Cardinal Virtues were paying tribute to the real
ruler of Milan, Lodovico Sforza. Jupiter gloried in having had the
power to send a Moor from heaven to earth who had the soul and

the mind of a god, and to bear out his words there was a Moor floating down with the angels.

Since the "paradise festival" Lodovico had had no further doubt of Leonardo's capacity to carry to completion the huge monument to his father. Leonardo, for his part, had learnt the limits of his power, and instead of dreaming of an unattainable perfection he had capitulated to reason. But his capitulation was a severe trial to him, and he expressed his despondency in the cryptic language of one of his puzzle pictures (now at Windsor): "Up to this time I have never achieved a single work." It was a bitter confession, and an injustice to a man on the threshold of the forties who could look back on a life full of laborious work. Then, however, he recovered his determination, and his indestructible capacity for vast hopes and dreams, and he followed the words of depression with these: "But I know that my present work will bring triumph."

Three months after the "paradise festival" Leonardo recorded under the date April 23, 1490, that he had completed another design for the monument—*ricominciai il cavallo*.[20] He was now no longer living with the de Predis brothers; Lodovico had assigned him a studio in the old part of the castle, the Corte Vecchia, for his work on the monument, and in addition to this studio on the ground level Leonardo had the use of a room in the top story, in which he carried out experiments which he wished to keep secret; he kept the room carefully locked. This upper room gave him access to the roof, which appears to have stretched as far as the old St. Gotthard Tower. From there Leonardo could look across to the cathedral with the scaffolding that still stood round the unfinished building. The sound of the masons' knocking and hammering came softly across to him. He watched, interested, as the workmen laboriously hoisted a statue to its niche or raised a pillar; he watched them sawing beams and putting up a temporary roofing; and constantly he noticed the inadequacy of the tools of his day, the rudimentary machines, and the waste of time and human energy. On his walks through the streets of Milan he would similarly stop and watch, wherever building or navvying was in progress; and he had many of these walks to the houses of acquaintances in whose stables he was making his studies of

horses; he had compiled a whole list of Milanese owners of specially fine horses. He would watch the work on churches and
houses under construction—everything connected with building
had an irresistible attraction for him. Constantly he would be
tempted to intervene with good advice and to show the hard-
pressed labourers how they could get better results with less effort,
even to lend a hand himself; but he would merely shake his head,
and on arrival home would sketch the correct grip in place of the
ineffective one he had observed, or a simplification of some need-
lessly complicated operation.

On one of the sheets on which he sketched what looks like a
recollection of something just seen—this time a Gothic window in
the usual Lombard style—Leonardo drew a series of tools, picks,
shovels, hammers, barrows for transporting soil, and so on, and
illustrated the right way of breaking up foundations.[21] Elsewhere
he sketched a design for an earth drill on the principle of the
modern corkscrew; this implement was introduced into practice
about 1580 by Bernard Palissy.[22] For handling heavy stones Leonardo invented a lifting-grab, the so-called "wolf," made of three
wedges connected together [23]; for lifting great pillars he designed
a crane working with screws and transmission gear; he designed
another crane, of slender construction, which was based on the
same principle as the derricks in use in building to this day,[24] and
a lift with which a heavy metal bell could be hoisted with ease to
the top of its campanile.[25] An invention which might have been
of exceptional importance for this epoch, in which all pipes for
water conduits were made by boring through tree trunks, was a
boring-machine on which the trunks were fixed perpendicularly
and bored upwards from below, so that the sawdust came away at
once. As the boring-tool turned, the platform from which it op-
erated moved up, carrying the workman with it [26]—a principle
first reduced to practice toward the end of the eighteenth century
by a Dresden engineer, Peschel. Roofing also presented a difficult
problem for Leonardo's time, and he made a soldering-stove of
the same length as the sheets of lead, which would weld them together in position by melting their edges. Furnished with this
arsenal of new machines and methods, Leonardo still waited for
some big constructional task to which he could apply them.

At last, in the summer of 1490, his opportunity seemed to have come. Lodovico had written to his secretary, Bartolommeo Calco, telling him to send the Sienese architect Francesco di Giorgio Martini, who was working in the building office of Milan cathedral, to Pavia in order to inspect the work on the cathedral of that city. In a postscript Lodovico, who was always of the opinion that three heads were better than one, added that Maestro Leonardo da Vinci and Maestro Giovanni Amadeo should also proceed on the same mission.

Experts had been contending for three years at Pavia over the plan of the cathedral. Cristoforo Rocchi, the cathedral architect—or, as he modestly called himself, the master modeller—had submitted to them a design which merely copied Saint Sophia at Constantinople on a smaller scale; this plan had been very well received by the people of Pavia. But Cardinal Ascanio Sforza, brother of Il Moro and bishop of Pavia, was contributing a large part of the funds for the building of the cathedral; on his travels he had seen the many great monuments of the new style, and he refused to put up with this feeble copy. Amadeo had therefore been commissioned to work out a new design, and in 1488 Bramante, who had been brought over from Milan, had proposed a number of drastic alterations in Amadeo's design. But the people of Pavia continued to favour their good master modeller and were disinclined to yield to the views of foreigners. Lodovico had himself been at Pavia and had taken the opportunity to intervene personally. Both the Sienese architect and Leonardo now hastened to comply with his request; Amadeo did not join them.

Leonardo had made innumerable sketches in preparation for his task. Like Bramante, he preferred the plan of the Greek cross for sacred buildings, and he sketched it in endless variation. On eleven sheets now in the *Codex Atlanticus* he drew one after another the most varied designs of crosses inscribed in a square, and in eight sketches in the MS B he worked at the same problem. He seems to have been particularly devoted to the system of a cupola resting on quartering pillars on a square substructure; to this he added apses on all four sides, with four corner towers in addition in one design. One of these designs, with quadrants roofing the apses to link up the domes on the four towers to the huge central dome, is amazingly suggestive of the perfect harmony of the original plan for Saint Peter's at Rome. He also designed churches on octagonal substructures, with eight identical chapels, reminiscent of Brunelleschi's Cappella degli Angeli in Florence, or Santa Maria in Pertica, in Pavia. In another drawing he shows a ring of chapels of varying designs, connected with a central octagon by semicircular niches; some of the chapels are octagonal, and some round and surmounted by belfries.

But Leonardo was aware that his patrons preferred the form of the Latin cross, which was customary in Lombardy; and he designed long churches closely resembling such well-known buildings as San Sepolcro or San Lorenzo in Milan; he gave them three similar apses,[27] or surrounded the great dome with a wreath of eight smaller ones.[28] This latter design agrees in many details with the wooden model made by Rocchi which is preserved to this day in the cathedral; it has the same cloister along the arms of the cross, and the elegant lantern on top of the dome.

It is no longer possible to discover how far Leonardo's designs and suggestions were turned to practical use. But for Leonardo himself this stay at Pavia was a source of new impressions and inspirations which he stored up for working out later; he intently observed everything, as was his wont, and noted odd characters and customs. Francesco di Giorgio Martini stayed only some ten days in Pavia; the two visitors put up at the Saracen Inn, and the building committee paid their bill, which came to no more than twenty lire. Leonardo stayed a short time longer. He had with him a pupil named Marco, probably Marco d'Oggionno, a youth of barely twenty years, whose young eyes Leonardo was training to observe properly.

Up to now Leonardo had not moved much about the world, except in fancy; he had seen no monuments by ancient sculptors, except in pictures. He saw now for the first time the ancient bronze statue of a horseman in the piazza in front of Pavia cathedral, supposed to represent the Goth king Gisulf, and popularly called the

Regisole. He went round and round the statue, thinking of his own equestrian monument, on which he had recommenced work just two months before. The king's horse at least stood firmly and securely on its legs; his own galloping dream horse, so wonderfully effective, existed only in the drawing. Leonardo now had one more argument with which to console himself for his first ill-success. "The movement in the Pavia monument is more admirable than anything else . . . the trot is almost of the quality of that of a free horse," he writes, and this "almost" forms the bridge which he built for himself between his aspiration and what was really within his power. Then he added—though through all his life he unceasingly urged artists to rely entirely on the study of nature, the mother of the arts—"The imitation of ancient objects is more praiseworthy than that of modern ones." [29] Was it his failure or the easy-going atmosphere of a tour that moved him to this abandonment of a little of his dogmatism?

At Pavia, Leonardo also saw for the first time the ruins of an ancient theatre, built for King Theodoric. But his new feeling for ancient art was not yet strong enough to fill him with unqualified respect for these ruins of a sunken world; entirely in the spirit of his own times, he felt fully able to make a harmonious adaptation of the remains to new purposes. He sketched a plan for converting this classic theatre into a "theatre for hearing mass." He worked out several variations of this odd idea. He added onto the ancient amphitheatre, with its rising rows of seats, a rectangular building divided into three naves and with an apse on either side of it.[30] In the centre of the arena he placed a tall fragment of a pillar, to serve as a pulpit; so bold was his fancy and so great his trust in the eloquence of the preachers of his day, that he had no qualms about the idea of a monk preaching from the middle of a pagan theatre. But he was not yet entirely satisfied with this reconstruction. It was not splendid enough, not sufficiently overwhelming. He added on three semicircular rows of seats, to be grouped as in an apse round a rectangular choir—and he proposed to surmount the whole with a cupola.[31]

Even then Leonardo could not tear himself from the sight of the ruins; they seemed to hold him spellbound. He made another restoration of them, placed a pillar in the centre of the arena, and made the rows of seats surround the stage as in a modern theatre in a three-quarter circle. The whole theatre, placed on a height to which radiating flights of stairs and covered ways led up, was roofed by a vast dome, a strange pagan-Christian pantheon, which Leonardo himself described as "a place for preaching," *locho da predicare.*[32]

To these grandiose and utterly unpractical dreams belongs one of the strangest and most enigmatical designs ever ventured on even by the hardiest of imaginative pioneers (Vallardi collection). Leonardo proposed to build a tomb for princes. He gave no indication of the occasion for the idea, or of the owner or the site he had in mind, if any, for his gigantic mausoleum. But if this is one more dream it is envisaged with such wakeful eyes, worked out so carefully in every detail, from the figures for its vast scale to the carefully drawn arrangement of the stone slabs, that it seems almost as if, at all events at the time when he was patiently elaborating the whole plan, he believed that it would actually be carried out. On an artificially elevated site there rose a pyramidal structure in the midst of an undulating landscape. As in his plan for the amphitheatre, gracious stairways rose from two sides to a platform, from which six entrances led through a circle of galleries into three vast death-chambers. The inside of the tomb was built of layers of stone slabs, apparently of granite, which would defy destruction by time or by the hand of man. These slabs were so cleverly advanced above one another, with their timber-like rounded edges, that they formed, in a mixture between the Mycenæan style and that of Leonardo's own time, a buttressed cupola of unexampled massiveness.

According to the measurements indicated by Leonardo, the diameter of these death-chambers at their base was some six hundred metres, and the elevation, for this breadth, was to be approximately that of the towers of Cologne cathedral. Above the platform a cone rose up until it was crowned by a circular temple surrounded by a spacious colonnade; and the dome of this temple, as with the ancient Pantheon, was open to the sun and sky—as though the heavens were the only fit crown for this splendid tribute to the dead.

The tomb would have sufficed for generations of princely families, with room for about five hundred funerary urns. But the rulers with whom Leonardo was associated were neither Pharaohs nor Etruscan princes. (The Etruscan tombs, strangely allied to Leonardo's design, still lay buried beneath the Italian soil.) They were men of ephemeral taste, caught between the day and its morrow, and their narrow, restless covetousness left no room for thoughts of eternal resting-places for their dead, or reminders such as this temple, soaring to the skies from the bowels of the earth, of the meaning of life and death. Thus one of the grandest designs that ever came from the brain of an architect vanished from view as completely as its occasion, if any, has done.

This was a period of his life during which Leonardo, who at times could entirely immerse himself in his concern of the moment, had no other interest than architecture; he thought and dreamed in terms of architecture, and every impression received from the day's experiences set him pursuing some architectural idea. When he strolled along the banks of the Ticino it was neither the landscape nor the play of light and shade that held his attention, but the work on the old city walls of Pavia.[33] Darkness fell; he lost his way in the maze of narrow lanes, and found himself pursued by the attentions of women in garish cloaks of coarse linen. He had the same aloof curiosity about everything, and must have followed one of the women to the house of ill fame popularly known as the Malnido, the "evil nest." There he must have looked round him with his coldly critical gaze, and what he saw was not the unlovely practices of the prostitute's profession but the very unpractical way in which the brothel was built. He found that nobody knew how to build even houses of this sort, and under the influence of his passion of the moment for architectural design, he sketched a plan of a well-organized bawdyhouse, with three entrances enabling respectable citizens to slip in unnoticed, while a system of well-arranged corridors protected them from indiscretions.[34]

But his practical bawdyhouse aroused no more interest than his colossal tomb for princes, and this plan too remained in his notebook, that cemetery of vain schemes for commissions, where it lay in the midst of elevations of churches and designs for domes. While he was sketching the plan of the bawdyhouse all sorts of other matters were running through his head, and he noted this medley of

ideas on the same sheet, as though they were all of the same interest as the sketch; he noted, for instance, the method of construction of the chimneys of the castle of Pavia, and mentioned a book
in the castle library which had made a great impression on him.

There was a great deal about the castle of Pavia that was better
worth notice than its chimneys. It was a gigantic square building
dominating the valleys of the Ticino, the Po, the Adda, and the
Olona, with four massive square towers flanking a huge façade
which, with its loopholes and crenellations, stood out sharply
against the dazzling summer sky. In the basement of the castle,
with its high barred windows looking out on the dark still water
of the moat, were the dungeons with their medieval apparatus of
torture and their cells for life-prisoners, popularly called *lunga
dimora,* "lodgings for permanencies." Above this sinister substructure were the banqueting and reception halls, vast rooms with
gaily painted little mirrors on the walls; the floors were covered
with rich mosaic; the vaulted roofs were painted sky-blue or
gilded, with a series of frescoes depicting the extravagant, pleasure-
loving life at the court of the Sforzas. Thus Galeazzo Maria had sat
at table opposite his own portrait at table; Bona of Savoy faced a
portrait of herself playing ball; their relatives and courtiers could
see themselves and one another *da naturale,* life size, portrayed
with their horses and dogs, and from room to room the duke and
duchess were to be seen riding through a deep green landscape,
through woods and groves, hunting deer, or angling for silvery
fish by the bright Ticino.

6

But the finest treasure of the castle was the ducal library, housed
in one of the towers. A marble staircase up which it would have
been possible to ride on horseback led to the great hall of the
library, the walls of which were covered with shelves full of illuminated parchment manuscripts, bound in richly dyed velvet or
damask, or gold brocade, and chained to their places on the shelves
by silver chains. This library was one of the wonders of Italy, and
a contemporary historian relates that a young savant visiting the

library fell on his knees at the sight of the unique works it had been his dream to see. Not only was this treasury of knowledge sacred in the eyes of the lay world; the procurator of the Carmelites at the court of Rome, Niccolò da Napoli, declared that he had felt it a greater happiness to see this library than the Holy Places at Jerusalem.

Leonardo must have held many of these manuscripts, their chains softly clinking, and their velvet covers nestling in his hands; one especially remained in his memory, because it was concerned with a new world of research on which he had just entered. "In Vitelone there are 805 conclusions on perspective," he wrote,[34] full of what he had found at his first reading; on another occasion he wrote: "look up Vitelone, in the library at Pavia." [35] The work of the thirteenth-century Polish savant Witelo on perspective was of special importance to Leonardo because he had begun the study of optics shortly before his visit to Pavia, in April 1490; his notebook C, which is devoted almost entirely to this subject, opens with the note: "On April 23, 1490, I began this book and made a fresh start with the horse." [36]

Leonardo made one more memorable visit during his stay at Pavia, to Fazio Cardano, whom he had perhaps met already at Milan. Cardano was a lawyer, physician, and mathematician, and lectured at the university of Pavia on mathematics, his favourite subject. He was one of those strange characters who had always exercised a special attraction over Leonardo. Fazio Cardano was the older of the two by only eight years, but with his bent body, his pale eyes that seemed to shine like a cat's in the gloom, and his trembling hands that moved unceasingly to and fro, he had the appearance already of extreme old age. The other professors all wore black, but Fazio Cardano was dressed always in a coat of flaming red, which gave him a rather gnome-like, uncanny appearance. His contemporaries regarded him as a miracle of learning; he lived a hard and strenuous life, showing no consideration either to himself or to those who lived or worked with him. He had nothing but contempt for the conventions and insincerities of social intercourse, and was entirely free from any sort of arrogance of caste or professorial pride; his best and most trusted friend for many years was a plain blacksmith.

Cardano put into Leonardo's hands a book which he had translated in 1482, the *Perspectiva Communis* of John Peckham. From it Leonardo copied these words:

"Among the studies of natural causes and reasons it is light that most enthrals the observer. . . . Accordingly perspective should be placed in the forefront of all humane disquisitions and disciplines. . . . In it you will find the glory not only of mathematics but of physics, ornamented with flowers both of the one and of the other." [37]

In that moment Leonardo had made up his mind to write a treatise of his own on this most exalted of mental disciplines. Perspective was the first great discovery in art made in the fifteenth century. The conscious creation of works of art had begun with wrestling with the problems of the representation of space. The most highly cultured among the older of Leonardo's fellow-painters had regarded it as their mission to transmit to posterity their new knowledge of the effect of distance, not only through their works but also in theoretical expositions. Leonardo refers to this wealth of existing treatises in the preface to his own work:

"Seeing that I can find no subject specially useful or pleasing—since the men who have come before me have taken for their own every useful or necessary theme—I must do like one who, being poor, comes last to the fair, and can find no other way of providing himself than by taking all the things already seen by other buyers, and not taken but refused by reason of their lesser value. I, then, will load my humble pack with this despised and rejected merchandise, the refuse of so many buyers; and will go about to distribute it, not indeed in great cities, but in the poorer towns, taking such a price as the wares I offer may be worth." [38]

It was in no spirit of false modesty that Leonardo described his own contribution as "refuse": in this work, the first which he proposed to place before the public, he was filled with anxiety lest his self-education should place him at the mercy of humanist arrogance; and he opened with an attempt to disarm criticism by candour and humility, before proceeding to attack his anticipated critics with energy and to reject any suggestion that as a man without education, *senza lettere,* he was not competent to deal with his subject. He called his treatise *Proemio di Prospettiva, cioè dell'*

Ufficio dell' Occhio—"An Introduction to Perspective, that is to say to the Function of the Eye." For all his statements to the contrary in his preface, he was confident that in his work he had entered a territory not yet fully explored, and as soon as he had overcome his initial diffidence in face of the savants he launched out boldly into an attack on the classic authors: "Now let the reader note how much faith we can place in the old writers." They strayed helplessly among barren speculations, while the things "which can be recognized and demonstrated from experience at any time have failed to be recognized or have been misinterpreted through so many centuries! The eye, which so clearly reveals its function, has been explained in one way by countless authors right down to my time; while I have found from experience that it must be explained in another way." [39]

However thorough they were in their discussion of perspective, Leonardo's predecessors had neglected optics, the actual theory of vision, or had contented themselves with the erroneous conclusions of classical science. The Platonic school held that rays emanated from the eye, which was convex and therefore less adapted for reception than for transmission; these rays brought back the image of an object, and the image then reached the consciousness in the soul. This "filament reception" theory, as it might now be called, was taken over by Euclid and Ptolemy, and was accepted down to Leonardo's time, as he states. It lasted even longer, for Bramantino, Bramante's pupil and follower, laid down that the eye sends out rays to the object on which it wants to fasten. Leonardo himself followed this theory for some time. "The eye," he wrote, "sends its image through the air to all the objects which are apposed to it" (or planted over against it), "and receives them into itself." [40] But after coming to grips with the theory of vision he rejected this hypothesis with the vigour that generally indicates a revulsion from errors of his own: "It is impossible that the eye should send out from itself, by means of the visual rays, the faculty of vision." [41]

Aristotle's theory was that light needs a medium for its transmission, as sound makes use of the air, and Leonardo adopted this theory: "Just as a stone flung into the water becomes the centre and cause of many circles, and as sound diffuses itself in circles in

the air, so every body . . . fills the surrounding air with infinite
images of itself"—so he wrote at the opening of his discussion of
the subject.[42] He took over the conception of images (*similitudine;*
he also frequently used the term *species,* Latin for "image") from
the Schoolmen, who attributed to objects the faculty of transmit-
ting their forms to the organs of perception; he imagined the air
as filled with these *species* or images, which the eye attracted to
itself as a magnet does.[43]

Testing and abandoning one error after another, Leonardo
gradually approached his theory of vision. His experiments made
him throw overboard the ideas he had acquired from reading. He
took a sheet of paper with a small hole in it, looked through the
hole at a source of light, and saw how the rays from the source
came together in a cone; when he allowed them to pass through on
to a white wall he noted how they spread out again. He manipu-
lated the sheet of paper with its pinhole for a time, made the hole
star-shaped, and enjoyed the pretty effects of perspective he thus
secured—*belli effetti di prospettiva.* He established as the first result of his experiments that light spreads in straight lines: "I ask
to have this much granted me—to assert that every ray passing
through air of equal density throughout, travels in a straight line
from its cause to the object or place it falls upon." [44] And to clinch
his argument he quoted Aristotle's theorem that every natural action proceeds along the shortest path, and that the shortest path is
the straight line.[45] At this period Leonardo seems to have been un-
acquainted with Euclid's *Optics* and *Catoptrics.* These works were
not printed until 1557, when they were published in Greek and
Latin in Paris; there he would have found the same conclusion expressed in different words.

Continuing his experiments with the pierced sheet, Leonardo
constructed a cubical box into which the rays of the sun could be
admitted through an opening in a thin iron plate, crossing to the
farther side of the box. He constructed a camera obscura [46]: this
apparatus had probably been mentioned already by the Arabs, and
may have been known to Alberti, but Leonardo was the first to
give it its final shape. Girolamo, son of his friend Fazio Cardano,
had only to furnish it with a lens in order to provide a complete
camera obscura. This was long regarded as a seventeenth-century

invention, and credited to Giambattista della Porta or Maurolycus. Yet Leonardo was himself familiar with lenses; while in Florence he had made use of a lens as the shutter of a lantern, "to produce a fine strong light." [47]

At this time, however, he seems to have concentrated entirely on the process of vision. The construction of the camera obscura had brought him much nearer the truth, confirming the uniformity of the process. All that he had still to solve was the problem of the way the double inversion is effected, producing the straightforward image—a problem to which neither Witelo nor the Arab mathematician Alhazen, who was Witelo's authority, could give him an answer. Leonardo proceeded to investigate the formation of the eye. His interest in optics dates from the same period as a new and absorbing interest which was to become, much later, the ruling passion of his life—the study of anatomy. At the beginning of 1489 he had started a special notebook for his anatomical researches; he wrote that "On April 2, 1489, [I started] the book entitled *De Figura Umana,*" and from then on the two interests ran parallel, or ran together, as at the time when he devoted himself to the anatomy of the eye. Of the various parts of the eye he distinguished the optic foramen, which he called the *pupilla,* the pigment layer (*uvea*), and the iris (*luce*), all of which were known to the Arabs; and, advancing far beyond his predecessors, he established the existence of the crystalline body in the eye, *sphera cristallina,* which Maurolycus took credit for discovering in his book published in 1575. In this crystalline body, in Leonardo's opinion, there took place the second inversion of the rays, which produces the straightforward image.[48] Like Maurolycus after him, he did not get beyond the threshold of the explanation of the function of the eye, which was first given by Kepler's demonstration of the inversion on the retina.

In the years that followed, Leonardo steadily continued his researches into the process of vision. He was the first to attack the problem of binocular vision and to explain the creation of the three-dimensional image of objects through the differing perspective produced by the different position of the eyes in the head. "Things seen with two eyes will appear rounder than are those seen with one eye," he wrote some four years later.[49]

Leonardo was also particularly interested in the phenomena of optical illusion. In a series of experiments, to which he returned again and again, seeming to find special pleasure in them, he corrected various errors which he had still shared at the time of his theoretical introduction to his studies. He occupied himself, for instance, with the question whether light requires time for its transmission, and, like his predecessors of ancient and medieval times, he concluded that it does not; he inferred this, as they had done, from the fact that the rising sun at once—*senza tempo*—fills our hemisphere with light. But the eye needs time to absorb impressions, and he found that when the impressions follow rapidly after one another they are falsified. To demonstrate this he took a pointed knife and threw it on a table so that it stuck, when it swayed to and fro and there seemed to be two knives. At a later time he adduced the example of a torch rapidly swung in a circle, when it seems to form a circle of light. For other optical illusions which find a place in the modern teaching of physics he gave the explanations still current: a body placed against a bright background seems smaller than it really is [50]; a brightly illuminated body seems larger than an identical one which is less brightly illuminated [51]; if one end of an iron rod of uniform thickness is made red-hot, it seems thicker than the other end [52]—phenomena of irradiation which Leonardo was the first to record.

He also knew the illusions created by reflections, and describes the effect of two persons standing in front of a mirror and one of them placing his finger on the reflection, as he sees it, of the eye of the other; "it will seem to the other person that you are touching your own eye." [53] He explained these illusions by the law of reflection, which he formulated in the way still customary: "The angle of reflection is always equal to the angle of incidence." As a demonstration of this he took a hollow spherical vessel, poured sand or a liquid into it from a funnel, and showed that the falling particles were thrown back at the same angle as that of impact. He had a special liking for examples of the similarity of natural phenomena, evidencing the identity of the laws of motion for light, sound, smell, and magnetic waves, and he collected many such examples at this period.

In addition to demonstrations, Leonardo was fond of definitions, which he would repeat in various forms if these seemed to him tc be apt. An instance is his sentence on the nature of light: "Darkness is lack of light; shadow is diminution of light." [54] He distinguished three sorts of shadow, depending on the intensity of light. He made countless geometrical drawings to illustrate his theory of "primitive" and "derived" shadows. He intended to develop his theory in seven books, and, when he had dealt with theory, to go on to practice.[55] Among his practical applications of his theory of light there is a comparison of two sources of light, the intensity of which is measured by the depth of their shadows [56]; in the drawing accompanying this comparison he anticipates Rumford's photometer of some three centuries later. Again and again in his work Leonardo was overwhelmed with admiration of the laws which he was discovering step by step; again and again he was astonished at his rich harvest of discoveries in the research into the process of vision: "Write in your Anatomy how in the tiniest space the image can be reborn or reconstituted in its full dimensions." [57]

He found the divisions of science continually becoming effaced. His anatomical investigations, running parallel with his optical research, may have hindered the publication of his first scientific work; he determined to complete this at some later time. But his early studies in anatomy had none of the pure spirit of research with which he was filled in later years. His interest was drawn to anatomy by the studies in the nude which he made for the equestrian statue of Francesco Sforza. He frequently refers to the statue and to his studies in the nude in the notebook A, which was probably started at the end of 1490 and continued in use for some years. In among these references he continued the many threads of his researches, taking up now one and now another, and an astonishing general picture of his versatility results. His studies in perspective are continued, and alongside them are notes on the muscular power of the human frame. His keen interest in architecture is still evidenced, and he sums up the experience he has gained in a treatise on the strength of building materials and the weight-bearing capacity of various structures. In this treatise he hoped to bring to a conclusion the investigations he had begun earlier into the stability of buildings and the causes that imperil them, beginning with the pressure on foundations and ending with the distribution of pressure on joists. But while many things got no further than the start, he brought some sections of his work to completion, including the discussion of the arch, which in his plastic style he called a strength produced by two weaknesses. And already we find mention of a new field of research, as if there were not enough and to spare already. "The beginning of the treatise on water," writes Leonardo at the head of a page of his notebook.[58]

The sheets of sketches of this period are also a confused miscellany; as Leonardo sketched, new ideas continually interrupted his work. Everything that occupied him at the moment found involuntary expression through his pencil, so that any one of these sheets would serve as a record of his amazing intellectual activity, a cross-section of his brain at work. Profiles of pillars thrust themselves between sections of arms and legs; ornaments for recesses fill the space between dissected larynxes; and on the edge of a sheet picturing the network of the muscles of the leg and the epiphysis of the vertebral column there suddenly appears a mausoleum in a curiously oriental style, as though Leonardo was still pursued by dreams of impossibly vast princely tombs in the midst of his research into the structure and functions of the human body.

Alongside these sketches, which were a sort of pictorial meditation, Leonardo made anatomical studies of the utmost delicacy of execution and perfection of detail, a labour of love; the strokes of his silver pencil give the effect of stipple. The sheets of this period, with the sections of skulls, the profiles of vertebral columns, disarticulated bones and empty eye-sockets, contain some of the finest of Leonardo's drawings, as though the task of exposition brought out the very highest artistic effort of which he was capable. The book on human anatomy seems to have been also intended for publication; but here again the completion of the work was prevented not only by the mass of his competing interests but even more by the vast scale of his plans. The programme he set himself at the very outset demanded a lifetime of unceasing study. His chief interest at this time was in a field which up to his day had been particularly neglected, that of the nervous system. He set out to describe the motor nerves of every part of the body—the nerve that knits the brows, the nerve that opens the lips in a smile, the nature of sneezing and yawning, of hunger and thirst, greed and sleep and weariness, and the origin of nerve affections, from shivering and cramp to paralysis and epilepsy.[59]

Toward the end of this year, 1490, Lombardy suffered from a hard winter, with driving snow and dull grey days. In order to devote long hours at night to his studies, Leonardo made a lamp which threw a brilliant light on the white sheets of paper on his desk. The smouldering torches would play games with the shadows, the candles would flicker incessantly, the wicks of the oil lamps would provide a yellow flame that struggled feebly with the darkness; only Leonardo's study was flooded with a clear, steady light. He had had a glass cylinder fitted in the middle of a big glass globe, and he filled the globe with water, so that the weak glimmer of the wick in its olive oil was magnified to an almost magical radiance.[60] The lamp must have created a sensation, for Leonardo made a second one—this time on a richly carved pedestal—in the form which continued to be employed until mineral oil came into use at the threshold of our own times.[61]

But it was not only the night hours that Leonardo annexed for his studies; every waking moment was put to use, in a methodical existence which was hedged about with considerations for his health—the swept and garnished existence of a man who was saving himself up for some great end. He wrote down rules of life for himself, borrowed from a popular verse of the period; their plain common sense harmonized with his own habit of moderation. "If you want to keep in health," the verse ran, "follow these rules: Do not eat when you are not hungry, feed lightly at night, masticate your food well, let it be simple food and well done, drink no wine between meals or on an empty stomach; have no sleep in daytime, and cover yourself up well at night; take no medicines, and never fly into a rage; avoid luxury, and keep to a regular diet." [62] His whole life was as well ordered as if he were a scientist with independent means, in a position to devote himself entirely to the tranquil pleasures of a scholar's life. At times, when he sketched out his big programmes of work for continually extending fields of study, he seemed to have forgotten that he was a painter in the employ of the court of the Sforzas, and dependent on the whims and moods of his employer.

Lodovico showed no inclination to adopt any of the ambitious plans which Leonardo was never tired of submitting to him; but he made use of Leonardo again and again in the organization of big festivals in Milan; he was ready on any occasion for extravagant display for the sake of its ephemeral prestige. One of these occasions came now for Milan; it was also a turning-point in Lodovico's life—his marriage with Beatrice d'Este. The marriage contract had been signed some time before, but the wedding had again and again been postponed on trifling pretexts. Giacomo Trotti, the envoy from the Este family, who had good eyes and sharp ears, told the court at Ferrara the reasons for Lodovico's delaying: "He is concerned for his mistress, who is living in the castle and is with child." But Trotti was also a man of judgment and experience, and added, for the comfort of Beatrice's parents: "Time, to which no man can do violence, will set everything in order."

But if Lodovico was unwilling to enter into this new bond, which had become necessary for political reasons, at the moment when his beloved Cecilia was about to bear him a child, his vanity would not permit his own wedding to be less magnificent than the duke's. In order to keep within his more modest state as regent of Milan, he adroitly arranged that his wedding should take place simultaneously with that of Anna Sforza, the young duke's sister, who had been betrothed as a child to Alfonso d'Este, Beatrice's brother. In the invitations he sent out he disingenuously wrote that the festival was not in honour of his own wedding but of his niece's and of the ducal house of Ferrara. After this it was possible to send a circular letter in the duke's name to all the cities of Lombardy, requesting their foremost painters to betake themselves at once to Milan, where profit and honour awaited them; if they failed to present themselves, they would be fined twenty-five ducats and would forfeit the duke's favour. Work now went on feverishly in the Rocchetta, where apartments were being prepared for the bride. The walls of the vast ballroom, 160 feet long, were covered with frescoes, in which the painters so urgently summoned portrayed Francesco Sforza's victories; and the vaulted roof was painted sky-blue and picked out with golden stars.

Now it was possible for the young duke to send invitations to all friendly courts for a tourney, and to invite the rulers to bring with them their bravest jousters. In order to give the guests an idea "of the quality of the participants in the tourney," the duke added that among the Milanese jousters would be Galeazzo da Sanseverino and his two brothers—as though this name was sufficient in itself to satisfy the most ambitious. Galeazzo da Sanseverino now went to work energetically with the preparations; and he entrusted the decorative side of the festival preparations, the arrangement of the masquerade, the decoration of the arena, and the designing of the costumes to Leonardo, who was unable to resist his flattering pressure.

Galeazzo da Sanseverino, the commander of the ducal troops, came from a great ducal family who had left their home in the south of Italy to place themselves, with their consummate skill at arms and their love of adventure, at the service of courts and republics all over Europe. But Galeazzo himself was something more than the jousting knight of rare muscular strength and amazing suppleness who was his contemporaries' ideal of heroic youth; he had the boldness and the rapidity of decision that would particularly impress men of slow reactions like Lodovico; and he had also a lively appreciation of art, a genuine interest in poets and painters, a love of fine pictures as well as of pedigree horses. His fascinating appearance gave him a confidence of manner with which there was blended a smiling good nature shown equally to all persons, without distinction of rank—the magnanimity of the successful. Like all men who regard themselves as fortune's favourites, Galeazzo could always get whatever he wanted, and the envoy of the Esti summed up his position at court in these words, not without a tinge of jealousy: "This Messer Galeazzo might just as well, it seems to me, be the duke of Milan himself, for he can do whatever he likes and get anything he takes a fancy to by just asking for it." In order to bind this man more closely to himself, Lodovico Sforza had married his daughter Bianca to him a year before this time (she was his daughter by a Milanese lady, and was legitimized shortly before the marriage), although the child was only eight years old and felt the good fortune of belonging some day to this knight of romance as a burden too heavy for her.

All was rush and hurry, with messengers coming in and riding away, and strenuous efforts being made to find accommodation for all the foreign guests. The private palazzi could not provide for everyone, and envoys had to be quartered in inns. Lodovico begged his guests to keep down the numbers of their suite, and even the bride's sister, Isabella d'Este, margravine of Mantua, found herself compelled, to her great annoyance, to reduce the 114 persons and 90 horses she had intended to bring with her to "50 mouths and 30 horses." Carts trundled over the snow-covered roads bringing meat and game, fish and fowl, firewood and boughs for decorating the lists; even horses, carts, beds, and carpets were borrowed from all around, in order to provide for the great influx of guests.

On an icy January morning of 1491 Beatrice d'Este entered Milan. The population crowded into the garlanded streets and acclaimed Lodovico, whose golden suit shone like a saint's casket. The endless procession of guests rode through the Via degli Armorai, and in honour of Lodovico the armourers had lined both sides of the street with weapons and suits of armour. Knights were shown on mail-clad horses, their visors lowered, and a glittering lance or bright sword held in mailed gloves that had no hands in them. Between these ghostly rows of headless knights, between the two lines of steel shining greyly in the faint winter sunlight, Beatrice d'Este rode into her future home.

She was still a young girl, scarcely over fifteen, this formally welcomed bride who had entered womanhood through impatient embraces in the castle of Pavia. She still had a soft, full-fleshed face, oval and peevish (a face likely to show flabby, hanging cheeks in riper years), with an obstinate bulging brow; the dark hair was smoothed tightly over the forehead and drawn past the stocky neck to fall in a thick, heavy plait well below the shoulders. Two locks had escaped from the smoothed hair to play on either side of the round, dark cheeks, giving the sulky childish face a touch of frivolity. The eyes lay in shallow sockets beneath the arched eyebrows— very black, rather prominent eyes, capable of flashing dangerously. A long nose projected from the pronounced indentation of the round forehead; it came to a surprising end in a perky tip that

DIVAE

PHOTO ALINARI Beatrice d'Este. By Christophoro Romano LOUVRE

Isabella d'Este

turned cheerfully and as though inquisitively upward. But, to belie the humour of the snub nose and link up with the flashing eyes, there was a large defiant mouth, with a protruding lower lip that seemed to add ill-temper to the contemptuous curl of the upper lip.

The ballroom, with its blue and starry vaulting, was entered through a painted triumphal arch bearing an equestrian portrait of Francesco Sforza, the work of Leonardo himself or a copy from his equestrian statue. Here Beatrice d'Este, duchess of Bari, had to yield pride of place to Isabella d'Aragona, duchess of Milan—and from this day the Milanese tragedy took its start. As yet, however, the two women could smile at one another; Beatrice, at her visit to Isabella, bent over the cradle of the newborn child. Lodovico, with a tactless display of pride in his virility, asked her whether she would like to have a babe like that, and the watching courtiers heard her very cool reply, as she waved her hand toward the cradle: "This one is enough for me."

No cloud came to disturb the festivities. The tourney in the vast Piazza degli Armi lasted three whole days; the most famous swordsmen of the day had come to Milan, and even the margrave of Mantua, who had stayed away from the festivities out of regard for the Venetians, in whose service he was, hurried to Milan, in order not to miss so splendid an event. He rode with his suite, a cavalcade in green velvet; a smile of satisfaction played round his thick red lips, and his ugly black face breathed such vigour and vitality that Isabella d'Este, the margravine, watched him with her proud eyes lit up with admiration.

The knights-at-arms were a medley of green and gold, blue and silver, red and white; spears and shields shone and sparkled. Resplendent above all were the golden symbols on the helmets—the terrestrial globe, an olive branch, a tiger, a snake, the figure of a nude woman, or clasped hands; the most popular choice of all was a Moor's head, in honour of the bridegroom; some of the competitors carried the compliment to the length of smearing brown paint all over their faces. But the most ambitious of the foreign princes were outdone in magnificence by the cavalcade of Galeazzo da Sanseverino. He galloped up on a wildly rearing horse, and behind him there came a boisterous procession of "wild men," in Tatar costume as imagined by the untravelled Leonardo. One of them, representing himself to be the king of the Jews, made a speech in which he referred to the previous year's "paradise festival," the news of which had reached even this distant race. The wild men played on strange instruments such as had never before been seen in Milan; they blew bent trumpets with goatskins attached to them, according to an astonished eyewitness; the description suggests bagpipes.

Galeazzo's wild horse wore a golden saddle-cloth painted with peacock's eyes, and peacock's eyes also decorated his golden mailed shirt. In the centre of his shield was a flashing mirror, and on his richly damascened helmet a peacock spread its tail over a golden ball. This ball, Leonardo explained in his notes, represented the earth; the peacock's eyes symbolized the enchanting beauty of those who are loyal servants; the mirror on the shield meant that he who truly desires favour must be mirrored in his virtues.[63] The illustrious hero Galeazzo won the first prize in the tourney, and he was acclaimed by a tremendously proud little child, the nine-year-old Bianca. The poor child was destined to a premature death. The young bride Anna Sforza, too, as she rode into her new home, accompanied by two hundred cavaliers, was radiant in the anticipation of her splendid future; and her eyes, too, had the over-brightness of one doomed to premature death.

The young margravine of Mantua also thoroughly enjoyed the festivities; after watching her husband's skill at arms for a while, she plunged into a passionate literary discussion with a fascinating Milanese courtier, Galeazzo Visconti. The controversy over the relative merits of those two famous knights of romance, Rinaldo and Orlando, lasted until her departure; her last word on taking farewell was a cry of "Rinaldo," and Galeazzo Visconti shouted in reply that Orlando was the only true hero. This literary controversy continued for a long time to excite the two courts, producing a busy correspondence and a host of sonnets and other contributions to the whiling away of many evenings.

No one was better satisfied with the festivities than Lodovico himself. He wrote a long letter to his brother, Cardinal Ascanio, in which he declared, in spite of "our natural modesty," that they had been of unique character; not for many years in Italy had so many lances been broken, and they were lances of a stoutness that no one would credit who had not seen them. He added that the Pope ought to be told what a splendid affair it had been.

Only Leonardo, who had contributed so much to the success of the festivities, had had to suffer a great deal of vexation at this time. At the end of July 1490, while he was at Pavia or after his return, he had taken as an apprentice a ten-year-old boy named Giacomo, the son of a certain Giovanni Pietro Caprotti, of Oreno. The father seems to have been too poor to pay the usual fee, but Leonardo was attracted by the boy's fine features, regular as a marble Greek god's, with a soft tangle of curly hair above his smooth forehead; and he took the boy for nothing. Little Giacomo was ill-dressed and half starved, and on the very day after his arrival Leonardo had to buy him a couple of shirts, a pair of trousers, and a coat. And the boy was so lively and active and so incessantly fidgeting that he used up in a year no less than twenty-four pairs of shoes. At the end of the year, in one of his fits of method, Leonardo added up what it had cost him to clothe Giacomo— a cloak and a lined coat, four pairs of breeches, three jackets, and the incredible array of shoes: the total came to a considerable sum.

But the boy whom Leonardo was so spoiling, while he was so frugal for himself, had been not only physically but morally neglected. The money that Leonardo had set aside in order to pay for his first purchases for Giacomo, disappeared from his purse; and although he questioned the boy closely, "it was impossible to wring a confession from him; yet I was quite certain" that he had taken it. On one occasion Leonardo took the boy with him to supper with his friend Jacopo Andrea da Ferrara. Giacomo was unused to such profusion of food, and ate everything ravenously; "he ate enough for two and did mischief enough for four"; the wine, which he can rarely have tasted before, went to his head; he broke three glasses during the meal, spilling the wine over the table.

Even this was not all. In Leonardo's studio Giacomo made himself a thorough nuisance, and he stole everything he could lay hands on. A fellow-artist in Pavia had made Leonardo a present of a piece of shoe-leather, but Giacomo purloined it. Leonardo made a list of all the tricks the boy had played on him, a careful list, as though they were serious events in his life; and he wrote at

the end of it: "He is thievish, lying, obstinate, and gluttonous."
His pupil Marco d'Oggionno missed a silver pencil; after a long
search it was found in a box in which Giacomo kept his few poor
belongings. A scolding brought no improvement; a little later another pupil, Boltraffio, missed a silver pencil that had been left
lying on a sketch, and again it was traced to Giacomo. During the
preparations for the tournament at Lodovico's wedding, Giacomo
found various things to do in the house of Galeazzo da Sanseverino,
and one day, when the costumes of the "wild men" were being
tried on, he slipped up to the bed on which the jackets had been
thrown, passed his nimble child's hands over them, and quickly
emptied a purse.

Leonardo was curiously sensitive to any annoyance inflicted on
him by those around him. He had become inured to disappointments and bitter injustice, to human harshness and lack of comprehension, and to the pains of creative labour, but he seemed to
have the thinnest of skins for the pinpricks of ordinary life, as
though little domestic irritations affected him more than fate's
hardest blows. He gave vent now to his wrath in a long letter of
complaint that might have been written by a public prosecutor, a
stern, humourless document in which he calculated to the exact
soldo the injury he had suffered from and the money he had spent
on this ten-year-old child. Yet he kept the boy with him, complete
stranger though he was, and Giacomo continued to sow his wild
oats, as though he were well aware that he could give play to his
worst instincts with impunity. Leonardo continued to indulge in
furious outbursts against the boy, and yet to spoil him and treat
him with far more consideration than was due to his position in
his house, as half apprentice and half servant.

8

Altogether Leonardo was not getting the peace he needed for
his work. Since Beatrice d'Este had come to Milan, she had been
the centre of a restless activity that had spread as far as the walls
of his quiet studio. Beatrice was still half a child when she came to

Milan. Her stiff, erect carriage in her dress of brocade, with chains of pearls surrounding the heavy plaits of hair closely coiled on her head, did not disguise the callowness of her dark face or the jerkiness of her movements, which lent her something of the fierceness of a spitting wildcat. This young girl now found herself in a situation with which it would have been difficult enough for the tact of older, ripened women to cope. The problems of a marriage with a man so much older would have been hard enough in any case, but she now discovered that her husband was deeply in love with Cecilia Gallerani. She took up the unequal struggle with all her native impetuosity; and where she was powerless as a woman she gained her ends by insisting on her rights as a wife. After some violent scenes she succeeded in having the lovely Cecilia forbidden to appear at court in the same style of dress of embroidered gold brocade as her own. Injured and resentful, she armed herself against her husband with a curt unapproachability.

The effect on Lodovico, who had no small knowledge of women and was accustomed to easy conquests, was the reverse of what she had intended. Quite early in the honeymoon Lodovico confided to the envoy of the Esti that he was "still enjoying Cecilia's company," since his wife would not make herself agreeable to him; she had only herself to blame, he added childishly. He busied himself with the preparation of a magnificent house for Cecilia, who in the meantime had borne him a son, Cesare. He ostentatiously invited the envoy to come to see the house.

From little more than a child, Beatrice had come suddenly to womanhood under the influence of her first disillusionment, and of the plunge from a child's sheltered existence to the hostile atmosphere that now surrounded her. She seemed to ripen suddenly and prematurely into a hardened, crusted, embittered maturity. Her early experience of the brutal side of sexual relations, and the humiliation of her husband's unfaithfulness, subjected her instinctive joy in life to the coarsening and demoralizing influences which were to bring her so early to a tragic end. Her childish pleasure in gaiety and splendour degenerated into a greed for luxury and possessions, her natural courage and unconcern into an hourly tempting of fate, a breakneck playing with perils. Thrown off her balance by her false start in life, she plunged into a whirl of pleasures and festivities, a daring huntswoman by day and a passionate dancer throughout the night.

Lodovico watched with amazement the development of this injured, peevish child into a capricious and reckless woman. He was himself cautious to the point of cowardice, a man of indecision and hesitations, but he was forced in spite of himself to respect her courage, her quick reactions, her headlong rapidity of decision. With him dissembling had become second nature, but he was impressed by her lofty candour. He was no great huntsman, and he would see this little woman racing off on a spirited horse in the midst of a pack of furiously baying hounds. One day he saw her rush up to a gigantic wild boar which was eviscerating the best of her hounds; she faced the tortured animal for a long moment before a courtier gave it the deathblow. On another occasion he saw a huge stag make for her with horns lowered. It tore her silk skirt, and a horn actually scratched her thigh; he hurried up, pale with anxiety, to find Beatrice erect in her saddle, her head thrown back in uncontrollable laughter. She seemed to him then to be almost beautiful, with the momentary colour in her cheeks like a reflection of the faint rose-colour of her dress, her irregular features shaded by her big silk hat with its waving aigrette. Her wild grace harmonized with the wildness of the landscape and the quick play of light and shade under the flying clouds.

Beatrice loved every sort of movement and activity and change; she fled from quiet and solitude as though she were driven by some inner unrest; perhaps she realized that her short, stocky figure and her characterless features owed their attractiveness to mobility. She was fond of her old home sport of running to catch a ball hit into the air with a racket of woven wire. Above all, she loved dancing and music and gay carnival processions and masquerades and the theatre. The court of Ferrara had been the first among the Italian courts to take a serious interest in dramatic art. It possessed a permanent stage, a stock of over a hundred theatrical costumes, and flesh-coloured tights for dancers and danseuses. Such classical comedies were performed as the *Menaechmi* and the *Amphitryon* of Plautus (these were performed in honour of the wedding of Anna Sforza and Alfonso d'Este); and a few years earlier Ferrara had seen the first performance of the first Italian

stage-play, the *Favola di Cefalo* of Niccolò da Correggio. Since
Beatrice's arrival there had been a great deal of theatre-playing in
Milan. A troupe of players had come from Ferrara, including
Ariosto, then a young boy, and before long, as Beatrice's secretary
wrote, scarcely a month would pass without a court poet producing "a pastoral play, a comedy, a tragedy, or some new performance." Beatrice had an experienced assistant at her side in Niccolò da Correggio, and though her father repeatedly invited him
to return to Ferrara she would not let him go; he was needed to
organize the carnival amusements for her first winter in Milan.
Niccolò was related both to the Esti and to the Sforzas, for his
mother, the beautiful Beatrice, was the natural daughter of Niccolò d'Este the Third, and her second husband had been Tristan
Sforza, a natural son of Duke Francesco. Niccolò da Correggio had
been brought up at court and had grown into the most perfect
courtier of his day; his clothes and his madrigals were alike copied;
his taste carried the day in every question; Beatrice called him in
to advise her whenever she ordered a new dress. In the ballroom
enviously admiring eyes were set on his supple elegance; and his
facile and charming rhymes lent enchantment to his conversation.

But Niccolò da Correggio had to divide his time between Milan
and Ferrara; he was also being pressed by the ambitious Isabella
d'Este to go to Mantua. Beatrice found herself compelled to look
round for young poets in Milan. The official court poet was Bernardo Bellincioni, a gifted man but servile and unscrupulous; he
was careless of dignity or principle so long as he enjoyed Lodovico's favour. Up to the time of Beatrice's arrival he had played a
leading part at the court of Milan; he wrote occasional verses for
Lodovico, describing him in one of them as Italy's true Messiah
(*"el Moro oggi è d'Italia el vero Messia"*), and he allowed himself
to be made use of in amatory intrigues and for little spying services. One day he was sent to persuade the young Duke Gian
Galeazzo that he was safe in Lodovico's hands, that all the rumours
were false, and that Lodovico's one concern was to do all he could
for his beloved nephew. Having succeeded with the simple-minded
boy, the astute Florentine continued the same tactics with Isabella
d'Aragona, who in her loneliness and thirst for life's joys was glad
of the company even of a man who was not ashamed to become

the court jester in order to please his exalted master. By his industrious subservience Bellincioni won the monopoly of Lodovico's favour, and frequently Leonardo found his path blocked by his fellow-countryman—even though Bellincioni praised Leonardo in his verses as a new Apelles.

Beatrice shared Leonardo's dislike of Bellincioni, knowing that he acted as intermediary between Lodovico and Cecilia and was constantly performing little services for the boy Cesare to please Lodovico, who was full of parental pride in the boy. She went elsewhere in her search for a substitute for Niccolò da Correggio, and took into her service the Milanese poet Gaspare Visconti. Visconti, as a poet and courtier, was dependent on the favour of the great; otherwise it would have been difficult to conceive how he could live in the immediate entourage of Il Moro, who had executed his father-in-law Cicco Simonetta. But he had no choice. He despised Bellincioni as a fatuous flatterer—"excelling a thousand histriones and a thousand Proteuses, since what he praises today he will abuse tomorrow"; but his profession required that he should angle in precisely the same way as Bellincioni for Lodovico's favour: Il Moro was "loved and honoured by all Europe," and was destined to turn his epoch "into the Golden Age." In a gush of classical allusions Visconti described Lodovico as a Julius Cæsar in war, an Augustus in peace, a Cicero in oratory, exceeding Trajan and Titus in clemency and uprightness, and, no doubt the main thing, richer than Crœsus.

Yet Gaspare Visconti was not without creative imagination; his lyrics in the style of Petrarch sometimes have the ring of genuine poetry; and he created that pair of lovers, Paolo and Daria, whose passion triumphed over family hatred, separation, and death: Paolo came back from a long journey to find Daria lying, to all appearance dead, in her bier in a monastery vault, and awakened her from her trance by his cries of despair—the first form of the story that was to be immortalized in *Romeo and Juliet*.

After his appointment as poet laureate to Beatrice, Gaspare Visconti dedicated to her a collection of sonnets, written in gold and silver on purple parchment and ornamented with miniatures; he wrote a play, *Pasitea,* and composed for her short masques and frivolous carnival pieces of the sort popular in Florence. For the performances of these Leonardo had to design the decorations and costumes and devise stage apparatus and little mechanical surprises. He enjoyed these tasks, and took them with the seriousness of an adult playing with children and entering well into the spirit of their game.

His sketches for these occasions passed from hand to hand, to the tailors and dyers, carpenters and mechanicians, and were swept away and burnt with the carnival rubbish. But here and there a note referring to one or another of these contributions to the entertainment of the court is to be found—a theatre curtain in blue and white check with a frilled border,[64] a cheaply made carnival costume with a patterning of grains stuck on to represent pearl embroidery,[65] birds that slip down cords to fill the theatre sky, and perhaps some allegorical figures, such as the girl with the unicorn, the symbol of the Esti, or the many glorifications of Lodovico in illustrations to the extravagances of Bellincioni and Visconti. It was a part of Leonardo's hard fate to be dependent now not only on a man of the very opposite type to his own, the narrow Philistine Lodovico, but also on the whims of a capricious girl who had neither understanding nor appreciation of his work.

Yet Beatrice, like her sister, had been carefully educated and given a thorough grounding in classical literature. Battista Guarino, son of the famous humanist, had been tutor to the two sisters, and they had read Virgil and Cicero and studied Greek and Roman history with him. Their mother had passed on to them the cultured traditions of the Neapolitan court, and they had grown up among poets and musicians, in an environment of song and the dramatic art. But while Isabella d'Este carried on this tradition with all the pedantry of the humanists and the dominating intensity of a beautiful and self-confident woman, making the court of Mantua an intellectual centre in spite of her foolish and flyaway husband and of the poverty of his state, the younger sister, at the outset of her married career, threw overboard the cultural interests of her childhood and plunged into a life of pleasure in her desperate effort to escape from the thought of her marital trouble.

She forgot those interests still more completely and finally when she found that in doing so she had won her husband's love. The day came, perhaps to his own surprise, when Lodovico discovered that this resentful young girl who so curtly rejected his attentions had grown into a very attractive creature, *molto piacevolina,* with a sensuous nature and not a trace of prudery if she was wooed in the right way. And now his easily awakened passion, variable as a weathercock, turned right round to her, and his tenderness and rather clumsy solicitude were lavished entirely on her. And as, in his vanity, he continued to make a confidant of Trotti, the ambassador of the Esti, Trotti was able to report to Beatrice's parents that Lodovico had no thought for anything else but making Beatrice happy, and that he told him every morning of the pleasure he had had in the night.

Beatrice had won her husband, and knew now how to keep him. He wanted her merry and pleasure-seeking, and that was all. She kept to that part; perhaps she thought it clever to play it, or perhaps it had become second nature to her. "If we want to see Lodovico Sforza now," wrote Trotti, "we always find him with his wife; he never tires of laughing and joking with her."

"All the things well worth doing that we could do with the wealth of the Milanese court," sighed Isabella whenever she came to Milan and observed her sister's frivolous life. "Would to God that we had the money, we who know so well how to spend it," was the continual refrain in her letters to her husband. But Beatrice merely shrugged her shoulders; she had no ambition left beyond the enjoyment of the day; no imperishable monument in bronze or marble would be created at her bidding, no work of art be traced to her inspiration, no picture be associated with her name.

Thus Leonardo the painter, sculptor, and architect found little employment from the new mistress of Milan; the only interruptions of his work on the colossal monument to Francesco Sforza that came from her were for her amusement. Nevertheless, he seems to have considered that as a courtier at the court of the Sforzas he was now assured of the success for which he had struggled for so long in vain. He had already made plenty of efforts to adapt himself to the atmosphere of the court. He had shrunk from no flattery and had had no hesitation in accepting the same mission as his countryman Bellincioni, though, perhaps, without sacrificing his personality; he had drawn allegorical pictures to set Gian Galeazzo's doubts at rest, and had tried to combat the rumours of Lodovico's ambitions and self-seeking. In numbers of sketches and designs of which no more than scanty notes of his are now extant, he carried on effective propaganda for the regent of Milan. He drew Envy holding out eyeglasses—symbol of clear-sightedness—to Il Moro, while a symbolically black Justice bore witness in the regent's favour (Bonnat collection, Bayonne). He drew a cock (*gallo*—symbol for Gian Galeazzo) with a pack of wolves pouncing on it, to the distress of a fluttering dove (the device of Bona of Savoy), while Prudence hurried up with the Visconti adder and the broom, Lodovico's favourite symbol, in her hand, to drive away the wolves (Christ Church College, Oxford). But though Leonardo industriously played variations on maligned virtue in the form of the ermine wading through mud, the young Gian Galeazzo seeking shelter under the "Moor's" cloak, or Fortune, in the shape of the Moor, driving away Poverty, he seems to have done this sort of work less successfully than the other professional flatterers at court. He continually found his way barred by creatures who were more skilled in working on Lodovico's vanity and weaknesses and were able to hold him in their power, as servile underlings can with a mistrustful ruler who is accessible to every breath of insinuation.

9

Lodovico's mind was able to entertain alongside one another the simple faith of his childhood and the absurdest superstitions, and he could combine the cynicism of the utterly ruthless with nightmare conceptions of the life to come. He was a realist with no moral inhibitions, and yet a man without peace in his soul; and as a true child of his age he took refuge in an occultism that provided sanctions for his every action. The humanist philosophers had rejected the religious notions of punishment for sin, but they believed in magic and in the casting out of evil spirits, as though in instinctive substitution for the chains thrown off. Such men as

Marsilio Ficino shared these superstitions, and even one of the most independent thinkers of the period, Pico della Mirandola, saw in the magician a man "who unites heaven and earth in marriage, and brings the nether world into touch with the powers of the world above." Strangely enough, the beginning of the influence of the natural sciences strengthened the belief in magic; the men to whom the wonders of nature began to be revealed, and the existence of natural forces and laws made evident, were unable at first to distinguish clearly between the possible and the impossible; the very strangeness of the knowledge they were gaining suggested the existence of mysterious unseen powers. Men spoke of natural magic as distinguished from demonic, even of "empirical" magic; and the more they added to their very imperfect knowledge of this world, the more they seemed to cling to the idea of a world beyond.

Magic and exorcism flourished especially at the court of Milan. Every charlatan who claimed to have relations with the spirits of the departed, every exploiter of human credulity, found easy access to court circles. One day a young man came from Ferrara to Milan, claiming "to possess the true art of magic and exorcism, and to be able to disclose the most occult secrets of nature," and he gained great influence over Lodovico. Leonardo hotly attacked these superstitions. "Of all the things men talk of," he wrote, "the most foolish is the belief in necromancy, the sister of alchemy." [66] He proceeded to demonstrate the absurdity of the belief in spirits and the reasons why spirits cannot possibly exist: if a spirit were an incorporeal quantity it would form a vacuum, and there can be no vacuum in nature—why a spirit cannot have a body like air: it would be torn to shreds by the winds—why a spirit cannot move and speak: without motion of the air there can be no sound, and an immaterial spirit can produce no motion. He brought argument after argument, and the latest results of his own research, to the attack on the belief in spirits; he trained on it the heaviest guns of physical laws.[67] He called almost despairingly for the aid of the certainties of mathematical science: "O ye mathematicians, bring light into this superstition!" and his fervour suggests the exasperation of personal injury, of loss suffered at the hands of the charlatans at the ducal court.

Yet, while with his supreme intellectual clarity and integrity he contemptuously tore every superstition to shreds, he was himself unable to resist the temptation to listen to the voice of the supernatural in regard to his personal fate, accepting for a moment the illusion that the veil of the future can be lifted; for among the spendings which, with characteristic method, he noted from time to time there is the shamefaced entry: *"per dir la ventura"*—"for fortune-telling"—*"6 soldi."* [68]

Even greater than the hold of magic over men's minds was that of the belief in the influence of the stars. Astrology united with magic to shape men's lives, and Marsilio Ficino developed this combination into a system embracing spirit and nature, the fate of the individual and the course of history. No decision was made, no journey undertaken, no marriage concluded, without first consulting the stars. Such servitude was an inconsistency in this age with its self-confident temper; now that man's environment had been extended without limit by new discoveries and new learning, and his intellect freed from fears and inhibitions and intellectual and moral shackles, it was absurd to put on fresh chains. But very few were daring enough to rebel against the tyranny of the constellations and their interpreters, or to declare, like Pico della Mirandola in his polemic against astrology, that the wonders of the mind are greater than those of the sky, and that destiny is the daughter of the soul—*sors animæ filia.*

All the sons of Francesco Sforza, from the domineering Galeazzo Maria to Cardinal Ascanio, who suddenly interrupted a journey because the configuration of the stars was unfavourable, conformed nervously with the doctrine of the influence of the constellations. Lodovico Sforza would pray first to God for help in his personal affairs; then he would consult the stars, as "second cause," in order, as he would say, "to be able to mitigate evil and follow the good." He determined the moment for his marriage by the horoscope. He waited for the pronouncement of a favourable constellation before swearing in his captains, and after waiting impatiently for the arrival of one of his diplomats he put off an interview with him because the month was under the sign of the extinction of the moon. He had installed four astrologers as professors at the university of Pavia, and one of them, Ambrogio da

Rosate, became his physician-in-ordinary and court astrologer, and the man whose influence over him was paramount. "Nothing is done here without consulting him," wrote a lady of the court of Isabella d'Este who was a curious observer of the happenings at Milan. So great was the reputation of this court astrologer that Pope Innocent VIII asked Lodovico to permit Ambrogio da Rosate to cast his (Innocent's) horoscope. Ambrogio da Rosate was not always happy in his intervention in other people's fortunes, but he was fully capable of building up his own, with or without the aid of the stars. Finding his professorial chair at Pavia insufficiently remunerative, he induced Lodovico to give him a prefecture, with customs and monopoly revenues; he was also ennobled by Lodovico in consideration of his medical services.

Leonardo mentions the name of Ambrogio da Rosate only once, but many of his tirades seem to be directed against that all-powerful personage. Leonardo was constantly inveighing against the absurdities of the medical science of his day, against "physicians who live on the sick," and against the remedies they prescribed, "a sort of alchemy." He urged men to take care of their health, as the best of all possessions, but he added that the best way to do so was to shun the physicians. He seems himself to have practised medicine occasionally; among his notes are a number of prescriptions; one is a means of dissolving stones in the bladder, an ailment from which one of the most influential of the ducal counsellors was suffering; a German physician had been brought to Milan to treat him, and had prescribed some strange decoctions.

Leonardo dismissed astrology with silent contempt. "Avoid the prescriptions of speculative persons whose arguments are not borne out by experience," he wrote.[69] To dependence on the configuration of the stars he opposed the one law he knew of—necessity, "the mistress and guide of nature, its theme and its inventor, its eternal curb and law." [70] This necessity, demonstrated by the exact sciences, harmonized with the contemporary sense of abundant vitality, and with the self-confidence of those who had this sense. For Leonardo the realization of this harmony was a source of happiness; when he was able to prove the connexion between cause and effect, the equality of force applied and work done, he exclaimed: "O wonderful justice of thee, Prime Mover, thou hast not permitted any force to lack the order and quality of its necessary effects!" [71]

10

This clarity of comprehension and intellectual integrity, which Leonardo acquired step by step, might seem to offer no bridge for reconciliation with the men who needed illusions of their own fashioning in order to find their way in a world in which a vast transformation was proceeding. There came, however, a time in Leonardo's life in which he was ready to build such a bridge himself, to renounce his absolutism, to leave out of account some of the things he knew, in order to make terms with the ideas of the society in which he was living. This time seems to synchronize with Beatrice's arrival at Milan, as though when his services were enlisted for her entertainment he found pleasure in the gay life of which she was the centre, and gradually accustomed himself to that alien atmosphere—as an adult is ready to forget his own age when he plays with children, and sets himself to be thoroughly silly. A compromise of this sort between his own certainties and the ideas of his time is to be found in the strange collection of animal fables which he completed in 1493 or 1494, after he had probably been telling these stories for a considerable time—that book for grown-up children, puzzlingly out of character with the rest of his work, which lies like a pile of medieval ruins across the path of his modernist research.

For his allegorical drawings in honour of Lodovico and his stage scenery and carnival costumes designed for Beatrice, Leonardo may have skimmed old editions of a Bestiarius or Physiologus in search of suitable animal symbols. These allegorical sketches, which almost entirely fill one of his notebooks, are something more than simple material for decorative work. The little notes which he makes here and there, "the salamander—for virtue," "the oyster —for betrayal," and so on, are plain evidence of themes he intended at some time to develop. The allegorical animal stories of which he made so large a collection were intended for the amusement and edification of his audience, and were adapted to its mentality. He told of the unicorn, which sleeps in the lap of a pure maiden and can be captured only in this way; he told how the salamander lives in the fire, how the chameleon flies above the clouds and feeds on air; and he combined these personifications of virtues and vices with maxims, some expressive, some banal: "He who seizes an adder by the tail will be bitten"; "there can be no greater mastery than of oneself"; "think little and err much"; "there can be no more single-minded advice than that given from a ship in peril."

Neither the allegories nor the maxims were of his own invention. They were all borrowed, things he had read, undisguised plagiarism. Many of them came from an anonymous collection, *Fiore di Vertù,* dating from the first half of the fourteenth century, from a poem, *Acerba,* by Cecco d'Ascoli, or from Pliny's *Natural History.* Leonardo scarcely troubled to alter their form; only once did he make a satirical addition of his own, when he was speaking of the peacock, the symbol of vanity, and commented: "This is the last vice to be overcome."

He seems, however, to have had good success as a storyteller, for in the years that now followed, his notes of this sort were multiplied, as though he had discovered a new field of activity. Beatrice d'Este had no desire for Leonardo to paint her a picture, even to paint her portrait, but she seems to have made him a talker and a courtier; she seems to have been responsible for his prose, in which he tried to suit his hearers and ultimately found amusement himself. The evenings were long in the court of the Sforzas, and it was impossible to be always dancing or playacting. And these long evenings were full of the tension of the enforced presence of people in one another's company, preventing one another from doing anything of use. Cards would be played—Beatrice was a keen player for high stakes and was very pleased when she won. The good conversationalists would outdo one another with the latest witticisms and amusing stories, or with the fables then so popular, with their simple and obvious morals. Many round games were played—*bulletini,* played with slips of paper; *cicirlanda,* played with crude mottoes in a "lucky dip"; a round game in which each player whispered a secret to his neighbour; and, the brightest of these amusements, a guessing-game, then very popular, in the form of prophecies of impossible things, referring to the most ordinary of everyday occurrences and dressed up in the most abstruse language at command.

There must have been a great deal of talking and laughter and noise in the great bare rooms of the castle of Milan, amid the dancing shadows from the flickering firelight and the honey-coloured light of the candles. The sparse, heavy pieces of furniture stood like sinister islands about the rooms; the tall chairs with their richly carved perpendicular backs gave little chance for sitting at ease; the stiff folds of the clothing stood out round the erect figures; and the unsteady glimmer of the lighting picked out the smooth, almost enamelled faces, the artificially bleached hair, the rippling gold embroidery on the clothes, and the flashing jewels. The duke of Milan would be sitting in the centre, his pale face looking whiter than ever in the dim light, his blond hair drawn tightly, like a frame of bright metal, round his lifeless features. He would sit brooding, sunk in himself, and if he closed his thin eyelids he "seemed to be of marble," like his own funeral monument, said one of those present. Ever and again Isabella d'Aragona would look at his expressionless face, her own expression betraying a haughty determination amid the bitterness of her humiliations, and a feverish desire stirred up by her husband's impotence. When she had stared long enough in contempt at his pale, immobile face, her gaze would pass on to fasten somewhere, anywhere, on one of the robust and handsome youths standing behind the ducal chairs; it would fix on the youth almost with shameless passion and abandonment. With this open surrender Isabella would pursue in front of the whole company her waking dream of a man with strong arms and firm thighs, who would not lie through the night like a lifeless doll—and a man who would not, like this silly boy, babble out every secret she told him, or draw back like a whipped dog, under Lodovico's severity or Beatrice's taunts, from the revolt she tried to inspire in him. So painful was it at times, wrote the ambassador of the Esti, to witness this waking dream of Isabella's that some third party would intervene to remove from the scene the youth whom she had thus singled out.

Even if she broke her silence, there was little gained, for she would begin every sentence with "At home in Naples . . ." with a side-glance at Lodovico. But Lodovico would seem scarcely to hear her. He would sit in his seat almost as stonily as Gian Galeazzo. All the life would seem to have left his strong, heavy features to concentrate in his eyes, which would slavishly follow Beatrice's every movement. Beatrice, meanwhile, with the light flowing along the golden stripes that ran the length of her dress, would flit chattering through the room, fighting with her high-pitched voice and her hearty laugh against the oppressive silence of the rest.

On such evenings must Leonardo have told most of his fables and jests, his riddles and prophecies. He told his symbolic animal stories to the men and women around him, with their shortsighted greed, their fratricidal envy, their petty jealousies and trickeries. Encouraged by his success, he went on to tell fables of his own invention; these he would laboriously draft and redraft before he finally gave them to his hearers. These fables had a single central theme, that of the punishment of pride, with the trite moral of the duty of modest contentment with the allotted sphere—a strange theme and moral for a man who could be content with nothing less than the supreme goal, and to whom nothing in this world seemed unattainable.

He would tell of the water that feels dull in the ocean and climbs into the sky, and then falls back as rain, and does penance for its pride in the dark custody of the earth; of the cedar, which despises all other trees, and, after its neighbours have been felled, is uprooted by the wind; of the flame, which is consumed in stinking smoke when it leaves the protection of the hearth; of the fig tree, which in its pride aspires to bear fine fruit, and is plundered and mutilated as soon as it attracts men's attention to itself; and, by way of contrast, of the little heap of snow that finds safety in descent from the towering peak into the valley, and there endures, because "those who humble themselves are exalted."

Did he tell these little stories in order himself to escape from the charge of arrogance; was he deliberately dissembling in order to placate the envious? His crude diplomacy, which often led him to adopt the most patent little devices in social intercourse, may have suggested this method to him. But it is more probable that he was almost entirely unaware of the incongruity, that in his completely impersonal way he did not for a moment apply the moral to himself, and was merely generalizing from his experience in intercourse with the mighty, from his disappointments and his practical experience of human ill-will. And as he spoke, so persuasively and effectively, he may have been nursing some dream of peace and happiness, of an obscure and sheltered existence—a dream which he nevertheless knew he was destined never to bring to reality.

But he was entirely in his element when he propounded riddles, casting them in the form of "prophecies." He took many of these from current popular sayings (the quick-witted Florentines were fond of this form of intellectual gymnastics); some he found in the writings of contemporaries; but most bear the unmistakable impress of his own personality. He made them the medium for many of his deepest reflections, and used them to take the sting out of his most violent satirical attacks on society and religion. It looks very much as if he made use of the freedom provided by this method in order to give expression to all the criticisms of the life around him for which no other outlet was possible. Just as a man who has donned a mask may feel free to speak without restraint, so Leonardo took advantage of this popular pastime to throw into the concise form of prophecies his denunciation of many of the things that distressed him or aroused his indignation, and used this form to mirror the true character of the men whom he was compelled to flatter, and of the world around them.

He could cleverly combine amusing plays on words with satire on the injustices of the world. The tone becomes sharpest of all when he draws upon the animal world for his subjects, as though he felt the suffering of dumb creatures to be more unendurable than the most eloquent complainings of men. "O Nature, why have you become partial, showing yourself a kind and compassionate mother to some of your children and the cruellest and most pitiless stepmother to others?" he exclaims; and the occasion is the thought of the donkey, which works so loyally for masters who brutally beat it. He prophesies that "the time of Herod will come again, for the little innocent children will be taken from their nurses"; he is thinking of the kids and calves and lambs that "die of terrible wounds" to satisfy the voracity of man. Man is surely the cruellest of all animals. "Nothing will remain on earth or under the earth or in the waters," writes the earnest vegetarian Leonardo, "that is not hunted or carried off or destroyed . . . and men's bodies will become a sepulture and means of transit for all the living things they have killed." Man is indeed the cruellest of all creatures: "O Earth, why dost thou not open and engulf him in the fissures of thy vast chasms and caverns, and no longer display in the sight of heaven so cruel and ruthless a monster!" [72]

When he turns to current customs he sometimes expresses views on matters remote from the normal interests of a bachelor. He protests, for instance, against the wrapping of newborn babies in tight binders; they can mourn their lost freedom only "by means of tearful complaints and sighing and lamentation." [73] Equally striking is his denunciation of the custom of providing brides with a dowry; he is so outraged by the practice that this "prophecy" is repeated in two different forms. "And whereas in the past young maidens could not be [sufficiently] protected from the covetousness of men and from rape either by the watchfulness of parents or by the strength of walls, the time will come when fathers and relatives of these maidens will pay a large price to men who want to sleep with them, even when the maids are rich and noble and most beautiful."

He adds in disgust: "There can surely be no question that Nature must desire to extinguish the human race as a useless thing and a destroyer of everything created."

In these indirect ways Leonardo's contempt of men breaks through his apparently cheerful acceptance of the existing order. With a clearsightedness astonishing for his epoch he singles out the struggle for property, the greed for money, as the basic social evil. Under the heading, "The Fear of Poverty," he writes: "A malignant and terrifying thing will spread so much fear among men that, in their panic desire to flee from it, they will hasten to increase their measureless powers." [74] And in another place, under the heading, "Of the Desire for Wealth": "Men will pursue the thing of which they are most in fear; they will live in want in order not to fall into want." [75] The sole blame for this human aberration falls upon gold, which is brought up from dark caverns and throws men into grief and anguish and toil.[76] The metals "will bring sufferings and dangers and death to the whole human race. To many who seek them they will bring delight after much suffering, but those who do not cling to them will die in misery and need. This will produce endless crimes; it will increase them and will induce bad men to kill and commit robberies and infamies. It will sow discord among the seekers, it will deprive free cities of their independence, it will rob many men of their lives, it will set men against one another through many artifices, deceptions, and betrayals. O monstrous animal, how much better it would be for men if all of these things should return to your cave!" [77]

Did Leonardo recite these "prophecies" in the castle of Milan—in the room adjoining Lodovico's treasure chamber, before men and women whose only thought was for luxury and amusement, who loved gold and jewels as their very life, and never for a moment devoted a thought to the source of their wealth and splendour or the labour and suffering of their fellow-men with which it was purchased? This truest and bitterest section of his "prophecies" was probably written for himself alone, as the conclusion of an investigation which began as a game and ended in an analysis of social abuses. The fanciful form of presentment gave him more freedom than he could have permitted himself in any direct approach, but his message would have been made of no avail by his hearers' entire lack of comprehension.

Leonardo ventured yet further, attacking something mightier even than the mighty of this earth. From social satire he went on to a castigation of religious usages. The polemic he carried on was by no means identical with the criticism of Rome's moral debasement, a criticism which was general in his time—a natural reaction among the most pious, and a product of deep and genuine religious feeling. That criticism could be ventured on from the pulpit and the market-place, though another Savonarola, Frate Giuliano da Muggia, who had dared in those very years in his sermons in Milan to praise the Ambrosian liturgy which severed Milan from "the vices of the sordid Babylon," had had to apologize for it, on his knees and with a rope round his neck, to the spiritual authorities in the presence of the assembled population. About this time Bellincioni wrote in a letter of the "flock of new Pharisees," the "greedy Roman wolves with their thousand spurious relics and impostures," and as this letter was addressed to Lodovico he must have been able to assume his master's tacit agreement with it.

The morality of the priesthood in Milan was no less debased than at Rome. There were prelates who lived under the same roof with their concubines and appeared in public with them, riding and hunting; there were friars who, even if they wore the cloak of the Umiliata, for instance, lived a gay life, and did not hesitate to place monastery jewels in pawn in order to satisfy the whims of their womenfolk. Still worse were the conditions in the convents, where abbots and confessors assaulted the young nuns; only in the most flagrant cases did the ecclesiastical authorities intervene, as in the scandal of the convent of San Nazaro di Belusco, where the abbess had already given birth to four children before the archbishop declared that her convent had "been conducted for forty years like a brothel."

Leonardo's criticisms were not directed, however, against the unworthiness of men who wore priestly garb, and when at one point he interjects: "Pharisees—I mean saintly brothers," it is not for any serious purpose. In his "prophecies" he refers to the misuse of the spiritual calling to place the priests in a special position at the expense of the workaday world. "There will be many men who will abandon the labours and pains and poverty of life in order to dwell in magnificent houses and in the midst of wealth, claiming that this is pleasing to God." Leonardo went beyond the abuses of the servants of the Church and dared to denounce the abuses committed by the Church itself. Like Huss before him and Luther after him, he turned with special vehemence against the traffic in indulgences. In one of his "prophecies," "Of the Sale of Paradise," he wrote: "A vast multitude will sell, publicly and unhindered, things of the very highest price, without leave from the Master of those things, which never were theirs or within their power; and human justice will not prevent it." Again, under the heading "Of Monks Who Sell Phrases and Acquire Great Wealth and Promise Paradise": "Invisible money will procure the triumph of those who will expend it."

Entirely in the spirit of the Reformation he denounced the pomp of the Church. He also attacked the extravagant expenditure on funeral processions, which were very popular in Milan—as though after a life that can scarcely have been pleasing to God men needed a really impressive recommendation to Him, so as to effect a reconciliation by main force. Citizens of special eminence might have as many as six thousand priests and monks in their funeral procession; an eyewitness reports that there were so many torch-bearers at one procession that all Milan seemed to be on fire. Leonardo must have had in mind a funeral of this sort when he wrote: "Simple people will carry a huge quantity of lights in order to light the journey of those who have lost their sight for ever."

He attacked the worship of the many saints with the same vehemence with which he had attacked indulgences. Treating "Of the Religion of the Monks Who Live on Their Saints, Who Have Been Dead Quite a Time," he wrote: "Those who have been dead a thousand years will defray the cost of living of many living men." And although he had provided the most wonderful of altarpieces for the devotions of the pious, he attacked the adoration of pictures of the saints: "And men will address men who will not hear them, who will keep their eyes open and not see; they will speak and receive no answer; they will ask for the compassion of one who has ears and hears not; they will light candles before one who is blind." He also attacked the institution of the confessional: "Of Friars Who Are Confessors"—"Unhappy women will, of their own free will, reveal to men all their sins and their shameful and most secret deeds." In the true spirit of the new faith, which had not yet divided the world, Leonardo, the painter of the most beautiful Madonnas, attacked the worship of the Holy Virgin: "Many who believe in the Son build temples only in the name of the Mother." And he went even beyond the attack on Mariolatry, directing his satire actually against faith in the Saviour: "In all parts of Europe great populations will weep for the death of a single individual, who died in the East."

All this Leonardo wrote in his easily decipherable cryptography, at a time when the Inquisition was beginning to move with energy. Alexander VI, the Pope who was most shameless of all in admitting his vices, had begun a vigorous campaign against heretics soon after he had succeeded, with the aid of Ascanio Sforza, Lodovico's brother, in attaining the papal office. The secular authorities in Lombardy were willingly assisting the Holy Inquisition.

Torture had officially been abolished, but it was continued for heretics, magicians, and witches. The tongues of blasphemers against God and the Holy Virgin were cut out; blasphemers of saints were stripped in a public place, before the eyes of the people, and three buckets of water were poured over their bared bellies. Lodovico, with his good business sense, had added to the spiritual penalties heavy fines payable to the secular authority.

Leonardo felt no call to a useless martyrdom, and while in the solitude of his study he elaborated his trenchant prophecies, outwardly he conformed; at the end of a paragraph intended for public reading he wrote: "Let there be no interference with the Holy Scriptures, for they are the supreme truth." But in spite of his caution, in the age in which he lived, with oral report as the one source of information and any gossip about men in high places all the more eagerly received, his attitude was bound to become known. Vasari, in the first edition of his *Life of Leonardo,* writes: "Philosophizing on nature, he tried to discover the characteristics of the plants; and he incessantly watched the movement of the sky, the phases of the moon, and the revolving of the sun. In the course of this he reached so heretical an outlook that he submitted to no religion, for he considered it a greater enterprise to be a philosopher than a Christian." Vasari characteristically removed this unqualified charge of heresy from his second edition, on his own initiative, as a painter will paint out of a picture a feature that falsifies the general effect. Nevertheless, Leonardo's contemporaries pictured him to themselves as a magician possessing supernatural powers, accustomed to converse with the stars, solving Nature's enigmas, and revolving dangerous thoughts behind his knitted brows.

11

But the secular and spiritual authorities did not venture to lay hands on him, for he had suddenly become famous. Some three years after he had abandoned his first ambitious design for the colossal monument to Francesco Sforza, the model was completed in its second, traditional form, in readiness for casting in metal.

When the gigantic model was first placed on public view, for all Leonardo's modesty it was an achievement that took men's breath away. The colossus had probably been brought to the courtyard of the castle in a wagon specially made to take it. Its vast, powerful silhouette stood out now against the red walls of the citadel. For all its quietness of outline, there was a tremendous energy of motion in the gigantic conception. It was like a triumphant shout of a force that had sprung from the very soil to storm the heavens— the triumph of that "force" (*sforza*) which the founder of the line, Attendola, the peasant's son, had taken as a surname, and which this armed figure on its colossal horse had bequeathed to a ruling family.

Lodovico, Francesco Sforza's lesser heir, knew that this statue laid a foundation for the fame of his house through all ages to come; or so he imagined in this hour of pride and exaltation. With his talent for stage management, he had arranged that the unveiling of the monument should be carried out during one of the magnificent festivals in which he allowed the pomp-loving Milanese to revel, in the service of his policy. And in his policy he was convinced that he had now made the critical move which would secure a firm basis for his ambitious plans for the future— his negotiations with Maximilian I. Of all the double games Lodovico played during his life, these negotiations were probably the most unscrupulous. He offered to the widower of Maria of Burgundy, from whom the king of France had snatched the wealthy Anne of Brittany, the hand of his niece Bianca Maria Sforza (cousin of the little Bianca Maria who was Sanseverino's childwife), and a dowry of four hundred thousand ducats—a huge sum for a man who was always in financial difficulties. But Lodovico attached one condition to the marriage—Maximilian must give a binding promise that as soon as he ascended the imperial throne he would invest the Sforzas with the fief of the duchy of Lombardy, thus establishing their claim to the duchy, which the house of Orleans contested. But the investiture was not to be in the name of Gian Galeazzo and his heirs, but in that of Lodovico and his issue. He may have regarded it as a particularly successful stroke to pay for this robbery of the young duke of Milan with the hand of the duke's sister and with the ducal funds.

Lodovico was so delighted with the secret treaty which he now had in his pocket that he furnished the insignificant Sforza princess with a trousseau which amazed courts thoroughly familiar with extravagant luxury. Her jewels alone were estimated to be worth forty thousand ducats, and she was provided with incredible quantities of underlinen, perhaps in order to impress the Germans, who were regarded by the Italians as a dirty and unkempt race. Her camisoles had sleeves that reached to the ground, and were embroidered with gold and silver; her bed linen was of the finest Cambrai, decorated with human and animal figures. Her toilet articles were of gold and ivory, and even certain receptacles serving the most prosaic of purposes were of solid silver. Maximilian was unable himself to be present, and the Milanese court was in deep mourning for the duchess of Ferrara, who had just died, but the wedding was celebrated with great magnificence: the carpets were brought out again to decorate the house-fronts; the triumphal arches were covered with evergreen creepers, and in front of the cathedral was an arch, the biggest and most magnificent of all, across which had been stretched a sheet of linen probably used at Lodovico's own wedding, with the equestrian portrait of Francesco Sforza.

The chariot in which the imperial bride sat was drawn by four white horses; the bride was dressed entirely in red satin, with a huge train, adding yet further slenderness to her slender figure. Her long sleeves spread out round her like wings of flame; and her unbeautiful face, with too pronounced a nose, too short an upper lip, and a receding chin, was bathed in the red glow of the satin. Next to her were the Duchess Isabella d'Aragona, also in red, gold-embroidered silk, and Beatrice, who at Lodovico's request had put off mourning, and wore a dark blue velvet with elaborate glistening arabesques of gold embroidery. Next in the procession came a long line of four-horse carriages with the ladies of the court; the quantity of carriages astonished the foreign guests as much as anything else, for at that time there were only three families in Paris who owned carriages, while in Milan there were sixty four-horse carriages and two-horse ones without number. Everything Milan had to display was displayed before the guests, from a crocodile, a sight absolutely new in Lombardy, to the great statue in the castle courtyard.

Lodovico's good stage management was of great service to Leonardo. The news of his amazing accomplishment went from city to city, from prince to prince, from studio to studio, and once the guests in Milan had seen the colossus with their own eyes everyone of importance suddenly became aware that Leonardo da Vinci had created the greatest, most glorious, most impressive work of art that had ever sprung from human hands. "I firmly believe, and I am not mistaken, that Greece and Rome never saw anything greater," wrote the Milanese poet Baldassare Taccone. For Leonardo no longer needed to ask friends to favour him with their lukewarm epigrams; poetic homage came now from all quarters, and a period addicted to superlatives outdid itself in its expressions of admiration. It was an epoch in which men went in search of record achievements, and they felt that they had found the supreme one in this colossal statue: none of the immortalized ancients, neither Phidias nor Myron, Scopas nor Praxiteles, could stand comparison with Leonardo the Florentine. Jupiter himself, according to an anonymous Roman poet, must yield the palm to the conquering Leonardo:

Vittoria vince e vinci tu vittore,

he wrote, with a play on Leonardo's surname—"Victory is victor and thou, O victor, hast the victory."

In this hour of fulfilment he felt the full sense of victory, with the universal recognition all the more tumultuous, perhaps, for being belated. Lodovico had entirely forgotten the day when, in doubt whether Leonardo would ever finish the monument, he had begun to look round for another sculptor; and Leonardo himself no longer remembered his own searching and experimenting, his doubts and agonized endeavour. Among sculptors "there is only one man of merit, Leonardo the Florentine, who is casting in bronze the horse of Duke Francesco," he wrote in a draft of a curious letter for the building authorities of Piacenza cathedral, sent for a friend to use.

The cavalcade accompanying the imperial bride to Germany included Leonardo's partner Ambrogio de Predis, who was later to paint so many portraits of the young empress and of her husband's aquiline features. Leonardo himself probably rode for a while in the company, for he made full notes on this journey. They went past Lake Como, where he noticed the streams, some running low, some in spate, driving millwheels. They went through the Valtellina, by the banks of the Adda, between high and formidable mountains, and through the valley of Chiavenna, with its precipitous mountainsides down which foaming waterfalls fell into the river. In spite of his great success he was as frugal as ever, glad to find a village inn in which he was boarded for four soldi a day; and he was no more conscientious in noting the wonders of the mountain country than in recording that in the Valtellina a pound of veal and a bottle of wine cost a soldo apiece and a pound of butter and a pound of salt each cost ten denari.

His partner went on with the company. After bidding him farewell, Leonardo surveyed his past life as he surveyed the valley from his mountain road. With the departure of Ambrogio de Predis he had reached the end of a period of obscurity and vain dreams. Now his path led upward like these steep mountain paths, up which men climbed laboriously, grazing their hands on the rocks. The path went up into snow-swept solitudes, where man is at peace and no longer desires communion with other men. He thought of the stone at rest on a mountain top that longs to join its brother stones, topples over, and rolls down to the highroad below, where it is trodden on by men's shoes and trampled on by the hoofs of animals and ground by the wheels of wagons, and sinks into the mud, full of repentance and longing for its squandered peace. And he added to this simile, with the bitterness of one who had suffered many wounds, some of them scarcely yet healed, from his life in association with men: "And so it happens to those who give up the solitary life of contemplation and meditation in order to live in cities, among a population that is full of infinite evil." [78]

CHAPTER FOUR

"One of You Shall Betray Me"

*Il giglio si pose sulla ripa del Ticino e la corrente
tiro la ripa insieme col giglio.*

The lily lay down on the bank of the Ticino, and
the current carried away the river bank and the lily
with it.

(H, 44 recto.)

CHARLES VIII of France crossed the Alps in 1494 like a
conqueror of ancient times. His white standards with the lily
and crown waved in the soft September wind, displaying the proud
inscription *Voluntas Dei: Missus a Deo*. The rattle of giant drums,
drums as big as hogsheads, heralded his entry into Asti in September. His infantry came marching through the streets, seventeen
thousand strong—archers and crossbowmen, spearmen and halberd-
iers, with short padded doublets, wearing the king's colours, and
Swiss footsoldiers with their short partisans. The cannon were
borne on heavy carriages—thirty-seven bronze cannon, together
with culverins and falconets—an artillery force such as the Italians
had never before seen assembled. The wagons were followed by a
deafening tramp of horses: seven thousand troopers rode past, a
glittering and seemingly endless procession.

Flute-players heralded the approach of the royal guards, eight
hundred horsemen in full armour of steel or gilded bronze, with
tufts of ostrich feathers that nodded above the shining helmets like
bright palm fronds as the heavy horses pranced past. After this
visible and impressive evidence of the king's power came the king
himself, riding on his famous black horse Savoia, under a golden
canopy between two files of velvet-clad pages and attendants, who
thrust back the gaping crowd.

Even without the golden canopy and the attendants in double

189

file, the king was recognizable at once by his glittering crown. It was fastened securely on his white hat, between black ostrich feathers, and held in place by a wide band passing under his chin. His long, flowing blue velvet cloak lent an appearance of massive dignity to his slight figure and concealed his thin, rickety legs; his breastplate under a doublet of gold brocade arched his sunken breast. His huge head, with its unhandsome, irregular features and long wry nose, sat close on his artificially broadened shoulders; his bulging eyes shone with an expression of self-satisfaction that was seconded by the inanely rapturous smile on his big twisted mouth; between that glance and grin the face looked as if it were covered with mucus.

A few days later Beatrice d'Este entered Asti, sitting erect on her rearing horse, "as straight as if she were a man," said one of the royal train. She had long been preparing for this visit, so as not to be put into the shade by the magnificence of the French court. The yoke of her green brocade dress glittered with diamonds and rubies, and the folds of her fine linen camisole rose like foam over the rich embroidery. The white linen welled out also through the slits in her narrow sleeves; the grey silk ribbons for tying up the sleeves reached to the ground. A cloak of crimson velvet, thrown well back, made a foil for her glittering figure. Her smooth, glossy hair was covered with a network of ropes of pearls, and she wore a tilted hat of red silk with six grey and red feathers. A French courtier remarked that the hat was "just like one of ours"; he did not know that Beatrice had arranged long before for the Milanese ambassador at the French court to send her a model of the hats worn by Anne of Brittany.

Beatrice had long been preparing for this hour; she had long been working also to assure its coming. She had given birth to a son in January 1493; the child was named Ercole after her father, but was later to be rechristened Maximilian in honour of the emperor. Since the boy's birth her frivolous existence had won a new meaning and her natural ambition a definite goal. The rivalry between the two mistresses of Milan, both of them women of more energetic temperament than their husbands, had begun as a struggle over the relative honour to be accorded to their first-born, over the shape of the cradles in which the children were laid, the duration of the peals of bells from the campanili, the number of their ladies in attendance, and the cut of their clothes. It continued on the chessboard of international politics, as an exertion of rival influences. Isabella d'Aragona's father had succeeded to the throne of Naples on the death of old King Ferdinand, and she wrote letter after letter to him, complaining of invasions of her rights and affronts to her dignity, and imploring him to move in her support. Meanwhile Lodovico had made representations at the French court, urging the king to assert his none too well documented rights to Naples, and working with promises and presents, persuasive words and persuasive coin, to secure the co-operation in his schemes of the "king's friends," who believed that they held the foolish young man in the hollow of their hands. Lodovico was fully capable of himself hatching his fatal plan of contriving French intervention, but he would never have carried it out single-handed, for he was prudent enough to bear in mind not only its direct advantages but its immediate risks. Even after he had carried it so far as the signature of a secret treaty of alliance between France and Milan, Lodovico tried to persuade himself and the world that the alliance was purely defensive, and when an envoy came from King Charles to speak "a word about the enterprise," Lodovico affected not to understand, and sent word to the king that he had nothing whatever to suggest. He would have continued to have nothing to suggest, or to venture out and then draw back, if he had not been continually urged on by his ambitious wife.

Beatrice had found a coadjutor, actuated perhaps by much the same motives as her own, except that his powerful intelligence clothed them in a masculine logic and gave them a tinge of idealism—Giuliano della Rovere, cardinal of Vincula. Milan had been witnessing the rivalry of two women; Rome had been the scene of the struggle between two men of forceful character, Rodrigo Borgia and Giuliano della Rovere. When Borgia became Pope the cardinal fled to the French court in order to encompass the removal of a worthless vicar of Christ in the name of an affronted Christianity. Later the same Giuliano, when he himself wore the tiara, was to lift his hand against the French as a soldier of Christ, in order to liberate Italy from these barbarian invaders.

All the promoters of this invasion had been moved by their own personal enmities and ambitions, their own interests and schemes. They had secured it against the opposition of the French court and the French people, against the warnings of Anne de Beaujeu and the passive disapproval of Charles's young queen. Etienne de Vesc, seneschal of Beaucaire, and the ambitious *surintendant des finances* Guillaume Briçonnet, who was not content with the real power in business of state but wanted cardinal's rank, had pursued the young king with their specious arguments; the king had listened, smiling inanely and staring glassily with his goggle eyes, but if they thought they had persuaded him he knew better what he was after. He had not crossed the Alps simply to procure the ducal crown of Milan for Beatrice, or the papal tiara for the future Julius II, or the cardinal's purple for Briçonnet.

What were their petty dreams beside his glorious one, their eager, officious counsels beside the overpowering call that he himself heard, the call of fame? That call set his young heart beating; so the hearts of knights had beaten as they rode out, against dragons or infidels, with their ladies' colours on their breasts, or vanquished giants, or rode through foreign lands in armour of solid gold, as he himself was now riding through the streets of Asti. His shallow young brain was seething with a medley of romances of chivalry, full of gallant exploits and supernaturally beautiful women's faces, and he felt like one of those heroes of romance whose purity of purpose was all-conquering and quite regardless of petty human laws. He knew that he too was destined to be a conqueror; the country through which he was riding was spread beneath his feet like a triumphal carpet. The battles ahead of him were surely no more than a prelude to the greater struggle to follow, the crusade against the infidels, the holy war against the Crescent. Of all this he thought in the first days of his contact with the new world that Italy was to him; his eyes moistened with the thrill of his own magnificence and his vast designs, and it was almost a voluptuous smile that spread over his hanging lower lip.

The smile became carnal, covetous, almost a grin, and a betrayal of his sublime mission, when he saw Beatrice and the handsome women in her train, the twenty-two ladies of the court, who drove up in six carriages lined with green velvet and gold brocade.

The ladies had ropes of pearls round their beribboned plaits, and the gold veils that fell over their painted faces waved as the wind caught them. Charles VIII loved pretty women, loved them at times more than fame, and desire ran even more furiously in his blood than the fever for great deeds with which the stories of chivalry had filled him. He loved women so well that he had cheerfully allowed eight hundred of them to come with his army, the majority collected from the streets of ill repute in the towns passed through. And he had himself had so little disdain of these cheap pleasures that at the very moment of his entry into Asti he bore within him the germs of a repulsive disease.

It was this sickness that gave the first check to the conqueror's triumphal procession through the country. Lodovico sent in haste for his own physician and astrologer, Ambrogio da Rosate, to treat the king's "smallpox," as it was discreetly called. Was it God's warning to the foolhardy? So hoped Alexander VI amid the cares that pursued him in Rome, and Isabella d'Aragona in her castle at Pavia.

At Pavia the young duke Gian Galeazzo himself lay sick, attacked by a painful and mysterious disease. He had been full of life and high spirits all the summer. It had almost seemed as though his father's wild blood had suddenly begun to course in the veins of the pale youth, in this last year of his life. He had become man enough to hold the affection of the woman he loved; strong enough to race for hours on horseback over the fields and meadows of Vigevano, tightly clasping Isabella in front of him on the saddle, his blond hair streaming in the wind, a radiant young god carrying off a nymph. Now he lay writhing with pain in his bed in the castle of Pavia. It was from his bedside that Ambrogio da Rosate was summoned to treat the sick king of France. Isabella d'Aragona had been full of the menace the invasion implied to her family in Naples and her own future, and had not noticed the still worse evil that threatened her; she had become aware of it only, perhaps, when Bona of Savoy had been sent for and, on coming to the duke's bedside, had broken into unrestrained weeping. Isabella then made a last desperate struggle for Gian Galeazzo's life, tending him with self-sacrificing love, as though she had at last discovered her true mission on earth.

Gian Galeazzo was no more ready for death than he had been for life. He fought blindly against his malady, refusing to admit that he was ill. He insisted that he could still ride, but when he was set on his horse the reins fell out of his nerveless hands. He shouted for wine, which the physicians had forbidden, and continued to shout for it until at last it was brought to him. He sent for fresh fruit—only to smell, he said with a child's disingenuousness—and ate it ravenously when he was unobserved, until he went into a fit. He had suddenly begun to play the master in the house, the strong man, now that he was on the threshold of death. He determined to receive the king of France himself—Charles had now recovered—and he got his way, although Isabella seized a dagger and passionately declared that she would kill herself before she would take the hand of the man who was seeking her father's life.

On October 15, Charles VIII stood at Gian Galeazzo's bedside. The patient had been sobered and no longer shut his eyes to the reality. With a new gravity in his voice he appealed to the king to give his support to his son Francesco. This new mood made an end of Isabella's impotent fury. She no longer raged and threatened but appealed to the king's compassion—not as duchess of Milan but as daughter of the king of Naples; she implored Charles to abandon the expedition against her father.

The king's dull features twitched and worked in his agitation. His dream of glory was visibly at issue with the dictates of chivalry towards a woman and a dying man. With the issue still undecided in his mind, he stammered that he could not in honour renounce the kingdom of Naples. He dwelt again and again on honour, though he no longer knew on which side honour lay, and he looked at Isabella in distress, as if he wanted her advice. Then he went away, awkwardly and still mumbling to himself, the helpless instrument of fate. Lodovico and Beatrice took charge of him at the door. The whole of the Milanese court had assembled in the castle of Pavia, for there was to be a theatrical performance in the evening, and the sounds of laughter and noisy conversation and music penetrated in mocking fragments into the sickroom.

Among those in Lodovico's train was Leonardo da Vinci, and while the fate of Milan was being decided in the castle of Pavia he strolled along the bank of the Ticino, watching the gold-washers sifting the river sand for gold. He asked himself why with the movement of the pan the lighter part of its contents collected on top or round the edge, and determined to investigate this physical law.[1] In spite of his lack of interest in political happenings he must have had some suspicion of the critical situation, and he may have foreseen the future more clearly than those immediately involved, or he was perhaps filled with forebodings on this walk, for he made a note of the theme of a melancholy parable: "The lily lay down on the bank of the Ticino, and the current carried away the river bank and the lily with it." [2]

Five days later Gian Galeazzo died, taking leave of the world as a child takes leave of a plaything. The revellers had left the castle; his mother, comforted by a deceptive improvement, had also gone. But it was not from his fellow-men that Gian Galeazzo felt it hard to part. After the priest had left the room, when the sick man knew that his last hour had come, he had his two favourite horses brought into the room, and painfully raised himself in order to stroke their silky hide once more with his delicate hand. Then he asked for his greyhounds to be brought to him. The pack stormed into the death-chamber, rubbing their pointed young snouts against the brocaded counterpane, and the last glance of the young duke of Milan fell on the moist brown eyes of the animals who were his only friends in the world.

The messengers rode out at once into the night, with a letter for Lodovico marked *cito, cito, cito,* in token of urgency, as was done on all state papers and reports of death. They reached Lodovico at Piacenza, and he set out there and then, in the utmost haste, for Milan; before the news had reached the city he had summoned the Grand Council to the castle. In usurping the throne he was careful to preserve as far as possible the appearance of legality, and at first—"as a matter of prudence," as his biographer wrote—he proposed that the legitimate succession should be adhered to. He had taken good care, however, that his supporters on the council should object that "the circumstances of the state are not such that small children could be entrusted with this dignity," so that he could allow the ducal crown to be pressed on him. Gian Galeazzo's dead body was still lying in the castle of Pavia, in a catafalque hung with cloth of gold, when the bells of Milan were ringing in honour of its new lord, and Lodovico was riding through the streets of the city amid acclamations from the crowd, and silent curses.

Beatrice now enjoyed her triumph to the full. Isabella d'Aragona was brought to Milan, by Lodovico's command, dressed in nun's clothing of the cheapest brown cloth—the material could not have cost more than four soldi the ell, commented the ladies of the court. Isabella's two children, both dressed in brown for mourning, clung shyly to her. Her haggard face was as if turned to stone; her crazily wandering gaze seemed to be seeking her dead husband, and her pale lips moved as she mournfully murmured his name.

Gian Galeazzo's death had been extraordinarily convenient for Lodovico, so much so that it was whispered in the entourage of the king of France that the rapid Italian poison had been at work, and that the king would do well now to seize the throne of Milan himself. Charles VIII wept over the young duke's death and had a mass said for the repose of his soul. For a while he hesitated between ambition and distaste for treachery to his host, between sympathy and suspicion; then life gained the day against death, and he continued his march of conquest.

It was a strange campaign. He was leading a powerful army which fought no battles: every city opened its doors to it; it marched unopposed and conquered unimperilled. Piero de' Medici hastened of his own accord to meet Charles and offer him the keys of his fortresses, and while the republicans of Florence swept away the hated Medici regime Savonarola in his pulpit acclaimed Charles as the sword of God, the new Cyrus and the new Redeemer.

Charles had conquered Italy with wooden spurs, said Alexander VI scornfully, but the Pope was gripped with terror when he saw from a window in the Vatican the red light of the torches that lit the way for the king of France as he entered the Eternal City with naked sword. The trampling of the horses thundered along the Via Lata (now the Corso), the heavy wagons rolled past, and the cannon shone grimly in the unsteady torchlight. "France, France!" shouted the crowd, and, in mockery of the Pope: "Colonna! Vincula!"—the names of his enemies. The French replied by shouting the words pronounced by Philippe de Commines: *"Dieu est avec nous!"*

Charles VIII came as the very embodiment of punitive justice; he had only to command, and the most worthless of all Christ's Vicars would be deposed, to the relief of all Christendom. But when Charles entered into negotiation with Alexander VI he was defeated in advance; he was no match for the worldly wiles of the unarmed Pope. While his troops plundered the Roman ghetto, extorted money from the rich Jews, and burned synagogues, the king allowed his triumph to be whittled away. When his troops marched on southward along the Via Latina, he had not even secured the promise of a papal investiture with the kingdom of Naples. He had brought away Cesare Borgia, cardinal of Valencia, as hostage, but the cardinal escaped two days later.

Yet once again Charles had but to chalk out his quarters, as Alexander VI said, in order to occupy them. Town after town capitulated to him; the smaller fortresses were invested and mercilessly reduced to ruins, or were handed over to him through treachery. King Alfonso, the father of Isabella d'Aragona, did not wait for Charles's approach; he transferred the crown to his young son Ferrantino and fled from Naples. Charles entered Naples in the style his romantic temperament prompted ("in bold emulation of the emperor of Constantinople," wrote his official annalist)—in a purple robe lined with ermine, with his heavy bejewelled crown on his head, the imperial orb in his right hand and the sceptre in his left, under a golden canopy carried by the principal nobles of the city; the gaping crowds in the streets imagined that they were witnessing the resurrection of a legendary ruler of Byzantium.

Lodovico Sforza, duke of Milan, and the king's ally, was now the mightiest prince in Italy. Was it not he who had summoned the king of France in order to make use of him as his tool? Had he not rid himself of his most powerful enemies, the house of Aragon; had he not humiliated the Pope, and seized the throne of Milan without a drop of blood being shed? The house of Aragon laid low, the Medici expelled by their populace, the Esti his allies—was he not now Italy's mightiest prince and the arbiter of her destiny? He was intoxicated with his power. He held out his hands, palms upward, with his short fingers spread out, and said to one of the ambassadors: "See—I hold peace in one hand and war in the other." He was lord of Italy's destinies, and of the world's.

But there was no lack of warning voices in Italy, describing the invasion of the country as a disaster. Men like Pistoia lamented the disgrace suffered by Italy's soil; he ironically addressed Lodovico: *"Ben puoi dir, Signor mio, Ho nelle mani il cielo e 'l mondo tutto sotto il manto"*—"It is easy for you, my lord, to say: 'I hold heaven in my hands and the whole world under my cloak.' "

The indolent Milanese took no interest in the course of events; they considered that they were personally unconcerned. In one of his poems Gaspare Visconti recorded a typical conversation between a foreigner and a citizen of Milan at this time.

"What are people doing in Milan?" asks the foreigner.

"Some filing iron, some hammering it; some mending shoes, or singing or making music; some building walls, some walking and some riding spurred; some doing ordinary things and some sublime."

"But what are they saying to one another?"

"Matins and morning mass, complin, tierce, sext, and nones."

"Devil take you—I mean, how are they arguing?"

"In the vulgar tongue or in Latin, in prose or in verse."

"But, seriously, have they nothing to say about the war?"

"What war? In Milan they talk of peace, everybody feels that he is in a peaceful country."

"Do they say nothing, then, about the king of France, who has crossed the Alps with more men than all Italy could raise?"

"Not a tongue stirs among them, but their country is in safety, since Il Moro does not disdain to take it under his wing."

2

A great deal of hammering and filing, building and pulling down, planning and completing, was going on in Milan, in private enterprise and at court. Some of the castle buildings were being reconstructed, and the fortifications were being further strengthened. Leonardo resubmitted old projects to Lodovico, and brought forward new ones in view of the changing technique of war. "Now that artillery has increased its former efficacy by three-quarters, it is necessary that the walls of the fortifications shall be given three-quarters more resisting power than has been customary in the past." [3] He had already proposed various improvements; he had made sketch plans of new work on the round towers,[4] and in order to facilitate the provisioning of the castle he had recommended the building of two flights of steps, crossing one another—an idea which may be seen carried out in the open staircase at Blois. "I am satisfied with all of this," he wrote after taking measurements of the thickness of the castle walls and the width of the moats; his only objection was to the plan of the secret passages connecting the castle with the artillery outposts; so soon as any one of these outposts had been put out of action, he pointed out, the enemy could take possession of the inner girdle of walls.[5] As a general principle he considered that the system of bastions had great disadvantages in comparison with the method of fortification customary in ancient and medieval times, and in a splendid drawing he sketched the plan of a polygonal system of fortifications.[6] Within a moat stood a rampart masked with shrubs, then moat defences, small semicircular buildings which commanded the moat with their guns; then the main rampart, with rooms in its thickness from which the assailants could still be fired on even if they had scaled the wall. Next came the inner moat and inner wall, with casemates throughout the whole length of this wall, probably intended as quarters for the garrison. A similar return to polygonal planning is to be seen in a drawing by Albrecht Dürer, dated 1527; but this system did not come into general use until its adoption by Frederick the Great in Prussia.

This fine drawing may have helped to gain attention for Leonardo's new ideas, but they do not seem to have found favour with Lodovico, who, like other men of his sort, used mentally to assign particular fields to each of his helpers, and had no trust in any of them if they ventured outside their assigned province. Occasionally Lodovico would himself entrust them with new tasks; thus in the summer of 1493 he had asked Bramante to report whether a castle which a Lombard nobleman intended to build near Domodossola was likely to be injurious from a strategical standpoint. When, however, Bramante had inspected the site and made his report, Lodovico commented that "Bramante cannot understand the subject as well as a soldier," and ordered a reconsideration of the question by an expert "better qualified by his professional knowledge of the science of war."

Bramante was by nature a man of infinite patience. He had been sufficiently hardened by poverty and privation not to be thrown off his balance by the whims of the mighty, and he had also a healthy good-humour and a ready wit that enabled him to put up with many a disappointment, besides winning him the friendship of men of higher culture than his own, such as Gaspare Visconti. But Lodovico's new insult was more than he would put up with. Without a word he left Milan, to seek elsewhere a more understanding employer and a less rigidly restricted field of work.

At once the absentee became of infinite importance and entirely indispensable in Lodovico's eyes; Il Moro instructed his ambassadors in Florence and Rome to seek out the artist; he had suddenly discovered that he had lost the collaboration of an outstanding personality, and he wrote at length to his ambassadors to say so. So busily was the search prosecuted, so urgently did Lodovico press Bramante to return, such promises had the duke become all at once ready to make, that Bramante soon returned to Milan—well aware though he was that, "to tell the truth, courts are like priests, with nothing to offer but water and words and smoke and froth, and anyone who asks more from them is offending against the rules."

Leonardo now collaborated with Bramante in the castle. At this time Bramante was nearly fifty, and though he had had most success as a painter he had done architectural work that contained the promise of yet greater things. He had many friends at the Milanese court; he was referred to with admiration by all the court poets, who never mentioned Leonardo. Leonardo himself seems to have been attracted to this man with the strong, rugged features, the high forehead, and the shrewd glance that shot keenly from his deep-set eyes. Leonardo sought his advice on architectural questions; he recalled Bramante's help in later years—"in the design of a drawbridge such as Donnino showed me." [7] But while at this period Bramante may have been the instructor in technical matters, the collaboration with Leonardo was to be fruitful for Bramante himself in a way of which he was perhaps unaware. It looks very much as if this matter-of-fact, self-confident man took over Leonardo's tremendous vision of architectural possibilities, as if he gradually approached Leonardo's vast conceptions. Some of the things the two discussed may well have sown seeds in Bramante's mind which after long germination came ultimately to astonishing fruition.

About this time the two had plenty of opportunity for discussion, for they were both occupied with work at Vigevano, the summer seat of the Sforzas. Lodovico had a special affection for Vigevano; it was his birthplace, and a primitive sentimentality in some recess of the soul of this calculating man made the place dear to him. He had the ugly old houses pulled down, wide streets and a spacious arcaded piazza laid out, and the new buildings so richly ornamented with multicoloured terra cotta that the square looked like a vast hall. The piazza was completed in 1494, not too late to be decorated with the arms of the duke of Bari, which may be seen to this day, with his significant device: *Ich hoff,* "I hope."

The old castle was also rebuilt. Isabella d'Aragona had complained bitterly of its discomforts in the first years after her marriage. Bramante built onto a wing of the castle the spacious Palazzo delle Dame, and filled the rooms designed for Beatrice with frescoes. He went to Pavia to copy the famous castle clock. Leonardo meanwhile worked out an estimate of the cost of the decoration of a hall, evidently a hall of great proportions, as he proposed to paint twenty-four scenes from Roman history, together with heads of philosophers and a number of other scenes, between pilasters of blue and gold. His estimated charge was modest enough—fourteen lire for each scene from Roman history and ten lire per philosopher; the paint alone, including blue and gold for the framing, would cost seven lire. This ambitious project does not seem, however, to have been carried out.

Leonardo was also busy with small tasks at Vigevano. He built a wooden pavilion for Beatrice, with a graceful fountain in it. He spent much of the spring of 1494 at Vigevano and on the adjoining property of the Sforzas, which Lodovico was trying to make

into a model farm. He studied the irrigation system which Lodovico had introduced there, and which had been so successful that
the poor soil at once produced a splendid yield. The Sforza canal
from the Ticino was being improved and extended from Sesia to
Vigevano—the extension was called the Mora in Lodovico's honour. Leonardo was full of admiration of the work that had been
done. He mentions the mechanism of the sluices, with 130 sluice
gates, by means of which the marshes were drained. "These sluice
gates," he writes, "were an example to me." He inspected the flour
mills, noted the time taken in milling, obtained information as to
grain and flour prices, and calculated the profit that would result
from expediting the work. "Water is Nature's wagoner," he wrote
in comment on his work at Vigevano.[8] He had long been interested
in the utilization of water power; during this radiant springtime
in Lombardy his interest grew into a passion which was to rule his
life for many years to come. He seemed to have some secret bond
with water; it was the element that most attracted him—constantly
changing and eternally uniform, transparent and yet reflecting
heaven and earth, protean and yet subject to unchangeable laws.
The rush of water ran through his dreams, he felt it break over
him in imagined disasters; if he sought similes or illustrations his
thought turned to sea or river; if he stroked a head of curly hair
he would smile and say it was like a wave.

The sense of the identity of the general laws governing all
phenomena was much in Leonardo's mind at this period. He was
attracted by every riddle of the universe, and the natural accompaniment of his searching spirit was a desire to bring unity into
the general conception of the world resulting from his observations—a conception which they were continually extending, filling
in, and complicating with discoveries of new phenomena and new
laws. He seemed to be afraid lest the very thoroughness of his investigations should dim his vision of the general picture. At this
period of his life he was more than ever tempted to reduce all
phenomena to a common denominator, sometimes at the cost even
of coming into conflict with scientific facts.

One of his most Procrustean generalizations, from which he
never succeeded in liberating himself though it falsified many of
the results of his studies, was the conception taken over from the

ancients of the parallelism of the microcosm and the macrocosm, of man and the universe. "Man is called by the ancient writers a world in miniature"—with these words he opened his treatise on water.[9] Among these ancient writers it was Seneca whom he found dealing at length with this idea. Leonardo's predecessors Brunetto Latini and Ristoro d'Arezzo insisted on this harmony of nature, and the idea dominated the thinking of many of his successors. Man, he explained, is formed like other created things of earth, water, air, and fire; his skeleton corresponds to the rocky frame of the world; man has within him the sea of his blood, which expands the lungs in breathing, and similarly the body of the earth has its ocean, which swells up and sinks back every six hours through the breathing of the world; and just as the blood vessels ramify through the human body, so countless veins of water pass through the body of the earth.[10] The water that comes rushing down in streamlets from the mountain tops "is the blood that keeps the mountain alive," trickling from a wound in the stone. The sap that rises in plants is also like blood that flows through the veins of men. At Vigevano, Leonardo watched the uncovering of the vine shoots that had been buried for the winter (he entered the date in his notebook—March 20, 1494), and saw how the shoots were trimmed, and he remarked that the sap that rises from the roots to the cut twigs is like blood that swells under the skin at some point in a sick body, which has to be cut open so that the blood may run out and be replaced by untainted blood, since Nature, "the helper of all living beings," sees to it that the life-preserving sap shall not fail.[11]

Attractive as the comparison seemed, Leonardo saw its weakness when he considered what sort of circulation it could be that drives the sap through the lifeless body of the earth, and carries the water to the mountain tops. In works of ancient and medieval writers— he seems to have had plenty of time for reading in these years—he found an explanation, but it did not entirely satisfy him. According to Aristotle's *Meteorology* the sea is imprisoned in the bowels of the earth; according to Pliny the Elder it circulates through the water-veins in the body of the earth and rises under the pressure of the earth and the force of the winds to the peaks of the mountains. Brunetto Latini believed that the sea lay higher than the highest mountains. Ristoro d'Arezzo supported this view with the argument that water is lighter than earth and therefore can remain up above. "Water will not move from place to place unless depth attracts it," says Leonardo, and if the sea had been higher than the mountains, as a "mistaken opinion" asserts, it would already have flowed away after so many centuries.[12] "I am not a little astonished at the opinion that has been formed, with the unanimous assent of all who have expressed a judgment, in conflict with the truth," he adds. He sets against the arguments in support of this view one single consideration: if the sea were higher than the earth it would inundate the globe as soon as the dams were removed. "In the universal mechanism of the earth that part is the lowest-lying which is flooded by the sea." [13]

Leonardo laid down another proposition which was by no means generally accepted in his time—that the level of the sea is the same everywhere, that "from its nature, no sheet of water can be lower than the surface of the sea." [14] But, accepting these truths as axiomatic, what was the explanation of the welling up of river sources? One step further, and Leonardo would have been on the verge of the true answer. But his vision was obscured by his favourite conception of the identity of phenomena in organic and inorganic existence. He sought to explain this flouting of the law of gravity by means of another physical law, that of heat, of which his time knew little and he himself was only beginning to learn something. "Where there is life there is warmth, and where there is the warmth of life one finds a movement of saps," he wrote. He proceeded to explain how heat drives aloft the water vapours from streams and marshes, and how in the colder atmosphere these vapours collect in thick clouds and then descend as rain.[15] But he was carried away from this correct hypothesis by his reading. Albertus Magnus held that sun and stars produce damp vapours under the earth, which rise up like an enclosed wind until they find a crevice inside the mountains; through this they pour out like a pot boiling over. Leonardo was caught by this idea, and in his explanation of the welling up of a spring he drew an alembic, a hemispherical vessel heated from above, with water pouring from an opening in its side. This combination of new experimental methods with the legacy of medievalism brought Leonardo to the completion of his similitude between the macrocosm and the micro-cosm: The same cause, natural heat, which drives the blood through the human body to the head, holds the water on the high mountain tops, working against the natural law; and just as blood flows out of a wound in the head, so the sea wells out of crevices in the mountains.[16]

Ristoro d'Arezzo had already opposed the theory of the vapori-zation of the inner sea, and Alberti had described the real origin of springs and their course through clefts in the rocks; but Leo-nardo was obsessed with the parallelism between man and earth, which was to prevent him from assimilating the new knowledge for a considerable time. The clash between the new and the tradi-tional continued to hamper Leonardo in other fields of thought; the struggle was often severe, assuming the character of a contest between feeling and experience, of the vain effort of a man to free himself from favourite notions.

"Motion is the cause of all life"—so Leonardo summed up his studies in mechanics in these years. Until his time the history of mechanics had been mainly that of statics; dynamics was in its in-fancy, and students drew mainly from the meagre heritage of Greek science.

The eventful period in which Leonardo was living seems to have left him plenty of leisure for study and research. As the result of countless observations he had discovered a number of laws, and he invented and applied all sorts of practical tests of them before proceeding to formulate them. What is movement? he asked him-self. "No lifeless object moves of its own accord; its movement is produced by others."[17] What is the force that sets lifeless objects in motion? he asked next. His definition was still influenced by the medieval metaphysics of movement. Force, *sforza* (later he used the word *impeto*), is produced by deficiency or excess; it com-pels all things to change their form and their position; it hastens full of rage to the desired death; it is born of violence and dies of freedom; and the greater it is the more quickly it uses itself up; it grows through efforts and vanishes in repose. The body to which it is applied has lost its freedom.[17] These generalizations date from a period which used the same terms for physics and philosophy, which knew no dividing-line between the exact sciences and mental science, and for which the movements in experimental space were identical with intellectual processes. Leonardo's artistic sensibility found special pleasure in the drafting of these generalizations, and several years passed before he threw overboard this ballast of philosophical definitions and reached the clarity of mathematical precision. But already there stood on the threshold of this metaphysics of the Schoolmen the elements of the dynamics of the future, which he found peacefully intermingled with these generalizations of the past.

He devoted much time to the problem of the centre of gravity, which he felt to be one of the fundamental problems of mechanics. He proceeded from his own personal observations; he noted that a man who is sitting down cannot stand up without the aid of his arms when that part of his body which is in front of his point of support is not heavier than the part behind it.[18] He watched skaters [19]; he noticed how a man who is lifting a weight with one hand stretches out the other and a man shouldering a burden bends his body in order to establish an equilibrium; he saw how a man who is slipping in one direction throws out his arm in the other; and from this mass of observations he came to the conclusion, formulated by no one before him, that it is sufficient for the maintenance of equilibrium if the centre of gravity of a body is not situated outside its base.[20] He recorded a number of paradoxical cases in which equilibrium is maintained—he drew a frame balanced on the point of a nail,[21] a rod supported at its extreme end and kept suspended by a counterweight [22]; it almost seems as if he had thought out these balancing feats simply in order to include them in his stock of conjuring tricks.

He steadily pushed on with his research into the problem of motion through the air. It had been held since the time of Aristotle that it is the air that maintains the motion; only William of Occam had ventured to oppose this generally accepted theory and to maintain that the continuance of motion is explained by inertia, the law of which was first formulated by Descartes. Leonardo took over from Albert of Saxony and Nicholas of Cusa the conception of driving force, with which, for instance, an arrow is filled as it leaves the bow; he sought to explain the continued motion of the arrow by the formation of circles in the air, which push on the arrow as the circles in water drive a boat forward.[23] He observed things for which he could suggest no explanation. Watching the flight of an arrow, he noted three stages in its motion—the first "rage" that drives it into the air, a slowing down, and the reversal of direction midway; and in making a faithful drawing of the trajectory he does not give it the form of a parabola, with identical upward and downward paths, but gives the falling curve much more steepness, as actually happens through the resistance of the air.[24]

Leonardo drew most of the suggestions for his mechanical studies from the work of a thirteenth-century philosopher, Jordanus Nemorarius, a pioneer of modern mathematical science. He took from this work such first principles as that "Every weight desires to drop to the centre [of the earth] by the shortest path," [25] and also the conception, new at that time, of work done, through which Jordanus explained the law of equilibrium of the lever. Another thirteenth-century work, also ascribed to Jordanus, the *Tractatus de Ponderibus*, is frequently mentioned by Leonardo; it led him to some of his most interesting conclusions. He worked out the law of movement on an inclined plane,[26] which was first made generally known by Simon Stevinus of Bruges some eighty years later. A remark on the acceleration of freely falling bodies led Leonardo to drop two balls simultaneously and then one after the other, and by this experiment he tried to obtain an exact formula for the relation of the increase in speed to the space traversed. He accompanied his text with a diagram showing horizontally the figures for the intervals of time and vertically the distances—probably the first graph known to the history of science.[27] He came near to establishing that the distance fallen varies with the square of the time, but did not succeed in finding a clear formula. He took account in his calculations of the factor of the resistance of the air,[28] and of the retardation of movement in a thicker medium, such as water—"You can demonstrate it by swinging a sword," he adds. He realizes, entirely in the spirit of modern research, the value of repeated tests. "I remind you that you must confirm your propositions by examples and not by propositions, which would be too simple; you will speak thus from experiment"—so he apostrophized himself a little later.[29] At another place he writes: "Before making a general rule out of this case, test it two or three times and see whether the experiments produce the same results." [30]

Thus his method of work complied with the requirements of experimental science, but as yet he had found no new language for the new conceptions. He had a dim sense of the principle of the conservation of energy; what he wrote was: "The weight is conquered by the force and the force by the weight; the more the weight falls, the more it increases; the more the force falls, the more it abates." [31] His practical experiments preceded his theoretical statements, and thus he grasped at once a corollary which Galileo was the first to formulate, that what is gained in power by the use of a machine is lost in time, and vice versa. His observations, probably made at the mills in Vigevano, led him to the conclusion that if a wheel is moved at a given moment by a definite quantity of water, and this quantity cannot be increased, "the same wheel can set a number of machines in motion, but requires correspondingly more time—and these machines will not do more work in the longer period than the first machine in one hour." [32] And when observing his beloved cogwheels in motion he notes: "The more the force is transferred from wheel to wheel, from lever to lever, from ratchet to ratchet, the more powerful it grows and the slower." [33] The conception of effective work was already dawning on Leonardo, and might have formed the conclusion of his treatise on motion if he had completed it. He mentions the chapters of this treatise several times, and it must have become known in part, since several of its suggestions are to be found in the works of his successors.

At this time he was equally interested in the science of hydraulics, which in his work is almost inextricably mixed up with dynamics. He notes, for instance, that when the piston of a water pump is pressed in a finger's breadth the water spurts out two ells' distance, and he finds the same kind of relationship, in velocity of rotation, between the circumference of a wheel and of its axis and that of the cogwheel which drives it. This comparison of relative transmission between water pump and gearing contained already the logic of Pascal's law, the fundamental law of hydraulics.[34] Leonardo tried also to discover how the pressure on the surface of a liquid is distributed,[35] and while his calculations are tentative and inexact, he shows a clear relationship between the pressure on a given surface and the height of the jet of water thrown up: "If eleven ells of stones are pressing on an ell of water, the jet of water will rise eleven times as high as when the pressure is only one ell." [36] The lifting power of water is subject to the same law as the raising of weights by a winch—"It is impossible for a falling weight to raise a weight equal to itself in no matter how long a time, even to the same height as that from which it descended. So be silent, you who propose to have a heavier quantity of water than the weight with which you press it," he writes, evidently to some engineer engaged on the waterworks. Liquids are subject to the laws governing heavy solids; in both cases the same relationship exists between force and distance and also between force and time. All movements in nature add up to the same sum: if a man jumps step by step down a staircase, the aggregate impact and weight of the jumps are the same as if he made one jump from top to bottom.

Leonardo next proposed to write a treatise on the motion and measurement of water—*Del moto e misura dell' acqua;* it was planned in fifteen books and subsequently extended to thirty-five. He had completed a number of sketches for his treatise; Lomazzo saw no fewer than thirty splendid drawings of mills. He watched the formation of waves in water, intending to devote one book specially to that subject. He threw two stones into standing water at a definite interval, and watched the circles ripple out, widen, intersect one another, and expand further round the centre formed by their particular stone.[37] The same movement takes place in the air: "As the stone thrown into water forms various circles, so a sound spreads in circles in the air." [38] These circles penetrate one another and maintain their own centre.[39] Leonardo was still busy with hydraulics when he began to think of investigating this similarity of wave motion in water and air. He writes that it is possible to determine the distance of a storm from the reverberation of the thunder; he made an apparatus with complicated gearing for this purpose,[40] and since "the wind in its motion entirely resembles that of water," [41] he designed a wind gauge, "for better recognition of the winds." [42] He invented a complicated apparatus, a graduated quadrant fixed on a board at the end of which there hung an iron flap, working as a pendulum and showing the force of the wind in arc measurement; a similar apparatus was to become known in England toward the end of the seventeenth century.

The effect of the magnet, says Leonardo, also spreads in wave-lines like the movements that go through water and air,[43] and he made for some unknown purpose a board with an arc and a compass needle, the first magnetic needle on a horizontal axis, an invention which was first brought into use half a century later.[44]

But his attention continued to centre mainly on the movement of water. He invented an instrument with which to discover whether the current in a river is faster at a depth or on the surface,[45] in the centre or at the sides [46]; and after observing the pressure exerted on the bank by the current he came to the changes in the river's course, a subject which was to form a particularly important chapter of his book.[47]

3

But he seems to have got no further with his studies at this time. Contemporary events and the troubles of everyday life began to demand his attention amid his painfully acquired leisure for study. Those who in these days had buried themselves in their work, and had had little contact with the outer world, found a completely changed Italy only a few months after the invasion of Charles VIII. Charles's triumph had enabled Lodovico Sforza to establish himself in power; but the very ease with which that triumph had been achieved had given Lodovico food for thought. The king of France, who had so successfully enforced the claims of the house of Anjou to the throne of Naples, might one day be equally successful in pressing the claims of the house of Orleans to the duchy of Milan. These claims were derived from the marriage of Louis of Orleans, brother of Charles VI, with Valentina, the legitimate heiress of the Visconti; and while that marriage had taken place a full hundred years earlier, Lodovico, the uneasy usurper, was only too well aware of the slenderness of his own pretensions. He felt strong enough now to break the tool he had used before it could turn against him, and decided to send home the king of France whom he had himself summoned across the Alps.

Lodovico accordingly collected together the dissatisfied rulers, and Charles VIII had not yet ascended the throne of Naples when he found that a league had been formed against France, headed by the Pope, Venice, the king of Spain, the German emperor, and the duke of Milan. Charles, with the heart of a knight errant and the brain of a simple fool, found it utterly incomprehensible that such treachery should be possible. In this critical situation, with his fate already sealed, his only reaction was a childish distress at the secret defection of his allies. "What a shame," he exclaimed to the envoy Domenico Trevisano, "when I always told you everything!"

He hastily set out on the retreat to France, and, being not only an innocent but a man with plenty of courage, he staked his own life in the battle of Fornovo, which the allied troops forced on the French army. He fought with the heedlessness of a sleepwalker, and with a sleepwalker's sureness he escaped from imminent death, and cut his way through to Asti, there to negotiate a precarious peace. A few months after the ceremonial crowning in Naples he had lost his Neapolitan kingdom; his tremendous dream had faded away. He returned to France as unconscious of the causes of his failure as he had been of those of his success.

Now Lodovico Sforza had indeed reached the pinnacle of his power—as conqueror of the forces he had himself conjured up. About this time he set in circulation in Italy an allegorical representation of himself as a Moor with a hand broom. Counting on his contemporaries' short memory, he had his praises sung as liberator of the country from the foreign barbarians.

But he had to pay out immense sums to consolidate this victory and his new accession of power. In addition to the huge dowry which he had given his niece, the frivolous Bianca Maria, he paid one hundred and twenty thousand ducats for his investiture by Maximilian, who in the meantime had become emperor; the ceremony took place amid great magnificence in Milan in 1495. In order to induce Charles VIII to undertake his Italian expedition, he had placed two hundred thousand ducats at his disposal, and he had now to spend enormous sums for his own armed forces. He

had gold medals melted down, and sent jewels to Venice as security for a loan of fifty thousand ducats, and he decreed new taxes
and levies until the people began to protest aloud and to hate their
new ruler. In order to defend himself against Louis of Orleans,
who had taken possession of Novara, he had to hire foreign troops;
and when his father-in-law, the duke of Ferrara, began to cast
heavy cannon Lodovico provided him with the metal required.
The cannon-founder of Este, Giannino Alberghetti, with whom
Leonardo had technical consultations at one time, sent for one
hundred and fifty thousand pounds of bronze to be dispatched by
water to Ferrara. This was the metal which was to have been used
in casting the colossal statue. Leonardo, to his bitter disappointment, saw the work of years brought to naught. He bore the hard
blow with his characteristic fatalism. "Of the horse," he wrote
later to Lodovico, "I say nothing, for I know what the times are
like."

Not only did Leonardo see his proudest hopes destroyed, but all
payments to him were stopped by Gualtieri, Lodovico's treasurer;
and he was faced once more with a struggle for bare existence.
And not only his own existence: he had to maintain his workmen,
his household, and the imp Giacomo—whom he renamed Salai,
"the little devil." "For thirty-six months I have fed six mouths,
and all I have got for it is fifty ducats"—so he summed up the results of three years' hard struggle.

He searched around for new commissions, and, hearing that the
cathedral authorities at Piacenza were looking for a sculptor for
the doors of the cathedral, he transmitted to a friend, probably a
man of influence, the draft of a letter in which, in his characteristically circumstantial way, he enlarged on the importance of a
work of this sort, which must make a special impression on travellers from foreign countries, and urged that such a commission
should not be placed in unworthy hands. He had heard, he wrote,
that a potter, a maker of cuirasses, a bell-founder, a bell-ringer,
and even a bombardier were offering to do the work; one of them,
a coarse, vulgar fellow, making use of his close relations with
the ducal building commissioner, had had the effrontery to obtain
a letter of recommendation from Lodovico himself. The draft concluded with a naïve indication that only one man was equal to

such work, "Leonardo the Florentine, who is making the equestrian statue in bronze of Duke Francesco, and who has no need
to bring himself into notice because he has work for all his lifetime, and I doubt whether he will ever complete the work, so
enormous is it." [48] It is a touching and pathetic letter in its mixture
of transparent cunning and proud confidence, and throws a light
on the difficulties with which Leonardo was wrestling at this time;
in any case it was a letter which was to fail of its purpose.

Other efforts to find important commissions also came to nothing.
Some years later Leonardo tried to secure the order for an altarpiece for the church of the Franciscans at Brescia. He actually
completed a plan for the saints' figures,[49] but this work also was
given to another artist.

Although Lodovico did not pay his artists, he required that they
should continue to work for him. In spite of the slump in the
ducal resources, he had alterations made in the castle and a number of small rooms, *camerini,* decorated for Beatrice. Leonardo
began the work, but it was not easy to paint cheerful decorative
subjects amid anxiety over his daily bread. He must have pressed
urgently for payment and have found himself balked by the arrogant incomprehension of prosperous ducal officials, who could
not imagine that a man who still dressed well and had lost nothing
of his confidence of manner was at a loss to know where to find
the morrow's livelihood.

"Perhaps Your Excellency has given no order to Messer Gualtieri in the belief that I had money," Leonardo discreetly inquired
of Lodovico. But discreet inquiries produced little, and no one
knew better than Lodovico how to turn a deaf ear. At last Leonardo lost patience and abandoned his work in the castle. The
officials were shocked at this outbreak in a man who had controlled
himself so long. "The painter who has painted our *camerini* made
something of a scene today, and left on account of it," wrote the
ducal secretary to Lodovico on June 8, 1496. There is no mention
of Leonardo's name in the letter, but it seems likely that the
scandal had reference to no less a personage, since Pietro Perugino,
who was now much in demand, was decided upon as the successor.

Detractors at court did their best to widen the breach between
Lodovico and his court painter by means of gossip and scandal-

mongering. Embittered already by his struggle for existence, Leonardo saw himself misrepresented by jealousy and ill-will, and the suspicion always latent in his mind broke out in a paroxysm of hatred against an unnamed enemy. Leonardo has left little record of attachment to any human being, but now, as at various points in his life, he wrote long letters telling the tale of all the mortifications he had suffered, letters full of a desperate and often unreasonable attack on human meannesses. Hatred alone seemed to give eloquence to him, silent and uncommunicative as he habitually was. "I know a man," he wrote, "who, having promised himself things from me which were far from being owed to him, and being disappointed in his presumptuous desires, has tried to deprive me of all my friends; and as he has found them wise and not pliable to his will, he has threatened me, saying that he has found reports that will deprive me of my benefactors. Hence I have informed Your Lordship of this . . . to the end that if he tries to make Your Lordship the instrument of his wicked and malevolent nature, he may be disappointed of his desire." [50]

This personal enemy must have been the same of whom Leonardo had written earlier: "All the evils that there are or have been, if he could set them to work, would not satisfy the lust of his evil soul. No matter how long I took, I could not describe this man's nature." [51] His grave financial anxieties, a world of enemies, and his vain efforts, famous though he was, to find commissions which his lesser colleagues obtained with ease, brought him to the desperate idea of abandoning art—a torn fragment of a letter contains the words *"la mia arte la quale voglio mutare"*—and entering the industrial field, where he hoped to make money out of his inventions. "Tomorrow morning, January 2, 1496, I will have the strap made, and the test," he notes, with the exact date, like a man planting a milestone by the wayside. He had invented a needle-sharpening machine, and had made a number of particularly careful designs for it; he calculated that it would bring him in a large sum. "A hundred times an hour with 400 needles each time makes 40,000 an hour, and in twelve hours 480,000. But let us say 4000 thousands, which at five soldi per 1000 gives 20,000 soldi, that is in all 1000 lire every working day, and with twenty days worked in the month it is 240,000 lire or 60,000 ducats a year." [52]

There is no record of this optimistically calculated result's being actually attained. But at this time and in the years that followed Leonardo continued to make splendid drawings, with carefully noted technical details, which look like plans for machine-constructors. He was well aware that the growth of the two great Milanese industries, metal and textile, was hampered by the slowness of manual operation, and he tried to mechanize production by means of a whole series of inventions. He invented a spinning-machine greatly superior in technical respects to Jurgen's spinning-wheel of 1530; and he well realized the novelty of his invention and the revolutionary effect it would be bound to have on the whole manufacture of textiles; in order to keep it secret he placed the machine in a box which prevented the spinning operative from seeing the works. The filament passed from the operative's hand to a beam visible from outside; the thread was twisted on a fork-shaped flier leg and then at once wound into a spool at the other end. The varying rates of turning of the two parts of the machine were achieved by Leonardo by means of two band pulleys of different diameter, which were set in motion by a crank handle. A notable element of his machine was the filament guide, which was first brought into use in England at the very end of the eighteenth century. In order to assure uniform distribution of the filaments, Leonardo built into his machine a small set of gearing which brought into operation a forked lever such as is used for spooling to this day in sewing-machines.[53]

Leonardo made dozens of designs of looms of various sorts, showing improvements in the parts and substituting machine for hand operation. The cost of cloth manufacture is greatly increased if the cloth has to be warped by hand, and Leonardo accordingly invented a cloth-warping machine in which four warping-banks were driven mechanically. The cloth was wound on rollers and drawn at full width over these banks, tightly stretched; the two cutters, worked by wires which were jerked tight by gearing, ran quickly over the rough surface of the cloth and shaved off every unevenness, while the warping-banks were slid backwards by means of tackle, to maintain even unrolling of the great cloth shaft.[54]

There is no report in Leonardo's papers or in any known contemporary documents of this invention being brought into use. It is the same invention which in England in the middle of the eighteenth century produced the rising against the machines, the revolt of dismissed and starving workers who with their own hands broke up the mechanical warping-banks and set them on fire—those monsters that were robbing them of their daily bread.

At a later date Leonardo invented a ropemaking machine, with spindles, arranged in a semicircle, which spun and twisted together fifteen thin strands. Another ropemaker's wheel with three spindles was notable especially for the fact that it contained the first belt-tightening device on record in the history of machine construction.[55]

Most of the processes in the iron and steel industry were just as slow and laborious as the manual operations of the textile industry. At the time when Leonardo was busy with his inventions in the field of military technique, he had already begun to design machines for improving these processes; his ideas had come as fast as the shavings from a plane. Now he took them up again, filled in their details, and added remarks which evidenced a wealth of practical experience. He designed rolling-mills, for the first time in the history of engineering, and long before the first ones were actually constructed; and he steadily improved his designs and increased the calculated output. One of his finest machine drawings is the design of a rolling-mill, driven by a turbine wheel, for rolling staves for guns.[56] Another design on the same sheet shows a draw-bench for reducing iron bars, which are drawn out to a length of twenty ells. This too is driven by a turbine wheel. Leonardo was now concerned mainly with the economic aspect, and adds the remark: "This machine must be driven by water, for if it were worked by hand power it would move so slowly that the labour would yield little result." He also converted his rolling-mills for general industrial use; in a volume dating from about 1497 he sketched a machine "for making thin and uniform tin sheets." [57]

Among Leonardo's earliest designs were grinding-machines, in which, as in the rolling-mill designs, he gradually increased the calculated output and aimed at a wide range of service. His designs grew more and more complicated, further stages of manufacture were mechanized, and he proceeded from simple grinding-machines to whole plants. There is, for instance, an apparatus for hollowing out cylinders; it is worked by a great cogwheel, and the upward and downward motion of the grinding-tool is achieved by a combination of a wheel of which half is cogged, a cogged nut, and springs.[58] It might well have been imagined that his first designs, many of which date from his early Florentine period, were separated from his latest plants not by years or decades but by centuries, so great is the technical progress shown by the latter.

He was particularly interested at all times in the transmission of motion. Again and again he returned to the problem of transmission by the most direct method and with the minimum expenditure of power. When he went on from theoretical to practical work he found a gap between his calculations and the actual work done. He began to investigate this loss of energy, and established the law of friction, which was still unknown in his day. He also observed that one sort of friction occurs in sliding motion and another in rolling; the latter he described in his metaphorical style by saying that the friction, "proceeding by infinitely small steps, consists of bumps rather than rubs." [59] He concludes from his experiments that on a smooth horizontal surface the resistance due to friction is equivalent for all bodies to a quarter of their weight; even this indiscriminate generalization was a first step on virgin soil. Now that he saw his machines in operation and not merely on paper—and his observations of this period all have the character of results of practical testing—he also observed that putting oil or grease on the machine parts reduced the frictional resistance, and so, for instance, he provided his wooden grinding-tool for hollowing out cylinders with small runlets through which oil flowed.

During this period of practical work, with his keen interest in gearing in no way diminished, he developed a new enthusiasm—for roller bearings. They drew from him an almost lyrical outburst: "This device gives circular motion a duration that seems marvellous and miraculous; a number of further turns are made after the motor has been shut off." [60] And after introducing roller bearings into a machine he writes: "These are marvels of the mechanical art!" [61] But, great as was his enthusiasm for research, and exhilarating as was the joy of invention, the material results obtained do not seem to have come up to his great expectations.

4

After the "scandal" Leonardo had aroused in the castle, Lodovico continued to try to get hold of Perugino. He promised him mountains of gold; but the shrewd Umbrian must have had a suspicion of the state of art at Milan, and was not to be tempted away from his remunerative work by the flatteries and urgencies of the Milanese ambassador. Leonardo, on the other hand, had grown used to Milan, or did not care to face the risk of trying his fortune elsewhere. In contrast with his intellectual adventurousness, he suffered from a certain inertia in practical matters, a difficulty of making up his mind, and once he had settled in a place he would never leave it except under some compelling circumstance or under the influence of a will stronger than his own. And so he resolved, with a heavy heart, to write a letter to Lodovico to bridge over their difference.

The letter gave him the utmost trouble. "It vexes me greatly," *assai mi rincresca,* he began three times, before he was able to find the rest of his opening sentence: "that having to earn my living has forced me to interrupt the work which Your Lordship entrusted to me." And as at this time his expectations had not all come to grief, he continued: "But I hope in a short time to have earned so much that I may carry it out with a mind at rest, to the satisfaction of Your Excellency." He proceeded then to make direct mention of the payments due to him for three years' work, and of his financial difficulties.[62]

But such reminders seem to have achieved nothing, and Leonardo drafted yet another letter to the duke. This draft [63] has been torn in half and only part of each sentence remains, but there is enough to tell eloquently of his despair:

"You are giving me no further commissions . . .

"I know, Sir, that at present your thoughts are turned in other directions . . .

"I should like to recall to Your Magnificence my poor services . . .

"And that my silence gave occasion for your dissatisfaction . . .

" . . . my life in your service, I hold myself in readiness to obey you . . . "

And then comes a bitter sentence in which he asks to be given at least some article of clothing, and refers to all the disappointments he has suffered and all the money that is owed to him. He threatens to change his art, and in the same breath reminds Lodovico that he can create "works of fame," "to show those who come after us that I . . . "

Either this submissive letter, or the difficulty of finding a successor to Leonardo, restored harmony between Lodovico and his court painter—the harmony that produced the "work of fame" which was to make Leonardo's name immortal.

No document exists to show when Leonardo received the commission to paint his *Last Supper*. The church of Santa Maria delle Grazie, the nearest to the castle among the churches of Milan, had always enjoyed Lodovico's special favour. It was there that he approached his personal God; there he found an island of peace amid his own worldly urgencies and preoccupations. He was on particularly friendly terms with the prior of the Dominican monastery attached to the church, and frequently after attending mass he would walk up and down the quiet monastery garden, which was like a bright green lake surrounded by arcades of golden yellow stone. There he would read his letters, or receive envoys with particularly important news; and often he would sit there for a long time meditating and drinking refreshment from the peace and seclusion of the place.

In joy and sorrow his thoughts were with this church and its monastery. The old church seemed to him too "plain"—*troppo positiva*—and in 1492 he had had the great nave and choir pulled down and had commissioned Bramante to rebuild the church, crowning it with a huge dome. He wanted also to confer a special pleasure on the silent monks in white garb whose noiseless movements had left him undisturbed in his meditation, and he had the refectory rebuilt, probably also by Bramante. It was a simple room of harmonious proportions. On its back wall he had a *Crucifixion* painted by a Lombard, Montorfano, a work with many figures, full of life; it was completed about 1495. The commission for the fresco for the front wall, on which all the light fell from the high windows, was given to Leonardo after his reconciliation with the duke. There was no hesitation about the choice of theme, for what subject could be more appropriate in a refectory than the *Cenacolo,* that Last Supper held in the "large upper room furnished and prepared"? It was also a favourite theme in Leonardo's native city; and it offered few difficulties, thanks to the existence already of its traditional elements. All that was needed was to range the figures of the apostles alongside one another, at a long table against a wall, in an architecturally harmonious setting. Each of the apostles was already a fixed Florentine tradition. The problem offered no difficulty—until the effort was made, as it was by Leonardo, to achieve both individual characterization and formal synthesis, to weld the multiplicity of reactions into a convincing unity.

Normally Leonardo would visualize a picture more quickly than words can be formed by a pen; but he had here a task of supreme difficulty. He began by setting down his ideas as they occurred to him and making a description of the picture:

"One who was drinking and has set down his glass and turned his head toward the speaker. Another, twisting the fingers of his two hands and with brows knitted, turns to his neighbour; this neighbour spreads his hands and shows their palms, raises his shoulders to his ears, and opens his mouth in amazement. Another whispers into his neighbour's ear; the listener turns towards him to lend an ear, holding a knife in one hand and in the other the bread half cut through; another, who has turned, holding a knife in his hand, upsets with his hand a glass on the table. Another rests his hands on the table and watches; another blows out his cheeks; another bends forward to see the speaker, shading his eyes with his hand; another draws back behind the one who leans forward and sees the speaker between the wall and the man who is leaning." [64]

This first idea for the painting gives a significant picture of Leonardo's brain at work. It records the reactions that primarily interested him, the manifold expressions of one and the same feeling in various types of men. Their formal arrangement, their grouping round a central point, interested him only in the second place; he left also until later the task of selection from among the subjects here picturesquely described, the sifting out and rejection of non-essentials and of the elements which formed no part of the deep emotion and agitation of the scene.

But the glimpses which, in this fragment and in other notes, Leonardo gives of the progress of his work on his *Last Supper* are not the only ones we have. He was no longer an unknown painter going his own way unnoticed; pupils and the curious now watched his preparations; the work on which he was engaged was too much in the centre of public interest for him to be able, as in the past, to bring it, slowly and hesitatingly, almost to completion before others saw it. Now there were observers watching over his shoulder as he drew or painted; men told one another about his methods of work; eyewitnesses wrote down what was said; fathers told their sons; suddenly the workings of Leonardo's brain had become visible to all. The creation of his masterpiece may thus be followed almost step by step.

It began with the search for human types, for figures that could be fit exponents of a particular emotional stress. "Leonardo," wrote Giovanni Battista Giraldi, "as soon as he prepared to paint any figure, considered first its quality and nature, whether it should be noble or plebeian, gay or severe, troubled or cheerful, good or malignant; and when he had grasped its nature he set out for places where he knew that people of that sort gathered together, and diligently observed their faces, their manners, their habits, their movements; and as soon as he had found anything that seemed suited to his purpose he noted it with his pencil in the little book which he carried at all times in his girdle. My father, who took great interest in these things, told me thousands of times that Leonardo employed this method in particular for his famous picture in Milan."

But Leonardo did not content himself with casual sketches; he brought models into his studio. Fresco painting, with its large surfaces requiring rapid fixing, was a method to which his painstaking, subtilizing work was ill-adapted, and he therefore carried his preliminaries as far as possible, making careful studies not only for the heads but for hands, for the feet visible beneath the table, and for sleeves and whole garments.

He began about this time to use a red chalk, with which he achieved effects of great delicacy. Instead of the jerky stroke of the pen he made use of the soft flow of the chalk, with lightly shaded surfaces, and many of his most beautiful studies belong to this period. There is the wonderful head of the apostle Philip (at Windsor), the head of a very young man, slightly bent, with long, lustrous eyes, soft, compassionate lips, and waving locks that fall gently beside the round cheeks—a head in which he captured the ideal type of his mature period, this Milanese period of his life. He was no longer painting Florentine youths with their short, straight noses and round eyes and a steep curve of the lips like a bow that is tightly drawn; the faces had become gentler, with round chin and a broad white pillar of neck. Leonardo also drew the type of ripe manhood, with square, massive brow, long and slightly bent nose, protruding underlip, prominent chin, and bull neck, as in the Windsor study for the apostle Bartholomew; and long-headed old men with drooping nose, toothless mouth, and upward-bent chin. These last he drew with no beard, so as to show their characteristics more clearly, only adding the beard, short and stubbly or round and jutting forward, when completing the figure.

He worked with steady energy and concentration; the great task monopolized his thoughts, and not only when he was sketching or painting; before he slept at night he thought long over what he had done during the day, his open eyes staring into the deepening gloom around him. He occupied a small room, saying that large ones interfere with concentration. Later he strongly recommended this habit of meditation in the dark, "for I have found in my own experience that it is of no small benefit, when you lie in bed in the dark, to recall in imagination, one after the other, the outlines of the forms you have been studying." [65]

His thoughts would be running on the picture again early in the morning; in his waking reveries the figures he intended to conjure up by the wall would file past; he dreamed thus, well into the morning, in those valuable early hours "when the mind is clear and rested and the body ready to take on fresh labours." Sometimes he was impelled to jump out of bed in the very early hours,

SANTA MARIA DELLE GRAZIE, MILAN

The Last Supper

when the sun had scarcely risen, and his room still had the uncertain radiance which he specially loved—the soft, transient radiance met with only at dawn or dusk—and he would plunge into his work in order to capture some vision that had passed before him in his dreams. The world around would vanish, as though he were stranded alone on his scaffolding as on a desert island; the hours would pass until one of his pupils would timidly remind him that it was time to eat; Leonardo would wave him impatiently aside. The refectory would be saturated with golden light, and the fresh colours would have the shimmer of enamel. Then the light would slowly grow pale, and only as the grey shadows spread from the corners and the contours faded would Leonardo lay down his brush, like one who suddenly awakes, and, with thoughts still far away, go slowly home.

After an orgy of work of this sort he would sometimes remain away for days; when he returned to the refectory it might be only to look at his work with folded arms, standing there sometimes for hours, silent and motionless; only his bright eyes would be at work, as if lit by cold flames. When he went away, with brows wrinkled almost as if in pain, sunk in himself and full of thought as if after a long conversation with the figures of his creation, it would often be without having once reached for his brush.

Sometimes, after he had been away for a period, calculating in his studio in the Corte Vecchia, or working on designs for the reconstruction of the castle or on studies of proportions in the human frame, he would suddenly jump up and rush out into the street, without noticing that the hot summer sun stood high in the heavens and the air was vibrating with the heat; he would hurry with unseeing eyes to the monastery, jump onto the scaffolding, seize the brush, make a few strokes, here more light, there a slight shading—and return at once, with the quiet, satisfied smile of a man who has done his day's labour.

Often some prelate of high rank would come to the monastery of Santa Maria delle Grazie, hoping to see Leonardo at his work; often Lodovico would come to the refectory after mass; idle courtiers would come in because it was the thing to do—they must keep abreast of the progress of the famous work. Leonardo's pupils would stand round him, curious visitors would stare at him.

Among the watchers was the prior's young nephew, Matteo Bandello, who wanted to be a poet and became a gifted writer of romances. He had bright eyes that took keen note of the world, and a gift of expression and of vivid description of what he saw. Now he watched Leonardo at work and listened to his sayings, and he transmitted the story to posterity.

Silent as Leonardo frequently was, he could be sociable and talkative. He would then gladly listen to the criticisms of those around him. "For," he says, "a painter should never refuse to hear the opinions of other people; we all know that even a man who is no painter is familiar with the appearance of other men. . . . We see that men are able to judge of the works of Nature; we should be all the more ready to admit that they may be able to judge of our mistakes. . . . Listen, then, with patience to the opinion of other people, reflect well on it, and consider carefully whether the adverse critic is right in criticizing you. If you find that he is right, make good the error; if you do not find so, then act as if you had heard nothing." [66] So he listened patiently to what intelligent observers had to say, and ignored the rest.

In spite, however, of his own precepts, he was too dogmatic himself to suffer fools for long. One day the old cardinal of Gurk came to the monastery. He was a Frenchman by birth, named Raymond Perauld, but held the rich bishopric of Gurk, in Carinthia, and was a favourite of Emperor Maximilian. The cardinal had heard of the great work, and wanted to watch the artist as he painted. The *maestro* stepped down from his scaffolding to greet the visitor. His Eminence was very gracious and condescending; he was a little puzzled at the atmosphere of veneration with which Leonardo was surrounded. With princely affability he asked what was being paid for the job. Leonardo was not inclined to tolerate condescension and still less the bumptiousness of priests, even when they had been stuck into cardinal's robes. What did a man of this sort know of creative effort; what did he understand of the greatness here revealed before his eyes? Leonardo knew that he could impress the cardinal (who was himself continually in want of money) only with some story of material prosperity as evidence of his ability. He had only recently been reduced to writing begging letters, but he now mentioned indifferently that he was receiving a pension

Study for the head of Philip

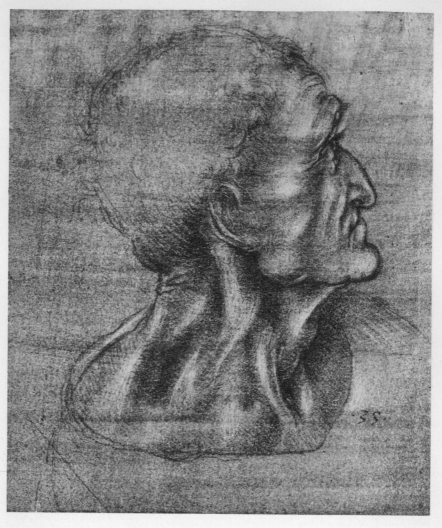

PHOTO MANSELL   Study for the head of Judas   WINDSOR COLLECTION

of two thousand ducats a year, apart from the presents the duke showered on him every day. The cardinal was greatly impressed and full of astonishment. On his departure Leonardo returned to his platform, remarking, as he went on with his painting, that great artists were always honoured even among barbarians. (So runs an old Florentine legend which Vasari quotes; no doubt there is not a word of truth in it.) Leonardo proceeded to tell how Filippo Lippi was in a boat one day with friends in the Marches of Ancona when they were attacked by Moorish corsairs and carried off to the country of the barbarians. There they were sent to the galleys and put in chains. Their sufferings would have been endless if Filippo had not picked up a piece of coal one day and drawn on a white wall a portrait of the slavemaster. This the barbarians regarded as a miracle, and they freed him at once from his chains.

The prior of the monastery, Vincenzo Bandello, complained to the duke that, while Leonardo's work was far advanced, it still lacked the two principal figures, Judas and Christ. Lodovico remonstrated with his painter, but Leonardo had a ready reply.

"What do the monks know of an artist's work? Can they paint?" he asked. "It is quite true that I have not been to the monastery for a long time," he continued. "Nevertheless, not a day passes but I devote at least two hours to the work."

"How can that be, if you do not go there?" asked Lodovico.

"Your Excellency is aware that Judas is missing. I cannot find features fit for so abandoned a character. I have been going every day, morning and evening, for more than a year to the criminal quarter, in which the scum of humanity live; but I have not yet found what I want. If I continue to search in vain I shall have to use the prior's head. It would serve well for the purpose. I have only hesitated to do this out of consideration for his feelings."

Lodovico's laugh boomed out at this answer. It was too good not to pass on, and the legend spread in after days that the prior had unwittingly served as model for Judas. In the end Leonardo found his model, a sharp-featured face which he sketched, without its beard, in profile (Windsor collection). He still lacked the head of Christ, and just as he had searched in the Barghetto, the criminal quarter of Milan, for the features of Judas, he now sought the radiant features of Christ among the aristocratic youths of the Milanese court. There is an old tradition that the search was vain, and that Leonardo expressed his despair to his fellow-artist Bernardino Zenale; Zenale replied that Leonardo had made the mistake of giving the apostles Philip and James the elder a divine beauty which could never be excelled; now there was nothing he could do but leave Christ's features unfinished—advice which Leonardo followed, giving only an indication of the figure of Christ, in evidence of human impotence in face of the superhuman.

But it was not in Leonardo's nature to rest content with half-solutions or to evade any difficulty, however great. The longer he searched for his figure of Christ, the more determined he grew to discover this consummation of divine humanity. And suddenly he exulted in a first success; he recorded in his notebook that he had found hands that he could use for his figure of Christ—those of Alessandro, of the Parma family of the Carissimi. The same notebook contains also the unintelligible sentence: "Christ, the young count —that of Cardinal del Mortaro." (*Christo giovan Conte, quello del Cardinal del Mortaro.*) [67] At last he had his model for the face of Christ.

Now the painting proceeded rapidly to its completion. When the scaffolding was taken away the painted wall seemed to reveal a miracle. Yet the first impression conveyed by Leonardo's pictured opening in the wall was of an extension of the actual world in which the Dominicans were living. The table stretching right across the picture was the same table at which the monks ate, and its cover, embroidered in blue, was copied from one in their linen chest and still showed the stiff folds of clean linen just spread. The room with its foreshortening in perspective also continued the plain architecture of the refectory. Through the three windows the eye could wander over wide skies and a familiar undulating landscape, with a bright stream zigzagging, and peaceful hills rising in a blue distance.

But the central window held the observer's attention. Here the stupendous entered. In front of the light streaming in through this window Leonardo had set the figure of Christ, as though framed in radiance. It was a device showing extraordinary technical skill, aimed at isolating this figure from the rest, at providing a clear

Christ

space for it amid the confusion of heads and arms, and immersing it in an aureole of light, as though it were no longer of this world.

The face of Christ is almost expressionless; the head is bent very slightly to one side; the heavy eyelids are half closed over the eyes, whose gaze has wandered far away and meets no human glance. The lips are firmly closed, as though the bitter truth he had just spoken, "One of you shall betray me," still weighed down the corners of his mouth. The two arms sink heavily to the table; the right hand is raised at the wrist, its inner surface involuntarily spread out in protection and benediction; the left hand, turned outward, has fallen to the table in a movement of sacrificial surrender: it is the hand of a man who accepts his terrible fate, a hand which says more eloquently than any words that that fate is now irrevocable.

But the words just spoken still work upon the emotions of all present, and the disciples see nothing of the silent acceptance in Christ's left hand. His neighbour on the left, James the elder, "opening his mouth in amazement," seems to be repeating Christ's words as men do who have not fully understood, and his broad, manly breast and his outstretched arms are like an involuntary refusal to understand and a shield offered to the Master.

The apostle Thomas, with his shrewd face, his pointed nose, and his thoughtful look, is raising his index finger; he is the eternal doubter, not to be put off with fair words. But another, who does not think but feels, the apostle Philip, has jumped up and is bending forward, his arms crossed over his breast, his eyes swimming with tears; his sorrowful mouth, and those hands pressed convulsively to his breast, protest his innocence. This group of disciples surges like a wave up against Christ's immobility.

On the other side the wave subsides in a dexterous interweaving of three figures. Bent as though mown down by grief is the head of the disciple whom Christ most loved. His hands are clasped together as though he had already lost everything; he no longer asks, no longer protests, he is carried away by a flood of helpless sorrow. Close to the passive sufferer is the man of action—Peter's strong, determined brow almost touches the lifeless martyr's face of John. His left hand is laid heavily in his agitation on John's shoulder, as though to shake and wake him out of his grief; and his right hand has involuntarily seized a knife as he suddenly springs up.

The painters of the *quattrocento* isolated Judas, like a man stricken with plague, on the opposite side of the table, as though all knew already of his treachery. Leonardo boldly set him next to the disciple whom Jesus most loved. In this Leonardo was a better psychologist than his fellow-artists; he knew that treason dwells close to trust, and can strike with such confidence only because it is embedded in faith and loyalty, was there for all to see but was observed by none.

Leonardo knew this from his own bitter experience; and he also had his own way of making the traitor recognizable in the midst of the company. He had immersed Jesus in light; he immersed Judas in shadow. The face of the Saviour was framed in radiance; Judas was thrust away from the source of light by his instinctive recoil from Peter's forthrightness, the almost imperceptible recoil of the bad conscience. His evil, vulture-like profile, with his shifty glance, stands out, as the only dark silhouette, so plainly that his identity is clear enough even without the evidence of the hand clutching the bag.

The movement surges up against Christ on the right of the picture, and falls away on the left. Leonardo the mathematician and architect sends it mounting again further left; it reaches its crest on the right against the figure of Philip, and Leonardo makes it fall away then, as though it were breaking against the wall. On the left the wave rises high along the outstretched arm of Matthew. He was one who must talk and discuss, and as he springs up he sweeps the air with his arm, for something must be done, and he appeals to the rest. "Can they let that happen?" he cries, turning to Simon Peter. His impetuous outburst is taken up with more restraint by Thaddeus, with his riper experience. The only answer the two receive in their agitation from Simon Peter is that of his outstretched hands with their shrewd tapering fingers, which insist that he has no idea of what has happened.

Leonardo's psychological subtlety in bringing the deep emotion of the company in this way up against an old man's readiness to rest content with ignorance, finds its counterpart in the formal completeness of the picture as its movement is brought to rest against the vertical of Simon's upright figure, with its hard profile and the pointed nose and drooping lips of a head on a Roman medallion. But Simon Peter has to meet more than the urgent entreaty of his neighbours. The apostle Bartholomew bends over to him from the other end of the table, in a fever of agitation, appealing to him with eyes aflame, his hands firmly resting on the table. And as these questionings psychologically unite the two ends of the table, so formally they set profile against profile, vertical against vertical.

Having thus harmonized the movement throughout, Leonardo, with consummate mastery, raises the tension on the left side of the picture to a climax, and then relaxes it. Against Bartholomew's fevered head he places the almost apathetic profile of James the younger; against Bartholomew's excited start from his seat the gentle gesture with which James the younger touches Simon Peter's shoulder. Then he provides a formal and psychological cæsura in the figure of the aged Andrew, whose eyebrows are raised as in inquiry, deeply lining his forehead, while his mouth, drooping at the corners, and his outspread hands declare his innocence.

The *Last Supper* in Santa Maria delle Grazie seemed a revelation to Leonardo's contemporaries. Here the bold attempt had been made, for the first time, to give twelve times over, true to the logical implications of each character, the psychological reactions to the common emotion. No unconcerned actor remained in the picture, no mere spectator, no simply decorative figure as in its predecessors. Leonardo had composed his work out of thirteen intimate personal dramas, welded into a unity. It was all familiar and within men's comprehension, and yet it was an event from another, a more heroic world, with which the everyday life had nothing in common. The room was the familiar refectory, the table and cloth were those used regularly by the Dominican monks, the plates and cups might have come from their own cupboards; the figures resembled persons met every day; yet these were figures of supermen, associated in their timeless garb with no epoch, heroic actors in an event which lay outside the pettier everyday life. They were familiar and yet remote, as everything in the picture was familiar and yet of heroic dimensions. Thirteen persons could never have sat down at that narrow table, and Leonardo knew it, just as the observers knew it; but it was entirely permissible to sacrifice reality for the sake of the effect to be achieved.

With this *Last Supper* the new age made its entry into art. Demigods and heroes took the place of frail humanity, and a wider vision replaced that of the everyday world. Leonardo, himself a son of the Florentine *quattrocento,* carried his art-epoch to its grave. Under his care the new art sprang into life and attained a radiant maturity. He prepared the way for all the demigods and heroes of the future; from his *Last Supper* came the prophets of the Sistine chapel and the philosophers of the *School of Athens.* But it was not only his own age that Leonardo so completely roused and unsettled; his influence was felt by many generations of his successors, a commanding influence to which the coming art could not but bow. This *Last Supper* was like the sudden gushing of a spring; everyone drew from it, drank of it wittingly or unwittingly; construction, types, gestures, draperies were taken over from it, copied, exaggerated, squandered, worked to death. The work was not merely a stupendous achievement like the colossal monument to Francesco Sforza; it was something unique, something inimitable, an achievement of which only Leonardo possessed the secret. His *Last Supper* was a legacy to posterity, a canon of the new beauty, a primer for artists to come. The profound impression created by the completed work spread everywhere and exercised an influence that lasted for centuries.

5

Leonardo himself realized the suggestive and educative elements in his work. He was led now by his ingrained love of teaching to interpret his silent lesson, to publish the conclusions to which he had been brought, and to educate a generation of artists who could be lifted above mere empiricism or copying of their teacher or pursuit of the tricks of their trade. He set out to write a *Treatise on Painting.* His book was born of a thoroughgoing contempt for the mere transmission of the craftsman's skill: "The painter who paints only by rote and by ocular judgment, without bringing his mind into play, is like a mirror which imitates all things put in front of it, knowing nothing of them"—*sanza cognitione d'esse*.[68] This undue elevation of the part played by the intellect, by *cognitione*, in creative art, runs like a leitmotiv through Leonardo's teaching. "Those who like to practise without knowledge," he wrote later, "are like a sailor who ventures on a ship without rudder or compass, and can never know where he will arrive." [69]

He admits that there may be branches of knowledge which cannot be transmitted as property can be bequeathed, and that painting is one of them, since the art cannot be inculcated in those to whom Nature has not given the faculty of exercising it; but almost in the same breath he says, apparently not realizing the inconsistency, that that science is the most useful whose fruit is the most communicable, and consequently a science is less useful according as it is less communicable, and the ultimate goal of painting can be conveyed to every generation of mankind.[70]

Leonardo, whose supreme passion was for research, whose desire for knowledge crowded out all other desires, and in whose mind every intellectual process had the vividness of actual experience, generalized from his own unique case, and identified intellect with inspiration, cognition with sensibility. "Painting is the supreme intellectual analysis," he remarks casually at one point,[71] not realizing how far this dictum is from describing the actual creative process. He is thinking of a unique type of man. At one point he heads a paragraph "Of the Life of the Artist-Philosopher in the Country"; later he strikes out the word "philosopher," but makes no change in his remarks, though in reality they have reference to an exceptional case.

Following the fashion of his day, Leonardo prefaced his great work on the theory of art with a long-winded introduction setting forth the superiority of painting over all other arts. This comparison—*paragone*—between painting, sculpture, music, and poetry was a dialectical trifling on the lines of the wordy duels that took place at the court of Milan between poets, painters, architects, engineers, humanists, theologians, and representatives of the exact sciences. One of these intellectual tourneys was the *duello* fought out on February 19, 1498, in the presence of Lodovico Sforza, and described by Fra Luca Pacioli, who mentions among the participants Ambrogio da Rosate, the unexcelled jouster Galeazzo da Sanseverino, and Leonardo da Vinci.

Idle as this comparison of the arts may seem, the *paragone* gives an idea of the *demostrazione così terribile,* the ruthless logic, which, according to Vasari, was characteristic of Leonardo. "If you despise painting, which is the sole imitator of the visible works of Nature, you will certainly be despising a most subtle invention, which regards in a philosophical and sensitive way the essence of all forms—seas and plains, plants and animals, grass and flowers— which are surrounded by light and shade. And this is truly a science and a legitimate daughter of Nature—for painting is an off- spring of Nature, or, more correctly, we may call it a grandchild of Nature, since all visible things are created by Nature; and, since painting springs from these created things, it is a grandchild of Nature, and related to God." [72]

Sculpture cannot stand comparison with painting. "I can judge of this without partiality," Leonardo claims, "since I practise both equally." His acute creative sensibility, the eternally vibrating alertness of every sense, finds expression when he says that sculp- tors "cannot represent either transparent or radiant bodies, either the reflection of brightness or bright surfaces like mirrors, either clouds or cloudy weather." [73] It is the sensitive, beauty-loving, slightly pedantic æsthete in him, disgusted by dirt and the sweat of labour, avoiding contact with all that is mean and ugly in life, and dreaming of cities in which the élite are segregated from the working populace, that comes into play when he condemns sculp- ture because it is an art so closely connected with manual labour. The sculptor runs with sweat as he stands in front of his work, his face is covered with white marble dust, his studio is dirty and dis- orderly, bits of stone cling to his hair and his clothes; the painter, dressed in carefully chosen raiment, and with hands well cared for, wields the light brush in a well-ordered room hung with fine pic- tures, carrying on his elegant art to the strains of music or poetry. The only advantage which Leonardo concedes to sculpture is the permanence of its works; but he adds at once that a picture painted on copper is just as durable as statuary.

Leonardo's arguments are particularly sophistical when he deals with poetry. He does not shrink from wild exaggeration when he gives examples, alleged to be from his own experience, of the effect of pictures. In the same lofty tone in which he told the cardinal of Gurk of his fabulous emoluments, he relates how he himself has seen babies in arms stretch out their little hands to a picture of their father, and the dog and cat rub against it; "it was wonderful to witness this spectacle." [74] He had also seen with his own eyes how dogs barked at pictures of dogs and swallows alighted on a representation of window bars. Painting, "which directly represents the works of Nature, needs neither interpreters nor commentators," he claimed, with a malicious side-thrust at the exegesis so industriously pursued in his day. "You have placed painting among the mechanical arts!" he exclaims, in anger at the intellectual arrogance of his epoch; and he adds a reference to the fact that poets were paid more for dedications of works of no outstanding merit than painters for their masterpieces. With a similar undertone of contempt he rejects the contention that poetry is more enduring than painting: "the works of a boilermaker last even longer, for time preserves them better than your works or ours." [75]

Some of his debating points are rather too far-fetched. "You may call painting dumb poetry, but the painter can retort that the poet is pursuing blind painting. Well, which is worse, to be dumb or blind? . . . Tell me, which is closer to the man, his name or his portrait? Men's names change from country to country, but not their form, except in death. . . . Write God's name in some place and over against it place His figure, and you will see which of the two is shown more honour." [75]

But Leonardo sets out to base his theory of æsthetics on something more than mere debating points, and he does not always notice that his philosophy of the beautiful sometimes contradicts the arguments he brings forward in favour of painting. When he represents painting as so exact an imitation of Nature that children, dogs, cats, and swallows confuse the picture with reality, and when he represents it as the supreme service rendered by painting that it gives the sense of vision, "the highest of all senses, the same pleasure as anything created by Nature," he does not at all intend to define the capacity of painting to create an illusion as the essence of the art, or to treat the enjoyment of art as equivalent to that of beauty in actual things; he uses these arguments in his battle of words, is caught by them and makes a note of them, and then, on reflection, rejects them. The supreme law of artistic creation—he calls it Necessity, as in his natural philosophy—requires the artist's mind to transform itself into the actual mind of Nature, *transmutarsi nella propria mente di natura,* becoming an interpreter between art and Nature, commenting on the causes of her phenomena and seeking to understand her laws. With his imagination the artist improves on Nature; he disregards her limitations, he selects from her indiscriminate offering, he concentrates the things she scatters, heightens the things she indicates, escapes from her dictation, seeks and finds what she fails to bring him, and makes a world for himself over which he rules as autocrat, thanks to the creative power that dwells in his hands.

"If the painter desires to see beautiful things that awaken love in him, he is their lord and can create them; if he desires to see a monster that appals, or a grotesque or ridiculous or really touching thing, he is their lord and god. If he wants to create landscapes and wildernesses, or shady or cool places on hot days, he represents them, and also warm places when it is cold. If he desires to see valleys before him, if he desires a wide landscape to spread out from high mountain peaks, if he desires that the sea shall appear on the horizon, he is their lord. And indeed all that there is in the universe, be it present in being or but an imagining, he has first in his mind and then in his hands; and these hands are of such perfection that they produce a simultaneous harmony of relationships, compressed into a single moment, which can be comprehended in a glance as with real things." [76]

Here Leonardo indicates his definition of the nature of art, and also his conception of the enjoyment of art, which he elaborates elsewhere. In his *paragone* between painting and poetry he tells how King Matthias was brought at the same moment a poem and a picture of his beloved, and he shut up at once the book he was reading and turned to the picture. To the enraged poet he said: "Do you not know that our soul is composed of harmony and that harmony is born only in those moments in which the full relationships of objects can be seen or heard? Do you not see, then, that in your science there is no proportionality produced in the same moment, but that one part is produced after another in succession, and that the succeeding does not come into existence until the preceding dies?" [77]

Not a deceptive imitation of Nature, but a selection from what she offers, a choice made with a view to harmony of proportions, is the first factor in the enjoyment of art; the second is the simultaneity—the simultaneous perceptibility or, as Leonardo says elsewhere, the rapidity (*prestezza*) of the sense perceptions: in other words, the synthesis, which is the condition and the outcome of the creative instinct. This conception of the nature of art and of the enjoyment of art, still only dimly formulated, still struggling for expression, lifts Leonardo far above the æsthetic outlook of his period, in which he was still half entangled, and of which the sole objective was the imitation of reality. What he hesitantly enjoined and deliberately practised was an overcoming of reality, a sifting and heightening of the real, which decreed the end of one art form and heralded the birth of another.

Leonardo indicated the effects at which this new art aimed when he said that painting gives more food for astonishment than all other arts; it is *di maggior maraviglia*. Elsewhere he said that sculpture is a less strenuous intellectual labour than painting, with less strain on the inventive faculty—*è di minore fatica d'ingegno*. This valuation on the basis of the intellectual difficulties overcome expressed Leonardo's entirely individual attitude to art, and from this personal attitude he deduced the artistic effect—the astonishment produced in the observer. He directed the new art to this purpose more by his example than by word. He did not know that in doing so he was sounding its death-knell, and opening the way to every conjurer and ropewalker of art, every juggler with mannerisms. To him this struggle was a wrestling to bring forth a miracle, an infinitely hard secret struggle, a battle with the material to be conquered, in which he engaged with the inward trepidation of creative genius, knowing that it is faced either with triumph or with crushing defeat.

He himself plainly defined this struggle, in a sentence which sets the keystone on his philosophy of art: "The painter wrestles and vies with Nature." Lomazzo, who had spoken with those most closely associated with Leonardo and with his disciples, added one small revealing word which completes the picture of Leonardo's creative wrestling: "Whenever Leonardo came to work on a picture he seemed to be filled with fear." In writing this Lomazzo little realized, perhaps, how near he had come to the truth. Again and again this fear came over Leonardo—as an unknown painter facing an empty canvas, and as a famous man surrounded with magnificence. Again and again it would take possession of him, a paralysing, suffocating incubus, with which he would wrestle almost as with a living adversary. Armed with his stupendous knowledge and with almost boundless gifts, he approached each new picture in the fullest consciousness of his purpose and under no vague instinctive impulse; and then he was overcome with this inner trembling, the sense of the greatness of the undertaking, and doubts of his adequacy to it. Often this fear would gain the upper hand, and he would then let his arms fall in the depth of despair, vanquished by his own purpose. All that the others realized of this despairing struggle was what Lomazzo wrote further: "And so he could finish nothing that he began, for he was filled with the sense of the nobility of art, so that he discovered errors in pictures which others acclaimed as wonderful."

But Leonardo himself knew that masterpieces are born of this fear and doubting. He tried repeatedly to formulate this idea. "It is a poor master whose work runs ahead of his intellect; the one who strives for perfection in art is he whose intellect towers above his work." [78] Elsewhere he expresses the idea in a slightly changed form, in the pregnant headline: "That painter who has no doubts will achieve little."

Living in the independence of intellectual isolation, testing everything by his own feeling and deriving everything from his own experience, Leonardo could not be expected to foresee that his generalizations in the theory of art, his collections of rules (and each rule, *regola,* that he formulated he invested with the force of a law), might lead, of all things, to the overcoming of the stress of creation, the removal of doubts, the lightening of intellectual labour, and the dominance of routine. Yet he may have seen something of this danger when he wrote: "If you try to apply the rules at the moment of composition, you will never get through with it and will only introduce confusion into your works." [79] This is no more than a casual warning, which he must soon have dismissed, for it would have robbed his work of its intellectual foundation. In that impulse to formulation which became more and more closely bound up with his impulse to research, he continued to draw rules from every field of knowledge, and to bring them to the service of the "godhead of the science of painting."

He was so engrossed in his own intellectual processes that he deduced laws and rules even from qualities which were purely his own, such as his personal sensibility and his wealth of imagination, and recommended the emulation of faculties which, if only it had occurred to him, he well knew to be virtually incommunicable, such as the gift of dreaming. He included among the rules for the guidance of his pupils a "new invention of speculation"; and at once the term seemed to him to be too ambitious and the invention, important as it was for him personally, difficult to formulate, like everything else that was strongly personal, so that he went on to say that the invention might seem "small and almost ridiculous, and yet it is of great value" as a mental stimulant: "It consists in this, that if you are looking at walls with all sorts of stains on them, or on a mass of rocks of many colours, and if you have to paint a landscape as a background, you may see in the stains and the rocks images of various landscapes, outlines of mountains, rivers, crags, trees, broad plains, and manifold valleys and hills. You may also see in them battles, lively gestures, strange figures, a quick play of human faces, apparel, and countless other things; for the same thing happens with these walls and rocks as in the pealing of bells, in the sound of which you may find every name and every word that lives in your imagination." [80]

So Leonardo himself dreamed in front of motley walls in the mild light that came from a cloudy sky, when the hard outlines of the shadows were effaced and the sun's glare mellowed. So he also dreamed when the pealing of the bells came to him on his solitary wanderings. Did his pupils see these same pictures in the formless splashes on ancient walls, did they hear the same call in the clang of bells borne on the wind? Were sound and colour, form and tone, so closely associated in their sensibility that the one recalled the other? Or did they merely stare at him with uncomprehending eyes, in a respectfulness that had a tinge of the sense of the unearthly and fearsome?

At this period Leonardo had a number of pupils, not only in order to initiate them into the art of painting, but also to add to his meagre income. He makes frequent mention of a pupil named Marco, probably Marco d'Oggionno, who grew into a hesitating painter fond of primitive bright colouring, and another called Gian Antonio—Giovanni Antonio Boltraffio, who of all those who learned directly from Leonardo was the best able to take over his artistic heritage. This young man was also probably the most akin to Leonardo in his receptiveness. Boltraffio came of a good Milanese family, so good and so old a family that it regarded the professional activity of its scion as beneath him, and took care to record on his tomb that he had pursued painting only for his own enjoyment. His close friend Girolamo Casio, the Bolognese poet, called him Leonardo's "only pupil"; Boltraffio was, indeed, the only painter who assimilated the sensuous surface charm of Leonardo's art, and acquired it so well that his masterpiece, *La Belle Ferronnière,* was regarded for centuries as a work of Leonardo's own. But with all his great gifts, Boltraffio had the outlook of his family: he approached painting in the spirit of a highly cultured amateur. He readily abandoned his work in order to serve on diplomatic missions or take up some public office; he would then, in his intervals of leisure, paint for his own enjoyment soft-limbed, effeminate figures of ephebi, lovely and suffering, like his *Saint Sebastian,* or in love with their own shapeliness, like his *Narcissus* in the Uffizi; or if he painted portraits of his friends—the poet Casio, for instance, with his long hair, sensuously curving lips, dimpled chin, and rounded feminine neck—he made his subjects, as Casio himself said, more beautiful than Nature had done.

Leonardo wrote his *Treatise on Painting* for his own pupils, and for many generations of disciples. It was a labour of love, the outcome of his desire to communicate his knowledge and experience, and of the pleasure of an older man in seeing the seed of his knowledge springing up in the minds of young and receptive followers. But, apart from the laws of painting and his technical instruction, he imparted to his pupils a rule of living which was the outcome of his experience, a lesson suited least of all to young men —his bitter teaching of avoidance and contempt of human society. He impressed on them that "The painter should be a solitary"; solitude is essential to creative art. "If you are alone, you belong entirely to yourself; if you have the society of even a single companion, you belong only half to yourself, and you will belong less and less to yourself in proportion as your social life makes more insistent claims on you." [81] Again and again he repeats this warning to them against wasting themselves in social life, this admonition to practise a jealous economy of their lives; and his own life was an impressive example of the way a man can immure himself in solitude in the midst of his dealings with the world.

Leonardo also set before his pupils the example of his own modest style of living. "You must understand," he writes, "that there is no need for a great deal of money in order to provide for more than all we require. If you use money in superfluity, you do not make full use of it, and it is therefore not yours; the whole of the treasure of which you make no use is just as much in our ownership; what you gain without putting it to the service of your maintenance is in other hands in spite of you, and is of no service to you." [82]

Leonardo was well entitled to write that not much money was needed for a man's maintenance, for his own housekeeping was of Spartan simplicity. He still noted every soldo he spent on bread, vegetables, or wine, or on meat for his pupils and assistants, and, to judge from his day-to-day expenditure (it was never, even at other times, more than 31 or 32 soldi), his housekeeping was that of a man to whom frugality had become second nature—and of a solitary man, who entertained little.

In these household accounts, women's names appear from time to time, pointing to their presence in this bachelors' home. A Lucia is mentioned, and Leonardo records that Caterina came to him on July 16, 1493. This Caterina fell ill, was taken to hospital, and died, and Leonardo paid for her burial. The expense was considerable; it was a fine burial, with four priests and four clerks and a great number of wax candles, and the funeral feast cost 120 soldi. The physician had cost only two soldi—it cost more to die

than to live in Milan. From the scale of this expenditure and from
the identity of name some writers have inferred that this Caterina
was Leonardo's mother, who had come to Milan to die in her
son's arms. This does not seem probable. Leonardo never mentions his humble origin and did not care to be reminded of it; he
had lost all connexion with his home and relations; but the family feeling of his time would have required that even the plain
woman of the people should not be denied the name of mother in
her dying hour. This Caterina was probably a housekeeper, one
of the simple womenfolk who served him with quiet loyalty. Of
these women, critical as he could be of his environment, he never
complained, and on his deathbed he thought of the last of them
with sincere gratitude.

In his quiet and modest household Leonardo was surrounded by
solitude; he belonged entirely to himself, as he demanded. Even
the belated recognition that came to him brought no change in
his misanthropic seclusion, no temptation to repeat his early social
success. Only one strange figure hovered on the edge of his isolation, as vague in its character as in its relation to Leonardo, the
boy Giacomo. He had now become the young man Salai; in the
years spent under Leonardo's roof he had shown no improvement,
and in the midst of his accounts Leonardo makes in 1497 the
laconic entry: "Salai stole money." He was still as spoilt by Leonardo as the little "tinker" of ten had been; he was given shirts
of the finest linen at ten soldi the ell, and a cloak of silver brocade
edged with green velvet and with lots of lacings. The boy who had
come to him starving and in rags had now grown pretentious. The
moment Leonardo accorded him a regular payment as one of his
staff, the boy asked for an advance, and spent it on a pair of
flounced pink breeches.

Salai attached himself to Leonardo's life like a soft and graceful
shadow. He went with him everywhere as when he was a child.
"In Milan," writes Vasari, "Leonardo took as his protégé the
Milanese Salai, an attractive, graceful, beautiful child, with lovely
rich curly locks which greatly delighted Leonardo." Two of his
drawings in all probability portray the features of young Salai.
The earlier one shows the boy at about seventeen. The line of his
smooth nose is continued upward without a break by the straight

forehead, and if only the upper part of the face had been visible it would have passed for that of a Greek god. But the nostrils are long and narrow, giving little evidence of sensitiveness, the upper lip is too short, as though it would not close over the teeth, giving the small, childish mouth a look of greed, and cunning lurks in the suggestion of a smile about the corners of the mouth. The strong rounded chin, a departure from the godlike profile, fits in with the almost stupid stare from the eyes, which are not very large, and with the soft cheeks and the rounded fullness of the neck. Around this ephebus's head, which vacillates between purity and sensuality, between dullness and spitefulness, is spread a confusion of short locks, soft, hazy, almost like clouds, through which a very small ear peeps out.

In the second portrait, made perhaps six years later, this profile has scarcely become any more manly. On the contrary, the suggestion of a double chin has lent it further weakness. The mouth curls in even greater self-satisfaction; only the look of obstinate stupidity has gone, giving place to a faint smile from under heavy eyelids, the experienced, enigmatic smile that was later to appear in the eyes of Saint John. The locks which earlier had spread out like smoke lay now like a wreath of short curling vipers along the rather long skull, and Leonardo's charcoal pencil carefully traced their convolutions.

In Salai, Leonardo found embodied the type of beauty of which he had always been in search. Whenever he took up a pencil and idly sketched a profile, it had always been the same profile, that of Salai—before Salai came into his life. But whatever this vain, cunning, spoiled, despised boy may have been to him, Salai did not enter into the world that was Leonardo's own, a world that became more and more definitely cut off from his outward life and his work as artist, the world of the great adventures of the intellect, to which Leonardo devoted all the passion that was in him. Every new research was to Leonardo the discovery of an unknown continent. Joy and sorrow, excitement and depression, pride and anguish, came to him only from incidents of his researches, and the great turning-points in his life were marked for him by the emergence of new fields of study.

The period in which he painted his *Last Supper* was that also of a new ardent research, a reawakened interest in mathematics. All his past studies had brought him step by step toward mathematics, but he had not the good grounding in the elements needed for the study of pure mathematics, and similarly his technical experiments sometimes went wrong or produced divergent results because his calculations contained some simple and elementary mistake.

Chance brought him into touch with a man who possessed the routine skill which he himself lacked, and who gladly helped him with his calculations or showed him, for instance, how to extract a root. This man was Fra Luca Pacioli, who had been appointed professor of mathematics by Lodovico Sforza. He was two years older than Leonardo and, like him, a Florentine, plentifully endowed with the Florentine alertness and practical sense. Luca Pacioli had realized at a very early date the advantage of friendship with important personages, and as a young man had joined Alberti, who took him to Rome and lodged him in his own house. When Pacioli was about thirty-five he became a Franciscan monk, for material reasons rather than in piety; all his life was guided by utilitarian motives. His lowly monk's cowl disguised a man of great attainments and still greater ambition, thirsting for worldly splendours, a man with sharp elbows with which to make his way in this life, and with no scruples or qualms to impede his progress. Within the austere frame of the cowl his face beamed with self-satisfaction. His eyes, set close together, looked out on the world with solemn gravity and not without a touch of craftiness; his mouth was separated by a long upper lip from the short, commanding nose; a double chin made the thin lips, tautened by a vain smile, seem no more than a thread.

"Fra Luca Pacioli," writes Vasari, "was one of those who cover their ass's skin with the fell of a lion," and he accuses him of having stolen the Latin writings of the blind and aged painter Piero della Francesca and published them as his own work. But Fra Luca Pacioli was so plausible, and the field in which he worked was so new, that in that world of esotericism and obscurantism he passed as a man of outstanding intellect and the expositor of a secret science. He was the first to succeed, thanks to his persuasiveness, in overcoming the reluctance of the printers to issue a scientific work, so that his *Summa de Arithmetica,* issued in Venice, was the first printed scientific work of his time.

Such a man would at once realize the advantage of association with Leonardo da Vinci. At this time he was at work on a book on geometry, to which he gave the pretentious title *De Divina Proportione,* and he asked Leonardo to draw the plates for this work. In his introduction to the work he describes Leonardo as "the most honourable of all painters, investigator of perspective, architect, and musician, a man furnished with all the virtues." Over and above this official collaboration with Leonardo, he made use of Leonardo's studies in proportion in his directions for the design of Roman type. A learned French printer, Geoffroy Tory, later charged Pacioli with having "secretly plagiarized" not only his (Pacioli's) system, but everything of worth in his book *De Divina Proportione,* "from the deceased Seigneur Léonard de Vinci, who was a great mathematician, painter, and sculptor."

Leonardo may have been deceived by Luca Pacioli or he may have seen through him and have been content to be exploited by him; in any case Pacioli was of real service to Leonardo, for he led him to the threshold of a new world. It was Pacioli who stimulated Leonardo's interest in the proportions of the human body. A famous drawing in Venice shows a male figure inscribed in a circle and also in a square, an early contribution to the study of human proportions. Leonardo recognized proportion as the law of the universe—"Proportion is found not only in numbers and measures, but also in sounds, landscapes, times, and positions, and in every sort of power." [83]

Pacioli's essential contribution was the new assurance with which he endowed the self-taught Leonardo, who found his conclusions confirmed in a field which specially attracted and at the same time awed him. Leonardo suddenly felt firm ground beneath his feet; he had attained the utmost certainty—*somma certezza.* His past discoveries now fitted together perfectly; he had attained clearness at every point, and he now swept away his own mistakes and the errors into which others had led him—"for no human inquiry can be called science unless it pursues its path through mathematical exposition and demonstration." [84] Without a word he threw overboard the ballast of medieval conceptions; his very lan-

guage acquired a hard, metallic ring; he cast off all philosophic
fetters, and, after the diffidence of the introduction to his first
work, with its apology for his lack of authority, he could now
write, almost in a spirit of arrogance: "Let no man who is not a
mathematician read the elements of my work." [85]

7

Leonardo became so engrossed in his mathematical studies that
he neglected the work he had begun in the refectory of Santa
Maria—the decorative frieze round the *Last Supper* and the figures
of the duke and duchess as founders which he was to add on
Montorfano's fresco of the Crucifixion. He was repeatedly admon-
ished, but went so grudgingly to work that Lodovico lost patience, and instructed his secretary to draw up a written agreement
with Leonardo in which the latter should undertake to complete
the work in Santa Maria delle Grazie by an agreed date.

Opposite the wall lit up by the bright colours of the apostles'
garments, alongside the hard outlines of Montorfano's figures, Leonardo now painted Lodovico and Beatrice d'Este, kneeling and
with their hands put together, in the traditional attitude of pious
founders, with their sons Maximiliano and Francesco. Beatrice
had now grown stout—"some day she will be as fat as Mother,"
wrote her sister Isabella in concern. She always wore clothes with
stripes down them, in order to appear more slender, and she was
dressed thus for Leonardo's portrait. But neither her portrait, the
first which Leonardo painted of her, nor that of Lodovico, resisted
disintegration. Leonardo had rapidly painted the two with unsuitable materials; and while Montorfano's work retains all its original freshness, only faded outlines or formless stains on a scraped
surface remain to tell of the ambition of the duke and duchess to
go down through all the ages with the masterpiece of the *Last Supper*. It is as if fate ruthlessly denied to these two, on whom Leonardo depended for years for his existence, an undeserved immortality in association with him.

About this time Leonardo received from Lodovico a commis-

Detail from the *Last Supper* (Judas, Peter, John)

Detail from the *Last Supper* (Thomas, James the Elder, Philip)

Lodovico Sforza. By Boltraffio

sion for a much more worldly picture, the portrait of Lodovico's mistress, Lucrezia Crivelli.

The fight Beatrice had made for the soul and the senses of Lodovico, which seemed to have been crowned with entire success, had ended with her defeat. Perhaps for the very reason that Lodovico had become so bound up with her, a reaction set in, and he sought refuge from his sexual and intellectual dependence on her in unfaithfulness. The atmosphere of the Milanese court also militated against constancy. "Spring does not bring forth in each new year so many flowers and boughs as women play tricks on their husbands," writes Bandello; "if these were all known and described, they would take up more volumes than the longest and most circumstantial digests of law." And Bandello uses the gentle term "tricks" to cover not only the deceiving of their husbands by these philandering women of Milan, but the removal of inconvenient husbands by poison or by the hand of a hired assassin. "The men pay back their wives in the same coin, with the result that one may place husbands and wives in the same category as highway cut-throats and bandits." Corio, the official historian of the court of Milan, gave this picture of the ethics of the court: "The husband would take his bride to her lover, and the father his daughter."

The lovely Lucrezia, lady-in-waiting to Beatrice, was herself married, but her husband was indulgent. So were her family; her brother, a priest, used his sister's position to gain advancement to the fattest benefices that fell vacant. At first Lodovico was careful to spare Beatrice, but before long his masculine vanity and egotism gained the upper hand. He had his mistress's portrait painted by Leonardo, and he was inordinately proud of the picture, to which the professional flatterers at court did honour in more or less neatly devised epigrams. One anonymous poet, for instance, wrote that the gods had showered their gifts on Lucrezia, had given her features of rare beauty, and had granted her the good fortune to be painted by Leonardo and loved by Lodovico, the first among the painters and the first among the dukes.

Beatrice was more successful in preserving her political than her wifely influence. While she was being set aside as wife she interfered more and more disastrously in business of state. No doubt she was trying to be politically of service in the hope that the worse the political situation became, the more her husband would need her. Milan was still menaced by the claim of Louis of Orleans to the ducal throne, and vague reports continued to come of prepa- rations by Charles VIII for a new campaign. At Beatrice's instiga- tion Lodovico now tried to induce Maximilian to intervene in Italian affairs, holding out the prospect of the crown of Lombardy; meanwhile Alexander VI, moved by the same apprehensions in regard to France, was holding out the bait of the crown of the Holy Roman Empire to induce Maximilian to come to Rome. The emperor set out in 1496 to intervene in the war between Florence and Pisa. But he brought inadequate forces into Italy, and at Livorno he came into a violent November storm. He turned back with nothing achieved, taking refuge under the excuse that he could not fight against God and man together.

This fiasco marked the end of Beatrice's political activities. Everything had been in vain; she had failed to win her husband, and she had failed to win power. Was there anything left in her young life (she was barely twenty-two) to make it worth while? Her agitation found expression in furious orgies of savage cruelty, and in a passionate and unmeasured lust for the pleasures of life that seemed almost like a desire for self-extinction. The winter's festivities had come round again, and in order to dissipate the ris- ing popular discontent in Milan they were celebrated even more noisily and boisterously than usual. Beatrice was again pregnant, for the third time; but Lucrezia was also, and Il Moro was con- cerned only for her child. In spite of her condition Beatrice danced more wildly than ever in this winter of 1496. Her black satin gown, embroidered with darting flames of gold, concealed her condition; her breast and back were covered with heavy embroidery studded with rubies, like spilt blood. She danced throughout the gay Mil- anese winter, squandering her unspent passion, the wild tender- ness that lay fallow in her. In the autumn she had lost one more consolation in the midst of the ruin of her hopes. Little Bianca, Lodovico's daughter, the child-wife of the handsome Galeazzo da Sanseverino, had constantly kept close to her stepmother, "like her shadow," said contemporaries—a pale, delicate shadow with the disarming cheerfulness of children whom death claims. And one day the child had suddenly died, like a shadow swallowed up by the darkness.

Beatrice went on dancing, day and night, in spite of urgent warnings from her physicians. And one night, in the midst of the dancing, her little brown face was suddenly overcast by a livid pallor, and with a wild cry she collapsed. The musicians continued to play, entirely unaware of what had happened, drowning her cries as she struggled for breath.

A grey winter morning dawned slowly, a January morning shrouded in damp mists, after a night of agony in the castle of Milan. The candles flickered in the faint daylight, no longer emitting any radiance. Hurried steps still echoed down the wide passages of the castle, but there was an oppressive stillness in the little room into which Beatrice had quickly been taken. Under the counterpane of gold brocade her slight frame lay extended and tragically motionless. The shadows fell on her pinched face, violet shadows against the pale reflection of gold. Her never-resting child-like hands had suddenly become still, closing over a cross which someone had placed between the unconscious fingers. Her mouth, with its short upper lip, was shut—in her life it had never quite closed over the sharp bright teeth. In death it had taken on an expression of curt, self-willed rejection, almost revealing that she had sought this death.

Lodovico had collapsed in remorse on her bed. Now that she was dead, and her premature babe with her, he imagined that he had loved only her. There dawned on him a sense of the connexion between her death and his neglect of her, a sense of his own guilt, and all his self-confidence and air of magnificence collapsed. He was consumed with grief, and gave way to it in a vehement sobbing. Meanwhile Beatrice's favourite jester, a misshapen dwarf, slipped out of the room, his small face lined and anxious; he stood about outside, like a piece of furniture no longer of any use. Later, in passing on the news of his mistress's death he took advantage of his jester's liberty to remark that few would regret her, for she had been as incalculable and vicious as a wildcat. That was Beatrice's official epitaph, written by Frittalla, her favourite fool.

The duchess of Milan was buried with Milanese magnificence, and it was a genuinely remorseful Lodovico that followed her

bier. He was a changed man, determined to have done with the
life of immorality which had brought his little "Toto" to her
end. He shut himself up in a room hung with black, dressed in
a long mourning cloak; he took his meals standing, and depressed
courtiers moved silently about him, lowering their voices and stepping softly in the echoing halls, as though there were still a corpse
in the house. "The Milanese court has changed from a merry paradise into a dismal hell," sighed Beatrice's secretary. Lodovico was
as violent and as unrestrained in his grief as at other times in enjoyment. He had a memorial tablet to his dead wife and her unborn child placed in the small room that adjoined the vaulted
banqueting-hall, a tablet of black stone, of the size of the lid of
a child's coffin; and the room was to be decorated by Leonardo
with symbols of mourning on a black ground—a private mausoleum for Lodovico and his grief. A hundred candles were lit daily
round the stone sarcophagus in which Beatrice lay in the church
of Santa Maria delle Grazie, and Lodovico prayed every day by the
coffin. "The duke has become very pious; he attends mass every
day, fasts, and lives in chastity," reported Sanuto, the Venetian
historian. Lodovico had now renounced all worldly lusts, and intended to live only for his children and his state; he hoped to avert
the wrath of God as men appease their angered fellows, by humility and presents. He made the monks of Santa Maria delle Grazie
the intermediaries between himself and his God, bestowing on
them brocaded fabrics and silver which had belonged to Beatrice,
and bequeathing to them her favourite estate, the Sforzesca. He
commissioned Leonardo to paint the ascension of the Virgin Mary
at the main entrance to this church of his private devotions, with
figures of himself and Beatrice as founders, himself commended by
St. Dominic, the patron saint of the order, to the Virgin, and
Beatrice next to St. Peter. It was an urgent commission, and Lodovico was so insistent on its rapid execution that Leonardo painted
it on linen, although it was exposed to wind and weather. It
quickly went to pieces, and the monks removed it and had it replaced by a copy, which has also been lost.

Lodovico's grief and contrition were exhausted by their own
extravagance. A few months later Lucrezia Crivelli bore him a
son, Gian Paolo, and Il Moro felt this to be a mark of Heaven's

forgiveness. Beatrice had scarcely been six months in her grave when the duke made a lavish gift to his mistress in recognition of the vast pleasure—*ingentem voluptatem,* said the official deed of gift—which he found in her society.

Leonardo had still to finish the little black room, the Saletta Negra, when he was commissioned to decorate the banqueting-hall it adjoined, the Sala delle Asse. Right alongside the quickly dismissed reminder of death, on the very next wall to the black stone plaque which was to preserve the memory of Beatrice and her unborn child, Leonardo now called into being in the banqueting-hall an apotheosis of Nature's prodigal increase. In recollection of the cupola of woven boughs which he had once erected, he spread a great arbour across the whole width of the room. Gnarled trunks ran along the edges of the vaulting, carrying on in painted relief the ornamental copings of the walls. The boughs were intertwined, and ribbons of gold threaded the leafy labyrinth.

This interweaving of boughs and ribbons was a colossal game, a vast joke on the part of this born mystifier. Leonardo was particularly fond of exercising his patience on decorative intertwining of this sort. A sketch dating from 1494 shows the beginning of one of these designs. Vasari possessed an engraving with this motif, inscribed LEONARDI VINCI ACADEMIA; this, together with other engravings with a similar inscription, gave rise to the erroneous idea that at one time there existed a Leonardo academy in Milan. "Leonardo," writes Vasari, "spent a great deal of time in actually drawing groups of knotted cords, carried by him from end to end and so arranged that they completed a circle."

Leonardo devoted immense labour to the tracery of the Sala delle Asse. He was principally interested at this time in working with circles and squares, and at the back of this preoccupation with labours that were half games there stood his thorough knowledge of the laws of growth, of the sap that accumulates under the bark, of the elasticity of young shoots, the make-up of leaves, and the setting of leaf in twig and twig in bough. He had gained his interest in tracery from Lombard decorative motifs. Bramante was fond of these *gruppi,* and Leonardo admired his execution of them; he mentions them several times. But these overarching leaves, with their purpose of creating an optical illusion, went far beyond the idiom of contemporary style. Just as Leonardo, in his *Last Supper,* had borne the *quattrocento,* the art of the fifteenth century, to its grave, so now he carried the style of decoration of the High Renaissance beyond the borders of his age into the still unborn world of the baroque.

The banqueting-hall was like a vast wedding-arbour when in April 1498 the scaffolding began to be removed, only one platform being left; in reply to his pressure Lodovico was told that "Maestro Leonardo has promised to complete it by the end of September." Lodovico was already thinking in secret of a second marriage, with Clara Gonzaga, sister-in-law of Isabella d'Este and widow of Gilbert de Bourbon, Count Montpensier. Clara Gonzaga was an excitable woman of whom it is related in the *Heptameron* that, "not content with the favour of the king, she had illicit relations with three noblemen, and subsequently with others; but she secured their silence through such solemn oaths that for a long time each of them imagined himself to be the only favoured admirer." After her husband's premature death she travelled all over Italy, pursued by never-ending financial cares and by incurable restlessness. Lodovico would have been a good match for her, and he, for his part, saw the advantages her French connexions might bring him. But this marriage project seems to have come to grief through the veto of Charles VIII, who is said to have warned the countess against letting her head be turned by so unreliable a man.

This was Charles's last intervention in Italian affairs. In April 1498 he was torn by sudden death from the midst of a round of pleasure—a fit ending to his wayward, hedonist existence. He was succeeded by his cousin, the Louis of Orleans who claimed the throne of Milan. Louis XII was no irrational dreamer, no knight errant like Charles. He was in frail health, and his tired nerves permitted no ambitious plans. At thirty-eight he seemed an old man. He had, however, a small stock of notions to which he clung tenaciously. He formally placed on record his claim to the Milanese throne by taking the title of duke of Milan at his coronation, and the ruler of Milan was never referred to by him except as Signor Lodovico.

At first he contented himself with the simple title, for he had to bring his domestic affairs into order. He wanted to obtain a divorce

from Louis XI's misshapen daughter Jeanne, in order to marry
Anne of Brittany, whom he had wooed in vain before her marriage
with his predecessor. For a time the destiny of the throne of Milan
hung on the marriage-bed of a poor plain woman.

At this point another actor came upon the stage in this tragic
comedy—Cesare Borgia, son of Pope Alexander VI and a cardinal
against his will. Since the mysterious death of his elder brother,
the duke of Gandia, who had been the Pope's favourite son, Cesare
had been in feverish pursuit of the secular power which Alexander
had reserved to the elder son. He sought an alliance with the
daughter of the king of Naples, but she spurned the idea of marriage with this perjured "priest and son of a priest," and she was
not the only Italian princess to do so. Cesare accordingly set out to
purchase an alliance with the French court with the offer of the
papal dispensation which Louis needed.

Now Lodovico's fate lay in the hands of some undefined petty
French princess, and depended on whether she could be induced to
sacrifice her moral principles. The choice fell on Charlotte d'Albret, princess of Navarre, and on the day when her assent was extorted by Louis XII, Cesare Borgia's worldly career was assured—
and Lodovico's fate was sealed. For Louis now had the papal bull
which enabled him to marry his *chère Bretonne,* and he could
pursue the Milanese ambition which, according to those in close
touch with him, had consumed his spirit from the first.

The struggle over the fate of the plain Jeanne, and Cesare's
search for a bride, had given Lodovico Sforza a breathing-space,
which he had feverishly employed in the effort to consolidate his
power. He had maintained his position for nearly twenty years by
dint of a complicated series of intrigues, playing off his enemies
against one another and holding them in check, until he had come
to feel that he had reached firm ground. Now he found in Louis
XII an adversary who was his match. He tried to induce Emperor
Maximilian to invade Burgundy; he made a pact with the Venetians, and at the same time incited the Turks against them. He
gained nothing by all this; on the contrary, his transparent intriguing made it easier for the king of France to assemble a European coalition against him. All too late Lodovico discovered that
his diplomacy had failed, and he began to take thought for the de-

fence of his own country. As in a deathbed repentance, he sought
reconciliation with his Lombard adversaries; he sought to make
good the injustices of years, and to settle long-standing debts of
gratitude.

In this critical moment, in which he tried to repair the errors
of a whole lifetime, he thought also of his court painter Leonardo
da Vinci. In the midst of his feverish activities he opened negotiations for the purchase of a vineyard near the Porta Vercellina from
its existing owner, as a present for Leonardo. The transfer of this
vineyard, sixteen rods in extent, to Leonardo took place at the end
of April 1499. This, the duke stated, would enable his court
painter to build a house on the property, and so would "strengthen
the bonds which already unite him with Our person."

For the first time in his life Leonardo found himself possessed
of an assured livelihood. For the first time he was in a position to
live on land of his own and under a roof of his own. In his happy
realization of this belated security, he scarcely noticed the wider
menace that made it illusory. He counted his money in hand, and
noted where it was kept, like one who takes a last look at rooms
in which he has long lived; and he noted, with a sigh of relief: "I
found myself with 218 lire on the first of April 1499." [86]

8

That summer of leisure, and of a material security at last won,
brought Leonardo the fulfilment of a dream that had pursued him
from his early youth: he climbed "Momboso," as he called it—
probably Monte Rosa. Not one of his notes of the great experience is dated, but the fact that he writes of it in the *Leicester
Codex,* which probably dates from the first decade of the sixteenth
century, indicates that he took his mountaineering holiday before
he left Lombardy, though the date may possibly have been later,
about 1511. The ascent of a mountain was a tremendous adventure
in those days, achieved only by outstanding men, who were thereafter the talk of their whole century, like Petrarch after his ascent

of Mont Ventoux, or Pietro Bembo after he had ventured up Mount Etna.

Leonardo had felt from early youth the fascination of the mountain tops, of squeezing through thickets and climbing over steep rocks, of breathless crawling up clefts and through ravines; but all his childish memories paled alongside the marvels revealed by a mountain top never before ascended. He forgot to mention the year in which his trip to the mountains took place, but he mentions the season—midsummer; it was the middle of July when he reached the peak, of which he proudly records that "no other mountain has its basis at such a height." The mountain chain divided two countries, France and Italy, from one another; the foot of the mountain produced four rivers, crossing Europe in the direction of the four cardinal points—the Rhine, the Rhone, the Danube, and the Po, thought Leonardo. But the pride of having climbed many thousand feet—how many he did not know—and of standing above the cradle of famous rivers (he had no means of verifying this) was forgotten in the awe inspired by the spectacle which spread out before him at that great height (over 3500 metres). Cloud masses floated below his feet, the solitary peak of the mountain towering above them; above it spread a darkened sky, as though it were the cover of darkness which, in the medieval conception, enclosed the sphere of fire. But in front of this vault of distant darkness there floated an azure radiance; many years later Leonardo tried to reconstruct this strange effect, which had remained indelibly impressed on his memory, by sending up wreaths of smoke in front of a curtain of black velvet.

Above him was a dark sky and around him a floating blue; the surface over which he was walking glittered like a blaze of diamonds, throwing up an almost painfully dazzling radiance. Never had Leonardo seen a light of such intensity—he noted that the sun never shone so brightly in the valleys—and this strong light was broken up on the frozen surfaces of coarse-grained hail, which was deposited in layers on the summit of the mountain. As he stood there, with a sense of being suspended between heaven and earth, Leonardo felt that he was remote from all that was real. The milky cloud-stream below him parted to reveal other peaks, the tops of a jagged chain of snow-covered mountains, with the glaring sun-light falling on them; and snowfields and bare rocks, with chasms steeped in shadow, passed into the same blue which pervaded the air (drawing at Windsor).

This unique spectacle led Leonardo into meditation on the strange colour effect, and he declares with satisfaction that he has discovered the explanation of the blue shade of the atmosphere: "I say that the blueness we see in the air is not the colour of the air but is caused by warm humidity which is evaporated in minute and insensible atoms, and which catches the sun's rays falling onto it." [87]

Leonardo had never been so cut off from contemporary happenings as in these months in which events were coming to a climax very close to him. At the end of July 1499 the news reached Milan that the French army had already invaded Lombard territory. Leonardo went on quietly with work on small commissions and with his studies. It may have been just at this time that he had an opportunity of fulfilling a request from poor Isabella d'Aragona (whom Lodovico had separated from her eldest son and had banished from the castle to the Corte Vecchia) for the installation of a bathroom in her new quarters. He went to work on the task as if there were no other cares to disturb him. Three parts of hot water to four of cold gave, in his calculation, the right temperature for the bath [88]; he sketched the apparatus for supplying and heating the water and the outflow arrangement [89]; and on one of the many designs he put the date August 1, 1499.[90] The world that was his world was tottering around him, but he scarcely noticed it. On the same sheet on which he entered the date he noted the fact, important for him, that on that day he had written on "Motion and Weight."

Meanwhile the duke of Milan was engaged in the final desperate struggle to maintain his menaced rule. With the French army already preparing for the invasion of Italy, he was fighting now to retain the allegiance of his people. Hitherto he had concerned himself only with winning over the mighty of this world, but now he was devoting all his subtle eloquence, his grave dignity, and the sensuous warmth that took the place of humanity in his character, to retain the support of a population who had been mercilessly taxed and subjected to the chicanery of a servile bureaucracy. He explained to the masses that it was only the continual menace from evil-intentioned adversaries that accounted for the oppressive taxation, and he implored the citizens of Milan, who must still have had a vivid memory of the triumphal reception given to Charles VIII, to defend their country against the barbarians. Pressing his hand against his heart, he implored the people to stand by their legitimate princes in the hour of trial. He had never been guilty of an injustice; he had been a father to widows and orphans. His voice quivered with suppressed emotion at the thought of his magnanimity. Never before had he spoken to the people in this strain.

But the only result was that the people divined the gravity of the peril that could wring such an appeal from their ruler; the appeal was itself his undoing. At the last hour some curious change had come over him. All through his life he had consistently deceived and broken faith, betrayed friend and foe alike; now he suddenly staked his whole future on the appeal for trust, like a cardsharper who had failed to realize that his were not the only marked cards. He was warned of the doubtful loyalty of the commander of the ducal army, Galeazzo da Sanseverino; he replied that he could not conceive of such ingratitude. But Galeazzo's brother had already come to terms with the French, and at the first clash with the French army Galeazzo himself, as defender of the fortress of Alessandria, lost his nerve and abandoned the fortress.

"The very men whom I have loaded with favours are those who have betrayed me," complained Lodovico, completely unable to comprehend such treason. After the fall of Alessandria he placed his sons and his treasure under the protection of his brother Cardinal Ascanio in Germany; and he prepared to flee himself. In spite of his bitter experiences he still clung to his faith in human loyalty. He entrusted the defence of the castle of Milan to a man whom he regarded as absolutely trustworthy, Bernardino da Corte. Against his brother's advice, he declined to take Bernardino's children with him as hostages. The castle was impregnable; it was amply supplied with munitions and food, and Lodovico hoped that the French would break their teeth on this fortress. This hope brightened the bitter hour of departure of a man who, after being for many years the absolute lord of his country, was now accompanied on his flight by the mocking cries of the people—*"Francia! Francia!"*

Four days later the Milanese opened the gates of their city to the French. Not a shot was fired from the fortress, though its towers and embrasures could pour forth a withering fire at any moment. In the night there was a strange coming and going to and from the castle. Letters were exchanged and sacks of gold brought in—Louis XII was applying now to the men in Lodovico's service the same methods with which Lodovico had won over Charles VIII's officials and the "friends of the king." And Bernardino da Corte, the truest of the true, delivered up the castle to the French, in strange agreement with the captains of the fortress. "From Judas to this day," exclaimed Lodovico, "there has been no worse traitor than Bernardino da Corte." After this the French soldiers called the knave at cards "Bernardino." The perjured castellan lived on in isolation with his bags of gold, avoided like the plague by friend and foe, until in the end, in his sense of degradation, he fretted himself to death.

All who had depended on Lodovico, and who had reason to fear the French, now fled from Milan if they could. Leonardo, too, slowly prepared to go, but hoped still to be able to remain, "though," as an eyewitness wrote, "the city was in unimaginable confusion, as though the Day of Judgment had come." He found himself suddenly caught up in a network of intrigues; as was often to happen to him later, his leisure for quiet work was ruthlessly cut into by the ambitions and urgencies of the mighty. Among the invaders of Milan was Louis de Luxembourg, comte de Ligny, who had accompanied Charles VIII to Naples on his Italian expedition. During the short period of French rule in Naples, the count had married the princess of Altamura, and after her death he had claimed the succession to her Neapolitan possessions. The count was used to positions of command, and could not reconcile himself to Louis XII's appointment of Gian Giacomo Trivulzio to the supreme command of the French troops, instead of himself, Ligny. He hoped to induce the king to undertake an expedition against Naples, and in the meantime he entered into negotiations of his own with the Venetian republic for financial support for his personal campaign to seize the principality of Altamura. The cautious Venetians went no further than to assure Ligny's envoy that they were most grateful for his confidence and found his plans extremely interesting; but the count was apparently making preparations already for the execution of his fantastic project. He proposed to fight his way through Florentine territory with his own forces, to get as far as Rome—did he hope for help from Cesare Borgia or the Pope?—and to stir up a revolt among the Neapolitans. For this private campaign he needed a man who was familiar with the country and people, who had knowledge of the Florentine system of defence, and who was skilled in the arts of war. He found him in Leonardo da Vinci.

On a sheet among Leonardo's papers there is preserved a note in a strange hand reminding Maestro Leonardo that an early report was awaited from him on the Florentine state, the condition of its fortresses, and the way they were manned and maintained.[91] It was not felt in Leonardo's day that there was anything improper in the suggestion that he should give information about his native country. The general view at that period was that any strong personality outgrew the narrow limits of petty states and became a citizen of the world. "Where any savant settles, will do well enough for a mother country for him," wrote Codro Urceo. Leonardo had no compunction about offering his services to either friends or enemies of Florence, since his native city had no use for his services. He also enjoyed the atmosphere of conspiracy with which Ligny surrounded his plans, and in addition to his habitual right-to-left writing he now made use of anagrams in noting down what he had to do next: *"Truva ingil [Ligny] e dilli che tu l'aspetti amorra [a Roma] e che tu andrai con seco ilopanna [a Napoli]"*— "Go to Ligny and tell him you will await him at Rome and will go with him to Naples." He had two large cases made for packing his few possessions, which were tied up in bed linen; whatever he could not take was to be sold. He made various purchases, mainly of clothing—cloaks, caps, stockings, four pairs of shoes, and leather for making new ones, for he intended to stop at Vinci on his way, and probably wanted to impress his relatives by his stock of clothing.[92]

Adventurous as were the plans into which he was entering, he did not forget to deal with practical matters of importance to him; he made use of Ligny, as he mentions in another anagram, in order to get Lodovico's grant to him confirmed by the king of France. But before he had concluded the preparations for his journey, the news reached Milan that Lodovico intended to regain his realm by force, and was enlisting Swiss soldiers for an invasion of the duchy. In Milan the French, who had at first been received with shouts of joy, had been making themselves thoroughly unpopular through their failure to adapt themselves to their surroundings. "The French," said Alexander VI contemptuously, "know a lot about conquering, but do not know how to hold their conquests."

Leonardo's best friend, the architect and engineer Giacomo Andrea da Ferrara, attempted to carry through a plot against Trivulzio; his plan was to introduce supporters of Lodovico into the castle by an underground passage. He was caught by the French guards in the act of filing through the iron bars of a grating. For Leonardo himself the situation grew more and more uncomfortable, used though he was to patiently awaiting the outcome of events. The approach of the French had compelled Ligny to abandon his plans for the moment, and Leonardo no longer knew which way to turn. He collected his resources, six hundred florins in all, and deposited the money with the Florence loan office; and at the end of 1499 he left Milan in company with Fra Luca Pacioli —and with his inseparable protégé, the curly-haired boy Salai.

On his journey Leonardo learned of Lodovico's return, his capture of Domodossola and Como, and his entry into Milan. Then came the news of Lodovico's disastrous fate, his destruction by a last act of treason, the cowardly treason of Swiss soldiers bribed by the French. Thinking over the tornado of events that had swept away the regime of the Sforzas, Leonardo noted the things which had most interested or moved him. His first thought was of the works of art destroyed and those in progress which were cut short —not his own works, but those of Bramante, the cupola of Santa Maria delle Grazie, the church of Sant' Ambrogio; and he wrote down "Buildings by Bramante." Then he recalled men he had known. "The castellan taken prisoner," he noted, and he recalled other friends, such as Galeazzo Visconti, who, in the words of a contemporary, had always been on the side of the winner; he was now treated with great harshness by the French, and was sent to a French prison. "Visconti carried off," writes Leonardo, "and then his son died." Other entries recall Leonardo's enemies at the Milanese court: Rosate, the all-powerful physician and astrologer—"Gian della Rosa was deprived of his money"; and the dilatory treasurer, Bergonzo Botta, of whom Leonardo writes in his enigmatic style: "Bergonzo started but did not want to go on, and so fortune deserted him." And then—only then—he thought of Lodovico: "The duke has lost his state and his possessions and his liberty, and has brought none of his works to completion." That is all that Leonardo had to say after sixteen years of close association with Il Moro—an epitaph written in unconcern on an enormously powerful prince who suffered an unparalleled downfall.

CHAPTER FIVE

The Unconcerned Observer

Decipimur votis et tempore fallimur et mors
Deridet curas; anxia vita nihil.

Our hopes are cheated and time foils us: death
Grins at our cares—life's struggles are in vain.

(MS L o.)

NICCOLÒ DA CORREGGIO, that perfect courtier, called
Isabella d'Este, margravine of Mantua, "the first lady in the
world." Her contemporaries, in their admiration and their love of
superlatives, set her on a special pedestal in her lifetime, and posterity surrounded her with all the colour and radiance that it
found scattered through her epoch. Isabella herself felt sure that
she was destined to become legendary, and she was not mistaken.
For centuries she was a symbol of intellectual activity, artistic ambition, and sensitive and fruitful understanding of contemporary
achievements. Posterity set her radiance against the dark spots it
found in her epoch, her dignified repose against its wild passions,
her beneficence against its enormities, her welcome for all that was
new in art against the survivals of barbarism around her, and her
exemplary life against the loose morals of her day. Simply to meet
her, her contemporaries felt, was to discover that there could be
virtue without tedium, seductive womanhood without sacrifice of
dignity, influence without force or wealth—in short, a victory of the
spirit over material circumstances. As time passed her figure grew
into a personification of inspiring womanhood.

This crystallization around a name was neither fortuitous nor
arbitrary. Isabella had chosen her course as men choose their profession; she had deliberately assumed her place in the cultural life
of her day much as an actor may have heroic parts specially written
for him. She had grown up with a determination to achieve fame,

and held to it throughout her eventful career. No life could have been more unswervingly consistent. She allowed neither disasters nor triumphs, neither her own feelings nor those of others, neither successes nor humiliations to divert her from her goal; she made no concessions either to life or to herself, and none on any account to those who would have helped her at that price. Although she was woman enough to be capable of strong, primitive emotions, to make quite vulgar and plebeian scenes with the stupid, ugly, and continually unfaithful husband whom she nevertheless loved, and to pull the hair of his mistress, she abandoned herself to her hate or her love only when she could do so safely and without disturbing her fixed plans.

Yet destiny itself seemed to conspire against her and against her instinctive urge to self-assertion. If Lodovico Sforza had wooed her a little earlier, she would not have become the mistress of a petty state, the wife of a soldier who would offer his forces now to the Venetian republic and now to its enemies; she would have reigned over the most flourishing realm in Italy. Often she beat her wings painfully against the bars of the narrow cage that was her sphere of activity, rebelling against the emptiness of her state exchequer, her husband's irresponsible expenditure, and the poor quality of her diplomats; often she had to threaten her husband that she would dress entirely in black if he insisted on pawning her last jewels; she was compelled to borrow, to humiliate herself, to let foreign princes pay for her journeys. Yet she set the fashions, invented new hats and new styles for the hair, and took her role of best-dressed woman in Italy so seriously that once, when on setting out on a journey she discovered that she had left a new hat at home, a messenger had to return many miles to fetch it. The malice of fate had bound her to Francesco Gonzaga while her plain and insignificant sister was able to play a part in world politics and to live in immense luxury; had granted her no male heir; had restricted her sphere and had humiliated her womanhood and even her wifehood. But her will triumphed over destiny itself.

Her petty state was no more than a pawn on the political chessboard, her husband reputed a mere condottiere and not even a reliable one—"You are rid of a great fool," said the Pope to the

Venetians when the margrave of Mantua left their service. But Isabella made up for her lack of material power by her strong personality, by an unexcelled diplomatic ability, by her knowledge of human weaknesses, and by a tireless cultivation of the friendship of the mighty. She was unable to offer any alliance of substance or any important loan to the princes whom she received; but at least she made sure that their beds were comfortable, gave them the food they liked and the wine they were used to, and even ascertained whether they preferred tapestry or paintings on the walls of their bedchambers. She knew everything that was going on in the world, watched for every opportunity of being of service to influential people, wrote the right letter at the right moment, and sent in due season the needed words of sympathy or of gushing congratulation.

She cleverly remedied every blunder of her husband's in his irresolution and his semi-betrayal of both sides—he did not get so far as complete betrayal. She had had a genuine liking for Lodovico, and did not deny it in the hour of peril; she knew, indeed, that it would have been useless to deny it. But when the French ambassador complained that she was a "pro-Sforza" she expressed an indignation that did not seem in the least feigned; she was now, she wrote, "as good a Frenchwoman as anyone could be, and dressed entirely in lilies," and she made such a parade of injured innocence that the ambassador made humble and profuse apologies for his "mistaken idea."

She could not pay their weight in gold for great works of art, or employ famous artists on that sort of basis; but she would keep on sending her envoys to one famous man or another, to place twenty-five ducats on his table, or some such amount, and go away. When the envoy returned a few weeks later the money would have been spent, and the artist would thus have placed himself under an obligation to the margravine. He would then be continually reminded of it, month by month and year by year, and finally threatened with prosecution. Giovanni Bellini was one of the artists treated in this way until at last he discharged his obligation. Isabella never forgot anything on which she had set her mind, and she never allowed others to forget.

Her strongest weapon was her overpowering, inescapable amiability. Her diplomatic correspondence reads like love letters. Every artist whom she reminded of his remissness was addressed as the one great genius who had all her admiration. She devoted the same energy to things of consequence and to trifles, and pressed each of her requests with such earnestness that it might have been supposed that her soul's welfare depended on its fulfilment.

Burning as was her collector's zeal, and simple matter of routine as her cultivation of celebrities had become, her pursuit of Leonardo, which continued in vain for years, had a deeper and a more personal quality. She had frequently met him during her visits to the Milanese court, and had realized his importance earlier and better than did Beatrice and Lodovico. Failing to get any picture from him, she borrowed his portrait of Cecilia Gallerani for a short time. Failing to tempt him to Mantua, she took up his friend and fellow-countryman Atalante Miglioretti, the singer who had gone to Milan with Leonardo; she even became godmother to Miglioretti's child.

Her admiration, too, of Leonardo seemed deeper and more genuine than the feelings she exhibited in other directions. It seemed to be felt not only for the painter whose works she wanted to possess but also for the man, whose quality she considered that she fully appreciated. "Leonardo, the painter, is our friend," she wrote, quite simply, on one occasion. She was used to dominating all who came into contact with her, but this man showed no sense of her superiority, and she treated him as an equal. She felt drawn to him, indeed, as, like herself, intellectually an exceptional person, and she felt that he and she were kindred spirits. It may be that she felt his thirst for knowledge to be a trait similar to her own bookishness, and his passion for research, which at times filled him to the exclusion of all else, to be the same quality as her persistence in pursuing her own ambitions; she may have regarded the universality of his genius as the same thing as her lynx-eyed efficiency, and have seen in her rapid rise above the intellectual level of her environment the counterpart of the isolation of a man whose environment was the universe.

When Leonardo, escaping from the disorders that followed the collapse of the Sforza regime, reached Mantua, Isabella received him as a friend. For a time Mantua was a haven in the worldwide storm, and for this security he was certainly indebted to Isabella. In the midst of this political storm, which could have swept away her petty state like a straw, Isabella had done her best to attract to Mantua the scattered artists of the court of the Sforzas. One of her most ardent desires was fulfilled when Leonardo, under the pressure of her admiring pertinacity, set out to paint her portrait. In the room which she had set apart as a refuge and decorated as an island of beauty in the midst of the urgencies and uglinesses of life, the *"studiolo"* which was to share her fame, these two were now face to face with one another, as though destiny itself had decreed that they should come together—the most outstanding woman of her time and the greatest man of his epoch.

The window of the *studiolo* looked out over the silvery surface of a lake, through a white haze beneath the low wintry sky. A wide landscape such as Leonardo loved, with a dim horizon hung mysteriously with veils of cloud, formed the natural foil for the portrait of Isabella d'Este. On one wall of the room hung Mantegna's picture the *Triumph of Parnassus;* the muse who led the dance had Isabella's features. Her full-fleshed face, with firm oval cheeks, was turned to the observer; her arched forehead, not too high, with rounded temples, was framed in a wealth of black hair; in her wide-open almond-shaped eyes was the eager radiance which beautiful women are able to assume with such deliberation, and the small, sensuous mouth blossomed like a discreet promise.

No doubt this was the way Isabella hoped to be painted by Leonardo too, as she sat there in triumph over this beginning of the fulfilment of her desire. She leaned back in her seat, sure of her own effectiveness, a little more silent than usual and a little more relaxed, for she was expecting soon to become a mother. But Leonardo did not sit down opposite to her; he seemed to be deliberately avoiding her direct, compelling gaze. From his seat he saw her unflattering profile, the rather long nose with thickened tip and fleshy nostrils, the dominating chin, already showing signs of becoming a double chin, and the protruding eyes. But he saw also the intellectuality of her arched forehead, now bent forward a little in thought. He saw the self-confidence with which she could carry her head, erect between the dark wavy locks that fell to her plump shoulders. He saw her in her shrewdness and subtlety; and he gave her the sensitive spiritual hands of an intellectual, emerging from the heavy fabric of the sleeves with such knowledge and eloquence that they seem entirely unused to resting on top of one another, and ready at any moment to be raised to point an argument. Only around the small and firmly outlined mouth, too small for the full-fleshed face, did Leonardo allow the famed charm of Isabella's beauty to appear, and with it a suggestion of humour, the one faint suggestion of humanity in an apotheosis.

The sketch which Leonardo completed in order to paint from it —the drawing in the Louvre shows the marks of tracing—was a remarkably close likeness, according to Lorenzo Gusnasco, the lute-maker, who saw it in Leonardo's possession a little later. But there is a coldness in the drawing, an almost malevolent coldness: it is the picture of a woman of importance, but not of a woman with whom he could ever have fallen in love, not even the picture of an admired friend. This was not the Isabella that her husband and friends wanted to see—robbed of her disarming sensuous charm, and reduced to the fundamentals of her nature, her active intelligence, her clearness of ambitious purpose, and the calculating coldness she concealed from her admirers beneath a semblance of spontaneous devotion. Francesco Gonzaga found this representation of Isabella so little to his taste that, to his wife's intense regret, he soon gave away the replica of the drawing which Leonardo had left at Mantua; for Gonzaga it was, apparently, something to be put out of sight.

A cold, unfeeling sketch, made yet cruder by another hand, a traced drawing for the portrait of a great lady, was all that remained of the meeting between Isabella d'Este and Leonardo da Vinci. The memorable occasion passed like any casual moment. From it there did not even come a lukewarm friendship, and scarcely as much as the draft of a masterpiece. Yet Leonardo was offered in Mantua many things of which he was fond, and was given some of which he had long been deprived. There was a great deal of music; Isabella herself had a fine trained voice, and played on a great lute made by Atalante Miglioretti, which she had managed to inveigle by flatteries out of Niccolò da Correggio. In the long evenings well-dressed, intelligent, leisured people came to-

gether for diffuse and discursive conversation, revealing or commenting on the treasures of their learning in carefully polished
sentences.

But Leonardo met not only the poets and musicians, the perfect
courtiers and knightly conversationalists of Mantua, but also his
fellow-artist Andrea Mantegna, who, long before Isabella's time,
had painted in the castle banqueting-hall a series of frescoes,
Cæsar's Triumph, which was shown to every visitor as the finest
thing in the castle. Isabella's pride, however, was in the *Triumph
of Parnassus,* which Mantegna had painted in accordance with
precise instructions laying down not only the choice and pose of
the figures, not only the composition and the landscape in the
background, but every accessory down to the very tips of the garments. Isabella was always ready to tell at length the story of the
making of this picture.

But Leonardo saw not only the picture but also the lined and
wrinkled face of the old painter, the face of a solitary thinker. He
heard from Mantegna, as well as from Isabella herself, how she
took advantage of her knowledge of art to dictate to the artists. At
that moment she was busy with the decoration of her *studiolo,* and
Leonardo heard of the characteristic way in which she proposed to
obtain masterpieces for it. Like many women who are protected
from temptation by their discretion, and fall only when they
choose to do so, Isabella was fond of banal moralizing, and she had
chosen as the subject of her series of pictures the struggle between
virtue and vice. Her learned secretaries supplied her with a draft,
the *invenzione*—pretty sophistical stuff it would be—and she added
details and then passed it on to some unfortunate painter to work
into a sketch. To prevent any mistake two tape measures were supplied, giving to the inch the breadth and height of the picture
ordered. The "invention," the sketch, and the two tapes were then
passed on to some great artist for attention. "I wish," Isabella
would sigh, if some picture thus ordered to measure did not arrive quickly enough, "I wish I were as well served by the painters
as by the poets; but I know it is a vain wish."

Leonardo was alone among the artists to whom she turned in
being spared from these meticulous instructions. Later, when Isabella suggested to him an idea for a picture—and, indeed, a delight-

ful idea—she hastily added that she hoped he would paint it with his own unique sweetness and charm: she wanted only to have a picture of his, any picture— "We would leave to you the invention and the date for delivery." But it may be that Leonardo feared something more than æsthetic tutelage. He may have been unable to endure her invasion of his hermit's peace. It may be that Isabella's intelligence and insight had come too late into his life, and were trying doors which he had bolted and barred behind him.

Leonardo had encountered a great deal of ingratitude and incomprehension in his life, and there is evidence of only one human being who lavished admiration on him and eagerly courted his friendship. That one human being was a woman, whose inexhaustible amiability was perhaps due to something more than mere admiration for his genius; and Leonardo rewarded her for this feeling with a bearishness that amounted to unkindness. For years Isabella continued to invite him at frequent intervals to come to Mantua, and he never obeyed her summons; for years she continued to press for the completion of her portrait and to allow herself to be put off with replies which sometimes went no further than: "Leonardo has nothing more to say." Yet in those years Leonardo found time, and a great deal of it, for painting the wife of an obscure citizen of Florence and making her immortal. For years Isabella begged and implored him to send her a picture, any little picture, promising him mountains of gold, sending ambassadors and agents and priests to him, inducing people in touch with him to put in a word for her; only after his death did she receive a work (no longer extant) which had been presented to her by Leonardo for her *studiolo*—as though her will had not been strong enough to move the living man but had overcome the dead one. Mantua was but a short stage in Leonardo's journey. The unusual resolution with which he broke away was suggestive of a feeling that he must flee, the one thing that can move the hesitant. His departure was the signal for a silent breach with Isabella d'Este, which he maintained year after year until at last even her pertinacity was worn down.

2

At the moment of his departure he had the excuse, which may have been genuine, that he was called to important business of state. In March 1500 he reached Venice. It was the first time he had set foot in "the most triumphant city I have ever seen," as Commines called it. "Rome was planted by men, Venice, you'll say, by the gods," say the Venetians—*Illam homines dices, hanc posuisse deos;* and the fair city does indeed rise from the blue waters like a dream dreamt by nectar-bemused gods. The March sunlight filters through the haze that floats over the sea, bringing from the water a silvery shimmer that streams back through the air as though a vast pearl oyster had opened to bathe earth and sky in an iridescent radiance. Golden and faint pink hues spread over the marble of the churches and palaces, over the tracery of their openwork windows, the harmonious colonnades, the delicately ornamented gables; and the domes of the churches float as though painted in the sky.

It was of this radiance diffused through the air that Leonardo had dreamed as he lay in bed in the morning, looking at the sun through half-closed eyelids and letting little rainbows play on his fair lashes. It was a light that saturated every colour, as though liquid silver or gold had been mixed in, a light that lent every shadow a transparent depth and softened every outline. It was this light that had made artists of the Venetians; and Leonardo, who had sought to capture it in his paintings before ever he saw it with his own eyes, would have felt it to be his own native element if he had had the leisure to observe it.

But he had come to the city at a moment of public excitement. The piazze, filled usually with a gentle hum of cheerful activity, orderly and restrained, were packed now by noisy and excited crowds, which were demanding that the council then in session should punish Admiral Grimani for his disgraceful defeat at the hands of the Turks at Lepanto. Leonardo heard them screeching their song of hate:

Antonio Grimani,
ruina d'Cristiani,
rebello de' Veneziani,
puostsi esser manza da canni—

"Antonio Grimani, ruin of the Christians, rebel against the Venetians—you should be food for the dogs!"

Leonardo listened to the confused rumours that flew to and fro among the crowd, intensifying the panic. The Turks had invaded Istria and Friuli; they were said to number twenty thousand—savage horsemen, the terrible spahis of Sultan Bayazid's army; they rode from village to village burning and murdering. The country lay defenceless, at the mercy of the invaders; no one had dreamt that they would penetrate from the continent into Venetian territory. The spahis had already reached the Isonzo. The prisoners whom they were carrying along in their train hampered them in the crossing of the river, and were being murdered wholesale. They were sowing such terror among the population that the houses were barricaded against them, and men preferred to starve with their wives and children rather than attempt to face the enemy.

The Venetian envoy, Alvise Manenti, had returned empty-handed from Turkey. Venice was still so filled with the illusion of her own power that Manenti had demanded the liberation of the prisoners taken and of the Venetian merchants; he had even demanded the return of Lepanto. "Better say nothing about prisoners," was the answer he received; "they will remain with us until peace is concluded, if there is a peace at all. Venice," Bayazid had added scornfully, "is no longer spouse of the sea; in future you will have to reckon with us—we possess more of the sea than you do." Never before had a Venetian ambassador been addressed in this style. Manenti returned to his own country, to report the failure of his negotiations to a government as perturbed as himself.

Leonardo had reached Venice about the same time as Manenti, while the Council were anxiously debating and the crowds filling the streets with uproar. His reputation as a military engineer had preceded him. He may have been recommended by comte de Ligny, whose relations with Venice were so intimate that he was

given a seat in the Council; or Fra Luca Pacioli, who knew how
to turn any situation to his own advantage, may have told his Venetian friends that Leonardo would be useful in their need. In any
case, he found himself from the moment of his arrival in a whirl
of negotiations, commissions, journeys on special service, and secret
reports. He could not follow his inclinations and stroll through
this new city as though it were an undiscovered world, applying
his rule *nota ogni cosa*—"take note of everything." He had no
leisure for observing the unique loveliness of Venice; instead, his
notebooks are filled with dark hints and vague suggestions of secret
preparations for resistance. An air of impending disaster hung
over Venice—and this tension filled him with imperturbable calm,
as though his nature demanded the clash of unleashed forces in
order to rise in lofty indifference above them.

The first and most urgent task was to protect the defenceless
hinterland from a new invasion in force, which might bring the
enemy right up to Venice; fortresses had to be built and measures
of defence planned for the points most exposed to attack. There
must still have been scattered bodies of Turkish troops in this
region at the time when Leonardo made a hasty tour of investigation; the conclusion at which he arrived was that the only route
for a Turkish invasion involved crossing the Isonzo. "I realize,"
he wrote in a report to the Illustrissimi Signori, of which, as usual,
he preserved a draft, "I realize that it is not possible to provide
permanent means of defence, but I cannot but point out that a few
men, with the aid of such a river, are equivalent to a large number. . . . I am of the opinion that no defence force can be so generally serviceable as if stationed along the said river." [1]

Leonardo travelled for a while through the valleys of Friuli,
along the Piave and the Tagliamento; he went as far as Gorizia.
On a rough sketch of the course of the Isonzo and the Vilpago he
noted: "Bridge of Gorizia-Vilpago—high—high." [2]

His earlier work, theoretical and practical, was of service to him
now in the task of planning sluices on the Isonzo, and there was
a touch of dogmatism in his communications with his employers:
"The more muddied the water is, the more it weighs, and the
more it weighs the faster it moves in its descent; and the faster a
body moves the harder it hits its object." He knew in advance the

objections which the Venetian experts might bring forward, and set out at once to parry them in his report. The current, with the wood and stones it would bring down with it, would not be able to destroy his barrage, as he intended to build it up to four ells, the average level of the water; and if floods came and the water rose above that level, tearing trees up in its course, it would carry them over the buttresses of his zigzag dam without hitting them.[3]

The Venetian authorities seem to have raised objections to the cost of all this, for Leonardo remarks ironically in a note: "The Venetians have boasted that they can spend thirty-six millions in gold in ten years of war with the Empire, the Church, the king of Spain, and the king of France—300,000 ducats a month." [4] The question of cost seems, however, to have been quickly settled, and Leonardo took the work in hand at once. Many years later, when he was constructing sluices in France, he recalled his Venetian contract—"and let the barrier be movable, as I arranged in Friuli, where with the opening of a sluice the water that passed through dug out the bottom." [5]

In this hour of need Leonardo was employed also as a gun-maker. A brief note shows that he gave orders for cannon-building —"Bombards . . . at Venice . . . on the lines I laid down at Gradisca." [6]

In the midst of these labours Leonardo put forward a daring plan which would enable the Venetians to deliver a crushing blow against the Turks. It was an idea which would only be entertained at all in a situation as desperate as was that of Venice. He formally set out the scientific principles underlying it, but no explanation could prevent it from appearing to his contemporaries to be a recourse to black magic. This foreign magician informed the Venetians, with the air of one who expounded something perfectly simple, that he had invented an apparatus by means of which the enemy ships could be approached under water and holed.

The idea of diving below the surface of water is a dream as old as that of rising into the air. It strongly attracted the imagination of the Middle Ages. The Alexander legend, into which there was poured for centuries the love of adventure of the men of the Middle Ages and their dream of escape from the allotted sphere, tells how Alexander the Great rose into the air, and how he dived to the bottom of the sea in a glass ball; and ivory-carvers, miniaturists, and tapestry-weavers bent all their skill and their fantasy to giving a credible representation of the crowned hero in his bell with its air-pipe, or crouching in a glass ball. Yet there had been a time when this medieval dream was a reality: in the period to which the legendary hero of romance was assigned, diving was so ordinary a matter that Aristotle casually compares the elephant's trunk to the pipe used by divers for breathing below water. Aristotle also writes of a diving-bell which the diver took with him; it was filled with air and floated over him as he worked on the sea-bed.

About the middle of the fifteenth century Leone Battista Alberti made an attempt to raise up the sunken Roman galleys in Lake Nemi. He sent to Genoa for divers, of whom it was said that they "swam like fish, and when they got to the bottom of the lake they were able to report the size of the ships and whether they were whole or damaged." The earliest drawing of a diving-dress is found in the work of a Sienese engineer of the fifteenth century, Giacomo Mariano, surnamed Taccola; but he contented himself with putting over his diver's head a cap provided with an airbag. An actual diving-suit was designed by an engineer, Gian Battista della Valle, who wrote in the first half of the sixteenth century a widely read book on military science. He was typical of the technicians of that time, men entirely without theoretical knowledge, who yet achieved astonishing results in practice. Della Valle's diving-suit had a helmet with glass eyepieces, and was fitted with an air-pipe reaching to the surface of the water. This "noble method of remaining under water," as della Valle called it, was also intended for holing enemy ships, and the drawing in his first edition, of 1524, bears a striking resemblance to a sketch made by Leonardo in his early days in Milan.

Leonardo probably got the idea for his invention from one of the travellers from the East whom he had met; they no doubt told him how pearl-fishers in the Indies used a special dress that enabled them to work under water. "This instrument," Leonardo wrote under his sketch, "is used in the Indian Sea for excavating pearls, and is made of leather with frequent hoops, so that the sea shall not compress it; and above there is a companion with a boat;

the diver fishes pearls and coral, and has eyepieces of snow-glass and a cuirass with spikes fixed in front of it," [7] probably for protection against big fishes. About the same time he designed a diving-dress for saving life at sea—"means of escape in a tempest from a wreck at sea."[8] It was a leather waistcoat with a broad hem reaching from the girdle to the knee, which could be filled with air through a tube of the thickness of a finger, fixed to the breast. For making swimming easier he designed a glove with fingers extended into webs like huge ducks' feet.[8] At a later period he designed many helmets, provided with a leather mouthpiece to which a long tube, stiffened with hoops, was attached; the upper end was supported above water by a disk of cork.[9]

But easily visible apparatus of this sort was entirely unsuitable for Leonardo's present purpose. His new inventions, which made it possible to approach the enemy unseen, he shrouded in deep secrecy. The diving-dress which he now designed he intended to manufacture in his own house (*fatti cucire la veste in casa*), with the help of a simple artisan, "preferably a simpleton." This suit, so far as he describes it, consisted of a shirt of plate armour; trousers, which even contained a receptacle for urinating; a mask with glass panes fitted into it; and provision for connecting nose and mouth with a huge skin or bladder, stiffened with hoops, fastened to the diver's coat and kept off his breast by means of a semicircular iron ring, so as not to hamper his breathing. The skin with the air supply was to be bound on only when the diver was at sea, "so that your secret may not be disclosed," Leonardo reminds himself. This skin or bladder was, Leonardo expressly emphasized, to be emptied of air when the diver, weighted with bags of sand, dropped into the water; Leonardo adds that it can be blown up again under water, with two or three other bladders which the diver is to take with him, in order to be able to return to the surface (this idea was employed in the modern diving-apparatus devised by Hersika); Leonardo must therefore have invented a method of supplying air below water, perhaps a sinkable air chamber; this might be inferred from one of his drawings, showing a diver fully equipped on a large floating body, which he describes as "cork resting between the two waters." [10]

In 1535 a second attempt was made to raise the galleys in Lake

Nemi; a certain Maestro Guglielmo da Lorena had invented a diving-bell which could be provided with an air supply and yet have no visible connexion with the surface of the water. This William of Lorraine exacted an oath from all present that they would keep his invention a secret, and he took the secret with him into the grave. Leonardo too refused to give away his secret. "Tell nobody and you alone will be distinguished," he wrote, in an access, unusual in him, of inventor's egoism.[11] Normally he would be lavish in his descriptions of his inventions to all and sundry, but would gain no attention. In this case, however, he had a special reason for preserving secrecy. Some years later he explained: "How and why I do not describe my method of remaining under water, or how long I can stay without eating; and I do not publish or divulge these by reason of the evil nature of men, who would use them as means of murder at the bottom of the sea, by breaking the bottom of ships and sinking them together with the men in them. And although I will impart others, in those there is no danger, because the mouth of the breathing-tube is visible above the water, supported on bags or corks." [12]

For the first and the only time since he had placed his infinite inventiveness at the service of the human lust for power, Leonardo was troubled by the thought of the possible consequences of his invention. He had described the most terrible explosive shells with a feeling of satisfaction, and had drawn them as lovingly as if all that mattered was the artistic effect; his cool indications of the method of using the most murderous cannon suggest that it simply did not occur to him that death on blood-soaked battlefields was a horrible thing; but now he felt that he dared not describe a weapon which he claimed to be specially effective in naval fighting. It almost seems as if he felt that death at sea was more frightful than on trampled fields, that it was incomparably more cruel to sink a galley than to mow down serried ranks of soldiers. Or had he realized now what he had not felt so vividly before, the cruelty of men, the unbridled lust for killing which can fill man's evil nature?

He was concerned now, however, with a defensive war against a merciless aggressor, and with means of bringing a naval war to an end by a smashing blow—and also with putting to the test a

pet invention of his. On the same sheet [13] on which he drew his
secret diving-dress, he explained the intended method of sinking
enemy ships. The diver was to swim up to the ship unobserved and
bore a small hole in its hull, if possible at the end of a plank.
He then set a two-foot or three-foot frame over the hole, and fitted
into the frame a screw with prongs attached to it. The prongs
would open out as soon as the screw had been screwed into the
hole. The frame thus made fast had a big hoop hanging from it,
which gave the diver support as he went on boring until the ship
was leaking beyond repair. The air supply with which Leonardo
furnished the diver was calculated to last four hours. The divers
were not required to sink the whole Turkish fleet by themselves;
they were first to destroy the principal galleys, and then to turn
to the others; but meanwhile, under cover of the dark, when the
watch had made its round, a small vessel was to come unobserved
up to the galleys and fire explosive shells from a gun.

In these hasty notes [14] of last-minute preparations, Leonardo
gives no details of the "small vessel" which could get close under
the bows of the big galleys without being observed. An invention
of an earlier date, the date to which most of his studies in military
engineering belong, is described by Leonardo as "a ship to be used
to sink another ship." [15] This resembled a huge round shield, with
room in its interior for one person in a crouching position. (A
sketch on a sheet now at Windsor shows this more plainly.) Above
his head is a raised round headpiece, for closing down like a lid.
This vessel could be submerged; as soon as its occupant entered
it, it sank into the water to the level of the raised part in the middle. Leonardo surrounded this invention of a primitive submarine
with further mystery; even in notes protected from indiscretions
by his right-to-left handwriting, he indicates its functions in an
enigmatic manner. "Remember before getting in and closing down
to push out the l——t," he wrote; the two letters stood for *alito*,
the air supply, obtained by a method, not explained, which Leonardo used for his divers' suits and proposed to provide for the
submergible vessel. Was Leonardo not the only person who dreamed
of a submarine, or did the fame of his mysterious inventions spread
beyond the boundaries of Italy? In any case Francis Bacon, in mentioning a diving-bell in his *Novum Organum,* writes that he has

heard also of the remarkable invention of a small vessel that could move under water for a time.

Having thus dealt with the preliminaries, Leonardo hints in cryptic notes at his plan of attack on the Turkish fleet. He would secretly arrange for the help of specially reliable officers to wait on shore for the completion of the work of destruction, provided with plenty of chains in order to capture the Turks as they swam in. He showed an unusual business sense at this time; perhaps he had a practical-minded adviser at his side: he would make sure in advance that he should be properly remunerated in the event of the enterprise being successful: "But first make an agreement in writing for one-half of the prize money to be yours without deduction." The man to whom he intended to entrust the financial management of the whole enterprise was Alvise Manenti, the Venetian ambassador to the Sublime Porte, who would be bound to bear a strong grudge against the Turks on account of the failure of his mission: "Let the delivery of the prisoners be in charge of Maneto and the payment made to Maneto—that is, of the said prize money." In his excitement over the adventurous plan he took success for granted—*guastero il porto!* "I shall devastate the harbour!" In imagination he heard already the shout of warning to the Turks: "If you do not surrender within four hours, you will be sent to the bottom!" Ideas came to him thick and fast, and he committed them excitedly to paper. He felt sure of victory, and of his huge reward and of immortal fame. He imagined himself sounding the horn he would take with him, in order to announce to the waiting throng that he had succeeded; far across the water sounded the shout of exultation that announced to Venice the destruction of the barbarians.

This foretaste of triumph was destined to remain unrealized. Did unforeseen obstacles crop up at the critical moment, did the final tests fail, did some technical error wreck the scheme? Not another word does Leonardo give to this Venetian enterprise; no contemporary report makes any mention of it; only Leonardo's circumstantial notes, his reports of journeys in the Isonzo region, evidencing his contact with the Venetian government, the names he mentions, and the drawings of the instruments he made, show that this was no mere dream, no new story of imagined disasters

The Virgin with Saint Anne

Niccolò Machiavelli. Artist unknown

elaborated in his studio. This frustrated plan of battle against the Crescent is one of the most mysterious episodes in Leonardo's life, throwing a vague and baffling light on the short period that lay between his departure from Mantua and his return to his native city.

3

A draft on his account with Santa Maria Novella shows that he reached Florence at the end of April 1500. It was sixteen years since he had left the city. He was now forty-eight years old, and still had the erectness and the great muscular strength of his youth. But his face had aged prematurely: the eyes lay deep in their sockets, surrounded by a network of fine wrinkles that reached up to the temples. The cold glance from his blue eyes was as penetrating as ever, but his vision had lost much of its keenness, and he now wore glasses. His nose, with its straight, strong bridge, had become long and pointed; two deep creases ran from the nostrils over the sunken cheeks, which were well covered by his fair, reddish beard. The powerful forehead turned sharply back over the deeply embedded temples, past which the thinning hair flowed down in long, wavy locks. Thus was Leonardo painted in profile toward the end of his time in Milan by a Lombard artist, probably his former partner Ambrogio de Predis. The painter had given him the dignity of age and the dignity of wisdom and already, so far as his resources permitted, an element of the legendary, as though this were no man of ordinary flesh and blood but a prophet or magician.

And a magician, familiar and yet aloof, was what Leonardo seemed to his fellow-countrymen to be. His clothes helped to heighten the impression of unusualness. They were carefully tended, and his whole exterior was carefully tended, with almost pedantic particularity, and with complete indifference to fashion. Leonardo had often made fun of the follies of fashion, and in his *Treatise on Painting* he had placed on record all the excesses he had observed. He recalled from the days of his childhood the universal pinking or scalloping, on clothes and caps and shoes, as though cocks' combs were starting out of everything sewn; he recalled the fashion of clothes that were so tight that "they burst on many people," and shoes so tight that "the toes were covered all over with corns"; he recalled the next fashion after this, of jerkins that went up so high that they reached above the head, and the next of dresses that were so scanty that they scarcely covered the shoulders. At a time when cloaks were being worn long and with many folds, so that, as Leonardo relates, men went about with their arms full of cloth in order not to tread on the hems, he wore short coats reaching only just to his knee. They were usually of pink cloth, which made his fresh complexion look fresher still and his carefully twisted moustache and long waving beard look a still brighter auburn.

Even stranger than his appearance, in the eyes of his compatriots, was his manner of living. When, many years later, Giorgio Vasari came to Florence in eager search of all available recollections of Leonardo, and collected the impressions which Florentines were able to give him, he obtained the picture of a man who had lived the careless life of a great nobleman: "Although he had next to nothing to live on and did little work, he always kept servants and horses, in which he took great pleasure." Nowhere did Leonardo's style of living create more surprise than in busy, hustling Florence. His cheerful leisureliness contrasted violently with the restlessness of his compatriots; to men who were always in a hurry about something, and continually talking of their work and plans and anxieties, his resolute drifting seemed simple idleness. Least of all could they understand his ostentatious indifference to the financial yield of his work; years afterwards they still remembered in talking to Vasari how imprudent and extravagant Leonardo had been in money matters, how he would maintain as his guest any friend who was able to capture his interest for a while, and how on one occasion, when his fee was offered in small change, he rejected it with the gesture of a *grand seigneur,* proudly declaring that he did not paint for pence.

The legend of his extravagant liberality stuck to Leonardo; the careful Florentines knew nothing of his close resemblance to themselves in his style of living, the meticulous care with which he administered his meagre budget, the note he took, just like the small

shopkeeper round the corner, of any small sum lent, and the insistence with which he demanded its return. A similar legend, perhaps deliberately fostered by Leonardo himself, was that of his
grand style of living. Probably he was rarely able to call his own
any of the horses in which he took such pleasure. No expenditure
on oats is to be found in his endless domestic accounts, except
when he was on a journey. The talk of his supposed hospitality can
scarcely have had any more substantial basis; usually he was himself in search of food and shelter, himself the guest of other people.

When he returned to Florence after his long absence, he had
first to look around for a roof over his head. He had left the city
because of the confusion of his family circumstances; on his return
he found still worse confusion. Ser Piero's third wife had died a
few years after Leonardo left Florence. The draft of a letter, the
only extant fragment of any correspondence between father and
son, mentions a letter received recently from the father, which
"brought me within its small compass joy and sorrow, joy because
I learned of your good health, for which I thank God, and sorrow,
because I learned of your misfortune." [16] This misfortune was
probably the death of Leonardo's stepmother. But it did not upset
Ser Piero's indestructible vitality. He was now sixty years old,
and he took as his fourth wife a girl of barely twenty-five, of good
family, Lucrezia di Guglielmo Cortigiani. Lucrezia, the impover-
ished orphan of a notary, probably saw in her marriage with this
much older man a means of escape from her family's financial
troubles. But Ser Piero still had at sixty the temperament and the
vigour of his youth; his young wife brought a child into the world
almost year by year, and when Leonardo came to Florence five little ones were romping in the house in the Via Ghibellina, in which
the sons from the third marriage were growing up; and a sixth
baby was expected shortly. There was no room for Leonardo in
his father's home.

His total savings, deposited with Santa Maria Novella, the loan
institution in which his father and grandfather had placed their
assets, amounted to a sum which under present-day conditions
would be about thirty thousand gold lire. This capital, the whole
yield of many years' hard work, Leonardo was determined not to
touch except in case of emergency, and he soon looked round him

for opportunities of earning. If he did not return from his wanderings a rich man, he brought with him at least an unchallenged fame, which smoothed the way for him even in his critical, sceptical native city. So great was his fame that a younger fellow-artist, Filippino Lippi, who had concluded an agreement with the monks of the order of the Servites for an altarpiece, withdrew at once when Leonardo, in the course of conversation, mentioned that he would have been glad to undertake a commission of that sort. The Servites hastened to conclude an agreement with Leonardo; they offered him board and lodging in the monastery, and so great was their eagerness that they agreed also to look after his inseparable companion Salai. After his months of unsettled existence, the monastery walls enfolded Leonardo comfortingly in their quiet seclusion.

The monastery with its silent occupants was an island of peace for him; freed from the cares of existence, he plunged into his work—his own work. As though all that had happened had been wiped out, and he were back in his studio in Milan, he returned to his interrupted geometrical studies, forgetting all about the commission which had procured him the monks' hospitality. Almost it seemed as if he meant to exact compensation for the months that had been wasted on men and events, to make up for his mistake in playing a part in the history of his times.

So absolutely did he shut himself off from the outer world that not a word reached his cell of the excitement that surged through the streets of Florence. The firebrand Cesare Borgia had risen on the political horizon and threatened to set the whole country aflame. He had driven out hereditary princes and captured impregnable fortresses, and was steadily closing in on Florence. There was universal agitation; every Florentine who regarded himself as a statesman and a coming ruler published abroad his plans for saving the state, denounced the existing confusion and the decay of commerce and industry, and prophesied the downfall of civilization. Meanwhile Leonardo occupied himself with planimetrical transformations, and helped his friend Fra Luca Pacioli, who had come with him to Florence, in his edition of Euclid's *Elements*. Three lines written by Leonardo as introduction to the *De Divina Proportione,* which was ultimately printed in 1509, reveal his en-

Saint Anne (detail from the Virgin with Saint Anne)

thusiasm for the "sweet fruit" of study which "nourishes the intellect" of the philosopher:

El dolce fructo vago e si diletto
costrinse già i philosophi a cercare
causa di noi per pasciar l'intelletto.

The Servites found their expectations disappointed. They had imagined that with Leonardo actually living in their monastery they would be better able to watch over the progress of his work, but they had had no idea of the difficulty of overcoming his bland imperturbability, of the uselessness of hints and suggestions, and of the passive resistance he could offer to a task which he regarded as a troublesome interruption of his studies. A considerable time elapsed before their loud complaints at last penetrated to his notice. Then he took up the commissioned work, an altarpiece for the church of the Annunciation.

He chose as the most suitable theme that of the Virgin with Saint Anne, a theme which had already occupied him at Milan. His earlier design, which he had brought with him, and which has been preserved in the cartoon in the Royal Academy, is similar in style and feeling to the *Madonna of the Rocks*. The juxtaposition of the women's heads seemed to Leonardo at that earlier period to be a useful means of heightening the effect, like a phrase repeated for clearness. At that time he still favoured the dialectical gesture of the raised forefinger, and still contented himself with the introduction of the diagonal, which rises above the back of Saint John and above the little benedictory arm of the Christ Child and terminates in the vertical of the Madonna's head. But for the creator of the *Last Supper* this design was no longer satisfactory. The theme of his new composition (which may be seen in the *Saint Anne* now in the Louvre) seems in its austerity almost to reflect his pleasure in the geometrical studies he was now pursuing. The group of three persons is built up as a steep pyramid, compressed into so narrow a space that Leonardo has had to resort to the unusual expedient of setting Mary on Saint Anne's lap. But his consummate knowledge of the human frame enables him to give the observer the impression that the expedient imposed on the artist was freely adopted and the natural course.

Saint Anne's head thus occupies the space above the group. Her headcloth rises to a point which crowns the pyramid—the mathematician Leonardo has admitted no accidental element into his calculation. From her out-turned elbows a slant passes by the head of the Christ Child and along the back of the lamb to the base of the composition. The other slant runs down with equal severity past Saint Anne's shoulder, past the cloak which spreads out from the Virgin's thighs, and past the garment of the seated saint. The deep intersection of the diagonals in the interior of the picture is produced by Mary's extended arms as she holds the Child, who is pushing away from her. The flow of her outstretched arms is followed by the forward bend of her head; the parallels of the two women's legs share in the movement on the left of the picture; they are emphasized on the right by the little arm of the Christ Child and even by the animal's curling tail, for nothing in the work is arbitrary and nothing is irrelevant. The movement from left to right is balanced by the leftward movement of Saint Anne's bent arm, the parallels of the Madonna's profile, the downward-flowing lines of the shoulders, and the bright folds of the garments. Then the landscape plays its part, taking up the bend of the Madonna's head, and rising from left to right to the dark, jagged silhouette of the tree, while the mountain peaks in the background emerge from the undulating valley to form a cone similar to that of the Holy Family.

It is the most carefully considered, the most balanced, one might almost say the most sophistical of Leonardo's compositions, and in the hand of any other painter it would have become a dry, formal work, a lifeless geometrical design. But Leonardo made human beings of flesh and blood, and women's bodies abounding in vitality, with soft, velvety shoulders and full throats in which the very breathing is manifest. The Madonna's long, lustrous eyes are full of the tenderness of a lover; a smile of almost swooning self-surrender hovers round her mouth; and her comely neck droops as though bent under the fervour of her devotion.

In defiance alike of tradition and of probability, Leonardo represents the mother of Mary as a woman of Mary's own age. Above the woman who is lavishing her love, Saint Anne's glance from beneath her arched eyelids seems to send out an imperceptible radi-

ance. Her face is dominated by a broadly arched forehead with
eye-sockets that are almost rectangular, as though the strength of
these broad surfaces were needed to calm the emotion of the smile
that passes through flitting shadows to melt away in the outline of
the cheeks that curve down to the pointed chin. Leonardo's geometrical design seems to exist only to lead to this smile, to allow it
to develop in solitude, a mystery raised aloft like a precious object.
It is a smile entirely of this world, ripened beyond devotion, a disturbing smile, working on the senses, a smile of comprehension,
full of indulgence for self-effacing womanhood, a smile of self-
preservation, heavy with disappointments overcome, a smile that
has left pain and happiness behind it, a triumphant smile that
knows the beginning and the end of all feeling, a smile that is
wise and yet powerless, with the impotence of experience that cannot be communicated.

Leonardo has himself described the effect this unsaintly smile
he gave his saints could have: "I have had the experience of making a picture representing something holy, which has been acquired by someone who fell in love with it, and desired to remove
the attributes of saintliness so as to be able to kiss it without fear.
But in the end conscience overcame desire, and the enamoured
person found himself compelled to remove the picture from his
house." [17] This saint who so disturbed a lover of art must have
smiled like Saint Anne; but if anyone who was at peace with himself and with the world, and firmly anchored in his faith, stood
before the picture, it would be a lovely, devout woman's face that
bent over him, with the promise of heavenly blessedness. It was
similarly possible to invest this Virgin and Saint Anne with whatever mystical ideas were in the observer's own mind. A learned
monk, the vice-general of the Carmelite order, Pietro da Novellara,
discovered in the unfinished cartoon when he saw it a profound
theological meaning: he thought that Leonardo intended the smiling saint to embody the triumph of the Church; for the lamb
which the Christ Child is trying to reach signifies his passion, and
while the Holy Virgin, in her mother's love and compassion, wants
to preserve her Child from his hard destiny, Saint Anne, the symbol of the Church, holds her daughter back, that Christ's passion
may be fulfilled.

The cartoon was finished about Easter 1501. The Servite brothers were overwhelmed by the design; they had forgotten their complaints, and no longer cared what had been the cost of maintaining Leonardo and his attendants, his *famiglia*. The Florentine artists looked in amazement at the immense *tour de force* of the composition, the filling of a narrow space with life-sized figures; and men and women of the people, old men and children, stood before the picture and found it a miracle: it had something to say to each one of them, for each one it was a personal experience. In their pride in the cartoon the Servites allowed the public to view it for a short period, and for two days all Florence passed by it; it was a procession, said Vasari years later, like those on high feast days of the Church. Leonardo had now awakened an enthusiastic response in his native city, that sudden loud chorus of unanimous praise into which a critical public can break, once its allegiance has been won.

The only one who no longer had any feeling for the picture, who had lost interest in it at the moment of its completion, was Leonardo himself. "Leonardo has lost all patience with the brush," wrote Pietro da Novellara to Isabella d'Este, "and is now working entirely at geometry." The margravine of Mantua had been waiting for more than a year for the portrait Leonardo was to have painted from the sketch he had taken with him. Now she had heard that he was in Florence and at work on a new picture, and she had accordingly sent to the vice-general of the Carmelites one of those letters in which she was so skilled, asking him to inquire as to what Leonardo was doing in Florence, the work on which he was engaged, and the length of time he would be staying in the city; and, with a discretion unusual in her, she had requested the vice-general, who was wholly at her service, to sound Leonardo cautiously, "as if on your own account," as to his readiness to paint a picture, any picture, for her studio, and when it would be convenient for him to do it. If he should prove obdurate, *renitente*— her woman's instinct had warned her to expect that he would —then Novellara must do his best to get at least a Madonna from him, "of his own devout, sweet sort."

"Leonardo, from what I hear, seems to be leading a very desultory, unsettled life, living for the day's whim," replied Novellara. The master was sick of painting and immersed in his geometrical studies; he had set his assistants to paint two portraits, to which he put his own hand only occasionally. All this the vice-general knew merely from hearsay; but he took his commission seriously. He made the acquaintance of Salai, and asked him about his employer; and in Easter week he was taken by a friend to visit Leonardo himself. He found that the rumours he had heard were not exaggerated. Leonardo's mathematical studies had so destroyed his interest in painting that he could not bring himself to take up the brush— *"non può patire il pennello."* But the priest was famous for his eloquence, and he brought all his persuasiveness to bear in Isabella's interest. All he could get, however, from Leonardo was the thoroughly non-committal statement that he would give the margravine preference over everyone else if he could get free from his obligations to the king of France without sacrificing the king's goodwill.

4

At the moment when Leonardo evaded Isabella's pressure with this unblushing subterfuge, his commitments to the king of France were of the vaguest and his assurance of the king's goodwill as definite as could be. The first meeting between Lodovico Sforza's court painter and the new lord of Milan took place at the time of Louis's triumphal entry into Milan in the late autumn of 1499. The conqueror regarded the city as his hereditary property by virtue of the family claims he had asserted, and had an inventory made at once of all the splendours of his new possession; and very soon he went with the gentlemen of his court to the refectory of Santa Maria delle Grazie in order to see the *Last Supper*. The king, a frail man with angular shoulders and sunken breast, put on all the airs of a conqueror, but he was far from looking his part. His small, narrow head was supported by a lean neck which seemed yet more haggard because of his great protruding Adam's apple. The outline of his thin, narrow-browed face descended past the bony cheeks to a pointed chin, and from these constricted surfaces the great bulging eyes and the wide twisted mouth stood out with all the more prominence.

But this man of such unkingly presence was the son of a prince who was also a poet of fine sensibility, and who amid the bitterness of exile had preserved all his warm humanity. As Louis XII looked at the *Last Supper* his thick lips parted in a smile almost of voluptuousness; for his enthusiasm was accompanied by the sensuous pleasure of those who have a true feeling for art. Leonardo's masterpiece so fired King Louis with desire—*"cujus operis libidine adeo accensum Ludovicum regem ferunt,"* writes Paolo Giovio, who may as a boy have been told the story—that Louis raised his long arm and with his narrow, childish hand traced a great rectangle in the air, asking those round him whether the fresco could not be removed from the wall and taken to France, at any cost, even if it meant pulling down the refectory.

One of the members of the king's entourage, Florimond Robertet, was a man of sudden decisions, and while Louis was considering his impossible plan Robertet went in search of the great painter. Robertet was in the habit of confining himself to the attainable but taking the shortest way to get it. He was of middle-class origin, and had made his way by setting out in one post after another to acquire the knowledge that would make him indispensable. He spoke English, German, Italian, and Spanish. His career at court had begun when he became secretary to the queen, Anne of Brittany; he accompanied Charles VIII on the king's Italian expedition, and with his unlimited capacity for work and his gift of keeping on good terms with whoever were in favour at court he won the confidence of Louis XII, who made him his secretary of state. Robertet as a merchant's son had recognized early in his career the strength of the new power which was to make an end of the privileges of the nobles as the ruling class. He exacted the full price of his influence—took tips, *mancia,* said the Italian representatives at the French court—and by marrying into the famous banking family of the Gaillards he secured the financial power which placed him on an equality with the foremost in the country.

In that Easter week of the year 1501 in which Pietro da Novellara looked with curiosity round Leonardo's studio, he saw there an actually finished little painting which was just the sort of thing that Isabella wanted, a Madonna full of piety and charm. The picture had been painted for the secretary of state to the king of France.

It was one of those everyday scenes which at once appeal to any observer, an intimate scene such as every happy mother may provide as she plays with her child. The Virgin was trying to reach some coils of yarn, to spool them, but the Child, in playful mood, was pawing with his little feet in her workbasket and had clutched laughingly at the yarn-winder, which his mother was vainly trying to get out of his little fist. But over this placid scene, full of child laughter and mother-love, there hung already the sacred sign of martyrdom, the cross of the yarn-winder, like a menacing shadow.

The picture has disappeared, but it has left its bright trace in pupils' copies, and in variants and imitations by later artists, showing the strong impression it made on contemporaries; it was destined to gain distant friends and admirers for Leonardo, and to exert an influence over his destiny of which he could have had no idea at the time.

Now, however, another man sought him out—Cesare Borgia. The two had met before, at Milan, at the time when King Louis XII entered the city under his golden fur-lined canopy, suppressing a smile of gratification at the magnificence of the procession which had come to welcome him. Dukes and cardinals, ambassadors and army commanders, Milanese dignitaries and French barons had competed in the display of their splendour in this procession; each reigning prince had had one hundred and fifty horsemen in his cavalcade; but the most magnificent of all had been the new duke of Valentinois, duke by the grace of the king of France— Cesare Borgia. His train had aroused astonishment as they rode in velvet clothes on horses caparisoned in gold and silver. The glare from the October sun, which seemed to be pouring forth additional radiance in honour of Louis XII, lit up the white damask that lay loosely round Cesare's broad shoulders, and made the rings sparkle on the delicate fingers of his hands as he rested them swaggeringly on his narrow hips. A black cap, with a white feather

drooping over its pearl-embroidered rim, shaded his high and narrow forehead and the bold upturned eyebrows above his strangely
wide-open eyes. A disfiguring disease had left its traces on his fair
skin and had upset the harmony of his fine, regular features; only
his mouth seemed to have escaped, a large mouth with a well-
arched upper lip that closed firmly on the short under lip, as in
one who was used to keeping his own counsel. These deep red lips,
left free by the auburn beard, and the dark, smouldering gaze that
seemed to fill the eyes, dominated the disfigured face. The gaze was
one that fastened resolutely on its object, seized and held it, a gaze
that never forgot and was never forgotten.

Cesare Borgia had no feeling whatever for art, but he knew the
value of enthusiasm when a powerful monarch lavished it on a
picture, and since the day when Louis XII had so openly admired
the *Last Supper* the name of Leonardo da Vinci had been impressed on Cesare's retentive memory. Three years after that meeting, in the spring or summer of 1502, he invited Leonardo to enter
his service as architect and military engineer. Machiavelli said of
Cesare Borgia that he knew better than any other man how to win
men's allegiance; and Leonardo did not withstand his attraction.
Yet at that time Leonardo had abandoned art and resolutely shut
himself off from men's society for the sake of the most abstract of
all sciences. It seemed a strange freak of destiny that led him to
serve a man of violence, one regarded in his own day and ever
since as the most insatiable schemer of all in an epoch of universal
greed for power.

Cesare Borgia was certainly the greatest adventurer of his epoch.
If he had been born in another clime and another age, he would
have been a robber knight, a navigator, a gold-digger, or in different circumstances a famous financier or great industrialist. His destiny had set him in what was a place apart even in his own time—
in the status of a papal bastard. This gave him eminence without
dignity of right, and yielded vast opportunities not entirely in
keeping with his true position. Moreover, his destiny had brought
him into the world as a younger son, and, born man of action and
fighter though he was, had invested him only with the indirect
spiritual power, reserving the secular power for his brother. A
hatred of society awoke very early in Cesare; perhaps he was born

with it—the hatred felt by the handicapped, the disinherited, the born rebel.

Cesare's hot-blooded father Rodrigo Borgia was a man of a sensuality that knew no inhibitions; yet he had no less sincere a regard for his high office than for his mistresses and his children, and in his most arbitrary excesses and his wildest outrages against morality he retained the human feelings of the ordinary man. Cesare was of a different type. He was no battlefield of incalculable emotions; his make-up was more deliberate—a gloomy, insane ambition, envy without satisfaction in possession, jealousy without the capacity for love. His most ruthless murders were committed with cold deliberation, his most execrated betrayals were mere magnifications of a petty trickiness. He attacked only the weak and defenceless, and if he mixed a poison or sent his ruffians in pursuit of their quarry it was after careful consideration of the consequences and without advancing a step beyond the limits of assured immunity for himself. In one of his outbursts of rage he wounded an attendant so close to the Pope that the man's blood splashed the pontiff's robes; but even in his most furious outburst he maintained sufficient self-control to make sure that there was none who would bear witness against him, or none that could not be got rid of.

He took credit for every success as of his own achieving, and blamed himself for every failure. The death of the Pope brought him sudden disaster, but he attributed his misfortune to his own lack of foresight, to a flaw in his calculations; he agreed with Machiavelli that he should have provided against everything, even against the chance of his own serious illness coming at the moment of his father's death. His egoism was completely unemotional; this man, powerful as his heraldic device, the bull of the Borgias, never gave himself up to a passion. He arranged orgies in the Vatican for the satisfaction of his father's senile lusts; he brought back a harem from his conquering march on Capua; but he knew only the cold and cynical sensuality of a despiser of humanity, only the joyless satisfaction of gratified covetousness. The gossip of his day described him as the lover of his sister and pursuer also of his sister-in-law, the frivolous and dissipated Donna Sancia; but never was Cesare genuinely drawn to any woman; even if the gossip was

well founded, his attachment to Lucrezia was probably only the
liking of the gamester for the highest stake he could play.

Even when he attained power Cesare Borgia continued to be
filled with resentment for the past. He was full of morose animosity against the powerful rulers whose favour he courted, and
against the ruling class to which he already belonged. His style of
living was that of the newly rich, ostentatious, pushing, sometimes
on the verge of the ridiculous. He kept meticulously to the rules
of Spanish etiquette, with the care of a plebeian watching his manners, accepting boredom as the price of his magnificence. He had
no feeling whatever for art, but surrounded himself with poets,
painters, and musicians, because his position required it. He was
never entirely at ease in his surroundings. Whenever he could escape from the social burden he had imposed on himself, he would
mix with the common people, wrestling with a soldier or felling a
bull with a single blow. He considered himself to be possessed of
the virtues of a ruler, and certain things he did possess: exceptional organizing and administrative ability, knowledge of the
needs of the common people, and a rare capacity for making use of
men of talent as items in his calculations.

One such item was Leonardo da Vinci.

5

By the beginning of 1502 Cesare had gained by force or fraud so
much territory in Italy, from Piombino in the west to Cesena and
its port on the Adriatic, and had made himself so secure in his hold
of the Romagna, that he was in a position to consider the planning
of fortifications and the creation of a capital worthy of himself
at Cesena. The Pope, who told all who would give ear that it had
once been prophesied to him that he would become Pope and
would have a king as his son, threw himself with enthusiasm into
plans for the building up of Cesare's future kingdom. The Mantuan minister at Rome listened as the Pope told enthusiastically
of the future splendour of the Romagna, of a new quarter in
Cesena round a castle that was to spring up almost by magic, of a

line of splendid palaces reaching from Cesena to Porto Cesenatico, and of a chain of fortresses that would make the new state impregnable.

Leonardo da Vinci arrived at Piombino in May 1502. The town was still full of the story of the Pope's visit: Alexander VI had made a point of personally inspecting Cesare's possession, and had travelled thither with all the pomp of Christ's Vicar, accompanied by cardinals and by his choir, and preceded by the *sedia gestatoria,* the symbol of his high office. The tough old man, who had now worn the tiara for more than nine years and declared that he meant to wear it for another nine, felt no diffidence about enjoying the pleasures of this world, and the people of Piombino talked still of the open-air ball for which Cesare had the most handsome women and girls of the district dressed in cloth of gold. Those who had been present particularly remembered the strange spectacle of the holy father looking on, with his ruddy face and sparkling eyes, at the dancing, a lascivious smile playing round his lips as he hummed softly to himself and wagged his big head in time with the music.

This memorable visit left a tangible trace in the immediate starting of work on various buildings and on the draining of the marshes that surrounded the town. Leonardo had drawn up an ambitious plan of reclamation, providing for a network of ditches emptying into two canals, one running round the marshes and the other crossing through them, to carry the water from the marshland into the sea. "The way to drain the swamp of Piombino," he wrote under his drawing for this scheme.

At this time Cesare Borgia was still in Rome, whither he had accompanied his father on his return; and macabre stories were being whispered coupling the rumour of a ghastly crime with Cesare's name. One day during Leonardo's stay in Rome the sodden corpse of the eighteen-year-old Astorre Manfredi (the blond, handsome lord of Faenza), pierced again and again by daggers, was brought out of the Tiber. Astorre had placed his realm and his own fate in Cesare's hands, and, lulled into security by Cesare's promises, had imagined himself safe in Rome. But he was too popular for Cesare to spare him. His terrible death shocked even that age of habitual violence. The murderer was named only in whis-

pers, for a Roman who had talked too loudly of Cesare's atrocities
was seized by the duke's bravoes, who hacked off their victim's
right arm and tore out his tongue. But it was not only out of fear
that the people of Piombino spoke little of this; these simple people
knew their duke only as a good and just ruler, who had placed no
foreigners but only good fellow-citizens of theirs in his service, who
respected their customs and usages, and who was now drying the
swamp that spread disease through the air with its poisonous stench.

If the rumours from Rome reached Leonardo at all, they were
drowned by the wash of the sea, on which he was concentrating his
whole mind, regardless of the world around him. He looked at the
waves as they rolled in from farther than eye could see, to break
at last on the beach. Many years later he recalled these waves, with
their broad snow-white crests. "The wave of the sea at Piombino," he wrote, "is all foaming water." At Piombino he watched
a violent springtime storm; he stood in the streaming rain by the
edge of the sea; he saw the rain pelting the fishing-boats while the
fierce wind roared round him, uprooting trees and carrying them
through the air. He saw the waves rise high like a wall of glass and
then plunge in swirling eddies. These hours passed amid the uproar of the elements impressed themselves deeply on his memory,
and finally, after many years, were the basis of his catastrophic
story of the Deluge.

It was not only the æsthetic pleasure in the natural forces unleashed that kept Leonardo by the seashore; he was beginning to
ask what were the forces that drove forward these vast masses of
water and what were the laws that governed ebb and flow. A sketch
of the breakers which he marked "drawn by the sea at Piombino"
is accompanied by a number of remarks on the clash and retire-
ment of waves.

But Cesare Borgia's military engineer had no time to go into
these problems. He soon left Piombino, travelling on by quick
stages. He scarcely had time to see the sights at Siena; his glance
dwelt awhile on the Mangia tower of the communal palace, which
dominates the hilly town; and he listened to the high tones of the
bells in the famous clock-tower. The only notes he made were reflections on the mechanism of the bells and "the place of the attachment of the clapper." [18]

When he reached the end of his journey, at the gates of Arezzo, he was in the camp of the bitterest enemy of his native city, Vitellozzo Vitelli. Vitelli had entered the service of Cesare Borgia as a condottiere, in order to avenge the death of his brother, who while in the service of the Florentine state had been accused of treason and executed. At the beginning of June the citizens of Arezzo had revolted against Florentine rule, and Vitellozzo had hastened to their aid. Leonardo joined his troops as they marched against the Tuscan army, and drew the map of the terrain which Vitellozzo required for his military operations. He completed the map with special care, the advice Toscanelli had given him in his early youth running in his mind; he hatched in the elevations, traced the fine arabesques of the streams, touched up the towns with warm sienna, lit up the wooded hills with emerald-green, and tinted the lakes a brilliant blue, taking pleasure in the work; not for a moment does he seem to have been disturbed by the thought that foreign soldiers were to march along the lines of white he had left for the roads of Tuscany, to fight his own compatriots.

The streets of Arezzo were thronged with an excited populace that shouted "Freedom! Freedom!" as Vitellozzo's troops marched in; *"Palle! Palle!"* answered occasional groups of supporters of the Medici. The gonfaloniere listened in the palace of the Priori to the tramp of the horses' hoofs, and wept for joy at the approach of the liberator. But the garrison remained faithful to the republic, and defended the citadel. Vitellozzo announced through a trumpeter that he would massacre the troops to the last man if they did not surrender within two days; Leonardo designed gabions for filling with earth for siege operations, and prepared a special mixture of blasting-powder.

A fortnight later the fortress surrendered; and all Italy was stirred to its depths. The Florentines were panic-stricken; they saw Cesare Borgia already at their gates. They turned to the king of France for aid, and found an ally in Charles d'Amboise, lord of Chaumont, the regent of Milan, who warned the king of the growing power of the duke of Valentinois, and advised him to send French troops to protect Florence, which he did. Cesare Borgia avoided a direct conflict with France by dissociating himself from his captains and declaring that Arezzo had been attacked without his authority. Vitellozzo, however, continued his campaign of vengeance against Florence. He marched against San Sepolcro and after a short struggle captured the town. In the midst of the thunder of cannon and the crumbling of the town's walls, Leonardo recalled that there was a manuscript in the town which Vitellozzo had promised to procure for him, and he wrote, as calmly as if he were sitting in his study: "Borges" (he meant Antonio Boyer, cardinal archbishop of Bourges) "will procure for you the Archimedes which was in the possession of the bishop of Padua, and Vitellozzo the manuscript which was in Borgo di San Sepolcro." [19]

While his captains were growling that he had left them in the lurch, Cesare Borgia had won a new realm by an outrageous trick —the duchy of Urbino. He had brought to bear his strongest weapon, more dangerous than the notorious white poison of the Borgias, his plausibility. The frightful end of Astorre Manfredi was still fresh in men's memory; but the weak Guidobaldo da Montefeltro, duke of Urbino, succumbed as easily as the lord of Faenza had done to Cesare's sinister gift of persuasion, and supplied him with men and guns on Cesare's assurance that he needed them for a campaign against a neighbouring territory. Guidobaldo idly awaited the issue of this pretended campaign, while Cesare's army was marching into the duchy of Urbino. The duke escaped Astorre's fate only by precipitate flight. After great hardships he reached Mantua in the disguise of a peasant, still asking himself in perplexity how anyone could be guilty of such insidious treachery. "This happened," wrote Isabella d'Este to her sister-in-law, Clara de Montpensier, "because he trusted the duke of Valentinois, who made professions of such brotherly love as would have entrapped any honourable man with no fraud in his nature."

Even those who stood nearest to Cesare felt that his treachery to the duke of Urbino was unspeakably brutal and heartless. Lucrezia Borgia thought of the welcome Duke Guidobaldo and his beautiful wife Elisabetta had given her and her husband in Urbino on their honeymoon, six months earlier, how they had placed the ducal palace at their disposal and had been unremitting in attentions and hospitality. But she had long been compelled to condone her brother's acts of violence, and only commented wearily that she would have given fifty thousand ducats to remain in ig-

norance of this one. The people of Urbino had had an affectionate
regard for their intelligent, high-strung duke, and especially for
his brave and beautiful wife. Anxiously they waited to see their
new ruler, who had installed himself in the palace; but all they
saw was an occasional company of horsemen galloping along the
steep mountain roads, accompanied by spotted leopards and a pack
of wild hounds; and every rider wore the same dress and black cap
with a white feather in it—and rode masked.

The castle of Urbino towered up as though it had grown out of
the rock; the people boasted that it had as many rooms as there
are days in the year. Leonardo, looking up at its "savage" flight of
steps,[20] pondered on the cause of their impressiveness, and noted
the dimensions of the steps and the relative thickness of the plinth
course and the walls above it.[21] Cesare Borgia was aware of the
precariousness of his hold, and took the precaution of removing
to a place of security the art treasures which Federigo da Montefeltro had collected with such loving care. He sent the famous
tapestries, representing the Trojan war, as a present to the cardinal of Rouen, who watched his interests at the French court; the
splendid library, on which thirty-four copyists had been engaged
in the past, he transferred to Cesena. Leonardo watched as the
famous Latin, Greek, and Hebrew manuscripts, and the precious
works bound in gold brocade, were packed and loaded onto the
backs of mules, and wrote one of his enigmatic "prophecies": "Of
mules that carry great quantities of silver and gold; many treasures and great wealth will be found on four-footed animals, which
will carry them to various places." [22]

The thoughts of the margravine of Mantua also revolved round
the plundered palace of Urbino. She had welcomed the exiled
duke and duchess to Mantua, and wept as she held her sister-in-
law Elisabetta in her arms. Then she went to her *studiolo*, locked
herself in, and wrote to her brother, Cardinal Ippolito d'Este, telling him that there were two ancient sculptures, a little marble
Venus and a Cupid, in the palace at Urbino, and asking him, as
the duke of Valentinois had no great interest in antiquities, to use
his influence with the duke to induce him to send her these two
works of art, and she would regard it as the greatest favour anyone
could do her. Cesare Borgia, the parvenu prince, was already try-

ing to arrange an alliance with the Gonzagas by betrothing his little daughter to Isabella's son, and he hastened to fulfil Isabella's wish. The little Venus and the Cupid (this was probably Michelangelo's spurious antique) were sent to the margravine; and even after Cesare's fall and Guidobaldo's return to Urbino she refused to return them to their rightful owner.

On the same day on which Isabella forgot family sorrows and her own cares in peaceful dreaming of her guests' treasures, Leonardo was no less peacefully strolling through the streets of Urbino, watching the pigeons plunge through the deep blue of the summer sky as swimmers plunge into the sea. He made a note of this hour of contemplation: "The dovecot of Urbino, July 30, 1502." [23] On the following day he went on to Pesaro, the former seat of Giovanni Sforza, whom Cesare had found means of divorcing from Lucrezia when he had need of a more influential brother-in-law. The brief happiness of that marriage was still recalled by the arms of the Sforzas and the Borgias, peacefully coupled on the walls of the palace of the exiled ruler. Cesare had not removed the library from this palace—the library which Alessandro Sforza had accumulated at such expense. It contained every Latin translation from the Greek, all the astrological, medical, and cosmographic works of the day, all the poets, all the writings of the Fathers of the Church, in short, as Bistizzi wrote, "every book that is worth possessing." Leonardo was very specially interested in libraries, and, as though his travel on service through Cesare's forcibly united possessions were the journey of a savant for his own edification, he wrote on the cover of his notebook: "On August 1, 1502, the library at Pesaro."

On the same cover he also wrote a strange couplet which is to be found inscribed on the sarcophagus of the archbishop of Squillace in Otranto cathedral:

> *Decipimur votis et tempore fallimur et mors*
> *Deridet curas; anxia vita nihil.*

Had Leonardo travelled at some time as far as Otranto, was he perhaps already in the service of Cesare Borgia in the summer of 1501, when Cesare accompanied the French army in its march of conquest to Naples; or had he found the couplet quoted in one of the manuscripts at Pesaro, and did he copy it with a thought of his new employer's restless life, of the rise and fall of the mighty, of life's disillusionments and of death that grins at human cares? *Anxia vita nihil* was his summing up of his experience of the most eventful period of his life. In the midst of this urgent journey and this period crowded with events, he stopped as if of set purpose to dwell on restful paintings and collect quiet and harmonious impressions, as though he needed something to counterbalance the feverish activity which had been imposed on him.

6

At Rimini, Cesare was strengthening and extending the fortress, and the houses that stood in the line of fire were being pulled down. Stone masons and sawyers and navvies were busily at work, carts bumped over the rough roads, foremen were shouting, and the air was full of din and dust. After inspecting the work Leonardo strolled through the streets of Rimini in search of a quieter spot. He stood a long time in front of a fountain, listening to the crystal tones of the water as it crashed after rising in strands of liquid silver; he noticed that each jet had its own individual tone, and that these tones blended musically, and this was the only impression of Rimini that he found worth recording: "Make a harmony with various jets of falling water like those you saw in the fountains of Rimini, those you saw on August 8, 1502."

When he wrote that, did he not know the conclusion to which all Italy had jumped—that Cesare Borgia's rule was nearing its end? Louis XII had reached Milan at the end of July on his way to defend his Neapolitan possession against the Spaniards; and the princes whom Cesare had driven from their lands besieged him with their complaints. Every rumour of Cesare's atrocities was brought to him, every tongue was loosed to describe this devil in human shape, who was now said to have murdered his own brother. Isabella d'Este warned her husband, who was then in Milan, to be cautious in speaking of Cesare, and to be careful what he ate and drank, "for a man who is capable of lifting his hand

against men of his own flesh and blood is capable of anything."
Gradually Louis himself grew suspicious. He advised Duke Guidobaldo not to abandon Urbino, of which Cesare was trying to legit-
imize his hold by the offer to Guidobaldo of a cardinal's hat; he
advised the Gonzagas not to betroth their son with Cesare's daughter, for, he said to their envoy: "God knows what may come; it is
impossible to trust Valentino's word or deed." All Italy breathed
more freely at this; for Cesare's power was built upon that of the
king of France, and if Louis XII withdrew his favour Cesare's
realm would collapse like a card castle. "The French now regard
the Pope as their adversary!" said the Venetians exultantly; they
had been giving shelter to all Cesare's victims who came to them.

Cesare, to all appearance entirely unaware of the peril in which
he stood, spent the first week of August at his sister's bedside; she
had brought into the world a still-born child. He held her fever-
stricken body in his strong arms until the physicians had bled her,
and he did not release her from his hold until a faint sign of life
returned to her pale, drawn face. Then he rushed to Milan for the
critical meeting with Louis. He sped through the Porta Romana
at dusk, and ran unexpectedly into the arms of the king as Louis
was leaving Trivulzio's quarters. His dark face lit up at once with
an innocent, trusting, genial smile; he addressed Louis with the
grave courtesy which was a legacy from his priestly career—and immediately there was an end of all the king's intended reproaches,
all his doubts and suspicions; Louis embraced Cesare like a long-
lost brother. When they reached the castle he gave him a room
next his own. At the evening meal he sent Cesare food from his
own table. He went himself in his nightshirt to make sure that his
guest had everything he wanted; he sent his servants on one errand
after another; he returned again and again right into the night, as
though he had twinges of conscience on account of his past suspicions. The courtiers listening at the door whispered to one another: "Never was guest so favoured." Cesare had made plain to
the king how necessary he and the Pope were to Louis in his Neapolitan enterprise, and how little the exiled princes could do for
him; and Cardinal d'Amboise, to whom Cesare had held out the
dazzling prospect of the papal tiara, solemnly nodded assent. Niccolò da Correggio, who collected every rumour that went round

the anteroom and took note of every reported gesture of the king, wrote to Isabella d'Este that Louis "could not have done more for a son or brother."

When Cesare went with his friend King Louis to Pavia, he felt sure enough of his power to start on the accomplishment of his most ambitious plans. It was from Pavia that he issued Leonardo's letter of authorization, attesting his official position; with his characteristic clearness Cesare Borgia instructed all his "deputies, castellans, captains, condottieri, officers, soldiers, and subordinates" to allow free passage to the bearer of the document, "the excellent and most beloved servant, Architect and Engineer General Leonardo da Vinci, who is commissioned by us to consider our places and fortresses in order that we may provide for them in accordance with their exigencies and his judgment." They were to give passage everywhere, free of all public payment, to him and his assistants and to permit them to see, measure, and form a good judgment of whatever they would. To this end labour was to be provided and every assistance, support, and facility given for which the engineer general might ask; every engineer was to get into touch with him and comply with his directions. And let no one presume to do the contrary if he were concerned "not to incur our indignation."

This unmistakable language smoothed the way for Leonardo wherever he went. Now he had the commissions for vast works of which he had long dreamed in vain; and he had at his back a ruler with the needed energy and authority to see that what he wanted was done. At Cesena, the capital of the Romagna, a new law court was to be built, the old government offices were to be remodelled in consonance with their new importance—and in the centre of the city a fountain was to capture the singing jets of water. But Cesare Borgia attached most importance to the development of Porto Cesenatico, which would assure him influence in the Adriatic; at present the port was slowly silting up. Leonardo proposed to connect the port with Cesena by a canal; in the plan he drew up for the construction of the canal he indicated the organization of his labour columns in the form of a pyramid. He drew a plan of the new quarter of the city, the *borgo integro* in which Alexander VI took so keen an interest. The plan showed the separate building plots, the layout of the streets, and the water conduits; the plan was complete on paper before a single house was built. Leonardo imagined the *borgo* as it would be when it was fully populated, with people who amid their daily tasks might forget essentials as people do, and he wrote on the margin of his plan: "Care must be taken that the tanks are kept full." [24] He arranged for the extension of the palace, and directed the work on the fortifications; he had the bastions placed well to the front, in order to protect the outer moats from artillery fire.[25]

In spite of his many official activities, Leonardo found time for his general interests. He wandered through the streets of Cesena, and on coming to a medieval palace with heavy battlements he sketched it in his notebook; he stopped a long time in the market-place, watched the peasants bringing in their grape harvest, and sketched the hooks on which they hung the heavy bunches. He made many journeys in the country round Cesena; he watched the grain just threshed being carried to the primitive mills, and considered how the force of the wind could be better utilized. Amid all the pressure and haste of these days he invented a wind-mill with a movable roof, supported on a solidly built round tower, and able to revolve and carry the sails with it. From the precise instructions he gives for the building of the mill, the situation of the millstones, and the details of the roof works, it seems probable that this mill was actually built—the first so-called "Dutch" mill of the type that came into general use fifty years later. In order to bring the mill to a stop he introduced a sort of band brake, a semicircle of wood into which the great cogwheel of the driving mechanism was jammed—an arrangement which has been retained down to the present day.[26]

During his strolls Leonardo observed the habits of the country people. He recalled later that he had once watched the herdsmen at the foot of the Apennines dig large funnel-shaped holes and place a small horn in the opening, which, "having become one with the cavity," gave out a loud sound.[27] There were many things he disliked in the primitive life of the people. He was vexed by the four-wheeled carts with small wheels in front and big ones at the back, throwing the main weight on the front wheels and so hindering progress. "The Romagna is the home of every sort of stupidity" was his final summing up.[28]

Perhaps his surroundings seemed so dull to him because his old dream of a journey to the East had been revived by the visit of a delegation from the Sublime Porte to Cesare Borgia—strange figures in gorgeous, exotic array. Leonardo was exceptionally well acquainted with eastern conditions; he was familiar through study with regions seldom traversed, with the course of the rivers and with towns curiously built which had been visited by very few explorers; he was so well acquainted with the customs of the Mohammedans and with their religious teachings that a legend arose later that he became a convert to Islam. He had entirely forgotten that quite recently he had been ready to fight against the Crescent. Bayazid II also seemed to have no prejudices against Christians who could be of service to him, and was trying to find an architect in Italy who would build a solid bridge between Pera and Constantinople to replace the wooden one, resting on heavy barges, which Mahomet II had thrown across the Golden Horn. On the basis of measurements which had probably been given to him by the delegation, Leonardo made a design for the bridge. "Bridge from Pera to Constantinople," he wrote at the foot of the drawing; "40 ells wide, 70 ells above water, and 600 ells long, 400 ells being above water and 200 resting on land; in this way it provides its own supports." [29]

Had Leonardo really negotiated with the Turkish envoys, or did he only dream at his desk of a summons from Bayazid II? Did he shrink at the last moment from the troublesome journey, or did he merely exercise his imagination on the bridge over the Golden Horn, in order to escape from the dullness of the Romagnoli? Some years later Michelangelo felt the same desire to escape from irksome conditions of existence, and after a quarrel with the irascible Pope he entered into negotiation with the Turks for the building of this bridge; but Julius II found him indispensable and induced him to remain in his service.

Cesare Borgia, too, was unable to do without his engineer general. Cesare's personal victory over Louis XII at Milan had given him only a short breathing-space. That astonishing reconciliation had dismayed his allies. His condottieri regarded his renunciation of Arezzo, and his promise to abandon his campaign of conquest and to make no attack on the Florentine possessions, as a ruinous blow at their ambitions for personal revenge or enrichment. They considered that Cesare had made use of them and then betrayed them. They met in secret at La Magione, near Perugia, and counted their forces. Finding that they had in all ten thousand men, they took the risk of open rebellion against him. They attacked his troops in the rear and defeated them. The way was now clear for the exiled princes to return to their states, and Guidobaldo entered Urbino amid the acclamations of his people.

At Mantua the nun Osanna had prophesied in a trance that "the Borgia will resemble a fire of straw," and it looked now very much as if the fire was going out. Every enemy Cesare had made joined the rebels. Francesco Gonzaga's brother Giovanni came into the field with the rest against Cesare, who was universally regarded as doomed; but Isabella d'Este, mistress of Mantua in her husband's absence, considered that it was too early to come out into the open; secretly she approved of her brother-in-law's action, but officially she denounced him.

The rebels closed in on Cesare from all sides; he was surrounded at Imola. But his banner still waved with its proud inscription, *Aut Cæsar aut nihil.* He had always regarded himself as an incarnation of his Roman namesake; as a cardinal he had had the words *Cum nomine Cæsaris omen* engraved on the pommel of his sword. He had, moreover, always been a gambler, ready to stake his own life on a single throw; the pommel carried also the words *Jacta alea est,* "the die has been cast." But at this moment he felt like a man who had thrown and lost everything; reduced to despair, he consulted the stars to ascertain his fate. He was filled with the sense of impending death. His disease was covering his skin with sores. No one was allowed to see him except his trusted aide-de-camp Micheletto; all orders were issued through Micheletto. Many of the Romagnole captains had never heard their commander's voice. He slept through the day behind drawn curtains; was he afraid that the sunlight would reveal the ravages of disease, or were his overtaxed nerves unequal to the strain of the day's clamour? Not until after dark, when all was still, about eight o'clock in the evening, did he jump out of bed and go at once to his desk. There he would remain at work, taciturn, morose, tense as an animal about to spring, until five or six in the morning. As soon as the grey dawn began to break into the candle-lit room, he would return to his bedroom and lock himself in. Through these waking nights he would sit bent over military maps. Leonardo had made him a splendid plan of Imola, showing all the approaches, the town walls in yellow ochre, the groups of houses within them russet-colour, the fields bright green with the river Salerno as a blue streak winding through them.

Already the conspirators of La Magione had many fortresses in their possession; the territories of Pesaro, Fano, and Rimini were in their hands, and in the north Cesare held no stronghold beyond Imola. In reply to his urgent request the king of France had agreed to send a relief expedition, but he did not feel that he could afford to rely entirely on this, and he decided on a course which he was the first Italian prince to adopt—that of summoning the population to military service, instead of using mercenaries. With his remarkable gift of organization he rapidly succeeded in forming an army recruited from the people.

7

"A state resting on mercenary armies will never be adequately safeguarded; for mercenaries are quarrelsome, ambitious, without faith or discipline, boasting in front of friends, cowardly in face of the enemy; they know neither the fear of the Lord nor loyalty to men." So wrote Niccolò Machiavelli later. Machiavelli, who was secretary to the Signoria of Florence, came about this time to Imola. The Signoria had had a perplexing problem to face when they decided to send him; they shared the general view that Cesare was already a doomed man, but among the conspirators was their mortal enemy Vitellozzo Vitelli, with whom there could be no parley. A mere secretary was not a really competent negotiator, but he was at all events a man on the spot who could keep them informed of events and maintain touch with Cesare. Machiavelli had only reluctantly undertaken this mission. He was a man whose single faith was hero-worship, whose divinity was the man of action, who knew of only one virtue, that of resolution; but for himself he preferred his ease, and it was with a heavy heart that he tore himself from the modest comfort and the peace and happiness of his home with his young wife. To add to the unattractiveness of his mission, he well knew the caution and the close-fistedness of his employers; they would entrust him with no positive proposals to make to the duke, and they gave him next to no money for his expenses. He was also well aware of the difficulties ahead of him; he had had earlier dealings with Cesare Borgia. He knew that the duke was not to be put off with voluble assurances; Cesare was himself a master of that art.

At this time, however, Cesare Borgia was in no position to pick and choose; he had to be thankful even for an obscure emissary from a half-hearted ally.

From the compromise made in this October of 1502 by an irresolute government with a great adventurer in a tight place, there emerged a new doctrine of the state and a new political morality, whose consequences were to affect men's lives for centuries to come. For at first Niccolò Machiavelli saw little of Cesare Borgia, and had all the more time to think about the duke, to interrogate the few men who could give information about him, and to learn the logic of his statecraft. Niccolò's quick glance, from eyes set wide apart, noted everything that went on; and he learned the more and with the more accuracy since Cesare's intimates and the duke himself did not take the Florentine secretary seriously, and did not consider him important enough to make it worth while to mislead him or to keep information from him. At first sight he looked much like any of the clerks in the service of the Florentine republic. His short, dark hair was brushed forward like any copyist's; it stuck in an untidy fringe to that massive forehead with its upturned eyebrows; the projecting ears made the broad face look still broader; the face then fell away abruptly past prominent cheekbones and lean, sunken cheeks to a receding chin. That brow, not falsified by the fringe, and the widely parted eyes and long and prominent nose would have made a striking, formidable head, reminiscent of the classical busts of the Roman heroes whom

Machiavelli so venerated. But the receding chin destroyed their effect, and still more so did the wide mouth with its smiling up-turned corners. This humorous, garrulous mouth, suggestive of easily satisfied lasciviousness, and this weak chin, converted the features of an actor in heroic parts into those of a comedian. And when the smile rose to the eyes and slanted them over the broad cheekbones, the physiognomy was revealed of a competent official who sought compensation for the dullness of his duties not only in his sense of humour but in undiscriminating amorous adventures.

Nothing that happened in those weeks at Imola was of more far-reaching consequence than the meeting between Niccolò Ma-chiavelli and his ideal. He had come from a city proud of its demo-cratic institutions, from the citadel of equality of persons and free-dom of speech and thought; but he knew the less admirable fea-tures of this undiscriminating equality, and those alone. He knew the disadvantages of the parliamentary system, with its continual challenge of authority, and those alone. In many years' service in a political secretariat he had seen the defects of parliamentarism at close quarters; he had seen the results of pusillanimous leader-ship; every document that came to him reflected the dread of re-sponsibility of leaders whose period of rule was limited and who, in everything they did, had their eye on their successors and their thoughts fixed on the reckoning that might be demanded of them. In all their negotiations he found that they were met with a mis-trust of a system under which many persons shared knowledge and participated in decisions. Both the duke of Valentinois and the king of France complained that if they confided anything to the Florentine envoy it became public knowledge at once.

Seen from his office, the democratic regime was the root of all evil. The representatives of the government with whom he was personally in contact seemed to him, when they came under his keenly critical eye, to have neither the qualities of statesmanship nor those of leadership. The serious results of changes of govern-ment were widely realized among Florentines of genuinely demo-cratic outlook, and it had been decided to remove them by the ap-pointment of a gonfaloniere as head of the Signoria, to hold office for life. A hotly contested election for this office had taken place barely a fortnight before Machiavelli reached Imola, and he was still full of the excitement of it. But the chosen gonfaloniere was Piero Soderini, so harmless a mediocrity that it had been felt that he could be trusted with the office. Machiavelli knew him well, and had no more respect for him than for anyone else he knew in democratic Florence.

He brought his excited imagination to play in studying the character of the inscrutable Cesare Borgia, *questo signore segretissimo,* in whose greatness of soul and lofty intentions he believed no less firmly than in his undoubted forcefulness and resolution, and whom he was later to represent as a model for all princes. But all his paragon was doing was to sit in his gloomy castle like a huge spider in his hiding-place, sending out sticky streamers to float in the air. "I am trying to gain time," he explained to Machiavelli, "watching events and awaiting my opportunity." Soon he caught his first silly fly, poor Paolo Orsini, who came one day in disguise to Imola.

Cesare continued his work of sowing dissension among the conspirators, playing them off against one another, and coolly and cautiously preparing a safe revenge. A cold winter had come suddenly, making the frozen roads of the Romagna impassable; a violent snowstorm cut off Imola from the world for a time. Then suddenly the oppression that had weighed on Cesare and his entourage seemed to relax, and the day came when the duke emerged from his seclusion. The French relieving force had arrived. He now had the support he needed before he could strike a blow.

In these winter months in the Romagna he had been surrounded by no more than a handful of confidants and collaborators, some of them, like Leonardo da Vinci, Antonio da Sangallo, and the sculptor Pietro Torrigiano, Florentines. Torrigiano was a big, gloomy man with beetling brows that betrayed his ferocity. Once in a spasm of rage he had broken Michelangelo's nose. He had fled from Florence, and was now serving Cesare Borgia as a soldier, out of simple love of adventure.

Cesare had recovered all his confidence in these winter months. There was no neighbouring ruler in the Romagna who needed to be flattered and hoodwinked, no prince left to watch what he was doing. It was a Cesare full of cheerful optimism who would go now on a Sunday with a few of his suite to one or another of the squares in front of the churches, and watch the citizens go by in their best clothes, all stepping gingerly in the slush. He would plant himself there with his legs apart and stir up one of the puddles of mud with his cane, his companions aping their lord as he did so, so that the Sunday clothes were splashed and the women fled screaming. Or amid the noise and gaiety of carnival nights he would suddenly have the doors of the palace of Imola opened; the people would crowd in, urged by a slightly shuddering curiosity, as far as the door of his sleeping-chamber. There they would see him at full length on his bed, lying in his ermine-lined cloak on the golden counterpane, motionless, a naked sword in one hand and his sceptre in the other—handsome, grave, terrible, as the little man imagines his prince. Or, no less characteristically, he would suddenly appear in one of the squares and vie with the peasant lads in wrestling or in jumping ditches; or with his carefully tended hands, which had a totally unexpected iron grip, he would break a fresh hempen cord which had defeated every one of the peasants. Then he would give a sudden laugh, plebeian and startlingly in character.

He was in high spirits during these Christmas weeks at Cesena. But there was something sinister about him. He gave a ball in the palace of the Malatestas, of a gaiety and magnificence such as the old walls of the palace had never before witnessed. His slender body swiftly threaded the rows of the dancers, with catlike grace, as though he were uplifted by some secret frenzy. Next morning passers-by were horrified to see the mutilated body of a man lying in the square in front of the citadel. His gold-embroidered coat was covered with blood; his head was stuck on a spear standing in the ground, and its distorted features were recognized as those of the governor of Cesena, Don Ramiro de Lorqua, most loyal and most ferocious of Cesare's officers. An inscription informed the horrified crowd that this man, so powerful the day before, had been executed by the duke's command because he had been speculating in grain and had driven up the price of the people's bread. This theatrical punishment captured the hearts of the population. A prince, says Machiavelli, must be careful not to interfere with the well-being of his people, for "men can more easily forget the death of their father than the loss of their possessions."

Cesare was now able to rely entirely on the loyalty of his Romagnole subjects as he set out to meet his repentant condottieri, his "dear brothers." In proof of his readiness for peace he sent away the French troops before the feast of reconciliation. He no longer needed foreign aid, he announced; to himself he may well have said that he had no use for foreign witnesses.

The condottieri met him at Sinigaglia, which they had reconquered for him. Only one of them, Vitellozzo Vitelli, who was in an advanced stage of the "French evil," was troubled with premonitions of foul play. Yet there was another one, Oliverotto da Fermo, who could hardly have failed to find something ominously familiar in Cesare's method of reception. The duke gave his returning friends a loud and hearty greeting, and then conducted them through the dark passages of the castle to a remote room, where they suddenly found themselves separated from their troops. Oliverotto himself, when staying at the palace of his uncle, Giovanni Fogliano, had chatted one day arm in arm with his uncle like this, getting him away from the other guests, and had then had him carried off to a remote room and butchered by hired assassins.

Next morning Cesare Borgia sent for the secretary to the Florentine republic and told him, with "the most cheerful air conceivable," *colla migliore cera del mondo*, that Vitellozzo Vitelli and Oliverotto da Fermo had been executed, and Paolo Orsini and his brother the duke of Gravina made prisoner. Taking Machiavelli's approval for granted, he exulted with him over this coup—*si rallegro meco con questo successo*. He also wrote to Isabella d'Este to inform her "of our progress." Isabella hastened to congratulate him, and as an expression of her pleasure she sent him a case containing a hundred carnival masks, for the duke's relaxation after all his "fatigue and exertion." These masks represented human faces, and Cesare, as he took them out of the case one by one, declared with his loud, hard laugh that they resembled this or the other of his friends.

When the news of this "delicious dupery," *bellissimo inganno*, as Paolo Giovio called it, reached France, Louis XII shuddered, and Francesco Gonzaga wrote to his wife: "The king himself revealed his disgust to me, though we all know that he usually hides his feelings." But the king recovered his composure, and later he was heard to say that the deed was worthy of a Roman. It was left to a woman to refuse to allow policy to complicate her simple woman's code of morals, or to let the accomplished fact override her judgment; Charlotte d'Albret, Cesare's wife, perhaps because she was the only woman who had really loved him, wrung her hands in despair, "both deploring and lamenting such cruelty and malignity," as Francesco Gonzaga wrote. Such was her horror that neither Cesare nor the king could induce her to return to her husband.

Shortly after the assassinations at Sinigaglia, Cesare went to Rome, where he later executed the Orsini brothers. Did Leonardo accompany him, as might be inferred from a later note, in which he records the withdrawal from the Custom House at Florence of a case sent from Rome? Or did he return to Florence with his countrymen, Torrigiano, Sangallo, and Machiavelli, in January 1503? He did not waste a single word on the event which his contemporaries long discussed with bated breath. Not until he was back in Florence once more, taking up the threads of his daily work, and entering his cares and concerns in his notebooks, did his thoughts return for a moment to Cesare; and they can have been neither unfriendly nor scandalized, for he asked himself, almost as though he regretted the interruption in their collaboration: "Where is the Duke?"—*Dov' è Valentino?*

CHAPTER SIX

The Great Bird's Flight

Piglierà il primo volo il grande uccello.

The great bird will make its first flight.

(Mz. o'.)

LEONARDO was walking through the market at Florence. Glancing over the heads of the jostling crowd, he listened intently for something in the midst of the loud shouts and laughter, the tradesmen's cries and the noisy haggling and quarrelling of buyers and sellers. Suddenly he heard a bird-seller crying his wares, to the accompaniment of desperate twittering. Thither Leonardo made his way at once. The little birds were closely packed in their small cages; they beat wildly against the bars, and from their tiny throats came short distracted cries.

The bird-sellers were familiar with this eccentric gentleman, who paid them whatever price they asked; and the strollers in the market stood still, for they knew what was coming. He would put his hand into a cage and carefully take hold of a bird's warm, protesting little body; then he would open his hand and let the captive fly away.

The crowd laughed at this whimsical waste of good money; but Leonardo did not see the jeering faces; he was intently watching the beating of the little wings. The bird, he reasoned, is an instrument working in accordance with a mathematical principle; and it must undoubtedly be possible to construct a similar instrument, to imitate the bird's movements. But the first thing needed was to discover the laws that govern the bird's flight, and to calculate the force a man would have to exert in order to maintain himself in the air.[1]

Leonardo had long been haunted by this dream of the man who would lift himself above the earth. It had been with him as long as he could remember—since his vision of the great bird that plunged down to the sleeping child. Another had dreamt of flight before him— "An instrument may be made to fly withal, if one sit in the midst of the instrument, and turn an engine, by which the wings, being artificially composed, may beat the air after the manner of the flying bird." So wrote Roger Bacon, Leonardo's great forerunner of the thirteenth century, the solitary pioneer of all scientific research. Leonardo had been reading Roger Bacon's works at about this time.

Again and again, whatever the work or research he was engaged on, Leonardo would return in thought to this most tremendous, most obsessing, most tyrannical of his dreams. He had pondered over the problem of the conquest of the sky even in his earliest days in Milan, when he was working out his ideas in military engineering and promising to secure dominance by land and sea for Lodovico Sforza. He did not content himself with a seer's visions, or even with a theoretical investigation of what might be possible in generations to come. At the time when he was caught by the fascination of engineering, revelling in the beauty of machine parts and feeling that a constructional workshop was an earthly paradise, he was already making his first experiments with flying apparatus.

In a note dating from those early days in Milan, Leonardo lays down the fundamental principle of movement through the air, later enunciated by Newton as the law of aerodynamic reciprocity: "An object exerts the same force against the air as the air against the object." [2] The eagle, writes Leonardo, is lifted into the highest and most rarefied atmosphere by the beat of its wings. "You may also see how the air moving above the sea, thrust back by the swelling sails, propels a heavily laden ship. From these examples and reasons given, a man with sufficiently broad and properly constructed wings could learn to overcome the resistance of the air and, by conquering it, subjugate it and rise above it." [3]

Later Leonardo described air as a sort of liquid, with a definite weight, elastic, compressible, and of great density in the lower strata, near earth and water; in his expressive way he compared it to a "feather pillow pressing on a sleeper." From the first he proceeded on the assumption that it is the alternating condensation and rarefaction of air that enables a bird to fly: a body heavier than air can be borne aloft only if the air is sufficiently compressed beneath the broad bearing surfaces of the wings to exert an upward pressure. "Unless the movement of the wing which presses the air is swifter than the movement of the air so pressed, the air will not become condensed beneath the wing, and in consequence the bird will not support itself above the air." [4]

He tried first to determine the bearing surface needed to lift a load of about 400 pounds.* He tested on a balance the lifting capacity of a wing in relation to the weight of the human body [5]; then he made an apparatus which enabled him to observe the rise of a wing twenty ells wide and twenty long when correspondingly loaded. "If the 200-pound board rises before the wing sinks, the test has succeeded." [6]

Leonardo's earliest aircraft had a tapering board with wings fitted at the broader end. The flier lay flat on the board, to which he was secured by iron hoops; he moved the wings by pulling with his arms and treading with his legs.[7] In these first designs Leonardo proposed to bind the framework together with iron fittings, but later these were replaced by the most flexible material he could get—young and elastic wood, reeds, or well-tanned leather. He considered the apportionment of the movements; the flier would lift the wings with one foot and lower them with the other.[8] Later he introduced hand cranks and added a rudder shaped like a bird's tail. This was fixed to the flier's neck; when he turned his head to the left the rudder moved to the right, and vice versa.[9]

Soon he experimented with a model of a different design, in which the weight of the flying mechanism rested mainly on the flier's shoulders and no longer on the board beneath him. This model was provided with a double pair of wings, which the flier worked partly by a sort of stirrups and partly by a lever.[10]

In his first attempt to make wings, Leonardo took a bird's wing as his model. He stretched a strong fabric across firm ribs of wood; on this he stuck feathers, and he lined it with raw silk; for safety he stretched netting over the whole. In view, however, of the dimensions he required he considered the long, rigid ribs to be unsuitable, and replaced them with jointed links, which permitted

---

* Florentine. The Florentine *libra* was about ¾ lb. avoirdupois.

the wings not only to move up and down but to revolve about their axis at the point of attachment.[11] After some time he came to the conclusion that the imitation of the bird's wing was impracticable. "Remember that your bird must imitate no other than the bat," he wrote, "because her web forms a framework, or, rather, the linking of a framework; that is to say, the connecting links of the wings. . . . The bat has the help of her web, which connects everything and is without holes." [12]

At about the same time as he found his definitive model for the wing, Leonardo rejected his past aircraft types entirely. He drew a thick line across the one of his earlier designs on which he had worked most. He went to work now on a third type, in which the flier stood upright between two posts in a sort of gondola of the shape of a shallow saucer; a double pair of wings was fixed to the posts. This apparatus, more or less resembling a helicopter, was set in motion by the flier by pedalling; the pedals were connected with the wings by cords passing over drums. The flier worked not only with his feet but with his hands and even his head. Leonardo made this calculation: "A man exercises a force of about 200 pounds * with his head, and a force which is also approximately 200 pounds with his hands, and this corresponds to a man's weight. The wings are driven crosswise as in a horse's gait, and I maintain that this process is better than any other." The apparatus was made of reeds and linen. The wings had a span of 40 ells (80 feet); the "boat" was 40 feet wide and 10 feet high.[13] To facilitate taking off, Leonardo provided for a pair of ladders, which were to perform the function fulfilled by a bird's legs in precipitating the bird into the air. During the flight they would be drawn up. These ladders were to be 12 ells long; for, he wrote, birds with short legs cannot fly up again so easily when they have come to earth.[14] These ladders ran out in arch formation; they would serve also to lessen the shock of landing and so to prevent damage to the machine—"and that is perfect," e questo è perfetto, added Leonardo contentedly.

"I maintain," he wrote as his conclusion from his experiments, "that it is more effective to stand up than to lie on the stomach." [15] His new model consisted of two horizontal surfaces fixed one above the other, and provided with the ladders. In his carefully executed

---

* Florentine; about 150 lbs. avoirdupois.

drawing,[16] to which many details of construction are added, the apparatus appears to be hanging from the ceiling of a large room, probably the room in the Corte Vecchia, above his workshop, which was placed at his disposal for his experiments.

"Block up the upper room with beams," he writes, "and make a big, tall model, and you would have room above on the roof, and this is a more suitable place than anywhere in Italy, in every respect." [17] On this roof, which probably extended to the St. Gotthard Tower, Leonardo was protected from the curiosity of the public. "And when you are on the roof by the tower," he adds, "they will not see you from the tambour" (of the cathedral dome).

"You will test this instrument over the water, so as to do yourself no harm if you fall," writes Leonardo under the design of this model, which he intended to put to a practical test.[18] There was an earlier machine [19] which he similarly proposed to test over a lake, providing himself with a lifebelt. But he had now made a discovery which would protect him still better from the dangers of crashing. "If a man have a tent roof of caulked linen 12 ells broad and 12 ells high, he will be able to let himself fall from any great height without danger to himself." [20] So he wrote in the concise, categorical style characteristic of him when he felt sure of the excellence of one of his inventions; and the tent roof does in fact represent a properly working parachute. More than a hundred years later the Venetian Veranzio, who may have been acquainted with Leonardo's manuscripts, prepared a square sail with ropes at each corner as a parachute; but a flat sail could not offer the same security as a tent opening slowly in falling; and nearly two centuries were to pass before Lenormand dropped from the Montpellier observatory with the first modern parachute and demonstrated its incontestable efficiency.

In order to improve the steering of his apparatus, Leonardo added an inclination gauge, consisting of a pendulum hung in a glass ball. "This ball within the ring," he writes, "will enable you to guide the apparatus straight ahead or aslant, as you wish." [21]

On the same sheet on which he designed the final model of his flying apparatus, he sketched, as though half dreaming, a map of part of Europe, with regional and national divisions indicated, as though his wings were already carrying him over distant countries.

But in the midst of this vivid imagining of the fulfilment of his dreams he was seized with doubts whether the machine would be able to lift itself into the air without mechanical power. Following out this point, he took a wide, thin ruler and twirled it rapidly in the air. He found that there was a strong pull on his arm in the direction of the axis of revolution. On the strength of this experiment he inferred that an air-propeller could be made with which it should be possible to lift oneself into the air.[22] This screw, with a radius of eight ells, would be driven by means of a strip of spring steel wound tightly round a drum. Leonardo gives no details, however, of the way he proposed to connect the screw to the flying machine, or what other practical purpose it was to serve.

After this came the years of important commissions, and he was caught by the fascination of architecture; for a time, with his work on the equestrian colossus and his many new lines of research, the dream of the conquest of the air faded away. About the time of his breach with Lodovico Sforza, when he was absorbed in industrial projects and for a second time under the spell of his researches in mechanics, the idea came to him of applying his new knowledge and the practical experience he had gained to the making of a flying machine. About 1496 he designed one, and provided it with mechanical means of propulsion. The motor—*fondamento del moto,* "foundation of the movement," he called it in a note on the edge of the drawing—consisted of two powerful elliptical springs fastened at the edge of the horizontal surface on which the flier stood. Two ropes connected to the springs ran over a roller and were wound on two reels on a transverse shaft. This shaft was set in motion by a parallel shaft; the motion was transmitted by ropes wound on drums of different diameter from that of the reels, so that they revolved at a different speed. The second shaft was set in motion by a crank of which the axis engaged in a cogwheel placed in the centre of the shaft. Two crank handles at the two ends of the shaft converted the uniform rotary movement by means of a connecting rod into the up-and-down movement required for moving the wings.

This design of a flying machine with mechanical drive represented only a momentary return to Leonardo's earlier dreams. Years were to pass before he plunged again into the work with renewed enthusiasm, with an absorbing passion that dominated all other interests. This was when, after his adventurous service with Cesare Borgia, he returned to Florence.

In the interim an event had happened which could not but make a deep impression on him. At the beginning of January 1503 the marriage was celebrated at Perugia of Pentesilea Baglioni, sister of the reigning duke, with the famous condottiere Bartolommeo d'Alviano, and special distinction was to be given to the festivities by the trial of a flying apparatus by its inventor, the mathematician Giovanni Battista Danti. It was an exciting spectacle for the invited guests when a heavy body like a misshapen bird broke away from the tower of the church of Santa Maria della Vergine. For a short time the machine hovered in the air, but as it sank to earth one of its wings caught in some projecting masonry, and its wooden rods split; a shriek of horror rent the air. Fortunately the wrecked machine landed on the roof of the church, and its inventor escaped with nothing worse than a broken leg.

Now Leonardo knew that he was not alone in the pursuit of his magnificent dream. He must concentrate on his researches if a rival inventor was not to be the first to succeed. While he had been making his cautious and tentative experiments with models, his rival had had the courage to put his rudimentary apparatus to the test; it had been at the risk of his life, but was not this an adventure worth any risk?

Danti's failure, and his own ill-success with experimental models which had gone wrong, or which he had not ventured to expose to the risk of actual test, showed Leonardo that the main problem in the conquest of the air was not a purely constructional one. He realized that the mechanical power of which he had been in search in his latest complicated designs could be replaced by the uplift of the wind. But the air currents which lift a body, the resistance of the air against which it must proceed, the eddies that can seize an apparatus, the whole problem, indeed, of atmospheric conditions, had not been sufficiently studied to be taken accurately into account. A man's strength should be sufficient to oppose the resistance of the air, for, as Leonardo ascertained from his observations, a man has in his legs double the muscular power required for standing upright.[23] The problem of flight was thus not one of

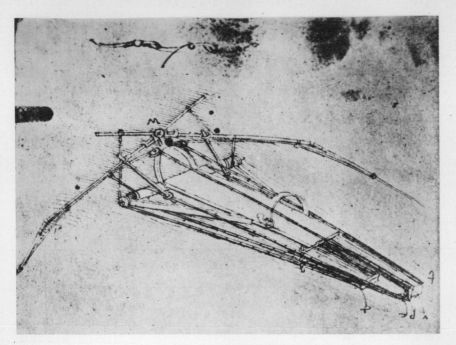

Design for flying machine CODEX ATLANTICUS

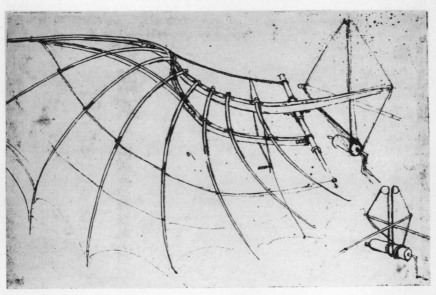

Design for wings of flying machine MS B.

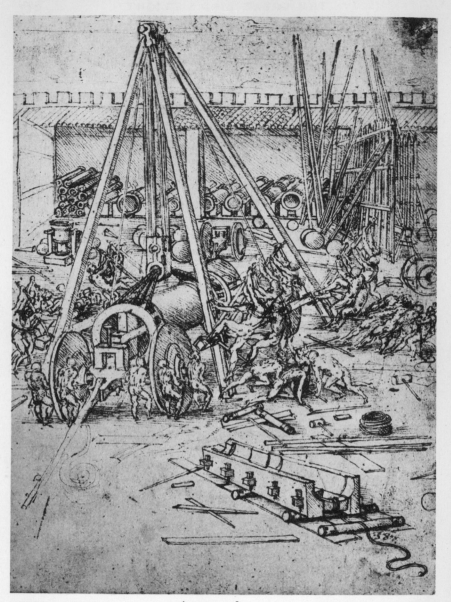

PHOTO MANSELL   An arsenal   WINDSOR COLLECTION

power but one of skill and of accurate knowledge of the air currents. After many false starts and premature experiments, Leonardo at last reached the only path that really lay open before him, that of the investigation of gliding.

The model for the human flier is the bird: Leonardo's new conception of his problem started from that briefly stated principle. Man can make the same movements which the birds make; he needs only exact knowledge of the laws of avian flight.[24] In experiments in human flight the relation between the weight to be borne and the span of the wings must be the same as in birds. Leonardo weighed various birds and found that the figure for the surface of their wings in ells was the square root of the figure for their weight in Florentine pounds. He came to the conclusion that if a man weighed 400 pounds he would need surfaces with a span of 20 ells to bear him aloft.[25]

But the essential thing, he considered, was to study the way birds are adapted to the effort they have to make. "You will perform the anatomy of a bird's wing," he wrote at this time.[26] He intended to carry out exact observations of the way birds fly, establishing from innumerable examples how they make use of the pressure of the air in rising, with wings outspread and almost motionless. He was as fond as ever of analogies that proved the unity of all phenomena, and he compared this rising in the air in semicircular flight with the rising of Archimedes' screw out of the water.

2

In these first months of 1503, in which Leonardo seems to have devoted himself entirely to his researches into the conditions of flight, his native city was involved in fresh hostilities with Pisa. This was to be a war of annihilation. The Florentine republic had recruited large forces; the fortune of war favoured them, and they advanced to within five miles of Pisa. The alarmed Pisans sought the aid of Cesare Borgia; and while they failed to get a definite answer in Rome ("the Pope," people said, "never does what he says, and Valentino never says what he does"), the Florentines already suspected that Cesare aimed at the conquest of their state. The common people were, however, beginning to grumble at the cost of the enterprise and to criticize the policy of their gonfaloniere, Piero Soderini. They complained also of the extravagance of his wife Argentina: she was having the balconies of the Palazzo della Signoria filled with flowering plants.

Was Leonardo at last summoned to the service of his compatriots at this critical time, perhaps at the instance of Niccolò Machiavelli? Or did he make use of Machiavelli's recommendation in approaching the Signoria? In any case, he placed before them a plan for the destruction of the power of Pisa for all time. It was so vast and so bold a plan that he could have obtained a hearing for it only in very grave circumstances. He proposed nothing less than the diversion of the Arno from its bed into two canals that would enter the sea at Leghorn. Cut off from its water supply and from access to the sea, Pisa would be reduced for all time to insignificance; never again would it become the fulcrum of a policy aimed against Florentine overlordship.

At the end of July Leonardo was commissioned by the Signoria to survey the ground. He was assigned, perhaps as a precaution, an assistant who was one of Soderini's trusted subordinates, Giovanni the Piper. Giovanni, who was the father of Benvenuto Cellini, was the official piper to the city, but he also dabbled in military engineering, and had often been employed on the preparation of models for bridges and for machinery. The two set out for the army headquarters near Pisa, in a carriage with six horses; their mission, as Giovanni described it in his account of expenditure, was "to survey the Arno in the neighbourhood of Pisa and to lift it out of its bed."

On this journey in the heat of the Tuscan summer, beneath a cloudless, sapphire-blue sky, Leonardo watched the country unrolling slowly like a map as they proceeded. He noted the bends in the shrunken river-beds, and the structure of the hills, to see whether the course the future canal would pursue would be through easily removed soil or through a rocky stratum. In the camp of the Florentines his project was welcomed with enthusiasm; a report was sent to the Florentine Balìa or war department that "when we had examined the plan with the Governor, I concluded, after many discussions and doubts, that the work would be of great service either if the Arno were in fact diverted locally or if it were led away altogether by a canal—this would at least prevent the hills from being attacked by the enemy."

During this preliminary consideration in the camp before Pisa, Leonardo placed his knowledge of military engineering at the disposal of his compatriots. He drew a bird's-eye map of Tuscany, which showed the towns and the principal fortified places, rising ground and roads, with the utmost clearness. It was a map intended purely for strategic purposes. On his return to Florence he went enthusiastically to work with the preparations for his new enterprise. He drew a second map of Tuscany, with regard chiefly to the watercourses, with their sluices and their windings, the entry of their tributaries and the lakes—a real masterpiece of cartography. The mountains were carefully shaded so as to throw the watersheds into relief; the sepia skimmed like the finest haze over the plains; the chain of high mountains piled up darkly; the sea shone in a brilliant enamel-blue.

An essential condition for the success of the enterprise was rapidity of execution. But Leonardo knew of a number of mechanical appliances for economizing time and labour. On a fine sheet of the *Codex Atlanticus* (1 v.a.), which is as full of colour as his map, he drew a huge mechanical navvy for bringing up earth out of the bed of the canal. A gigantic treadmill, worked by a number of men, lifts up two buckets by means of a crane-like device at each end, tipping them at the top. On the margin of the drawing Leonardo has calculated the output of the machine in comparison with that of the traditional process. When the soil is loosened by mattocks, they must be driven in six times in order to fill a wheelbarrow, for 18 pounds is as much as a man can put into a wheelbarrow at one stroke, and a wheelbarrow can take 112 pounds; but the buckets have the capacity of twenty wheelbarrows, as they will hold 2240 pounds.* In the wake of the buckets Leonardo proposed to use an automatic crane which would move forward on beams laid on the bed of the canal and would permit work to be carried on at two levels, being fitted with jibs of different length, which would take the buckets filled by the workmen and empty them.[27]

---

* The figures Leonardo gives are 25,150 and "about 3000" pounds (Florentine).

Leonardo was centuries ahead of his day in his concern for time-saving; he also considered the replacement of labourers, cheap as their services were in his time, by draught animals. Alongside a sketch of a mechanical navvy which could be placed on the bank of the canal to lift stones out of the canal bed with its derricks,[28] he made two very curious drawings of a revolving crane working in conjunction with a lift. A wide and easy stairway leads up to a lift on the ground level; a driver is urging an ox up this stairway to the lift. As soon as the ox gets into the lift, the lift sinks, bringing up a case full of earth by means of a rope. A crane empties the case, and the ox is driven out of the lift, to repeat the operation. Leonardo calculated that the animal must make four hundred round journeys in the day; and, as though he already possessed the modern sense of the value of any saving of time or energy, he remarked that it would give an increase of efficiency if the stairway turned on itself, so as to begin and end by the two exits from the lift, as this would save the animal a mile and a third in the day. The technical execution of his idea was as modern as its principle; it was carried out in almost identical form in France in the middle of the nineteenth century on the suggestion of Coulomb.

Leonardo also devised various appliances for levelling ground, sketches of which are to be found among his notes both of earlier and of later periods. In order to level a very extensive surface, he proposed to place lamps on alinement posts at regular intervals of 400 ells.[29]

In his estimate of cost Leonardo calculated the exact duration of each part of the work; he knew every motion involved. A shoveller worked with six movements, sometimes four, but not continuously in the latter case—"I have counted," he wrote. A navvy could dig four square ells in two days.[30]

But in spite of his exact knowledge of methods of working, and in spite of the equipment he designed, the work did not progress as quickly as he hoped. There was soon friction with the commanding officers—the inevitable tension between military and civil authorities. Machiavelli had to intervene with the whole authority of the Signoria on behalf of Leonardo in order to make it clear to the commander of the Florentine troops in the field that the Florentine government was determined to carry through the enterprise. "We hereby reiterate our request," he wrote at the end of August, "since our resolve is fixed and we desire that you shall by all means carry it into effect; and it is therefore necessary that in addition to giving practical assistance in this matter you should assist it with goodwill. This is communicated to you because, if there should be with you any condottiere who does not realize this, we desire that you should be able to make him understand what is our intent, and that we are united in desiring that it shall be furthered by words and by deeds."

This letter had the desired effect, and the command went to all the surrounding communes to send a sufficiency of labourers. Under Machiavelli's instructions exceedingly high wages were fixed—ten soldi a day. In order to get the best results, experienced foremen were brought from Ferrara. Soldiers were assigned for the protection of the work from any attack.

Leonardo spent much time on the scene of the operations, and had still many difficulties to contend with. But the peaceful beauty of the river scenery enthralled him. This was something more than a brief escape from the hated city life; he wandered by the threatened river as though eagerly taking his fill of the unspoilt peace and beauty, soon to be destroyed by the invasion of spade and pickaxe and by their work of disfigurement. He watched the morning mists as they moved up the hillsides in swaths. The sky did not yet become blue—*non azzurreggia*—and there was no blueness in the atmosphere, which was of a shimmering white like that of clouds on a clear day; the green of the landscape was overhung with grey; the outlines of the distant church towers rose indistinctly above the horizon. Only slowly did the brilliant blue penetrate the thinning haze.[31] "But in fine weather, when the sun is high at noon, the landscapes are of the loveliest blue." The air was swept free from all moisture; the sun-drenched green shone brightly; deep shadows lay beneath the thick foliage of the trees. Leonardo would lie down in the pleasant shade and look up at the crystal-clear sky. As he lay there, sheltered from the glare of the sun, the leaves on the outer boughs had the translucency of green glass; and when a breath of wind fluttered the leaves so that their white underside was lit up, it was as if a silvery radiance rippled along the boughs.[32] There would be other days on which heavy clouds hung over the landscape; objects would then be scarcely distinguishable from one another; the shadows would be few and faint, and their outlines would dissolve like smoke—*il lor termini se ne vanno in fumo.*[33]

He studied the landscape so closely that every tree acquired an individuality of its own for him. He saw that the green of fir and pine and cypress shades into black, and that there was a suggestion of yellow in the green of walnut and pear, and a great deal of silvery white shimmering through the green of olive and willow. And as autumn came in he noted the trees which were the first to take on a russet hue as the leaves withered. He proposed to describe the landscape when winds sweep the valley, when rain pours down, when the sun comes out or disappears behind clouds, and when it gives them a deep red and sends a glowing rim of light along their fringes. He determined to devote a separate chapter in his *Treatise on Painting* to the changing face of the countryside. Again and again on his walks he would open his notebook in order to make some entry about the play of colours and the magic of light; and at times he would take a long rest in order to sketch some part of the landscape. Every one of these small drawings was made into a finished picture. With a delicate, filmy stroke, almost suggesting colour, he caught the river with its bends, indicating the surface current by a line like a wisp of hair; he caught the gleam of marshes dotted with islands of tufa, and drew crags with the stream rushing past them, and a tiny bridge over the swishing waters, and a little house clinging to the ledge of a cliff. Sometimes he drew just a sheet of water with a ferryboat working along a rope, slowly and cautiously, over the rushing water towards a bushy bank; or just a couple of trees washed by the river, each of them as individual as a human face (Windsor collection).

3

When autumn had reddened the leaves of the service trees and cherry trees and vine shoots, Leonardo returned to Florence. Important political events had given the Florentine republic a new security and diverted its attention for a time from the destruction of Pisa. In August Pope Alexander VI had died, suddenly and mysteriously, from an attack of malaria, though the symptoms suggested that he had accidentally drunk poison—by Heaven's judgment, men said. The same malady seized Cesare Borgia, and though he recovered he was unable to prevent the final collapse of his power; only the slow-witted peasants of remote corners of the Romagna still expected their duke to return. The Florentine republic was freed from its most powerful enemy; and as, soon after this, Piero de' Medici also died, men felt that the republic was at last firmly established and safe for all time from external and internal perils. They were as elated as if their victory had been of their own achievement. The decent, ordinary men who ruled the city were filled with confidence by their good fortune. They felt that they were now called to great things, and began to hatch vast plans. Piero Soderini, the gonfaloniere or life-governor of the city state, was filled, like most naturally timid men, with boundless optimism by success; he was accessible now to any ambitious scheme, and devoted his thoughts to the means of winning glory for the state.

This seemed to Leonardo to be the moment for pursuing his own efforts to achieve great things, and the boldest ideas took shape in his mind. He put them forward in cool and precise proposals, carefully worked out in full detail. In harmony with the changed circumstances he converted his original plan of diverting the Arno into that of building a canal from Florence to Pisa, turning a war measure into a peaceful and constructive one. Lorenzo de' Medici had discussed with the father of the architect Luca Fancelli the cutting of a canal from Prato to Signa, to be fed by the Bisenzio. But Leonardo's project went far beyond this. He proposed that the lower Arno should be regulated from above Florence and a canal cut from it to pass through Prato, Pistoia, and Serravalle, emptying into the sea through the Stagno marshes, near Leghorn. Realizing the importance of industrial support, Leonardo approached not only the official authorities but the representatives of the guilds with his plan. "The wool weavers' guild should make this canal, and receive the revenues from it." [34] He enumerated a whole list of other industries which would benefit by the canal: corn mills could be built beside it, and a silk-spinning mill which would give employment to a hundred workwomen; ribbon-weaving sheds, forges, mills for grinding saltpetre, knife-grinding works, paper mills, water-driven potters' wheels, fulling mills, water-driven saws, and arms-polishing factories.[35]

Leonardo hoped also to interest the towns lying along the route of the canal. "The canal will benefit the countryside; Prato, Pistoia, and Pisa, as well as Florence, will gain 200,000 ducats a year therefrom, and will lend their assistance in labour and money for so beneficial a work; so will the people of Lucca." [36] He was a poor calculator on his own behalf, but found unending economic arguments with which to appeal to the imagination of the people whose support he hoped to get—clinching arguments in their appeal to small men's greed of gain. "If the Arno is guided above and below, all who will may find treasure in every acre of soil." [37]

To facilitate the financing of his project and bring down his estimates of cost, Leonardo proposed to pay wages of only four soldi a day instead of the ten which Machiavelli had authorized. He also proposed to make use of the cheap labour available between the middle of March and the middle of June, when the peasants could be spared from the work in the fields.[38]

"I shall lead this canal through Prato and Pistoia, cut through Serravalle, and make an outlet into Lake Sesto, for I shall have no need of locks or supports, which do not last and so will always be giving trouble in working at them and maintaining .them." So wrote Leonardo in his original plan. But at Serravalle he came to a rise of some 470 feet, through which he could not cut with the technical equipment of his day. He accordingly designed a huge suction-pump, which was to carry the canal up in a zigzag through locks ten ells deep and eight wide. "Any big river can be carried over the highest mountains by applying the principle of the pump," he categorically declared. He proposed to use the power generated by the fall of the water from the top to work the suction-pumps which brought water from one lock up to the next.[39]

This zigzag canal would not be navigable, but perhaps Leonardo was thinking of a solution which he once recommended in Lombardy: two tunnels were to be cut and connected by a vertical shaft; a sluice would be placed at the entrance to the upper tunnel and a trapdoor at the bottom of the shaft, through which the water would slowly flow away, enabling river craft to fall gradually.

Leonardo had once more been caught by the fascination of engineering. He dreamed of vast natural forces tamed by the hand of man; it seemed to him to be a simple matter to lift a river out of its bed or carry it over a mountain. He thought only in terms of pumps and cranes and gigantic iron structures, and he drew his machine monsters with the tenderness of a lover and the zeal of a sectary. "And every day," writes Vasari, "he made models and drawings to show how to move mountains with ease or to cut through them in order to pass from one level to another; he showed that with levers and capstans and screws heavy weights could be lifted and drawn along, and he described how harbours could be emptied and how to lift waters from depths—so that that brain never rested from whimsicalities."

It is probably to this period, at which nothing seemed to Leonardo to be beyond human achievement, that the project belongs which seemed to his contemporaries to be the absurdest of all his "whimsicalities"—that of lifting up the Battistero, the old church of Saint John the Baptist in Florence. This jewel of early Florentine art had lost much of its effectiveness through the proximity of the great mass of the new cathedral dome, which dwarfed it. Leonardo had the idea of providing a substructure for the church, without disturbing a single stone of the building. He proposed to lift up the Baptistery with the aid of enormous hydraulic windlasses, and then to build the substructure, which would consist of a circle of inverted arches supported on upright arches.[40]

It was objected that the building might develop cracks and collapse; Leonardo replied with a whole arsenal of scientific arguments. He had occupied himself for years with the question of the strength of building materials, the load capacity of bearing surfaces, and the source of defects in walls, and now he thought of giving the results of his investigations, which he had begun in Milan, in a treatise "on the generating causes of breaches in walls." Armed with his superior knowledge, he discussed his plan with every member of the Florentine government, disposing of the objections offered and stressing the many precautions he would take; and, says Vasari, "he brought forward such strong and persuasive arguments that the plan seemed practicable, although everyone knew for himself, the moment Leonardo had gone, that the enterprise was impossible."

4

While Leonardo was brooding over projects which were to remain beyond human achievement for centuries to come, he lost sight of his own material needs, until their pressure roused him from his dreams. He had cut down his household expenditure to a minimum—he was looked after at this time by a housekeeper named Margherita—but he found himself compelled to draw again and again on his savings in Santa Maria Novella. Since his return from the service of Cesare Borgia he had had no income, and every three months he had withdrawn fifty florins (equivalent to 2500 gold lire) from his account. Under the pressure of urgent financial necessity he returned once more to painting, as at other times when all his plans came to nothing. In October 1503 he rejoined the Florentine guild of painters.

His decision to do so was connected with the plans which the Signoria were considering, at this time of general exultation over perils averted. They wanted to give outward expression to their newly consolidated power, and decided that their council chamber should be decorated with frescoes recalling heroic deeds of Florentine history. Leonardo asked them to give him the commission for this. The Florentines might shake their heads over his weird schemes and abstruse occupations, but they could not turn away so famous a man. There is a suggestion, however, of petty annoyance with the Milanese court painter, and of surreptitious malice, in their choice of a subject for the frescoes. They asked Leonardo to celebrate the victory of the Florentines over the Milanese in 1440 in the battle of Anghiari.

Among Leonardo's papers is the official Florentine version [41] of the battle. The handwriting is not Leonardo's; it strongly resembles Machiavelli's. It is a historic legend of the usual type—the heroic struggle of the Florentines and their allies against Niccolò Piccinino's superior force. Saint Peter himself appeared above the clouds to announce to the Florentines that God was on their side;

the enemy troops were routed, "and there began a great slaughter of men, none escaping save the first to flee or take hiding." The battle of Anghiari was in truth a turning-point in Florentine history, for, as Machiavelli subsequently showed, the defeat of the Florentines would have delivered over all Tuscany to the duke of Milan.

The enemy had made a surprise attack on the Florentines, who had thrown down their arms in the heat of the day; but the Florentines had the advantage in strategic position, and fortune had favoured them in other ways, so that, long and bitter as the struggle was, it cost only a single life, that of an insufficiently skilled rider who fell from his horse and was trampled to death by the fleeing cavalry. Such was the story told later by Machiavelli the historian, differing substantially from the account given by Machiavelli the propagandist.

But Leonardo took little heed either of the official version or of historic facts. He painted a battle in which he deliberately omitted the prescribed representation of the intervention of heavenly powers; and instead of a battle episode in which Florentine citizens could glory he simply painted the wild fury of war as it is. A passage of his *Treatise on Painting* is headed "Of the Way of Representing a Battle"; a battle, he wrote, should be shown taking place amid clouds of dust and in the reflected light of a distant glow; it should be a maze of frenzied horses and fleeing men, a scene of horror, with wildly yelling combatants and with victims whose eyes are filming in death; "and do not leave any level spot that is not trampled and soaked with blood." [42]

Filled with this vision of war as madness let loose, Leonardo went in search of the elements of horror out of which he would build up his picture. The Signoria had assured him complete leisure for his task and set him free from financial cares, and had had some rooms in Santa Maria Novella, including the unused Sala del Papa, put in order for his use. He began work by making countless studies of horses—galloping horses, their heavy bodies one surging wave, their long necks stretched out, their nostrils distended; horses rearing perpendicularly, with their hind legs deeply planted in the soil; horses biting one another; fallen horses, with necks desperately writhing on the ground; fleeing horses with stout, panting sides flecked with foam, and with every muscle swelling beneath a hide stretched almost to bursting.

He went on in his usual methodical way to sketch a series of male nudes, with sturdy legs firmly planted, and with arms on which the muscles stood out like cables; then he set these muscular bodies on his massive horses, and plunged man and beast, as though they were one being, into the eddy of furious movement.

He searched long and carefully for suitable models for his fighters. He found an old bald-headed man with hooked and drooping nose, wide loose mouth, and a nut-cracker chin; when the man opened his mouth wide to shout, streams of wrinkles ran over his lean cheeks. As he drew this old man in all his hideousness, Leonardo idly pencilled on the edge of the sheet, under some unconscious impulse of revulsion from his subject, the small firm mouth and soft round chin of Salai. He had found a model for a soldier in the flower of manhood, a bull-necked, square-headed man with a straight nose and thick arching eyebrows; he drew him with eyes blazing and the thick bridge of the nose wrinkled in fury. He also made many sketches of a youth with round cheeks and a strong, firm chin, his mouth opened wide for a yell; sometimes he sketched the youth in profile, with head turned away, between the heads of horses with snorting nostrils and gnashing teeth; on the same sheet he drew a lion's head in profile, with its jaws parted for a savage roar, and he made man and beast uncannily like each other. He tried again and again to capture the bloodthirsty yell he wanted; on one sheet there is a blot of ink round which Leonardo has drawn a human face, with the blot serving as a mouth opened wide in a furious roar.

After some considerable time he had wrested the utmost intensity of expression from his models, and had them fixed in splendid, finished red-chalk studies; there are two examples at Budapest. And finally he reached the stage at which he could begin to plan the composition. He thoroughly disliked rapid working on the surface of a wall, and intended first to complete his design in a large coloured cartoon. In February 1504 the Signoria gave the order to a carpenter to make a scaffolding in accordance with Leonardo's directions. It took the form of a flying bridge, the wonder of contemporaries: it rose when the boards were pushed together and sank when they were pulled apart.

The painting no longer exists, but it appears from contemporary accounts that the wall in the council chamber on which it was to go was broken by windows and did not offer Leonardo sufficient continuous space for the whole savage scene of carnage; he took account, therefore, of the windows in his composition, spanning them by a steeply arched bridge, which had played an important part in the real battle of Anghiari. This device enabled the fresco to be split up into three groups of fighters, as the sketches show— the cavalry surging forward, the struggle for the flag as climax and formal centre, and as conclusion the confused hand-to-hand struggle of the infantry, with fleeing cavalry in the background.

The work would have completely disappeared except for the hints of it given in rough sketches (in the British Museum, in the Academy at Venice, and at Windsor), had not a young Fleming named Peter Paul Rubens, travelling, like so many of his countrymen, as a student in the Promised Land of art, visited Florence nearly a century later and there discovered the cartoon for the fresco. Rubens, the fair-skinned northerner, bursting with energy, hungering for experience of life, and almost infinitely receptive, a man of easily awakened sensibility combined with indestructible moral and intellectual balance, had not come like his older, more stolid fellow-artists in search merely of formal beauty; he was alive to the appeal of all that had vigour and intensity of life, all that overflowed with a passion akin to his own fury of artistic effort. In the cartoon of the battle of Anghiari he found ideas that were most stimulating. With rapid, skilful strokes he copied in chalk on a large grey sheet the central scene of the struggle round the flag; then he shaded in his drawing with sepia.

It is the climax of the battle that Rubens has saved from Leonardo's great work—an almost inextricable tangle of horsemen fighting each other to death. The standard-bearer's horse rears up in the centre of the picture, slantwise; its rider, his back bent and his head pressed against his horse's neck, is clinging with both arms to the flagstaff, which a young horseman is trying to wrest from him. A third rider, with a high, old-fashioned cap, probably the

Milanese condottiere Niccolò Piccinino, is pressing forward in the centre of the picture. He has come so close to the man who is trying to seize the flag that their horses' legs are entangled and the two animals, gnashing their teeth, have crashed head to head. An old man with a turban has jumped to the young man's assistance; the short broad swords have crossed high up in the air. On the ground, beneath the heavy bodies of their horses, lie riders who have fallen; two on the left are engaged in a mortal struggle with each other, and on the right a soldier who has half risen is trying to protect himself with a round shield from a horse that is trampling on him.

It is a picture of furious, raging strife, of the agony of death and the lust for murder. Man and beast thrust and strike and trample on one another in a blind rage of destruction, with gnashing teeth and shouting and howls of pain. The sword-blades gleam as they wave in the air, the horses' manes fly up, and the corners of every cloak flap and twist in the air amid the excitement. And, as though there were not enough of whirling and swinging and tortured lines and surfaces, the very decorations on the arms play their part in the confusion. One rider's helmet is made of gleaming spiral shells. The standard-bearer's helmet rises in spirals to a surprising cock's comb; his coat of mail is carried over the arms by shoulder-pieces which are half starfishes and half lizard's paws, and a ram's head with twisted horns stands out from the middle of his breastplate. Leonardo had set out to represent the utterly bestial insanity—*la pazzia bestialissima*—of war, and Peter Paul Rubens faithfully copied his work, reproducing every imaginative detail.

But what Rubens noticed less was the strict geometrical arrangement on which even this picture, the most agitated of all Leonardo's works, was based. This section of the cartoon was contained within an almost pedantically executed rhomboid. The main part of the movement proceeds between two sharply defined diagonals, the one on the left side of the picture being formed by the rearing horse and passing along the fluttering flag to meet the one on the right, which is formed by the arm of the assailant with his raised hand and sword. The base of the rhomboid runs past the horses' firmly planted hind legs and the head of the fallen soldier; higher up in the picture a parallel line is provided by out-turned elbows and drawn swords. The tangle of human and animal forms is in reality a firm construction, a rigidly consolidated unit. All is confusion within the rectangle placed slantwise in the picture, but the intersecting lines are drawn with mathematical precision, the centre of gravity is rigidly preserved. There is something almost uncanny in the clearness with which, for instance, in the centre of the picture the dying man's head as it falls backwards, the intertwined legs of the horses, the angrily turning horse's neck, and the condottiere's arm, are harnessed to an inner diagonal.

During his preliminary work for the cartoon for the battle of Anghiari, Leonardo seems himself to have been caught in the furious storm that raged through his picture. Everything he painted, drew, or sketched during this time was heightened as if by autosuggestion into the savage, cruel, and infuriated. The horses which he continually sketched jumping or falling turned gradually under his pencil into monsters with sirens' tails and covered with matted hair or with scales; he added ram's horns and lion's beards to the gnashing snouts, and step by step he carried them away from reality, turning them into fire-breathing dragons. Leonardo was entirely in the grip of this dragon motif for some time. He gave his fabulous monsters a bat's wings, a crocodile's gaping jaws, and a lion's claws; he made them attack one another or showed them as despairing victims of knights in armour. These chimeras of his fancy attain their most frightful effect when he puts in the middle of the grotesque face a ridiculous snub nose, or sets below a mass of tangled horns two staring human eyes, giving an uncanny familiarity to a mosaic of accumulated hideousness.

Man, beast, and the elements were grotesquely mixed together during this stormy period of his imaginative work. A friend of his, the rich Florentine merchant Antonio Segni, a man of artistic taste, had a love of allegorical pictures; it was he who had ordered from Botticelli the *Calumny of Apelles*. Leonardo gave him a drawing, no longer extant, of Neptune in his car, drawn by seahorses. A sketch for this drawing, now at Windsor, shows the bodies of the rearing horses, suggesting by their rhythm the high waves of a stormy sea.

As though unable to break away from the subject, Leonardo studied the element of madness in every sort of passion; and the further his work progressed the more fully he grasped the bestiality and repulsiveness of the bloodthirsty fury to which he was giving visual shape. He realized with inexorable clarity the grotesqueness and absurdity of whipping up warlike instincts. There is a sketch at Windsor which has the effect of a grim parody of the heroism he was commissioned to celebrate. It shows a confused mass of tiny human beings fighting, while above their heads mountainous elephants and monstrous headless animals furiously charge at one another.

In the midst of this period of preoccupation with phantasms of violence and horror, Leonardo seemed to begin, perhaps unconsciously, to hunger for peaceful beauty; in the midst of rapid sketches of galloping horses there suddenly appears a figure of an angel with raised arm, the first bright trace of the sexless saints or gods which found their culmination in the *Saint John*. On another sheet Leonardo marked out a small square and filled this frame with the figure of a kneeling woman, the first glimpse of that pæan of voluptuousness, his *Leda with the Swan*.

This new need for compensation was sensed by a woman who knew him better than he himself might have been ready to admit, and who never tired of the effort to invade his solitude with her sympathetic understanding—Isabella d'Este. In May 1504 she sent her ambassador at Florence, Angelo del Tovaglio, to Leonardo to present to him once more her unwearying request for a work of his; this would provide a refreshing change for him when he was tired of working on the great battle picture. She followed up this message with a personal letter to Leonardo, reminding him of the engagement he had entered into—*l'obligo della fede che havete cum noi*. Since he could not now paint her portrait, would he not make good his promise with some other picture? "If you would satisfy this supreme desire of ours, you may know that, apart from the payment, which you yourself will fix, we should remain so indebted to you that we should have no other thought but of being of service to you, and from now on we should be ready to do anything for your ease and pleasure."

The subject Isabella proposed for a little picture met the need which Leonardo repeatedly felt for escape from the thraldom of his task. There rose before him as he read her letter the vision of

Leonardo's studies of horses' heads for the *Battle of Anghiari*

The Battle of Anghiari. Rubens's drawing from Leonardo's cartoon

Study of hands

the Christ Child "at the time of his life when he questioned the doctors in the Temple—done with that sweetness and gentleness of expression which you have in the highest degree as your peculiar gift." Isabella never received the picture she suggested; but Leonardo made one painting of Christ as a fair-haired boy, perhaps among the doctors in the Temple, judging from the many studies for heads of bearded old men, or as the young Saviour, with the globe in his left hand and his right hand held up in blessing, as in the many copies made by his pupils from an original that has been lost. The subject seemed so attractive to Leonardo that he gave the Mantuan envoy the promise asked for. But Angelo del Tovaglio was a man with experience of life, and after he had got into touch with Perugino at Isabella's request and secured a similar promise from him, he wrote to her: "I have a strong suspicion that the two will now enter into a competition in dilatoriness; and while I do not actually know which of the two will excel the other in this respect, I feel certain that Leonardo is destined to be the victor."

Just at this time it had become generally known in Florence, where the acoustics were perfect for all rumours, that the Signoria were very annoyed at the slow progress of Leonardo's work and had taken energetic steps to overcome his dilatoriness and desultoriness. He had received 35 florins, it was complained at a sitting at the beginning of May 1504, and not even the cartoon was yet finished. They refused to put up with these delays any longer; either the cartoon must be delivered by February 1505, or Leonardo must refund the advances he had received and hand over his design as it stood. This decision was embodied in a notarial agreement prepared for Leonardo's signature; the terms were to be complied with "without exception or quibble"—*ogni exceptione et cavillatione rimossa*. He signed the document in good faith, as though he had still to appreciate the irresistibility of his manifold interests.

The relatively long time Leonardo was allowed may have been due to the resumption of the work on the canal, of which he had not lost sight amid the fever of creative activity. His studies for the battle of Anghiari are interspersed with designs of pumps and turbines; horses tearing along and men's faces distorted with fury are to be found on the same sheet as great suction-pumps and conduits, and among his notes there are continual references to works to which he wanted to refer for the theoretical basis of his practical work—the Latin translation of Archimedes' work on floating bodies, *Archimedes de insidentibus in humido* [43]; or the *Pneumatics* of Hero, available only in manuscript, from which the model of a siphon came.

But at the very time when Leonardo was making his surveys of the upper basin of the Arno (there are many indications that it was in this early summer of 1504), there lay in wait for him one of those tremendous adventures of the mind which sidetracked all his practical work and made him forget even his immediate obligations. During these journeys he was impressed once more by an observation which had amazed him in his youth, when in the cave at Vinci he had discovered the skeleton of a huge monster, petrified remains of the mysterious life of past ages. In his Milan years he had examined the rock formations of Lombardy, and had been struck by the presence in them of petrified shells, and one day, when he was working on the "great horse," peasants had brought him a sackful of curious stones, for everybody knew that he was interested in every unusual natural object; these stones, collected in the mountains between Parma and Piacenza, contained closed shells and vermiculate corals, still in a good state of preservation.[44] The excavations for the canal in the valley of the Arno between Florence and the Gonfolina defile revealed no trace of fossil shells, but on the rocky slopes through which the upper Arno winds Leonardo discovered a quantity of marine crustaceans, as though a wave had carried them up to these heights and they had then turned to stone.

The ancient writers had noted the deposits of shells on mountain slopes, and had recognized their association with the bed of the sea; but in Leonardo's time they were generally regarded as freaks or caprices of nature. Some supposed that the Creator Himself had taken pleasure for a time in placing imperfectly formed creatures in the world before He created those which exist today; others talked of plastic powers of the earth, which they credited with attempting to imitate the forms of nature. The Italian school which subordinated everything to the influence of the stars considered that the shells had been magically conveyed by heavenly powers to the tops of the mountains. Those wise heads who could not deny the organic origin of the fossils because they found it laid down by classic writers, declared that these crustacea had been swept up to the heights by the Deluge.

Under the heading "Doubt"—*Dubitatione*—Leonardo wrote: "Here a doubt arises, whether the Deluge which came in Noah's time was universal or not; and it will appear that it was not, for the reasons that will be given. We learn from the Bible that this deluge consisted of forty days and forty nights of incessant and universal rain." [45] But, he asks, if the Deluge covered the whole earth up to the tops of the highest mountains, how did the waters subsequently subside, considering that water can only move downwards? "And in the absence of natural explanations," he adds ironically, "we must bring miracle to our aid in solving this problem, or else must say that all this water was evaporated by the heat of the sun!"

He attacked the problem with all his equipment of scientific knowledge and dialectical skill. He wasted little time on those who ascribed the formation of fossils to the influence of the stars: they were babblers—*di troppo discorso*.[46] In the treatise he proposed to write he would confine himself to the refutation of the Deluge theory. "In this work you have first to prove that the shellfish at a height of a thousand ells were not carried there by the Deluge." [47] He proceeded then to argue at length that shellfish cannot swim, but dig a furrow in the sand with the sides of their shells, and that they move only three to four ells a day in their furrow, so that they could not have covered the distance of 250 miles from the Adriatic to Lombardy, where he had seen them with his own eyes, in forty days. Nor could they have been carried by the waves, since they are heavy and move only on the bed of the sea; these were not empty shells which might float on the water, for they were closed as with living shellfish. Nor could the eddies of the Deluge have driven them forward, for in that case they would have been whirled about and intermingled, not left lying one above another in layers. He carefully considered the sorts of shells found in the rock, the backbones of fishes, and the animal and vegetable remains with which they were intermingled, and established that they were crustaceans that can live only in salt water.

As his gaze wandered over the landscape, there unfolded before his eyes a vision that seemed like a fable to the men of his day, with their superstitions and their imperfect knowledge. Once these valleys and mountain slopes were covered by the sea. "At first schools of fishes swam above the plains of Italy, above which flocks of birds now fly." The Mediterranean was far more extensive than now; it covered the basins of the great rivers of Africa, Asia, and Europe, and its waves washed the upper slopes of the mountains that surround them; the peaks of the Apennines stood out of the ocean like islands.[48]

He must have met with a great deal of incredulity, with ignorant objections, as he writes, and with the assumption of better knowledge on the part of the book-learned. Scholars told him that if what he said had been true it would have been recorded by the old writers. He replied, with a quiet confidence which might have suggested that he had a whole school of disciples at his back, instead of standing alone: "Since many things are much more ancient than written records, it is no marvel if, in our day, no records exist of the extension of the seas over so many countries; and even if the records had existed wars and conflagrations and inundations, and changes of tongues and of laws, would have obliterated every vestige; but sufficient for us is the testimony of the living beings born in salt water which we find on high mountains, far removed from the seas of today." [49]

Many years were still to pass before a man of Leonardo's own unerring vision, Bernard Palissy, swept away all the confused interpretations of the fossils, bringing his practical experience of pottery to his investigations, the results of which he published in

1580. Leonardo's researches, while reliable because based on actual observation, suffered from the restricted field of his observation. The rock formations which he studied were almost all tertiary deposits, and the fossils they contained were too like the forms of life still existing, so that he had no opportunity of discovering, as Palissy did, that these were the survivors of species that had died out. The restricted field of Leonardo's observations also prevented him from fully realizing the extent of the modifications that have taken place in the earth's crust.

Aristotle had raised the question whether parts of the continent had not at one time formed the bottom of the sea; but he did not think that this exchange of surfaces between land and sea had been extensive. Strabo had realized the great transformations of the surface of the earth, and had attributed them to volcanic forces, aided by water. The Middle Ages drew their knowledge of the face of the earth mainly from an Arabian manuscript, *De Elementis*, which was believed to be a work of Aristotle (it combated the theory of changing surfaces of land and sea), and from a treatise on minerals, part of which was erroneously attributed to Aristotle and part, perhaps rightly, to Avicenna. This treatise contained traces of Strabo's doctrine, but attached less importance to the effect of earthquakes than to that of erosion by water.

This latter explanation harmonized better with Leonardo's general conception and with the observations he had been able to accumulate. In imagination he had explored the remotest regions of the earth, but he had never been outside central and northern Italy, and had had no personal acquaintance with volcanic formations. Etna—called Mongibello in his day—and Stromboli were to him scarcely more than examples of a mysterious force of which he knew only by hearsay and which did not interest him greatly. "There is no part of the earth which is uncovered by the wear of flowing water, which has not already been a surface of the earth seen by the sun." [50] In this brief and happy phrasing, adopted to express his fully ripened ideas, Leonardo summed up the evolution of the earth. But in his description he was led astray by his passion for the study of water power and by the comparison, to which he was still inclined, of the earth to a living organism. At this time he was completing his great treatise on water, that life's work of his, to which he was always adding; he summed up its contents anew as follows: "These books treat in their first section of the nature of water itself in its movements, and in others of the effects of its currents, which change the world in its centre and its shape." [51] Following the classic conception of the specific weight of the elements, Leonardo considered that the parts of the globe which were full of rivers and were eroded by water became lighter, while the other parts, in which the material carried away by the water was deposited, became heavier, so that their relation to the centre of the earth changed.[52] But rivers have not only "cut apart and divided the limbs of the great Alps, as may be observed from the arrangement of the stratified rock"; they have also hollowed out the interior of the earth to such an extent that the crust has fallen in. "The great elevations of the peaks of the mountains above the sphere of the water may be attributed to the falling in of a large part of the earth, which was filled with water, toward the centre of the earth, after it had been riddled by the veins of water, which continually eat away the soil through which they run." [53]

Leonardo explained in this way the destruction of Sodom and Gomorrah and the origin of lakes and inland seas. A fallen mountain might have closed the outlet of the Red Sea and another narrowed that of the Mediterranean. "For we have seen the same thing happen," he added, "in our own time, when a high mountain collapsed, closed a valley, and made a lake out of it." [54] He spent a considerable time in the effort to fill in the details of his picture of the prehistoric world. He thought that the Mediterranean was connected with the Red Sea until the Strait of Gibraltar opened and the Mediterranean poured its waters into the Atlantic.[55] He supposed that the Adriatic took in the whole valley of the Po, that Tuscany was once crossed by two great lakes, and that the Black Sea covered the present Danube valley.

In connexion with these premature and inadequate efforts to identify the past face of the earth, Leonardo asked his friends in distant countries for information concerning the course, rapidity, and outlet of their rivers and the ebb and flow of their seas. He went to work with passionate tenacity to determine the nature of the millennial process of change, and to gain an insight into the mysterious working of the forces which had been reshaping the earth down to his own time. He even imagined that he had discovered a world-soul at work, a "spirit of growth" inhabiting the body of the earth. "Nothing grows in any place where there is not sensitive, vegetative, rational life. . . . And so we may say that the earth possesses a spirit of growth (*anima vegetativa*), that the soil is its flesh and the rocks which form the mountains are its bones . . . and the waters its blood. . . . The ebb and flow of the ocean is its breathing. . . . The dwelling of the spirit of growth is in the fires which burst forth in various parts of the world in hot springs, in sulphur mines and volcanoes, in Mongibello [Etna] in Sicily, and in many other places." [56]

Fantastic ideas like this and practical inspirations centuries ahead of his time so jostled one another in Leonardo's brain that this very conception of his of the fires that are the warmth of the world's soul led him to the investigation of an unknown force which had never been applied or measured—steam. In his time and for more than a century after him, no distinction was made between steam and hot air. Leonardo himself had no sense of any distinction between the two: during his early studies of military engineering he proposed to use steam to fire a gun; later he suggested driving turbine wheels by hot air, and devised a plan of drawing water from the trough of a fountain up the conduit pipes by means of the pressure produced by heating air and letting it cool.[57]

Not until the time of his intensive geological studies did he concern himself scientifically with the problem of steam. He then made the first measurements of steam production, "in order to make the experiment and to lay down a rule for the amount by which water increases when it turns into steam." He fitted a bag of calfskin into a cubical vessel, open at the top; the bag was half filled with water and then tightly closed; it took up only part of the vessel containing it. On top of the bag he placed a lid fitted with a piston, which was pressed down by a weight. As soon as steam was raised by heating the vessel, the bag swelled and drove up the lid, enabling the volume and pressure to be measured.[58] The experiment does not seem to have satisfied Leonardo; he tried again, this time with the water in the cubical vessel itself, to measure the volume of steam in proportion to the quantity of water turned into steam.[59] The experiment was not attempted again until about a century later, when Giambattista della Porta carried it out—for the first time, it was supposed.

At this time Leonardo was developing at greater length and with more examples than ever his mistaken theory of the uniformity of the organic world. But he had already begun to pursue an investigation which, with the many years of thought he had already given to the theory, was to free him from his error. It is a curious fact that he came to a right understanding of the composition of the earth through the insight he gained into the laws of the universe in the course of his study of the heavens.

While he was completing his treatise on water, in which he proposed to impart the whole of his knowledge, including even the inventions for submarine warfare with which he had refused to endow men's wickedness,[60] his gaze rested on the great river Arno, as though he meant to wrest its last secret from it. He watched it in the blazing sunlight, and noted that on the days on which the water is disturbed the reflection of the sun seems bigger than when the water is smooth; and he thought of the similar case of a lute-string on which the light of a candle falls: if the string is still, it reflects only a point of light; if it is vibrating it seems to be all of woven gold. He also watched the river during one of those hot moonlit nights which powder the violet dark with silvery radiance. He saw how the light lies like scales on the almost black water, caught by the crests of the waves and deflected in the trough (it occurred to him that the same thing happens with the surface of a fir-cone); so the image of every reflected object is multiplied in the water more times or fewer according to the curve of the waves.[61]

This simple observation led Leonardo on to the study of the nature of the moon. His first conclusion, which he defended with great energy, was erroneous. He considered that it was the seas and waters of the moon that reflected the sunlight, and the moving waters that multiplied the reflected rays. He entered into a controversy with a contemporary, Maestro Andrea da Imola,[62] who contended that the light of the moon was not due to the countless reflections from its waters: "All my opponent's arguments to say that there is no water in the moon." [63] He considered that the maculæ on the moon, of which he made careful drawings, were "clouds rising from the waters of the moon." [64] Mistaken as this idea was, it represented an advance over the many explanations which must have been known to Leonardo; for the spots on the moon have always exercised men's imagination. All sorts of theories were put forward in the Middle Ages. "One sees in them a man on the gallows, another two men tearing each other's hair out . . . others claim to see Cain and Abel . . . and there are some who see a bull or a horse, as is often the way with ignorant people," wrote Ristoro d'Arezzo scornfully, and he added his own interpretation: in the full moon there is a human face, because this is the most perfect object which can be inscribed in a circle.

Plutarch, in his *De facie in orbe lunæ*, describes the changing spots of the moon as shadows thrown by the sun, and the unchanging ones as hollows in the surface of the moon, which he held to be a thick, solid body radiating light borrowed from the sun. But medieval astronomy was baffled by the idea of a thick, solid moon. It took over from Aristotle the doctrine of the four elements: earth, water, air, and fire. It also took over from him the doctrine of the division into the sublunary and the heavenly world. According to the Schoolmen the sublunary world was formed of a corruptible and finite substance and subject to straight-line motion, while the substance of the heavenly bodies was neither heavy nor light, neither fruitful nor corruptible; it was subject to circular motion, the most perfect of all motions, and moved round the immovable central point of the earth.

Leonardo had unquestioningly accepted the Aristotelean doctrine of the four elements of the sublunary world. But while he was thinking about the reflection of light from water, he was led on to the confident conclusion that the moon radiates light borrowed from the sun, and all at once it struck him that the phenomena in the earth and in the sky are identical. So unusual was the intellectual path of this self-taught man, and his intuitive reaction to the traditional, that he upset the contemporary view of the universe at the very point at which his experimental method was least applicable, in the distinguishing between earthly and heavenly material. "The moon solid and heavy—solid and heavy as the moon is," he wrote on the first page of the notebook which he was using at this time; he made the entry as a man may note an amazing idea which has suddenly come to him as an illumination. He went on to note something like the heads of a line of argument. "Nothing light is opaque. Nothing light remains among less light things. Whether the moon has its seat within its elements or not. And if the moon has not its special seat like the earth in the midst of its elements, how is it that it does not fall into the midst of our elements? And if it is not in the midst of its elements and does not fall down, it must be lighter than all other elements. And if it is lighter than all other elements, why is it solid and not transparent?" [65]

There is something of the "ruthless logic," the *terribile demostrazione*, which Vasari praises in Leonardo, in this set of questions. "It is manifest that the moon is clothed by its elements, that is to say, water, air, and fire, and so maintains itself in itself and through itself in that space, as our earth does with its elements in this other space; and that heavy things in its elements fulfil the same function as do heavy things in our own." [66]

With this argument of the identity of elements and of functions Leonardo destroyed the whole edifice of scholastic philosophy. If the moon was clothed with its own elements and possessed its own centre toward which all heavy things tried to move, then the earth could no longer be held to be the centre of the universe as the men of the Middle Ages thought, with the infinite arrogance of their claim to be made in the image of God, and the infinite humility of their acceptance of sinfulness from which redemption was granted them. The whole metaphysical system of the Middle Ages, based on man and his relation to the Creator, also fell to pieces.

Did the sun really revolve round the earth, was it no more than a planet like the moon, Jupiter, Venus, Saturn, Mars, and Mercury? "The sun does not move"—*il sol non si muove*—so Leonardo had written, in unusually large letters, on a sheet covered with rough sketches dating from his Milanese period. This discovery had come to him like a flash of lightning, and like a flash was swallowed up again in the darkness of traditional ideas. Now he was once more tentatively approaching the same revolutionary discovery. He proposed to write a treatise on the nature of the moon, *della essentia della luna.*[67] It was to be the introduction to his astronomical studies. He set about his preparations for researches as extensive as if his moment of leisure could be prolonged to infinity. He erected a sort of observatory beneath the roof of the house in which he was living, and had an instrument placed under the skylight. His reference to this instrument is brief and enigmatical: "Make glasses for seeing the moon magnified." [68] He had already invented a telescopic tube; had he now placed magnifying lenses in it and made the first telescope? He adds, in any case, instructions for its use, explaining how the apparatus has to be directed at any time to a star in order to ascertain its nature; and in his notes of the time there is a suggestion of the excitement of a man who was conscious that he had reached an important stage in his life.

6

Engrossed in his work, Leonardo was deaf to all that went on around him. Yet news came to him in these summer days of 1504 which might well have aroused him if he had not been so deliberately aloof from everyday life. Among the notes of small sums given to Salai or spent for the household, there is this short memorandum, written in a firm hand that reveals no sign of any emotion: "At 7 a.m. on Wednesday, July 9, 1504, Ser Piero da Vinci, my father, notary to the Podestà, died, at seven in the morning. He was eighty years old, and left ten sons and two daughters." [69] Leonardo gave the dead man's title and office as though he was a distinguished friend of whose acquaintance he was proud; and, just as if they were but slightly acquainted, he had the age wrong. Ser Piero was at most seventy-seven when he died. Moreover, July 9 was not Wednesday but Tuesday. The error may have been due to Leonardo's absence from Florence at the time. The hour of death was repeated, perhaps a sign of repressed emotion. On a sheet of the *Codex Atlanticus* is another record by Leonardo of his father's death. Was he so moved by the news, or had he merely forgotten that he had mentioned it once already?

An old gentleman, a stranger, the notary to the Podestà, had died—a man with whom he was associated only by the chance of his birth. No painting or drawing by the notary's famous son exists to show what the father looked like, and only the two short notes of his death remain as evidence from Leonardo of the relationship between the two men. Leonardo had been left with bitter contempt of everything connected with family relationship, with a poisoned scepticism concerning the relations between parents and children, a feeling that they were natural enemies. Ser Piero's indifference to his illegitimate son had turned the son into a misanthrope and an enemy of the family system. Uncommunicative as he was about personal matters, there was one occasion, many years later, on which his hatred of family ties found expression, in eloquent witness of the sufferings of his youth. His half-brother Giuliano, who had also become a notary, had written to him to convey the happy news of the birth of a son. To this news Leonardo replied in a way which must surely have been unprecedented, with a letter which could have been sent only by a man who welcomed the opportunity it gave him to express the bitterness that rankled in him. "I learned from your letter," he wrote, "that you have been given an heir. I learned how extraordinary a pleasure it was to you, and as I think you are an intelligent man I realize that I am far from having the same good opinion of intelligence as you; for you have rejoiced over having provided yourself with an active enemy whose one desire will be for the freedom which cannot be his until you are dead." [70]

After Ser Piero's death his many legitimate children quarrelled violently over his estate. The elder children tried to cut down the share of the younger ones, who were represented by the stepmother. Leonardo took no part in this ugly squabble; his father had left him nothing, either because he was alienated from Leonardo or because he assumed that the famous painter could no longer be in need of material assistance. Leonardo had only one friend in this family, his uncle Francesco, the friend of his early youth. Uncle Francesco, who loved him and felt that his father had unjustly passed him over, still lived and took his ease at Vinci. Soon after his brother's death Francesco da Vinci made his own will, and as though to right the balance he left everything he had inherited from his parents to his beloved nephew Leonardo, ignoring Ser Piero's other children.

About the time when his father was assuming that he could pass over the prosperous son, Leonardo drew yet further on the savings he had brought from Milan. In the spring he had drawn another fifty florins, although he was receiving advances from the Signoria for the cartoon of the battle of Anghiari. He may, however, have been expecting at that time that he would receive much more for his work on the Arno canal. The work had made such progress that it was now possible to make the first attempt to divert the river. The experiment was favoured by the Arno's being in flood, and for a time its waters flowed into the new artificial bed. But unusual autumn heat gradually reduced the level of the water, and one day the river suddenly returned to its old bed; the canal dried up.

The Florentine captains complained of the employment of their troops on the guarding of a useless undertaking; the commander of the troops in the field, Antonio Giacomini, angrily demanded to be recalled. In Florence the sceptics revived their arguments against the plan, and the Council of Ten described it as a mad one —*piuttosto ghiribizzo che altro.* But Soderini held fast to the plan, with the tenacity which undecided men can show on occasion, and Machiavelli, who was not always in agreement with him, brought all his inescapable eloquence to the support of the gonfaloniere. At the end of September the Council of Eighty were convoked to consider the question, and after long and heated discussions they decided, in spite of doubts and of the growing difficulties, not to abandon the work but to continue it with redoubled energy. Machiavelli communicated this decision to the captains in emphatic terms, and watched over the progress of the work. In October he was glad to note that there remained only a last section to complete, the final outlet of the canal, planned to have a breadth of 55 ells along its 80 ells of length.

Now, however, violent autumn storms set in; the heavens themselves seemed to be falling to earth in a wall of rain. The workmen refused to stay in the workings, and abandoned their task. Finally there came a storm more furious than any of its predecessors. Three galleys, commanded by the Neapolitan condottiere Don Dimas de Requesens, were stationed at a sheltered spot near where the canal was to enter the sea. They were struck by the storm; their masts broke, the sails ripped, and the three vessels capsized; the shrieks of the drowning mingled with the howling of the wind. Eighty sailors lost their lives.

The curse of God seemed to lie on the enterprise. The Florentines were aghast. Experts came from Ferrara to try to calm them, but no one ventured any longer to advocate the continuation of the work. The troops guarding the canal were recalled. The Pisans rushed to the abandoned workings and filled them up again, amid the rejoicings of the hungry population of the city. By the end of October 1504 nothing remained of the great enterprise but broken soil. It lives in contemporary accounts as the ridiculous dream of an eccentric. "The Florentines," wrote Muratori, "flattered themselves that they could wrest the Arno from Pisa; such fine promises did they receive from their architects and engineers. But the river laughed at those who would legislate for it, and continued to flow in its broad course as in the past."

Not a word did Leonardo write about the heavy blow which had destroyed his high hopes. Only, as always when he had suffered a set-back or when proud plans had merely brought humiliation, he plunged furiously into his work as an artist and devoted himself once more entirely to painting—less for any consolations of his art than in order to make up for a defeat by a success on which he could count.

7

But beneath the renewed energy with which he now went to work on his cartoon for the battle of Anghiari there lay another motive besides that of returning to the shelter of his art. He was putting forth all his powers for a tremendous contest, a competition with a great rival who faced him in enmity, with the advantages of youth, ruthless energy, and singleness of purpose—Michelangelo Buonarroti.

The first meeting between the two had taken place at the end of January 1504. The Signoria had summoned all the eminent artists of the city to a meeting in Michelangelo's studio for a discussion on the place of erection of his marble statue of David. The fence with which the sculptor had jealously surrounded his work had just been taken down, and the figure of the young champion, hewn out of the marble, rose before the spectators with the stark power of a natural phenomenon. The lean, sturdy legs had been stretched to their full length, and the firm trunk of the powerful body was tautened from the narrow hips upwards. The currents of force passing through the youth's frame were concentrated in his broad shoulders. The arm with the sling, looking like a bundle of twisted cables, was tense in every muscle up to the exaggerated column of the neck with its tightly drawn sinews; the other arm, with the rough and disproportionately huge hand, had dropped like a cudgel. Above this turmoil of exertion within the youth's still immature body stood his small head, with a tangle of rumpled hair over the low brow, the big square eyes, and the almost painfully twisted eyebrows, between which rose two angry forked lines. Only about the handsome mouth with its sensuously arching upper lip was there a charm that offset all this violence.

The young champion stood like a challenge before the assembly of artists. Some of those present were painters of an older generation, some contemporaries of the sculptor, but almost all felt in the face of this work that they belonged to an art epoch whose knell had been sounded. Alongside this giant, Botticelli's figures were fragile as glass; Perugino's saints had become empty and superficial; Pollaiuolo's realistic austerity had the effect of filigree work: Filippino Lippi, Piero di Cosimo, Lorenzo di Credi saw their art being swept out of existence. Silently they asked themselves if this was beauty.

There was a long and heated debate over the situation to be assigned to the David—whether in front of the palace of the Signoria, where it would be visible from all quarters and an honour to the city, or in the Loggia dei Lanzi, the great hall used for public ceremonies. In most minds there was a secret wish to allow the statue neither of these places of distinction and to set it within some church; it was pointed out that in the Loggia dei Lanzi it might be in the way during public festivities. Amid this atmosphere of unspoken fears, concealed envy, and a desire which none ventured to confess for the denial of the prominence the work deserved, Giuliano da Sangallo spoke fairly and dispassionately, recommending that the work should be put under cover in the Loggia dei Lanzi because of its easily damaged material.

During the discussion Leonardo looked long and earnestly at the statue, and sketched it in his notebook, as he did everything that aroused his interest. He was at work at this time on the cartoon for the battle of Anghiari, and had no reason to regard this achievement by a fellow-artist either with apprehension or dislike. He had no need to fear the rivalry of younger masters—his own fame was assured. Did he sense the unevenness of the execution of the work, which was best viewed from the front and less able to stand inspection from other sides? Or was he influenced only by Sangallo's sensible recommendation? In any case, he expressed his agreement with it, saying that the *David* would be best erected in the Loggia, in such a way as not to interfere with the Uffizi palace festivities.

In this assembly of the most eminent artists of their epoch, it was left to a little-known goldsmith named Salvestro to declare the artist's right to determine the fate of his own work. He considered that the man who had created the statue would know best where it should go. That, said Michelangelo's friends, was the only just solution. Michelangelo himself, suspicious, hypersensitive, imagining himself to be surrounded by the envy of lesser men and the jealousy of the accepted masters, was eager to secure the most prominent position for his work, and was young enough to prefer a momentary triumph to the protection of his work through the years to come.

The controversy over the site for the *David* was transferred from the artists' meeting to the streets of the city. All Florence listened breathlessly to hear the destiny of the work. Michelangelo's friends stood guard over the statue as it was enclosed in a framework of heavy beams in readiness for transport—for, said Giovanni the Piper, it would be easy for some envious person to damage it. And one night stones were actually thrown at the statue in its framework, strengthening suspicions which Michelangelo had already harboured that an organized conspiracy against it was afoot. The people of Florence were unanimous in their praise of the sculptor and his work; they seemed to see in it a symbol of their own heroic strength and energy. The "Giant," as the common people called it, was dragged in a solemn procession, lasting three days, through the streets to its destination, and the event became a landmark in Florentine history; for years afterwards every trader referred to past transactions as having taken place before or after the erection of the Giant.

His triumph did not dissipate Michelangelo's ill-feeling towards his fellow-artists. Perugino had made sarcastic remarks about him; in the presence of witnesses he called Perugino a rough, ignorant man, a painter without any sort of talent. Perugino depended for his living on his reputation as an artist, and summoned Michelangelo before the Council of Eight; but Michelangelo so ably demonstrated the complainant's artistic shortcomings that, says Vasari, Perugino "emerged from the case with little honour."

But Michelangelo's anger seems to have been chiefly directed against Leonardo: he felt that Leonardo's expression of opinion had amounted to a cold refusal to acknowledge the greatness of his work. He laboured at all times under a sense of persecution, interpreting entirely innocent phrases as uttered in malice, with intent to humiliate him. One day some of the most prominent men in the city were seated on a bench outside the Palazzo Spini, in the Piazza della Trinità, busily discussing a passage in Dante, with the portentous gravity of men to whom disputation was one of the principal things in life. At the climax of the debate Leonardo happened to cross the piazza. He was the very man they wanted, a man redolent of scholarship and well known for his pleasure in nice points. They asked his opinion of the correct interpretation of the passage. It happened, however, that at that moment Michelangelo appeared at the other side of the square. He was immersed in thought, looking down and disdainfully ignoring all who passed him. Did Leonardo seize on this meeting as an opportunity of evading the idle discussion, was he merely out for a joke, or was he actually trying to placate his disgruntled fellow-artist? In any case, he pointed to the young sculptor, who was known to be an ardent student of Dante, and said:

"You had better ask Michel Agnolo; he will expound it to you."

Michelangelo started like a man who has suddenly been wakened—and flushed at once with anger.

Leonardo had come dressed, as always, like a great noble, with carefully twisted moustache, a metallic gleam in his beard, and meticulously tended hands. Michelangelo's clothes were crumpled as if he were in the habit of lying fully dressed on any bench for a couple of hours' sleep; the folds were full of marble dust, and clay stuck to his roughened hands; his short, tumbled hair fell untidily over his frowning forehead. Leonardo at fifty still had regular features untouched by the hand of time, and a fair-skinned face framed in the matt sheen of his long hair; the big forehead and cold, keen eyes seemed waiting to give short shrift to folly, and there was an arrogant furrow between the bushy eyebrows. Michelangelo's young face was worn and tormented, and the nose that had been broken by Torrigiano's fist—that brand of Cain, as Michelangelo himself called it—had distorted the whole face; his eyes were fevered with the tension at which he worked, and on the rugged forehead throbbed the prominent artery of the easily aroused. Always on the watch for insults, he felt Leonardo's remark as a direct challenge. "Explain it yourself," he shouted, "you who made a model of a horse to cast in bronze, and then could not make the casting and cravenly abandoned the work!"

Leonardo was dumbfounded by this burst of ill-will. It was Michelangelo's outlet for his unending resentment at his own fate, and, like everything he did, it went far beyond the occasion for it. The sculptor passed on, but turned back to hurl one more sarcasm: "And those fat geese of Milan trusted a task like that to you!"

Not a word passed Leonardo's lips; only the blood rushed into his bright cheeks. Amid the dismayed silence of all who had witnessed the scene, he went away, erect and master of himself even under this humiliation. "There can be no greater or lesser mastery than over oneself"—*non si può avere maggiore ne minore signoria che quella di sè medesimo*—said Leonardo once. Though he noted so many troubles in his records, he never made the slightest reference to this public incident; only, about this time, he wrote as an admonition to himself, and a reminder to arm himself yet better against the malice of men:

"Patience protects us from wrongs just as clothes do against cold; and do you, just as you heap on clothes with the growing cold so that it shall do you no harm, likewise increase your patience in face of great wrongs, and they will then be powerless to vex your mind." [71]

Yet Michelangelo's thrust had hurt him more than the aggressor imagined, for it was a reminder of the tragic destiny that hung over Leonardo's creative work, as though fate herself had sworn to defeat all his efforts toward perfection. As far back as he could remember, his life's path was strewn with the wreckage of plans that had failed and with masterpieces left unfinished, from the *Adoration of the Magi* to the Sforza monument—burst bubbles of dreams, discoveries only half made. The colossus still stood ready for casting, exposed to wind and weather, in the castle square; day by day it had crumbled, and now it was serving as a target for the Gascon archers quartered in the castle. After Lodovico's fall Ercole d'Este, duke of Ferrara, had tried to arrange for it to be cast in bronze—"a good and desirable thing," he wrote to his ambassador at Milan. Cardinal d'Amboise had expressed his readiness to meet the duke's wish, but he had to wait for the king's consent, and Louis XII delayed his answer, perhaps hoping to do something himself. So the duke's request was forgotten, until the monument had become weatherworn beyond saving. Was it only blind fate, or time, consumer of all things, that was answerable for the destruction of all his highest aims? Once, at a moment of depression, Leonardo admitted to himself his own responsibility for the tragedy of his life: "The highest happiness becomes the cause of unhappiness, and the fullness of wisdom the cause of folly." [72] How many plans he might have carried to completion if they had not been too vast and too amazingly bold; how many discoveries he might have passed on to humanity if he had not always been wrestling for flawless accuracy of formulation and absolutely complete demonstration; how many masterpieces he might have finished if he had not striven after utter perfection!

Michelangelo's shouted charge of incapacity was all the more unjust because the casting of the Milanese colossus had been prevented only by the disturbed times and the scarcity of metal; yet if the monument had not been designed on so immense a scale the metal would have been available, and even in a time of stress the casting could have been carried out. But at the back of Michelangelo's explosion there was something besides personal resentment, something of which he was scarcely conscious—the hatred of a fanatic for an apostate. Michelangelo, whose absorption in the exercise of his art amounted almost to dæmonic possession, felt instinctively that Leonardo had not this exclusive loyalty, that for Leonardo the essential things in life lay outside artistic creation. That dissipation of energy seemed to Michelangelo to be a betrayal—the reprehensible frivolity of a dilettante frittering away vast powers.

Michelangelo entrenched himself in his sombre animosity against Leonardo, as though to justify his outburst. All he knew, moreover, of Leonardo was the legend of his luxurious and convivial existence, made up wholly of idle hours dreamed away, and with this legend he contrasted his own austere youth, sacrificed to work. As though in order to prove his own mastery and to indemnify himself for his sacrifices, he determined to enter into competition with Leonardo in a field in which the elder man had demonstrated his unquestioned mastery, a field which to Michelangelo was still unfamiliar. Michelangelo was primarily a sculptor, and had done little painting; what he had done looked like reliefs transferred to a smooth surface. Two years later his enemies induced Julius II to entrust him with the decoration of the Sistine chapel, in the hope that he would shrink from undertaking the work; Bramante, who would have been very glad to be rid of this extremely formidable rival, said with a grin that he knew Michelangelo would not dare to accept the commission.

But nobody really knew the fanatical determination of which Michelangelo was capable. He made up his mind now to enter into rivalry with Leonardo's battle of Anghiari, and sought the commission for a fresco on the wall in the council chamber facing that reserved for Leonardo's work. The Florentine councillors did not venture to oppose the popularly revered creator of the *David*, and in the autumn of 1504 Michelangelo received the commission he wanted.

This was in itself a set-back for Leonardo, who some time before had been promised the decoration of the whole chamber. There now started in Florence a contest such as the world of art had never before seen—a competition between these two for the expression of the highest that was in them, fought out by each in lonely and strenuous wrestling with himself.

A large room was cleared for Michelangelo in October in the dyers' hospital of Sant' Onofrio, a scaffolding was built for him, and the pasteboard prepared for his cartoon. He plunged passionately into his task, and the very subject that he chose was a challenge to Leonardo. To Michelangelo, whose relief of *Centaurs and Lapithæ* dated from his early youth, the fury and confusion of battle which Leonardo had captured in his design were subjects so familiar and so much his own that he might even regard Leonardo's work as an invasion of his own sphere. In any case, he now entered a sphere in which Leonardo was an undisputed master; he set out to paint beautiful human bodies in various attitudes, opposing an almost idyllic scene to the fury of the Anghiari battle. He proposed to celebrate the city's heroic past by painting a genre scene—the soldiers at Anghiari surprised while bathing. The Florentine councillors made no objection.

In the dyers' hospital of Sant' Onofrio and in the Sala del Papa at Santa Maria Novella, the duel went on, amid the excitement of all Florence and of every art community in Italy. Florence had become the world's school: everywhere students of painting left their teachers, and young artists their unfinished pictures, to make the pilgrimage to Florence. One day, late in the autumn of 1504, a young man came to the Sala del Papa in order, like many other young men, to watch Leonardo at work—the young painter Raffaello Sanzio, from Urbino. He was only twenty-one and looked like a boy, with his slender, supple figure, his narrow shoulders, the soft outline of his long, pale face, and a childish dimple still in his chin. His forehead, too, was smooth and round and unmarked as a child's, and the pale lips, the lower one thrust forward purposefully, were those of a youth. Only the long, almond-shaped eyes beneath the strong, bold, deep black arch of the eyebrows were strangely mature, with a precocious resoluteness that contradicted the softness of the features and the agreeable smile round the mouth. From behind the warmth with which these eyes beamed alike on men and things there broke through an insistent hunger for life.

The young Raphael, son of a painter and at this time a pupil of Perugino, had come to Florence in the spirit of one who had been sent there by an inner voice which he was in the habit of obeying. He was still wholly under the influence of his master; he painted the same saints with flat, empty faces supported like flowers on the delicate stalks of their necks, and with a gaze fluttering up to heaven. Though he knew much better than his master how to give them life and motion and how they should be articulated, he did not parade his knowledge but gave them gestures which all the world could understand; an air of contemplation runs through his pictures like a gentle melody.

In Florence a new world, a world of which his young ambition had never yet dreamed, opened before him. After his first meeting with Leonardo he knew that he must throw overboard as useless ballast all that he had brought with him. Painfully and laboriously he liberated himself from things learnt which blocked his progress and his path to fame. "Gradually, with great effort," writes Vasari, "he abandoned Pietro's style." Two overmastering influences, Leonardo's ripe but not easily communicable art, and Michelangelo's overwhelming strength, adored by all the youth of Florence, competed for possession of the young artist, but Raphael did not hesitate a moment in his choice. "When he saw Leonardo da Vinci's works he was altogether dumbfounded and amazed, and as Leonardo's style pleased him better than any other that he had ever seen he set himself to study it, and tried his utmost to imitate the said Leonardo's style." Such is Vasari's substantially accurate but rather naïve story of this turning-point in Raphael's artistic career.

With his infinite natural receptivity the young man drank in this revelation. He was the better able to do so since he made no mental reservations whatever. On the other hand, with a remarkable sureness of instinct he adopted only those elements which he was able to assimilate completely, with the result that they became so much a part of his own manner that he would soon be entirely unaware of his indebtedness. This instinct for the things that

LOUVRE

Mona Lisa (*La Gioconda*)

could assist his own development, this sense of what could be useful, was a factor of his creative work. Michelangelo, who considered that he owed everything to himself and energetically repudiated all indebtedness to his teachers, was unable to comprehend the young painter's capacity for adaptation of his art, and later, when Raphael had reached success and fame, Michelangelo said he owed his rise not to talent but merely to industry. Raphael, however, went his way unperturbed.

8

Raphael had come to Florence to study the cartoons for the frescoes in the council chamber, and, with the thoroughness that had made him a favourite student, he copied a group of horsemen from the cartoon for the battle of Anghiari. But he was to have more to thank Leonardo for than the knowledge of the movements of man and beast, the mastery of chaos, and the art of arranging groups and of relating them to one another. For at this period of ferment in Leonardo's life, when he was torn between the fever of artistic creation and the urge to flee to the beloved world of his studies, this period of accumulated disappointments and of the harassing rivalry of Michelangelo's ambition, Leonardo was also at work on the portrait of La Gioconda.

Leonardo had probably been at work for some time on this portrait of Mona Lisa, the young wife of the rich Francesco del Giocondo. It may be that the portrait was ordered at the time of his return to Florence, when he was compelled to look round for commissions. Even the name attached to the picture has only traditional authority, and the story of its subject is as fragmentary as the history of the picture. It was in any case a commonplace story. Francesco del Giocondo, rich and growing old, had been twice a widower when he married this dowerless girl, twenty years younger than he, the daughter of a Florentine named Antonio Maria di Noldo Gherardini; she, like Leonardo's successive stepmothers, had looked on her marriage as a sort of refuge for the needy. This is all that was known in Florence of Messer Giocondo's wife, Madonna Lisa (Mona Lisa for short, or alternatively, after her husband, La Gioconda)—this, and that a little daughter was born to the couple but died young; they seem to have had no other children.

When Leonardo began her portrait, Mona Lisa was something over twenty-four years of age; when she last sat to him she was nearly thirty and, in the eyes of people of that time, a woman past her prime. The people of her day liked slender women with girlish faces poised on long, slim necks, fragile figures with sloping shoulders that seemed too weak to carry the heavy folds of their brocade dresses or the weight of their strings of glittering jewellery. But Mona Lisa was a robust, well-developed woman; marriage and motherhood had filled out her figure, and her face had broadened. As the fashion required bright complexions, her firm skin was stretched like gleaming satin over her full cheeks. Her face was, moreover, a commonplace one, the product of a commonplace existence—a face that revealed perfect health and imperturbable calm, the face of a woman whose senses had been dulled by the lazy flow of her existence and who whiled away her days with little to expect or desire.

And yet this thoroughly bourgeois woman, ripened and not very happy and not particularly unhappy, had been able to fascinate Leonardo more than any other woman he met in all his life. He spent many years painting her portrait; and during those years many commissions were waiting for him, pressed on him; Isabella d'Este was begging in vain for her portrait; vast plans and unhappy failures threw his life into disorder. Yet he went on with this one work with steady persistence, and years after the sitter's husband had ordered the picture he still declared that it was not yet finished, as an excuse for taking it with him on his further wanderings.

Mona Lisa's name does not appear a single time in Leonardo's notebooks, which are so sparing at all times of personal notes. There is not a suggestion anywhere of anything that could be connected with the portrait, not a word or figure or detail of any sort. Nor is there the slightest vestige of any contemporary studio gossip connecting Mona Lisa with her painter, or of any fanciful connexion of the two in the works of the sensation-seeking biographers of the great, of which there were so many in the generation that followed. But many years later, when the respectable Messer Giocondo was virtually forgotten and only his wife's name remembered, there were still many contemporaries of Leonardo who vividly remembered the circumstances under which he painted her portrait, apparently treating it quite differently from any other that he ever painted. While he worked on it he arranged for readers and musicians to come to his house, and he surrounded the portrait with an atmosphere made up of everything that he himself loved, an atmosphere full of all the pulsations of light and colour and music that harmonized with his own spirit.

A name associated almost casually with the picture; the description of the manner of its painting; and the picture itself—that of a woman like many other women, with a history like many others, and yet a unique work, never excelled, never even approached, which has delighted and disturbed all observers through hundreds of years, preserving its vitality as on the first day it appeared in spite of being discussed and described and interpreted to death—such is the enigma of Mona Lisa. Whatever he was doing, Leonardo returned again and again to this portrait as to the fount whence he drew his inner repose, his refreshment after the trials of everyday life, and the calm and composure of which he stood in need. In the midst of the feverish work on the Anghiari cartoon, when he was getting too obsessed with the rage-distorted faces of his shouting warriors and the glazing eyes of the dying, and when dragons and demons were crowding in on his imagination, he would leave all this to spend a few quiet hours on the portrait of Mona Lisa.

In his *Treatise on Painting* Leonardo had recommended painters not to work on portraits in the hard light of a bright day, but when the clouds hang low and a pale light filters through; when rain pours down in silver streams; or when the bluish dusk effaces every hard gleam, enticing the shadows and giving men and women the unreal charm of faces seen between dreaming and waking. In such hours of subdued light he painted Mona Lisa. The room would be filled with the unusual tones of musical instruments of his own making. (At this time he made many new instruments, of strange richness and peculiar timbre, like a voice floating in from another world.) Meanwhile one of the readers would recite the verses of great poets of the past. Mona Lisa sat resting with folded hands in her chair, with the poise of any Florentine woman of good family. She wore nothing that indicated her husband's wealth. Her dark hair was parted in the middle and fell unadorned past her cheeks, making her face look even broader; a veil passed over her head, falling away on either side. Her dress, with no other decoration than a narrow embroidered border, was drawn tightly over her full breast. No flashing stone or chain broke the pearly surface of the full and firm neck that rose from her deep-cut gown. Her hands were equally free of jewellery, and had a strange bareness as they stood out from the brilliant zigzags formed by the crisp folds of her sleeves.

What was going on beneath Mona Lisa's broad, soft face in these hours of festal ceremony? In the portrait the expression is vividly alive and yet remote, as though it were that of a person living a life alien to her and uncomprehended. A broad forehead lies above these regular features, a broad and cheerful forehead never touched by fevered thoughts or torturing doubts. Entirely unexpectedly, however, there breaks from the almond-shaped eyes, between the heavy, fleshy lids still weighted by slow-moving dreams not yet fully dreamed, the quick light of a smile, apparently born of the moment. The smile passes down the broad face to the firm little mouth, whose upper lip closes tightly over the coral-red lower lip as in women who are used to silence and are good listeners.

Was it this smile that Leonardo was determined to capture during the years of his wrestling with Mona Lisa's portrait? Did he see it flit over her face when some phrase recalled memories or some harmony aroused emotions perhaps never before felt? Or did Leonardo first see it in a dream, palpable and yet elusive? Once he asked in regret: "Why does the eye see a thing much more clearly in dreams than when in wakefulness it tries to visualize it?" [73] Or did Leonardo implant the smile of the closed mouth and the questioning glance in this woman's face out of the great store of his own knowledge? Did the same thing happen to him as to many other painters, of whom he says that they impress their own physical features on the most dissimilar models, giving the model their own characteristics of body and soul, and burdening the ideal figure of their invention with their own faults and shortcomings?

"I have known painters," he writes in his *Treatise on Painting*, "who made every figure they created an exact copy of themselves, giving their subject their own gestures and movements." [74] Painters with a natural gift of liveliness would give their subjects their own vivacity, the pious ones their own heavenward gaze, and a painter who disliked a strenuous life would make his figures look like the embodiment of laziness.

Leonardo considered that this tendency to mould in one's own image was as old as the power of discernment itself. The soul, which rules the body, forming man's exterior from within, also determines his power of judgment. So strong is its influence that "it guides the painter's arm and makes him reproduce himself, since it appears to the soul that this is the best way to represent a human being. . . . And if the soul finds a being that resembles the body which it has built for itself, it finds that figure so pleasing that it falls in love with it." [74]

Did this creative process of investing the model with the artist's personality, this tyranny of the formative ego, which Leonardo thus tentatively analysed, determine also the character of Mona Lisa's portrait? Did Leonardo unconsciously assimilate Mona Lisa's features to his soul's ideal? Is it his own gaze, burdened with some unfathomable problem, that peers from her eyes; is it his own smile, a smile of consciously superior knowledge, that flits round her firm little mouth, expressing a haughty inaccessibility that has nothing in common with her good-natured face? "The painter who has clumsy hands will paint similar hands in his pictures," wrote Leonardo. Are Mona Lisa's hands, with their strong wrists, their long, firm backs, and their sensitive finger-tips, these hands that seem to be enjoying the softness of the silk they are stroking—are these the hands of the plump and placid wife of a wealthy Florentine merchant?

In any case, Leonardo was familiar with Mona Lisa's smile long before her portrait was commissioned by Francesco del Giocondo. It had flitted across the women's lips in his early terra-cotta busts, no longer extant; and it flickered round the mouth of his *Saint Anne*. And some suggestion of the magnetism of Mona Lisa's glance appeared in the eyes of the angel in the *Madonna of the Rocks*, a suggestion fully developed later in the strong, mysterious appeal in the almond-shaped eyes of John the Baptist. That glance and that smile were intimately associated with Leonardo himself, they were his own personal possession and not his model's. Did they now come most startlingly to life in Mona Lisa because they were brought into intimate association with authentic womanhood, a womanhood balanced and self-sufficing, accepting its earthly lot, absorbing every emotion only to suppress it? In Mona Lisa's portrait Leonardo laid special stress on this majestic imperturbability.

Behind the woman's harmonious and carefully finished silhouette he put a rough and broken country, crossed by zigzag paths and winding streamlets, full of rising swaths of mist that moved to and fro between steep mountainsides. And the light that poured over the landscape, seeming as if it were sifted through moving water or greenish glass, a light like that at the bottom of the sea or beneath thick sunlit leafage, opened up a troubled infinity beyond Mona Lisa's calm.

The paint of this picture cracked and peeled, and other hands tried to stem the fading of the skin's radiance; the red colour deadened to a violet blue, the yellow passed into green, the blue into a grey dullness; the varnish, yellowed and grown dirty, sucked up the last beauty of the colours; yet Mona Lisa's smile still floats victorious over devastation and decay, as though it could endure a thousand deaths.

For Leonardo's contemporaries this portrait was the starting-point of a new art. His fellow-artists were still painting reality with all its hardness and crudity, its chance beauty and its incidental ugliness, as a faithful record for friends and relations; Mona Lisa's portrait swept away all the springlike sharpness and the frail charm of reality and substituted for it a new conception of beauty, a new human type, full and radiant, raised above personal destinies and maintaining itself on the canvas as though it were the centre of the world.

To this day Mona Lisa's portrait remains a solitary masterpiece on the threshold of a new epoch. But the young Raphael was soon able to see it, and his fresh and ardently receptive mind appreciated the marvellous character of the work, even if he did not fully grasp it. He carefully copied Mona Lisa's self-possessed silhouette,

her upright posture and slight turn, the sensuous restfulness of her
hands, and the glimpse of a landscape in the distance. At about this
time he was commissioned to paint the portrait of Messer Doni
and his wife, and with his impulsive, ambitious, not very scrupulous temperament he assimilated every element of Leonardo's
work which he could turn at once to account. He produced a portrait which had the touching and slightly comic character of the
over-zealous work of an altogether too imitative disciple. Round
the fat, empty face of the prematurely stout Maddalena Doni he
placed hair and veil exactly as in Mona Lisa's portrait; the dull
glance from her round eyes he allowed to wander out of the picture and fasten mildly on the observer; the little mouth between
the already flabby cheeks he closed with a firmness that ill suited
her garrulous lips. To make a job of it, he placed her stubby
hands, with their fat sausages of fingers, on top of each other, but
he loaded them with heavy rings, and he hung a very solid neck-
lace round her thick neck. And yet this picture, with its array of
dissonances, proclaims the heir who was to carry Leonardo's heritage, the immense heritage of the art of portraying human beings,
into the new age. But Raphael assimilated more than this while he
openly followed Leonardo step by step during this period of the
great master's most fruitful activity.

For Leonardo the portrait of Mona Lisa was an essay in the representation of woman. His disciples and imitators, who painted a
naked Mona Lisa in this identical attitude, an absurd and irritating picture, followed the master's ideas with dull incomprehension. Beneath Mona Lisa's individual features Leonardo was in
search of the eternal mystery of womanhood. That unspoilt, un-
subdued womanhood, with its healthy, animal, slightly sleepy sen-
suousness, which he found in complete self-surrender and yet in
complete self-mastery in the wife of Francesco del Giocondo, had
been a revelation to this man, no longer young, who knew so little
of women. To his own unresponsive senses, the experience was like
that of witnessing a natural phenomenon; he was thrilled as by
the spectacle of an external force in fateful action, a force that left
him untouched.

After his portrait of Mona Lisa, Leonardo set out to embody the
fate that is woman in the full-blooded, drowsily sensuous nude fig-

ure of Leda, rising from the ground amid a profusion of flowering plants, with the warm outline of her exuberant hips pressed against the great swan, a bewildering, breath-taking trinity of plants, bird, and woman.

Raphael similarly appropriated the preliminary ideas for the *Leda*. He copied Leda's grave bent head, with the hair wound in strangely intertwining coils and lying like scaly snakeskins, or shining snailshells, or the shoots of exotic plants, over her broad-browed, pointed face. He also took note, with his glance that registered everything, of the disturbing outlines of the woman's well-developed body, though at the time he had no opportunity of making use of these details; he used them many years later in his *Galatea*.

Leonardo, however, got no further in this Florentine period than the first designs for the *Leda*. He had delivered the battle cartoon by the stipulated date, and set to work now to transfer the design to the wall of the Sala del Consiglio. At the end of February 1505 he had a platform on wheels erected by Giovanni the Piper. He was anxious to achieve something quite special, and had thought out a process which should add substantially to the brilliance of the colouring. He had, indeed, no liking for the technique of fresco painting, with the broad, rapid strokes of the brush, which could not be modified in any way; the uniform progress required was also incompatible with his desultory method of working, with days of feverish activity followed by long intervals of reflection. At Santa Maria delle Grazie he had covered the wall with a layer of resin, after which he had been able to treat the surface almost like a panel. Now he believed that he had found a still better medium for his method of painting, and one which would also give something of the brilliance of oil colours to the rather dull tones of tempera. In one of the ancient writers—Pliny, according to an anonymous contemporary—he had found a description of the encaustic method of painting, and, following the ancient recipe, he had prepared a binding medium which he had employed with very good results in the cartoon; he had lit a big fire in the room which had quickly dried the medium without injury to the enamel-like brilliance of the colours.

After this successful experiment he had the wall in the Sala del Consiglio coated with the same mixture. To help him to make progress with the work, the Signoria had given him two assistants, the painter Raffaello di Biagio and a young Spaniard then studying in Florence, Ferrando de Almedina. Tomaso Masini, the friend of Leonardo's youth who had taken the name of Zoroastro da Peretola, was commissioned to mix the colours according to the master's directions, and a young pupil of Leonardo's named Lorenzo (perhaps Lorenzo Lotto of Bergamo), then seventeen years old, gave such help as he could.

But it would take some time for the priming to dry on the wall so that the transferring of the design could be begun. Meanwhile spring had come, and after his strenuous winter's work Leonardo felt more weary of town than ever. He took advantage of the interruption of his work to accept an invitation from the canon of Fiesole, Alessandro Amadori. Amadori was proud to call himself Leonardo's uncle, although he was only the brother of Ser Piero's first wife. But until her early death she had taken the place of a mother to Leonardo, and he had a grateful recollection of her, and a kindly feeling also for her brother.

9

Spring in Fiesole is like a festival. The young, cheerful green everywhere ripples down the slopes of the valleys; the fresh breezes shake the tops of the olive trees, and a silvery foam seems to be blown over the emerald-green meadows; the cypresses rise darkly erect from the golden ribbons of the paths; the pines reach out with their long, irregular branches to the deep blue sky. The sunlight has not yet the hard white glare of summer; it is like gold shot with blue; the dews of early morning seem still to cling to it. There is still a vestige of coolness in the air on the heights, gradually giving way to the warm scent of the wild flowers. The rarefied, perfumed air goes to the head like a light wine gulped down too quickly. And as if the radiance and fragrance had really been too much for him, Leonardo would stand motionless, looking steadily ahead or up to the cloudless sky. Then he would pull out his notebooks and busily cover the sheets with sketches and voluminous notes.

The notes were concerned with his lifelong dream, the dream of the great human bird that would lift itself into the air. In the first free moments he found, he took up his researches at the point at which he had had to break them off—his thorough study of the flight of birds. This incurable worker, in whom his contemporaries saw a dreamer and waster of time, turned his holidays in Fiesole into weeks of intensive observation and thought, weeks in which he collected, sifted, and correlated the results of his observations and tested their serviceability for human attempts at flight. In the radiant spring sunshine at Fiesole Leonardo worked at a comprehensive treatise on the flight of birds, planned to contain four books, treating of forward motion with and without the beating of wings, and giving a general account of the flight of birds, bats, and insects, and a description of every detail of its mechanism.[75]

His account of the flight of birds was based on the results of innumerable prolonged and painstaking observations. No man before him had ever seriously tackled this problem, and nearly two hundred years were to pass before Borelli published his *De Motu Animalium* (1680), which dealt with the laws of motion in all animals, and two hundred more before, almost at the end of the nineteenth century, J. B. Pettigrew dealt in a series of monographs with the mechanism of flight. Yet Leonardo, a pioneer in an entirely unexplored field, dependent entirely on his sharp eyes, and equipped with only the primitive science of his age, sketched a picture of the flight of birds which, in spite of various errors, anticipated many elements of the modern theory of avian flight.

He penetrated farthest in his observation of gliding flight—flight without the beating of wings. Birds with big wings lift them and wait, gently circling, for the upward thrust of the wind, "like the bird of prey, the vulture, which I saw on my way to Fiesole, above the village of Barbiga, on March 14, 1505"—so he writes, giving the precise date as for a memorable event.[76] A scarcely visible fluttering of the wings maintains the bird's balance; then it allows itself to be slowly carried up in a semicircle by the impact of the wind on the under surface of its wings; for a while it moves on under this thrust, and then it sinks again, describing another semicircle, until a fresh puff of wind lifts it further and drives it on.[77]

Proceeding purely from things seen, from facts repeatedly observed, Leonardo discovered fundamental laws of mechanics as if by chance, and then casually mentioned them, as though he had stumbled upon too many such discoveries, and had ventured too far into the wilderness of research, to trouble to set up signposts along his path. Thus, in connexion with gliding flight, he described the way a bird acts in suddenly reversing the direction of its flight: it pushes the tips of its wings toward the tail in the direction desired, and this sudden thrust automatically carries the bird round against the pressure of the wind—because "every movement tends to maintain itself; or, rather, every body in motion continues to move so long as the influence of the force of its motor is maintained in it." This principle, the law of inertia, was first formulated by Galileo in 1638, in his *Discorsi e Demostrazioni Matematiche,* and is described in the history of the sciences as his discovery.

The chief problem that engaged Leonardo's attention—always with a view to practical application—was that of equilibrium, which depends on the relation between the centre of gravity and the centre of resistance; he invented an instrument which enabled him to determine the centre of gravity of a bird's body.[78] His observations were accordingly directed in the first place to ascertaining how a bird is able by opening and closing its wings to shift the centre of resistance. "When the bird sinks, the centre of gravity is moved beyond the centre of its resistance . . . and when the bird wishes to rise the centre of gravity remains behind the centre of its resistance." [79]

In the course of his observations he was filled again and again with admiration for the perfection of the mechanism within the bird's body; of this mechanism he tried to identify the various functions. "Beginnings of things," he wrote, "are often the cause of big results. Thus we may see a small, almost imperceptible movement of the rudder turn a ship of astonishing size, loaded with a very heavy cargo, and this, too, amid such a weight of water as presses on its every timber, and in the teeth of the boisterous winds that fill its mighty sails. So in those birds which can support themselves above the course of the winds without beating their wings, a slight movement of wing or tail, serving them to enter either below or above the wind, suffices to prevent their fall." [80]

Leonardo also drew special attention to the fact that on approaching the earth a bird will lower its tail and spread out the tail feathers, stretch its head upwards, and give little beats with its wings, to reduce the speed of descent and make a gentle landing. He recognized that landing was one of the chief dangers to the flying apparatus, and in order to study the process he made an artificial bird with movable tail and tested the regulating effect of the tail feathers, with the bird's body hanging freely.

He dealt in advance with the objections that might be made to the application of observations of the flight of birds to human attempts to fly. It was true that a bird's muscles and nerves, and especially the breast muscles, were strong out of all proportion to those of a man. But, he contended, the strength birds have is much greater than they need for simply flying; they need to be able to escape from a pursuer and themselves to pursue their quarry, and often they have to carry a heavy load in their claws. Men, too, themselves have more strength in their legs than they ordinarily exert; this fact Leonardo demonstrated by a simple experiment. He measured the depth of the footmarks of a man standing in soft earth, then the depth when he stood with another man on his shoulders, and then when he came down after jumping as high as he could. From the increasing depth of the footmarks he drew the conclusion that a man has twice as much muscular strength in his legs as he needs in order to stand upright. [81]

He was in line with modern flying technique in recommending the flier to rise to a great height, "since this will be his safeguard." When flying high the apparatus would be better protected against air currents and eddies than when flying low; the flier would have less difficulty in maintaining equilibrium, and would be better able to manœuvre so as to land gently. [82] The great birds of prey, he wrote, fly very high for reasons of a similar order: "If their flight were low . . . they would be unable to find any shelter by reason of the fury of icy blasts among the narrow defiles of mountains, and unable to guide themselves with their great wings so as to avoid being dashed against precipices or tall crags or trees." [83]

Leonardo was aware of the inadequacy of contemporary knowledge of atmospheric conditions, but at this time he was able to make only superficial investigations; not until some years later did he enter thoroughly into this problem, which he recognized as the "first condition of knowledge concerning the winged creatures in the air." [84] He hoped, however, that even now he had collected sufficient experimental data, and had acquired a sufficiently accurate knowledge of the laws of flight, to proceed with the building of the "great bird," as he called his apparatus.

The model to which he now adhered was designed on the principle of the glider. The bearing surfaces were copied from bats' wings; for their sinews, as he called them, he proposed to use ropes of pure silk, and strong tanned leather for the joints. The flier was placed in a sort of air gondola, for, as Leonardo stated at this time, "the flying man must be free from the girdle upwards, so that the centre of gravity in him and in the machine may be shifted according as necessity demands." [85] A flying apparatus was exposed, in Leonardo's view, to two chief risks—its supports might break, or it might overturn when canting. He sought security from the former risk in the special strength of his chosen material, and from the latter by separating the centre of gravity and the centre of resistance widely from each other. For an apparatus 30 ells (60 feet) wide he provided a distance of four ells between the two.

Leonardo now felt that all the difficulties in the way of the production of his flying apparatus had been overcome. In this radiant springtime in Fiesole the dream of his life seemed to be within reach, and more vividly present than the realities around him. Between the undulating heights that reached up to the sparkling skies there rose a bare hill, some 1300 feet high, popularly called Monte Cecero, or Swan Mountain, on account of its peculiar shape. Leonardo determined to attempt a flight from the crest of this hill; he did not for a moment doubt his success. All his past hesitations and disappointments and failures were forgotten in the exultation that now filled him. Once more he assumed that his dream was on the eve of fulfilment, and savoured in advance all the joy of triumph. He returned to Florence and to his work like a man under an enchantment, wrapped in his great secret. Hastily, and preserving secrecy even with himself, he entered in his notebook: "From the mountain that bears the name of the great bird, the famous bird will take its flight and fill the world with its great fame." But this seemed to him too tame and ordinary to convey his happiness and excitement, and he wrote again, this time on the cover of the book in which he had entered his observations concerning the flight of birds, these almost lyrical lines: "The great bird will make its first flight—upon the back of its great swan —filling the whole world with amazement, filling all records with its fame, and bringing eternal glory to its birthplace." [86]

So he dreamed of his fame. It was not through his creative work that he expected to confer eternal glory on the place of his birth, not through immortal works that his fame was to fill the whole world and all records; this longing for fame, with which he was filled, he had scarcely ever hoped to satisfy through a painting; and the bitterness of the denial of recognition that he suffered in his younger days, which found expression in the ardent desire for recognition by his native village, seems scarcely ever to have come over him when he stood facing a fresco or a panel. Often as Leonardo the painter thought of fame, he never promised himself immortality as a painter. Great inventions, unique discoveries, new results of research, or victories won over elements—these were to carry his name far over the world, beyond frontiers and down the centuries. And all his unsatisfied ambition, all his festering humiliations, all his hunger for recognition as a vindication before his contemporaries, poured now into his dream of the human bird that would lift itself with widespread pinions into the air.

He returned to his work in the Sala del Consiglio like a man torn by wretched professional ties from the only activity that mattered to him. The varnished surface took the colours splendidly. With the aid of his clever young helpers the transfer of the design proceeded rapidly. In the course of the winter the central scene, the struggle for the flag, was completed. The bloodthirsty faces of the warriors were lit up as though bathed in the reflection of a distant glow, and in the more than life-sized representations of beasts and men there was a wild splendour.

But these colours, brilliant as enamel, obstinately retained their sticky dampness. The wonderful binding medium which Leonardo had invented required more time for drying than he expected. There seemed to be something wrong with the mixing. In his impatience Leonardo set out to repeat in the Sala del Consiglio the experiment of artificial drying which he had made with the cartoon. A huge brazier was placed in the council room, and waves of heat surged up against the damp and shining picture. Suddenly, as the flames were stirred up, some colours began to trickle down from the upper edge of the painting over its surface; runlets of colour merged with one another, and a horrible work of destruction went on steadily before Leonardo's eyes. All that remained of years of labour was a striped surface broken by ghosts of figures. Once more Leonardo had destroyed a unique achievement, a triumph of his art, by his search for utter perfection.

At the time of this disaster Michelangelo had returned to his cartoon. A few months after beginning it he had had to interrupt the work because Pope Julius II summoned him to Rome. But in May 1506 he had quarrelled with the Pope. Two obstinate temperaments had clashed, and Michelangelo had returned to Florence in a furious rage. He did not know which way to turn: he sought a reconciliation with the Pope, he considered entering the service of the Turks, and meanwhile he worked like one possessed on the cartoon of the bathing soldiers. In the past Florence had been split into two camps. Now Michelangelo found support from the young with their cult of the new, and from the half-hearted and hesitant whom Leonardo's ill-success had discouraged. He had the support of the gonfaloniere; Soderini accorded him the palm in the rivalry of the artists. "We can aver that Michelangelo is a man of distinction, the first in his craft in Italy, even, perhaps, in the whole world," he wrote to his brother. And Soderini had the tolerance of which limited and obstinate men are capable when once a man's worth has dawned upon them: "If we speak kindly to him and treat him gently we can get anything from him. All that is needed is to let him see that we like him and are well disposed towards him; then he will do amazing work."

In face of the gonfaloniere's scarcely concealed hostility, of the reproaches of the Signoria, and of his own bitter disgust, could Leonardo possibly take up his task anew? Only a tremendous success, an unparalleled triumph, could extricate him from this galling defeat. Spring had come again, and again he was at Fiesole, the guest of his adoptive uncle Alessandro Amadori, who was so proud of his influence with his pseudo-nephew. In this spring of 1506 Alessandro Amadori was made use of, in his capacity of an influential advocate, by Isabella d'Este. But neither Isabella nor his uncle could prevail on Leonardo.

The time had come for the great bird to take flight. The slopes of the Swan Mountain rose bare amid the fragrant blossoming of the Tuscan spring. With this hill there is associated a legend which has been carried down from father to son through generations, and has been as firmly believed as if it was attested by a credible eyewitness: one day there rose up from Monte Cecero a huge bird, as though the Swan Mountain had lifted itself into the air; and suddenly the bird disappeared as though swallowed up by the skies.

Something happened in the solitude of that spring. Did Leonardo complete his "great bird," provide himself with parachute and bladders, and himself hazard the flight? He was already in the fifties, but his hands had still the strength that had once broken iron bolts and horseshoes. Did he now attempt the flight, preserving the secret with a conspirator's jealousy, and did he fall unhurt amid the wreckage of his apparatus? Or was only a dream shattered, before he could venture to attempt its realization?

No eyewitness ever spoke. No word was written by Leonardo himself after his exultant prophecy of his flight. But from now on he never again wrote of the "great bird" as a tangible reality, never again saw himself rising in the air to fill the whole world with his fame. Something crashed in this spring at Fiesole, an apparatus or a hope. Many years later, long after Leonardo had died, when there was no longer any reason for those who were in the secret, if any there were, to fear to speak, Girolamo Cardano, the son of Leonardo's friend Fazio Cardano—revealing a secret, or merely repeating a rumour?—wrote with the easy superiority of the successful:

"Both those who have recently attempted to fly came to grief. Leonardo da Vinci also tried to fly, but he, too, failed. He was a magnificent painter."

CHAPTER SEVEN

Man, the Work of Art

*Ancorachè lo ingiegno umano faccia inventioni
varie, rispondendo con vari strumenti a un medesimo fine, mai esso troverà inventione piu bella, nè
piu facile, nè piu brieve della natura, perchè nelle
sue inventioni nulla manca e nullo è superfluo.*

The genius of man may make various inventions,
encompassing with various instruments one and the
same end; but it will never discover a more beautiful, a more economical, or a more direct one than
nature's, since in her inventions nothing is wanting
and nothing is superfluous.

(An. IV, 184 a [7].)

BEYOND the Porta Orientale, the eastern gate of Milan, lay
a wide stretch of open country, and through this there ran
a rapid, sparkling streamlet, popularly called Acqua Lunga—the
Long Water. Here Leonardo proposed that a palace should be
built, with a loggia 21 ells long, 10½ wide, and 8 high. It was usual
to make these loggias of equal width and height, "but," wrote Leonardo in his notebook, "it seems to me that this gives a melancholy
effect, since at that height they are gloomy."

This palace was to be made bright and airy, and thus cool on
summer days when an oppressive heat hung over Milan. Leonardo
proposed that the cool water of the stream should be carried
through the building and made to rise in silver threads from fountain basins. With his irrepressible fondness for practical joking, he
proposed to place traps here and there, where visitors, stepping un-
suspectingly on a certain spot, might be doused with water sprayed
from all sides; he grinned as he pictured the behaviour of fine
ladies caught in one of these shower-baths.

Broad, easy steps were to lead down to a great park, irrigated to enable orange groves and avenues of evergreen cedars to be planted and, beneath these, a profusion of rare plants to be cultivated, their flowers flickering like little coloured lights under the deep green foliage whenever a breeze passed over them. As the water rippled through the narrow ditches it was to be caught in big ponds, filled with silvery fish darting to and fro, peace-loving fish that would not eat their lesser brethren; nor must they cloud the surface of the water, through which the bottom of the ponds must be clearly visible, with a good growth of water plants springing from between the pebbles.

The air must not be allowed to become still and sultry in this park. "I shall create a wind at all times in the summer by means of a mill," wrote Leonardo, and he proposed that his mill should set various instruments in motion, making music which the scented wind would carry through the park. The glamour of this enchanted summer palace would not be complete without the fluttering of bright birds' wings in the shimmering sunlight, and the singing and chirping that must mix with the sound of the lutes; accordingly he proposed to spread a net of fine copper wire over the whole park, in order to hold captive a plentiful company of singing birds. "Many different sorts of birds," he wrote, "and so you will have music all the time, with the scent of flowers, cedars, and citrons." [1]

This enchanted garden, remote from the stress of the day, was intended for the French ruler of Milan, Charles d'Amboise, Sire de Chaumont and *Grand-Maistre* of France, and all the loveliness that Leonardo heaped up to make this midsummer dream was simply the expression of an aspiration, in his deep gratitude for this French nobleman's great kindness to him. It appears that in the midst of the tragic mishaps of this spring of 1506 Leonardo received a pressing invitation from the Seigneur de Chaumont to come to Milan, an invitation that afforded him a welcome opportunity of escape from his trying dilemma.

He had first to overcome the opposition of the gonfaloniere and the Signoria, who were much annoyed with him for abandoning his task at so critical a stage. But it was difficult for the gonfaloniere to resist a desire expressed by the viceroy of the king of France, whose protection Florence enjoyed. Before, however, he assented to Leonardo's departure he drew up a notarial agreement which Leonardo signed on May 30, 1506, and by which he undertook to return to Florence within three months, and to deposit a security of one hundred fifty florins which he would forfeit if he did not recover it in person from the office of the Signoria. In any case, Leonardo had now secured a short breathing-space before he need deal with the damage to the mural painting of the battle of Anghiari. The disappointments of recent years weighed heavily on him, the nagging he had endured from his fellow-citizens and the mocking contempt they had poured on him after his ill-success had been hard to bear, and at fifty-four years of age he came to Milan no less bitterly humiliated and perplexed than when he first came there at thirty.

At this moment of accumulated anxieties, Leonardo was suddenly, as by a miracle, brought the tribute of discerning friendship and sympathetic appreciation. The viceroy of Milan received him in his house as a distinguished visitor whose acquaintance he had long wanted to make and who he knew in advance would become his friend. "The magnificent works," he wrote to the Signoria, "with which your fellow-citizen Maestro Leonardo da Vinci has endowed the cities of Italy, and especially Milan, have aroused a particular love for him in all those who have seen them, even in those who have never met him. And we too confess that we were among those who loved him before ever we knew him personally."

The Sire de Chaumont, nephew of the all-powerful Cardinal d'Amboise, had been appointed the king's lieutenant-general at twenty-five years of age, and when Leonardo met him Chaumont was already loaded with honours and offices; he was marshal of France and grand admiral of the French navy. During his viceroyalty in Milan, Chaumont amassed vast wealth by rather doubtful methods. He had one of his inherited properties, the Château de Meillant, rebuilt with great magnificence, and the wits whispered that *"Milan a fait Meillant."*

Behind his broad, square forehead the Sire de Chaumont was revolving ambitious plans; he dreamed of a Tuscan dukedom, taking in Lucca, Pisa, and Piombino, and only the objection of his uncle, who was aiming at the papal tiara, prevented him from carving his duchy out of Italy, in the debilitated condition of the country, by force of arms. In expectation of a glorious future, Charles d'Amboise lived a carefree life of boisterous gaieties and erotic adventures; he was, said the Milanese chronicler, "a friend of Venus and of Bacchus," and his pleasure-seeking was the more reckless and determined the more frequently he was attacked by the malaria which drove him, in spite of all his strength and vitality, to an early grave.

As though he had a foreboding of the shortness of his allotted span, Charles d'Amboise caught eagerly at all the pleasures, not only of the senses but of the intellect, which life offered him. His conversations with Leonardo opened out a new world of undreamed-of opportunities of activity, astonishing and unimagined vistas, and vast projects such as had never entered into his most ambitious dreams. He discussed with Leonardo bold constructional projects, the cutting of canals, the dredging and regulation of rivers to make them navigable, and military inventions; and in talking with Leonardo he felt that the artist's masterpieces revealed but a small section of the vast scope of his genius. "After our conversations with him and our experience of his many excellences," he wrote to the gonfaloniere of Florence, "we see in truth that the fame he has won through his painting is as obscurity to the praise he deserves to receive in other respects in which he is of the highest excellence; and we wish to confess that in the proofs he has given in whatever we asked of him in design and architecture and other things, pertinent to our situation, he has satisfied us in such a way that we have not only remained satisfied with him but have acquired an admiration for him."

Chaumont had no intention of letting so valuable a man go away again after three months; and Leonardo himself did his utmost to postpone his return to Florence, for he could not bring himself to begin all over again with the work that had ended in failure, now that the inner flame was extinguished and the joy of creation a thing of the past. Chaumont accordingly asked the Signoria to consent to a prolongation of Leonardo's leave of absence. His request was taken very ungraciously; the Signoria wrote brusquely to Geffroy Carles, the vice-chancellor of Milan, that they could grant only one month more: Leonardo might remain in Milan until the end of September. They would have no objection to his remaining longer if he would return the money he had received for his work, which had scarcely got beyond its initial stage.

A regular battle over Leonardo now developed between the Signoria and Chaumont. The viceroy sent another urgent message to the gonfaloniere, asking him to grant Leonardo a further three months, and mentioning that this was the express desire of the king. He received from Soderini a petty and ill-tempered reply. "Leonardo da Vinci," wrote the gonfaloniere, "has not behaved as he should to this Republic; for he has taken a good sum of money and has scarcely more than begun an important work which he was to do."

Geffroy Carles, too, warmly espoused Leonardo's cause. This man, whom Louis XII called his "beloved and faithful counsellor," was not only an eminent administrator, president of Dauphiné and now vice-chancellor of Milan, but also a scholar, who had gained a doctorate at Turin. He had a formidable aquiline nose, the effect of which was largely destroyed by the round and receding chin of the good-humoured. He was a collector of valuable manuscripts, interested in the natural sciences and in music, and a poet whose praises were gratefully and assiduously sung by the men of letters privileged to forgather freely in his house and to make it their cultural centre. His friendship for Leonardo was misrepresented in Florence by the malicious gossip of the envious; Soderini added to his reply to Carles that for his sake Leonardo had acted as a spy—*"e per amore della Signoria Vostra si è comportata da delatore."* He concluded his letter with a definite refusal: "We desire that there shall be no further requests, since the work is for the satisfaction of the community, and we cannot allow it to be further delayed without failing in our duty."

The viceroy shared his uncle's opinion of the commercial spirit of the Florentines. Cardinal d'Amboise once flung it in the face of their ambassador: "You Florentines," he exclaimed, "can never get anything done! You haggle for ever over men and money." But Chaumont replied with diplomatic courtesy, and with no more than an undertone of irony, to Soderini's offensive communication. He wrote warmly of his admiration for Leonardo, as though he needed to open the eyes of the Florentines to their fellow-countryman's greatness, and added: "And if it is necessary to commend a man of such qualities to his own people, we commend him to you with all our heart, and certify to you that you can never do anything for him either by increasing his possessions and his well-being or by bestowing honour on him, without giving us as well as him a singular pleasure."

Even this outspoken homily was not enough to divert the short-sighted gonfaloniere from his insistence on Leonardo's return. The dispute over Leonardo threatened to develop almost into an affair of state, with the king himself intervening. And at this time the Florentines had special reasons for making sure of the king's favour. Louis XII had recovered from a grave illness after his life had been despaired of; and he was now preparing for a new Italian expedition. The Florentines had special reasons, too, for gratitude to him, for he had prevented Ferdinand the Catholic from intervening against them in their war with the Pisans. "But now," said Louis to Francesco Pandolfini, the Florentine ambassador, "it is time for your Signoria to do me a favour. Write to them that I desire to make use of the services of Maestro Leonardo, the painter, who is now in Milan, as I wish to have some works of his; and see to it that the Signoria authorize him to enter my service at once, and to remain at Milan until I arrive there."

Louis knew enough of life and of human nature to be aware that even a ruler must make it clearly understood how real is his desire for the fulfilment of a request, and he added: "And write to Florence in such a way that it shall have effect, and do it at once, and let me see the letter."

Pandolfini informed the Signoria of this conversation; he seemed amazed that Leonardo was so much in favour. He added in explanation, in the air of one who was familiar with the irrational whims of the great: "And all this has happened in consequence of a small picture of his which was recently brought here and is regarded as a very admirable work." Pandolfini had been curious to learn what sort of commission the king intended to give Leonardo: the king, with his thoughts full of the smile hovering on the lips of the Madonna with the yarn-winder, painted for Florimond Robertet, had replied: "Some picture of a Madonna, or something else—whatever occurs to me; perhaps I shall ask him to paint my own portrait."

To make sure, Louis himself wrote to the Signoria, in the middle of January 1507: "We have particular need of Maistre Léonard de Vince, painter, of your city of Florence, and we intend to command from him some work of his hand, as soon as we reach Milan, which will be shortly, with God's help. And as soon as you receive these letters, write to him that he is not to move from Milan until our arrival."

2

Louis soon had a serious reason for the proposed journey to Milan. For some months Genoa had been in ferment. The populace had revolted against the regime of the aristocrats, and the struggle between the classes soon developed into a revolt against French rule. French hesitations had assisted the Genoese in their struggle for independence; they had interpreted as weakness the French habit of waiting until the critical moment before coming to a decision.

In spite of his advisers' warnings, of the queen's anxiety, of the Pope's appeals, and of Maximilian's threats, Louis got his way; if any man in the world, he declared, tried to stand in his path, he would give battle to him. Wherever the French army came in its march, adventurous young cavaliers joined it, seeking a glorious death or a life of honour and plenty beyond the Alps. Before the reckless daring of these young warriors, who were led by such men as La Palice and Bayard, the Genoese capitulated in spite of the good fortifications and the strong natural situation of their city.

After the formal occupation of Genoa the king entered Milan, on May 24, 1507. The populace and the clergy of Milan came out to meet him. Youths in glistening doublets of blue silk, heavily embroidered in gold with the fleur-de-lis, lined the road along which he came, and the procession of his knights rode in their shining armour, with the king at their head, through three triumphal arches. The largest of the arches was surmounted by a representation of a hill strewn with countless gold pieces, and on the hill stood Christ scourged, with Saint Ambrose, the city's patron, on one side and on the other a statue of the king of

France, which looked down from a seat of gold brocade upon its living model.

Amid the festivities which began with the king's arrival at the castle, many people who had been familiar visitors in the past re-emerged like their own shadows. Lodovico's son-in-law, the gallant and handsome Galeazzo da Sanseverino, who was as successful in conquering the king's favour as he had been in the past in gain-ing that of Il Moro, had now become *grand écuyer de France,* Louis's master of the horse; over his richly embroidered doublet he wore the glittering écaille chain of the order of Saint Michael. Lodovico's brother-in-law, Francesco Gonzaga, was also there; he had entered the service of the king of France and had helped him to crush the Genoese revolt. And Isabella d'Este had hastened to Milan at the king's special desire; she appeared at a ball which took place in the room in the Rocchetta onto which the death-chamber of her sister Beatrice opened. Memories were short in her day, and hearts were insensitive to the vicissitudes even of those who stood nearest to them; none thought of the duchess who had died in her youth or of the duke who languished in a gloomy dun-geon at Loches and scribbled on its wall, as well as he could in a tongue that was strange to him, *celuy qui ne pas contans*—"he who is not content."

Isabella d'Este created a great impression among the French—*une belle dame qui danse à merveille,* was the remark of a grave monk, the king's official chronicler, Jean d'Auton. She was in-toxicated with her triumphs, and full of the fact that the king came personally to meet her as she entered the castle. The French court was the most magnificent in the world, and she knew how her much-travelled friends would envy her.

The past was erased from men's minds by the new splendour. Galeazzo da Sanseverino gathered fresh laurels in the tourney which took place in the piazza outside the castle. Leonardo re-sumed his function of organizing brilliant entertainments; he designed scenery for theatrical performances, and comedies were played beneath skies through which his artificial birds floated to and fro on invisible wires. But if the company that gathered round the new ruler was the same as of old, a new spirit played havoc with the castle ceremonial; etiquette was ignored, there was no longer the old jealous observance of rights of precedence, and the great French nobles addressed one another as man to man. Isabella complained that amid the new confusion "it is quite impossible to distinguish one personality from another." The king's own high spirits threw into confusion the strictly ordered Italian ceremonial. At the ball the old wine and the loveliness of the young women of Milan turned his head, and his most Christian majesty went to the length of compelling the four younger cardinals to join in the dancing, to the delight of the spectators.

Among the dancing cardinals was one who had been among Lodovico's most faithful friends, his brother-in-law Ippolito d'Este. The cardinal had remained at Lodovico's side up to the last minute, and had actually taken up arms on the duke's behalf, in spite of an express prohibition from Ippolito's cautious father, the duke of Ferrara. The young cardinal's relations with Lodovico's court painter probably dated from the time when Lodovico was in power; but the first mention of him as a trusted patron in Leonardo's notes dates from after the ceremonial entry of the king of France into Milan.

Ippolito d'Este was tonsured, in Ferrara cathedral, at the age of six; nobody asked the child whether that was what he wanted. He was a bright and handsome boy, with the charming lordliness of children born into high estate. Destiny imposed on him at a very early age a life of fabulous magnificence and of vast opportunities, even by the standard of his spacious epoch. When Ippolito was seven, Matthias Corvinus, king of Hungary, who had married the boy's maternal aunt Beatrice d'Aragona, made him archbishop of Gran and primate of Hungary. The archbishopric yielded a revenue of thirty thousand ducats a year. Ippolito's aunt took him with her to her distant home, and the child grew up amid incredible magnificence and a naïve adoration; he was idolized for his handsome face and his precocious cleverness. He was barely fourteen when Alexander VI invested him with the cardinal's purple, and at eighteen he assumed one of the most coveted dignities in Italy, the archbishopric of Milan.

Had Ippolito d'Este been able to follow his own inclinations, he would have exchanged the purple for shining armour and his assured revenues for warlike adventures; for he was at his best on the battlefield. Spoilt by nature herself and robbed of all self-discipline by the servility and flattery that surrounded him, he grew up as good and as bad, as brutal and as generous, and as reckless and incalculable, as his unique fortune was likely to make him. His name was associated with particularly scandalous episodes; but his extravagant munificence was also legendary. He was ardently and jealously in love with the beautiful and capricious Angela Borgia, cousin of his sister-in-law Lucrezia. One day the girl, with the provocative Borgia smile on her lips, talked of her admiration of the fine eyes of his half-brother Giulio; the young cardinal threw himself upon his rival and gouged out those hateful eyes. But he had also the quick sympathies of the hasty-tempered, and when his aunt Beatrice d'Aragona was driven out of Hungary and deprived of her Neapolitan inheritance he settled on her half of the revenues of one of his archbishoprics. He was regarded as a patron of all artists and scholars, and he also had the education proper to his position; but Ariosto, who immortalized him in *Orlando Furioso,* where he is praised as the pattern of all worldly and other-worldly virtues, used regretfully to tell his friends that all that was needed to please the cardinal was to be able to wear the spurs well and to carve a capon. Leonardo, too, seems to have received no commission from Ippolito d'Este, either as painter or as architect; but their relations must nevertheless have been intimate at this period, for a little later Leonardo turned to the cardinal in a purely personal matter, in evident reliance on this powerful friend.

For the second time in his life Leonardo was enjoying on Milanese soil a success which had been denied him in his own country. For the second time he was building up a career with the aid of patrons who were not his countrymen. He had again become entirely at home in Milan, where he was still the guest of his patron, the Sire de Chaumont. Some days before the arrival of the king of France he had had the remainder of his credit with the Santa Maria Novella transferred to a deposit account. The amount, one hundred and fifty florins, corresponded to the sum he was due to pay to the Signoria in compensation for his absence. He had now discharged his obligation and destroyed his last link with Florence.

About this time came an event which was to bind him even more strongly to Milan—his meeting with young Francesco Melzi, who came to him as a pupil and was to play an important part in the life of this ageing and essentially solitary man. The Melzi were a distinguished Milanese family, and the boy was probably nòt intended to have more than an amateur's acquaintance with painting. He had a little talent, much patience, and plenty of imitative skill, but as he grew up in the position of a leading citizen he would doubtless have abandoned painting before long as a youthful fancy, if the meeting with Leonardo had not opened out a wider life before him.

Leonardo was strongly attracted by the boy's personal charm, his regular features and natural gracefulness, and his freedom from any sort of adolescent uncouthness or awkwardness, just as in the past he had been caught by the outward attractiveness of the young scapegrace Giacomo. But it was not a case this time of a neglected and demoralized child whose precocious instinct told him that he could impose on Leonardo's good nature: this boy had a straightforward and transparent character, though unformed and ill-defined, as was to be expected of one whose childhood had been carefully watched over and whose existence no shadow had disturbed. Francesco was a pliant and obedient boy, with an inborn goodness of heart and so equable a temperament that even the sudden gift of this amazing friendship failed to excite him.

In this strange association of a prematurely ageing man and a young boy, a man who had absorbed the whole of the knowledge of his time and a child who accepted the world around him as unquestioningly as a mirror, Leonardo was by no means the only giver. With the intuition of a boy on the verge of adolescence, Francesco Melzi began very soon to have some idea of his famous friend's loneliness: he saw through the misleading glamour of the legendary fame that was Leonardo's into the great thinker's utter isolation. And very soon his idolization of the master began to be mingled with a touching solicitude for his welfare in the small matters of everyday life, such as a young son will sometimes show for a father who is an unpractical man of genius.

As the years passed, this practical helpfulness developed in Francesco Melzi into a virtual sense of responsibility, and ultimately into a feeling that this was a sacred mission which destiny had laid on him. Long before Leonardo realized how indispensable to him his young friend was to become, he accepted the young man's devotion as an unhoped-for gift, so late, from life.

3

The happier atmosphere in which Leonardo now lived quickly took the sting out of the misfortunes he had had in Florence. Barely a year had passed since he had almost fled from that city rather than face the task of remedying his own failure, but already he was able to shake off these evil memories, and felt strong enough to take up the cudgels against the Florentine authorities in the defence of his own personal interests. He carried the struggle, indeed, into the enemy camp, with a pugnacity that suggested the influence of a grievance now years old.

About the middle of 1507 his uncle Francesco da Vinci had died, as unnoticed in death as he had been in life, so that not even a death certificate has been preserved. But this unsatisfactory son of a pushing and industrious family now came to his own, attracting more attention by the will he had made than by anything else he had done in his life. With his independence of outlook he had had eyes for the material difficulties and the hurt susceptibilities of his famous nephew, and he had left him the bulk of his property. Apart from the practical benefits of this legacy, it was an admission of Leonardo's membership in the family and made up for his father's neglect in that respect. The rest of the family, headed by Ser Giuliano, who had followed the family tradition by becoming a notary, contested the uncle's will, and Leonardo now retorted by claiming a share of his father's estate. He went personally to Florence, furnished with letters of recommendation from his patrons, including the king himself; Louis XII threw the weight of a conqueror's power into the scales in this action between commoners. He, "Loys, par la grâce de Dieu Roy de France, Duc de Milan, Seigneur de Gênes," wrote on July 26, 1507, to the gonfaloniere and Priori of Florence:

"Very dear and great friends, We have been informed that our dear and well-beloved Léonard de Vince, our painter and engineer in ordinary, has some dispute and litigation pending at Florence against his brothers over certain inheritances; and inasmuch as he could not attend properly to the pursuit of the said litigation by reason of his continual occupation at our side and in our entourage; and also because we are singularly desirous that the said litigation should be brought to an end in the best and briefest delivery of justice that may be; for this reason we have desired to write to you on the matter. And we request that you will cause this litigation and dispute to be settled in the best and briefest delivery of justice that may be, and you will give us very great pleasure in so doing."

As though this plain indication of the king's favour was not enough for him, Leonardo approached the viceroy of Milan with a request that he would use his influence with the Signoria on his, Leonardo's, behalf. Charles d'Amboise wrote to Florence on August 15 that the king had been very unwilling to part with Leonardo because the painter was at work on a picture for him; accordingly he must settle his Florentine affairs and return to Milan as soon as possible.

Eighteen months earlier, Leonardo had left Florence with a breach of contract on his conscience; now he was returning as painter and engineer to the king of France. He had armed himself, however, against any unpleasant incident to which he might be exposed in Florence. Excessive caution of this sort was strangely mingled in his nature with an occasional lack of practical sense; fits of shrewdness seemed to alternate in him with periods of incapacity for the ordinary affairs of life. He now left no stone unturned in trying to influence a decision in his favour. His energy seems to have been due to a desire to find compensation for all the humiliations of the past. On arrival at Florence he learned that his case was being argued before one of the Priori, Raffaello Hieronimo, and he soon discovered that this magistrate was on particularly friendly terms with Cardinal Ippolito d'Este. He had had no compunction about enlisting the king's interest in his private dispute, and he had none in asking the cardinal to intervene. "I arrived here from Milan but a few days since," he wrote, "and find that my elder brother refuses to carry into effect a will made three years ago when my father died. Although my case is good, I esteem it most important to make sure that I shall succeed in establishing it, and therefore I cannot forbear to crave of Your Most Reverend Highness a letter of recommendation and favour." He asked the cardinal to write to Ser Raffaello in "that dexterous and effective manner which Your Highness can use ... and I have not the least doubt, from many things that I hear, that, Ser Raphaello being most affectionately devoted to Your Highness, the matter will issue to my desire."

Feeling that he had done everything in his power, Leonardo patiently awaited the issue. This time he was the guest of the sculptor Giovanni Francesco Rustici, in a house which Piero di Braccio Martelli, a wealthy scholar and patron of artists, had placed at the sculptor's disposal. It was a strange household into which Leonardo entered with his inseparable companion Salai—the household of an eccentric, and entirely to the taste of Leonardo, with his interest in the grotesque. Rustici shared Leonardo's liking for all sorts of strange beasts. The place of a house-dog was taken in his house by a porcupine, which sometimes stuck its quills into the legs of guests at meals; when they shrieked and rubbed their wounded calves, their host would be convulsed with laughter. A tame eagle flew freely about the large rooms, as though it had forgotten the boundless heavens. Suddenly there would come from some corner, in the midst of a conversation, a shrill croaking voice, hoarse and uncanny, uttering wise saws, and a raven would alight on the table with flapping wings, glance sideways at the speaker, and open its beak to make some remark that suggested a human soul imprisoned by magic in its black body. The sculptor believed that his animal pets had undergone some mysterious metamorphosis. He was also a believer in necromancy and magic; he brewed strange mixtures in retorts, liked to surround himself with magicians and alchemists, and wasted his money on vain attempts to freeze quicksilver.

But this unusual young man, who surrounded himself with queer animals and still queerer human beings, and who shunned the fine society to which he belonged by birth, was something more than a mere blasé despiser of the ordinary. He had great gifts as an artist, which had impressed Lorenzo de' Medici when Rustici was little more than a child; at Lorenzo's instance he had entered Verrocchio's studio. Leonardo was then no longer with Verrocchio; he left Florence when Rustici was no more than ten years old. But the boy must have seen Leonardo's early sculpture and drawings, including studies of horses, in which he himself was especially interested; he must have heard of Leonardo's researches, of his mastery in every field, of his way of life, his obedience to an incomprehensible law of his own; and he made Leonardo his pattern, to the extent of his own talent and of such control as he kept over a rather aimlessly spent life. Vasari is careful to point out that the young sculptor worked at his art more for pleasure and out of the desire for distinction than in order to earn money, since he was of noble birth and had enough to live on. From time to time he would summon up the energy for some big achievement, from the feeling that he must give tangible evidence of his powers.

Leonardo reached Florence at the time of one of these spells of creative work. The merchants' guild (*arte dei mercatanti*) had decided a year earlier to remove the crumbling marble figures over the doors of the Baptistery and to replace them by groups in bronze, of more than life size. The commission for one group, Saint John between the Pharisee and the Levite, had been given to Rustici, and it was one of his earliest important commissions. Leonardo's arrival just at this time seemed to Rustici to be a special dispensation of fate. He devoted himself to providing in every way for the comfort of his venerated guest and anticipating Leonardo's every wish. Behind his host's surface frivolity Leonardo could see the young man's profound goodness of heart. Rustici kept money always ready in an open basket, so as not to have to turn away any who should ask for alms at his door; and he made his less fortunate friends share his subsistence. Yet he would pretend to have little belief in the honesty of his fellow-men. One day, after resting in a wood, he forgot to pick up his mantle; when it was brought to his house he exclaimed humorously: "The world is getting too perfect; the end must be near!"

Leonardo could also see with what seriousness of artistic purpose Rustici approached his big commission, and he lent patient and sympathetic aid in the preliminary work, although he himself had at this time an important commission to complete for the king of France, and Charles d'Amboise had also been kept waiting a long time for a picture. Malicious gossip went round the Florentine studios about the way Leonardo put up with being exploited; Vasari notes the story that was still told in his day: "Leonardo was so attached to him . . . that he did at all times exactly what Giovanfrancesco desired."

In spite of the twenty years' difference in their ages, the two had the same pleasure in practical joking, often of a grim sort, in hoaxing their contemporaries, in mechanical devices, and in surprise effects. Giovanfrancesco Rustici belonged to a group of young artists who called themselves the "Brothers of the Cauldron"—*compagnia del paiuolo*—and who met regularly at the house of one or other of their members. One day when Giovanfrancesco was host the guests found the dining room turned into a vast copper cauldron, which he had had made out of a giant vat. In the strange light that filtered down from the round handle over their heads, the guests' faces looked as if they were under water. At a nod from the host a tree suddenly sprang up through the floor, and its branches spread over the table, bearing plates of food to the guests. After the first course the branches collapsed and disappeared, reappearing with further courses; a hidden band of musicians drowned the noise of the mechanism. With this invention Giovanfrancesco outdid the best of his guests' ideas. One had brought a roast goose made up as a boilermaker, another veal cutlets prepared in the form of an anvil; the painter Domenico Puligo had brought a small boiled pig dressed as a scullery maid.

4

Some of these mechanical marvels may have been worked out by Leonardo and Rustici together, or Leonardo may at this time have initiated Rustici into inventions of his own; for he had now settled comfortably into Rustici's house, with all his papers and sketches, not in the spirit of a man awaiting the issue of a lawsuit while urgent tasks await him elsewhere, but in that of one who had at last reached a haven of peace in which he could survey all his scientific work of the past.

He put in order his loose papers, read through the small note-books in which observations in the most various fields were mixed up together, struck out repetitions and mistakes, copied passages that pleased him, leaving them virtually unaltered, placed together things that were related to one another, and felt, at the end of all this, that, if the collection of material did not form a completed work, it was still publishable as it stood. In any case, he now wrote the introduction to the proposed edition of his writings:

"Begun at Florence in the house of Piero di Braccio Martelli on the 22nd day of March 1508. And this is to be a collection without order, taken from many papers which I have copied here, hoping to arrange them later each in its place, according to the subject of which they may treat. But I believe that before I am at the end of this task I shall have to repeat the same things several times; for which, O reader, do not blame me, for the subjects are many, and memory cannot retain them all and say: 'I will not write this be-cause I have written it before.' And if I wished to avoid falling into this fault, it would be necessary in every case when I wanted to copy a passage that, not to repeat myself, I should read over all that had gone before; and all the more since the intervals are long between one time of writing and the next." [2]

He had been thinking for some time about the printing of his works. On one occasion he calculated how many letters there would be in a work of one hundred and sixty pages,[3] and after he had begun to take an interest in printing he planned the issue of one of Roger Bacon's works, and made a similar estimate.

He designed an improved printing press, one of the earliest de-signs extant; it consists of a press in which the flat-bed runs down on an inclined plane as soon as the platen has been lifted, so that the printed sheet may be easily removed and a fresh sheet placed in position. A large cogwheel, working in the spindle of a huge screw, then draws the flat-bed back under the platen; a leather strap provides the required pressure, enabling a clear impression of the letters to be produced.[4]

But Leonardo seems to have considered that he had gone out too soon to gather in his harvest, and apparently he quickly abandoned the idea of publishing his work. Perhaps he felt that he had not sufficiently established his conclusions; or it may be that his overmastering love of research once more claimed his whole time. He returned now to a field on which he had entered tentatively twenty years earlier, subsequently returning to it again and again with evident pleasure the moment he was able to spare a little time for it—that of anatomy. He had approached it repeatedly and from all sides—when he was studying the human figure in Verrocchio's studio; when he was pursuing his studies of human proportions; when he was occupied with optics; when he was investigating the fundamental laws of mechanics and their application to human movements; when, in his disgust with the charlatans at the court of Milan, he sought to demonstrate the incapacity of physicians; and when he came from hydraulic engineering to the description of the terrestrial globe, falling into the erroneous theory of the identity of organic and inorganic existence.

It was not an entirely untrodden field. Among the ancient classics preserved were the studies of Hippocrates and, above all, those of Galen. Few could read Galen, as Greek had become a dead language; but the results of his researches were preserved in Arabic works, particularly the *Canon* of Avicenna, the handbook used in Leonardo's day by all students of medicine. Under the influence of Arab scholars Frederick II of Hohenstaufen had decreed as long ago as the middle of the thirteenth century that no physician or surgeon should be admitted to practice unless he had studied medicine for five years and anatomy for at least one, and was thoroughly familiar with the works of Hippocrates, Galen, and Avicenna. In the latter half of the thirteenth century lectures on anatomy were given at Bologna; and this new science was then brought, probably for the first time in history, into the service of the law courts, the Bolognese professor Guglielmo da Saliceto being instructed to dissect the corpse of the nephew of Marquis Umberto Pallavicino in order to establish the cause of death. In succeeding years there were several trials in which anatomy played a similar part to that of modern toxicology, and a number of surgeons were called upon to establish by means of autopsy of the intestines whether a dead person had been poisoned. Toward the end of the century, at the time of a very serious outbreak of plague in Italy, a heroic Lombard physician dissected the bodies of victims in the hope of identifying the cause of infection amid the bubonic pus.

In 1300 Boniface VIII issued the bull *De Sepulturis,* which threatened with excommunication "those who eviscerate the bodies of the dead and barbarously boil them in order that the bones separated from the flesh may be carried for sepulture into their own country." The bull was directed against a custom which had crept in during the Crusades, but it was interpreted in France and some other countries as a general prohibition of anatomy. The Italian scholars seem, however, to have understood it more correctly, or to have deliberately ignored it; the Milanese anatomist Mondino de' Luzzi, who was also a professor at Bologna and who in 1316 wrote a handbook of practical anatomy, claimed to have dissected three corpses, two of them of women.

But prejudice and superstition and religious scruples were still so strong among the population that it was very difficult to procure corpses. Only those of persons who had been hanged, of members of foreign races, and of slaves were permitted to be used, and in Bologna, where the interest in anatomy was particularly strong, and the rector of the university was allowed two corpses a year, a man's and a woman's, it was laid down that these must not be those of Bolognese citizens or of any persons born within thirty miles of the city.

In the period in which the scientific investigation of the proportions of the human form began in Italy, some of the high enthusiasm for this advance was caught by the general public, and silenced the objectors. About the middle of the fifteenth century a professor at Padua remarked that he had witnessed fourteen dissections. In Florence the study of the human form was promoted mainly by the artists, and as a young man Leonardo saw Antonio Pollaiuolo at work on anatomical studies of corpses which Pollaiuolo had himself dissected. A Florentine anatomist of that time proudly claimed to have publicly dissected twenty corpses, apart from private autopsies; and only once in his life, he added, had he been refused permission to make a private autopsy. In their thirst for knowledge the Florentines desired to share the insight that was being gained into the structure of the human body; in 1505 a pub-

lic dissection took place, and these dissections grew into a social
event. A man named Bernardino Belladonna was hanged for theft;
his corpse was publicly transported to the anatomical theatre at
Santa Croce. There the professors had a mass read at their expense
for the salvation of the dead man's soul; the corpse was then laid
on a wooden table, and the staff proceeded to dissect it, while a
professor lectured on the subject and a demonstrator pointed with
a little rod to the parts referred to by the professor. This continued
twice a day so long as the condition of the corpse permitted it. The
public gathered round open-mouthed, anyone being permitted to
attend the lecture if his nerves were good enough and if he had a
taste for the gruesome.

In view of this public curiosity the prohibition of the use of
corpses of persons who had died a natural death was evaded in
Florence, especially by those artists who could take liberties owing
to their popularity. Michelangelo worked between 1503 and 1506
in a room placed at his disposal in Santo Spirito, and the prior
allowed him access to the mortuary and even helped him in dissecting. The artist would have been able to work there unhindered
for a long time if he had not committed the indiscretion of using
his scalpel on the body of a Corsini, on which the scandalized family raised an indignant outcry.

About the time when Leonardo was making his studies of movements for the battle of Anghiari, he began his researches into the
part played by the muscles as motor agents. Corpses were dissected
in the hospital of Santa Maria Novella, close to where he was living, and he may have witnessed dissections at that time and may
perhaps have attempted some himself. In his first breathing-space
between the work that had then crowded on him and the counter-
call of his manifold interests, this new passion lay in wait for him
and took entire possession of him. Years earlier he had set out a
comprehensive programme for his anatomical studies, beginning
with embryology, encompassing every stage of development from
infancy to old age, and even penetrating into pathology. Now he
proposed to unriddle the ultimate mystery of being. With the ecstatic pride of the investigator, which led him into excited outbursts in spite of his dislike of any display of emotion, he declared:
"I am revealing to men the origin of the prime and perhaps the

secondary cause of their being." [5] He was aware of the vastness of the enterprise: "I want to work miracles!" *voglio far miracoli*, he exclaimed; and he poured scorn on the "alchemists, the would-be creators of gold and silver, and engineers who would have dead water stir itself into life and perpetual motion, and those supreme fools the necromancer and the enchanter," whom he had been meeting in the house of his friend Rustici—all the misguided persons who were blind to the true miracles. He knew also how much labour and renunciation was necessary if he was to attain the goal he envisaged. He cheerfully dispensed with prosperity and position: "It may be that I shall possess less than other men of more peaceful lives, or than those who want to grow rich in a day." [6]

Since he had been engaged on the cartoon for the battle of Anghiari, Leonardo had kept in touch with the monks of the hospital of Santa Maria Novella, and they had given him the same permission which the prior of Santo Spirito had given Michelangelo, to dissect the bodies even of persons who had died a natural death. He watched the sick persons whose lives were despaired of, and waited for them to die so that he could place them under the knife. He sat by the bed of a very old man who particularly interested him, because he was dried up and withered, "free from fat and juices which interfere with the recognition of the various parts." The old man's small, wrinkled head, covered with yellowish-brown skin, lay like a shrunken chestnut on the pillow. He was still fully conscious, and in his cracked, bleating voice he told this distinguished stranger, who was so surprisingly interested in him, that he was just a hundred years old, and was in no actual pain, only very, very weak, and often so cold that he simply could not get warm. Leonardo was able to sympathize; he had himself become very sensitive to cold as he grew older, and had recently got a fur chest-protector. The strange gentleman's kindly attentions brought a last ray of warmth into the old man's destitute and solitary existence. One day, when the two were together, isolated now by the death of all the patients in the other beds in the room, the old man sat upright, with a poor little smile round his toothless mouth, and "without making another movement or any sign that aught was amiss, passed away from this life."

Some time before this, Leonardo had had a specially fine saw

made for sawing bones, *sega da osso di sottil dentatura*, and now he
went calmly to work, with a steady hand, and dissected the body
in order to ascertain the cause of "so gentle a death"—*et io ne feci
notomia, per vedere la causa di si dolce morte*. The muscles were
wasted and dried up; thanks to the absence of fat, dissection was a
simple matter.[7] In the veins he found calcifications (*pietre*) as big
as chestnuts; they were of the colour of truffles and were bound to
the veins in bags like a gizzard. The full description Leonardo
gives of the result of his autopsy is the first report in the history of
medicine of a death from arteriosclerosis.

In another patient he found a nut-like encrustation in the bron-
chi: "in the interior were dust and aqueous humour" [8]—clearly a
case of pulmonary tuberculosis. On another occasion he records:
"I have removed the skin from a man who was so shrunken by disease that the muscles had been consumed until they looked like
a thin membrane, so that the sinews, instead of being converted
into muscles, were turned into broad strips of skin."

He dissected the body of a two-year-old boy, and found "everything the opposite of the old man's." Alongside the crooked,
twisted, coarsened network of the arteries in the old man's arm he
drew the straight, supple lines of the blood-vessels in the child. He
also dissected the little body of a baby four months old, and he regarded it as a special piece of good fortune when he was able to
dissect a woman who had died in pregnancy; in her uterus he
found an almost completely formed fœtus. Under the programme
he had drawn up years earlier, his treatise on anatomy was to "begin with the conception of man, and describe the nature of the
womb and how the fœtus lives in it; also its growth" within the
mother's body.[9] A few years later he stated that he had dissected
ten corpses with his own hands; and toward the end of his life,
when he was surveying the extent of his researches, he mentioned
with particular pride that in his efforts to fathom the mysteries of
the structure of the human frame he had dissected thirty corpses.

In the hot Italian climate corpses quickly decompose, and cannot be kept more than three or four days for dissection. The medieval students had sometimes made use of embalming preparations, but Leonardo would not do this because of the organic

changes that resulted from their use. At first, especially with bones, he used a method of dissection after steeping, but he found it unsatisfactory in studying blood-vessels and nerves: "I warn you that the anatomy of nerves will disclose neither their system of ramification nor the muscles into which they branch if you study them in bodies which have been steeped in flowing water or lime water." [10]

Under these circumstances dissection had to be carried out rapidly. In the long nights in the mortuary an uncanny stillness lay over the place where Leonardo stood alone with the dead. The unsteady light threw his shadow, magnified to giant proportions, on the cellar vaulting; it flickered over the flayed and dismembered corpses, and the flickering shadows created a ghostly atmosphere. Leonardo's alert and over-excited senses registered all the grisliness of the experience, the indescribably repulsive appearance of the hacked limbs and protruding entrails, the solitary dissonant breach of the stillness made by the crunching under the bone-saw, and the disgusting smell of putrefaction, growing more oppressive hour by hour until a wave of nausea overcame him and he had to restrain himself from vomiting. "And if you had a love for such things," Leonardo warns his readers, "you might be prevented by loathing, and if that did not prevent you, you might be debarred by the fear of living in the night hours in the company of these corpses, quartered and flayed and horrible to see." [11]

But though time did nothing to diminish his keen sense of the gruesomeness of the work, his iron will held him to his research at the dissecting table—his will and the sense that he was fulfilling a mission for which no other was so well qualified as he. With self-control and the necessary skill it was possible to probe the secrets of the structure of the human frame. But much more was required to enable this knowledge to be passed on to others; that could be done only by pictorial representation. "And even if all this did not prevent you," Leonardo reminded his readers, "perhaps you might not be able to draw so well as is necessary for such a demonstration; or, if you had the skill in drawing, it might not be combined with knowledge of perspective; and if it were so combined, you might not understand the methods of geometrical demonstration, and the method of the calculation of forces and of the function of muscles; patience also may be wanting, so that you lack perseverance." [11]

This is one of the very rare occasions on which Leonardo made any reference to his artistic powers. He mentions them here as one of the many qualities that constitute his special fitness for the practical study of anatomy. He develops his argument very effectively: "O writer, with what words will you describe the entire configuration of objects with the perfection that the drawing gives? If you are unable to draw, you will describe everything confusedly and convey little knowledge of the true form of objects; and you will deceive yourself in imagining that you can satisfy your hearer when you speak of the configuration of any corporeal object bounded by surfaces. I warn you against entangling yourself in words, unless you are speaking to the blind; or if you desire that your words shall reach men's ears but do not intend to present anything before their eyes, speak of the essence of things or of the phenomena of nature, and do not attempt to convey to men's ears things which are apprehended by the eyes; for you will be far surpassed by the work of the painter." [12]

The earlier anatomists were well aware of the need for illustrations in order to explain the structure of the human body. But the first drawing that showed any actual observation of the reality was one dating from the middle of the fifteenth century, a drawing of a skeleton, which formed the frontispiece to a German translation of a treatise on surgery by Bruno of Pavia. Until then the conventional representations had all been reproductions of an unknown and grotesquely unhelpful original, which was copied time after time simply because there was nothing better to be had. The first printed illustrations appeared in a collection of medical papers, *Fasciculus Medicinæ*, published in 1491 by Johannes Ketham, a German living in Italy. A few years later there followed editions of an early treatise by Mondino; these and the German anatomical works of the last years of the fifteenth century were accompanied by a considerable number of plates, but the plates are no nearer reality than the work of children playing with a pencil.

Leonardo, the great pioneer in the true representation of the human figure, was also the first to make records of the internal structure of the body, in drawings which were not excelled in accuracy for centuries. His fellow-artists studied the structure of the human frame in order to place this new knowledge at the service of their art; Leonardo devoted his unique artistic mastery to the service of anatomical science, as if it could fulfil no more exalted purpose. He planned nothing less than an illustrated encyclopædia of human proportions. "The true knowledge," he wrote, "of the form of any body can be won only by its representation under the most various aspects. In order, therefore, to give a knowledge of the true form of any part of the body of man, that first beast among the animals (*prima bestia infra le animali*), I shall make it a rule to provide four representations, from four sides, of every part. And of the bones I will provide five, by cutting them through the centre." [13]

These transverse sections, usually of bones, which Leonardo made with knife and saw, were an innovation that anticipated modern scientific methods. Some of these osteological studies, such as the drawings of the skull, are among the most beautiful products of Leonardo's hand. The skull drawings date from about 1489, when he set out to write "the book of the human form"; they are made with a fine silver pencil and look like copper engravings.

But apart from the unexcelled mastery of the representation, in his investigation of the human skeleton Leonardo made discoveries which constituted an immense advance in the study of anatomy. He was the first to make accurate drawings of the curves of the spine, and of the inclination of the sacrum, through which the weight of the upper part of the body is duly distributed over the lower part; he also described the rounding and sloping of the ribs, an essential contribution to the understanding of the mechanism of breathing. He was the first to recognize the true situation of the human pelvis; centuries passed before this was discovered afresh. The investigation of the static and dynamic laws of the upright skeleton also dates back to Leonardo. In his drawings of skulls and his sections he showed for the first time the configuration of the frontal and sphenoid bones; he drew the lachrymal canal, through which, he wrote, "the tears rise into the eyes from the heart"; he was the first to demonstrate the various cavities, including the cavity in the superior maxillary bone, which was rediscovered in 1651

by Highmore and named after him "the antrum of Highmore."
In the anatomy of the hands, especially, the painter of the hands
of Mona Lisa attained the utmost perfection. He proposed to represent the hand, as seen from its back, in no fewer than ten drawings, and in ten more from the inner surface.[14]

He proceeded at intervals spread over a number of years with
his programme of representing the various parts of the human
skeleton. "Begin the anatomy," he had written, "at the head, and
finish it at the sole of the foot." [15] He then proposed as his further
programme: "First draw the spine of the back; then clothe it by
degrees, one after the other, with each of its muscles." [16] Galen had
left a very thorough description of the anatomy of the muscles, but
it was based almost entirely on dissections which he had carried
out on apes. The medieval writers were chiefly interested in the
muscles contained in the three main cavities of the body, those of
the head, breast, and stomach; they neglected the leg and arm
muscles.

In his investigation of the muscles Leonardo was especially concerned with the discovery of their function. The teleological principle which the Arabs took over from Aristotle, and which the
medieval writers had not ventured to challenge because it was in
harmony with the teachings of the Church, found an echo in Leonardo's habit of demonstrating the usefulness of every phenomenon and of finding a common basis of significance for all phenomena; and he made it the starting-point of his studies, in which
it often hindered him or led him astray. "Of nature, which of necessity creates the vitally important instruments in the proper and
necessary form and positions; and how necessity is the companion
of nature"—in these words,[17] as a true son of his age, with its apotheosis of necessity, Leonardo summed up his programme. Contemporary science had not reached the stage of distinguishing between
anatomy and physiology, between structure and function, and this
made it possible for Leonardo to hold to the traditional doctrine.

For Leonardo a muscle was an organ that served a definite purpose and could not be properly understood until that purpose had
been determined. In order to obtain a correct grasp of the action
of the muscles, he decided to illustrate it by means of cords; "thus
you will be able to represent them on top of one another as nature

has placed them, and to name them according to the limb they serve." [18] On one occasion he proposed to make a model of a skeleton with the muscles represented by wires attached to the bones and "bent into their natural form," and he drew a system of wires on a sheet on which he carried out a comparison between the hip and thigh muscles of man and horse.

He laid down as his first general principle: "The function of muscles is to pull, not to push, except in the case of the muscles of the sexual organs and the tongue." [19] When a muscle contracts, its counterpart expands [20]: with this further generalization he anticipated the law of reciprocal excitation by the nerves, elaborated by Sherrington. In his day the conceptions of nerve reflexes and nerve inhibitions had not dawned on men's minds; but Leonardo had something of the conception when he wrote of automatic muscular spasms in cases of paralysis and epilepsy, where the sufferer's soul is unable, in spite of every effort, to restrain the twitching of his limbs.[21] On one occasion he observed a stallion that could scarcely move for utter tiredness; catching sight of a mare, it rapidly recovered, chased the animal, and overtook it.[22] Had the nerves supplied all the wind needed for this rapid recovery? he asked himself; and he was unable to find an explanation. The question that interested him above all was "whether the muscles receive their motion from the brain or not" [23]; and Leonardo the painter decided to search for "the source of the movements that become visible in the skin, the flesh, and the muscles of the face." He was mainly occupied with the motor function of the muscles, and thus his studies proceeded farthest with the muscles of leg and arm: but at all times it was the painter that dominated the scholar in him, the draughtsman that proved superior to the expositor.

Leonardo had at all times to bear the burden of much useless ballast of tradition. Again and again he was hampered by the conception of power or energy as something separate from matter. According to Galen it was the pneuma that supplied the organs of the body with the needed energy; but Leonardo rejected the conception, bound up with this idea, of the differing functions of the venous and arterial blood, the former supplying nourishment to the body and the latter mixing with the pneuma in the left chamber of the heart. But what went on in the heart if this differentiation could not be accepted? The mystery strongly interested Leonardo. He wrote under a drawing of the heart a sort of involuntary exclamation—"A wonderful instrument, the invention of the Supreme Master." [24]

He wanted to discover what happened at the moment when death brings the heart to a stop—"does the heart change its position at its death or not?"—and as he was unable to test this on a human body he tried to find out through experiments on animals. The customary method of slaughtering pigs in Tuscany provided him with the opportunity he wanted of solving his problem. The animal, struggling desperately and rending the air with its squeaks, was thrown on its back and held fast by an assistant while the butcher, with practised hand, plunged deep into its heart a stiletto of the type used for broaching casks of wine. Leonardo watched the operation with the greatest interest. He noticed that while the animal lay already motionless on the earth the handle of the stiletto continued for a while to move to and fro, coming to rest only when the body was almost cold. He waded through blood and mire, quickly cut open the body the moment the heart had been pierced, and took careful note of the spasms of the wounded organ. "I have watched this several times," he wrote, "and have noted the measurements, leaving the instrument in the heart until the animal was ripped open." About the middle of the nineteenth century Schiff made experiments with a needle to test the nerve control of the heart. Rudolf Wagner used the same method for counting the beats of the heart; finally the experiments begun in the barbarous Tuscan slaughterhouses led to the invention of the modern cardiograph.

A little later Leonardo made a glass model of the aorta in order to watch the blood currents. He filled the aorta of an ox with wax, took a plaster impression of it, and then blew glass in. When the plaster mould was broken up he had a replica of the aorta in glass, in which he could observe the circulation of the blood.[25] He also proposed to fix a membrane within the glass tube to represent one of the semilunar valves.[26]

Leonardo was especially insistent on the value of artistic representation, as conveying information beyond the range of any verbal description, in the investigation of the action of the heart.

"With what words will you describe the heart," he asks in the introduction to his proposed treatise on anatomy, "without filling a whole book? And the more thoroughly and comprehensively you write, the more you will confuse the mind of the reader." In his efforts to make the most faithful representation of the heart he came to the conclusion, substantially in advance of the traditional ideas, that the heart is "a vessel formed by stout muscles, vivified and nourished by arteries and veins, as are also the other muscles." [27] His observations also enabled him to obtain a correct conception of the function of the semilunar valves. He realized that the powerful bundles of muscles at the root of the aorta approach one another during the diastole in order to produce a firm closure; and he explained from his studies of hydrodynamics the opening of the valves under the influence of the eddies produced in the bulbus aortæ. He drew the valves with their papillary muscles and the "nervous sinews" (corde nervose), which, he said, are clothed in the tenderest of flesh—sottilissima carnosità; he thus discovered the endocardium, a membrane unknown until then.

In order to maintain the conception, to which he clung, of the ebb and flow of the blood-stream, Leonardo was obliged to adopt Galen's theory of the movement of the blood through a porous membrane between the ventricles. This membrane he named septum ventricolorum, "the sieve (cholatorio) of the heart," and he erroneously gave the vena cava and the vena pulmonalis direct outlets into the ventricles, overlooking the passage through the auricles.

His first dilemma came when he found himself required to assume the existence of a mysterious warmth with its seat from the beginning of time in the left ventricle of the heart. His positivist outlook made it difficult for him to assume the existence of any supernatural intervention, and he compromised with tradition by replacing this calor innatus by the hypothesis of the production of heat by friction, "the rapid and continuous motion of the blood producing friction with the cellular wall of the upper ventricle. ... Thus the blood is heated and subtilized so that it can penetrate through the pores and give life and spiritus to the members." [28] The adoption of a mechanical principle was an advance from tradition (the true explanation was made possible only by the much later discovery of oxygen), but it prevented Leonardo from reaching the great discovery of the circulation of the blood. He came so close to it that in his next sentence he almost enunciated it, declaring in opposition to Galen's theory that "all the veins and arteries arise from the heart," [29] and added: "The heart is the nut which gives rise to the tree of the veins." He then stated that the blood which returns to the ventricle is not the same as that which closes the valves; and after comparing the evaporation and condensation of moisture with the rise of the juices in the human body he adds that the blood courses in a permanent circulation.

Leonardo was particularly proud of his knowledge of the blood-vessels and his research on them: "To obtain a true and perfect knowledge" of the veins, "I have dissected more than ten human bodies, destroying all the other members, and removing the very minutest particles of the flesh by which these veins are surrounded, without causing them to bleed, excepting the insensible bleeding of the capillary veins; and as one single body would not last so long, it was necessary to proceed step by step with several bodies, until I came to an end and had a complete knowledge; this I repeated twice, to learn the differences." [30]

He also missed no opportunity of studying the ramification of the blood-vessels. He proposed to make a sketch one day of the arm of Francesco the miniaturist (his friend Francesco Vente, from whom he once borrowed money), "because it shows many veins." [31] Most of his drawings appear to have been made from animal, not human dissections, but they show various details of the vascular system, such as, for instance, the bronchial arteries, which Leonardo was the first to identify.

His theory of blood-heating by friction received, he thought, confirmation in the part played by the lungs, into which he found that the blood flowed through the vena arterialis, and in which it cooled. He accepted the traditional theory that the lungs were a single organ with two wings; they interested him most in connexion with the process of breathing—the lifting of the ribs by the muscles, and the sinking of the diaphragm, producing a vacuum in the thorax and a consequent stream of air into the lungs to fill them. He regarded the whole process as a purely muscular activity.

Similarly with the organs of digestion he was primarily interested in function—the mechanism of the emptying of the stomach and intestines. He denied that in expelling its juices the stomach moves of its own accord; he ascribed the rhythmical expulsion to the alternating constriction of the walls of the stomach and to the motion of the diaphragm in breathing. He gave, as was his wont, a teleological interpretation of the situation and form of the stomach and intestines: "Animals without feet have a straight intestine, for they are always lying down. But man is erect, and his stomach would quickly be emptied were it not for the coiling of his intestines; and if the intestines were straight, not every part of the food would be touched by the intestines, and thus much would remain undigested and unabsorbed by the intestines." [32]

Traditional, medieval conceptions (those, that is to say, which fitted in with his rather arbitrarily fashioned philosophy) mingled strangely in Leonardo's mind with others centuries ahead of his day. Alongside his primitive teleology he had inklings of the eternal process of metabolism, which he tried tentatively to formulate: "The body of anything whatever that takes nourishment constantly dies and is constantly renewed. . . . And if you do not supply nourishment equal to the nourishment which is gone, life will fail in vigour, and if you take away this nourishment the life is entirely destroyed. But if you restore as much as is destroyed day by day, then as much of the life is renewed as is consumed, just as the flame of the candle is fed by the nourishment afforded by the liquid of this candle . . . until a brilliant light is converted in dying into murky smoke." [33]

This search for controlling laws made the greatest breaches in the body of traditional ideas. Again and again Leonardo asked himself where was the seat of motion, the cause of all life. He experimented on a frog, cutting out one after another its brain, its heart, and its entrails, and he observed that the body continued to twitch, although "the frog died at once when its spinal cord (*midolla della schiena*) was severed; until then it could live without head, heart, entrails, or skin. And it seems, therefore, that it is here that the seat of movement and life is situated." [34]

He was sceptical about the Greek traditional theory that the heart was the seat of the soul; this, too, he sought to investigate experimentally. "Follow the reversive (vagus) nerves," he wrote, "as far as the heart, and see whether these nerves give movement to the heart or the heart moves of itself; and if the movement comes from the reversive nerves, which have their origin in the brain, then it will be clear to you that the soul has its seat in the ventricles of the brain, and the vital spirits have their origin in the left ventricle of the heart. And if the movement of the heart springs from itself, then you will say that the seat of the soul, as well as that of the vital spirits, is in the heart." [35]

While he was handling saw and scalpel, and moving step by step toward the discovery of the nature of the human body, he was suddenly seized with the sense of unlimited power. Everything seemed discoverable and demonstrable. It must be possible to find the seat of the soul somewhere in the midst of this wonderful fabric of delicate veins and filmy membranes. "For it is not all-pervading throughout the body, as many have thought. Rather is it entirely in one part. Because, if it were all-pervading, and the same in every part, there would have been no need to make the instruments of the senses meet in one centre and in one single spot." [36]

This centre, the sensory nerves, Leonardo located in the "middle" ventricle of the brain. "The soul seems to reside in the judgment part (*nella parte juditiale*), and the judgment part would seem to be seated in that place where all the senses meet; and this is called the common sense (*senso comune*)." [36] In order to be able more effectively to observe the ventricles of the brain, which he assumed to be the seat of the soul, Leonardo determined to fill them with liquid wax as follows: "Make two air-holes in the horns of the greater ventricle, take melted wax with a syringe, make an opening in the ventricle of memory, and fill through this opening the three ventricles of the brain. And then, when the wax has solidified, dissect the brain, and you will see the form of the three ventricles distinctly." [37] Not until Harvey's discovery of the circulation of the blood, in the seventeenth century, did the custom begin of making injections into the blood-vessels, and this method of demonstration was not applied to the ventricles of the brain until recent times. The experiment requires exceedingly careful management, as the roof of the ventricle can easily be broken through; this seems to have happened with Leonardo's experiment, since he wrongly represents the form of the third ventricle.

At the time of his early anatomical studies, when he ascribed almost every process to the brain, Leonardo thought that the sperm had its origin in the brain; in confirmation of this view he quoted the opinion of Hippocrates, which he had read in a Latin translation, *De Semine,* then existing only in manuscript: "Hippocrates says that our seed has its origin in the brain, the lung, and the testicles of our parents, where it undergoes the final synthesis." [38] At a later period, when he began to be specially interested in the formation of the sperm and the structure of the organs of reproduction, with the object of "disclosing to men the prime cause of their existence," he assumed that the sperm is produced in the blood. His personal observations, which he has recorded in such masterly drawings, represent an immense advance over the theories transmitted from classic and medieval sources. His interest in research was so keen that he examined the sexual organs of men who had been hanged [39]; on one occasion when he dissected a hanged man he found the penis full of blood.[40]

Leonardo was the first to give a correct representation of the organs of reproduction. He believed that the male organ had a life of its own: "This animal often has a soul and an intelligence which are independent of the man." [41] After considering the part played by the testicles in the formation of the sperm and the production of subjective heat,[42] he declared that they are the seat of emotional energy, and in evidence of this he pointed out that all castrated animals are cowardly and whole herds of them will flee from a single uncastrated animal.[43] He also gave the first correct representation of the female sexual organs. The medieval scholars assumed that an animal had as many subdivisions in its womb as it had mammary glands, so that in a sow's womb there must be seven compartments and in the human womb two. Leonardo drew the womb as a single organ, and he also drew the ovaries with fair accuracy, though he made the mistake of connecting them with the womb, following the traditional assumption that both the testicles and the ovaries produced seeds, which united to form the embryo. He mentioned, as bearing this out, that "In Ethiopia the Negroes are not made black by the sun; for if a Negro makes a Negro woman pregnant in Scythia she brings a black child into the world, and if a Negro makes a white woman pregnant she gives birth to a grey child. And this shows that the mother's seed has the same potency in the embryo as the father's." [44]

A series of splendid and impressive drawings showing the fœtus crouching in its mother's womb [45] prove by their accuracy that Leonardo had dissected the corpse of a woman in an advanced state of pregnancy. With intense interest, almost with excitement, he investigated the connexion between the mother and the unborn child. He supposed at first that the blood of the mother and of the embryo must be entirely separated, but beneath one of his finest drawings he wrote, as if his own representation had brought him to the instinctive realization of the union: "And the same soul rules the two bodies, and desires and fears are common to this being and all the other members of the woman's body . . . hence it is to be inferred that one and the same soul controls both bodies, and that the same body nourishes both." [46]

Elsewhere he wrote: "The mother's soul produces in the womb the form of the human being, and awakes in due time the soul that is to dwell therein; that soul at first sleeps in the protection of the mother's soul, which nourishes it through the vein of the umbilical cord and instils life into it." [47]

The further Leonardo progressed in his research into the human frame, the more deeply was he filled with veneration for the marvellous adaptation of the human organism, that most perfect of nature's achievements, to its ends. And, curiously, it was only now that he acquired a sense of the preciousness of human life, and only now that he was filled with horror at the thought of its destruction. Friends and pupils must have looked over Leonardo's shoulder, full of admiration of the artistic powers of the man who was revealing to them the secrets of the human body; and to one of these he replied with all the force of his new faith in the sanctity of human life:

"And you, O man, who will consider in this labour of mine the wonderful works of nature, if you think it would be a criminal thing to destroy this her work, reflect how much more criminal it is to take the life of a man; and if this, his external form, appears to you marvellously constructed, remember that it is nothing in comparison with the soul that dwells in this structure; for that, indeed, be it what it may, is a thing divine. Leave it then to dwell in His work at His goodwill and pleasure, and let not your rage or malice destroy a life—for, indeed, he who does not value it, does not himself deserve it." *

In the past, Leonardo the military engineer had designed the most murderous machines with the same loving care with which he now made drawings of the internal structure of the human body. But now he seemed to have broken entirely with that past, and henceforth machines designed for massacre never again appeared in his papers, as though his knowledge of the human form had produced compassion for tortured humanity and a longing for peace on earth.

Marvellous, however, as was the mechanism of the human body, nature had produced other beings yet more perfect in some respects. While Leonardo was amplifying his research into the human body by means of the dissection of animals more accessible for his experiments, he arrived at the conviction that various animals have greater powers than man's. "I have found that in the composition of the human body, as compared with the bodies of animals, the organs of sense are much duller and coarser. Thus it is composed of less ingenious instruments and of less capacious surfaces for sense-impressions." [48]

He came to a decision which called for vast labour and years of uninterrupted research—to follow his treatise on human anatomy with one devoted to comparative anatomy. After his discussion of "the first beast among the animals," he would write "of such creatures as are of almost the same species, as apes, monkeys, and the like, which are many." [49]

A special section of the new treatise would describe "the movements of animals with four feet; among which is man, who likewise in his infancy crawls on all fours," [50] and when grown up moves his limbs "crosswise after the manner of a horse in trotting; that is, if he puts forward his right foot in walking he puts forward, with it, his left arm, and vice versa, invariably." [51] What he

---

* E tu uomo, che consideri in questa mia fatica l'opere mirabili della natura, se giudicherai essere cosa nefanda il distruggerla, or pensa essere cosa nefandissima il torre la vita all' omo, del quale, se questa sua compositione ti pare di marauiglioso artifitio, pensa questa essere nulla rispetto all' anima che in tale architettura abita, e veramente, quale essa si sia, ella è cosa diuina, sicchè lascia la abitare nella sua opera a suo beneplacito, e non volere che la tua ira o malignità distrugga una tanta vita, che veramente, chi non la stima, non la merita (W., xxix).

proposed to write was by no means a mere description of the various species of animals, but a comparison between them and an examination of the similarities and differences to be found. "You will represent here for a comparison the legs of a frog, which have a great resemblance to the legs of man, both in the bones and in the muscles. Then, in continuation, the hind legs of the hare, which are very muscular, with strong, active muscles, because they are not encumbered with fat." [52]

He dissected a bear, and in four beautiful silverpoint drawings he represented a bear's paw [53]; he dissected an ape [54]; and he proposed then to demonstrate "the extent of the differences between the foot of the bear or ape and the human foot." [55]

In Florence, where the lion was the popular symbol of the republic, opposed to the *palle* of the Medici, symbol of an authoritarian government, lions were kept in cages behind the Palazzo del Capitano; they were gifts to the city from friendly states. One day Leonardo was enabled to dissect the body of a lion, and he went to work with specially keen interest. He found that the "king of the beasts," as he called this cruel and voracious beast of prey, was furnished with much keener senses than man's. The sockets of the eyes occupied a comparatively large part of the head, and the optic nerves, which in man are thin, long, and weak, were intimately bound up with the brain; the organ of smell was also given much more space in the lion's skull.[56]

Leonardo included birds, fishes, and insects in his programme of comparative research. Everywhere he set out to make the comparison with man, pointing out differences, and carrying out what he called the "second demonstration, interposed between anatomy and life." He had travelled far from the fancifulness of his *Book of Animals,* his *Bestiarius,* thoroughly medieval in spirit, of twenty years earlier; he had advanced to the threshold of modern conceptions of natural history. But he got no further than the first preliminaries. The vast projects he would have liked to carry out were more than could be coped with by a single human being in his lifetime, even if he were not hampered by the professional obligations of which Leonardo was very glad to be forgetful on occasion. He felt the burden of the never-ending insufficiency of time for his needs, and at the close of the introduction in which he enu-

merated the qualifications an anatomist must possess he wrote: "As
to whether all these things were found in me or not, the hundred
and twenty books composed by me will give verdict Yes or No. In
these I have been hindered neither by avarice nor by negligence,
but simply by want of time." [57]

5

Leonardo's stay in Florence was approaching its end; judgment
was about to be delivered in his action against his brothers. He
had no further excuse for prolonging his stay in Florence; and his
patron in Milan, Charles d'Amboise, seems to have become irri-
tated at his long absence and to have left his letters unanswered.
"I have had the feeling," Leonardo wrote, "that the small return
made for the great kindnesses I have received from Your Excellency may have made you annoyed with me" [58]; he sent the letter
by Salai, who was to say that Leonardo would arrive about Easter.

As though gradually reawakening to realities and anxious to
make up for his period of immersion in his studies, Leonardo energetically took up the threads of his affairs once more, trying
feverishly to get them into order. He sent letters in all directions,
urging his friends to do things for him. He inquired of Chaumont
whether the pension granted him by the king had begun to arrive,
for he did not want to continue to be a burden on the count's hospitality. Louis had granted to Leonardo a gift of dues on river
water taken, and had confirmed that these were payable even during Leonardo's absence from Milan; but there had been a severe
drought during the summer, and the arrangements in connexion
with the metering of supplies had not been completed, so that
Leonardo had been unable to present his claim. He now asked his
patron Chaumont to use his influence with the president of the
water commission. At the same time he wrote direct to the president. Letters of this sort were a trouble to him, and he made several drafts of both of these.

Francesco Melzi, too, had left him a long time without news.
"Good day to you, Messer Francesco," he wrote. "Why, in God's
name, of all the letters I have written to you, have you never an-

swered one?" But, easily as Leonardo could be put out of humour
as a rule, he took the boy's neglect good-naturedly: "Now, wait till
I come, by God, and I shall make you write so much that perhaps
you will become sick of it." Melzi, too, was to press the matter
with the members of the water commission: "take the trouble, for
the love of me, to urge the president a little." [59]

As the most effective means of ingratiating himself with his
friends and patrons, Leonardo mentioned that in Florence he had
painted two Madonnas, of different sizes, intended for the king.
So he wrote in the first draft of a letter to Chaumont; in a second
one he diplomatically amended this to "for our most Christian
king or for whomever else Your Excellency shall please."

While he was painting these pictures (in one of his letters he
wrote that he had *begun* to paint them, and that may be nearer
the truth), Leonardo was surrounded by young men who, though
they may not have received regular instruction from him, learned
at all events from watching him and listened to advice from him
which affected their whole careers. One of those who were with
him at this time must have been the thirteen-year-old Jacopo Ca-
rucci, whom Vasari calls his pupil. Jacopo was a precocious child
with a gentle, bright face, surrounded by a cloud of fair hair, and
with big round eyes that reflected the loneliness of a child or-
phaned in tender years. He was the son of a Florentine painter
and had a natural artistic talent; born in the village of Pontormo,
he was sent as an apprentice to a shoemaker, from whom he ran
away in order to train in the studios of Florentine painters; he had
just bolted from his latest master when Leonardo came to Florence.

None of the pupils who came under Leonardo's influence had
more brilliant potentialities or attained mastery at an earlier age
than Jacopo, but his meeting with Leonardo entirely wrecked his
anticipated career of effortless achievement. If their paths had
never crossed, Jacopo da Pontormo might have been a master in
his own style, a painter of works of luxuriant beauty and rich
colouring like those of Andrea del Sarto, who was also one of his
masters. If he had been able to work longer with Leonardo and
accompany him in his journey through life as Salai and Melzi did,
he might have developed into the heir to that great spiritual herit-

age. But the period of association was too short for this—and too long to fade away as a simple episode. The boy caught the infection of the man's effort to achieve utter perfection; and it never left him in peace. Jacopo da Pontormo remained a dissatisfied artist to the end of his life—a searcher who threw away the object of his search as soon as he attained it. His natural mission would have been to achieve pleasure-giving works, in rich, bright, cheerful colouring and intoxicating loveliness of form; instead of this he wrestled desperately with one vast problem after another, tried to attain a depth of significance that was beyond his range, and shattered his gentle and amiable art in a sort of frenzy of self-torture.

Another young artist came into touch at this time with Leonardo—Baccio Bandinelli; Leonardo encouraged him in his career as a sculptor. Bandinelli, too, was infected with a spirit of deep unrest and a boundless artistic ambition; and if he was not the berserker who, according to Vasari, cut into pieces Michelangelo's cartoon of the *Soldiers Bathing*, his life was at all events a wild and furious fight against Michelangelo's hopelessly superior powers.

It seemed to be Leonardo's destiny to unsettle the young artists who crossed his path; only colourless and second-rate minds withstood his influence. Those of his followers who, like Andrea Solario, Bernardino Luini, Gianpedrino, and Sodoma, imbibed something of his personality without losing their own, had escaped his disturbing influence, his pregnant generalizations, his overmastering individuality. Andrea Solario left Milan in 1507, summoned by cardinal d'Amboise to the Château de Gaillon. Luini, that amiable and competent craftsman, who knew how to assimilate everything that it was possible for Leonardo to pass on, had probably never worked directly under Leonardo; nor had Gianpedrino, or Sodoma, the most gifted of Leonardo's imitators; Sodoma had already completed important work when he returned to Milan in 1508. And yet Leonardo had often dreamt of fruitful educative activity, of founding an academy of artists who would be grouped round his name; he toyed with this idea as one who from his youth had had a veneration for the very conception of the academic; and on one occasion when he drew a maze of ribbons he saw in imagination the realization of this dream, and filled a space in the middle with the inscription: "Ac. Leonardi Vinci."

But the young men who came to him when he finally settled in Milan after his return from Florence were not of the calibre needed for an academy or community of disciples. The names of the pupils who figure in his housekeeping books are names of unknown artists, of mediocrities who carefully kept well within the limits of their powers while slavishly adopting particular elements in Leonardo's instruction. The most conscientious of them was Cesare da Sesto, who tried with almost artful tenacity to assimilate Leonardo's technique. However exact his copies of paintings, he betrays himself at once by his reddish surface colouring, but as a draughtsman he made sufficient progress for his drawings to be confused for centuries with those of his master.

Of the pupil who worked longest under Leonardo, and in this Milanese period was already an independent artist, Salai, not a single accredited painting remains, but a number of rather feeble works which reveal a certain kinship with one another in their ill-defined contours might be ascribed to this man, on whom Leonardo vainly lavished his teaching. Salai still lived near Leonardo, and though he was earning a livelihood he knew how to exploit Leonardo's generosity for himself and his family. His father had taken a lease of Leonardo's vineyard by the Porta Vercellina, and when his sister married Salai borrowed further from his master. "On October . . . 1508," writes Leonardo, "I received 30 gold thalers. I lent 13 to Salai, to make up his sister's dowry, and had 17 left"; and he adds a jingle of humorous warning: "Lend not! If you lend you will not be repaid; if you are repaid it will not be soon; if it is soon it will not be good coin; if it is good coin you will lose your friend!" But chaff fell from Salai's back as easily as Leonardo's wrath had done in the past; all he troubled about was how to make the most for himself out of his famous friend's improved fortunes.

With his return to Milan there began for Leonardo a period of greater freedom from material cares than he had ever known. The payments from the king of France came in regularly; he kept a conscientious account of them.[60] And, as if fate intended to compensate him for the long years of adversity, he now received a commission which promised not only large material reward but the opportunity of something to set against the destruction of his masterpiece, the equestrian statue of Francesco Sforza. The commission was for a monument to Marshal Gian Giacomo Trivulzio. The marshal belonged to one of the oldest of the Milanese families; as a loyal servant of Galeazzo Maria Sforza he had been banished from Milan by Lodovico. Of all the precautions taken by that uneasy usurper, this was certainly one of the most fatal. Trivulzio, torn from his native soil, became a knight errant with an unquenchable longing to return to his homeland; he was ready to enter the service of anyone in the world who was Lodovico's enemy, and to take part in any conspiracy hatched against the duke. He was a born soldier; several times he had nearly bled to death on the battlefield; his body was a mass of scars; nowhere did he sleep better than amid the bustle of a camp or the thunder of cannon. He took part in every armed struggle fought out in his day. He sought a command under the king of Naples, and when Lodovico played false with Charles VIII Trivulzio entered the service of the French king. He was a plain, downright man, and a man of strong feelings, and his hatred of Lodovico dominated all else in his life. But this hatred, far from distorting his vision, preserved his sense of values even in exile.

Louis XII was only too familiar from his own experience with the feelings of the dispossessed and disinherited, and with the tactics of the struggle for the recovery of power. He was glad to take advantage of Trivulzio's knowledge of men and of the country, and he enabled him to fight for the duchy of Milan with a sense of personal property in it, by promising him the viceroyalty of the duchy when he had conquered it. The king also allowed Trivulzio to feel that the French victory, when it came, was the marshal's personal triumph; he allowed him to march in as conqueror at his side, and thereafter to do as he pleased in the duchy, furnished with powers "as extensive as he cared to demand."

But after living only for this day Trivulzio found himself robbed of the substance of his dream in the moment of its fulfilment. He had no sooner returned to his own state than he was filled with disgust by the arrogance of its alien conquerors. A knight of Picardy had taken liberties with a lady of Trivulzio's own family; he had the knight hanged. Trivulzio also alienated the Milanese nobles by his own unbounded arrogance; he recognized no one as his equal, rode roughshod over his peers, and showed signs of genuine humanity only in dealing with the common people. Louis XII astutely permitted his viceroy to fritter away his reputation and popularity, and when both had been exhausted he set him aside, his place being taken first by the comte de Ligny and then by Chaumont. When Trivulzio retired in dudgeon to France, the king played cleverly on the exile's nostalgia, finally, with all the air of conferring a favour, granting him permission to return to Milan, without rank or title.

Trivulzio's one remaining desire was to die on his native soil and be buried with pomp and magnificence; and, as he did not trust his heirs to make due provision for these posthumous honours out of the fortune his greed had amassed, he decided to see to his own monument while he still lived. When he had made his ceremonial entry into Milan with Louis XII, Leonardo's colossus had still dominated the great courtyard of the castle, a striking symbol of the hated power of the Sforzas; he had observed it with envy. Now that wind and weather had destroyed it, he turned to Leonardo to immortalize the Trivulzi in a new colossus.

Leonardo's new patron was a man worn out with reckless pleasure-seeking and with the hardships of his many campaigns, and ravaged by a disease which was regarded as incurable; yet he still gave the impression of unimpaired physical powers. His stocky, broad-shouldered frame supported a powerful head, ruddy-faced, with a large, wide nose given prominence by his weathered cheeks. Such a figure might have been hewn by a sculptor out of some hard, coarse-grained stone—formidable, unfinished, with no more than roughly indicated features. And it was as a conqueror even over death that Gian Giacomo Trivulzio wanted to be represented on horseback above his tomb. "A charger of life size with a man riding it," was the first note Leonardo made on his drawings for the statue. His precise estimate of cost and a series of sketches give an idea of the magnificence of the proposed monument. A massive foundation supported the heavy stone slab with horse and rider, and eight allegorical figures united the architectural element with the actual monument. The sarcophagus, bearing the recumbent figure of the dead man, was placed in a niche; this, in one of his sketches, Leonardo surrounded with a colonnade reminiscent of Bramante's Tempietto at Rome. A frieze, on which the marshal's victories were celebrated, surrounded the sarcophagus. The intrados of the niche was decorated with rosettes; the Doric capitals of the pillars were of cast bronze. Broad steps led up to the monument, with iron harpies bearing candelabra. The architrave was hung with heavy clusters of flowers. The profiles were in full relief. Every surface was covered with ornament in harmony with the new style of a period that surrounded its dead with as much commotion as if they had already risen from the grave.

Leonardo had calculated the cost of the monument down to the last soldo. For the making of the model he set down 432 ducats; but the materials—metal, and wood and charcoal for the casting— were to cost 700 ducats, and the labour for polishing the statue when cast 450. Leonardo put the fee for his own work "for the statue of the deceased, to do it well," at 100 ducats, but marble and bronze ran to 389. The total came to 3046 ducats.[61] The amount does not seem to have alarmed his patron, for Leonardo began his preliminary studies shortly after completing this estimate.

In his first sketches, as in those for the Sforza monument, Leonardo drew a horse rearing, with its fore feet resting on the shield of a fallen enemy. He held fast to his old dream of representing a horse in full career, and hoped that this time, on a smaller scale, he would be able to realize it. His horse was a true war-horse, with a massive body, its powerful neck sharply bent, looking down at the enemy. In later sketches the prostrate man was almost under the horse's hooves, and pushing with one leg against the heavy body of the animal as it swept over him; this filled gaps left in the first sketches, and gave greater concentration. But once more the horse in motion was no more than a dream set down on paper. More realizable was a trotting horse, with its fore legs supported by an overturned vase; one of the hind legs was planted on a tortoise.

Leonardo's sketches for this memorial, all at Windsor, differ from the silverpoint sketches for the Sforza monument in being done in thick chalk strokes, which are given precision at times with a pen or heightened with red pencil. The general silhouette, moreover, is stronger and more self-contained. The sharp bend in the horse's head, bringing it close to the neck, produces more concentration. Horse and rider are more firmly bound together; in the Sforza monument the "great horse" was created independently, the rider being seated on it later.

The new sketches were also quickly liberated from dreams of the impossible; they were conceived and visualized in bronze. Leonardo devoted a great deal of attention to the connexion between the rider and the architecture. In one case he designed an almost two-story construction, in another a triumphal arch in three sections; then he extended the arched niche by a projecting base, placing on either flank of the niche, between the base and the cornice bearing the rider, captured slaves, naked youths in chains, who provided a wealth of contrasting movement which united the statue with the monumental architecture.

This last sketch is no more than a rough suggestion, but it is a striking representation of massive naked figures, with muscular backs turning this way and that, taut, firmly set, strong limbs, and a great display of energy serving no definite purpose, existing apparently for its own sake, as with Michelangelo's youths in the Sistine chapel, who bring every muscle into play in order to support light wreaths of flowers.

Leonardo had been drawing horses from life for thirty-five years —his studies date back to his *Adoration of the Magi*. He had captured every possible attitude in countless sketches. He was thoroughly acquainted with equine anatomy. But when he began to work on his sketches for the Trivulzio monument he sketched once more from life, drawing every detail, the play of the muscles under the skin, the folds over the bent joints, right down to the hooves.[62]

He proceeded with equal care, taught by his earlier misfortune, with the preparation for the casting. The model was to be built up "on legs of iron, strong and well set on a good foundation." The mould was to be "made in sections," so that it should be easily removed from the "well-greased wax" after casting. He devoted specially minute care to these instructions to himself, and he showed such concern for economy that he proposed to "make the outside mould of plaster, to save the expense of wood," and to return the unused wax to the dealer.[63]

But even this work, so carefully calculated and thought out down to the smallest detail, was never brought to completion. The unsettled times, and Leonardo's continual employment on other duties, made it impossible for him to finish the preliminary work before the whole project fell through, owing to the collapse of the French rule in Milan.

6

While he was at work on his studies for the Trivulzio monument, Leonardo was also busily occupied with canalization work in Lombardy. This time his personal interests were involved, and during this period, the most carefree period of his life, he was more successful in looking after his interests than at any other time. In the past he had patiently waited for years for the arrears due to him from Lodovico, but now he entered industriously into correspondence to secure his income from the canal of San Cristoforo. It was pointed out to him that the king himself would lose seventy-two ducats of revenue if Leonardo were paid, but Leonardo replied vigorously that it would not be the king that suffered but the water stealers who had enriched themselves through the regulation of the canal—*i ladri,* these thieves, and the incapable engineers who were determined to do everything as they thought fit.[64] He set out to show what ought to be done, and while he was still at Florence he tried to secure the favour of the president of the water commission by making promises in a letter to Chaumont to do various things: "I pray your lordship to remind the president of my matter; and on my return I hope to make there instruments and other things which will greatly please our most Christian king." [65]

Canalization was already well developed in Lombardy when Leonardo first came to Milan. The use of locks was known as early as the beginning of the fifteenth century, when the last of the Visconti had them built at various spots. In a period of thirty-five years over fifty miles of canals were built, with twenty-five locks. On his first arrival in Milan Leonardo took pains to acquaint himself with the methods of upkeep of canals. He mentions sending for a foreman "well acquainted with water" to explain to him what is done to prevent damage by water, what the maintenance works cost, and all about "a lock, a canal, and a mill in the Lombard style." [66] But soon he knew more than his instructor, and he put before Lodovico a plan and detailed estimate for the regulation of the Martesana canal.[67]

Now, however, he had reached the stage of describing the Milanese engineers as incapable. He put forward new proposals for the canal in which he was interested, that of San Cristoforo. A particularly fine drawing, showing a section of a canal with six locks placed in three pairs one above the other, bears the laconic inscription: "The canal of San Cristoforo, Milan, May 3, 1509." [68] He also made improvements in the design of locks. He drew the locks with cheek gates, which Alberti mentioned as early as the middle of the fifteenth century, and he provided them with various devices for closing. In one drawing the gates are lifted by two chains which are wound on a windlass fixed on the bank and can easily be set in motion from the watchman's house.[69] In others he designed a trapdoor moved by an oblique draw-bar,[70] or made to tip by heavily laden vessels.[71]

At this period Leonardo returned to another problem which had occupied him in Lodovico Sforza's time, that of rendering the Adda navigable. He proposed that a huge dam should be built on the Adda, connecting the crags known as Tre Corni. He suggested a canal between Brivio and Trezzo, which would shorten the passage by two miles; he brought all his eloquence and some impressive economic arguments to the support of this idea: "If it is not announced that this is to be a public undertaking and the land has to be purchased, the king will be able to pay the price out of the dues received in a single year."

For the work on this rocky stretch, with its steep gradient, Leonardo proposed to set up three great siphons and six windlasses at various levels. "It will be necessary to begin from above, so that the material may be brought down to one level. . . . Each windlass will be placed by the section of the canal to be dug, and it must not be moved . . . for it is easier to lengthen the towing rope than to move the machinery." [72]

He also made play, in advocating his plan, with the fame such a work would bring, and promised to put up a memorial tablet at the outlet of the canal at Brivio.[73] But his efforts were in vain, and the canal Leonardo planned was built by another engineer, Bartolommeo della Valle, under Francis I. Leonardo's great hydraulic engineering projects came to nothing almost without exception, being taken up again years later and carried through by others; and his inventions remained unapplied. He now proposed that they should at least be transmitted to posterity. He was especially concerned to prove the practical value of his theoretical knowledge: "When you compile the science of the movements of water, remember to add after each proposition its practical advantages (*li sua giovamenti*)." [74] After reflection he decided to separate the study of water from that of hydraulics; otherwise "you would have to mix up practice with theory, which would produce a confused and incoherent work." Meanwhile the practical section of his work had grown to forty chapters—*40 libri de' giovamenti*.[75]

In sifting his theoretical material he observed that the important was mixed up with the unimportant. "First write of all water, in each of its motions . . . and let the order be good, for otherwise the work will be confused. Describe all the forms taken by water, from its greatest to its smallest wave, and their causes." [76] But this time there was more to do than the mere arranging and completing of the constantly growing material for his treatise on water. In the few years that had passed since his geological studies, he had meditated long on the problems they presented, and gradually he had revised his ideas. In the course of his astronomical research he had upset the conception, so dear to the men of the Middle Ages, of the central position of our world in the universe; and this had entailed the abandonment also of the traditional conception of the similar nature of the organic and the inorganic world. For years Leonardo had held fast to the idea of the identity of nature of the macrocosm and the microcosm. He had represented this idea in countless imaginative similes, with a warmth that betrayed how wedded he was to the idea. It weighed on him like a relic of the Middle Ages, hampering his freedom of thought. If the universe was not centred in man the earth could not be the image of man, that most perfect of created beings. If the moon was a world, and our world like many of the stars, the explanation of the phenomena of the human body could have no relevance to the organism of the universe. Leonardo's profound anatomical studies, his increased knowledge of the organs of the human body, gave the deathblow to his pet idea; and one day he silently abandoned it, as one gives up childish beliefs—not without a little shame at one's past credulity.

Abruptly, without a word of mention of the long and circuitous paths by which he had arrived at his new beliefs, Leonardo now denied the existence of a "sea of blood" in the body of the earth, circulating through its water-veins and rising to the tops of the highest mountains as the blood rises to a man's head. If, he now argued, the water on the mountains came from a sea that lifted itself above the highest summits, why did not the water that touches the air rise through the atmosphere, where it would find fewer obstacles on its path? He added in self-mockery, or in forgetfulness of his past error: "And you, who have found such hypotheses, go back to nature to learn from her." [77]

He now proposed to write a special chapter, "Book 42, Of Rain"—"How clouds form, what cause lifts the water vapours from the earth into the air, and the cause of fog, and the cause of snow and hail." [78] In this research he was brought up against the problem of the formation of drops, which had escaped his attention up to then. "Every elastic and fluid element has necessarily a spherical surface," he wrote [79]; "every orb even of the smallest fragment of water becomes the container of the fragment within it"; but this spherical form had nothing in common with that of the ocean, which was attributable to gravity. With this distinction Leonardo drew a dividing line between the two branches of theoretical physics—the hydrostatics of liquids which are subject to gravity, and the capillary theory—in a first tentative anticipation of the development of modern science.

Alongside these fruits of a research now pursued in freedom from the fetters of tradition, his practical work produced new observations and discoveries. He occupied himself with the draining of marshes: "How with the aid of running water the soil should be brought from the mountains into marshy valleys to render them fertile and the surrounding air salubrious." [80] In section 6 of the ninth book of his *Hydraulics,* he described the causes of marshy estuaries, and he recommended dumping soil into the marshes, "purging" the air and producing arable land.[81] But these were methods in use in Tuscany as early as the twelfth century, and Leonardo must have been familiar with Alberti's description of them. His personal contribution consisted of the recommendation of apparatus which he invented at this time, depending on the principle of centrifugal force, of which he was the discoverer. "If the water in a half-filled vessel is stirred with the hand, a whirling current is produced which will expose the bottom of the vessel to the air; and when the force that produced it is no longer applied, the current will continue in motion, but will continually diminish in speed until the impetus given by the force ceases." This was the principle of his centrifugal pump "for draining marshes bordering on the sea." The current mentioned in his experiment was produced in a huge vessel of which the only inlet was a "hole in the bottom, where the water enters only through the pipe led to it from the marsh." He produced the current with a beam the axis of which was fixed in a fly-wheel set in motion by a turbine. The vessel was so placed as to raise the water above the sea level. Water flowed through a pipe into the vessel and out to the sea, and the centrifugal motion that raised the water from its lowest level sufficed for the complete draining of the marsh.[82] Leonardo was very proud of his invention, and determined to keep it a profound secret. "In use the secret of the siphon and the whirl must be hidden and walled in"—in the drawing a wall is to be seen between the marsh and the sea—"and cut off from the sea."

On the back of a sheet on which Leonardo grappled with the theory of the production of artificial currents and eddies of water, he drew a screw with sixteen blades lying in a canal and supplying power by means of gearing to a machine not represented. Not until the eighteenth century were screws used for the propulsion of ships, and little progress was made with this method until at the beginning of the nineteenth century the Austrian Joseph Ressel invented the screw propeller.

Genuinely interested though Leonardo was in the practical side of his hydraulic studies, it was the multiplicity of the motions of water which he observed, the currents and rapids and natural and artificial eddies, that caught his imagination and fascinated him. His papers of this period are covered with winding streams, rapidly whirling eddies, intertwining currents, turbid, bubbling, splashing waters—as though all the world had been swallowed up for him in a wild dance of the waves. He found no release from the obsession of this turmoil until he had given it imaginative form in his series of drawings of the Deluge. And from now on the strokes of the soft crayon which he used almost exclusively took on an element of restless curving and waving, which remained with him to the end of his life.

As though the eddying waters were not enough for him, Leonardo proposed to devote Book 43 of his treatise to "the motion of air imprisoned beneath water." To the commotions of water there succeeded those of air. "I have seen," he writes, "movements of the air so furious that they have carried, mixed up in their course, the largest trees of the forest and whole roofs of great palaces, and I have seen the same fury of the air bore a hole with a whirling movement, digging out a gravel pit and carrying gravel, sand, and water more than half a mile through the air." [83] He was attracted again and again to the subject of violent motion in water, air, sand—"Describe the motions of shifting deserts; that is to say, the formation of waves of sand borne by the wind, and of its mountains and hills, such as occur in Libya. Examples may be seen on the wide sands of the Po and the Ticino, and other large rivers." [84]

Everything Leonardo did at this time was dominated by the idea of motion, of the circling and eddying which had now become for him a law embracing all phenomena. He devoted special attention to his theory of the blood currents that swirl up to the heart; it was now that he made a glass tube in the form of the aorta, to assist him in observing these movements. He pushed on with his anatomical studies, trying to procure such books as *Anatomica sive Historia Corporis Humani,* published by a physician, Alessandro Benedetti, a few years earlier in Venice. He had a work by Avicenna translated. He proposed to study the human body in motion and repose: "Go every Saturday to the vapour baths, and you will see naked men." In order to verify the proportions of the

body he tried to procure an edition of Vitruvius; Messer Ottav
ano Pallavicino promised to get it for him. He proposed to do
some more dissecting, and bought "knives from Bohemia" to this
end. Feeling that his studies of the process of breathing were still
in the rudimentary stage, he resolved to inflate the lungs of a pig
"to see whether they expand laterally and longitudinally, or only
laterally, diminishing in length." This list of things to be done,
which, as usual, Leonardo entered on the cover of the notebook
in use, gives the clue to the labyrinth of his intellectual activity at
this period. He was no longer being pursued by a patron's impatience, no longer disturbed in the midst of his studies by the
thought of material needs, no longer prevented by written agreements and fixed time limits from devoting himself to a peaceful
life of scholarship. Leonardo the artist, who all his life had wrestled with Leonardo the scholar, had now yielded him the palm,
and Leonardo the man felt that he had won his enfranchisement.
He copied a facetious verse that expressed the satisfaction of a man
who at length had escaped from the slavery of the daily round of
duties: "Human liberty, how dear art thou! Alas for him who lives
in dependence!"

He now had justification for the hope that he would be able to
bring some sections of his studies to completion, and he proposed
to get on with his astronomical studies. His notes open with the
mention of concave mirrors which he needed for his experiments
in breaking up the sun's rays. Most of the books he hunted down
were mathematical and astronomical works—the *Meteors* of Aristotle in an Italian translation; Archimedes' *On the Centre of
Gravity,* the classic work on statics; the books of Giovanni Marliani, the Milanese physician and mathematician, with whose sons
Leonardo was on terms of friendship. Some of the books he read
and dismissed with contempt—"Marliani's science is wrong." [85] He
pursued any hint, however vague, of works unknown to him:
"Horace wrote on the rate of motion of the heavens," he wrote on
one cover of a notebook, and on the other: "Posidonius composed
books on the size of the sun." [86] The book that made the strongest
impression on him was the *Questiones in Aristotelis Libros de
Cœlo et Mundo,* by Albert of Saxony, which he probably read
with the aid of a dictionary, since he secured at the same time a

Latin-Italian vocabulary (*Vocabolista Volgare e Latino*). The influence of that great scholar, born in Helmstedt, and prominent at the Sorbonne about the middle of the fourteenth century, is plain in all the notes made in the notebook Leonardo was using at this time.

Leonardo now threw over a whole series of errors of his own or from other sources. He used the same arguments as Albert of Saxony to combat the Pythagorean idea, so popular in the Middle Ages, of the music of the spheres, which was supposed to accompany the circling of the heavenly bodies with waves of crystal-clear, superterrestrial melody. He also combated, as though it had been an error of his own, the idea that the spots on the moon are caused by rising water vapour.[87]

Enriched by new knowledge and liberated from some illusions, Leonardo took up his astronomical studies at the point at which he had interrupted them, the identity of the elements and the laws of nature on earth and in the heavens. A chapter of his proposed treatise on astronomy was devoted to the "Demonstration that the earth is a star." He was fully aware of the extent to which this demonstration would play havoc with tradition, and added with characteristic irony: "In your discourse you must prove that the earth is a star much like the moon, and the glory of our universe; and then you must treat of the size of various stars, according to the authors"—*secondo li autori*.[88] His impulse to generalize, his instinctive tendency to assume the unity of the laws of the universe, led him to extend this demonstration of the similarity of moon and earth to the stars in general, which in his view merely reflected the light of the sun as the moon does. "Some say that they [the stars] shine of themselves, alleging that if Venus and Mercury had not a light of their own, when they come between our eye and the sun they would darken so much of the sun as they could cover from our eye. But this is false." [89]

Filled with the idea of the minuteness of our earth, Leonardo looked up at the heavens. On one occasion he looked at the stars through a convex lens.[90] On another he held to an eye a sheet in which he had made a pinhole, in order to eliminate the twinkling of the stars, which he recognized as an optical illusion. Even Galileo, decades later, ascribed the twinkling of the stars to their

"vibration with the native splendour of their intimate substance."
Seen through the pinhole, the stars looked inconceivably tiny, and
yet many of them were infinitely larger than the star which is
our earth with its water: "Consider, then, how this our star would
appear at such a distance, and reflect on the number of the stars
that lie up and down between the stars which are strewn through
the darkling heavens."

And was it to be supposed that our earth, this tiny point in the
universe, was the centre around which the sun and stars moved?
Once before, at the outset of his astronomical studies, Leonardo
had thrown doubt on this hypothesis, writing in unusually large
letters: "The sun does not move." But now, after studying many
astronomical works, he did not venture so far, in spite of his poor
opinion of some of "the authors"; he did not venture to discard
the traditional theory of the structure of the universe, in face of
the mass of arguments that had been brought to its support. He
continued, however, occasionally to give indirect hints of his conviction that the earth moved: "Let the earth turn on which side
it may, the surface of the waters will never move from its spherical
form." [91] But in writing this it was possible to imply that the
earth turned on its own axis (as Nicholas of Cusa had already declared that it did), without disturbing the medieval conception of
the earth as the centre of the universe.

While it is impossible to establish beyond question what was
Leonardo's actual view, all his arguments ended in a glorification
of the sun as the all-powerful controller of the universe. "I cannot
but censure the many ancient writers," he declared, "who state
that the sun is no greater than it appears to us." He intended to
deal with this statement in the fourth book of his treatise on
astronomy. He had probably seen its attribution to Epicurus in
the *Vitæ Philosophorum* of Diogenes Laertius. He read also that
Socrates had described the sun as an incandescent stone, and had
severely commented: "The one who opposed him as to that error
was not far wrong." [92]

The sun, too, was formed of the same substance as the earth and
the stars. It had been contended that their white radiance proved
that the stars were composed of some ethereal matter. Leonardo
replied, thinking of his own experience of bronze casting, that

liquid bronze also gives out a white glow, which becomes still brighter as it is further heated.[93] In an exordium headed *Laude del Sole,* "Praise of the Sun," he wrote what sounds almost like a pagan invocation:

"I only wish I had words to serve me to blame those who are fain to extol the worship of men more than that of the sun; for in the whole universe there is nowhere to be seen a body of greater magnitude and power than the sun. Its light gives light to all the celestial bodies which are distributed throughout the universe; and from it descends all vital force, for the heat that is in living beings comes from the soul; and there is no other centre of heat and light in the universe, as will be shown in Book IV; and certainly those who have chosen to worship men as gods—as Jove, Saturn, Mars, and the like—have fallen into the gravest error, seeing that even if a man were as large as our earth, he would look no bigger than a little star which appears but as a speck in the universe; and seeing again that these men are mortal, and putrid and corrupt in their sepulchres." [94]

Some men, when caught between two passions, begin to despise the earlier one as soon as they have made their choice for its successor. So did Leonardo look back now with depreciation on his old enthusiasm for man, the work of art.

At this time his only interest outside his astronomical research was in his mathematical studies. All his life he had tended to lose interest in external happenings, and this tendency had now entirely gained the upper hand; it was in his work that he now met with the shattering or heartening events of his life, the torture of doubt, the exhilaration of certainty. These adventures of the spirit he noted as signposts on paths which only he could recognize.

On Sunday April 30, 1509, during a quiet evening after the day's labour, he had an experience that made it a red-letter day. "I had long been trying to square the angle with two curved sides; at this moment of the vigil of the month of May, about the 22nd hour on Sunday, I discovered the following. . . ." [95]

After that eventful night Leonardo lay, as was his wont, meditating in bed until late in the morning. Suddenly the stillness of this May Day of 1509 was broken by firing close by. The streets of Milan were then invaded with an unaccustomed sound, the resounding tramp of soldiers marching in, the rattle of arms, and the shouting of the spectators, perhaps in welcome, perhaps in protest—it was impossible to say. And the gunshots continued to boom, until suddenly there came the thunder of an explosion, the echoes of which were drowned by the panic cries of the fleeing crowd. Louis XII had entered the city and salutes had been fired in his honour; but the cannoneers had been overzealous and a cannon with an excessive charge had exploded. A nobleman in the king's suite was buried beneath a shower of fragments of iron, and a little boy who had gone too near was blown to pieces. A bad omen for the king's enterprise, whispered the superstitious Italians.

It was, indeed, a strange enterprise that had brought about Louis's new intervention in Italy—the war against Venice on which the League of Cambrai had resolved. It was a war in which France was allowing herself to be misused as the instrument of the papal ambitions. Louis's adviser, Georges d'Amboise, cardinal and papal legate, was an able man, and so well aware of his ability that his self-assurance imposed respect. But he used to think he knew well what sort of man was Cardinal Giuliano della Rovere, now Pope Julius II, and consequently he was unable to understand what was the Pope's present aim. One ambassador at that pleasant assembly at Cambrai described the papal aim as "to be lord and master of the intrigues of this world." At Cambrai the Pope had been the invisible wirepuller behind the negotiations.

In addition to this invisible opponent of his own intricate political game, the astute cardinal found another opponent, who was also fully his equal in ability and influence—a woman, Margaret of Parma, who was quite capable, as a contemporary said, of "coming to blows with him"; and who, moreover, had suffered a gross and wounding insult at the hands of France which, in spite of her protests of friendship, not all the years that had since passed could efface from her memory. She had been betrothed to Charles VIII and had then been unceremoniously sent back to her father, Maximilian of Habsburg, like a consignment of rejected merchandise. In face of the Pope's secret ambition and this woman's secret lust for revenge the French were bound to be the losers, to serve merely as auxiliaries made use of in a campaign of conquest in which the Pope was out to recover the ecclesiastical city states of which the Venetians had taken possession, the Emperor the Venetian provinces, and France herself no more than parts of the former duchy of Milan.

Under the subtly framed agreements of the League of Cambrai the French had opened hostilities in April 1509 the moment Julius II had hurled his ban of excommunication against Venice, and Charles d'Amboise had already been fighting with varying fortunes against the powerful Venetian army before the king himself came into the field. This war against their old opponent, the arrogant Venetian republic, was popular among the Milanese; hundreds of nobles offered their services to the king, arming troops at their own expense, and they rode in shining gold brocade in the king's train when, after a short rest in Milan, he set out from the city, clad entirely in white as though for a festival. There also rode in the king's train the engineer to the king, Leonardo da Vinci.

At the castle of Cassano, on a hill above the Adda, Charles d'Amboise received the royal troops with the magnificence he loved to display. A war council was held in the castle; the king was for striking a blow at once, but his commanders tried to persuade him to await the approach of the Venetian army. Meanwhile Leonardo examined the country and the nature of the river banks, to ascertain whether it would be possible to establish a port here for river traffic; in his notebook he made the brief entry: "Porto di Cassano."

Trivulzio urged and implored the king not to advance, declaring that it would mean the total destruction of the French army, but Louis was not to be moved. Next day light bridges were thrown over the Adda, and the great army crossed unhindered; the Venetians kept to the heights on which they held fortified positions. After the crossing Trivulzio, a good loser, turned to the king and acknowledged his error: "Sire, the victory is now ours." Louis, with vague memories of ancient history and a taste for heroic gestures, ordered the bridges to be destroyed, so that his troops might rely only on victory at arms, with flight impossible. He advanced rapidly and with decision—and with brutality: the unfortunate countryside was devastated, villages were burned down, the living were robbed and the graves of the dead desecrated; the army advanced inexorably, leaving a trail of misery and horror. At Agnadello the French troops met the Venetian army, which attacked with the cry of "Italy and freedom!" But the Venetian attack crumbled beneath the superior French force; after a raging battle the field was covered with 16,000 dead, lying with glazed eyes in the red glow of the setting sun; and most of them were Venetians.

Encouraged by his victory, Louis next laid siege to the fortress of Caravaggio; his artillery blew up the powder magazine and compelled the fortress to surrender. The French army then marched in the direction of Lago d'Iseo. Leonardo quickly made sketch maps showing the marching route, and when the king decided to capture Bergamo Leonardo sketched the lower course of the river Serio, which wound through the valley through which the troops had to pass. Another map is connected with the taking of Bergamo, and on a further sheet the region between Bergamo and Brescia is sketched. These were fertile and well-watered valleys, and Leonardo was particularly interested in the course of the rivers and the merging of their tributaries, and in the outlines of the lakes, as though he hoped to be responsible for the development of the waterways of this region; but it remained for so short a time in French possession that it became popularly known later as Francia Corta, "brief France." Most of these sketches were roughly made, as by a traveller passing rapidly through the country. Leonardo could ascertain the names of the towns and villages only by inquiry of the inhabitants, and he noted them phonetically, as they were pronounced to him in the harsh Bergamask dialect.

It was mainly hydraulic development that interested him while he took part in Louis XII's expedition, and he discussed this subject at a chance meeting with the engineer in the enemy camp, Fra Giocondo da Verona, a Dominican friar. Fra Giocondo, a man already well into the sixties, had the same multiplicity of interests as Leonardo. His contemporaries called him a library of ancient and modern knowledge; he possessed a large collection of codices, and on his many journeys he went continually in search of new manuscripts; finally a happy chance led him to the discovery in Paris of a codex of Pliny the Younger. He was an archæologist and followed the profession of architecture. As a military engineer he had built the fortifications of Treviso, and as a hydraulic expert he had diverted the river Brenta, which had become a menace to the lagoons of Venice. It was only by chance that he was now in the enemy camp, for he had been in the French service; he had returned to Venice shortly before hostilities broke out. In Paris he had built the bridge of Notre Dame, and perhaps also the Petit Pont de l'Hôtel-de-Dieu, the palace of the Chambre des Comtes, and the Golden Room for the Paris Parlement. War had overtaken him in Venice while he was engaged, by command of the Emperor, on the erection of the Fondaco dei Tedeschi, the German merchants' headquarters.

Fra Giocondo had also done work in the castle of Blois, and Leonardo was interested in the plan of the waterworks for the castle; his colleague explained to him the system of pipes and pumps, and Leonardo made a rough sketch of it.[96]

True to his habit of gaining all the information he could from the specialists he met, Leonardo also watched his friend Jean Perréal, court painter to Louis XII, at work, and proposed to acquire his technique of miniature painting, in which Jean Perréal was eminent. "Learn from Gian di Paris the art of dry colouring, and how he makes the white salt and prepares the paper, double-folded paper; and his paintbox; learn from him the skin colours in tempera, and how gum-lac is dissolved. . . ."[97] Jean de Paris, as Perréal was called in his time, was a shrewd adventurer with unlimited self-confidence. He was painter, engineer, architect, and valet de chambre to the king, and had served Charles VIII in these varied capacities during the Italian expedition; Leonardo's acquaintance with him dated back to that period, and they must have been on fairly intimate terms, for Jean Lemaire, the court poet, whom Jean Perréal kept to sing his praises, in the fashion of a petty prince, sang also those of Leonardo, *"qui a des grâces suprêmes."*

At this time, however, it was principally in astronomy that Leonardo was interested, and he noted with pleasure that Perréal, who considered himself something of an adept in the theory and art of mathematics, had offered to procure for him the measurement of the sun.[98]

Meanwhile Louis XII had captured Peschiera, and was waiting for the arrival of the Emperor. But in spite of the most solemn promises the Emperor delayed coming until in the end Louis lost patience and returned to Milan.

He arrived there much earlier than had been proposed, and the gilded chariot was hastily brought out and white horses harnessed to it; it was to be followed by persons dressed up to represent the five conquered cities. But the king rather spoiled the programme by refusing to enter the chariot: he had no desire to proceed through Milan, splendidly escorted, like a Roman general celebrating a triumph. He was too serious-minded to care for empty theatrical display, and it may already have dawned on him that, unquestioned as was his victory at arms, he had been less successful in the political manœuvring.

There were further festivities, however, in these days of July 1509 in Milan, and a vast crowd collected in front of the cathedral to see a mechanical lion—one of the giant toys Leonardo enjoyed making—scare a dragon out of the sea and drive it ashore, where the Gallic cock, with feathers bristling, gouged out its eyes. Meanwhile the Venetian republic, wasting no time on mechanical toys or symbolism, was busy already with diplomatic preparations for making up for its defeat, and was in negotiation with Julius II.

After the king's departure from Milan Leonardo was no longer directly concerned with the war. His pupils worked in his studio as before on parts of pictures of his designing. Some of the groundwork of the *Saint Anne with Two Others,* which Leonardo had sketched years earlier in Florence, was probably painted by Cesare da Sesto, the women's faces, the soft folds of the veils, the sheen of the silk garments, and the fading outlines of the distant landscape being Leonardo's own work.

His *Leda* was also slowly maturing—a picture of sombre, oppressive voluptuousness, a gurgling cry of sensuality, rising from its triple harmony of woman, bird, and landscape. Leda's figure rests on her firmly planted right leg; the outline passes along the well-turned curve of the leg and the little knee-cap and swells into a semicircle round the massive arched hip—a wealth of firm, rosy flesh, the lines of which are strongly emphasized by the brilliant white edging of the swan's wing, which follows the woman's form in a disturbing parallel. The left leg, with its straightened knee and its long, firm thigh, whose glistening skin is thrown into high relief against a shadow, is being gently planted on the ground, giving a twist to Leda's belly, which has the slightly rounded surface usual in a woman who has already conceived and given birth to a child. The round, sloping left shoulder is turned sharply forward from the bend at the hip, creating a suggestively shaded fold in the flesh; the strong upper arm reaches forward past the breast and completes a semicircular outline, in harmony with Leda's bent head. It is as if the long wave of the thigh were submerged in the shadow of the hip, to re-emerge in a stronger curve, subsiding more quickly, and then to swell again for the third time in the roundness of the cheek and twining strand of dark hair, finally subsiding as though from a foaming crest over the crown of Leda's head. The wave passes away along the outline of the backward-thrown right shoulder past the breast, ultimately finding its outlet in the wave of the hip embedded in the swan's wing. The movement to and fro of the deep shadows and the strong light further emphasizes this wave-motion of the outlines, like a stream rippling over Leda's body, or like silky, glistening eddies passing over deep water.

The firm hemispheres of the breasts and the muscular outstretched arm provide the link between the incoming wave of the outlines on the right and the ebb on the left. They also incorporate the swan in the picture as, in a physical similarity that is almost horrifying, it presses its smooth round breast against the woman's figure. Leda's hands are placed on the swan's curved neck; the almost angry turning of the neck provides on this calmer, quieter side of the picture a balance for the waves of the woman's form on the left.

Leda

Pope Leo X. By Raphael

Leonardo bound woman and bird in an indissoluble formal unity. The bird's ugly beak rises past the projection of the small breast and past the challengingly withdrawn shoulder. The open beak is given the expression of an almost human ardency. Leda's head bends back before the beak's advance, with a lazy movement that is full of a tempting assent; the finely chiselled feminine face, with its smooth round forehead, the large curving eyelids, straight, slender nose, and pointed chin, droops in demure surrender, while a smile that confesses partnership in guilt plays round the mouth —a significant smile heavily charged with memories. Her glance passes over her own form as though in tired contentment.

In addition to the formal unity of the composition, this conscious indulgence, this surging and recoil of desire, unite woman and bird, producing the almost painfully exciting atmosphere that fills the picture, as though with a heavy, oppressive scent. Perhaps it was necessary for a man to have Leonardo's inaccessibility to the lusts of the senses in order to create this symbol of sensual temptation and voluptuous surrender; perhaps it was necessary for a man to be so unmoved by the mystery of the female form in order to paint it so excitingly surrendered to an embrace.

The original of the picture has disappeared, and it is known now only from copies or imitations made by pupils, one of them probably by Sodoma. These have not the strong light or the satin sheen of the woman's skin, and they are rather too crudely naturalistic, indefinably overstepping certain limits.

This perturbing *Leda with the Swan* managed to blossom amid Leonardo's studious leisure as though escaping through a crevice from walled captivity; he was still in the thrall of his astronomical research. And then the thraldom was suddenly broken, perhaps by a meeting which took place toward the end of the year or the beginning of the new one, reawakening the old passion for anatomy which Leonardo thought he had overcome.

Marcantonio della Torre was then less than thirty years of age, but already he was looked upon as the first of living anatomists, and was ranged with Pico della Mirandola as a marvel of scholarship. Until the autumn of 1509 he had been a professor at the university of Padua, surrounded by a group of passionately devoted pupils, and his lectures were attended by crowds of listeners curious to hear him. He was born of a princely house, and lived amid the adulation which his contemporaries habitually accorded to gifted men belonging to rich and distinguished families. Yet he remained completely unspoiled, a scholar immersed in his special subject, but applying to all human activities the same high standards as to his scientific research. To Marcantonio an error due to negligence, or a misrepresentation of facts resulting from insufficiently thorough investigation, was a crime. He learned one day that one of his colleagues, Gabriele de Zerbio, had been dissected alive by the command of a Dalmatian prince; he dryly commented that a scientist with so many errors on his conscience well deserved his penance.

Amid the excitement aroused by the League of Cambrai this scholar, entirely wrapped up in his studies, was accused by the Venetians of intriguing against the state, and was threatened with arrest. Utterly horrified, and disgusted with this revelation of a spy-mania quite incomprehensible to him, he fled from Padua and settled in Pavia.

Leonardo was so deeply impressed with Marcantonio's devotion to science that he now determined to get on with the completion of his anatomical studies. "In this winter of 1510," he wrote, "I hope to master the whole field of anatomy." [99] He may at this time have attended some of della Torre's lectures and practical demonstrations at Pavia, in order to correct and complete his material. But the atmosphere of the university was unfavourable to serious study; the students had been affected by the political events of the early years of the new century—the struggles between unpopular rulers and foreign invaders, the continually changing loyalties, and the internal discords produced by external insecurity. As always during periods of warfare, with the resulting general unsettlement, the students, distracted by political perplexities and harassed by constant uncertainty as to what the morrow might bring, found their protracted and arduous studies unendurable. They protested noisily against the tedium of the lectures on anatomy and the laborious practical work required of them, and left the lecture room shouting abuse at the professor.

The students then developed a sort of systematic brigandage, rioting and attacking peaceful citizens in the streets. Meeting with no interference, they invaded private dwellings, plundered stores, and broke up the workshops of helpless artisans. Finally bands of students forced their way into the palazzi of the rich, and at this the outraged citizens called on the authorities to intervene, complaining that the students' associations were bodies "whose only studies are of looting and disorderliness of every sort."

As at all times of relaxed morality and belief, these young men readily imbibed crude mystical doctrines; they were more interested in the supernatural than in the structure of the human body. Leonardo, with his passion for exact knowledge, found these youths incomprehensible, and thundered against their unintelligence: "O human stupidity, do you not perceive that though you have been with yourself all your life, you are not yet aware of the thing you possess most of, that is, your folly? And then, with the crowd of sophists, you deceive yourself and others, despising the mathematical sciences, in which truth dwells. . . . And then you occupy yourself with miracles, and write that you possess information of those things which the human mind is incapable of grasping and which cannot be proved by any instance from nature."

He was particularly scornful of the crude popular compilations, setting out to explain all that was worth knowing in simple language, which had a great vogue among the students: those "impatient spirits . . . fancy they are losing such time as they employ usefully in studying the works of nature and the deeds of men. Let them remain in the company of beasts; let dogs and other beasts of prey be their associates. . . . Of what use, then, is he who abridges the details of those matters of which he professes to give thorough information, while he leaves behind the chief part of the things of which the whole is composed? It is true that impatience, the mother of stupidity, praises brevity, as if such persons had not need of a whole life in order to acquire a complete knowledge of any single subject, such as the human body; and then they want to comprehend the mind of God, in which the universe is included, weighing it minutely and mincing it into infinite parts, as if they had to dissect it!" In his emotion Leonardo added these self-revealing sentences: "The love of anything is the offspring of knowledge, the love being the more fervent in proportion as the knowledge is more certain. And this certainty is born of a com-

plete knowledge of all the parts which, when combined, compose
the totality of the things which ought to be loved." [100]

That dictum, "Love is the offspring of knowledge," stands like
a signpost pointing down Leonardo's whole life. From all the
winding paths it investigated, his intellect emerged to make
straight for the one goal of his passionate search, that of the pro-
motion of knowledge. His destiny was determined by that spiritual
urge, by his unceasing refusal to rest contented with what he had
acquired, his unceasing pressure on the boundaries that confined
his powers of intellectual conception and activity. He was now
nearly sixty years of age, and about this time he began to be affected with a slight impatience that was the outward expression
of a fear of being unable to complete his works within his allotted
years of life, of failure to bring his manifold partial achievements
to a conclusion.

His Anatomy must at least be published, with its magnificent
illustrations. Of their value he was well aware; he returned once
more to that point: "This briefest method of representing the various aspects will convey true and full knowledge, and in order that
this advantage which I am giving to men may not be lost, I am
teaching the way of properly printing, and I beg you, my successors, not to allow avarice to induce you to leave the printing
un—" The sentence was left unfinished, as if this moving appeal to
the good sense of his heirs had been cut short by some unforeseen
event.

8

He may have heard sounds like distant thunder, and seen
through his window the reflection of a distant conflagration in the
pale winter sky. He drew in red chalk rolling clouds of smoke, lit
up by the flickering glow of a fire; and underneath he wrote: "A
sound is often heard from the apparent direction of its echo and
not from the true source—*sito del voce reale*—and this happened
at Ghiaradadda, where the fire that broke out in the air loosed
twelve apparent bursts of thunder in twelve clouds, and their
origin was not recognized."

This acoustical problem, which Leonardo investigated in complete unconcern, as though it were a harmless natural phenomenon, was in reality the forerunner of a storm which was gathering menacingly on the political horizon, the prelude to new hostilities that threatened to destroy Leonardo's livelihood and leisure for work. Such conflagrations were multiplying, but Leonardo apparently had no idea that they might closely affect himself; he noted them, with date and hour, and then returned to his own work: "On the 10th day of December at 9 a.m. fire was set to the piazza. On the 18th day of December 1511 at 9 a.m. this second fire was kindled by the Swiss at Milan." [101]

It was not the first time that the Swiss had invaded Milanese territory. A year earlier they had pushed as far as Varese, but Chaumont, the viceroy, had known how to hold back the invaders without bloodshed: "they were fought with gold pieces (*escuz au soleil*), by the method taught by Grand-Maistre Chaumont." [102] But now they were being incited to attack the French by gold pieces from the Vatican. Julius II had been responsible for the triumph of French arms through his formation of the League of Cambrai, but when the news of their successes reached Rome the veteran fighter in the tiara became uneasy. He sought furiously for any possible means of checking them, and as he had all the unscrupulousness required for a refusal to accept the consequences of his own action, he came to the sudden decision to go over to the support of Venice. "If Venice did not exist," he said, "another one would have to be made." Some time before this, in February 1510, he had lifted the ban of excommunication against Venice, and shortly after that he had concluded an alliance with the Swiss, whose military support Louis XII had trifled away through French parsimony.

With all his intelligence, Louis XII was no better able to comprehend this sudden misfortune than the far less able Charles VIII had been when Lodovico betrayed him. Louis's advisers were equally nonplussed, and scarcely concealed their astonishment and perplexity. "Since France first existed, however good a face messieurs the French put on in their determination to defend themselves, they have never been so astounded as they are now," wrote one of the agents of the Emperor.

The League of Cambrai had become yesterday's indiscretion and the holy league against France today's reality. Chaumont now held the Pope at his mercy in Bologna, the city to which he had once hastened as the Pope's ally and to which he was now laying siege. He could easily have captured God's perjured vicar if a vestige of respect for the head of the Church had not crippled his resolution. On his escape from this peril Julius II marched against the French. He had for years been a guest at the French court, spinning his intrigues while he lived on their favour; now he marched against them in the name of Italian liberty, of Italy's outraged independence. He went himself, a gouty old man suffering from the sequelæ of the disease the Italians called the French malady, leading his army against the barbarians. With the aid of the Venetians he overcame them at Correggio, where young Chaumont died, weakened by malaria and by chagrin at his defeat, and exhausted by the hardships of the winter campaign.

Chaumont was succeeded as viceroy of Milan by Gaston de Foix, nephew of the king, a champion hardly emerged from boyhood, one of those tall, slim youths who have shot up while quite young. He marched out, full of youthful ardour, against the dogged old Pope. "I will wager a hundred thousand ducats and my tiara on top of them," said Julius II, "that I shall drive the French out of Italy."

The king and his advisers were no more perplexed by the Pope's change of front than were the common people outside Italy, who were least of all able to comprehend what this struggle could be about—this struggle between the most Christian king and the head of Christendom. The Pope had excommunicated seven cardinals who supported the king against him; Louis summoned the seven to a council, held first at Pisa and then at Milan, where, led by the learned Bernardino di Carvajal, they declared the Pope to be unworthy to hold his office.

At about the same time the Swiss crossed the frontier, with a red banner on which the scene of the Passion was painted. But they were thrown back by Gaston de Foix. Soon after this the young champion went out to meet the papal and Spanish troops in an encounter that should be decisive. A sanguinary battle was fought at Ravenna against the superior forces of the allies. The Spanish general and military engineer Pedro Navarro brought powerful artillery into action, and he sent against the infantry battle cars armed with murderous sickles, cars which, according to contemporary accounts, bore a striking resemblance to Leonardo's early inventions, brought now into use through some mysterious happening for the destruction of the troops of the king whom Leonardo was now serving.

The battle ended in a great victory for the French forces. Fifteen thousand dead were left on the battlefield. The enemy were driven to panic flight. But the young hero of the day, Gaston de Foix, himself lay among the dead, with eighteen wounds—a premature end to a career that had seemed destined to incomparable glory. The French victory had been overwhelming; the enemy were in the utmost fear and confusion, only the old Pope preserving unbroken courage; but this youth's death on the blood-soaked field of Ravenna seemed to have robbed the French dominion in Italy of its mainstay. Plague had broken out in Milan, introduced from Brescia, and was raging in the city. Tired troops entered the city, and the hospitals were filled to overflowing with wounded. A brooding unrest lay over Milan, and the populace knew already that they would soon change masters once more: they looked askance at the French as already an alien and odious element.

Leonardo awaited the issue of events, as he had done a dozen years earlier. Once more he had established a foothold only to find the soil slipping once more from beneath him. He shut himself off this time yet more determinedly from the world around him, remaining obstinately blind and deaf to external events. Men he had loved had died or become the victims of the catastrophic times. His patron Chaumont was dead; his friend Marcantonio della Torre had succumbed to fever; fortune had turned against the king who had paid his pension so punctually and had lifted him out of material cares: and now Marshal Trivulzio, whose monument he was to have erected, left Milan to go a second time into voluntary exile, accompanying the French on their retreat to their own country.

The French were already fleeing over the Alps by June 1512, the troops mocked by the pursuing Swiss and cursing the king who had led them into this disastrous adventure. Leonardo still re-

mained in Milan, waiting, perhaps he knew not for what. The
Swiss were the victors of the moment; with them came German
troops, and the Emperor, now assured of victory, brought the Milanese a new ruler, Lodovico's eldest son, whose godfather he was.
The court painter to the king of France looked on at the entry of
the young Maximiliano Sforza as the court painter to Duke Lodovico had looked on at the entry of the king of France. It was as
stately a procession as the entry of each new ruler into Milan had
been; the young duke, who had grown up in the distant north, rode
now in the cloak of white satin, heavy with its glittering gold embroidery, through the familiar yet half-forgotten streets of the city
which he had had to leave as a child.

Whether held by the French or by the Swiss and Germans, by
the house of Orleans or the house of Sforza, Milan meant to Leonardo the home he lived in with its scented garden, the vineyard
in which his grapes ripened, and the study in which white sheets
lay under the bright circle made by his oil lamp.

Somewhere in the neighbourhood of Milan the fighting continued. In May 1513 the French once more crossed the frontier, and
the young duke, remembering his father's dreadful fate, fled into
Switzerland. Julius II, *pontefice terribile,* the great enemy of
France, had died, and after the death of the "terrible pontiff"
Venice and France had come to an agreement, dividing the penin-
sula—on paper—between them. The Milanese no longer knew to
whom to give allegiance, whether to the French or to the fugitive
duke; they looked down the streets to see what ruler would now
come in white and gold through the city gates.

The Swiss unfurled their standard again and marched in anger
across the Alps. They had put the young Maximiliano on the
throne and intended to keep him there. In their righteous indignation they hurled themselves so furiously against the French at
Novara that they speedily won the day. Yet again the beaten
French had to retreat to their own country, their troops half anni-
hilated, and much of their heavy artillery left in the hands of the
Swiss.

Once more the heavy tread of Swiss mercenaries sounded on the
streets of Milan, once more the harsh German accents and the
noise of arms invaded Leonardo's ears. But the blue skies of sum-

mer still floated over Lombardy, and his garden was fragrant as in peacetime. The French garrison still remained in Milan castle, holding out against hunger and discouragement, and waiting for help from over the frontier.

On September 19, 1513, the exhausted garrison abandoned the castle, having been promised an unmolested withdrawal. There did not seem any likelihood of an early return of the French. For the second time Leonardo had lost a patron's support and the home of his choice. And now, after long months of uncertainty, he decided his next step. What it was is shown by a laconic entry on the first page of his new notebook:

"I left Milan for Rome on the 24th day of September 1513, with Giovanni, Francesco de' Melzi, Lorenzo, and il Fanfoia." [103]

CHAPTER EIGHT

The City of Disillusion

Non si debbe desiderare lo impossibile.

We should not desire the impossible.

(E, 31 v.)

NOT one but countless cities was Rome, *æterna urbs*. They were jumbled together within the girdle of its medieval battlemented walls, as in any other fortified city; and it was no very extensive girdle, for a Frenchman with the leisure and patience had walked round it about this time and counted his steps—16,000. He had also counted the towers, and made the number 360. But the moment one came within the walls, the city broke up into countless contradictory and heterogeneous elements, which might well have been brought together by pure chance. The district at the foot of the Capitol, with its labyrinth of irregular lanes, and the thickly inhabited Trastevere quarter, still bore their wholly medieval character; the little houses with narrow latticed windows were crowded closely together, and their projecting upper stories, reached by external flights of stairs, shut out the light from the narrow streets and multiplied the reverberations of their noises. Above the roofs, which sloped in every direction and at all sorts of angles, there rose square medieval towers, whose silhouettes mingled in the distance with gently curving gables and here and there one of the cupolas of the new age, which were beginning to be placed above the churches and palazzi.

But the new age, although it was still young, was well established already in the masonry of the façades, the filigree work of the loggias, and the harmony of arcades that dissolved the austerity of bare walls in a magic of shadow and light. The new age had cut through the winding streets, shifting the wreckage of ancient Rome out of the way or making use of the marble blocks; some-

440

times it burned the lime out of sculptured limestone slabs or columns, sometimes irreverently incorporated them in its walls or colonnades. Fragments, however, of ancient Rome still endured, squeezed between the medieval and the new age, some now harnessed to everyday uses, some left alone amid the indiscriminate destruction.

From the Forum there rose the grunting and squeaking of pigs, penned for sale between the remaining pillars and among the ruins of the temples. Triumphal arches were walled up into towers in which customs guards exacted octroi on the cattle brought in by peasants from the environs. The monastery of Santa Maria Nuova nestled for security against the arch of Titus. Wagon builders worked in front of the temple of Faustina and the arch of Septimius Severus, making two-wheeled carts and wooden yokes for oxen; near by was the cattle market.

The column of Marcus Aurelius was still partly buried; the uncovered part, richly sculptured, was chipped and rubbed by the shafts of wagons, which could scarcely avoid striking it as they wound along the narrow space between the houses. Pigs had annexed the Forum Romanum; goats seemed to regard the Capitol as their kingdom; they had even given it a new name, for the Mons Capitolinus had become Monte Caprino, the Hill of the Goats. They ran about between the pillars and stone blocks on the edge of the Tarpeian Rock, climbed over the ruined walls of ancient homes, and ventured as far as the Senators' Palace, with its formidable towers, which had been built on a space cleared of ruins.

Round the vast halls of the thermæ of Diocletian a forest had grown; it served now as a deer-park and papal hunting ground. The seeker after lost glories of ancient Rome would meet the inquiring gaze of a group of animals among the great arches of these ruined public buildings.

The ancient world was in sole possession of the Palatine hill; its ruins battled here only with the vegetation. Pines grew among the great columns of the septizonium of Severus, ivy climbed its redbrown walls, dog-roses spread over the fallen pillars, and shrubs protected the remains of altars. There were carved marble gates still standing, surrounded by laurel trees, and on the remains of the walls there still gleamed frescoes recording in undiminished brilliance the daily life of the Romans of so many centuries earlier; scholars came from all countries to examine them and to lament a lost civilization.

No less multifarious than the aspects of the city were the varied and discordant elements of its daily life. The Via Giulia, which Julius II had cut through the narrow lanes of the bankers' and court functionaries' quarter, was one of the main arteries of the new life which, since the elevation of Giovanni de' Medici to the papal see as Leo X, had brought countless Florentines and sight-seeing foreigners and ambitious scholars to Rome. From the gleaming new palaces, full of light and air, there emerged young men in velvet shoes, with their caps worn jauntily sideways over their fair or brown hair, while their posse of servants pushed aside the gaping loiterers. In the Via Giulia the young men passed women covered with jewellery and moving amid a cloud of perfume, with the arrogant bearing of the ladies of Rome, of whom a contemporary said that they looked "as if each one of them was soon to mount a throne." This provocative display of the rich aroused black looks from ill-favoured passers-by of the sort that gave the easily aroused populace its evil reputation. *Roma santa, ma il popolo cattivo,* "Holy the city, vile the people"—so the saying went. All too frequently the turbid current of the Tiber would bring down a swollen corpse, some victim of jealousy or vendetta, of a quarrel about nothing or of robbery under arms.

Amid this unsocial wealth and resentful poverty came pilgrims from far countries, their broad hats drawn down over their northern faces and their heavy staffs held tightly in their hands; they crawled up the steps of Santa Maria in Aracoeli on their knees, and poured into the seven churches to which their pilgrimage was directed. They would frequently meet grave men sunk in contemplation whose backs were turned to the basilica of the Lateran; the gleaming mosaic of a church façade was nothing to these scholars; it was the equestrian statue of Marcus Aurelius, or some marble slab on which the pilgrims trod indifferently, that they had come to see. Pilgrims and scholars would eye one another with no friendliness—fanatics of rival faiths.

Princes of the Church, resplendent in purple, rode out to the chase in gay and lively cavalcades, with packs of baying hounds and an army of beaters, falconers, musicians, and versifiers; they rode through the damp and narrow lanes, past women haggling with Jewish sellers who offered clammy, floundering fish on ancient marble altar tables; they rode past ancient tombs, and past houses of ill fame out of which half-clad prostitutes leaned to look on at the fine procession.

The travellers from the north entered the city through the Porta del Popolo, and here they found a first example of the work of the new age in the church of Santa Maria del Popolo, with its smooth and as yet insubstantial early renaissance façade and its delicately fashioned gable. Soon they came into sight of the pyramidal mausoleum which had become popularly known, on no discoverable authority, as the tomb of Nero's mother. They passed by the cattle grazing alongside the tomb of Augustus; and then they were swallowed up by the narrow lanes, in which poor artisans lived between semi-derelict medieval palaces that threatened to collapse on top of them.

But all this was not the Rome that was the world's stage. The city the pilgrims had come to see lay on the other side of the Tiber, beyond the great castle—half ancient tomb and half embattlemented citadel—of Saint Angelo. There lay the city of the Popes, with which no temporal capital in the world could stand comparison. Swiss guards, big, ruddy-faced men in uniforms of white, green, and gold, kept watch at the entrance to the Vatican; the light flashed from their bright halberds and the gold-embroidered devices on their breasts. An older part of the basilica of St. Peter's was still standing, with mosaics centuries old thrown up by the flickering light of candles; but the foundations were already to be seen of the new building, which was intended to be the largest and most magnificent church in all Christendom.

The foreigner bent his steps first of all toward the Vatican, and round the complex of papal palaces there were numbers of inns, mostly Swiss and German, whose landlords hung out gaily painted signs to attract their fellow-countrymen. At one of these inns Leonardo put up with his pupils and his servant, while rooms were being made ready for him in the Belvedere. He seemed at last to be entering a period of success and recognition: the preparations made for his stay in Rome suggested the arrival of a personage of acknowledged eminence. For most of his life he had lodged in any quarters he could find; now he was being given accommodation among the splendours of Rome, in surroundings of exquisite beauty.

The Belvedere, a luxurious summer palace built on the top of the Vatican hill, resembled a miniature fortress, with battlemented walls, placed on a massive substructure, as though it had to be able to withstand a siege. Its windows looked out over the wide plain of the Campagna to where distant undulating hills faded into the deep blue of the horizon. This prospect was terminated on one side by the sharp outline of Monte Soracte; then there came into view the papal gardens in their autumn green, and the shady and commodious arcades which Bramante had built to connect this palace with the Vatican.

The corridors of the palace were faced with brightly coloured majolica tiles. The rooms were decorated with views of famous cities, Venice, Milan, Florence, and Rome, painted "in the Flemish style" by Pinturicchio. The quarters assigned to Leonardo had probably been long unoccupied, for the rooms were almost entirely bare of furniture, which had to be procured for him. He also had various alterations made, partitions and wainscoting put up, a kitchen arranged, windows changed and raised in order to provide a good top-light, and a terrace built and paved. A trucklebed was ordered for him, and a trestle table for meals; and cupboards and chests, benches and chairs, and even a stand for mixing paints; for he settled into the Belvedere as if it was to be his home to the end of his days.

The Belvedere had not only wide spaces and a distant view, but something more. A broad marble stairway leading from the grounds up to a thickly wooded height ended in a strange sanctuary, a glade of peace which Julius II had opened at a time when, in the midst of his life of restless conflict, he had been overcome by a longing for quiet meditation. This garden of the Belvedere, the Giardino delle Pigne, was regarded as one of the wonders of Rome; Vasari called it the most beautiful thing the world had seen since the golden age of antiquity. White marble gods stood out from the dark green of the laurel hedges and the metallic sheen of the orange trees—statues recently recovered from the soil that had buried them; with them was the powerful *Laocoön* group which so strongly appealed to the imagination of the men of this time. A magnificent young *Apollo* was there, his delicate head surrounded by a confusion of interwoven locks in Leonardo's own favourite style. There were also a massive *Tiber,* an *Ariadne* of late design, and *Venus Felix,* earliest of all the excavated goddesses. The soft light that came through the boughs of the pines seemed to give momentary life to the white marble figures. No profane step crunched the gravel paths: an inscription forbade the general public to enter the sanctuary. Only the wind shook the boughs against one another, water plashed in the marble basins of the fountains, and the song of birds joined enchantingly with wind and water to complete a reality that eclipsed the magic garden of Leonardo's dream.

There were other wonders that attracted Leonardo to Rome besides the pagan sanctuary of the Giardino delle Pigne. In the plantation on the slope of the hill Leo X had placed his great menagerie, and Leonardo had never seen so many unfamiliar species of animals brought together in a single collection. Kings and princes had sent lions to the Pope from all quarters of the globe as his namesakes; there were also spotted panthers and leopards restlessly moving to and fro in their narrow cages; chameleons, and apes; and parrots, whose hoarse cries mingled with the roars of the carnivora. The greatest wonder of all, Rome's idol and big toy, was a white elephant sent to the Pope by the king of Portugal, a light grey mountain of an animal, with little eyes that blinked so slyly in between the thick folds of skin that the simple folk were positive that it understood everything people said. The Pope himself never tired of watching the animal, and when it set its vast body awkwardly in motion Leo would shake with laughter. He was so concerned for the animal's welfare that he assigned it a special keeper. But the elephant could not stand the climate of Rome, or else it suffered from too much attention; it soon died, to the grief of the Pope, who commissioned Raphael to paint its portrait on a wall of the Vatican.

Leo X had also laid out a botanical garden in the Belvedere, and sent for the rarest plants from all over the world. The sight of the exotic flowers reawakened in Leonardo his old keen interest in the plant world, to which he had never yet devoted any thorough research. He found himself now surrounded with everything in which he was interested on this earth. In one of the oldest wings of the Vatican palace, whose windows gave onto the inner court of the Belvedere, was the library established by Sixtus IV. Leonardo found there various manuscripts for which he had sought all his life in vain. He came to Rome as to a Promised Land—the city of a thousand facets, the city of fulfilment.

Yet, if he but looked round the Belvedere, with eyes not dazzled by the unaccustomed magnificence, he could not fail to find in that very place a warning which another before him had left in a symbolization of his disappointment. The story was still told of Andrea Mantegna's experience of working at the Vatican. Pope Innocent VIII had had great difficulty in persuading Isabella d'Este to lend him her court painter for a time. Mantegna was received with open arms, and praised to the skies. He set to work on the decoration of the papal chapel in the Belvedere. But fair words were all the payment he received, and he failed even to secure recoupment of his out-of-pocket expenses. He had painted the four cardinal virtues of Plato, Prudence, Justice, Fortitude, and Temperance, and the three Christian ones, Faith, Hope, and Charity, and with bitter irony he added a virtue of his own invention, that of Discretion. The Pope took the allusion in good part. "Now add Patience," he said, and permitted Mantegna to return to Mantua.

But even if Mantegna's experience had given Leonardo food for thought, he would only have considered, as so many others did, that such things belonged to the past, and that a Pope of the family of the Medici would act very differently. Had not the golden age returned, was not Apollo to reign after the protracted rule of Mars, as Pasquino phrased it in proclaiming the hope with which all intellectuals were filled? Every humanist who had reaped honour or neglect anywhere in the world felt that his hour had come when Cardinal Giovanni de' Medici emerged victorious from the Conclave. Every struggling artist in Italy thought he had found a Mæcenas in Lorenzo de' Medici's connoisseur son. Every Florentine felt personally honoured and elevated by this election. Merchants and bankers streamed to Rome; poets and musicians left wife and children, employer and assured post, and made like moths for the light that streamed over the world from Rome. Leonardo was himself a countryman of the Pope. Lorenzo de' Medici had given him his opportunity in life when he sent him to the court of Lodovico Sforza with the silver lute; and Leo's favourite brother, Giuliano de' Medici, was particularly friendly to Leonardo. The two had come into touch, apparently, at some time during the exile of the Medici, and Giuliano remembered Leonardo now when destiny overwhelmed him with gifts and glory. Rome seemed to be offering Leonardo a belated fulfilment of his aspirations; and Giuliano de' Medici seemed the ideal of a discerning ruler, and a friend and patron such as he had rarely encountered in his life.

Giuliano was merely the grandson of a self-made adventurer, but he looked like the listless scion of a long line of noble ancestors. His father used to say that he had a mad son, Piero, a wise one, Giovanni, and a good one, Giuliano. But the mad son seemed to have inherited so much of Lorenzo's pride and ambition and craving for power that there was very little of their father's forceful character left for the younger sons to inherit. The Magnifico was plebeian, massive, and ugly; Giuliano had scarcely a distant trace of family resemblance to him. His nose was long and crooked, with a fine, slender bridge that contrasted with its broad and bulky tip; he had Lorenzo's bushy eyebrows, but instead of strongly arching over the blue eyes they faded away ineffectively; the eyes were long and melancholy and looked out dreamily and indifferently over men and things. Giuliano's whole appearance was refined and blasé —a cloud of soft hair framed his irregular features, a downy beard half concealed his narrow, sensitive mouth, the Adam's apple stood out from his long neck, and his long hands with pointed fingers folded lethargically over each other as though expressing a slight disgust. His narrow, pointed shoulders bent forward as though the weight of brocade and silk was too much for them; his toneless, dragging utterance slowly elaborated his thoughts, and though he was not yet thirty-five, his movements seemed slow and tired; he appeared too worn out to complete each faintly indicated gesture.

Giuliano had come into the world as one who had nothing more to conquer or strive for, nothing that even needed energetic maintenance, in a security that seemed entrenched for all time; he seemed born only to enjoy life. But early in life he made the acquaintance of fortune's caprice, of the perishable nature of the trappings of power and the insecurity of all possessions. He made the acquaintance also of the fickleness of popular favour and the faithlessness of friends. If nature had endowed him with more ambition, he would have been filled with the embitterment of all sensitive persons who have fallen from great power.

He had inherited his father's impressionability and also Lorenzo's inclination for indiscriminate indulgence; he passed the years of exile in a succession of short-lived amorous adventures, each of which he enshrined in its place in a charming cycle of sonnets. He was now prematurely worn out, and lived only for his interest in an intellectual world beyond the range of the classic authors, with whose works he had been well acquainted from his youth—his interest in the unexplored mysteries of natural science, of which he dimly sensed the vastness and by which he was strongly attracted. But he had not the strength for continuous intellectual exertion. Any long discussion tired him; his pale face would become yet more bloodless, the heavy lids would fall over his lustreless eyes, and he would be forced to lie down for a time before he could resume the conversation. It was as if he hammered feebly for a while against iron gates beyond which he knew there were worlds to conquer, but then realized his impotence. He would seek refuge then in a return to devout and simple faith, and for a while would ardently engage in religious exercises. Soon, however, he would be overtaken again by scepticism and resume his quest for knowledge.

For a time he dabbled in alchemy and came under the influence of magicians and necromancers; then he began to be utterly tired of life, and dwelt on the idea of suicide as the only way out of his spiritual perplexities. He wrote a sonnet in justification of voluntary death: "It is no cowardice, nor the result of cowardice, if, in order to escape from the yet worse horrors that await me, I have spurned life and longed for its ending."

Giuliano de' Medici and Leonardo, the young man and the old one, were united in their emergence beyond the life of the senses; the dilettante and the insatiable worker were alike pursued by curiosity about worlds unexplored, about ultimate and impenetrable mysteries; both were weary of society with its restless superficiality;

and the ailing nerves of Giuliano and the infinitely delicate perceptions of Leonardo were alike drawn to all that was beautiful, surprising, or in any way uncommon.

A workshop was set up for Leonardo in the Belvedere, and a German artisan, who received seven ducats a month, was appointed to work exclusively in his service. So far as can be inferred from obscure allusions in his letters and his notebooks, Leonardo was employed mainly in the manufacture of burning mirrors or distorting mirrors for Giuliano de' Medici. He invented at this time a number of machines for his workshop, mainly draw-benches of various sorts for making large metal concave mirrors. One of these draw-benches supplied him with long, uniform strips of copper, which he required for soldering up the mirrors. It was the first machine of this type in industrial history. It was worked by a crank handle and could also be driven by a water wheel.[1]

Giuliano de' Medici provided Leonardo with the means of living in summoning him to Rome, and did so with the liberality that was characteristic of him. He allowed him 33 ducats (about $82.50) a month, an ample sum, for a pair of capons cost four carlini or 60 cents in Rome (15½ carlini went to the ducat), and eggs were about four cents a dozen. Giuliano also paid for the fitting up of Leonardo's quarters in the Belvedere. His income amounted to 60,000 ducats a year, and he had not the miserliness in providing for others with which rich persons often make up for extravagance in their own living. Giuliano's lavish generosity was the common talk of needy artists, mendicant friars, and charlatans.

Leonardo also used a large number of metal screws, a rarity in his time, the current means of securing objects being then the wedge or the rivet. Heavy wooden screws were used in ancient times for wine presses, and there were cases on record of metal screws having been cast by the Romans, but until the end of the seventeenth century small metal screws seem to have been little used, their manufacture being very troublesome. The best the medieval goldsmiths could do was to solder a metal wire firmly round a pin and another wire in a bored hole to receive it. Later the thread was laboriously made with a file. Leonardo had thought earlier of casting bronze or brass screws in a wooden mould, turning them afterwards in iron thread-cutters, "first in the larger hole and then in the second one, and in this way you will avoid the labour of filing." [2] Thread-cutters of this sort were introduced into Europe from America at the beginning of the nineteenth century, and are still used.

This process, however, no longer satisfied Leonardo, and he now made a screw-cutting machine which could make long screw rods; his method is used to this day. The material to be threaded was fixed in a sliding carriage fitted with screw stocks. As soon as the middle wheel was set in motion, screw rods on either side moved the sliding carriage evenly forward, larger or smaller cogwheels, according to the thread needed, being fitted on the screw rods. "This is the way to make a screw," Leonardo wrote on his drawing.[3]

For each of these inventions Leonardo made extremely careful drawings, complete down to the last detail. He was also working at this time on unusual metal alloys, of quicksilver, copper, and iron. He did not venture to give their composition even in his right-to-left handwriting, but described the components as Mercury, Venus, or Jupiter, as if he was concerned to protect his notes from the eyes of the indiscreet. In one case copper appears as *erenev—* Venere (Venus) reversed. Various chemicals seem to have been used in these experiments; Leonardo entered a list, including saltpetre, vitriol, alum, sal-ammoniac, quicksilver, sublimate, arsenic, and verdigris; he made no mention of the purpose they were to serve. He wrote still more mysteriously of a mould or pattern which he frequently mentioned in the notes of this period; he called it a "sagoma," and it was made of copper, iron, or lead; it could be "frequently placed in its mother's lap"—that is to say, probably, in the fire.

The ultimate purpose of the work Leonardo did for Giuliano de' Medici cannot be discovered from the notebooks. Giuliano, with his keen interest in alchemy, must have made use of Leonardo's inventions for various occult purposes. His morbidly excited mind was probably set on trying to tamper with inviolable natural laws; for there is a warning in the notebook containing the references to the "sagoma"—"O speculator on things, boast not of knowing the things that nature ordinarily brings about; but rejoice if you know the end of those things which you yourself devise." [4]

But whatever might be the tasks on which Giuliano employed Leonardo da Vinci, and however amply supplied Leonardo was with the means of existence, Rome meant more to Leonardo than an assured livelihood and mysterious workshop experiments. Rome was the city of unique opportunities for gaining immortal fame. No secular prince in the world could give such commissions as those of Christ's Vicar. Leonardo found in Rome old friends of his, and old enemies, at work on tasks such as he had only dreamed of, tasks only conceived and only possible in this city.

At the head of the artistic world in Rome stood Leonardo's collaborator at the court of Milan, Donato Bramante. When Lodovico Sforza's rule in Milan was tottering, Leonardo had waited and hesitated, finally setting out on a journeying without definite goal; Bramante had made straight for Rome, and there he had at last found his spiritual home. He was then about sixty years of age, but he had the capacity of the true artist to break entirely with the past as soon as he had found his true mission, and at sixty he plunged energetically into the study of the architecture of Rome in order to assimilate all that it could teach him. With every task he undertook his own abilities grew and ripened, and in face of this unexpectedly late crop of creative opportunities his great self-confidence increased until he felt there was nothing that was beyond his power. Against the opposition of all Rome, and to the indignation of all Christendom, he was able to induce the Pope to pull down the thousand-year-old basilica of St. Peter's. As though he was only at the outset of his life, he shouldered tasks the very idea of which would have daunted anyone else. For the rebuilding he marshalled a whole army of stone-setters, masons, foremen, inspectors, accountants, builders, architects, and sculptors, and rapidly brought foundations and superstructure into view. He built boldly, quickly, and with no great care, using any material that came into his hands—spurred on by his own impatience to see results and by the feverish ambition of Julius II.

When Leonardo reached Rome, Bramante had left the Belvedere, in which he had lived at first; he had long ceased to be "the patient son of poverty," and now possessed a fine palace in the Borgo Vecchio, in which all in Rome who desired to attain success and reputation used to gather. His square, powerful head, which might well have been hewn into shape with a chopper, was now bald on top, but surrounded by a broad garland of wavy, silvery hair; his bull neck, roped with muscles, stood out like a wrestler's, and an imperious glance came from his deeply embedded eyes, as in the portrait painted by Raphael in the *Disputa*. Bramante had developed into a real dictator in the world of art, for he was not only architect of the basilica of St. Peter's and of the Vatican, but the actual administrator of the fine arts in Rome, suggesting to Julius II the architects, sculptors, and painters whom he should employ.

Bramante seemed entirely to have forgotten his old friendship with Leonardo. Not once in his notes of the Roman period does Leonardo mention this man, whose name appeared so often among the notes of the Milanese years. But Bramante may already have been suffering from the malady to which he succumbed in April 1514; and, in any case, he then had room for only one protégé amid his ambitions and his unceasing pursuit of power—Raphael, whom he was training, with an exclusiveness that savoured of the jealousy of a father, to be his successor. The fortunate boy—*fortunato garzon,* as his fellow-artist Francia, who met him in Rome in 1508, had called him—had run straight into the arms of his destiny when he came to Rome, a destiny that bore the features of Bramante. Raphael was Bramante's fellow-countryman, and, indeed, a distant relation of his; and he had the mixture of confidence and modesty that characterize the gifted heirs-designate to exalted posts.

As Bramante gradually monopolized power he may at times have had fears for the durability of his hastily built structures; he was always on the alert against envious rivals who might be watching his work narrowly, and he showed almost equal ingenuity in pushing himself to the fore and in preventing others from doing so. But Raphael's youth and charm were disarming and inspired confidence. Round his mouth there played the smile of the fortunate who are troubled neither by envy nor by jealousy; in his velvety eyes was the touching expression of the grateful who do not forget their indebtedness. When Bramante took him under his wing in order to protect himself from troublesome rivals, the older man was already so powerful a protector that Raphael, though barely twenty-five and with only a local reputation, was entrusted with the decoration of the reception rooms in the Vatican. When Leonardo reached Rome the Stanza della Segnatura, the room in which the supreme ecclesiastical court met, had already been given the frescoes of the so-called *Disputa* and the *School of Athens,* and Raphael was world-famous.

In Rome Leonardo also found his great rival Michelangelo. About a year earlier Michelangelo had finished the ceiling of the Sistine chapel, and Leonardo now critically examined the work. The display of huge naked limbs, the exaggerated play of the muscles, and the violence of the motions were disturbing to his sense of proportion. At this time he was correcting and completing his *Treatise on Painting,* perhaps with a view to publication, and in the course of it, under the influence of his observation of Michelangelo's work, he not only recommended artists to study anatomy as "extremely important and extremely useful," but also warned them against exaggeration: "O painter-anatomist, take care not to become a wooden painter through too strong an emphasis on bones, muscles, and sinews." [5] He added, as in a faint echo of the old contest in Florence, a remark that has a suggestion of irony, about "naked figures which display all their feelings."

Apart from this allusion, there is no mention, either in Leonardo's notebooks or in any contemporary report, of any meeting between Leonardo and Michelangelo. The latter was living at this time in a house of his own in the Macel dei Corvi, near the Capitol, where he was at work on another big commission, the tomb of Julius II; he was expecting yet more important commissions from Leo X.

If so many immortal works by Bramante, Raphael, and Michelangelo had been made possible by Julius II, that warrior in the tiara, who had refused to be painted with a book in his hand and requested Michelangelo to give him a sword instead, what a field Rome would offer under a Medicean Pope, and one who said of himself that he was born in a library and might have added that he was brought up in a museum! What commissions might lie in wait for the Pope's countryman and the protégé of his favourite brother! And what, indeed, were Leonardo's 33 ducats a month in comparison with the 3000 ducats allowed to Michelangelo for the ceiling of the Sistine chapel, or the amounts Raphael earned— 12,000 ducats for each room in the Vatican?

Leo X himself thought that the golden age of art and science was dawning with his accession, and that under him Rome would at last begin really to fulfil its historic mission as a cultural centre. A great company of gifted artists of every sort, filled with boundless hopes of opportunities for achievement, thronged the rooms of the Vatican, which had never before seen so much life. Artists, poets, and scholars mingled with prelates and ambassadors who often had to wait hours for an audience, and the luxury and magnificence which the new Pope had introduced seemed to justify their great expectations. The visitors to the Vatican walked on luxurious carpets past richly carved tables and windows; past golden bowls studded with semi-precious stones that lit up the polished wood with their reflection; past canopies of silk and gold brocade whose folds acquired a shimmering radiance at every movement. When, after passing through hall after hall, they were admitted to audience with the Pope, the spectacle presented to them almost took their breath away. They saw a big, heavy man, majestic in appearance, seated motionless on the throne, his great bulk rigid as a statue; the only life was in his excessively soft hands, which the Pope held before him like some precious jewel. His round, disproportionately large head sat close on his powerful shoulders, almost without any neck. His face was alarmingly pale, standing out with its vast double chin almost eerily above his purple robe, as though floating independently through space like a moon. The Pope was barely thirty-seven, but his face was unearthly—lifeless, sickly, and so full-fleshed that it might have been of some flabby sponge. The broad, puffy cheeks, which almost hid the small lascivious mouth, were dominated by a huge fleshy nose. The tense, nervous glance from the goggling, shortsighted eyes seemed out of harmony with that masterful nose, but the Pope was in the habit of quickly closing his eyes and listening so, a habit which heightened the impression he gave of an uncanny aloofness.

But sometimes this expressionless, inscrutable face would light up with a very candid smile, compounded of profound knowledge of human nature, easily moved sympathy, a true feeling for spiritual values, and an innate good humour. Then the fat features would suddenly brighten, and the surprisingly fine and harmonious voice would carry to the listener a finely phrased and thoughtful message, all the more impressive for its romantic unexpectedness. Every artist or scholar whom Leo X received in audience felt like a prodigal son welcomed home, and thereafter waited in complete trust for the fulfilment of the miracle of the papal favour.

If the best minds of the time so trusted the Pope, the reason lay partly in his own sense of his many virtues. He knew his freedom from all the varied faults of his predecessors, from the warlike ambition of Julius II and the nepotism of Alexander VI, and from the lusts of the flesh and the worldliness with which so many priests alienated their flocks. Like other men of blunted susceptibilities, he regarded his many limitations as so many virtues—his insensibility to temptation as moral superiority, his lack of interest in men and events as pure spirituality, the moderation in eating and drinking necessitated by his feeble constitution as virtuous abstinence, and the lavishness that sprang from his desire to please as the outcome of an inborn generosity of spirit.

His hesitating policy, and his abhorrence of making decisions that involved a choice between two friendships, were dictated by the same desire to please, and it was this desire that made it impossible for him to endure disappointed faces around him. Accordingly he was profuse in promises which, if he had given them honest thought, he must have known he would never be able to fulfil. He had learnt the art of dilatoriness, which is the strength of the weak, and he slowly tired out all those of whom he could make no use.

He tried to hinder Michelangelo in the completion of the vast monument to his predecessor; he did not want to be pestered with giving him new commissions. "Michelangelo is terrible—you can see for yourself that there is no doing anything with him," said the Pope on one occasion to Sebastiano del Piombo, throwing up his fine white hands in apparent despair.

Leo could not disregard his brother's special protégé, and soon gave him a commission to paint a picture, on which Leonardo set to work with his usual circumspection. About this time, probably through living just by the botanical garden, he had begun to make studies of plants, and he now tried to distil a varnish from plant

juices, hoping to find it exceptionally durable. But the walls of the
papal palaces had particularly sharp ears; the *famiglia* of Leo X
was about four times as numerous as those of his predecessors,
counting no fewer than 683 functionaries of all ranks, and each one
of these spied on his neighbours, in order to get hold of strange or
malicious stories to carry to the Pope. Leo thought it highly amusing that Leonardo was occupying himself with the varnish before
he had begun to paint the picture. "Alas!" he exclaimed. "This
man will never get anything done, for he is thinking about the end
before he begins." The story is told by Vasari, and seems entirely
in keeping with the Pope's mentality. What did he know of the
strange, intricate paths along which Leonardo's spirit travelled?
He had no idea that Leonardo had his work fully visualized in its
final form before he lifted a brush, that his problem was the
creative act of conception rather than the execution, or that his
delay in transferring his ideas to the canvas was the direct result
of the finality with which they were realized in his studies. But this
story of the varnish, so easily given an uncharitable twist, supplied
the Pope with the opportunity of getting rid of a man whom he
could not entirely understand and who was not always entirely
tractable. The Pope was ever inclined to shake off the inconvenient with a witty phrase that amounted to their dismissal. "This
man will never get anything done"—*costui non è per far nulla*—was
the phrase that ended Leonardo's artistic career at the papal court.

The Pope, moreover, was quite able to do without Leonardo,
and without Michelangelo, for he had found in Raphael a man
entirely to his taste, as well as one with whose thoroughly sound
work he felt morally entitled to rest content. If the Pope had demanded of fate his ideal of a court painter, that ideal would have
been in Raphael's image and would have had Raphael's characteristics. Leo X felt that this charming and affable young man was
a gift from his lucky star.

Raphael was now thirty; he still preserved his youthful slenderness of figure, and his oval face with its pointed chin had scarcely
grown any fuller. He carried his well-formed head high; from beneath the round forehead with the boldly arching eyebrows the
warm, velvety eyes looked out into the world with an expression
of naïve satisfaction and self-confidence. The small, sensuous

mouth had a boyish, captivating smile, half apologetic and half impudent—the smile bequeathed by a youth free from cares and doubts. Bramante, on his deathbed, had recommended this young painter to the Pope as his successor, with the irresponsible egoism of a parvenu who had seized all he could for himself and his protégés without asking himself whether they were equal to their great responsibility. This recommendation from so eminent an artist gave Leo X a welcome excuse for passing over better qualified men, and the Pope referred to Bramante's request, as though he needed that justification, in the *breve* entrusting Raphael with the direction of the building of St. Peter's.

Now Raphael was conferring daily with the Pope, as he wrote to his uncle with a touch of youthful vanity; and he was juggling with figures of undreamt-of magnitude: Leo X had assigned 60,000 ducats a year to the building operations. Raphael listened without demur to whatever the Pope might propose. Not a trace of annoyance appeared on his smiling face if he was called away from the most important tasks for unending discussions of the arrangements for a festival, the design of a coin, the scene-painting for a play, the decoration of some vessel, or the painting of a portrait, of more than life size, of the dead elephant. Here was a man who never said no, never kept the Pope waiting for the execution of an order, never showed dismay or tried to argue a point; the Pope sent for him as a matter of course for anything he wanted done. Raphael, equally as a matter of course, accepted every task imposed on him as the price of his high and magnificent estate.

Whenever Raphael thought of his trials, he recognized that the compensations were ample. After Leo X had shown him such unreserved favour, in a way very unusual with the Pope, his example was followed by every toady and flatterer, every courtier and patron in Rome, and Raphael was borne high on the tide of success. Suddenly he had become the one recourse of artistic Rome—he and his pupils and friends. No court was ever more at the mercy of current fashion in art than that of Leo X. Everybody who had a commission to give for a painting, not for his artistic enjoyment but from the motive of worldly ambition, gave it to Raphael.

Agostino Chigi, the first financial magnate in the modern sense, a self-made man and parvenu who had built up a vast banking trust, formed with his own resources and entirely dependent on them, felt that he owed it to himself and to his position to employ no other than Raphael on the decoration of his villa and private chapel, even if the overburdened Raphael left a large part of the work to his pupils to carry out. Chigi was a shrewd patron, spending only for display and spending cautiously. At his receptions he would have silver services thrown into the Tiber—where nets lay hidden to recover them.

Another of Raphael's patrons was Bernardo Dovizzi, surnamed Bibbiena after his birthplace, Cardinal of Santa Maria in Poetian, the most powerful man at the Roman court. He had been brought up with the children of Lorenzo de' Medici, and his gift of entertainment and his discretion in his relations with these princely playmates had combined to make him indispensable to the young Giovanni. When Giovanni became a candidate for the papacy the Conclave had doubts about the election of so young a Pope, and Cardinal Bibbiena did much to secure his election by spreading a rumour at the last moment that Giovanni was suffering from an incurable fistula. The cardinal was now the Pope's chief political adviser. Bibbiena was less discreet in the use he made of the services of his friend Raphael: he made him paint erotic pictures on the walls of his bathroom. He was also embarrassingly anxious for Raphael's social advancement, for he proposed to give him his own niece in marriage. Raphael's ambition grew rapidly, however, with his success, and soon overleaped this plan of marriage with a rich bride, though it was carefully discussed with his family. Meanwhile he enjoyed his wealth and fame with almost naïve exuberance; and he collected offices and titles—that of papal chamberlain, for instance, and that of knight of the golden spur—which placed him on terms of equality in the aristocratic circles in which he liked to move.

He was an indefatigable worker, sitting late into the night over his sketches for paintings, wrestling anxiously with the problems of the foundations of St. Peter's, to which Bramante had given entirely inadequate attention, climbing from one scaffolding to another, hurrying from one building to another, himself taking a hand in the work, and sometimes pale to the lips from superhuman exertion. But he liked to appear to be living the life of a gentleman of leisure. When he passed through the streets of Rome he was as magnificently dressed as the most eminent of his patrons, and always escorted by a number of his pupils as if by a body-guard. One day he met Michelangelo, who, supersensitive, humiliated by the Pope, and now neglected, felt this magnificence as a piece of insolence and a personal affront. He planted himself in Raphael's path, with a scornful smile, as though demanding an explanation, and shouted wrathfully: "There you go with your escort, as if you were a general!" But envy and contempt struck in vain at Raphael's impregnable self-assurance. He replied to Michelangelo with the readiness of the successful: "And there go you, all alone like a hangman!" From his young companions there came a devastating roar of laughter, the hard laughter of those who side with fortune's favourites.

Michelangelo saw conspiracies against him everywhere, and he furiously attacked Raphael's reputation. Many years later he was still declaring that "all he knew of art he had from me." But Raphael could afford to be fair and magnanimous, and when Michelangelo's sarcasms were retailed to him he replied that he thanked God that he was born in the day when Michelangelo was living. Raphael showed the same ready magnanimity in regard to Leonardo, whom he had so venerated a few years earlier; he even passed on small commissions to him, like crumbs from the rich man's table; for Baldassare Turini, of Pescia, the papal Datario or head of the chancery for patronage, a close friend of Raphael and the executor of his will, ordered two small pictures from Leonardo, a *Madonna and Child* and a *Child Christ,* "a wonder of grace," wrote Vasari; both have disappeared save for countless disciples' imitations.

But Raphael's influential friends had not his generosity: they could not deny the genius of his rivals, but they represented them as impossible for one reason or another. Michelangelo, who never forgot a grievance, complained years later that Bibbiena once called him a madman. Leonardo, too, was regarded as an eccentric. One of the most cultivated men at the papal court, Baldassare Castiglione, a man of intelligence and good feeling but with the narrow judgment of those who have made conformity their first rule, later referred to Leonardo in his *Cortegiano:* "Another one among the foremost painters in the world despises that art, in which he is of the rarest excellence, and has addressed himself to the study of philosophy, in which he has such strange conceits and new fantasies as he could not depict with all his art."

Supplanted in art by Raphael, Leonardo met in Rome with the same lack of understanding as in Florence in his younger days. A trivial obstacle shut him out from the immediate entourage of the Pope—his insufficient knowledge of Latin, the current language of the court. He kept up his efforts to learn the language almost to the end of his life; his grammatical exercises continue into his late notebooks, spasmodic efforts to make good his youthful lack of opportunity; but, as Francis I said later to Benvenuto Cellini, Leonardo never got beyond "a slight knowledge of Latin." The Pope's immediate entourage were a varied company, ranging from scholars to clowns, from prelates to idiots, from musicians to Latin-chattering grooms; but neither Bramante nor Leonardo nor Michelangelo was admitted there, and Raphael was the only great artist allowed to join the company assembled in the papal hunting lodge, the Villa Magliana, where court ceremonial was cast aside.

It was not only their lack of Latin that put the artists at a disadvantage with any schoolmaster who had a stock of classical clichés and any rhymester who was master of the traditional technique. Humanism was losing ground in some of the cities of Italy, but it was still all-powerful in Rome. Erasmus, passing through Venice in 1508, found a good many scholars refusing to talk to him in Latin, although they were thoroughly familiar with the language; and here and there philology had been superseded by the study of the natural sciences, *la natura delle cose occulte*. But Leo X had grown up in the intellectual atmosphere of the Platonic Academy of Florence, and among the many things in which he was mildly interested his taste for classical studies was relatively keen. His first act after his election as Pope was the foundation of a Greek university in Rome, to which he summoned well-known Hellenists who had been friends of his father. This foundation, like everything he started, was only half-heartedly organized, and furnished with no secure endowment; and he soon lost interest in it. One thing, however, remained and entrenched itself—the active clannishness of a clique of scholars with the same intellectual arrogance which had poisoned the life of young Leonardo in Florence.

The gift that was idolized by the intellectual élite which set the tone and laid down the law at court was that of rhetoric, in uncritical imitation of classic models. Rome was ruled by the phrasemongers. Tommaso Inghirami, secretary to the papal curia or administration, was a capable negotiator in diplomatic issues, but he owed his fame and his office less to his classical scholarship than to the sensational feat he once performed of reciting impromptu Latin verses at a dramatic performance; from that day he bore the nickname of Phædra. The most famous preachers were esteemed largely for the quantity of classical quotations they could cram into their sermons. The humanists of Rome carried on heated controversies over a word or a phrase; under Leo X these literary vendetttas were as noisy as the clash of arms under Julius II. The events of the time aroused less interest than disputations between Ciceronians and partisans of other classical writers.

Versifiers were far better rewarded for their indifferent productions than were artists. Raphael received for his arduous work as intendant of the building of St. Peter's three hundred ducats a year; a poet of Ferrara, Lucrezia Borgia's secretary Tebaldeo, was given five hundred ducats by the Pope for a Latin epigram in his honour, and a schoolmaster of the Trastevere quarter who concocted a Latin work in honour of Giuliano de' Medici was appointed to the Collegio Mediceo with a big salary.

Music made the best headway at the papal court against this exaggerated valuation of classical culture. Leo X had inherited from his father a genuine love of music; he could listen for hours with closed eyes to the stringed-instrument players, nodding his unshapely head in time and softly humming to himself. Often he could be heard late at night playing in his bedroom on one of the many instruments hung on its walls; sometimes his fine voice rose above the sound of the strings. No one ventured to disturb him at these times. Like his father, he had a full appreciation of musical talent; he cared little about the antecedents of singers and luteplayers so long as they were gifted. A singer named Gabriel Marin, who had a remarkably beautiful voice, was made archbishop of Bari, and a German Jew named Giammaria, a lute-player, was appointed castellan of Verrucchio castle and permitted, as a mark of especial papal favour, to take the name of Medici. Pietro Aaron, a Florentine Jew, was appointed conductor of the Vatican orchestra.

But rewards and benefices were lavished above all on those who could keep the Pope amused. So fat that he moved with difficulty, and avoiding everything that might be troublesome or trying, Leo suffered from boredom in the resulting emptiness of his days. And he had set out to enjoy life, quietly and without effort, innocently and without risks; he is said to have remarked to his brother Giuliano, and the remark entirely fits his character: *Godiamoci del papato poichè Dio ce l'ha dato,* "Let us enjoy the papacy, since God has given it to us." Life was exertion enough in itself for a man with weak legs and so heavy a body that he could get out of bed only with a great effort and had to have two servants to lean on. The master of ceremonies, Paris de' Grassi, was continually in despair at the Pope's lateness for every ceremony, no matter how many people were kept waiting. To restore himself after these labours, Leo X surrounded himself with people who could make him laugh, including those whose eccentricities or greed or vanity he could mock to his heart's content.

About a year after his arrival in Rome, Leonardo had an object lesson on the sort of successes it was possible to reap at the papal court. Leo X had for some time been revelling in the spectacle of the vanity of the aged poet Cosimo Baraballo, and finally he determined to crown him in the Capitol as *Poeta laureatus.* The distinguished old man was urged by his countrymen not to allow himself to be made the plaything of the Pope's caprice, but he was unable to believe that a ceremony beginning with prayers in the papal chapel could be intended as a farce; and when at the banquet that followed, with the Pope and many of the cardinals present, he was praised as a rival of Dante and Petrarch, and a cosmos of learning and talent, he smelt no rat. Then Bishop Lang, the Emperor's ambassador, placed a laurel wreath on the old poet's white hair, and amid the bawling of the crowd the heavy old man was laboriously hoisted onto the back of the white elephant, the only creature that seemed to see nothing amusing in the stupid affair; it refused absolutely to carry its painted, screaming, ridiculous burden across the bridge of Sant' Angelo.

This joke at the expense of an old tradition and of Cosimo Baraballo himself was but a mild example of the follies of the papal court. Wherever he looked, Leonardo saw either strange figures of doubtful sanity or competitors in folly in the service of the Pope's love of gaiety. Separated from him in the Belvedere only by a partition which was put up on his arrival, lived Giovanni Lazzarro de Magistris, chamberlain to the Pope and keeper of the privy purse, an ugly little man with such shrivelled, convulsive limbs that the wits declared that he was once carried up the chimney when a fire was being blown up, and that since then the Pope had furnished him with lead-soled shoes. Actually he slipped like a shadow through the rooms, and only his high-pitched, droning voice betrayed his presence. His real names had long been forgotten; he was known as Serapica ("midge"). He merely smiled subserviently, knowing that he was the most important man at court. In his youth Serapica had been employed about the kennels. "He began by leashing the hounds, and then he became Pope and ruled the world," wrote Pietro Aretino of him. His annual salary was 100 ducats, but he made about 90,000 a year. The Pope had strictly enjoined him to admit none but amusing persons into his presence, but for due payment he would admit anybody, instructing him how to behave. Then he would announce some grave scholar as a clown or a rival of Cosimo Baraballo. Leo only laughed at the trick played on him.

A heavier step than Serapica's was that of Fra Mariano, a grotesque figure of a monk, waddling along on his misshapen legs. He called himself the leader of the lunatics, *capo dei matti*. His fat face was distorted in a permanent grin; his belly jumped up and down under the cowl. His booming voice would break into a squeak in laughing. But the little eyes embedded in his fat face blinked astutely at his fellow-men. This chattering court jester, who seemed to babble out like an innocent any secret he got hold of, was the most reticent and reliable man in the world, and Lorenzo de' Medici, whose barber he had been, kept him as his confidant even after the barber, under Savonarola's influence, had become a monk, although Lorenzo used to say that there were three things in life to beware of—an ox from in front, a mule from behind, and a monk from both.

After Bramante's death in April 1514, Fra Mariano was appointed *Piombatore* or Keeper of the Seals. The office carried a salary of eight hundred ducats a year, and he lived in the Vatican in the Uffizio del Piombo, with a golden chain in front of his door, "just right for a madman," he commented.

Fra Mariano set no less store by his reputation as a guzzler than as court jester. The Pope liked to have men with vast appetites feeding at his board, and from his own table, set on a dais, he would watch them through a magnifying lens. Fra Mariano was said to have polished off four hundred eggs on one occasion, and to have eaten twenty capons at a meal. Once the Pope had a jerkin baked in a pie for him, and on another occasion a rope served him in a *sauce piquante*. Fra Mariano declared to the laughing guests that the rope was the symbol of the bondage the kitchen imposed on its devotees, and that he preferred to swallow it rather than suffer it.

The Pope's buffoon-in-chief was at bottom a philosopher. He owned a little house on the Quirinal, with a wide view of the Campagna. It had been furnished in a quiet, unostentatious style, and decorated with frescoes by Caravaggio. The fat, noisy monk was also a poet and a sentimentalist; the Pope despised him, but he loved the Pope, and did his best to keep at a distance from him the sycophants and real buffoons who brought the papal court into disrepute—such men as the "archipoeta" Camillo Querno, who competed with Fra Mariano in guzzling. Sometimes the "arch-poet" would come in disguise to the papal banquets—once he came as a veiled Venus—and would engage in a duel in Latin versification with the Pope. "Buffoonery is the life and soul of the court," wrote Aretino.

Another competitor in buffoonery was Cardinal Bibbiena, the most influential diplomat in Rome. His face had a comedian's mobility, and he could distort it in an infinity of grimaces. His mouth went up at the corners in a perpetual smile; he had a keen eye for the comic aspect of everybody and everything, and could make the most extravagant stories credible. Isabella d'Este called him *moccicone*, "the brat," in affectionate derision. Paolo Giovio relates that Bibbiena was able to make the gravest of men so furious that they made fools of themselves.

The infection of these follies interrupted Leonardo's studies. His latent interest in the grotesque and the mystifying sprang into life again, and here he could give it full vent. He prepared all sorts of surprises for his neighbours, with the aid of his knowledge of natural phenomena, his inventiveness, and his inexhaustible patience. He moulded bits of wax into queer little animals, carefully inflated them, and sent them up into the air during his strolls in the Vatican gardens; the little monsters would sail for a moment before the wind and gradually sink to the ground like withered leaves. One day he found a curiously formed lizard in a vineyard near the Belvedere; he asked the vigneron to let him have it, and took it home, full of an enthusiasm that made the peasant stare. With endless patience he covered the little body with scales, fixed on it an untidy beard and big horns, and made its eyes protrude. When anyone came to see him he would open the box in which he kept it imprisoned, and the little beast would dart about, its scales bristling and its horns wobbling, to the dismay of the visitor.

On another occasion he procured some well-cleaned sheep's entrails; he showed them on his open hand to his visitors, in the style of the professional juggler, and then took them into an adjoining room, used as his workshop. Here he inflated them with a bellows until they began to come through the open door. As he went on pumping they uncannily crept on, gradually filling the room. The visitors flattened themselves against the farther wall to get away from the formless, transparent monster, and found the joke a little uncomfortable. Leonardo then came back calmly to them—a magician for whom the powers he had conjured up made way; he explained to the company with a smile that he was only introducing them to a symbol of virtue, which at first may be relatively insignificant but is capable of infinite growth.

Stories were told for many years by dwellers in the Vatican of the strange tricks Leonardo the eccentric used to play; nobody realized that in these tricks with little waxen animals and inflated entrails Leonardo was investigating another phenomenon, the expansion of the air when heated, and the possibilities of its utilization. He may have had visions of the alternative which the distant future was to oppose to his "great bird," the flight of vessels lighter than air. But he does not seem to have pursued this idea, which would have brought him back to the starting-point of his study of flight.

While he was throwing his little wax objects into the air in the Vatican grounds, Leonardo had begun to observe the trees and bushes and the plants that lined the paths, and soon he was engrossed in a field of investigation comparatively new and unfamiliar to him, that of the plant world. In the botanical garden laid out for Leo X he had the opportunity of studying exotic species and of realizing the uniformity of the laws to which vegetable life is subject. He was a firm believer in the rational purpose of every form created by nature, and the first thing that struck him now was the astonishing efficiency with which the boughs and leaves of plants were exposed to the life-giving rays of the sun and the nourishing moisture. With his keen vision and his gift of observation he discovered botanical laws entirely unknown to his epoch. He found that different species of plants have their leaves differently arranged on the bough, and that the leaves "have four modes of growing one above another." They are arranged spirally, so that "the sixth always emerges over the sixth below; or the two third ones above are over the two third ones below; or the third above is over the third below"; or, as in the lilac, "two and two are placed crosswise above one another"—so as not to rob the lower ones of sunlight.[6] These laws of phyllotaxis were rediscovered about a century and a half later by Sir Thomas Browne, and published in 1658 in his *Garden of Cyrus*. Since the boughs also spring from the axillary buds between the leaves, they too must be subject to the same serviceable arrangement, and Leonardo enumerated no less than eleven types of grouping which facilitate the access of air and light.[7] His knowledge of the laws of plant growth enabled him to lay down that the age of branches and trunks is given by the number of rings they show in section.[8]

One day he brought home a gourd, and carefully removed all its roots but one, in order to be able to study it better. He placed it in a pot in the sun and patiently watched it as it grew and acquired leaves and fruited; he proudly counted the fruits. He saw how the stalks strain upward, and how the leaves try to turn to the sun; and, while continually changing the position of his plant

Plant studies

Study
of fruit and leaves

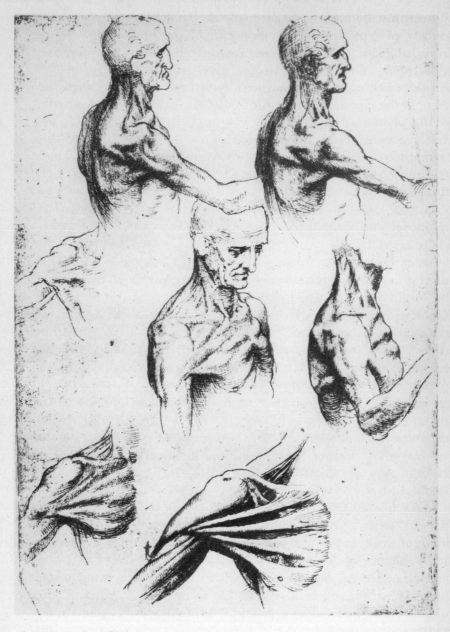

Anatomical studies   **CODEX ATLANTICUS**

and continually finding that it made the same movements, at first scarcely perceptible, he hit upon two of the fundamental tendencies of plant growth, the negative geotropic and the positive heliotropic. "The sun," he wrote, "gives spirit and life to plants, and the earth nourishes them with moisture." [9] He explained the rising of the sap, in apparent contradiction with the law of gravity, by the phenomenon of capillary attraction, which was rediscovered by Stephen Hales in the middle of the eighteenth century. But Leonardo's continual search for unifying laws in natural science led him into the effort to find parallels between plant and animal life, as well as between the organic and inorganic world, and he placed the rising of the sap in the same category of phenomena as the movement of the blood in the human body and of the waters in the earth.

Leonardo's interest in the plant world was curiously unlike his interest in other fields of study in not being abstract. In other cases the original motive which led him to start a research would be forgotten and the research then pursued for its own sake. In his walks through the Vatican grounds he devoted principal attention to the colours and forms of plants and to the changing light, and though he made a number of important scientific observations his interest centred more and more in purely æsthetic ones, as though the painter's eye had won more attention than the scholar's thirst for knowledge. Contact with nature reawakened his old passion for landscape, and the notes he now made were suggestions for the painter, advice to those pupils who did not wish to confine themselves to the representation of the human body but aimed at Leonardo's own universality.

Every tree, he pointed out, has its own individual colours and shades. "Remember, O painter," he wrote, "that the variety of depth of shade in any one particular species of plants is in proportion to the rarity or density of their branches." [10] Every part of a landscape changes its expression with the light as a human face does. "When the sun is in the east the trees are darker toward the middle, while their edges are light." [11] The leaves become almost transparent in the light, and the meadows are of a most beautiful green.[12] "The grass in front of the shadow of plants has its stems lighted up on a background of shadow." [13] But if the sun is in the

west the green of meadows and trees darkens; the moist air lies
heavy and depressing over the landscape, bereft of radiance and
grey as ashes.

Yet, as in portrait painting, Leonardo best liked a landscape beneath a clouded sky, when the trees absorb the mild, filtered light,
and spread wide surfaces of uniform shadow over the grass.[14] Seen
from a distance, the sharpness of projecting boughs is lost in the
haze, and the form of the trees becomes almost spherical near the
horizon.[15] When one paints a landscape in winter, "the mountains
should not be shown blue as in summer, since those will seem
bluest which are in themselves the darkest, and when the trees are
stripped of their leaves they will look grey in the distance." [16]
Leonardo gives instructions as to the painting of towns when the
sun is in the east or is declining in the west; when the roofs rise
dark against the bright sky, or when the brilliant sunlight plays on
them and lights them up against the shadowed walls of houses;
when mist envelops a town, or a cloud of fine dust is sweeping
through it; when the smoke ascends—the more deeply tinged with
red, the denser it is—or disappears in the fading light from the
west.[17]

Even the laws of phyllotaxis which he demonstrates are brought
to the service of the painter; and it is to the painter that he turns
at the end of his scientific observations: "O painter, if you do not
know these rules, strive to draw everything exactly as it appears in
nature, in order to escape from the criticism of those who have
knowledge; and do not despise study, as those do who are eager
only for gold."

These notes on landscape painting were intended for the *Treatise on Painting,* of which Leonardo was now considering the publication. In the revision of the work he found other gaps, and passages with which he was no longer satisfied. He resumed his studies
of perspective of more than twenty years earlier. But he was more
concerned with surveying and arranging his material than with
fundamental revision; his chief desire was to achieve a clear and
effective formulation of the laws of perspective. Everywhere he replaced diffuse explanations by brief, concise statements. Twenty
years earlier he had written: "Every portion of the surface of a
body is varied [in hue] by the [reflected] colour of the object that

may be opposite to it," and he developed this thesis at great length.[18] Now, at Rome, he wrote tersely: "The hue of an illuminated object is affected by that of the luminous body"—*Il colore del alluminato partecipa del colore dello alluminante*.[19]

Again and again he emphasized the importance of theoretical knowledge, as though in justification of his lifelong devotion to research: "Of the mistake made by those who practise without knowledge.—Those who are in love with practice without knowledge are like the sailor who gets into a ship without rudder or compass and who never can be certain whither he is going. Practice must always be founded on sound theory, and to this Perspective is the guide and the gateway; and without this nothing can be done well in the matter of drawing." [20]

Most of the additions to his *Treatise on Painting* accumulated at this period Leonardo marked "Pichera" (*Pittura,* painting), in order to identify them in his masses of notes. He wanted to have not only the book on painting but other nearly completed works printed. He was spurred on by the example of old Fra Giocondo, who published the second edition of his Vitruvius with Filippo di Giunta, of Florence, in 1513, dedicating it to Giuliano de' Medici. Leonardo wanted to pay his patron a similar compliment: it was one which the Medici, with their pretension to the intellectual leadership of their age, particularly appreciated. He was continuing the geometrical work which he had begun at Pacioli's suggestion, and at the foot of one of his geometrical demonstrations he wrote, as though to remind himself of his indebtedness to Giuliano: "Finished at 23 o'clock on July 7 in the Belvedere, in the studio assigned to me by the Magnifico in 1514." These geometrical studies took up a great deal of his time. But he seemed to have plenty of time at Rome; the clamour of the city's restless pursuit of work or pleasure did not penetrate into his quiet studio in the Belvedere. Bramante and the aged Fra Giocondo, and later young Raphael, had been concerned with the greatest task Christendom had to offer, the building of St. Peter's. Leonardo was himself at work on an architectural design [21] in Rome, but it was only for the rebuilding of a stable, for Giuliano de' Medici—a great stable for one hundred and twenty-eight horses, at the Palazzo de' Medici. While he was engaged on this stable-masterpiece he had before his eyes the ancient dome of the Pantheon, near the Medici palace. It was like the embodiment of his dream of some conqueror's mausoleum or of an amphitheatre for demigods, and he must have felt bitterly the gulf between his early ambitions and present realities.

He was passed over not only for great commissions but for high offices. While the post of Piombatore, one of the most remunerative and usually given to great artists, was conferred by Leo X on his chief jester Fra Mariano, Leonardo was commissioned only for such tasks as the designing of a die for the papal coinage. This was the first attempt at an improved apparatus for stamping coin, which until the end of the fifteenth century had been struck almost entirely by hand. With Leonardo's die the coin could, he pointed out, be "cut perfectly in roundness, size, and weight, saving the worker who cuts and weighs the coin and another who rounds it. The coins thus pass only through the hands of the examiner and the stamper, and are especially fine." He added that "all coins whose edge is not perfect should be rejected as not valid." [22]

His fortunate rival Raphael had developed his studio into a whole industrial quarter, and was at a loss for time to complete all his commissions; Leonardo was entrusted only with small tasks and small commissions for pictures. His fame lived still among the foreigners who came to the city; an eminent visitor from Naples, Costanza d'Avalos, duchess of Francavilla, ordered her portrait from him. It is no longer extant; it showed a dignified woman in widow's dress, and, according to the description given by a contemporary poet, the grave, lovely face, seen through the folds of a widow's fine black veil, "excelled art and was victor over itself," *supero l'arte e sè medesimo vinse.*

His best friends and most ardent admirers seem to have forgotten him. Isabella d'Este, whose son lived at the Vatican half as a hostage and half as an idol of the Pope and the people, came to Rome in October 1514. Leonardo might now, perhaps, have been induced to paint her portrait—she was still a beautiful woman—or to fulfil her wish for a work of his hand. But Isabella was in Rome for the first time in her life, and her entry in company with Giuliano de' Medici and with her old friend Bibbiena was made a veritable triumphal procession. She visited the ruins of the ancient city, displaying her classical culture and testing that of her friends;

she took part in the hunts arranged in her honour in the thermæ of Diocletian; she danced, masked, through the Roman carnival; she made pilgrimages to all the churches and ran up debts with all her friends and acquaintances. From time to time her thoughts turned to her husband, who lay sick of the evil French disease at Mantua; but she seems not to have troubled in the slightest about Leonardo. There is no mention in his notebooks of a meeting at this time with the duchess of Mantua. Isabella had a keen sense, however, of the things that mattered, and made a point of ordering a picture from Raphael.

Isabella's brother, the handsome and luxury-loving Cardinal Ippolito d'Este, took an active part in arranging these lively entertainments for her. He had once been Leonardo's patron, but now ignored him as his sister had done. He similarly ignored Ariosto, the poet who had made him immortal. Ariosto, disappointed and humiliated, and disgusted with court life at the Vatican, returned to Ferrara, whence he launched bitter satires against Rome.

Leonardo, neglected and forgotten, continued to live in the Belvedere. About Christmas, his brother, Ser Giuliano, came on business to Rome. Giuliano's wife Alessandra reminded him in a postscript to a letter to remember her to his brother Leonardo, "that man of unique distinction"—*uomo excellentissimo e singularissimo*. But Alessandra seems to have been one of those women who, living dull and commonplace lives, cherish the memory of any meeting in the past with famous or exceptional men. This letter, the only family document still extant which bears any friendly reference to Leonardo, has a note written later by another hand: "Alessandra lost her reason and became a victim of melancholia." [23] Dreamers with half-clouded intelligences were the nearest in spirit at this time to Leonardo.

His only dependable friend in this city of merciless oblivion was the tired and ailing Giuliano de' Medici, his patron. Giuliano was believed to be only at the outset of a career of splendid promise, from which Leonardo might hope to profit. He was the Pope's brother, and was rumoured to be dreaming of the crown of Naples. In reality Giuliano was without ambition and without even the capacity to make his way, and the Neapolitan scheme was imposed on him by his friends and hangers-on, who hoped for the pickings from his future power. All Italy, and the king of France, and in apprehension the king of Spain, believed that Giuliano was thinking of the conquest of Naples, and was influencing the papal policy accordingly; meanwhile he lay on his sofa, his heavy lids half closed over his tired blue eyes, his narrow lips twisted awry, as he laboriously chiselled a line of some amorous sonnet.

Leo X, like his brother, did not so much himself initiate these schemes as accept them when placed before him. He was well aware that his brother was not of the stuff of which conquerors are made. He entrusted Giuliano with the leadership of the papal troops and his nephew Lorenzo with the supreme command of the Florentine forces; but he commented pessimistically to a friend: "I have appointed two *capitani* who have not the slightest experience; if they are faced with any important task, I do not know how they will tackle it." But the Pope loved Giuliano as he loved few other men in the world, loved him for his good-heartedness and his weakness, his fine intellect and his practical incapacity; and he was true to the Medici tradition of watching over the family heritage. Yet love and family pride might have been insufficient to overcome his lethargy, once the pressure from those interested was relaxed (such pressure came later from Lorenzo de' Medici and his imperious mother Alfonsina Orsini), but for his fears of Spanish supremacy on one side and of French hegemony on the other. His policy oscillated between pro-French and anti-French attitudes, according as the nightmare of Spanish power approached or faded away; and Giuliano's Neapolitan succession tossed to and fro on these uncertainties.

Meanwhile Giuliano received the ecclesiastical possessions over which France and Milan were struggling, the cities of Modena, Parma, Piacenza, and Reggio. On his instructions Leonardo went to Parma, probably in order to inspect the fortifications. His notebook contains the brief entry: "At Parma, at the Bell Inn (*alla Campana*), September 25, 1514." [24] He also travelled along the coast south of Rome as far as the region known as the Pontine Marshes. He found craters of extinct volcanoes all over this country, dotted with deep lakes or shallow meres surrounded by thick growths of tangled underwood. Through some of the lakes flowed rivers which passed on to the sea. Many other streams, big and little, meandered through the plain, disappearing in sand or volcanic slime or among reed-beds and peaty grassland, to reappear laden with mud, which accumulated to form dunes on the coast, so that their turbid waters occasionally flooded the country.

In hot summers a fever-laden air drifted from the Pontine Marshes over Rome, a poisonous miasma whose infection could suddenly lay low the strongest men. Leo X, who with his un-healthy fatness so suffered from the heat that in all church cere-monies he had to be continually mopping the sweat that trickled down his face and drying his damp hands, had the true egoist's panic fear of disease, and he had always before him the spectre of the dreadful end of Alexander VI. At the very outset of his pontif-icate he considered the question of the draining of the Pontine Marshes. One of the first plans laid before him seems to have been for the diversion of the water from the higher coastal ground by the deepening of the Rio Martino. Giuliano de' Medici was full of enthusiasm for this beneficent plan, and as he knew his brother's habitual irresolution he declared himself ready to bear the cost of the work. Under his instructions Leonardo travelled through the marshy region, and there he made a remarkable sketch map, in blue and sepia, with the names entered plainly in normal left-to-right script, as was his habit when preparing maps for his employ-ers. His plan for draining the marshes went beyond the first proj-ect of the papal engineers. He proposed that the standing water should be drained away not only by enlarging and regulating the bed of the Rio Martino but also by cutting an artificial outlet to the sea from the river Livoli (Ufente) in the neighbourhood of a place called Badino, which is twice mentioned in holograph letters from the Pope dated July 7 and December 14, 1514. Leonardo's map showed the river Livoli winding through countless turns across the plain and then making a wide curve as it passed Monte Circeo to reach the sea. This river he also proposed to regulate, its short-ened course and increased gradient enabling it to carry off the ma-larial lakes and standing water. "The draining of the marshes will be effected," Leonardo wrote, "by conducting turbid streams through them. But in these marshes the river must enter by a deep and narrow channel, and it must leave them by a broad and shal-low outlet. . . . The marsh will be filled up with soil by receiving

turbid water at a low level and running off water from the surface
at the opposite end of the marsh." [25]

The inhabitants of the small town of Tarracina, on the edge of
the Pontine Marshes, presented Giuliano with the land, in itself
worthless, through which the proposed canal would pass; the canal
was to be named after Giuliano. Some years later part of the Pontine Marshes was drained at Badino on Leonardo's plan; a Lombard engineer, Fra Giovanni Scotto, of Como, was entrusted with
the work, and adopted Leonardo's proposal. The water ran rapidly
to the sea and wide stretches of land emerged. The inhabitants of
Tarracina then laid claim to the restored soil. Giuliano de' Medici
was no longer alive, and his heirs contested the claim to the land;
the litigation continued until the work was suspended and finally
abandoned.

Some months after Leonardo's return from his survey of the
Pontine Marshes, his patron prepared for a distant journey. An
alliance was planned with the French court, as a step toward the
realization of the ambitious dream of a kingdom for Giuliano; it
was hoped to cement the alliance by his marriage with Philiberta
of Savoy. Louis XII did everything to further this marriage with
the Pope's brother. After the death of Anne of Brittany he had
married Mary Tudor, sister of the king of England, in spite of his
age and his feeble health, in order to seal the Anglo-French
alliance; and he furthered the new union in the hope of gaining
the adhesion of the hesitating Pope to the league that had been
formed between France, Venice, Florence, and Ferrara against
Spain, a league which aimed at recovering the duchy of Milan for
Louis and gaining the throne of Naples for Giuliano. At this period the Pope was on terms of friendship with Spain, but he
warmly supported his brother's marriage with Philiberta of Savoy,
which would bring prestige to the Medici. Philiberta was a thin
girl with a pale, pinched face, and almost a hunchback, but her
royal blood commanded a high price, and the Pope promised her
a dowry of 100,000 ducats, 30,000 of it in fabrics, clothes, and jewellery.

Early on a grey December morning Giuliano de' Medici, pale
and weary from sleeplessness, set out reluctantly from Rome to
meet his pale, deformed bride. An enormous sapphire, the Pope's

parting gift to him, blazed on the long, thin, sickly hand with which he waved to his friends. He himself looked limp and lifeless; he seemed to be saying "farewell for ever." But his friends sped him on his journey with pleasure; they hoped that his young bride would infuse new life into the papal court. As Cardinal Bibbiena said, this court needed only the presence of women to set things humming.

Only Leonardo, on this grey morning, went back filled with a strange feeling of oppression to his workshop in the Belvedere. He feared that he was to be abandoned by his patron, and felt that this was a sad day in his life. And soon he learned that on that same day his great friend the king of France, to whom he would have been able to turn as a last resort in time of need, had suddenly died. Obsessed by dark forebodings, he wrote in his notebook: "The Magnifico Giuliano de' Medici left Rome on the 9th of January 1515,* just at daybreak, to take a wife in Savoy; and on the same day fell the death of the king of France." [26]

After Giuliano had gone Leonardo began to be pestered by petty troubles in his work. His assistant Georg, the German artisan, who received seven ducats a month from Giuliano's banker, suddenly claimed an increase in his wages, and when Leonardo confronted him with his contract he made every excuse he could think of for getting away from his work. Leonardo had suggested to Georg that he should live in the workshop; he wanted to teach the man Italian, so as to be able to do without an interpreter. But Georg preferred the company of his young compatriots to that of the eccentric old man. He also preferred to have his meals with the Swiss of the papal guard; they must certainly have fed better than he could with the economical Leonardo, who was aghast at the German's huge appetite. When he had eaten and drunk his fill, Georg would wander about the ruins with the Swiss, shooting birds, to Leonardo's disgust. One day Leonardo tried to put an end to this, and sent his pupil Lorenzo after the man; Georg sent back the impudent message that he objected to having so many masters, and that anyhow he was doing some work for Giuliano. He kept away for two months. Then Leonardo happened to meet Giuliano's foreman, and learned from him that Georg had

---

* The date by the Florentine calendar.

been lying; all he had had to do was to repair a couple of shotguns. Leonardo sent for Georg, who flew into a rage, tore out of the workshop, and shut himself in his bedroom, where he continued to make an uproar. When one of Leonardo's men went into the room Georg rolled his eyes and growled unintelligible curses with such fury that no one else ventured near him.

The man's impudence vexed Leonardo as only petty things could. He magnified it into an affair of state, seeking the motive for this rebelliousness and characteristically believing that he had unearthed a whole conspiracy. "At last I have discovered," he wrote triumphantly, "that it is Messer Giovanni degli specchi"— Johannes the mirror-maker—"who is at the bottom of it all." Messer Johannes, who was furious with Leonardo for supplanting him in Giuliano's favour, now did his best to urge on his fellow-countryman. The two sat together all day long, talking in their uncouth foreign tongue which nobody could understand. Worse still, Johannes watched everything Georg did. Leonardo gave his mechanic sketches only of parts of his apparatus; Georg now demanded the complete wooden template. The Germans wanted to steal Leonardo's invention. Then they went about the Vatican telling everybody that Leonardo knew nothing about mirrors although he was supposed to be making them for Giuliano; Giovanni degli specchi was the only true master of this art.

His troubles with his German artisans were too much for Leonardo. He could always adjust himself to fate's heavy blows and to serious disappointments; his philosophical scepticism had armed him against bitter experience at the hands of his fellow-men. He could see his hopes crash and still remain calm. But he was unable to endure the petty warfare of everyday life, the quarrels that wore him out and made him unable to work, and this constant and determined interference from stupidity and malice. His armour of equanimity had this one wretched crevice.

He had been morally worn out by the humiliations he had suffered in Rome, and the quarrel with his German workmen made him ill. He was now more than sixty, and his health and physical strength, which he had used up all through his life as if there was no demand he could not make of them, now for the first time gave way. In this winter he fell ill and had to send for a doctor. In his papers there is an address, not in his writing, of a physician in Rome.[27] It may have been the first warning of the malady which in the end killed him, a forerunner of the seizure that crippled his hand. It was only a transitory warning, and he took no further notice of it. The news of the return of Giuliano de' Medici to Italy roused him from this unaccustomed atmosphere of depression and malaise.

But Giuliano himself lay ill in Florence, tired out by his journey and by the long series of festivities, and upset by the change in the habits of a lifetime involved in his marriage with a young wife. When his condition improved, the news made Leonardo feel that he had himself recovered. "I was so greatly rejoiced, most illustrious Lord," he wrote to Giuliano, "by the desired restoration of your health, that it almost had the effect that my own illness left me." He apologized for his inability to complete the tasks entrusted to him, "by reason of the wickedness of that German deceiver." Four times he began this letter, struggling to express himself, revising and rejecting and finally returning almost exactly to his original words, in giving Giuliano the story of all the misdeeds of the German mechanic.[28] The fragments of this letter grew into a whole charge sheet, the longest document existing on Leonardo's relations with those around him. Numbers of outstanding men of his epoch crossed his path; yet the only careful psychological description from his pen is that of Georg, the stupid and impudent German workman. Apart from this there is nothing but the slight sketch of the wild young Salai.

Georg the German soon made off. Messer Giovanni degli specchi took possession of the workshop in which his fellow-countryman had worked. There he made mirrors wholesale, sending them out to every market; soon he had the whole of the Belvedere filled with mirror shops. Leonardo waited impatiently for his patron's return in order to make an end of these scandalous proceedings. But Giuliano's improvement did not last; his prematurely exhausted constitution held out with difficulty against his illness. Leonardo had plenty of time now to devote to his scientific work; and his own illness had increased his desire to bring his researches to a conclusion. He was like one who hurries to gather his harvest before it is too late—the great harvest of his life, scattered and inaccessible in the desert of his papers. There were a number of studies, pursued through many years, taken up and dropped again, which now, he thought, needed little more revision to make them ready for publication.

Now, in the closing period of his life, he was filled with a cheerful confidence in the great superiority of his experimental method in natural science and his mathematical demonstrations over the humanist mental science, the introspective philosophy which he had combated even as a young man. He expressed this superiority in one of the terse and neatly phrased generalizations which were at his command at this period: "There is no certainty in science where one of the mathematical sciences cannot be applied." [29] He went through his notes on mechanics, intending to collect them into a treatise; instead of a preface he proposed to open with this apophthegm: "Mechanics is the paradise of mathematical science, because here we come to the fruits of mathematics." [30]

But, in the course of the collecting and arranging, he discovered many things which, returned to now after years had elapsed, needed revising and completing; and he found himself drawn into new studies and experiments. Many of the most astonishing results of his research in statics and dynamics date from these last years.

He arranged part of his observations under the heading: "Of the science of heavy bodies in relation to the force of their motor." [31] He compressed an earlier lengthy exposition into this generalization: "The nature of a heavy body is threefold: one [element] is its simple and natural gravity, a second is its accidental gravity, and the third is the friction it produces. The natural gravity is unalterable; the accidental gravity associated with it varies continually with the force, and the friction varies according to the nature of the medium in which it originates." [32]

He now experimented afresh, as though he were doing it for the first time, with a pair of scales. While considering the conditions of equilibrium, he noticed that in explaining them he could make use of the theory, already familiar to him, of the elbow lever. He filled many pages of his manuscript with attempts at the solution of his problem; later he struck out some passages and wrote in the margin: "This is better expressed three pages further on." [33] At last he arrived at a perfectly clear conception of the composition of a force as the resultant of components acting in different directions. This theory was one of Leonardo's most important contributions to the science of mechanics. He returned to it in the revision of his earlier investigations of the laws of gravity, and declared that a heavy body descending obliquely distributes its weight between two different "aspects." [34] In order to observe the path of bodies falling freely, he dropped a number of weights from the top of a tower, and noted that, contrary to all expectation, they did not reach the earth vertically below the point from which they were dropped. He repeated his experiment several times, and believed that he was able to detect a slight eastward bias; he attributed it to the rotation of the earth about its axis. High as was the tower he had ascended, it seems scarcely conceivable that he should have been able to make this observation with so relatively short a drop. But what he thought he observed led him to the discovery of the influence of the rotation of the earth on the path of falling bodies. The body retains the tangential velocity at the point from which it starts, a higher velocity than that of the surface of the earth. Galileo sought in vain for the explanation of this deviation from the perpendicular, and the true explanation was not found until Gassendi gave it in his *De Motu Impresso a Motore Translato,* published in 1642. The resolution of the motion into a rectilinear and an elliptical component, to which Leonardo's experiment led him, occupied him for a considerable time.

A child spinning his top was the starting-point of long-continued research. Leonardo looked on spellbound at the movement of the toy, with which children have played in all ages, and then began to spin tops himself, patiently drawing their path up to the moment when they spun no more and fell over. He was so fascinated by the problems raised by the top that he proposed to collect his exhaustive notes into a special chapter on composite motion, in which he would include a definition of "hemispherical" and spiral motion.

His great interest in curves of motion was connected with two other branches of study which he was energetically pursuing at this time. A relatively large space is taken up in his papers by work on the planimetrical transformation of curvilinear figures and on geometrical equivalents. He often gave this work the heading *De*

Ludo Geometrico, which he also proposed to use as the title for a treatise on the subject. A large number of sheets of the *Codex Atlanticus,* covered with these transformations, date from this time of enforced and bitterly resented leisure. They bear plain traces of Leonardo's recent illness. The stroke that had been so delicate and often no more than a breath now dug deeply into the paper, as though the hand that made it had suddenly grown heavy; the writing, once like copper engraving, was now hurried and blurred, and at times it seems as if the writer's vision had lost its past acuteness.

Leonardo had been wearing spectacles for some years, and now he reflected on the decreasing strength of vision in men of advancing age.[35] He had stronger lights hung from the ceiling, and in order never to be without light he contrived an oil lamp in which the wick rose as the oil was consumed.[36] He also made glasses filled with water, so that "the eye shall not see remote objects greatly reduced as is done by natural perspective." [37]

But, though he complained of his failing sight, he now took up studies for which he had to rely entirely on clearness of vision; for the manuscripts he set out to complete included his treatise on the flight of birds. He proposed to add to the observations noted years earlier by taking advantage of his subsequent practice in dissection, working now on the anatomy of birds' wings.[38] In spite of thickened and slightly blurred strokes, the sheets on which he noted the results of his dissection show all the old mastery.[39] On several pages of the notebook E, which he was using at this time, he described the construction of the wings and of the breast muscles in various species of birds. He did not confine himself to birds; he described the flight of bats,[40] butterflies,[41] and "other insects which fly with four wings" [42]; and he studied with special attentiveness the flies that suddenly hover in the air at a particular spot, with a rapid beating and humming of the wings.[43] In addition to describing the various motions of flight, he tried to verify from the flight of living creatures the laws of mechanics which he had discovered. When he observed the flight of birds in the wind, and resolved into its components the expenditure of energy with which they overcome the resistance of the air, he found his propositions confirmed, and commented with satisfaction: "Nature does not break her own laws." [44]

But a real understanding of the movements of birds in the air would depend on an understanding of the nature of winds. This could be obtained by considering the movements of water. "This knowledge will be a ladder leading to the understanding of flying creatures in the air and the wind." [45] Leonardo set out to investigate the currents of air. "The wind," he wrote, "exercises the same force on a bird as a wedge lifting a weight." [46] Thus the air exercised no motive force, contrary to the Aristotelean theory which attributed to it the maintenance of movements; all it did was to set up resistance to moving bodies. "The air is condensed in front of bodies which push rapidly through it, with greater or less condensation according as the speed of the moving body is greater or less." [47] "Its capacity of condensation or rarefaction approaches the infinite." [48] These generalizations are set at the beginning of Leonardo's observations on the elasticity of the air, the principles of which were first made known through Borelli's works, published in the seventeenth century.

In this effort to complete each section of his life's work Leonardo advanced in a relatively short time far beyond his earlier conclusions. It might have been supposed that he had sufficiently shaken off the fetters of medieval thought to be able to make rapid progress along the paths of modern research; but he was still obsessed by the notion of the unity of all natural phenomena, and this idea determined the course of his studies. Again and again he drew parallels between air and water. "The air moves like a river, and carries the clouds along with it just as water carries along everything that is supported on its surface." [48] In setting out to explain the nature of air by that of water, the characteristics of which he and his age knew better and were better able to demonstrate, he was led to the revision of his treatise on water, which he had regarded as finished.

Each one of Leonardo's new discoveries was confirmed by those that had preceded it, or brought them fresh confirmation. In his own phrase, they were steps by means of which he proceeded from one "science" to others. The treatise on water, the work to which he most frequently returned, reflects all the successive stages of his development. The programme which he now laid down under the heading "The Order of the First Book on Water" was influenced by his latest studies on mechanics: "Define first what is meant by height and depth; also how the elements are situated one inside another. Then, what is meant by solid weight and liquid weight; but first what weight and lightness are in themselves. Then describe why water moves, and why its motion ceases; then why it becomes slower or more rapid." [49] As in many other instances, he completely ignores earlier errors of his own: he demonstrates that "the ocean does not penetrate under the earth," [50] but "water rises through the heat of the sun, and then falls again in rain." [51]

At this time he made some experiments in order to test the applicability to hydraulics of his new discoveries in mechanics. These experiments proved that in communicating vessels the levels of different liquids are in inverse proportion to their density. Pursuing this research further, he found that the equation between motive impulse and resistance which produces equilibrium in solids is comparable with the equation between the upward pressure of fluids and the downward pressure applied to them. This identity between the laws governing solids and liquids is part of the field of modern research, and this identity between all natural laws took the place in Leonardo's philosophy of his earlier conception of the identity of the organic and inorganic worlds. But though he no longer drew his picturesque comparisons between man and the body of the earth, with warmth and breath as its spirit, he did not easily break away from his earlier fixed ideas, and continued to try to harmonize the parallelism of the microcosm and the macrocosm with his new observations.

But Johannes, the German mirror-maker, had made up his mind to get this troublesome old man out of his rooms in the Belvedere by making his life in Rome a burden to him. "He hindered me in anatomy, blaming it before the Pope; and likewise at the hospital," wrote Leonardo in complaint to the ailing Giuliano de' Medici.[52] Interest in the study of anatomy had been steadily growing in Italy; artists and savants more and more made a practice of dissection, and the enlightened Leo X cannot have taken seriously the innuendoes made to him by the German mechanic. Leo was careful, however, to conceal his own indifference in matters of faith, and accordingly set great store by outward observance of the canons of the Church; he permitted ample licence to his friends in confidential talk, but was inexorable in putting down every infringement of religious prohibitions. He also had the humanist contempt for experimental science, and believed that the classic writers had transmitted to posterity all that was worth knowing. And as he always kept out of the way of anything that might arouse scandal, and also carefully avoided anything troublesome, he sacrificed Leonardo without a qualm to the scandal-mongering German.

Giuliano de' Medici still lay sick in Florence, and Leonardo had no friends in Rome who could speak up for him with the Pope. Isolated, neglected, and now defamed and hindered in his work, Leonardo fought with every means at his disposal for the recognition that was slipping away from him. As though he wished to prove the injustice of the German's accusations, and the absence of every element of heresy or scandal from his anatomical studies, he quickly collected his notes on the structure of the mouth, the larynx, and the trachea, and expanded them into an inquiry into the mechanism of human speech, which he entitled *Trattato de Vocie*. He hoped that Rome, where every dialectician was welcome, and Vatican circles, with their exaggerated respect for the artist in words, and the Pope, with his keen sense of the beauty of the human voice, would be specially interested in his exposition of the physiological laws of sound and word formation.

Proceeding from the anatomy of the larynx and the vocal cords, he set out to describe the anatomy of the trachea, in which, in his belief, the human voice contrived its changes of tone, rising or falling; and then to show the infinite multiplicity of the muscles of the tongue (a splendid sheet showed the interior of the cavity of the mouth and the root of the tongue), and the motor muscles of the lips, which in man are much more numerous than in other animals: "this is due to the need for the many operations continually carried out by the lips, as in the four letters of the alphabet *b, f, m, p*." [53] The creator of Mona Lisa's smile devoted special attention to the pair of muscles "which distend the mouth and prepare it for laughing." He then dealt step by step with the development of the sounds sent out from the trachea into vowels and consonants. He showed the membrane on which the air impinges when the Italian vowel *a* is formed, the cavity in which the vowel *u* is formed as the lips are contracted and thrust outward, and the way the lips open for *a* and come nearer together for *o*.[54]

This formation of intelligible sounds, and the origin and development of speech, were for Leonardo a miracle at which he never ceased to marvel: "Consider how by means of the movement of the tongue, with the aid of the lips and the teeth, the pronunciation of all names of things becomes known to us; and the simple and composite vocables of a language reach our ears by means of this instrument; the which, if all the workings of nature had a name, would extend to the infinite in common with the infinity of things done by nature or capable of being done. And the languages themselves are subject to oblivion and are mortal, like other created things; and if we assume our world to be eternal, we shall say that such languages have been and furthermore must be of infinite variety through the infinite ages which are contained in infinite time." [55]

There is a note showing that Leonardo delivered the *Treatise on Speech* on December 14, 1514, to Battista dell' Aquila,[56] the privy chamberlain to the Pope. But Messer Battista seems to have paid no particular attention to the work. The manuscript entrusted to him, with its splendid drawings, disappeared, and only a few sheets, preparatory sketches, and notes bear witness to this effort of Leonardo's to establish his position at the papal court.

The effort was as vain, however, as others had been. Leo X, like all lazy men, placed his own comfort before all else, and once he had made up his mind he would not take the trouble to change it. But, even if he had tried to interest himself in a research that was remote from his own concerns, or to take thought for another man's fate, he would not have had the opportunity; for the storm aroused by his own vacillating policy now broke over him. He had deliberately reversed the policy of his bellicose predecessor; he had sought peace at any price by means of successive alliances, first on one side and then on another. Now he found himself drawn into war. His first concern had been for equilibrium of the Italian powers; now he was faced with the inevitable collapse of any weak and equivocal policy. In February 1515 he had signed the protocol of a treaty of coalition between the papacy, the Emperor, the king of Spain, Milan, Genoa, and the Swiss. In March he offered a secret treaty to Francis I of France, who had succeeded Louis XII. Francis curtly declined, for he was dreaming of the reconquest of Milan, and was not to be dissuaded by an eleventh-hour effort from Rome. Leo X, however, was as determined to maintain peace as Francis was to go to war. When Rome's mercenaries were already on the march against the French army of invasion, the Pope was still negotiating with France; before long the enemy were actually at the gates of Rome, but Leo was still out for an understanding at any price.

Soon Leo found the French demanding Parma and Piacenza. He exclaimed that he would rather lose his mitre than those cities. In the end he was forced to face a war. He appointed Giuliano to the command of the papal troops. But Giuliano's improvement had been no more than a last flicker of his exhausted vitality. On the way to take up his command he collapsed, and now he was struggling with death. His nephew Lorenzo undertook the defence of Parma and Piacenza against the French.

Fearing an attack from the sea, the Pope considered the strengthening of the port of Civitavecchia, where great fortification works had been begun by Bramante in 1508 and were being continued by Giuliano Leno and Antonio da Sangallo. The Pope now went himself to Civitavecchia in order to inspect the circle of bastions which were being built to Sangallo's design and which were to make the port impregnable. At this hour of need Leo X may have thought of Leonardo's knowledge of military engineering, or Giuliano may have mentioned Leonardo to him; at all events, Leonardo went once to Civitavecchia from Rome, and in all probability his visit took place at this critical time.

Leonardo looked round Civitavecchia with his accustomed interest in the picturesque. By the harbour there still stood the ruins of a colonnade, thick truncated pillars "to which ships were once moored"; between the pillars there emerged from the soil here and there a mosaic paving "with various designs, leaves and scrolls of stones of various colours." He stood on the steps leading from the colonnade down to the seashore, and in imagination he saw the ruined arcades, probably the remains of an ancient market, in their original state, and the worn mosaic in its first bright splendour. At Civitavecchia there had once been a summer palace of the Cæsars. Actually it was on a hill, with a fine view of the town and harbour; but Leonardo thought it had stood by the harbour, with steps leading down to the sea, and he tried to restore the scene in its past magnificence. Many years earlier he had suggested rebuilding the ruined ancient theatre at Pavia; now, with his old capacity of dreaming in stone and marble, he erected in imagination over the remains of a colonnade a palace of the Cæsars. His pillared palace had three stories. Above its colonnades there opened a spacious loggia; the third story, set back, was crowned with a triangular gable.[57]

Not only the palace of the Cæsars rose before his eyes; he imagined also the harbour piers on their ancient foundations. But he drew piers advancing further into the sea and more completely enclosing the harbour than when he saw them, in order to provide a protected entry for ships. Behind the harbour rose the town, surrounded by walls, not zigzagging as in his own and in medieval times but in a massive square, the ancient *castrum,* within which the town was made up of straight streets crossing at right angles, in the classic style. This was not the Civitavecchia on which his gaze rested. His vision carried him back to an epoch of ancient splendour, and this man without classical education achieved what the humanists only rarely and timidly attempted—with his rapid strokes he reconstructed an ancient port on the strength of its extant ruins.[58]

While Leonardo was dreaming of a vanished world, the news reached the Pope in Civitavecchia that Milan was once more in the possession of the French. Francis I had set out at the beginning of August with an army of 35,000 men, an army that far outdistanced in its splendour those of Charles VIII and Louis XII. Alongside the king rode army commanders whose very names sounded in the ears of the Italians like a shout of victory, even if these commanders had not escaped defeats in the past—Trivulzio, Trémouille, and Bayard, the *chevalier sans peur et sans reproche.* And as they were well acquainted with the country the young king followed their advice. On Trivulzio's suggestion he chose the Col d'Argentière, which was generally regarded as impassable, for his crossing of the Alps. He invaded Italy without warning, destroyed the Milanese cavalry, and gave battle at Marignano. The fighting was so long drawn out and so sanguinary that Trivulzio, as he crossed the battlefield on the evening of his victory, sadly declared that the eighteen battles he had fought in his life were all child's play in comparison with this massacre.

Maximiliano Sforza's rule in Milan collapsed like a card castle, and the French pushed on to Rome. Leo X, like his father before him, saw that he had lost; and just as Lorenzo de' Medici had intervened in person to bring to an end the disastrous war between Florence and Naples, so Leo now resolved to use the prestige of his high office to secure peace with France. With his mind, for once in his life, definitely made up, he overrode the objections of his entourage and went to Bologna to meet the king of France, in order to come to terms personally with him.

Did Leonardo accompany the Pope? Was he present at the triumphal entry into Florence and at the Pope's visit to the palace of the Medici, where Giuliano lay dying? And did he first meet Francis I at Bologna, where the king, young and handsome and ready in his success to be provocative, kept the Pope waiting some time before he would see him? Attus, the king's paymaster, was in the king's train, and there exists a portrait sketch of him, probably by Melzi, which seems to attest Leonardo's presence at the meeting at Bologna. At about the same time he sent a letter from Milan, no longer extant, to a certain Zanobi Boni, who was administrator of his vineyard at Fiesole, perhaps an inheritance from his uncle Francesco. Whether he was in Bologna or in Milan, Leonardo tried to keep afloat on the current of events, and with as little success as ever. There exists at Windsor an evident attempt of this sort, one of the flattering allegories which at that time were so effective a means of securing the attention of princes. It is a curious sheet, representing a reconciliation between the temporal and spiritual powers. A boat is pushing its way through stormy waves; a wolf is at the helm, steering with a paw. The wind is blowing strongly and swelling the sail; the mast is a tree with green spreading boughs, a tree that can withstand any storm. Moving toward the boat, dancing on curling waves of the sort Leonardo was particularly fond of drawing in the closing years of his life, was a globe on which a crowned eagle was enthroned. Between the shaded lines on the globe the date 1516 seems to be distinguishable. Did this drawing of the meeting between the Roman wolf, the symbol of the Church, and the crowned eagle, a symbol of empire, celebrate the concordat concluded at Bologna between France and the Pope? Did the traditional symbol of the Emperors, the eagle within the rising sun, represent the victorious young king of France? At this time he was revolving plans of a vast crusade, considering himself to be called to the defence of Christendom against the infidel, and perhaps dreaming of the crown of the Holy Roman Empire, which he claimed two years later.

Whatever may have been Leonardo's intended explanation of the Windsor allegory, whether he hoped to win with it the favour of the Emperor or of the Pope, all his efforts failed. These years of Leonardo's life are shrouded in darkness, as if, famous though he was, he had been forgotten by his contemporaries. There is no record of any commission, no contemporary record of any sort, to show whether at this time he was in Milan, Florence, or Rome. It seems probable that he returned to the Belvedere, for there is a dated note of the proportions of St. Paul's church,[59] made for some unknown reason, perhaps simply as a matter of curiosity, and this suggests that he was still in Rome in August 1516—waiting for some new turn of events, for some powerful prince's interest, for some important commission; or, perhaps, for the Pope's decision on the competition he invited in 1515 for the façade of San Lorenzo in Florence. In this competition Michelangelo, Raphael, Giuliano da Sangallo, and Andrea and Jacopo da Sansovino took part, and also, apparently, Leonardo.

He waited in the twilight of semi-oblivion, just as he had waited in his youth, though a whole lifetime of fame and achievement had intervened; he was overcome by the same loss of confidence as in his youth, when he had accepted the philosophy of abnegation, the dull, pessimistic philosophy, foreign to his true nature, of acceptance of the inevitable. It was now an old man, tired and disillusioned, with lined forehead and lips drooping at the corners, who sat at his desk completing his observations on the relation of shadows to the form of the source of light. One day he was carefully drawing the outlines of the shadows thrown by a variously lighted body, and in the midst of the hatching and sketching he broke off to write in a minute script, unusually small, as though he were a little ashamed of his idea: "We should not desire the impossible," *non si debbe desiderare lo impossibile.*[60]

Amid this loss of confidence, the result of his narrowed circumstances, Leonardo began to dream as he had done years before—wild, fevered dreams of elemental catastrophes, visions of the end of the world. This time he set out to give his dreams a scientific foundation; he incorporated them in his studies of the elements, his long-continued studies of the movement of water and air; and he gave them the form of a manual for ambitious painters in search of a subject—as if there could be any young and ambitious painter who would venture to attempt such a subject as this unchaining of the elements. For many years he had been strongly attracted by rushing and eddying waters, as if he felt a kinship with them. For years he had also been pursuing research into the motion of the air, and lately he had been making more and more frequent notes of observations of the winds, of the formation of mists in the air, and of storm-laden clouds. But his dreams went beyond this research; they pictured landscapes shaken by the fury of the elements, and plagues visiting a petty and timid humanity, as though he sought imaginative compensation for his enforced inactivity in the contemplation of a universe in chaos.

The disasters he pictured on his solitary walks, or at his desk, he set down in the form of a description aimed at assisting diligent young painters to represent the Deluge. As once he told his story of eastern travel in a succession of paragraphs that steadily heightened the picture, so now he sketched a programme, stage by stage, of the destruction wrought by the Flood. "The Divisions," he wrote, as headings for his own use, "darkness, wind, tempest at sea, floods of water, forests on fire, rain, bolts from heaven, earthquakes and the collapse of mountains, overthrow of cities . . . people on trees which are unable to support them; trees and rocks, towers and hills covered with people; boats, tables, troughs, and other means of floating. Hills covered with men, women, and animals; and lightning from the clouds illuminating everything." [61] Leonardo proceeds then with all the ghastly details of his description, under the heading "Description of the Deluge": "Let there be first represented the summit of a rugged mountain with valleys surrounding its base, and on its sides let the surface of the soil be seen to slide, and descending ruinous from these precipices let it dash along and lay bare the twisted and gnarled roots of large trees overthrown, their roots upwards; and let the mountains, as they are scoured bare, discover the profound fissures made in them by ancient earthquakes. . . . And into the depth of some valley may have fallen the fragments of a mountain forming a shore to the swollen waters of its river, which, having already burst its banks, will rush on in monstrous waves; and the greatest will strike upon and destroy the walls of the cities and farmhouses in the valley." [62]

As if he felt the written word inadequate to represent the scene he imagined, Leonardo broke off again and again from his description in order to set in the margin of his sheet, or between the lines, like extensions of the flourishes of the writing, rough sketches of bare rocks hurtling down, rivers rising against an obstruction, water swirling down, eddies and whirlpools and foam-flecked waves that beat against city walls. He set these sketches in the midst of the text, like keywords, intelligible only to himself, which he intended to elaborate into elements of the tragedy. He continued:

"Then the ruins of the high buildings in these cities will throw up a great dust, rising up in shape like smoke or wreathed clouds against the falling rain. But the swollen waters will sweep round the pool which contains them, striking in eddying whirlpools against the different obstacles, and leaping into the air in muddy foam."

In order to bring this picture vividly before his own eyes, Leonardo recalled the storm he had witnessed at Piombino, the uprooted trees, the wrecks tossed on the frothy sea, the sheets of rain whirled along by the wind: "The waves of the sea which break on the slope of the mountains that bound it will foam from the velocity with which they fall against these hills; in rushing back they will meet the succeeding waves as they come, and after a loud report they will return in a great flood to the sea whence they came. Let great numbers of inhabitants, men and animals of all kinds, be seen driven by the rising of the deluge to the peaks of the mountains in the midst of the waters aforesaid." [62]

Leonardo kept to the fiction of scientific description of a suggested subject for painting, though, carried away by his imagination, he pursued his dream far beyond the limits of possible representation:

"The fields covered with water showed its waves in great part strewn with tables, bedsteads, boats, and various other contrivances made from necessity and the fear of death, on which were men and women with their children, amid sounds of lamentation and weeping, terrified by the fury of the winds, which with their tempestuous violence rolled the waters under and over and about the bodies of the drowned. . . . And all the waters dashing on their shores seemed to be battering them with the blows of drowned bodies, and killed those in whom any life remained."

Leonardo seemed to forget his role of painter; his ears were filled with the unearthly sounds of nature's massacre: "Ah, what dreadful noises were heard in the air rent by the fury of the thunder and the lightnings it flashed forth, and how many you might have seen closing their ears with their hands to shut out the tremendous sounds!" In his vision the tragedy of the world's destruction moved inexorably to its end:

"Others were not content with shutting their eyes, but laid their hands one over the other to cover them the closer, that they might not see the cruel slaughter of the human race by the hand of God. . . . Others, in desperate act, took their own lives, hopeless of being able to endure such suffering; and of these some flung themselves from lofty rocks, others strangled themselves with their own hands, others seized their own children and violently slew them at a blow; some wounded themselves with their own weapons; others falling on their knees recommended themselves to God. Ah, how many mothers wept over their drowned sons, holding them upon their knees, with arms raised towards heaven and with words and various threatening gestures upbraiding the wrath of the gods! Others with clasped hands and fingers clenched gnawed them and devoured them till they bled, crouching with their breast down on their knees in their intense and unbearable anguish. . . . Already had the birds begun to settle on men and on other animals, finding no land uncovered which was not occupied by living beings, and already the dead bodies, now fermented, were leaving the depth of the waters and were rising to the top. . . . And above these judgments, the air was seen covered with dark clouds, riven by the forked flashes of the raging bolts of heaven, lighting up on all sides the depth of the gloom." [63]

Leonardo had now become engrossed in his picture of the retribution wreaked on sinful mankind. He seemed to have entirely forgotten the convention of a manual for painters under which he had begun his description, so that it no longer mattered to him that the howling of the winds, the shrieks of the drowning, the wailing of mothers, could not be represented. He also forgot that he had once brought scientific arguments to bear, so far as he could without coming openly into conflict with religious belief, to combat the theory of the Deluge. Any pretext sufficed now for calling up this picture of retribution, in which he found compensation for his despair and impotence and humiliation. He could not tear himself away from the subject; again and again he set out to represent it in sketches.

He drew a sky overcast with rolling clouds from which torrential rains were pouring. Flames descended upon an ant-heap of human beings in headlong flight; rocks burst asunder; city walls gave way under the pressure of falling earth; towers leaned drunkenly as the earth shook and heaved beneath them. Another sketch on the same sheet showed a cloud wreathed in flames suspended above a crater spitting fire, and from the opened earth spectral skeletons climbed up, with gravestones slipping from their backs as they raised their bony arms to heaven. In another sketch the flames from heaven chased fleeing manikins in whose midst there stood a man towering up, like a tree with storms raging about it.

The first sketches closely followed the text, as if Leonardo had set out simply to illustrate it. On one sheet he drew the hurricane he was describing, as it swept over the agitated waves on which the poor improvised means of floating were driven before it, or tore trees out of the earth and flung them after fleeing riders, or unhorsed the fugitives and tossed them into the air. As though he sought especially to impress this drawing on his contemporaries, with their cult of the classics, by elaborating his meaning in the fashion popular in the humanist circles of Rome, he drew gods of the winds with puffed-out cheeks among the heavy clouds, combining pagan symbols with his representation of the Biblical visitation. But he soon abandoned such facile devices, and he also cut adrift from his own narrative; ultimately his representation of the welter of natural forces became entirely dissociated from the petty existence of mankind. In the series of representations of the actual Deluge on nine sheets now at Windsor, he leaves the unchained elements to tell their own tale; as though his powerful imagination and artistic genius enabled him to make the disembodied comprehensible, he pictures the final stage of the destruction of the world as a battle between rushing waters and howling winds. Vast eddying currents of water beat against splintering basalt cliffs and rebound from them; the picture is filled with the turmoil of raging waters. A wind-tossed group of trees in the foreground is the only living thing left in the sunken world. A cyclone descends upon a city like a vulture on its prey. Torrential rain streams from piled-up clouds; a cliff falls apart, and rocks breaking from it are falling on the ruins of towers and on toy houses that sway and totter as the flood sweeps against them.

On another sheet Leonardo shows floods sweeping past a wooded hill, tossing uprooted trees before them as though they were straws; each tree is turning in its course in a vain struggle against the current that is sweeping it away. Somewhere between earth and heaven there had once been a mountain city; the curtain of dense clouds lifts for a moment to reveal its utter destruction. A fortress built by man on a tall spur, impregnable against any human attack, is now being overwhelmed by enormous cataracts of water, which are falling inside its girdle of ramparts. The water sweeps away towers and bastions as though they were dust, plunging them into the flood that rises from below.

On another sheet a solitary tree still stands against the power of the elements, wildly torn to and fro by the wind; it clings desperately to a rock, but the whirling water is sucking it down with its rock, which is already separating from it. Already the earth is saturated with water; it spits towering pillars of water against the threatening clouds, and caught up in these whirling pillars are wretched remnants of what once were human possessions. The sea itself sends its foam-crested waves up to the skies, low skies that are sinking toward the earth. Clouds and sea are wrestling together. In this hand-to-hand struggle of the elements the last trace of life has disappeared, and only horror remains, alone in space.

As soon as all is swept away, destroyed and swallowed up, the interior of the earth breaks open and throws up vast basalt blocks and streams of water like tongues of flame; angry waves hiss past the cliffs as though the earth were advancing with clenched fists against the heavens, which, themselves grown to a sea in turmoil, are crashing down on the bursting crust of the earth. Amid this chaos a poor little patch of bushes is being tossed on the edge of the waters, solitary reminder of a vanished life.

While Leonardo was dreaming his dream of the annihilation of mankind, more vividly and compellingly than any who had preceded him, while he was seeking refuge from a joyless and narrowed reality in his powerful visions of disaster, the material basis of his existence collapsed. In March 1516 Giuliano de' Medici died, and with him the last of the hopes with which Leonardo had come to the Eternal City.

He hesitated for a while, with his old unwillingness to move; he clung to vague prospects, perhaps only in order to justify his remaining in Rome to himself. He may still have had some hope of winning the competition for the façade of San Lorenzo; he thought, perhaps, that this time he might triumph over his old rival Michelangelo. Many years later Vasari was told that Leonardo left Rome when Michelangelo was given that commission— so great was the enmity between the two. It may have been no more than studio gossip, the outcome of the tendency of his contemporaries to dramatize; but there is this to support the story, that Leonardo's departure took place at the time of a short visit Michelangelo made to Rome; he may have left the city rather than run the risk of a meeting.

Before he left Rome Leonardo, like all men who are leaving the scene of long activity, meditated on his past life. He thought of the outset of his career, when Lorenzo de' Medici sent him to Milan with the silver lute, and that meaningless gesture from a powerful man was lit up as he recalled it by the glamour of the opportunities which came later and to which it had led. He thought of Lorenzo with emotion—and then he thought of the cold hostility of the son of Lorenzo who was now Pope, the Medicean Pope whose elevation was supposed to herald the coming of the golden age of the arts. Lorenzo's help and Leo's coolness may have sprung from the same source, indifference and incomprehension; but Leonardo did not know this when he was comparing his past success with the collapse now of all his recent confident hopes. Filled with bitterness, the bitterness of an ageing man with little time left in his life for remedying plans that had failed and years that had brought no fruit, and weighed down with a hopelessness that redoubled the burden of his years, Leonardo, who had never complained to a patron, now complained to himself of the injustice done to him, as he cut himself off finally from Rome and from his own country: "The Medici made me and broke me"—*li Medici mi crearono et distrussono*.[64]

CHAPTER NINE

"I Can Go On"

L'un caccia l'altro.
Per questi quadretti s'intende la uita e li studi
umani.

One pushes down the other.
By these little blocks are meant the life and the
efforts of men.

(G, 89 recto.)

FRANCIS I was fond of masked balls and fancy dress, and of imagining himself in strange characters. "The king and certain young noblemen who were his favourites and confidants used to disguise themselves almost every day in strange and motley garb, with masks over their faces; they would ride through the city and go to some house to play and amuse themselves." [1] The king was also fond of tourneys with knights magnificently arrayed. As a child he had galloped on spirited horses, and as a boy he often returned home in rags from romps with his companions. He liked now to vie with the best horsemen of his court, on foot and on horseback, with lance and sword.

The king and his princes and knights and the young noblemen in his entourage had all fought hard battles on fields that had run with blood; they had all seen the glazed eyes of the dying, and had themselves bled from almost mortal wounds; they had had in their nostrils the stench of putrefying corpses and had chased off the swarming flies from their own oozing blood. Yet when they met together for pleasure and recreation they entered into mock battle on equal terms, using up their surplus energy in attacks on imag-

Francis I of France. By Jean Clouet

Charles VIII of France. Artist unknown

inary enemies and combats for imaginary possessions. They would
fight over a woman's glance or a woman's love already bestowed,
and set out to emulate the knights of the Round Table of whom
women dreamed.

His people were ready to credit the king with any qualities he
liked to assume. When he galloped up on his impetuous horse his
tall, robust figure was all radiance and resonance, with jangling
harness and equipment, and feathers and ribbons flying, and the
gleams of gilded steel vying with the sparkle of his jewels. This
excess of ornamentation, of gold chains and feather tufts, spoke of
the appetite for magnificence of a young man who was not yet satiated with his new power and unaccustomed luxury. But his proud,
handsome face countered any impression of theatricality. It was
the face of a man predestined to power, a long, tense face with a
prominent, square chin and a long, narrow, sharply projecting
nose; the small eyes, slightly slanting and not deep-set, were filled
with a luminous brown. In this kingly face men saw the reflection
of a boundless ambition and an ardent pursuit of greatness. They
credited Francis with sincerity and with high ideals in spite of his
hedonism. They credited him with the will power expressed in his
tense, twitching cheeks, and the sensitiveness shown by his fine
nostrils, as well as the love of power implicit in his large, white,
excessively beringed hands, and the consuming sensuality revealed
by his warm, gurgling laugh.

Like the king and his companions, the ladies of the court were
fond of dreaming that they lived in an imaginary world of austere
surrender to imperishable emotions; while they went from one
crudely sensual adventure to another, they dreamed of deeds of
heroism, of the joys of the bucolic life, and of great sacrifices and
abnegations in the service of an indissoluble union of loving souls
untainted by the deceits of this world. Men and women of the
court freely indulged in the pleasures of the senses, but felt a constant longing for the things that endure. They expressed it in lyrical outpourings (for everyone at the court dabbled in versification), and in a continual change of scene from one end of the
country to the other, with endless masquerades and festal processions and tourneys.

Leonardo da Vinci, whom the king had brought with him from

Italy to be his court painter, has captured this world of restless desire in his sketches for masked costumes and festal processions. His papers of the period are covered with legendary figures, god-like youths on the uncertain boundary between dream and waking, between legend and reality, solidly planted on their muscular legs and with an elastic vigour in their long, firm thighs. Their broad breasts are covered by scale armour, or by chain mail that falls jaggedly over their narrow hips; golden chains or cords are wound round their slender bodies. But, firmly as these young heroes seem to be planted on earth, they have the appearance of being lifted up by invisible wings, and in the current set up by their flight the long ribbons flutter and the flame-like fabrics of their sleeves twist and turn, and their hair floats out behind them in a bright cloud or in beribboned plaits or coils sweeping past their shoulders. Sexless faces look out from the clouds and twists of hair, with short noses running straight from the forehead, and the trace of a fleeting smile round their disproportionately small mouths—half archangels in armour, half dreaming shepherds, holding their lances with their delicate fingers like osier switches. They are dream figures dreamed for others, but yet are strangely akin to the youths' profiles which Leonardo had been absent-mindedly sketching since his own earliest youth.

While he was taking in the strange world around him, with its restless search for amusement and for escape from the tedium of existence, he drew, as though under the influence of this environment, the strange vision, now at Windsor, which shines as a beacon pointing the way to a world of unfathomed mystery. The drawing, begun as a sketch for a masked costume, developed for him into a symbol. With faint, hazy strokes of the crayon he captured an ethereal female form apparently floating on the clouds of her diaphanous drapery. The woman's keen eyes are fixed on the observer as though summoning him to follow the imperious beckoning of her hand. Her round face, with irregular, mobile features, is grave and tense, but around her almost lascivious mouth there hovers a smile. This dancing woman's figure is delivered up to every sensual pleasure; her long, firm legs are laid bare by the folds of the drapery as far as the voluptuous curve of the hips. Meanwhile, following a mysterious call, she strains to escape from her own pleasure-seeking, her eyes opened wide in the throes of unearthly longings.

Leonardo's dancing woman may have come from the paradise of sensitive souls described by the poetess Anne de Graville, the king's friend, that dreamland in which the women, like this dancer, went barefooted and clad in diaphanous drapery, gliding over the soft cool sward to the sounds of gentle music—sentimental nymphs fleeing from the amorous illusions and the false vows of the world they lived in. But Leonardo's dancer does not seem simply a creature of contemporary poesy. She looks like a very definite personality, as though this irregular face had not merely been dreamed but seen, as though this design for a costume was based on a familiar model whose features it almost involuntarily retained.

The drawing is the loveliest of this late period of Leonardo's life. If the dress was really designed for one of the ladies of the king's immediate entourage, it may have been intended for Marguerite de Valois, the sister of Francis I. At the beginning of October 1517 the king held a great festival in the castle of Argenton, where Marguerite was living, bored and discontented, with her unloved, ill-tempered husband, the duke of Alençon. Capable and witty, alert and of sound judgment, with a passion for culture and a surprising capacity for the most austere intellectual exercises, the cleverest (said an Italian ambassador) not only of the women but of the men of France, Marguerite de Valois might have played a decisive part at the French court and in European politics if she had been of less passionate character. Like the sunflower, which she took as her device, Marguerite turned all through her life to a distant light. She spent herself in vain emotions, in mourning for the young hero Gaston de Foix, and in passionate admiration of her brother and anxious concern for that sun of her existence. As though this self-surrender and self-sacrifice, against her better judgment and against the instinctive resistance of her strong personality, were the inescapable law of her life, she returned from every transitory amorous adventure to emotional dependence on some object of her care, until in the end she found the way to God in a faith that demanded martyrs, and, looking back on her youth, lamented that she had "loved her soft and fragile flesh more than her salvation."

From time to time her "sun on earth," her "only kingly king," remembered her longing for him, and then he would invade his brother-in-law's home. He would invade it with plenty of clamour and brilliance, as if he wanted to smash its grey existence into little fragments of brightness.

At the beginning of October the royal cavalcade burst into the castle of Argenton; behind it came uncounted wagons, loaded with carpets and tents and with surprises for the coming festivities. A tourney took place in the castle courtyard, to which the knights were summoned by a horn—it might have been Roland's horn of ivory summoning Charlemagne's paladins. The first horsemen in the land took part, but, reported an Italian who was present, the most Christian king surpassed them all.

The tourney was followed by one of the very popular stage-plays, crude and coarse, like the naïve woodcuts sold at village fairs. But the action in the play betrayed the hand of a master who was acquainted with all the mechanical devices of the stage. A hermit with a long flowing beard suddenly appeared in the centre of the banqueting-hall, knelt before the king, and recited a long speech, full of well-turned phrases, in which he said that God had revealed to him, the pious hermit, that the king had come into the world with the mission to rescue humanity from a savage lion. The hermit was still describing the prowess of this man-killer, which no one had ever dared to face, when the lion itself appeared in the open door and paced, with stiff, mechanical steps, between the courtiers, who involuntarily shrank back. Its mane was bristling and its jaws opened so threateningly that there were cries of horror from the women, a mild horror combined with pleasurable anticipation. The king rose to his full height, broad-shouldered and well balanced on his slender hips, an entirely convincing young hero at the approach of a real peril. He took firm hold of the magic wand which the old man handed him, and three times struck the monster. At that the huge body of the lion split in two, and from its opened breast, turquoise-blue inside, the colour of the French arms (turquoise-blue for love, whispered the courtiers), white lilies fell slowly at the feet of the king, with a silken rustle amid the breathless silence.

The story of this spectacle was spread far beyond the borders of

France. An Italian present, the monk Anastasio Turrioni, sent a full description of it to young Federigo Gonzaga, who had inherited from his mother Isabella d'Este her curiosity about any strange happening in the world. Yet he made no mention whatever of Leonardo as organizer of it all. But the young Francesco Melzi had accompanied his *maestro* to France, and faithfully recorded Leonardo's belated triumphs. "Leonardo Vinci," wrote the painter Lomazzo many years later, "according to what his pupil Signor Francesco Melzi related to me, once made a lion, with wondrous artifice, and sent it pacing through the banqueting-hall up to Francis I, king of France; the lion then stood still and opened its breast, which was full of lilies and other flowers."

As always at this period of insatiable pleasure-seeking, the festivities in the castle of Argenton continued for several days. On the following evening, at the end of a sumptuous banquet, when the guests were heated with wine and in boisterous mood, there suddenly appeared in the wide-opened door of the banqueting-hall a knight clad entirely in gold, Guillaume de Montmorency, holding high in front of him, like a sacred relic, a huge golden heart. He deposited his burden before the king, and the heart opened as the lion's breast had done; from the shimmering background of the golden interior there emerged a hybrid creature, poised on a globe. One side of its body was stout and robust and clad entirely in golden armour; the other side was lean and in rags, with tears running down its dismal cheek. The king's guests speculated on the meaning of this strange dual creature. Did it represent the double aspect of love, with happiness and suffering grown up together, or covetousness, *cupidine,* made up of false splendour and bitter repentance, as Frate Anastasio Turrioni wrote to young Federigo Gonzaga?

In this case also the Italian said not a word, in his full description of the event, about his great fellow-countryman. But in Leonardo's papers there is an allegorical drawing which seems to be closely connected with this cryptic symbolical figure. "Pleasure and pain"—*piacere e dispiacere*—"are represented as twins," writes Leonardo in explanation of the drawing, "since there never is one without the other; and as if they were united back to back, since they are contrary to each other. . . . Clay, gold . . . If you choose pleasure, know that he has behind him one who will deal you tribulation and repentance. . . . They exist in the same body because they have the same basis, inasmuch as the origin of pleasure is labour and pain, and the various forms of sinful pleasure are the origin of pain." [2] This is the austere sermon which the old man conveyed to the young people in the midst of their revels. And these young people with their reckless and unrestrained gaiety were strangely accessible to the warning from this wise man from abroad. He stirred up their secret longings, the doubts they did not want to admit, their anxiety in face of the transiency of good fortune. They were profoundly moved by the deep earnestness of this symbolic message. "Many ladies," adds the conscientious Italian observer, "made gestures revealing grief or penitence."

2

The young king was particularly responsive to Leonardo's moral teachings. Many years later Benvenuto Cellini heard him say, in the presence of the king of Navarre and the cardinals of Ferrara and Lorraine, that "he did not believe that any other man had ever been born into the world who knew so much as Leonardo, not only in sculpture, painting, and architecture, but still more in that he was a very great philosopher." Francis I was no profound thinker or searcher after eternal verities. In his childhood he had spent much more time tearing about on horseback than bending over his books; living amid the narrow conventionality of a minor court, with the precarious glories of a presumptive heir whose hopes of the succession to the throne were threatened by each one of Anne of Brittany's many pregnancies, he had sated his hunger for life with erotic adventures which had yielded material for popular lampoons and for the gossip and ribaldry of the stage-plays of the Place Maubert in Paris. He had whiled away his period of anticipation by wasting his energies in a reckless practice of the arts of seduction, instead of jealously saving himself for a great future. But, idolized and spoilt in his childhood by his passionately ambitious mother and his self-effacing, adoring sister, he had accumulated a great store of self-confidence, and with it, in place of depth of comprehension, he had an unerring instinct—the instinct that falls more readily than reflection into sympathies and antipathies, hatred and love. He also, like all who have had great expectations which were less than certainties, had a well-developed sense of opportunities and a keen eye for anything that could be serviceable to him, even if he did not appreciate its full value.

In this instinctive knowledge he sought Leonardo's friendship when they met, either at Bologna or Milan, sought it with the charming lordliness his sister so admired, and with the radiant smile that parted his lips as though expressing the desire to please the friend of the moment above all others. Leonardo, disheartened by long years of vain waiting, worn out with plans that had come to nothing and researches that seemed unending, embittered against his fellow-countrymen, and anxious about his means of existence, was particularly accessible to these advances; but he would have been unable to resist them even in happier circumstances, as he had been unable to resist Cesare Borgia and other invaders of his studious solitude. He had always been reluctant to move, even from a house in which he was a guest, and always inclined to put off the moment for departure. He had been a great traveller in imagination, but had always hated the pother of even a temporary transplantation. Now he was old and ill, but for the first time in his life he brought himself to go right away from his native soil, never to return.

Francis I was not descended from patrons of the arts, and had not the much-lauded artistic knowledge of the Medicean Pope; but he showed due honour to his guest and furnished him with the means of existence with royal liberality. Benvenuto Cellini stated that the king allowed Leonardo 700 crowns a year; the court account books show annual payments to Leonardo of 1000 *écus de soleil* (gold crowns), with a pension of 400 crowns for Francesco Melzi, "the Italian nobleman in the company of the said Maistre Lyonard," and a single payment of 100 crowns to "Salay, servant of Me Lyonard de Vince . . . for his services."

About this time, at the end of 1516 and the beginning of 1517, the king made frequent visits to Amboise, and he settled the old *maestro* in the neighbourhood of his palace. It was at Amboise that Francis had spent his youth, amid certain humiliations but with great hopes, and he still thought of it with the sentiment to which he was prone; later, for a similar reason, he avoided it. Amboise had been the favourite residence of Charles VIII. The castle rose frowning above the peaceful Loire like the realization in stone of some dream of that fantastic dreamer. Its round battlemented towers spoke still of its original purpose of defence of the plains beyond; the bastions extended grimly from the thick ramparts at the steep entrance. But once the visitor had passed on horseback or in his carriage through the entrance tower and had reached the winding drive within, he saw in the buildings that covered the summit the meeting of two worlds. The rectangular chapel of St. Blaise on the edge of the ramparts, the castle church of St. Florentin which formed the centre of the great complex of buildings, the Gothic turrets with their finials, which stood above the ogive windows like frozen flowerstalks, and the tangle of Gothic ornamentation, all belonged to the world which Charles VIII had abandoned when he experienced the revelation of the new art. Charles himself appeared now above the porch of the chapel of St. Blaise, sculptured in relief, kneeling with Anne of Brittany at the feet of the Madonna, with a broad cloak over his narrow shoulders and a heavy crown on his over-sized head, his thin hands devoutly folded, in the primitive realism of all the church porches of his country, symbol of an age that was passing.

But Charles had brought new life to Amboise. Though at Fornovo he had lost countless wagon-loads of booty, as well as pictures of women conquered or coveted, he had saved enough from his lost provinces for other wagons to come day after day to Amboise, loaded with sculpture and pictures, carved fireplaces and marble panelling, fragmentary foreshadowings of a new artistic outlook and new ideas of form. In addition to these specimens he had admired and torn from their environment, Charles VIII had brought from Italy craftsmen he had seen at work, gardeners from Naples who made gardens in which, as he wrote, only Adam and Eve were wanting to complete an Eden; architects (*deviseurs de bastiments*, "building devisers"), sculptors in marble, "alabaster turners," velvet weavers, jewellers, and many others, "to build and work to his order and pleasure in the Italian fashion." When this daydreamer, perhaps imagining that he was passing through a triumphal arch, knocked his head against a lintel and died, and Louis XII made new plans of conquest, realistically and with due thought, building and carving *à la mode d'Ittalie* began anew at Amboise; the Gothic masonry with its ogive windows was replaced by Renaissance façades, smooth as parchment; and with the Gothic turrets still pointing aloft from the gables great horizontal bands were carried along the broad surfaces, accentuated by the strong rectangles of broad windows.

The Italians brought over by Charles throve in their new home, and many of them returned to Italy and came back with their families. Louis XII brought more Italians to Amboise to work *à son devis et plaisir*. Leonardo's most famous predecessor at Amboise was the old monk Fra Giocondo da Verona. The round carved keystone of the arch supporting one of the towers shows a fat face framed in a rectangular, patriarchal beard, which resembles the traditional portrait of the learned monk, and a Renaissance building known as the Hôtel Joyeuse is traditionally regarded as his residence. In addition to architects, painters, and sculptors, skilled craftsmen of every sort came from Italy to Amboise, and the court account books show payments to an Italian "jeweller and inventor skilled in hatching and breeding chickens," a velvet cutter *"à l'Italienne,"* "makers of perfumes and musk waters," and a parrot-keeper. When Leonardo reached Amboise his ears were greeted by the familiar Italian speech amid the unintelligible foreign sounds, and his eyes by familiar motifs in the midst of the strange architecture; and in the Italian garden, laid out by the Neapolitan Dom Pacello, the first mulberry tree had been acclimatized and the first oranges had ripened to gold amid the metallic green of their foliage.

Yet he found an entirely strange world around him. Even the sky was different from the familiar sky of his own country, a paler blue, as though it were faded, with shimmering clouds passing by like white fabrics. The flat countryside was an insubstantial green, as if the trees and bushes were translucent; and the broad river reflected its islands with their undergrowth so faithfully on its slow-moving silver surface that land and water passed imperceptibly into each other. The soft porous stone used for building in this country seemed also to absorb the light, and even when the sky was overcast a gentle silver glow still went out from the castle of Amboise. The air was soft and mild, neither crystal-clear as in Florence nor blue and shot with gold as in Lombardy, but filled with hazy gleams that made all the shadows seem faint and transparent and smoothed away the sharpness of the outlines.

But on this alien soil and beneath this alien sky Leonardo found a home such as had seldom been granted to him in his life. He had almost always and everywhere been a guest, with someone sharing his quarters who had as good rights there as he had, if not better; scarcely ever had he been privileged to feel that he was master of a house of his own, in which he could do what he liked. He had had to be careful to close every door in order to shield himself from the curious and the intrusive, and when he left his room to go for a walk in a park or garden he had met unknown faces on his way, some looking searchingly at him, some watching open-mouthed to see what strange thing he was doing. At Amboise Francis I assigned him the villa of Cloux as residence. In this year 1516 the villa belonged for a time to the king's brother-in-law, the duke of Alençon; then the duke's mother acquired it. It was a house in a style unfamiliar to Leonardo, of brick with white sandstone borderings, and with the pointed roofs which had particularly struck him in the architecture of the country.

The house had been built for himself by Etienne le Loup, Controller of the Household to Louis XI, in the unobtrusive style that fitted the discreet servant of a great lord. It could not go beyond a certain degree of ostentation, and yet it was built to meet the needs of a powerful man, and so it had developed into a compromise between the style of a gentleman's house and a palace. The covered passage above the entrance, which formed the oldest wing, was a modest construction of beams and brickwork, but in the tower, which commanded a wide stretch of country, the owner had placed a mortar, by the king's permission, as if for the defence of a manor of which he was lord.

Then Cloux fell to the Crown, and under Charles VIII a chapel was built within the right angle made with each other by the two wings—a chapel with an octagonal turret, such as was indispensable in any nobleman's residence. Niches surmounted by finely carved baldachins, ogive windows with angular sections, balconies covered with Gothic ornamentation, loose scrollwork over the door-lintels, delicate turrets and gable-ends, broke up the plain brick surfaces, and the light attracted by the porous carving fringed the building with a faint silvery radiance.

The little château was closely surrounded by trees that isolated it from the world. But it stood at the top of a gentle rise, so that it had a view above the treetops over wide stretches of verdant country, merging in the distance in the silvery lustre of the horizon. Between the meadows flowed the Amasse, a tributary of the Loire, its shallow banks thickly covered with shrubs and boughs that stretched far across its slow-moving waters, so that in the sunlight it became a long zigzag line of emerald. A mill driven by an artificial waterfall stood in the grounds of Cloux, and also a large and strongly built dovecot. The stillness was broken only by the rippling of water from across the meadows, the fluttering of the wings of the doves, like the tearing of silk, and the exultant trilling of countless birds. After his long pilgrimage Leonardo had at last reached a haven of peace.

3

The rooms of the little château were large, with whitewashed walls; the tall narrow windows had bull's-eye panes of glass through which the light came in a mild and tempered radiance. Soft shadows, which the strongest sunlight could not chase away, played among the strong beams of the ceiling. On these alien walls, in the unaccustomed light, hung pictures which Leonardo had brought with him, loved friends from which he would not part. Mona Lisa's portrait was there, although it no longer belonged to him; Francis I, with his weakness for lovely women even in picture, had bought it. (The astute Bibbiena, well aware of this weakness, had ordered from Raphael a portrait of the beautiful Giovanna d'Aragona, in order to assure the king's lasting favour with this present.) The completed painting—completed at Milan with the aid of pupils—of the *Madonna with Saint Anne* shone in the gentle light, the flickering blue depth of its background standing out from the whitened wall as though a window had been thrown open to reveal the rocky, aqueous landscape that Leonardo loved.

Even more part of himself than the smile of Mona Lisa and the light of a familiar landscape was the compelling summons in the eyes of *Saint John the Baptist*, the last picture he had been painting before age and illness overtook him. The vision Leonardo captured in this late half-length of the Baptist had first appeared to him more than ten years earlier; in the midst of the chaotic fury of his sketches for the battle of Anghiari he had conceived the idea of the quietly radiant face of the young John. At that time the figure had the semblance of an Angel of the Annunciation, with one hand pointing obliquely across his breast to indicate his tremendous message. The small sketch which Leonardo had then jotted down, as a first idea crossing his mind, he must have worked into a design on the lines of which he or his pupils had completed the picture of an Angel of the Annunciation, for Vasari saw in the palace of Duke Cosimo de' Medici "the head of an angel who is raising one arm aloft, foreshortened from the shoulder to the elbow as it comes forward, while the hand of the other arm overlaps the breast."

But Leonardo was not concerned merely with the many intersecting lines and the strong contrast of light and shade which struck Vasari in the picture. As though he wanted to indicate the imparting of some mysterious message, to discover the definitive representation of a summons of great importance, he tried again and again to give shape to his youth with the pointing hand. The popular Florentine tradition or a chance commission gave him the idea of painting a Saint John; and now he could no longer escape from the vision, as though he had at last discovered the great mission of his life.

He made several half-length sketches of the saint, which his pupils industriously copied. But he went on meditating on the representation of a Saint John, with the soft beauty of an ephebus, still half-angel but already half-Adonis, until he saw him as the magnificent naked figure of a youth in the midst of a rich, open landscape. The picture set out to represent the Preacher in the Wilderness, tired from his wanderings, resting by a jutting crag. But he painted neither the Christian martyr nor the preacher of

Saint John the Baptist

Bacchus

repentance, but a young god with the full sense of his powers and his triumphant beauty. The glowing naked flesh of this Saint John had never experienced a shudder of contempt for his own body. These round, soft, almost feminine shoulders had never bent under the burden of doubt, the slender, shapely hands had never beaten the broad, swelling breast in the fervour of mysticism and penitence; the thin and springy legs had never knelt in the sand of the wilderness, and these dancer's feet had never been grazed by sharp-edged rocks.

Nor was John surrounded by an arid, hostile wilderness in which his cry would die away unheard. The soil on which he stood was covered with a profusion of grasses and plants, a bit of earth full of the same life-force as this magnificent young god. The cold, dark crag against which he leaned threw up his rosy, full-blooded flesh; the rugged surface of the stone contrasted with the soft glow of his velvety skin. This crag, in whose crevices the roots of the trees that had scaled it had hooked themselves, a triumph of fertile and inventive nature over an inhospitable soil, resembles the rocks from which the figure of Leda is rising in the copy in the Spiridon collection. But the two pictures are connected not only by the similarity of the immediate background, and the similar glimpse of a wide landscape, before which stands a single young tree like a shout of exultation ringing through a blessed world; the treatment of the naked bodies, the play of light and shade, and the atmosphere suggestive of restrained desire, is common to both. It is as if Leonardo had had the heretical idea of making his Christian saint a pendant of his heathen Leda, setting alongside the hymn of voluptuous womanhood the glorification of the perfect body of a young man.

After Leonardo's original, or after one of the sketches, one of his pupils, in all probability Cesare da Sesto, painted the picture now in the Louvre. As with another of his pictures, Cesare da Sesto must have called in the painter Bernazzano to help him, for the treatment of the plants is characteristic of Bernazzano. In spirit and in composition the picture is entirely Leonardo's. Until the end of the seventeenth century it was included in the royal collection as a Saint John in the Wilderness. Then came an age that was scandalized by this young naked hero with a cross in his hand;

a leopard's skin was wound about his slender hips, a vine-wreath placed on his long, curly hair, the cross to which he so emphatically points was replaced by a thyrsus, and in the eighteenth century the Louvre picture was named a Bacchus—as uncritically as if the scant clothing provided and the slight change of attributes were enough to convert Leonardo's not entirely convincing saint into a genuine pagan god of pleasure.

The radiant ephebic beauty of the Bacchus-John had survived unmolested in the half-length which Leonardo had taken with him on his journey to France. It was a late work and not entirely his own; apparently his powers were no longer equal to its completion. The hand of a pupil, perhaps the timid art of Melzi, is betrayed in the metallic sheen on the tangled locks, the hard lines of the eyelids, and perhaps even the overpainting of the background, for a copy by Salai now in Milan shows the saint in front of an opening revealing a distant landscape. Yet Leonardo showed it to his visitors at Cloux as his own work, for in spite of the small weaknesses it represented to him the last important example of his art that he had to bequeath. As if he knew or felt that he was painting the last work of his life, he brought to this picture his ripest experience, and incorporated in it every tried device of his mastery in achieving the utmost intensity of effect.

The small space of this picture is filled with life and movement; and though it is only the half-length of a youth turning round a little, infinitely more seems to be suggested. The strong forward reach of the arm is the controlling feature of the composition; the diagonal of the forearm with the hand pointing up is emphasized by the parallel of the sloping shoulder. The upper arm, which is swung forward gently and loosely from the shoulder, cuts almost at right angles across the two diagonals, and this quadrilateral, placed entirely within the picture, and reinforced by the shaded shoulder and the hand reaching forward out of the dark, opens up a depth in the picture which attracts and holds the observer's attention.

The thrust of the diagonals continues up to the saint's head, the slight inclination of which is paralleled by the outline of the upper part of the body, as though this upward movement from left to right on one side of the picture were meant to be firmly balanced by the rising of the diagonals from right to left. The mathematically calculated composition carried through by Leonardo in his *Saint John* has sacrificed nothing of its customary rigidity, though it is particularly complicated and elaborated, as if he still felt all his old enjoyment in the geometrical transformations which had occupied him for so long in the past.

The wealth of intersections is equalled by the wealth of light and shade, as if Leonardo had at last attained his ideal of plastic arrangement, the full intensity of relief. The invisible source of light is the main dramatic factor in this picture. The head, slightly inclined, emerges from the shade into the bright light, throwing a shadow itself on the breast, above which the arm and the pointing, brightly lit hand are poised. Strong light pours down on the young man's broad forehead, which is surrounded by a tangle of rather too exuberant locks. The bright light streams along the straight bridge of the nose, which continues from the forehead without any indentation; there is a concentration of light on the high cheek-bones, and light plays round the smiling mouth. The sockets of the eyes, long and almost rectangular, are in shadow; out of this warm darkness the saint's glance falls earnestly on the observer, with the urgency of a personal summons. The heavy, sensuous eyelids are half closed, as though to capture a smile. Yet in these eyes that follow the observer there is an insistent appeal, in which blessedness and sorrow are mingled. This urgent appeal is seconded by the smile round the moist, feminine mouth, a rather too intimate, too pressing smile, one that knows the weaknesses and the frailty of men, a seducer's smile that in the act of allurement tastes the fruit of possession. That smile hovers in the shadows of the full cheeks, sets the fine nostrils vibrating in pleasurable anticipation, and nestles exultantly in the dimples of the square chin.

Not one of the Greek gods, not the triumphant Apollo Belvedere, not Apollo Sauroktonos, the lizard-killer, with the coquettish bend in his soft, feminine hips, is so filled to the brim with pagan voluptuousness as this youth whom Leonardo presented as the Baptist. Half-man and half-woman, related to every one of the figures which Leonardo had furnished with their immortal appeal in the past, to the eyes of Mona Lisa, the moist lips of the angel of the *Madonna of the Rocks,* the voluptuous flesh of the *Leda,* sexless and yet strangely exciting, it emerges as the last vision conjured up by one who was dead to earthly lusts and whose hand had begun to fail.

Even more perturbing than the saint's actual form is the message he has to convey. The meaning gesture of his pointing hand, the dialectical gesture of the steeply raised index-finger, of which Leonardo was so fond, directs the gaze to the scarcely distinguishable cross in the background, lifted gently like a flowerstalk by the left hand. The cross is there to interpret the meaning of the smile and of the summons in the almond-shaped eyes, that sensuous smile, that summons to earthly bliss or perdition. It hovers, alien and almost distressing, over the youth's figure with its soft, light-drenched surfaces of naked flesh. Yet in this picture, in which everything is deliberate and intentional, like the last will and testament of a man in full possession of his mental faculties, the symbol of the cross is no mere concession to tradition, made with almost cynical indifference. The cross stands spectrally in the shade like a warning of the death that lives in the heart of enjoyment, the doom that lies in wait for all who prosper on this earth, the nearness of desire to dissolution.

Thus did the ancients picture Death, as a tempter offering bliss, as the last illusion of the desire that is in men—as a beautiful youth with a smile that is a lie, a youth under whose silent tread the torch of life is extinguished.

Was Leonardo familiar with the Greek tradition, or was he, in his pagan worship of beauty, so near to the Greek spirit that in the evening of his life he had the vision of this young, sexless god with the sign of the cross as an eternally smiling warner of man's end? To his contemporaries, at all events, living as they did under the spell of the reawakening of the ancient sense of beauty, and inspired more or less consciously with the idea of a conciliation of Plato with Christ, the message of this Saint John, who could be turned so easily into a Bacchus or an Apollo, seemed unmistakable, and they took the picture as it stood, without any puzzling over its meaning, as an unsaintly saint who spoke not to the soul but to the senses.

4

About this time, in October 1517, an Italian cardinal, Luigi d'Aragona, saw this painting in Leonardo's studio at Cloux; he and those who were with him simply accepted the fact that it represented John the Baptist as a youth. The cardinal was staying at Amboise on his way through France, and had made a point of visiting Leonardo. He was a man of cultured and luxurious tastes, with a genuine love of music, and was reputed a liberal patron of the arts, but in Rome he does not seem to have taken any particular notice of Leonardo; no mention of his doing so by Leonardo or by any of his contemporaries is on record. But a fellow-countryman who enjoyed high honour abroad, and who had been granted a small château as his residence by the king, was entitled to the courtesy of a visit: he had now become a "very distinguished painter of our day," *pictore in la età nostra excellentissimo.*

It fortunately happened that the cardinal had brought with him a young secretary, Antonio de Beatis, who had a full appreciation of the cultural value of travel, and who kept a conscientious record of everything that seemed to him to be worthy of note. Of those who met and talked with Leonardo, Antonio de Beatis was the last to take the trouble to write an account of the meeting, and to him posterity is indebted for the principal account of the great artist in his last years. Leonardo met others of his fellow-countrymen at the French court, but this visit, or the opportunity it afforded of a long talk with men with a knowledge of art, seems to have given him special pleasure, for he spoke freely and had many things to say about his life, as is usual with men who feel their isolation. Antonio de Beatis listened and looked on attentively, and while he was scarcely alive to the importance of the occasion he noted down everything with the very useful particularity of a matter-of-fact person.

The travellers found themselves in the presence of a very aged man, certainly over seventy, thought Antonio de Beatis. So soon had Leonardo become old, so worn out was he with never-ceasing mental strain and exertion, although he was no more than sixty-four. His illness, too, which had at last got the better of his great powers of resistance, made him seem much older than his years. A stroke, severer than the first warning attack at Rome, had crippled his right hand, which now hung heavily and lifelessly at his side. The cardinal's secretary knew nothing of Leonardo's left-handedness, and assumed that he could no longer paint but only instruct others. He looked at the pictures which one of the pupils, from the Milanese (was this Melzi or Salai?), *chi lavora assai bene,* who was doing quite good work, was painting under Leonardo's guidance; and he looked with great interest, as though the circumstances had given them particular value, at Leonardo's own works shown to the cardinal, the *Saint John,* the *Madonna with Saint Anne,* and a third which had a history, "the portrait of a certain Florentine lady, painted from life at the instance of the late Magnifico Giuliano de' Medici."

Had the visitors seen a work no longer extant, the portrait of a woman whom Giuliano de' Medici had loved, a portrait of which by some strange chance the gossips of the Florentine studios had never heard; or was it the *Mona Lisa?* This is much more probable. The portrait of Mona Lisa went straight from Leonardo's home to the royal collections. Antonio de Beatis may have mixed up unrelated scraps of conversation, and may, in spite of his unimaginativeness, have guessed at a romantic relation between Mona Lisa and Giuliano: or he may perhaps have been in possession of little-known information about the secret of the *Mona Lisa,* and transmitted it to posterity in this discreet way.

Did Giuliano love Mona Lisa in her girlhood, before he was exiled from Florence? In the midst of his life of disappointing adventures and vain pursuit of elusive pleasures, did he think with longing of her, now that she was married to Messer del Giocondo, and had he commissioned Leonardo to paint her portrait? Or was the ill-balanced Giuliano, always in flight from reality, the connoisseur mentioned by Leonardo who had fallen under the uncanny spell of one of his pictures? Recalled for a moment by a passing allusion, these two persons who had been close friends of Leonardo, Mona Lisa and Giuliano, reappear in association. For a moment the two shades, the woman whose secret Leonardo tried for years to unravel and the ailing, understanding friend of whom death robbed him too soon, are conjured up in association with each other by a piece of tittle-tattle; then the secret of their relation, if ever there was any, is buried again. Antonio de Beatis said much too little, or a little too much, and the riddle of Mona Lisa is left more insoluble than ever.

But there was so much to see at Cloux that the conscientious scribe was put to it to assimilate and retain everything. Leonardo brought out of his chests countless sheets with anatomical studies, and spread them out before the cardinal, explaining each one— drawings of bones and muscles, nerves and veins, the joints, the intestines. His astonished visitors saw for the first time the internal structure of the human body, represented as it never had been before. Leonardo proudly mentioned that he had dissected more than thirty corpses in his life, corpses of men and women of all ages. He made a special point of this, as though he wanted to make the cardinal thoroughly realize the wide range of his studies, so that he might tell it in Rome.

Leonardo's eagerness in showing his treasures to the cardinal was partly the desire of an ageing man to communicate his knowledge, and partly a desire to secure an authoritative witness of his labours and achievements, who could pass on the news of them in the homeland that had given Leonardo such scant honour. Antonio de Beatis divined this, and added that they had seen all these things "with our own eyes," *oculatamente*. Leonardo spoke to the cardinal of his great treatise on water, of his various inventions, and of the machines he had made, and with a glance at his manuscripts he added that they had accumulated to "an infinity of volumes." "They are all written," reported Antonio de Beatis, "in the vulgar tongue, and if they come to light they will be valuable and very delightful."

The secretary's thoughts returned to the old *maestro* in Milan two months later, on his return to Italy. At the end of December he stood in front of the *Last Supper* in the church of Santa Maria delle Grazie, and looked with emotion at that "most excellent" work. But already the process of decay had set in, and he asked himself whether the damp that was breaking through the crevices in the walls was responsible or whether some mistake had been made. The masterpiece was peeling away in the artist's own lifetime. Leonardo must have seen the damage during his last stay in Milan, and with his expert knowledge of defects in masonry, on which he wrote a special treatise, he must have been unable to conceal from himself the fact that this one great completed work of his was steadily and irreparably disintegrating.

His masterpieces destroyed or decaying, his vast knowledge unutilized, the immense mass of scientific material he had been collecting all his life preserved only in chests and boxes, in incomplete records written in a secret script and, in their existing form, quite inaccessible to mankind—"if they come to light," wrote de Beatis, and Leonardo began to ask himself whether they ever would come to light. He no longer nursed the illusion that he could complete his many works for publication in his lifetime. He began to admit that he had attempted a superhuman task, to realize that he was defeated. He knew the forces that had defeated him —the wearing struggle for existence, the maze of chance influences and events that pull a man this way and that, the arbitrariness of fate.

Sunk in thought, he mechanically drew on a sheet a series of little rectangles, each one of them symbolizing a particular aspiration or high intellectual enterprise. He drew them first upright and then falling down on one another like a child's bricks knocked over. "One pushes down the other," he wrote beneath the drawing; and with the hopelessness of one who bows to the inevitable, who has capitulated before the blind arbitrariness of fate, he added in explanation: "By these little blocks are meant the life and the efforts of men." [3]

5

The blind life-force that brought down the stones of his life's work now bore the features of Francis I, handsome, elongated, tense features whose youthful freshness as yet showed no sign of the flabbiness and coarseness of later years. This life-force looked challengingly at Leonardo out of its slightly oblique eyes, and smiled at him with its ingratiating, wooing, commanding smile. Again and again the young king burst in on the quiet of Cloux like a tornado

—graciously but inexorably upsetting everything, as inexorably as life itself. The king was possessed by a restlessness of spirit that drove him from place to place, as though he were not yet used to the endless opportunities opened up by his own power, and constantly feared missing something that was going on somewhere else at the moment. He seemed unable to endure any environment that had lost its novelty. The court had always to be ready to start off, to pack and go at any moment; special wagons were kept loaded with travelling equipment, carpets, tapestries, all the requisites of the luxury on which the king insisted even if he put up for the night at some remote country château. A special army of servants kept everything ready for immediately setting off post-haste along the highways when the king's restlessness began to show itself.

A path leads over the hills from Amboise castle down to Cloux, with a hand-rail which was set up at one time for the king's children and their nurses, to prevent them from slipping on the steep incline. Francis I often took this path in order to have a talk with Leonardo—a talk in which, like all superficial men, he would be a bad listener. With the quick perceptions and facile emotions that took the place in him of depth of understanding and acquired knowledge, the king was eagerly—too eagerly—receptive of the information which Leonardo tried conscientiously to pass on to him. This information, so painfully acquired by the older man, the young king would consider he had grasped long before Leonardo had finished his careful explanations. The king was less interested, indeed, in the accuracy or completeness of his grasp than in the stimulus provided for his own mental processes. He enjoyed being able to discuss all sorts of things of which until lately he had had no notion, and he also enjoyed hearing his own voice, with an inner applause of which he had an inexhaustible supply.

In these long talks with Leonardo, in which Francis I was able to feel that he excelled himself, the restlessness that continually pursued him was stilled for a while; but Leonardo's leisure for work was destroyed the moment the royal caravan invaded Amboise with its noise and bustle. The young king, spoilt and inconsiderate, monopolized Leonardo's time; perhaps he thought he was doing the old artist a kindness in enabling him to share the brisk and varied life of a young ruler. "And inasmuch," wrote

Benvenuto Cellini, "as Leonardo possessed so vast a genius in such abundance, having also some knowledge of Latin and Greek, King Francis was most strongly enamoured with his great virtues, and took such pleasure in hearing his discourse that there were few days on which he parted from him." So Cellini learned, years later, when he came to the French court. But he also caught a faint echo of the old man's complainings about the way he was hindered from completing his works by this masterful royal admirer, and he sensed the grief with which Leonardo saw the last of his powers being uselessly frittered away: "Such were the causes of his being unable to bring to completion his wonderful studies, pursued with such diligence."

Rome had had no adequate tasks to offer Leonardo; Francis I overloaded him with commissions. Full of energy himself, and anticipating a long and active life, Francis liked to get the most out of himself and everyone else. He would hatch vast plans, which would interfere with one another; he was content if he kept himself and everyone else thoroughly busy. Leonardo himself had all his old readiness for splendid dreams and vast plans, and it was stimulated by the king's unceasing flow of ideas; but in these dreams there was now an undercurrent of apprehension; time was passing, was slipping through his hands, and he saw the end inexorably approaching. Yet his habit of attempting the impossible was so deep-rooted that he still could not resist the fascination of great projects, as though even now he had not learnt by bitter experience what was practicable and what was not.

Amboise Castle, with its confusion of incongruous styles, unified only by the gentle glow of the sunlight on its fair white stone, disturbed Francis's newly awakened artistic sense. On his triumphal march through Italy he had seen princes' castles and private palaces of unified design, brought into existence by the controlling genius of some master of the new age. He determined to have this castle pulled down and a new one built *à la mode d'Ittalie*. Leonardo entered into the king's idea with an enthusiasm that had in it an element of desperate resolve, like a last love or a last hope. He had built so many palaces on paper, had planned whole cities at his desk, his papers were filled with projects beyond counting, and still he had not given up the hope of seeing his ideas at last realized in stone. Perhaps his opportunity had at last come for putting to use his wealth of experience, and for providing humanity with a better environment than that with which his contemporaries had had to be content.

He and his young king were united in their new ideas of comfort and convenience, in their need, which their contemporaries found it difficult to understand, of cleanliness and hygiene, and their sensitiveness to the roughness around them. Things that had disturbed Leonardo in Italy, he found still worse in France. Italians travelling through France, themselves cleanly in their habits and proud of it, complained again and again of the stench that poisoned the atmosphere even in the most magnificent courts, and the lack of cleanliness even of the highest in the land. Handkerchiefs were almost unknown; courtiers blew their noses between their fingers. One of the many observers in the service of Isabella d'Este reported to his mistress, who was much above doing without a handkerchief and liked to be reminded of the fact, that the French ladies "are rather filthy, with a little itch on their hands and certain other deposits of filth"—*un poco sporche, con un pochetto di rogna alle mane et cum qualche altra compositione di spurcitia.*

With Francis I there came into court circles a new mode of living, or, as it seemed to contemporaries, a new luxuriousness. The king's ample supply of fine linen and his quantities of embroidered handkerchiefs aroused general astonishment. His requirements for his living quarters, and for the beds he slept in, were regarded as the whims of a very spoilt young man, and one more example of his wild extravagance.

Leonardo thoroughly enjoyed showing Francis I how easily the drawbacks of living quarters of the old style could be removed, and not only more comfort provided but more security for human life. His plans for the reconstruction of Amboise—the plans of a man who was often charged by his contemporaries with too easily losing sight of realities—were directed primarily to practical improvements. The great rooms intended for balls and festivities were to be placed on the ground floor, for, he said, "I have seen many rooms collapse and bury numbers of dead." For the same reason, every wall, however thin, was to have its foundations in the earth or resting on well-supported arches; Leonardo may have been thinking here of the Vatican loggias hastily built by Bramante, which very soon developed dangerous fissures. He also went carefully into the question of fire prevention. All timbers—beams, oaken chains, and wall supports—were to be bricked in, to prevent any conflagration from reaching them. Leonardo proposed to combat evil smells by a variety of special devices. He proposed to install a large number of closets, all on the same side of the castle, connected together and provided with flushing channels inside the walls and ventilating shafts reaching up to the roof; and as people are apt in carelessness to leave doors open, counterweights were to be fitted to keep the doors automatically closed.

He seemed to be insisting that a château should be above all a pleasant and comfortable residence; only after dealing with all these practical matters did he pass on to the question of architectural design. In order to give the building its full effect, he proposed that there should be a large open space in front of it. The inner court was also to be very spacious, and surrounded by an arcade. It should extend, he considered, at least to half the length of the façade, and he calculated its dimensions at 160 feet in width and 240 in length. He took account of the king's interest in games, and arranged for a large sheet of water in which tourneys and water sports could take place. This idea seems to have surprised and greatly interested the king; Leonardo suggested that the jousters should fight one another from boats.[4]

While Leonardo was dealing in endless detail with the plans for the future castle of Amboise, Francis I was pushing on energetically with the work on the castle of Blois, which had been begun when he ascended the throne. At the time of Leonardo's arrival in France, the French architect Jacques Sourdeau was at work on Blois Castle. He was already building in the popular Italian style, closely following the designs of Italian palaces, probably working to plans prepared by a *deviseur de bastiments,* one of the architects whom it was then customary to bring in from Italy. They were paid specially, so that their names should not appear in the court accounts, and they are consequently now unknown. Sourdeau was doing good and conscientious work at Blois on the new principles. The new wing which he built contains all the elements of High Renaissance art, which had found ready appreciation in France. Blois Castle would have been just one of the many Italian palaces scattered over Europe, a notable transplantation of a foreign art, if its remarkable openwork spiral staircase tower had not suddenly been added, to make it unique. It was not unusual in France at that time, and especially in Brittany, to build a spiral staircase of stone or wood within a house, turning more or less closely on its axis; Leonardo's former patron Florimond Robertet had one in the magnificent house he built for himself at Blois after Lombard models. But the architectural form of the staircase at Blois is entirely unique. It looks very much as if someone had come when the building was finished, and, finding that it was no longer possible for him to give it a flight of broad Italian steps leading up to the entrance, had hit upon the idea of splitting the façade in the middle (for originally the staircase was in the centre of the wing), in order to build out from it this virtually independent openwork staircase tower. It is an unparalleled piece of architectural audacity, such as only one who possessed great influence and was regarded as an unrivalled master could venture on. It owed its form to no conventional architectural principle; it had taken its model from nature, rising organically like the spiral of one of the conch shells which the Italians meet with at every step on their north-western shore, whereas they were unlikely to be familiar to dwellers in the heart of Touraine. A curious feature of this staircase of Blois is that it turns left, as though it had been designed by a man who was naturally left-handed, and who at this time no longer had the use of even his right hand.

The man who not only had often given close attention to the forms of shells, not only loved all winding and intertwining shapes in nature, but was better able than any other to work the soft stone of these stairs into the semblance of smooth leaves, was living at this time in close proximity to Blois Castle, riding along the high-road to Blois, as his own records show. Yet, while every indication and every psychological probability argues for Leonardo's active participation in the designing of this staircase, no report, no note of his own, no sketch in his papers connects him with it. Was it a simple chance that this unique structure at Blois was erected in his time? Did the French architect get some suggestion for it from him? Or, with Leonardo's chests heaped up with projects that came to nothing, has there disappeared, by the caprice of fate, every trace of the one architectural masterpiece he actually brought to completion?

The new castle of Amboise, with its modern sanitary arrangements and its pool for medieval games of chivalry, also remained no more than a project. The young king was full of ideas, and made many demands on the *maestro,* but he quickly tired of past ideas and threw them over for new ones. He came and went with his big train of followers, and the old man with his crippled right hand, which could no longer hold the reins, had to go to and fro with the king, at the mercy of bad roads and rough conditions, spending the nights in primitive tents or in hastily prepared quarters in castles or hunting lodges.

On one of these journeys—to the royal hunting lodge of Romorantin—Leonardo put forward his plan, a bold one for his day, of constructing movable houses, their parts being made in the towns and rapidly put together wherever they were wanted, with the aid of a few wooden connecting pieces. These transportable houses, he added, could be used by some of the country population when the court was absent.[5]

In the summer heat and in the fogs or icy winds of winter, these journeys along the rutted highways were particularly trying for the older and less robust of the entourage, and Leonardo found grateful supporters when he suggested to King Francis that a water route should be established between the royal castles. He proceeded to make a close inspection of the course of the Loire, its bends and branches, the islands in mid-stream, and the rate of flow at low water and in flood.[6] If the Beuvron, a tributary of the Loire, were regulated and led into a canal, a connexion could be made with the Sauldre near Romorantin. "If the affluent of the Loire were turned with its muddy waters into the river of Romorantin, this would fatten the land which it would water, and would render the country fertile to supply food to the inhabitants, and would make a navigable channel for merchant shipping." [7]

The river (Beuvron) he added, would deepen and cleanse its own bed with its increased flow, and so would protect the country from flooding; he quoted the ninth section of the third book of his treatise on water, in which he showed that the faster the current the deeper a river will scour its bed. In order to secure a more rapid flow, he proposed to place movable floodgates—"as I arranged in Friuli," he wrote. The resulting falls had a double advantage, not only keeping the river clear but driving mills erected beside them.

Leonardo proposed a further connexion, beyond Romorantin, of the Sauldre with the Cher. He found that the bed of the Cher was lower than that of the Sauldre; but "where one river by reason of its low level cannot flow into the other, it will be necessary to dam it up, so that it may acquire a fall into the other, which was previously the higher." [7] He drew the plan of the weir, in which the turbid water would be led away to drive four mills, while the clear water of the centre of the stream descended near Romorantin into the Sauldre. With his alert eye for detail he recommended that the retained water should be used for fountains to be placed in all the squares at Romorantin.[7] The work "may be done by the inhabitants," he added, "and the timber of which their houses are built may be carried in boats to Romorantin." [8]

From Romorantin Leonardo went through the Sologne. Unlike the prosperous Touraine, he found it to be a poor and depressing region, with wretched peasant hovels, and subject to frequent inundations that destroyed human lives and the crops; in summer the marshland sent out pestilential vapours. He had planned the draining of the marshes of Piombino for Cesare Borgia, and he had elaborated a vast plan, which had not been treated quite seriously, for averting the peril from the miasma of the Pontine Marshes; now he hoped to reclaim this foreign soil, where he had been so hospitably received.

On his return from Romorantin to Amboise after parting from the king, he dreamed of further schemes for regulating and constructing waterways. On the same sheet on which he wrote of his return to Amboise, he made a rough pen sketch of the connecting waterway he proposed, as though he could not drag himself from the subject.[9] Once again he drew the course of the Loire and of the Cher, and considered the situation of the towns of Blois, Amboise, Tours, and Montrichard. At the end of the direction taken by his great waterway he wrote the Italian name of Lyons—Lione. He dreamed of a blue ribbon of water passing through wide regions of this country, past cities which were but names to him, through districts he had never seen, as far as Italy—a real bond between France and his own country, which had known France mainly as the sender of invading armies over the mountain passes. Pursuing this great dream, he wrote at the end of his notes: "You will make a plan," *Farai saggio.*

6

The times encouraged these peaceful dreams. After the Italian wars of ambitious adventurers, glorious or disastrous essays in expansion, had come the respite of fat years filled only with memories of past glories or dreams of new ones. "The kingdom of France," writes a contemporary chronicler, "was in great peace and tranquillity; at this time there was neither noise nor rumour of war or divisions or partisanship. Merchants journeyed with their goods in great security, both by land and by sea, and French, English, Spaniards, Germans, and all other nations of Christendom, traded peacefully together, which was a great mercy granted by God to the Christian people." Leonardo, who had so often been caught up in wars and revolutions, struggles for power and campaigns of conquest, lived now in his last years amid a peace and security that seemed to be impregnably established.

The peace of the country appeared to be doubly assured now that the succession to the throne was guaranteed. Plain, deformed little Queen Claude had borne Francis two daughters, of whom one had died at two years of age; then, at the end of February 1517, the long-desired son was born, and the king felt that he had been confirmed as his country's ruler by the decree of the Almighty.

A year later the baptism of the Dauphin was celebrated "with the utmost triumph"; the Pope himself stood godfather. But Francis seemed still to think that the great event had not been sufficiently honoured, and he resolved to have a second celebration. This took place simultaneously with the festivities in honour of the marriage of the Pope's nephew, Lorenzo de' Medici. Lorenzo had been sent by the Pope to be his proxy as godfather; but the Medici were not in the habit of conferring honours for nothing, and the real object of Lorenzo's visit to France had been to find a bride. All he wanted was to settle down with a woman of property in a small realm of his own, where he would be safe from the fickle favour of the Florentines. Scion as he was of an imperious race, son of an insanely arrogant father and a cold, ambitious mother, in Lorenzo the appetite for power seemed to have been stilled together with the passions and the passionate spirit of his ancestors. Warned by the example of his father's stupid and aggressive vanity, he resolved to live without giving cause for offence, "in order to afford an example of living with clean hands." His reflective temperament protected him from indiscretions, and he proved far superior to the rest of his family in uprightness and firmness of character, although he had neither their fire nor their talents nor their energy.

Lorenzo's mother and the unscrupulous Pope had procured for him, by force and treachery and ingratitude toward tried friends, the duchy of Urbino; and the king of France had now been seeking for years in the French court for a bride for Lorenzo. For a while Cesare Borgia's daughter was considered; that name was of evil repute, but it was not expected that it would offend the Vatican. The daughter of the wild and handsome Cesare was, however, small and ill-favoured, with a birthmark on her forehead and the misshapen nose of children with a tainted heritage, so that this clever and intelligent girl had the appearance of a dreadful example of the visitation of the sins of the fathers upon the children. After a long search a suitable party for the dowry-hunting Lorenzo was discovered in Madeleine de la Tour d'Auvergne, the daughter of Count Jean de Boulogne and Catherine de Bourbon.

In May 1518 the double celebration of the baptism of the Dauphin and Lorenzo's marriage took place at Amboise. Now that peace reigned securely, with no sign anywhere of any threat of war, a fictitious war was arranged as the chief attraction of this festival—"the finest tournament ever held in France or in all Christendom." A huge triumphal arch was built on the great square in front of the castle, bearing the king's favourite device, the salamander untouched by fire, with the motto *Nutrisco el buono, stingo el reo* ("I nourish the good and destroy the bad"), alongside the queen's emblem, an ermine, with the motto *Potius mori quam fœdari,* "Death before dishonour." Round the square were placed the platforms for arbiters and for ladies, "the gentle young ladies for the love of whom it is all happening." For the sake of his bride, "who was too much more beautiful"—*trop plus belle*— "than her husband," Lorenzo did his best in the tourney, but once more it was the king in his glittering gilt armour, with a storm-cloud of black feathers on his helmet, who carried off all the honours. The shouting spectators were quite unperturbed when on a Sunday morning a handsome young knight fell headlong from his horse, killed by a lance-thrust at his head.

The jousting continued for a whole week, and it was no more than the prelude to the main festivities. Early one morning, when the guests awoke, they found the castle square changed beyond recognition. Tall boards covered with painted linen had been set up all round it, to represent an embattled rampart with its turrets. Beyond the castle moat the painted scenery was continued on a wooden framework, representing massive bastions and grim towers; in between the towers and through the embrasures were to be seen the menacing barrels of guns. A whole citadel of wood and linen had sprung up in the night, a fortified city "true to life." Then there began a thunder of firing from towers and embrasures; the black mouths of the wooden cannon spat huge balls "as big as the bottom of a cask."

But the balls hopped merrily across the square; they were gigantic hollow playballs; "it was amusing to see the leaps they made," wrote the Seigneur de Fleuranges, who was among those present. Even the Italian guests, who had been rather spoilt in their own country, considered the spectacle "a novelty and very ingeniously carried out." Yet they did not say a word about their compatriot Domenico da Cortona, "valet de chambre and carpenter" to Anne of Brittany, who had erected the scenery, or about the actual organizer of this entertainment, who was manifestly a master in his province. Leonardo seems, for the last time in his life, to have placed at a ruler's service his great knowledge and skill in the military arts; but under the blue sky of Touraine the work of the inventor of tanks and shrapnel, flame-throwers and poison gas, ended in a peaceful parody of warfare.

Francis, however, and his guests took the game in dead earnest, as though the great cannon balls were sowing real death and the linen ramparts were of granite blocks. The king himself, his large, heavy figure made mountainous by his bulging armour, his long, square face within the shining helmet reddened with genuine fighting ardour, urged on his soldiers, exhorting them to do their duty and distinguish themselves in the sight of their ladies, and so to earn the favour with which they would reward the bravest. As he said this he looked across at the ladies' pavilion. But it was not the mother of the son he had longed for that his eyes so eagerly sought, not the little queen, already growing very stout, with her uncomely face, her fleshy nose, and her dull protruding eyes. At this double celebration the romance of Françoise de Foix, wife of Jean de Laval, Seigneur de Châteaubriant, had begun as a simple flirtation, later to end most tragically. But as yet Françoise knew nothing of the day to come when she would be abandoned and exiled from court, with some bad verses and a cynical "Requiescat in pace" as the king's last heartless attentions. She was sunning herself in the radiance of the king's young love; her dark eyes sparkled in her colourless face, and round her hungry red lips there played the confident smile of a woman who knew the power of her attraction.

Before the happy surrender of her eyes the fight for the stage town went on. The besieged soldiers, led by the duke of Alençon, made a sally from the fortress; and if the ramparts were no more than stage properties the hand-to-hand fighting was so real that there were footsoldiers actually killed and many wounded. "It was the most splendid combat ever seen, and the nearest to actual war," wrote the Seigneur de Fleuranges, friend of the king and playmate of his childhood. Fleuranges bore the scars of many wounds on his lean body, and his pale, twitching face bore the traces of the hardships of his last campaign, and of the warlike adventures of his own seeking which had earned him the nickname of "Le Jeune Adventureux."

The festivities at Amboise went on for weeks—weeks of excitement and high spirits, in which the young king kept his guests and his entourage continually busy with his many ideas and his restless pursuit of pleasure. Even Leonardo's peaceful home was drawn into the whirl of the royal merrymaking. One evening—it was now the nineteenth of June—Francis, who so quickly tired of his surroundings, brought his whole great company of guests to Cloux. In Touraine the warm June nights come slowly after the day, closing in as though reluctantly over the late glow; in a bright sky of the shade of frosted silver, copper streaks remain long after the sun has gone down. On this evening the guests, as they came down to Cloux by the hill path from the castle above, saw while they were still at a distance a strange radiance, as though white fringes of light shone above the dark walls surrounding the château. When they came through the arched entrance, they found themselves in an enchanted world. The square court of the château, sixty feet wide and a hundred and twenty feet long, was covered with a wooden flooring, on which carpets with the king's device were spread. Beyond this improvised ballroom was a colonnade whose white pillars of imitation marble were garlanded with ivy. Behind the pillars and above the colonnade was sky; not the Touraine sky of frosted silver but a deep blue sky, as though the guests had suddenly been transported to another clime and into broad daylight. Leonardo had stretched a dome of blue fabric over the full width of the court. In this artificial sky the stars twinkled, round its edge moved the planets, on one side was a bright sun and on the other a silvery moon.

Leonardo had no hesitation about repeating himself and reproducing his inventions of the Paradise festival, organized so long ago in honour of the unhappy Isabella d'Aragona. Those present thought they were witnessing a new and unique spectacle; even the Milanese Galeazzo Visconti was full of admiration of this "wonderful entertainment," at which "night seemed to have been chased away." He gave a full description of it, but, like all the Italians present at the French court, he made no mention of the host and organizer of the entertainment.

The magic night at Cloux brought the festivities at Amboise to an end. The king left Amboise, and Lorenzo de' Medici, pleased but exhausted by the excitements of the French court, returned to Italy with his "too beautiful" young bride. Soon after his return

Lorenzo, who had hoped for a long life of peaceful domesticity, fell sick of the malady which the Italians called the French disease. His young and delicate wife died in childbirth, and scarcely a year after the splendid festivities at Amboise Lorenzo himself, the great hope of the Medici, died in pain and misery. The baby Caterina, then only three weeks old, lived on, to survive not only her parents but her husband and her sons. The day came when, as Catherine de Médicis, queen of France, she visited the castle at which her parents' wedding had been celebrated with such magnificence.

7

After the guests' departure the peace of the hot summer days descended upon the little château of Cloux. The noise and bustle of the festivities and the clash of arms in the mock warfare gave place to a stillness in which all that was to be heard was the croaking of the many frogs in the early morning, the chirping of crickets in the white glare of noon, and the happy song of the birds. Leonardo returned to his desk, dismissing the memories of these weeks of wasted labour. Before the scaffolding had been taken down and the bales of painted fabrics rolled up, he had buried himself once more in his long-neglected volumes. He made the entry: "June 24, 1518, Saint John's Day, at Amboise, in the palazzo of Cloux," as if to mark a fresh start, and beneath it he wrote: *Io continuero*—"Now I can go on." [10] Filled with new hopes, he was making a last stand against the events that threatened to overwhelm him, a last challenge to his own fading strength. It might be that months and years of peaceful work lay ahead of him, that he would experience the happiness of further research, and the satisfaction of arranging and completing his collected works. It might be that he had in front of him a long period of peaceful and gradual approach to the end of his days. Life had dealt hardly with him, but he challenged it with that cry of hope—the last his papers showed, and a last declaration of his unconquerable will to work.

The warm and fragrant autumn, with the lavish glories of woods that flamed like gold and purple torches, was followed by a long

winter. The wind howled round the solitary château, fogs came
up in waves from the meadows like the breath of the ice-bound
earth, and a pale, diluted sunlight came thinly through the tall
narrow windows into the big rooms. In the huge fireplaces, like
little houses built in the walls, with roofs that projected into the
rooms, the thick logs flickered and crackled, mixing their red glow
with the pale winter light. The old man felt bitterly cold in this
winter in exile, and he wrapped himself closely in his good cloak
of black cloth with its fur lining.

He was surrounded by silence; the noisy, exuberant Salai had
apparently left France some time before this and returned to Italy,
where he built himself a house on Leonardo's estate. But all that
this solitary man still loved in this world was embodied for him in
the fine tranquil face of Francesco Melzi, who watched him full of
admiration and solicitude. Melzi must have felt that they had not
long to be together; he committed every detail of their existence
to his memory. Other loyal helpers were around Leonardo, caring
for him quietly and unobtrusively, in the way he liked—his servant
Battista de Vilanis, whom he had brought with him from Milan,
and a woman with the French name of Mathurine, who looked
after his household with the silent devotion he had received all his
life from the simple women of the people.

During this winter his strength seems to have been failing fast,
and he saw with a merciless clearness, which left him not the slightest possibility of self-deception, that his vital energy was fading
away. All through his life he had been unable to take due thought
for his own welfare; now he deliberately and carefully prepared
for his end. He took early steps to secure the king's permission to
make his own arrangements as to the disposal of his property, since
the French law laid down that the possessions of any foreigner dying in France reverted to the Crown. When the spring sunlight began to invade the rooms at Cloux and drive out the winter shadows, Leonardo realized that the time had come for him to make
his last dispositions; in his long sleepless nights of illness he had
thought out every detail. "In consideration of the certainty of
death and the uncertainty of the time of it," he sent on April 23,
1519, for Guillaume Boureau, the royal notary of Amboise, to take
down his will in the presence of witnesses.

In this hour of death in exile he put away from him every feeling of resentment, forgot the wrongs done to him, and was the more thankful for all the good things he had received from life. He put from himself the thought of his bitter controversy in the past with his brothers over the family inheritance; he forgot that he had never really been admitted to his family, and, except for his uncle Francesco, had never received any sign of affection from them; like a man of property conscious of his family liabilities, he bore in mind his "brothers in blood (*fratelli carnali*) domiciled in Florence," and bequeathed to them 400 ducats which he had deposited at Santa Maria Novella; later he added the bequest to them of his property at Fiesole.

His executor and the sole heir of his intellectual estate was the young man who was now the one human being to whom in his solitude he gave all his love. He did not forget in his will to mention Melzi's noble origin and give him his full title: "in remuneration for the services rendered by him in his kindness in the past" he bequeathed to "Messer Francesco de Melzo, nobleman of Milan," his whole artistic and scientific property—"each and all of the books which the said testator has at present and other instruments and portraits connected with his art and occupation of painter."

"To remunerate him for his salaries, vacations, and labours that he may have in the execution of the present Testament," Leonardo left to Melzi all the ready money in the house, and all payments due to Leonardo up to the date of his death from the king's treasurer. His clothing he also left to Melzi, except the "cloak of good black cloth lined with fur" and a cloth cap, which Mathurine received for her faithful services, with a final indemnification of two ducats.

His servant Battista de Vilanis was richly rewarded for his services. He received the rights granted to Leonardo by Louis XII in the dues for water taken from the canal of San Cristoforo, together with one-half of Leonardo's property situate without the gates of Milan. Leonardo placed Salai on the same footing as de Vilanis; both are called his servants in the will. Salai was left the other half of the Milanese property, on which he had already settled with his family.

The pale rays of the April sun that came through the long, narrow windows of Leonardo's bedroom, and lit up the sick man's bed, fell on a group of men in black priests' robes or monks' cowls. Apart from Francesco Melzi, who, as principal heir and executor, swore that "in his comings and goings he will say and do nothing contrary" to the will, the witnesses were all clergy—the vicar of the church of St. Denis at Amboise, two priests, and two Franciscan friars. It was strange company for a dying man who throughout his life had heaped scorn on the clergy as Pharisees and, as Vasari put it, preferred to be a philosopher rather than a good Christian. But Leonardo wanted to die at peace not only with men but with his God. "In the end, when he had become an old man," writes Vasari, "he was ill for many months; and, finding himself near to death, he turned diligently to the study of things Catholic and of our good and holy Christian religion, and then, with many tears, he confessed in penitence; though he could no longer stand upright, he then, supported in the arms of his friends and servants, got out of bed in order devoutly to take the Holy Sacrament."

He commended his soul "to God our Lord and Master and Ruler," *nostro Signor Messer Domine Dio,* "to the Glorious Virgin Mary, to Monsignore Saint Michael, and to all the blessed angels and saints of Paradise." Then he arranged, in meticulous detail, for his burial ceremonies. High mass was to be read three times in the castle church of St. Florentin, where he wanted to be buried; and on the same day thirty low masses in the churches of St. Denis, St. Grégoire, and the Franciscans, were to be said, in the light of many thick wax candles, whose weight he carefully prescribed: ten pounds. His body was to be carried from Cloux to Amboise in the presence of the whole chapter of the church of St. Denis and of the Franciscans; his coffin was to be borne by the chaplains of the castle church, and behind the coffin sixty poor people were to walk, each carrying a burning torch. The distance was not great, and Leonardo, calculating economically even for his burial, added that after the ceremony the unburnt torches were to be distributed among the four churches.

How far away was the time when he had satirized the simple people who light the way for those who have entirely lost their vision! * But, meticulously as he ordered his burial, Leonardo wrote not a word to say how he should lie in state or what should be the design of his monument. Apparently this dreamer of princely mausolea and vast memorial statues had not given any thought at all to the marking of his own last resting-place with sculpture, carving, or inscription. All earthly vanities had fallen away from him at this hour, in which he gave thought to his duties to the few people who had been with him in life, and to the salvation of his soul, that he might die at peace with the world beyond.

But now he waited in vain for the long rest, the deep sleep to follow his day's work. Sickness and old age had come upon him too soon, and he could not reconcile himself to death; his premature end seemed to be robbing him of fulfilment. His dying was full of distress and torturing self-accusation. He reviewed his life and saw it as misspent and squandered, with nothing but fragmentary achievements from all its immense effort. There was nothing on which he could dwell with pleasure; in all he stood condemned.

Francesco Melzi witnessed the despair of Leonardo's last hours, and his accounts of them to his nearest friends must have reached Vasari's ears. Vasari put his own construction on this grievous end. He described Leonardo as lamenting on his deathbed, full of repentance, that "he had offended against God and men by failing to practise his art as he should have done." Vasari, for whom there was nothing that mattered outside art, nothing, indeed, outside painting, and to whom Leonardo's enthusiasm for research was a sin against his creative genius, interpreted those dying regrets as regrets for unpainted pictures.

Thus was the grandest effort ever made by any man to explore and interpret the universe defeated by this man's mortality. His unique career, a lifetime devoted to research in every field of knowledge, ended without the publication even of fragments of his conclusions. Mankind was to have to discover afresh what he knew already, to explore afresh the paths he had trodden and mapped, to fall into his errors after he had recognized them, to struggle out of the traps he had evaded.

---

* *I semplici popoli porteran gran quantità di lumi per far lume ne' viaggi a tutti quelli che integralmente hanno perso la virtù visiva.*

This he knew in the hour of his death, when the tears ran down his lined and lifeless face, the most poignant tears of impotence ever shed by any man over his past abundant powers.

In the silence and solitude of Cloux, in the apprehensive silence that falls on rooms which death is about to enter, Leonardo fought his last fight to the end. On May 2, 1519, his gaze rested once more on those around him, on the familiar face of a young man whom chance had attached to him and on that of a hired servant who had gone with him into voluntary exile. Then his eyes closed for ever, eyes that had looked out in vain over the Land of Promise.

8

He departed from life unnoticed, an old man dying away from his country and his disciples. The only mourners who followed his coffin were a few simple people who had lost a good master, and the paid poor of the village, who waved their torches and made their lament for a stranger of whom they knew nothing except that he had directed that they should each be paid seventy Touraine sous.

But because this was so obscure an end to so great a life, Leonardo's contemporaries embroidered the story of his last hours, and Vasari describes how the king himself was present during the death struggle and supported the dying man's head with his own exalted hands. "And his spirit, which was most divine, knowing that it could have no greater honour, breathed its last in the arms of that king." Francis, however, was far away from Cloux when Leonardo died, for on the preceding day Claude of France had borne him a second son, at the castle of Saint-Germain-en-Laye.

When Francesco Melzi conveyed the news of Leonardo's death to the king, Francis, who in his young life had known only life's pleasures and not its burdens, was overcome by deep grief; he wept for a man whose death made a gap in his eager, restless existence. Melzi later told his friends how overcome the young king had been at Leonardo's passing; and as these were the tears of a king, Lomazzo devoted to them some feeble lines:

Pianse mesto Francesco re di Francia
Quando il Melzi che morto era gli disse
Il Vinci. . . .

(Francis, king of France, wept in sorrow when Melzi told him that Vinci was dead.)

To the young Francesco Melzi, though this was the expected and natural death of a much older man, it came as an irreparable loss, and his grief was keen and profound. He knew, too, how much poorer the world had become through this loss. In his sorrow the handsome, gentle, lighthearted youth gained a new dignity, and found eloquent words to describe his own bereavement. It was nearly a month after Leonardo's death before Melzi at last brought himself to send the news of it to the brothers in Florence. "To me he was like the best of fathers," he wrote, "for whose death it would be impossible for me to express the grief I have felt; and so long as these my limbs endure I shall possess a perpetual sorrow, and with good reason, since he showed to me day by day the warmest love and devotion. It is a hurt to anyone to lose such a man, for nature cannot again produce his like."

These were the words of a young man of scarcely more than average gifts, but they worthily express the loss humanity suffered in the death of Leonardo—*la perdita di tal uomo quale non è più in podestà della natura.* But fate pursued Leonardo with destruction even after his death. A storm soon broke over the alien soil in which he rested, over the quiet castle chapel of Amboise, where he lay between the remains of French princes and their courtiers, as though he were one of them. Under the banner of their confession brothers fell upon one another in enmity, sacrificing their earthly existence for the sake of their eternal salvation. Churches were stormed, tombstones smashed, the dead pulled out of their coffins; between the gravestones fresh blood trickled down to the corpses. The castle of Amboise became the scene of fighting and of the great assize held upon the leaders of the new movement, until the luminous white stones were soaked in blood and terror.

Even if Leonardo's grave escaped destruction in the Huguenot wars, his remains were accorded no more than a temporary immunity. The storm of the French Revolution attacked the princely graves anew, churches were destroyed and their dead disturbed once more in the name of new rights. Little is known of the fate of the chapel at Amboise in the time of the great Revolution. But if Leonardo's forgotten grave also weathered that storm, it fell victim at last to the picks and hatchets that brought down the crumbling, weatherworn chapel, no longer safe to use, in 1808. The vandals who did the work of destruction sold the marble slabs and gravestones and even melted the lead of the coffins. The chapel became a heap of ruins on the castle hill, on which children played with the bones of the dead, playing ball with the grinning skulls until they disintegrated. One night a gardener collected the scattered remains and buried them together in the dark. Destroyed and scattered like so much of his own work, Leonardo's mortal remains were mixed with those of other men and with the soil beneath the sward of Amboise park, to be trodden upon for decades thereafter by indifferent visitors.

In the age of the Romantics, who knew what they owed to their dead, a French poet, Arsène Houssaye, made a search for the dead and forgotten Leonardo. Among skeletons of unknown persons he found the bleached bones of a tall man, and a large skull which might be assumed to have once contained the brain of that great genius. Houssaye reverently collected together the remains that seemed to belong to this skeleton, and buried the corpse in the chapel of St. Blaise, the chapel above whose porch little King Charles VIII prays in his great crown, with his thin hands folded. On the simple gravestone which now covers the mortal remains perhaps of Leonardo, perhaps of another person, an inscription was placed which continues for his death the uncertainties about his life, delivering these remains to the same play of beliefs and suppositions to which his own career and works are subject:

> Under this stone
> rest bones
> collected during the
> excavations in the former
> royal chapel of Amboise
> among which it is surmised
> that there are the mortal remains
> of Leonardo da Vinci

*(Sous cette pierre
reposent des ossements
recueillis dans les
fouilles de l'ancienne
chapelle royale d'Amboise
parmi lesquels on suppose
que se trouve la dépouille
mortelle de
　　Léonard de Vinci)*

NOTES

BIBLIOGRAPHY

INDEX

Notes

Abbreviations used in referring to Leonardo MSS:

A, B, C, D, E, F, G, H, I, K, L, M—MSS in the library of the Institut de France. Published by Ravaisson-Mollien, Paris, 1881–1891.

An.A, An.B—anatomical MSS A and B, in the Windsor Castle library. Published by Theodor Sabachnikoff, Paris, 1898, and Turin, 1901.

Ash.—MSS in the library of Lord Ashburnham, Ashburnham Place, Sussex.

B.M.—the MS marked Arundel 263, in the British Museum. Published by Danesi, Rome, for the Reale Commissione Vinciana, 1923–1930.

C.A.—the *Codex Atlanticus*, in the Ambrosiana library, Milan. Published in facsimile in eight folio volumes, for the Reale Accademia dei Lincei, by Ulrico Hoepli, Milan, 1894–1904.

C.V.—*Codice sul Volo degli Uccelli e Varie Altre Materie (Codex on the Flight of Birds and Various Other Matters)*, in the Royal Library, Turin. Published in facsimile by Sabachnikoff, Paris, 1893.

Leic.—MS in Lord Leicester's library at Holkham Hall, Norfolk. Published by Gerolamo Calvi, 1909.

Ludwig—the edition of the *Trattato della Pittura (Treatise on Painting)* published in three volumes by H. Ludwig, Vienna, 1862. Based in part on the MS *Cod. Vat. Urbinas 1270*, in the Vatican Library.

Mz.—MS in the possession of Count Manzoni, Rome.

O—MS in the library of Christ Church College, Oxford.

Q.A.—*Quaderni d'Anatomia*, anatomical drawings by Leonardo, published in six volumes by Vangensten, Fonahn, and Hopstock, Christiania, 1911–1916.

S.K.M.—MSS in the Forster Library, Victoria and Albert Museum, South Kensington. Under publication by Danesi, Rome, for the Reale Commissione Vinciana.

S.K.M. II, III—the second and third MS volumes at South Kensington Museum.

T.P.—*Trattato della Pittura (Treatise on Painting)*.

Tr.—MS in the Trivulzi Palace, Milan. Published by Luca Beltrami, Milan, 1891.

W.—collection of drawings in the Windsor Castle library. A *Catalogue* by Sir Kenneth Clark, Director of the National Gallery, London, was published in two volumes (text and plates) by the Cambridge University Press in 1935.

W.L.—fragment of Pompeo Leoni's collection, in the Windsor Castle library.

I 2, 40 v. means the back (verso) of folio 40 of volume 2 of the MS I.

In general, numbers relate to folios; r. and v. mean recto, verso. Many of the folios of the *Codex Atlanticus* are in two or more pieces, and these are quoted as a, b, c, d. Thus C.A., 342 r.a. means the front (recto) of the first piece of folio 342 of the *Codex Atlanticus*.

The marks o and o' mean outside and inside cover of the MS quoted. Thus Mz. o' means the inside cover of the Manzoni MS.

CHAPTER ONE

1. C.A., 161 r.
2. Leic., 6 v.
3. B.M., 115 r.
4. B.M., 156 v.
5. B.M., 156 r.
6. T.P., par. 421.
7. C.A., 120 r.d.
8. C.A., 380 v.a.

9. B.M., 156 r.
10. C.A., 12 v.a.
11. G, 84 v.
12. T.P., par. 60.
13. C.A., 380 r.b.
14. S.K.M. III, 73 v.
14a. C.A., 76 r.a.
15. C.A., 4 v.b.
16. An.A, 80.
17. C.A., 9 v.b.
18. C.A., 12 r.
19. C.A., 71 r.a.
20. B.M., 156 v.
21. B.M., 155 v.
22. B.M., 156 v.
23. C.A., 71 r.a.
24. T.P., par. 58.

25. *Diario,* 24, 25.
26. C.A., 4 r.b, v.b, 34 v.a.
27. C.A., 9 v.b.
28. C.A., 34 v.a.
29. C.A., 56 v.a.
30. C.A., 40 v.b.
31. C.A., 50 v.a.
32. C.A., 28 r.b.
33. C.A., 34 v.b, 49 v.b.
34. C.A., 32 v.a.
35. T.P., par. 328.
36. C.A., 71 v.a.
37. C.A., 71 r.a.
38. C.A., 4 r.b.
39. C.A., 117 r.
40. C.A., 119 r.

CHAPTER TWO

1. G, 49 r.
2. C.A., 391 r.a.
3. B, 23 r.
4. C.A., 16 v.
5. C.A., 15 v.
6. B, 30 r., 21 r.
7. B, 59 v.
8. B, 75 v.
9. B, 33 v.
10. B, 55 r.
11. B, 56 r.
12. B, 64 r.
13. B, 59 r.
14. B, 50 r.
15. B, 37 r.
16. B, 31 r.
17. B, 67 r.
18. B, 51 v.
19. B, 10 r.
20. B, 24 v.
21. B, 33 r.
22. C.A., 2 r.
23. B, 32 v.

24. C.A., 317 v.
25. Tr., 68.
26. C.A., 324 v.
27. C.A., 344 r.
28. C.A., 324 r.
29. Tr.
30. C.A., 289 v.
31. C.A., 223 r.
32. An., 241 r.
33. C.A., 116 r.
34. C.A., 337 v.
35. T.P., Ludwig, par. 16.
36. Tr., 34 v.
37. Tr., 33 r.
38. C.A., 76 r.
39. Tr., 6 r.
40. C.A., 119 r.
41. Tr., 46 v.
42. An. IV, 184 r.
43. T.P., 33.
44. Tr., 39 v.
45. Tr., 41.
46. C.A., 145 r.a.

CHAPTER THREE

1. B, 28 v.
2. B, 4 r.
3. C.A., 270 r.c.
4. C.A., 303 r.
5. C.A., 76 r.
6. C.A., 65 v.
7. C.A., 394 v.c.
8. B, 53 r.
9. C.A., 89 v.
10. Tr., 17 r.
11. Plati Platino, *Epigrammaton* (1502).
12. B, 54 v.
13. B, 20 v.
14. C.A., 356 r.
15. C.A., 5 v.a.

16. C.A., 14 r.a.
17. C.A., 4 v.a.
18. B, 50 v.
19. C.A., 355 r.c.
20. C, 15 v.
21. C.A., 295 v.; B, 66 v.
22. B, 65.
23. C.A., 359 v.b.
24. C.A., 49 r.a.
25. C.A., 365 r.b; B, 71 r.
26. B, 47 v.
27. B, 52 r.
28. MS 2037.
29. C.A., 147 r.
30. B, 52.

31. B, 55 r.
32. Ash. II, 8 v.
33. B, 66 r.
34. B, 58 r.
35. C.A., 225.
36. C, 15 v.
37. C.A., 200 r.
38. C.A., 117 v.
39. C.A., 119 r.
40. C.A., 136 r.
41. Ash. I, 32 v.
42. A, 9 v.
43. A, 27 r.
44. A, 8 v.
45. A, 10 v.
46. C.A., 126 r.a.
47. C.A., 9 v.b.
48. O, 36.
49. H, 49 r.
50. C, 24.
51. C, 1.
52. C, 12 r.
53. C.A., 141 r.b.
54. C, 14 v.

55. B.M., 171 r.
56. C, 22 r.
57. C, 345 v.
58. A, 55 v.
59. An. I, 6.
60. B, 13 r.
61. C.A., 80 r.a.
62. C.A., 78 v.
63. B.M., 250 r.
64. B, 4 r.
65. I 2, 40 v.
66. An. II, 242 v (N).
67. C.A., 187 v.
68. C.A., 319 v.b.
69. B, 4 r.
70. S.K.M. III, 49 r.
71. A, 24 r.
72. C.A., 362 v., 1134 v.
73. C.A., 143 r.
74. C.A., 36 r.
75. I, 342.
76. C.A., 37 v.
77. C.A., 362 r.
78. C.A., 172 v.

CHAPTER FOUR

1. H, 88 v.
2. H, 44 r.
3. C.A., 48 v.a.
4. B, 69 r.; C.A., 281 r.b.
5. B, 36 v.
6. C.A., 41 v.a.
7. M, 53 v.
8. H, 95 r.
9. A, 55 v.
10. A, 55 v.
11. H, 77 r.
12. A, 56 r.v.
13. A, 59 v.
14. A, 60 r.
15. A, 55 v.
16. A, 56 r.
17. A, 34 v.
18. A, 28 v.
19. A, 21 v.
20. C.A., 153 v.b.
21. A, 1 v.
22. A, 33 v.
23. A, 43 v.
24. A, 4 r.
25. A, 22 r.
26. A, 52.
27. M, 44 v.
28. A, 36 r.
29. A, 31 r.
30. A, 47 r.
31. A, 35 r.
32. A, 30 r.
33. A, 35 v.
34. A, 57 v.

35. A, 15 v.
36. A, 45 r.
37. A, 61 r.
38. A, 9 v.
39. A, 61 r.
40. C.A., 249 v.a.
41. A, 60 r.
42. H, 100 r.
43. C.A., 126 r.a.
44. A, 20 r.
45. A, 42 v.
46. H, 84 v.
47. A, 59 r.
48. C.A., 316 v.
49. I, 107 r.
50. C.A., 380 r.
51. H, 3, 89 r.
52. C.A., 318 v.a.
53. C.A., 393 v.a.
54. C.A., 397 r.a.
55. C.A., 2 r., 2 v.
56. C.A., 2 r.a.
57. I, 48 v.
58. C.A., 291 r.a.
59. C.A., 195 r.
60. I, 58 r.
61. I, 57 v.
62. C.A., 308 v.
63. C.A., 335 v.a.
64. S.K.M. II, 2, 2r., 1 v.
65. T.P., Ludwig, 67.
66. T.P., Ludwig, 75.
67. S.K.M. II, 78 v.
68. C.A., 75 r.

69. G, 8 r.
70. T.P., Ludwig, par. 7.
71. T.P., Ludwig, par. 40.
72. T.P., Ludwig, par. 14.
73. Ash. I, 10 v.
74. T.P., par. 8.
75. T.P., par. 19.
76. T.P., par. 13.
77. T.P., par. 27.
78. T.P., par. 57.
79. C.A., 218 v.
80. Ash. I, 22 v.

81. T.P., par. 50.
82. T.P., par. 61.
83. K, 49 r.
84. T.P., par. 1.
85. An. IV, 163 v.
86. C.A., 284 r.
87. Leic., 4 r.
88. I, 34 r.
89. I, 28 v.
90. C.A., 104 r.b, v.b.
91. C.A., 230 v.c.
92. C.A., 247 r.a.

CHAPTER FIVE

1. C.A., 234 v.
2. C.A., 231 v.
3. C.A., 234 v.
4. C.A., 218 r.
5. B.M., 270 v.
6. C.A., 79 r.
7. B, 18 r.
8. B, 81 v.
9. C.A., 7 r.a, 386 r.b.
10. C.A., 333 v.
11. C.A., 33 v., 346 r.a.
12. Leic., 22 v.
13. C.A., 333 v.
14. C.A., 333 r.
15. B, 11 r.

16. C.A., 62 v.a.
17. T.P., par. 25.
18. L, 336.
19. L, 22 r.
20. L, 40 r.
21. L, 19 v., 20 r.
22. L, 91 r.
23. L, 6 r.
24. W., 12686.
25. L, 66 v.
26. L, 34 v., 35 v., 36 r.
27. K, 2 r.
28. L, 72 r.
29. L, 66 v.

CHAPTER SIX

1. C.A., 161 r.
2. C.A., 381 v.a.
3. C.A., 382 v.
4. C.A., 161.
5. C.A., 381 v.a.
6. B, 88 v.
7. C.A., 276 r.b.
8. B, 74 v.
9. B, 75 r.
10. B, 79 r.
11. C.A., 32 r.a.
12. Mz., 12 r.
13. B, 80 r.
14. B, 89 v.
15. C.A., 276 v.b.
16. B, 89 v.
17. C.A., 361 v.b.
18. B, 89 r.
19. B, 74 v.
20. C.A., 381 v.a.
21. C.A., 31 r.a.
22. B, 83 v
23. M, 13 r.
24. C.A., 161 r.
25. C.A., 302 r.b.
26. C.A., 45 r.
27. C.A., 1 v.b.
28. C.A., 8 r.b.

29. C.A., 131 r.a.
30. C.A., 210 v.b.
31. B.M., 169 r.
32. B.M., 113 v.
33. B.M., 114 v.
34. C.A., 398 r.
35. C.A., 289 r.
36. C.A., 45 r.
37. C.A., 284 r.
38. C.A., 46 v.
39. C.A., 108 v.a.
40. C.A., 293.
41. C.A., 73 r.
42. Ash. I, 4 v., 5 r.
43. C.A., 153 r.
44. Leic., 9 v.
45. C.A., 152 r.
46. Leic., 9 v.
47. Leic., 3 r.
48. Leic., 10 v.
49. Leic., 31 r.
50. C.A., 45 v.a.
51. Leic., 5 r.
52. Leic., 10 r.
53. Leic., 36 r.
54. C.A., 321 v.
55. Leic., 31 r.
56. Leic., 34 r.

57. C.A., 5 r.a.
58. Leic., 10 r.
59. Leic., 15 r.
60. Leic., 22 v.
61. B.M., 104 v.
62. Leic., 1 v.
63. Leic., 36 v.
64. B.M., 19 r.
65. B.M., 54 r.
66. Leic., 2 r.
67. B.M., 94 r.
68. C.A., 187 r.
69. B.M., 272 r.
70. C.A., 202 v.
71. C.A., 115 v.

72. C.A., 39 v.
73. B.M., 278 v.
74. Ludwig, 108.
75. K, 3 r.
76. C.V., 2.
77. C.A., 308 r.b.
78. C.V., 1 b (15 v.).
79. C.V., 8 (7) v.
80. C.A., 308 v.b.
81. C.V., 17 (16) r.
82. C.V., 7 (6) v.
83. C.A., 308 v.b.
84. E, 54 v.
85. Mz., 3 r.
86. Mz. o'.

CHAPTER SEVEN

1. C.A., 271 v.a.
2. B.M., 1 r.
3. C.A., 225 r.
4. C.A., 358 r.b.
5. An. I, 51 v.
6. An. IV, 167 r.
7. An. B, 10 v.
8. Q.A. I, 13 v.
9. An. II, 36 r (21).
10. Q.A. I, 2 r.
11. An. IV, 167 r.
12. Q.A. II, 1 r.
13. An.A, 1 v.
14. Q.A. I, 2 r.
15. An. IV, 21.
16. An. II, 76 v.
17. An.B, 217.
18. An.A, 18 r.
19. An.B, 29 r.
20. An.A, 15 v.
21. An.B, 2 v.
22. An.A, 18 r.
23. An.A, 13 v.
24. An.B, 12 r.
25. Q.A. II, 12 r.
26. Q.A. IV, 11 v.
27. An.B, 33 v.
28. Q.A. I, 4 r.
29. An.B, 34 v.
30. An. IV, 167 r.
31. An.B, 10 r.
32. An.B, 14 v.
33. An. II, 43 v.
34. Q.A. X, 21 v.
35. Q.A. IX, 7 r.
36. An. II, 202 r.
37. Q.A. V, 7 r.
38. S.K.M. III.
39. Q.A. II, 7 r.
40. An.B, 2 v.
41. An.B, 13 r.
42. Q.A. III, 3 v.
43. An.B, 13 r.

44. Q.A. III, 8 v.
45. Q.A. III, 7 r., 7 v., 8 r., 8 v.
46. Q.A. III, 8 r.
47. Q.A. IV, 10 r.
48. An. IV, 173 r.
49. An. I, 173 v.
50. E, 16 r.
51. C.A., 292 r.
52. W., xxiv (55).
53. Q.A. V, 11–14.
54. Q.A. V, 21 v.
55. An.A, 17 r.
56. An.B, 13 v.
57. An. IV, 167 r.
58. C.A., 310 r.
59. C.A., 364 v.
60. C.A., 192 r.a.
61. C.A., 179 r.
62. W., 12503.
63. W., xi.
64. C.A., 93 r.
65. C.A., 310 r.
66. C.A., 222 r.
67. H 2, 43 r.
68. C.A., 395 r.
69. C.A., 33 v.a.
70. C.A., 7 v.b.
71. C.A., 46 v.b.
72. C.A., 236 r.b.
73. C.A., 233 r.
74. F, 22 v.
75. F, 23 r.
76. F, 87 v.
77. F, 72 v.
78. F, 35.
79. F, 26 v., 27 r.
80. F, 14 r.
81. F, 17 v.
82. F, 13 r.
83. F, 37 v.
84. F, 61 r.
85. C.A., 204 r.
86. F o'.

87. F, 84 r.
88. F, 56 r.
89. F, 57 r.
90. F, 25 r.
91. F, 22 v.
92. F, 4 v.
93. F, 34 r.
94. F, 4 v.
95. W., 19145.

96. K, 100 r.
97. C.A., 247 r.a.
98. C.A., 225 r.b.
99. An., 17 r.
100. An. III, 241.
101. W., xxviii.
102. *Mémoires de Fleuranges.*
103. E, 1 r.a.

CHAPTER EIGHT

1. G, 70 v.
2. C.A., 367 v.a.
3. G, 70 v.
4. G, 47 r.
5. E, 19 v.
6. G, 29 r.
7. T.P., 813.
8. T.P., 820.
9. G, 32 v.
10. E, 18 v.
11. G, 22 v.
12. G, 20 v.
13. G, 9 v.
14. G, 19 v.
15. G, 26 v.
16. E, 19 r.
17. G, 22 v., 23 r.
18. Ash., I r.a.
19. G, 37 r.
20. G, 8 r.
21. C.A., 96 v.
22. G, 43 r.
23. C.A., 287 v.
24. E, 80 r.
25. E, 5 r.
26. G o'.
27. C.A., 114 r.a.
28. C.A., 243 v., 278 r., 179 v.
29. G, 95 v.
30. E, 8 v.
31. E, 58 v.
32. E, 54 v.

33. E, 77 v.
34. G, 45 r., 76 r.
35. G, 90 r.
36. G, 41 r.
37. E, 15 v.
38. E, 51 r.
39. Q.A. IV, 1 v.
40. G, 83.
41. G, 64 v.
42. G, 65.
43. G, 92 r.
44. E, 43 r.
45. E, 54 r.
46. E, 41 v.
47. E, 70 v.
48. E, 47 r.
49. E, 12 r.
50. G, 38 r.
51. E, 12 r.
52. C.A., 179 v.
53. Q.A. IV, 10.
54. An. IV, 184 r.
55. W., 19045.
56. C.A., 287 r.
57. C.A., 63 v.b.
58. C.A., 271 r.
59. C.A., 172 v.
60. E, 31 v.
61. W., 158 r.
62. W., 158 v.
63. W., 158 r.
64. CA., 159.

CHAPTER NINE

1. *Le Bourgeois de Paris.*
2. O, 2 r.
3. G, 89 r.
4. C.A., 75 v., 221 r.
5. B.M., 270 v.

6. B.M., 269 r.
7. B.M., 270 v.
8. B.M., 269 v.
9. C.A., 336 v.b.
10. C.A., 249 r.

Bibliography

Alazard, Jean: *Le portrait florentin*. Laurens, Paris, 1924.

Pérugin. Laurens, Paris, 1927.

Antoniewicz, Boloz J.: *O wieczerzy Leonarda da Vinci* [*Leonardo's "Last Supper"*]. Anzeiger der Akademie der Wissenschaften in Krakau, 1904.

Swietynia zagadkowa Leonarda da Vinci [*The Mysterious Temple of Leonardo da Vinci*]. Lwow, 1910.

Auton, Jean d': *Chroniques de Louis XII. Ed. par R. de Maulde La Clavière*. Paris, 1889.

Baldacci, Antonio: *L'adolescenza di Leonardo da Vinci e il mondo verde. Raccolta Vinciana*, fasc. XIII, 1926–1929.

Baratta, Mario: *Curiosità vinciana*. Fratelli Bocca, Turin, 1905.

Leonardo da Vinci ed i problemi della terra. Fratelli Bocca, Turin, 1903.

Beltrami, Luca: *Documenti e memorie riguardanti la vita e le opere di Leonardo da Vinci*. Fratelli Treves, Milan, 1919.

Il castello di Milano sotto il dominio dei Visconti e Sforza. Hoepli, Milan, 1894.

L'aeroplano di Leonardo. Conferenze Fiorentine. Fratelli Treves, Milan, 1910.

Berenson, Bernhard: *The Florentine Painters of the Renaissance*. G. P. Putnam's Sons, London and New York, 1896.

The Drawings of the Florentine Painters. G. P. Putnam's Sons, London, 1903.

Bertaux, Emile: *Rome*. Renouard, Paris, 1905.

Blum, André: *"Léonard de Vinci, graveur." Gazette des Beaux-Arts*, Paris, 1932.

Bode, Wilhelm: *Florentiner Bildhauer der Renaissance*. Cassirer, Berlin.

Bodmer, Heinrich: *Leonardo. Des Meisters Gemälde und Zeichnungen. Klassiker der Kunst*. Deutsche Verlagsanstalt, Stuttgart and Berlin, 1931.

Bosseboeuf, L. A.: *Clos Lucé. Séjour et mort de Léonard de Vinci*. Tours, 1893.

Bottazzi, Filippo: *Leonardo, biologo e anatomico. Conferenze Fiorentine*. Fratelli Treves, Milan, 1910.

Burckhardt, Jacob: *Die Kultur der Renaissance in Italien*. Alfred Kröner Verlag, Leipzig, 1919.

Der Cicerone. Seemann, Leipzig, 1910.

Calvi, Felice: *Il castello di Porta Giovia e sue vicende nella storia di Milano. Archivio Storico Lombardo*, vol. III, anno XIII, Milan, 1886.

Calvi, Gerolamo: *I manoscritti di Leonardo da Vinci*. N. Zanichelli, Bologna, 1925.

Il manoscritto H di Leonardo da Vinci, "Il Fiore di Vertù," e "l'Acerba" di Cecco d'Ascoli. Archivio Storico Lombardo, ser. 3, vol. X, anno XXV, Milan, 1898.

Contributi alla biografia di Leonardo da Vinci. Archivio Storico Lombardo, ser. 5, anno XLIII, part 2, Milan, 1916.

Vecchie e nuove riserve sull' "Annunziazione" di Monte Oliveto. Raccolta Vinciana, fasc. XIV, 1930–1934.

Abbozzo di capitolo introduttivo ad una storia della vita e delle opere di Leonardo da Vinci. Raccolta Vinciana, fasc. XIII, 1926–1929.

Spigolature vinciane dall' archivio di stato di Firenze. Raccolta Vinciana, fasc. XIII, 1926–1929.

Leonardo. 1936.

548   BIBLIOGRAPHY

Cartwright, Julia: *Isabella d'Este*. Murray, London, 1903.
    Beatrice d'Este. Dent, London, 1903.
Carusi, Enrico: *Ancora di Salai*. *Raccolta Vinciana*, fasc. XIII, 1926–1929.
    Un codice sconosciuto (il Vat. Cat. 3169) dell' opera de A. de Beatis. *Raccolta Vinciana*, fasc. XIV, 1930–1934.
Cassirer, Ernst: *Individuum und Kosmos in der Philosophie der Renaissance*. B. G. Teubner, Leipzig, 1927.
Castiglione, Baldassare: *Il cortegiano*.
Cermenati, Mario: *"Le roi qui voulait emporter en France la 'Cène' de Léonard de Vinci."* *Nouvelle Revue d'Italie*, Rome, 1929.
Chledowski, Kazimierz von: *Rom*. Georg Müller, Munich, 1912.
    Der Hof von Ferrara. Georg Müller, Munich, 1919.
Clark, Kenneth: *A Catalogue of the Drawings of Leonardo da Vinci in the Collection of His Majesty the King at Windsor Castle*. Cambridge University, 1935.
Clausse, Gustave: *Les Sforza et les arts en Milanais*. Leroux, Paris, 1909.
    Béatrice d'Este. Leroux, Paris, 1907.
Coleman, Marguerite: *Amboise et Léonard de Vinci à Amboise*. Arrault, Tours, 1932.
Conti, Angelo: *Leonardo pittore*. *Conferenze Fiorentine*. Fratelli Treves, Milan, 1910.
Credaro, Luigi: *"Quelques pensées pédagogiques de Léonard de Vinci."* *Nouvelle Revue d'Italie*, Rome, 1919.
Croce, Benedetto: *Un canzoniere d'amore per Costanza d'Avalos*. Accademia Pontaniana, Naples, 1903.
    Leonardo filosofo. *Conferenze Fiorentine*. Fratelli Treves, Milan, 1910.
Dannemann, F.: *Grundriss der Geschichte der Naturwissenschaften*. Leipzig, 1896–1898.
Delaborde, H. F.: *Expédition de Charles VIII en Italie*. Firmin-Didot, Paris, 1888.
Delvincourt, Claude: *"Léonard de Vinci et la musique."* *Nouvelle Revue d'Italie*, Rome, 1919.
Dina, Achille: *Lodovico il Moro prima della sua venuta al governo*. *Archivio Storico Lombardo*, vol. III, anno XIII, Milan, 1886.
Dorez, Léon: *"Léonard de Vinci et Jean Perréal."* *Nouvelle Revue d'Italie*, Rome, 1919.
Duhem, P.: *Etudes sur Léonard de Vinci*. Hermann, Paris, 1906.
Favaro, Antonio: *Leonardo nella storia delle scienze sperimentali*. *Conferenze Fiorentine*. Fratelli Treves, Milan, 1910.
    "Les difficultés que présente une édition des œuvres de Léonard de Vinci." *Nouvelle Revue d'Italie*, Rome, 1919.
Feldhaus, Franz M.: *Leonardo, der Techniker und Erfinder*. Diederichs, Jena, 1913.
    Die Technik der Antike und des Mittelalters. Athenaion, Wildpark-Potsdam, 1931.
Ferrero, Leo: *Léonard de Vinci, ou l'œuvre d'art*. Kra, Paris, 1929.
Frati, Lodovico: *Un cronista fiorentino del quattrocento alla corte milanese*. *Archivio Storico Lombardo*, ser. 3, vol. III, anno XXII, Milan, 1895.
Freud, Sigmund: *Un souvenir d'enfance de Léonard de Vinci*. Annoté par la Princesse Marie de Bonaparte. Gallimard, Paris, 1927.
Frey, Karl: *Michelangelo Buonarroti*. Curtius, Berlin, 1907.
Gauthiez, Pierre: *Luini*. Renouard, Paris, 1906.
Ghinzoni, P.: *Un prodromo della riforma in Milano*. *Archivio Storico Lombardo*, vol. III, anno XIII, Milan, 1886.
    Alcune rappresentazioni in Italia nel secolo XV. *Archivio Storico Lombardo*, ser. 2, vol. X, anno XX, Milan, 1893.
Giacomelli, Raffaele: *I modelli delle macchine volanti di Leonardo da Vinci*. Rome, 1931.
    Gli scritti di Leonardo da Vinci sul volo. Bardi, Rome, 1936.

Giulini, Alessandro: *Di alcuni figli meno noti di Francesco Sforza. Archivio Storico Lombardo,* ser. 5, anno XLIII, Milan, 1916.

Gregorovius, Ferdinand: *Geschichte der Stadt Rom.* Stuttgart, 1886–1893.

Grimm, Hermann: *Das Leben Michelangelos.* Spemann, Berlin and Stuttgart, 1899.

Guicciardini, Francesco: *Storia d'Italia.*

Hart, Ivor B.: *The Mechanical Investigations of Leonardo da Vinci.* Chapman and Hall, London, 1925.

Herzfeld, Marie: *Leonardo da Vinci, der Denker, Forscher, und Poet.* Diederichs, Leipzig, 1904.

  Ueber ein Skizzenblatt Leonardo da Vincis. Mitteilungen des kunsthistorischen Instituts in Florenz, Band IV, Heft 1.

  Bemerkungen zu einem Skizzenblatt Leonardo da Vincis. Mitteilungen der Gesellschaft für vervielfältigende Kunst, Vienna, 1928.

  Noch einmal Leonardo und Ligny. Raccolta Vinciana, fasc. XIII, 1926–1929.

  Zur Geschichte des Sforzadenkmals. Raccolta Vinciana, fasc. XIII, 1926–1929.

Heydenreich, Ludwig Heinrich: *Die Sakralbau-Studien Leonardo da Vincis.* Dissertation, Vogel, Leipzig, 1929.

  "Leonardo da Vincis Artilleriestudien." Die schwere Artillerie, January 1934.

  Studi archeologici di Leonardo da Vinci a Civitavecchia. Raccolta Vinciana, fasc. XIV, 1930–1934.

Hildebrandt, Edmund: *Leonardo da Vinci.* Grote, Berlin, 1927.

Hill: *"Chaffrey Carles." Numismatic Chronicle,* ser. 5, vol. VI, 1929.

Horst, C.: *L'ultima cena di Leonardo nel riflesso delle copie e delle imitazioni. Raccolta Vinciana,* fasc. XIV, 1930–1934.

Houssaye, Arsène: *Histoire de Léonard de Vinci.* Paris, 1876.

Lebengarc, Johannes: *Die Anatomie und Physiologie des Herzens in Leonardo da Vincis anatomischen Manuskripten.* Dissertation, A. Barth, Leipzig, 1926.

Legendre, Louis: *Vie du cardinal d'Amboise.* Rouen, 1724.

Ludwig, H.: *Leonardo da Vinci. Das Buch von der Malerei.* Braumüller, Vienna, 1882.

Lungo, Isidoro del: *Leonardo scrittore. Conferenze Fiorentine.* Fratelli Treves, Milan, 1910.

Luzio, A., and Renier, R.: *Delle relazioni d'Isabella d'Este con Lodovico e Beatrice Sforza. Archivio Storico Lombardo,* ser. 2, vol. VII, anno XVII, Milan, 1890.

  Isabella d'Este e Cesare Borgia.

Malaguzzi, Valerio Francesco: *La corte di Lodovico il Moro.* Milan, 1913–1915.

Marcolongo, Roberto: *I centri di gravità dei corpi negli scritti di Leonardo da Vinci. Raccolta Vinciana,* fasc. XIII, 1926–1929.

Maulde La Clavière, R. de: *Louis d'Orléans.* Paris, 1889–1891.

  Histoire de Louis XII (deuxième partie: La Diplomatie). Leroux, Paris, 1893.

  Louise de Savoie et François I. Perrin, Paris, 1895.

McCurdy, Edward: *The Mind of Leonardo da Vinci.* Cape, London, 1932.

McMurrich, J. Playfair: *Leonardo da Vinci, the Anatomist.* Williams and Wilkins, Baltimore, 1930.

Möller, Emil: *"Wie sah Leonardo aus?" Belvedere,* Vienna, 1926.

  Salai und Leonardo da Vinci. Jahrbuch der kunsthistorischen Sammlung in Wien, neue Folge, Sonderheft 16, 1928.

  Aggiunte e chiarimenti al tema: La Madonna coi bambini che giuocano. Raccolta Vinciana, fasc. XIII, 1926–1929.

  Leonardo e il Verrocchio. Raccolta Vinciana, fasc. XIV, 1930–1934.

Mongeri, G.: *Il castello di Milano. Archivio Storico Lombardo,* ser. 2, vol. I, anno XI, Milan, 1884.

Motta, E.: *Ambrogio Preda e Leonardo da Vinci. Archivio Storico Lombardo,* ser. 2, vol. X, anno XX, Milan, 1893.

Müller-Walde: *Leonardo-Studien*. Munich, 1889–1890.

Müntz, Eugène: *Léonard de Vinci, l'artiste, le penseur, le savant*. Hachette, Paris, 1899.

Raphaël. Sa vie, son œuvre, et son temps. Hachette, Paris, 1881.

Nicodemi, Giorgio: *La luce di Leonardo. Raccolta Vinciana*, fasc. XIII, 1926–1929.

Orestano: *"Léonard philosophe." Nouvelle Revue d'Italie*, Rome, 1919.

Paris, Paulin: *Etudes sur François I, roi de France*. Techener, Paris, 1885.

Pasolini, Pier Desiderio: *Caterina Sforza*. Loescher, Rome, 1893.

Pastor, Ludwig: *Geschichte der Päpste im Zeitalter der Renaissance*. Herdersche Verlagsbuchhandlung, Freiburg im Breisgau, 1909.

Péladan, Joséphin: *Epilogue. Conferenze Fiorentine*. Fratelli Treves, Milan, 1910.
La dernière leçon de Léonard de Vinci. Sansot, Paris, 1904.

Pélissier, L.: *Louis XII et Ludovic Sforza*. Thorin, Paris, 1896.

Perrens, F. T.: *Histoire de Florence*. Quantin, Paris, 1888.

Pfister: *Leonardo da Vinci*. Recht Verlag, Munich, 1923.

Popp, A.: *Leonardo da Vinci: Zeichnungen*. Piper, Munich, 1928.

Porro, Giulio: *Nozze di Beatrice d'Este e di Anna Sforza. Achivio Storico Lombardo*, anno IX, Milan, 1882.

Portioli, Attilio: *La nascita di Massimiliano Sforza. Archivio Storico Lombardo*, anno IX, Milan, 1882.

Ravaisson-Mollien, Charles: *Les écrits de Léonard de Vinci*. Paris, 1881.
Pages autographes et apocryphes de Léonard de Vinci. Paris, 1888.

Renier, Rodolfo: *Gaspare Visconti. Archivio Storico Lombardo*, vol. III, anno XIII, Milan, 1886.

Reumont, A. von: *Lorenzo de' Medici, il Magnifico*. Leipzig, 1874.

Reymond, Marcel: *Verrocchio*. Librairie de l'Art Ancien et Moderne, Paris.
L'éducation de Léonard. Conferenze Fiorentine. Fratelli Treves, Milan, 1910.
Bramante. Laurens, Paris, n. d.

Richter, Jean Paul: *The Literary Works of Leonardo da Vinci*. London, 1884.

Ronna, M. A.: *Léonard de Vinci, peintre, ingénieur, hydraulicien*. Renouard, Paris, 1902.

Rosenberg, Adolf: *Leonardo da Vinci*. Velhagen and Klasing, Leipzig, 1898.

Schaeffer, Emil: *Das florentiner Bildnis*. Munich, 1904.
Leonardo da Vinci: das Abendmahl. Bard, Berlin, 1914.

Séailles, Gabriel: *Léonard de Vinci, l'artiste et le savant*. Perrin, Paris, 1892.
"Le génie de Léonard de Vinci." Nouvelle Revue d'Italie, Rome, 1919.

Segard, Achille: *Sodoma*. Floury, Paris, 1910.

Seidlitz, W. von: *Leonardo da Vinci, der Wendepunkt der Renaissance*. Bard, Berlin, 1909.
Ambrogio Preda und Leonardo da Vinci. Jahrbuch der kunsthistorischen Sammlung des allerhöchsten Kaiserhauses, Band XXVI. Vienna and Leipzig, 1906.

Semenza, Guido: *"L'automobile di Leonardo da Vinci." Archeion*, vol. IX, no. 1, 1928.

Sirén, Osvald: *Léonard de Vinci, l'artiste et l'homme*. Van Oest, Paris, 1928.

Sizeranne, Robert de la: *César Borgia et le duc d'Urbino*. Hachette, Paris, 1924.

Solmi, Edmondo: *Studi sulla filosofia naturale di Leonardo da Vinci*. Modena, 1898.
Nuovi studi sulla filosofia naturale di Leonardo da Vinci. Mantua, 1905.
Le fonti dei manoscritti di Leonardo da Vinci. Loescher, Turin, 1908.
Leonardo da Vinci e la Repubblica di Venezia. Cogliati, Milan, 1908.
Il trattato di Leonardo da Vinci sul linguaggio, De Vocie. Milan, 1906.
Frammenti letterari e filosofici di Leonardo da Vinci. Barbèra, Florence, 1904.
La festa del paradiso di Leonardo da Vinci. Archivio Storico Lombardo, Milan, 1910.

Su una probabile gita di Leonardo da Vinci in Genova.
La resurrezione dell' opera di Leonardo. Fratelli Treves, Milan, 1910.

Spinazzola, Vittorio: *Leonardo architetto. Conferenze Fiorentine.* Fratelli Treves, Milan.

Stein, Wilhelm: *Raffael.* Bondi, Berlin, 1923.

Steinmann, Ernst: *Rom in der Renaissance.* Seemann, Leipzig, 1908.

Suida, Wilhelm: *Leonardo und sein Kreis.* Bruckmann, Munich, 1929.

Taylor, Rachel Annand: *Leonardo the Florentine.* Richards Press, London, 1927.

Tomasini: *Machiavelli.* Loescher, Rome, 1911.

Toni, Giovannı Battista de: *Le piante e gli animali in Leonardo da Vinci.* N. Zanichelli, Bologna, 1922.

Torre, Antonio della: *Accademia Platonica.* Florence, 1902.

Tourette, Gilles de la: *Léonard de Vinci.* Albin Michel, Paris, 1932.

Valéry, Paul: *Introduction à la méthode de Léonard de Vinci.* Paris, 1895.

Venturi, A.: *Studi del vero.* Hoepli, Milan, 1927.
"*Léonard de Vinci à la fin de la première période florentine.*" *Nouvelle Revue d'Italie,* Rome, 1919.

Verga, Ettore: *Bibliografia vinciana 1493–1930.*
Storia della vita milanese. Nicola Moneto, Milan, 1931.

Vulliaud, Paul: *La pensée ésotérique de Léonard de Vinci.* Grasset, Paris, 1910.

Walser, Ernst: *Gesammelte Studien zur Geistesgeschichte der Renaissance.* Benno Schwabe, Basle, 1932.

Werner, Otto: *Zur Physik Leonardo da Vincis.* Internationale Verlagsanstalt, Berlin.

Index